BEHAVIOR SCIENCE BIBLIOGRAPHIES

ETHNOGRAPHIC BIBLIOGRAPHY OF NORTH AMERICA

4th EDITION

Volume 2:   Arctic and Subarctic

GEORGE PETER MURDOCK
and
TIMOTHY J. O'LEARY

with the assistance of

JOHN BEIERLE   ALLISON BUTLER MATTHEWS
SARAH T. BRIDGES   JOHN MUSGRAVE
DONALD HORTON   JOAN STEFFENS
JOHN B. KIRBY, JR.   FREDERICK W. VOGET
BARBARA A. YANCHEK

HUMAN RELATIONS AREA FILES PRESS
NEW HAVEN
1975

Compilation of this volume has been
financed in part by grant GN35418 from
the National Science Foundation.

LIBRARY OF CONGRESS CATALOG CARD NUMBER: 75-17091
INTERNATIONAL STANDARD BOOK NUMBER: 0-87536-207-9

CONTENTS

PREFACE TO FOURTH EDITION   vii

PREFACE TO THIRD EDITION   ix

GENERAL INTRODUCTION   xiii

LIST OF ABBREVIATIONS   xxxvii

01   ARCTIC COAST   1

   Ethnic Map   2
   Introduction   3
   01-00   Arctic Coast Area Bibliography   5
   01-01   Aleut   32
   01-02   Baffinland Eskimo   40
   01-03   Caribou Eskimo   44
   01-04   Copper Eskimo   48
   01-05   East Greenland Eskimo   54
   01-06   Iglulik Eskimo   60
   01-07   Labrador Eskimo   64
   01-08   Mackenzie Eskimo   73
   01-09   Netsilik Eskimo   75
   01-10   North Alaska Eskimo   77
   01-11   Polar Eskimo   86
   01-12   South Alaska Eskimo   90
   01-13   Southampton Eskimo   94
   01-14   West Alaska Eskimo   95
   01-15   West Greenland Eskimo   104
   01-16   Yuit   112

02   MACKENZIE-YUKON   119

   Ethnic Map   120
   Introduction   121
   02-00   Mackenzie-Yukon Area Bibliography   124
   02-01   Ahtena   134
   02-02   Beaver   135
   02-03   Carrier   135
   02-04   Chilcotin   138
   02-05   Chipewyan   139
   02-06   Coyukon   143
   02-07   Dogrib   144
   02-08   Han   146
   02-09   Hare   146

   02-10   Ingalik   148
   02-11   Kaska   149
   02-12   Kutchin   150
   02-13   Mountain   153
   02-14   Nabesna   153
   02-15   Sarsi   154
   02-16   Satudene   155
   02-17   Sekani   156
   02-18   Slave   157
   02-19   Tahltan   158
   02-02   Tanaina   159
   02-21   Tanana   161
   02-22   Tsetsaut   161
   02-23   Tutchone   162
   02-24   Yellowknife   162
   02-25   Northern Metis   163

11   EASTERN CANADA   165

   Ethnic Map   166
   Introduction   167
   11-00   Eastern Canada Area Bibliography   169
   11-01   Abnaki   177
   11-02   Algonkin   182
   11-03   Beothuk   184
   11-04   Cree   186
   11-05   Malecite   198
   11-06   Micmac   201
   11-07   Montagnais   206
   11-08   Ojibwa   217
   11-09   Ottawa   241

   Arctic-Subarctic Ethnonymy   245
   General Ethnic Map of Native North America   257

SCHEMATIC TABLE OF CONTENTS
FOR
COMPLETE BIBLIOGRAPHY

VOLUME 1: General North America (contains expanded area bibliographies)

01	Arctic Coast	1
02	Mackenzie-Yukon	35
03	Northwest Coast	53
04	Oregon Seaboard	77
05	California	87
06	Peninsula	107
07	Basin	117
08	Plateau	131
09	Plains	147
10	Midwest	181
11	Eastern Canada	195
12	Northeast	209
13	Southeast	225
14	Gulf	245
15	Southwest	251
16	General North America (with five subject bibliographies)	299

VOLUME 2: Arctic and Subarctic (contains ethnic bibliographies)

01	Arctic Coast	1
02	Mackenzie-Yukon	5
11	Eastern Canada	65

VOLUME 3: Far West and Pacific Coast (contains ethnic bibliographies)

03	Northwest Coast	1
04	Oregon Seaboard	65
05	California	93
06	Peninsula	141
07	Basin	173
08	Plateau	211

VOLUME 4: Eastern United States (contains ethnic bibliographies)

10	Midwest	1
12	Northeast	49
13	Southeast	139

VOLUME 5: Plains and Southwest (contains ethnic bibliographies)

09	Plains	1
14	Gulf	163
15	Southwest	175

Preface to the Fourth Edition

This, the fourth edition of the *Ethnographic Bibliography of North America*, is intended to provide a basic coverage of the published literature on the Native Peoples of North America through the end of the year 1972. This edition differs in a number of ways from the third edition, which was published in 1960. The most obvious change is that the bibliography is now appearing in five volumes. As with every other discipline in the last twenty years, Native American studies has had to cope with an information explosion. Some idea of the magnitude of this explosion can be gained from the fact that while the third edition contained approximately 17,300 bibliographic entries in one volume, the present edition contains close to 40,000 entries in five volumes, most of this increase pertaining to the fourteen-year period 1959-1972, inclusive. Part of the increase, however, also comes from the increased span of coverage of the present edition, which includes a number of subject areas not covered previously.

Another obvious change is in the format of presentation. With one major exception, full bibliographic information has been given for each citation in the bibliography where it has been available. Each citation gives the author's full name, the full title and subtitle, place of publication, publisher, date of publication, etc. If the citation be from a journal, the name of the journal is given in full. This is a major change from previous editions, where such information was compressed as much as possible, using abbreviations for journal names and using short or abbreviated titles wherever possible, all with the idea of saving space so as to be able to include the whole bibliography in one volume. This compression was not necessary in the present edition, since we realized before we started the compilation of citations that there would have to be more than one volume. The major exception noted above is that whereas we have expanded the citations listed in the third edition whenever we could (giving full titles of books, the names of journals in full, etc.) we found it impossible to do a full and thorough job on this expansion, since it would have meant verifying each and every citation in the original. This could not be done with the time and funds allotted to us for the preparation of this edition of the bibliography. As a result, there are some inconsistencies in citation format in the bibliography that follows. It is hoped that for the next edition, all of the pre-1959 citations will have been verified and full information given for each.

The number of ethnic groups covered by the bibliography has been expanded somewhat, especially in the North Mexican area, in order to have the ethnic groups covered in the bibliography correspond more closely to the groups covered in the forthcoming *Handbook of North American Indians*. Also, we have dropped the general use of the word "tribal" when referring to ethnic groups, since many of the groups named in the bibliography are not "tribes" in the traditional sense.

Another major change from the third edition is that this is a computerized bibliography, based on a variation of the Human Relations Area Files Automated Bibliographic System (HABS), which has been developed over the past ten years (see Koh 1973). This computerization will make the preparation of future editions much less expensive, less time-consuming, and far easier to accomplish. Once the bibliographic information has been correctly put into machine-readable form, this inputting should never have to be done again. In addition, with a change in the programming of the computer, new formats can be used and special bibliographies can be printed without the laborious compilation process that was previously necessary. Several people were involved in the adaptation of the HABS for the purposes of this bibliography. HABS programming development has been by John Dow. Programming and computer operations were accomplished by Richard Hart and Joan Steffens. The computer used for the arrangement and printing of the citations was the IBM 370/158 at the Yale University Computer Center. The actual printing was performed with the use of a special IBM print train (developed with the aid of the American Library Association), which carries most of the pertinent diacritics used in a bibliography of this type.

Since the publication of the third edition of this bibliography, a number of individuals have written to us, offering suggestions, additions, and corrections. Such contributions are essential to an undertaking like this, since one individual or organization can neither hope to comprehend all of the requirements of the anticipated users of the bibliography nor control the diversity of the published materials relevant to the purpose of the bibliography. Therefore, we are very pleased to acknowledge the assistance of Lowell John Bean, David M. Brugge,

Harold C. Conklin, Alan Cooke, Gordon M. Day, Alan Dundes, May Ebihara (and her class), James L. Fidelholtz, Don D. Fowler, Stanley A. Freed, Robert F. Heizer, James H. Howard, Dell Hymes, Ira S. Jacknis, Janet Jordan, Luis S. Kemnitzer, Herbert Landar, William S. Lyon, John Moore, Vernon H. Nelson, Wendell Oswalt, Nancy J. Pollock, Bert Salwen, Claude E. Schaeffer, Samuel L. Stanley, Omer C. Stewart, Willard Walker, Margaret Wheat, and Richard B. Woodbury.

Special notes of thanks must go to two people. William C. Sturtevant has been a constant source of encouragement from the beginning of the project, taking time out from his very strenuous duties (among others of editing the forthcoming *Handbook of North American Indians*) to note new books and sources of information, errors in the previous editions, people to contact, etc. June Helm has been of great help in the preparation of the Northern Athabascan bibliographies (Area 2), sending on new versions of her own ongoing computerized bibliography as they became available. They, and the other scholars noted above, receive our most grateful thanks for their assistance. Naturally, they are in no way responsible for whatever deficiencies may remain in the bibliography, but they are very definitely responsible in part for whatever merit it may have for the user.

Most of the actual compilation of this bibliography was accomplished at various libraries within the Yale University system. Our particular thanks go to Harry P. Harrison and the staff of the Circulation Department at the Sterling Memorial Library at Yale, to Robert E. Balay and the staff of the Reference Department at Sterling Memorial Library, and to the staff of the Yale Anthropology Library for courteous and efficient assistance and many kindnesses throughout the period of research.

The compilation of this bibliography was financed in part by a grant (GN-35418) from the National Science Foundation to Frank W. Moore and Timothy J. O'Leary as co-principal investigators. Moore provided institutional coordination and general supervision of the project. O'Leary was responsible for the overall compilation and supervision of the project and for the final printed bibliography. He was very fortunate to be assisted in the compilation by John Beierle, Sarah T. Bridges, John B. Kirby, Jr., Joan Steffens, and Barbara A. Yanchek, all trained researchers with an interest in Native American studies. The data processing of the citations, i.e. the keypunching, proofreading, and editing, which for this bibliography proved to be a far more intellectually demanding task than had originally been envisioned, was very ably carried out by a team under the supervision of Joan Steffens, consisting of Ella Gibson and Lillian Ljungquist, with the assistance of Mary Elizabeth Johnson and Victoria Alexander. Frank W. Moore, who prepared and drew the maps for the 1960 edition, revised them where necessary for this edition.

Our very special thanks, finally, go to George Peter Murdock, who, while not actively engaged in the preparation of this edition of "his" bibliography, has constantly made his influence felt through the guidelines and the general level of excellence he established in the previous editions. While the current set of volumes may present a considerably altered face to the world, in its essentials it has followed the basic pattern of search, selection, and classification that was so ably established by him forty years ago. We certainly hope that he will look with favor on this edition of the bibliography.

Timothy J. O'Leary
New Haven, June 1975

Koh, Hesung C. HABS: a research tool for social science and area studies. Behavior Science Notes, 8(1973):169-199.

Preface to the Third Edition

[This preface is reprinted unchanged from the third edition (1960) in order to give the reader a brief historical background to the compilation of this bibliography. The reader should note that a number of basic changes have been made in the format of the bibliography, and therefore should not take as a guide to the new edition the statements contained in this Preface. The new format is described in the Introduction beginning on p. xi.   TOL]

Some thirty years ago the author began systematically to assemble bibliographical references on primitive and historical cultures with the object, partly of directing distributional and other studies in the classroom, partly of recommending library purchases, and partly of preparing for a projected study which later materialized as the Cross-Cultural Survey at the Institute of Human Relations.[1] By utilizing odd moments of time between appointments, useless for consistent research, to verify references in the Yale University Library, he was able over a period of years to prepare a classified worldwide ethnographic bibliography of considerable size.

This bibliography proved exceedingly useful, to the author and to others, in directing dissertations, making classroom assignments, surveying the existing literature preparatory to field work, and providing ready access to the relevant sources for topical and regional studies of all kinds. A considerable demand was expressed that at least the portion on aboriginal North America be made generally available by publication. The present work in its several editions represents a response to that demand.

The principle of classification by tribal groups having been adopted as the most serviceable to modern anthropologists, the first task was to determine the groups to be used. As a compromise between the segregation of all tribes bearing traditional names, which would have increased the bulk and cost of the work by necessitating frequent repetition of the same references for adjacent peoples, and a classification into a few large areal groups, which would have reduced the usefulness of the volume, it was decided to adopt as a norm the nationally self-conscious tribes of regions with some measure of political development, e.g., those of the Plains. For regions with less extensive political integration, groups of approximately the same degree of linguistic and cultural homogeneity were formed by arbitrarily uniting a number of tribelets or local groups, usually under the name of one of them. Thus under Snuqualmi were lumped the Salishan Dwamish, Nisqualli, Puyallup, Samamish, Skagit, Snohomish, Snuqualmi, and Squaxon of Puget Sound; under Massachuset, the Algonkian Massachuset, Nauset, Nipmuc, and Wampanoag of southeastern New England; and under Wailaki the Athapaskan Kato, Lassik, Mattole, Nongatl, Sinkyone, and Wailaki of Northwestern California. In this way, all of North America as far south as Tehuantepec was divided into 277 tribal groups, a manageable number.

The second task was to prepare a map showing the location of these groups. This was done in 1937 with the cooperation of the students in a graduate class in Systematic Ethnography. The map, which is appended to the present volume, shows, with approximate boundaries, the location of the various tribal groups as of the period of their first extensive contacts with Europeans.[2] It is thus not valid for any single period but represents a shifting date-line, which becomes later as one moves from south to north, from east to west, and from coast to interior. Since the locations of many tribes did not remain constant over three centuries, the shifting date-line made necessary a number of compromises in the fixing of boundaries. Careful mapping by a series of predecessors, notably Kroeber on California, Spier on the Plateau, Osgood on the Mackenzie-Yukon, and Sauer on Mexico, proved of invaluable assistance. Probably the least satisfactory area, because of severe early territorial dislocations, is the Midwest, despite aid generously given by the late Truman Michelson. It is gratifying to note the very high degree of correspondence between our map of North America and those prepared independently by Kroeber and by Driver, et al.[3]

In the selection of names for our 277 groups, established usage was followed in most instances. A few adjectival tribal names, e.g., Costanoan and Salinan, were changed to their nominal forms. Diacritical marks were eliminated. Where several well-known tribes were grouped together, the name of the most important or most familiar was usually given to the cluster. The only radical decision was with regard to names like Apache, Paiute, Shoshoni, and Sioux, which are ambiguous because applied, although commonly with qualifying adjectives, to several different tribal groups. Except in the case of the Eskimo, where it seemed impracticable, such names were either eliminated entirely or confined to a single group. In a few instances this has resulted in a certain arbitrariness in naming. Thus the traditional Coast Miwok have been called Olamentke, the Eastern Dakota are termed Santee, the Owens Valley Paiute of Steward have been grouped with their western congeners as Mono, the Western Apache are dubbed Coyotero, and the Western Shoshoni are named Panamint from their best known sub-group.

The preparation of the map prevented subsequent changes in our groupings, even when clearly advisable. Thus the Eyak, discovered by Birket-Smith and de Laguna, have been classed arbitrarily with the Ahtena (II-1) even though they deserve an independent classification.

The map does not divide the tribal groups into culture areas, but this has been done for the presentation of the bibliography. We have distinguished sixteen areas, adding Oregon Seaboard, Peninsula, Basin, Midwest, Eastern Canada, and Gulf to the ten proposed by Wissler.[4] The decision as to allocation has been close in several instances. Thus the Caddo might well have been placed in the Southeast instead of the Plains, the Klamath in the Plateau instead of in California, the Nanticoke in the Southeast rather than in the Northeast, the Sarsi in the Plains on the basis of culture instead of in the Mackenzie-Yukon on the basis of language, and the Seri in the Southwest rather than in the Peninsula. Mexico, an area embracing 24 tribal groups, though shown on the map, has not been included in the bibliography for the sole reason that pressure of other research has prevented the author from bringing this section of North America to a sufficient degree of completeness to justify publication at the present time. The bibliography therefore covers only 253 of the total of 277 tribal groups distinguished.

The work is organized by areas and within each area by tribal groups arranged in alphabetical order. Under the areal headings are included regional studies, geographical and historical sources, travel accounts, and other works presenting little specific original information on individual tribes. Under the tribal headings are included works pertaining directly to the particular group or its sub-groups. The order of arrangement of items under each heading is alphabetical by author's surname and thereunder by title. One exception is to be noted: standard monographs covering large segments of a tribal culture, or, in default thereof, other general works of considerable scope, are placed ahead of the alphabetical list of other sources. An appendix includes references to works on North America in general or on a number of areas; this list is very incomplete since no special effort was made to assemble such items.

To compress a classified bibliography on a whole continent into a single volume requires selectivity and compactness. The former has been achieved by including only such references as seemed likely to prove of value to an anthropologist desirous of discovering what is known about a particular culture. Works in which the tribe is barely mentioned or in which no new information of value is given have in general been excluded. Compactness has been sought through a standard system of abbreviating references. Space is saved by giving initials rather than full names of authors, by omitting unimportant information such as name of publisher, by using abbreviations for journals, series, and collections which recur frequently,[5] by omitting subtitles except when necessary to indicate the content of a work, and by shortening titles themselves wherever words or phrases could be deleted at the end of a title without loss of meaning or obscuring of content.

Pages have been indicated for all periodical items as a rough indication of quantity of material. For books, similarly, the number of volumes or of pages has been noted in most instances, although frequently the particular pages on which the most relevant information occurs are indicated instead. Diacritical marks are omitted except for a few standard accents. Within a serial volume, the number is noted only when it is separately paginated. Where the indicated date of a volume differs from its actual published date, the former is usually given preference. A few inconsistencies have arisen as a result of changes in the procedure of notation over a period of years. In the earlier years of compilation, for instance, the number of pages of single books was not noted, and the date of actual publication was preferred to the indicated date of a volume in a series. Since these inconsistencies did not seem serious, it was decided to ignore them rather than undertake the vast labor of checking back over all previous work.

Approximately seventy per cent of the works cited have been personally examined by the author, and most of the rest have similarly been seen by his assistants in the course of amassing the references. Perhaps five per cent of the references, including all those that are incomplete, have not been personally assessed—most of them works listed in other bibliographical sources but not available in the Yale University Library.

Effort has been exerted to make the tribal bibliographies as complete as possible on all ethnographical subjects. Works on physical anthropology and linguistics, and on archeology where pertinent to a known historical culture, have been listed whenever obtained in the search for ethnographic items, but no extended canvass for them has been made and the coverage of these subjects, particularly in regard to earlier works, remains incomplete. Complete runs of most of the serials listed in the Key to Abbreviations have been searched for pertinent materials. No consistent search, however, has been made of United States Congressional documents and series, and references to these appear in the Bibliography only when they were obtained incidentally in the search for ethnographic materials. The Bibliography is restricted to published materials, and no reference is made to unpublished manuscripts, dissertations, etc. For such materials, researchers should consult the standard reference works.[6]

In general, fugitive materials and items appearing in popular journals have not been included in this Bibliography, except in cases where they seemed to be of some importance. The cut-off date of this third edition was originally intended to be December, 1958, and the Bibliography is reasonably complete as of that date. However, an effort was made to include materials in the major anthropological journals and important books which have appeared since that time. Coverage of materials appearing in 1959 and early 1960 is, therefore, very incomplete.

Mistakes are inevitable in a work such as this. The frequent recopying incidental to compilation introduces typographical errors which escape even careful proofreading. Important references are overlooked, lost, or misjudged and excluded, and errors of allocation occur in areas with which the author is not especially familiar. The present volume pretends to be only so accurate as reasonable care and effort can make it.

Fortunately there is a remedy for errors and omissions. In future editions, corrections can be made, newly published titles added, overlooked sources noted, the Mexican area included, the general North American appendix expanded, and the archeological, linguistic, and physical anthropological literature covered as exhaustively as the ethnographical. To accomplish really satisfactory revisions, the author must have the cooperation of his anthropological colleagues. He, therefore, requests that users of this work call his attention to errors and omissions in areas familiar to them.

The first edition of this Bibliography appeared in 1941 as Volume 1 of the Yale Anthropological Series. The second edition appeared in 1953 as a Behavior Science Bibliography published by the Human Relations Area Files. In terms of number of entries, the first edition had approximately 9,400 and the second edition about 12,700. The present edition contains more than 17,300 entries.

The author received valuable assistance from Donald Horton and Frederick W. Voget in the preparation of the first edition, and from Mrs. Allison Butler Matthews and John Musgrave in the preparation of the second edition. In regard to the present or third edition, he is indebted to many colleagues who have supplied new references, and especially to William C. Sturtevant of the Smithsonsian Institution for generous advice and assistance. Its actual compilation is almost exclusively the product of the devoted effort of Timothy J. O'Leary.

Yale University
June, 1960

George Peter Murdock

NOTES

1 See G.P. Murdock, "The Cross-Cultural Survey," *American Sociological Review*, V (1940), 361-70.

2 Only 276 groups are actually located. The Seminole of the Southeast, having originated subsequent to intensive white contact, do not appear on the map.

3 See A.L. Kroeber, "Cultural and Natural Areas of Native North America," *University of California Publications in American Archaeology and Ethnology*, XXXVIII (1939), Map 1A; H.E. Driver, et al., "Indian Tribes of North America," *Memoirs of the International Journal of American Linguistics*, IX (1953), end map.

4 C. Wissler, *The American Indian* (2d edit., New York, 1931), p. 219.

5 A key to abbreviations, which precedes the text, presents the full titles and places of publication of these serial works.

6 E.G., F.J. Dockstader, "The American Indian in Graduate Studies; A Bibliography of Theses and Dissertations," CMAI, XV (1957), and W.N. Fenton et al., American Indian and White Relations to 1830, Chapel Hill, 1957.

General Introduction

Background

During the thirty-five years since the publication of the first edition in 1941, this bibliography has served as a standard reference work on the Native Peoples of North America — for the anthropologist in particular and, in general, for all those with a factual interest in learning about the ways of life of these peoples. The bibliography has continuously been expanded in its various editions, both in the types of information included and in the number of works cited, until this fourth edition is more than four times the size of the original. This growth reflects both an expansion of interest by writers and scholars in these peoples and an increase in the efficiency of the reference tools that attempt to control the literature on them.

This bibliography is a selected bibliography of published factual books and articles describing the cultures of the Native Peoples of North America. These peoples are considered to be the Eskimo of Greenland, northern Canada, Alaska, and eastern Siberia; and the Indians of Alaska, Canada, the United States, and Mexico north of the northern boundary of Mesoamerica (the area of "high cultures" in Mexico and Central America). It does not include citations to publications on immigrant ethnic groups settled in this area. For this reason, the title of the bibliography might more properly be reworded as an "Ethnographic Bibliography of the Native North Americans." However, as the present work has been known under its title for so many years, it will remain so in this edition.

The primary focus of the bibliography is on the ethnography of these peoples, i.e. on the description of their cultures and ways of life. The bibliography is restricted to citations of published books and articles. It does not contain references to unpublished manuscripts, to maps, or to sound recordings, films, or other audiovisual materials. An attempt will be made later on in this introduction to provide guidance for those who are interested in locating such materials. In spite of the extent of these volumes, this is a *selected* bibliography, more stringently so for the earlier materials. Many more citations were examined than are listed. Most of those dropped from consideration were peripheral to the scope of the bibliography or were ephemeral in nature (e.g. newspaper articles, broadsides, articles published in commercial house organs, etc.). The bibliography is limited to factual accounts; no fiction about these groups

is knowingly listed, except in the very rare cases where experts have agreed that the fictionalized account was in accord with ethnographic fact. These few cases should be obvious on examination.

While the primary focus of the bibliography has remained ethnographic, other subject areas have gradually been added through the various editions until the present one tries to include references to published materials on all subjects relevant to the study of the Native Americans, such as history, psychology, and human biology and medicine, among others. Because of this expansion through the years, not all fields of interest are covered equally thoroughly. Basic ethnographic description remains the most completely covered field, followed by linguistics, by archeology, and then by history, relations of the ethnic groups with the federal governments, education, medicine, human geography, urbanism, and Pan-Indianism. It is to be hoped that eventually all of these subject fields will be covered to the same extent. However, the primary focus will still remain ethnographic description.

In the remainder of this introduction, we will discuss more extensively the subject, area, and ethnic group coverage of this edition; the new format of the bibliography; and the search plan used for its compilation. We will also attempt to provide introductory guides to the location of the types of materials not included in the bibliography, such as most government publications, manuscripts, maps, and audiovisual materials, and also to the use of the Educational Resources Information Center (ERIC). The ERIC will be discussed because of its function in making generally available the results of much research on the Native Americans. Finally, we will provide a brief general discussion of some of the tools used in keeping up with the new literature as it is published, and of going beyond this bibliography in search of older published works.

Coverage

The citations in this edition of the bibliography are restricted to published materials on the Native Peoples of North America issued up to and including the year 1972. It is intended that the bibliography be as exhaustive as possible of those materials which are considered to be of professional quality or which contain valuable data not otherwise available. An effort has been made to have the individual ethnic group bibliographies as complete as possible on the traditional ethnographic subjects. Works on physical anthropology, linguistics, and on archeology where pertinent to a known historical culture have been listed wherever possible. In the earlier editions, no special effort was made to include materials on ethnic history, psychology, education, and other fields peripheral to ethnography. However, for the compilation of this edition we have tried to include everything published during the period 1959-1972 that relates to Native American studies. This broadening of coverage helps to account for the radical increase in the size of the bibliography.

An attempt was made to cover publications in all Western languages, including the Slavic languages. Publications in non-Western languages, however, are covered very sparsely. On the whole, the literature in these latter languages is not very large, although there is a growing body of good ethnographic material in Japanese which has been almost completely missed, since there was no easy way for us to get at it. There may also be material of equal value in other literatures whose languages the compilers were not capable of handling. It is to be hoped that such materials can be included in future editions of this bibliography.

The total number of individual ethnic group bibliographies presented is now 269, compared to the 253 in the earlier editions. The new bibliographies are included so as to make the coverage of the total bibliography more congruent to that of the forthcoming *Handbook of North American Indians* (which will be discussed briefly at the end of the introduction). The additional bibliographies are on the Northern Métis, Red River Métis, Sioux (as a whole), Oklahoma Indians, Middle Atlantic States Mestizos, Lumbee, Southeastern Mestizos, Acaxee, Cazcan, Tepehaun, Totorame, Zacatec, Chichimec, Pame, Cora, and Huichol. They are not as full as those for other ethnic groups in the bibliography, for we did not have the time to make a thorough search of the earlier literature. However, we hope that we have included enough citations to make at least some research on these groups possible.

As in previous editions, no consistent search was made of United States, Canadian or Mexican government publications, and such materials are generally included only when they were obtained incidentally in the search for ethnographic materials. An exception was made for the various publications of the Smithsonian Institution, the Bureau of American Ethnology, and the National Museum of Canada. The field of government publication is the great gap in both this and other bibliographies on the Native Americans. From the sampling we have made during the compilation of this edition, we estimate that

the size of this bibliography would have been nearly doubled if a search of all relevant government publications could have been made and the citations included. However, these publications are generally poorly controlled bibliographically, and very difficult to locate in toto. For the convenience of the users of this bibliography who may want to do research in this field, a brief introduction to locating such publications is given later in the introduction.

It was hoped that citations to films, sound recordings, and maps relating to the Native Americans could be included in this edition, but because of the unexpectedly large amount of printed literature encountered, this part of the compilation process had to be abandoned—with reluctance. We have, however, included a brief discussion of sources of these types of materials.

Neither fugitive materials nor items appearing in popular journals have been included, except in cases where they seemed to be of some special importance. As far as possible, all materials listed in the bibliography have been seen by the compilers. In the case of those not seen, an effort was made to verify the citations by locating them in at least two independent indexing tools. For books and monographs not seen, the standard source for verification was the *National Union Catalog* in its various cumulations. (Unless noted otherwise, titles given in italics will be discussed later in this Introduction.)

Search Pattern

In compiling this edition of the bibliography, a standard search pattern was evolved and followed. Using as a base the list of periodicals in the 1960 edition, as well as lists found in several other bibliographical tools, such as the *International Bibliography of Social and Cultural Anthropology* and the *Social Sciences and Humanities Index*, a search was made of the holdings of periodicals, as well as books, contained in the Yale University library system. Yale University has one of the largest libraries in North America, and it possesses strong holdings in fields related to Native American studies. Searches were also made of several printed library catalogs for materials not encountered in the search of the Yale University Library. These included, among others, the *Library of Congress Catalog. Books: Subjects* for the period 1958-1973, the Harvard Peabody Museum Library catalog, the research catalog of the American Geographical Society, the catalog of the Edward E. Ayer collection of the Newberry Library in Chicago, and the catalog of the History of the Americas Collection of the New York Public Library. Also checked as sources of citations were continuing bibliographical serials, such as the *Arctic*

Bibliography, the *International Bibliography of Social and Cultural Anthropology*, the *Bibliographie Américaniste*, and the *Index to Literature on the American Indian*. A search for relevant citations in *Research in Education, Dissertation Abstracts International*, and the current indexes discussed later in this introduction was also made. Also used as sources of citations to be verified were bibliographies and references contributed by individual correspondents and bibliographies on specific groups, areas, or subjects that had been published during the period 1959-1972.

The citations found during the search were transferred to individual worksheets, verified where necessary, edited, and transferred to keypunched cards for computer manipulation. Approximately 14,000 worksheets were completed during the course of compilation, of which approximately 11,000 were finally utilized. The remainder were withheld for a number of reasons, the two basic ones being a lack of real relevance to the purpose of the bibliography and the presence of obvious inaccuracies that could not be rectified in time for inclusion. These additional worksheets will remain on file at the Human Relations Area Files for further reference and analysis, should this prove necessary. It is estimated that each of the citations included on the worksheets appears twice on the average as an entry in the bibliography (some of the citations contain material on more than twenty groups). This total, when added to the more than 17,000 entries in the 1960 edition, gives the estimated total of 40,000 entries in the present edition that is referred to in the Preface. (It should be noted that the general bibliographies for each of the fifteen culture areas appear twice, once in the general volume and once in a regional volume.) Thus, the present edition is more than twice the size of the 1960 edition.

Format

General Discussion

When preliminary estimates gave the figure of approximately 2,000 pages for the bibliographic entries alone, without introductory materials, maps, or ethnic group lists, it became obvious that the bibliography would have to appear as a multivolume publication. We decided that, while no specific division is ideal, a five-volume format should meet the requirements of most users. The first volume is a general volume, covering all of North America, while the others divide North America into four regional volumes that are approximately equal in size in terms of the number of bibliographical entries—except for the larger final volume, which includes entries on Areas 9 (Plains), 14 (Gulf), and 15 (Southwest).

The first volume includes the general sections from each of the fifteen major areas in the bibliography, which are equivalent to culture areas (e.g. Southwest, Plateau). Into each of these major area bibliographies we have integrated the individual monographs and articles that we feel give the best cultural descriptions of the individual ethnic groups covered in each of the areas. Also included as Area 16 is the bibliography on General North America, which appeared as an appendix in previous editions. This general bibliography now also includes individual bibliographies on Pan-Indianism, Urban Indians, United States Government Relations with the Native Peoples, Canadian Indians in General, and Canadian Government Relations with the Native Peoples. Since these bibliographies are new to this edition, they are not as complete retrospectively as the other bibliographies in the volume. Also included in the first volume are ethnic group maps for each of the areas and the general ethnic group listing that was used in compiling and classifying the bibliography. We hope that this volume can serve as a general introductory bibliography on North American Native Peoples for users who do not feel the need for the finer classifications and more exhaustive listings found in the regional volumes.

Within each of the other four regional volumes is a set of area bibliographies, including detailed bibliographies on individual ethnic groups within the areas, corresponding to the fifteen culture areas established by Murdock (see the Preface to the Third Edition, p. vii). Each of the regional volumes contains bibliographies on a set of contiguous culture areas, which combine to form a major area of North America. Thus, Volume 2, on the Arctic and Subarctic, contains bibliographies covering Area 1 (Arctic Coast), Area 2 (Mackenzie-Yukon), and Area 11 (Eastern Canada). Together, these cover a block of land which forms the northern part of North America. In similar fashion, Volume 3 covers the Far West and Pacific Coast; Volume 4, the eastern part of the United States; and Volume 5, the Plains and Southwest. (See the frontispiece maps and the schematic table of contents for more detailed contents of each volume.) As a result of this regional grouping of bibliographies, the order in which the bibliographies are presented in this edition does not always correspond to the way in which they were presented in earlier editions, but we do not believe that this arrangement will present any grave problems to the user.

The general culture classification closely follows that devised by Murdock for the previous editions. The major difference is that several ethnic group bibliographies have been added for groups or conglomerates of peoples not previously distinguished (e.g. Sioux, Oklahoma Indians, Southeastern Mestizos). In addition, several ethnic group bibliographies have been added to Area 15 (Southwest), so as to have the southern boundary of that area correspond more closely to that used in the *Handbook of North American Indians*. There is a sketch map for each of the fifteen areas, showing the general boundaries and location of groups for which bibliographies have been compiled. As in the previous editions, these maps show the location of the ethnic groups as of the period of their first extensive contacts with Europeans. Since, in addition to the Seminole listed in previous editions, a number of the groups added for this edition of the bibliography originated subsequent to the period of extensive European contact, they are not included on these maps. These ethnic groups are the Northern Métis, the Red River Métis, the Middle Atlantic States Mestizos, Lumbee, Southeastern Mestizos, and the general inclusive category of Oklahoma Indians. The Sioux and the Chichimec also are not located on the ethnic group maps, since the materials included in their respective bibliographies refer to a number of component groups scattered over a large area. An indication of their location is given in the relevant area introductions, however. These latter introductions provide a brief sketch of each area and some information on each of the peoples covered in the individual ethnic group bibliographies, including location, linguistic affiliations, and important monographs and bibliographies which have appeared since 1972, as they are known to the compilers.

In these regional volumes, each areal set of bibliographies contains first a general bibliography pertaining to the culture area as a whole. This general bibliography includes regional studies, general geographical and historical sources, travel accounts, and other materials not specific to any group within the area. The individual ethnic group bibliographies follow in alphabetical order by name of unit, except where new bibliographies have been added (e.g. Lumbee follows Yuchi in Area 13, Southeast). Within each individual bibliography, the entries are arranged in alphabetical order by author's name (surname first). Where an author has more than one entry following his name, they are arranged alphabetically by the first word in the title (*not* by date). Where there is more than one entry for an author, the author's full name is repeated for each entry. Within each individual ethnic group bibliography, any cited bibliography which pertains to that ethnic group has been placed at the beginning of the listing, separated from the main body of entries. In addition, a limited number of works which have been considered by Murdock and/or O'Leary to give a good, basic description of the culture have been asterisked

This separation of bibliographies from the main listing and asterisking of basic cultural descriptions represent major changes in format from previous editions. Formerly, works presenting basic cultural descriptions were placed at the head of each bibliography, and bibliographies as such were not given any special treatment. We have made these changes in the present edition because we felt that bibliographies are important resources, which warrant further checking, since they generally represent viewpoints and present materials not always agreed with or used by the present compilers. We admit that this viewpoint may be debatable, but feel that no essential information is lost, since the basic cultural descriptions are tagged by the asterisks.

So far as the basic cultural descriptions (now asterisked) are concerned, we should note that some reviewers of the previous editions misunderstood the reason for the separate placement, usually noting that "important" works have been separated from the remainder of the listing. That was not the point. While "standard monographs covering large segments of a tribal culture" are certainly important, there are numerous other works in the bibliography not so designated that are certainly "important" as well, but perhaps for different reasons. Examples of these would be Casagrande's "Comanche linguistic acculturation," Lounsbury's "A semantic analysis of the Pawnee kinship usage," and Mead's "The changing culture of an Indian tribe."

Each regional volume concludes with an ethnic group synonymy (or ethnonymy), which pertains to the groups covered in that volume. This ethnonymy is derived from the complete ethnonymy used in the compilation of the bibliography, which may be found in Volume 1. No attempt has been made to list the numerous variant and obsolete spellings for the names that are included. For fuller listings, see Hodge (1910) and Swanton (1952). At the end of each volume is a map of North America, showing the total ethnic group coverage of the complete bibliography.

Formats for Individual Citations

There is a considerable difference between the citation formats used for the third edition of the bibliography and those used for the present edition. In the third edition, because it was desirable to keep the bibliography to one volume, compactness of citation form was a great desideratum. Therefore, a standard system of abbreviating references was followed. Authors' given names were represented by initials; the names of book publishers were omitted; abbreviations were used for the titles of journals, series, and collections that recurred frequently; subtitles were generally omitted; and titles themselves were often shortened.

In this edition, both because it was obvious that it would be impossible to issue the bibliography as a single volume and also because of the impracticability of using the old system for a computerized bibliography, it was decided to present the citations with as full bibliographical information as it was possible to obtain. This meant that the citations in the third edition had to be expanded as fully as possible to correspond to the new citation formats. Since resources were not available for rechecking each of the 17,000 entries in the third edition and thereby making their formats completely consistent with that of the new citations, it was decided to make use only of the information already available. As a result, of the three major citation types in the third edition—i.e. book, book chapter, and journal article—the book citation format is almost identical in the third and fourth editions, while the others show varying amounts of expansion. The expansion has been accomplished mainly by replacing the abbreviations used in the third editon with fuller information. For instance, MA is now given as Minnesota Archaeologist, and MAH as Magazine of American History, etc. This simple replacement procedure does not, of course, take into account the name changes that many of the journals have gone through. However, library catalogs generally cross-reference these varying titles to each other, so we feel the user will not be greatly inconvenienced by this transformation.

As an illustration of the types of format changes that were involved for these citations from the third edition, we will give some examples of the same citations in the two formats. The third edition format will be presented first, then the expanded format for the same citation, as used in this edition.

Book.

Dobbs, A. An Account of the Countries Adjoining to Hudson's Bay. 211 pp. London, 1744.

Dobbs, A. An account of the countries adjoining to Hudson's Bay. London, 1744. 211 p.

Note how little the book citation format changed. The differences lie in the capitalization of words within the title, the use of the abbreviation 'p.' to indicate pages, and the moving of the page count to the end of the citation.

Journal article.

Sapir, E. The Na-dene Languages. AA, n.s., XVII, 535-58. 1915.

Sapir, Edward. The Na-dene languages. American Anthropologist, n.s., 17 (1915): 535-558.

Note how this citation format changes. Where we knew the first name of the author, it is now generally given in full. Only the first word and proper nouns are capitalized in the title. The name of the journal is written out in full; Roman numerals are changed to Arabic; pagination is given in full; and the year is enclosed within parentheses.

Chapter in a book.

Service, E. R. The Canadian Eskimo. PPC, 64-85. 1958.

Service, Elman R. The Canadian Eskimo. In his A Profile of Primitive Culture. New York, 1958: 64-85.

Again the author's full name is given. The title of the book from which the chapter is taken is spelled out, with all significant words having initial capitals, and being preceded by the underlined words "In his," which indicate that the author of the book was Service. The inclusive pagination is moved to the end of the citation.

Within the present volumes, two types of citation format are used in addition to the above. The first is restricted to this introduction. We have used this format, which includes the use of italics, because it provides a visual emphasis of the various titles that are being discussed in the introduction. This emphasis is not needed in the main body of new bibliographic citations in the remainder of the volumes, and, therefore, a different format has been used for these citations. While still fairly compact compared to many other citation styles, these latter formats are much expanded over those used in previous editions of the bibliography. In addition, a fourth citation format type, that for an article in the proceedings of a conference or a congress, has been added. These new individual formats are discussed in order below.

Citation format for books.

Smith, G. Hubert. Like-a-Fishhook Village and Fort Berthold, Garrison Reservoir, North Dakota. Washington, D.C., National Park Service, 1972. 12, 196 p. illus., maps. (U.S., National Park Service, Anthropological Papers, 2)

This is an example of a monograph which was published as part of a series. The author's name comes first, with the surname and given names reveresed to facilitate alphabetizing. Following the name is the title, which ends with a period. After the title comes the imprint, which consists of the place of publication, the publisher, and the date of publication. Following the imprint comes the collation, which in our format includes the pagination (in this case including both introductory pages and the main body of text), the fact that the monograph is illustrated, and that it contains maps. The phrase within parentheses is the series statement. This indicates that the monograph was the second in the series called Anthropological Papers, which are issued by the U.S. National Park Service. Where applicable, the format may also contain information on the edition cited (if not the first edition by the publisher), on multiple authors, on editors, and on translators. Some other examples of this format are:

> Moziño, Jose Mariano. Noticias de Nutka; an account of Nootka Sound in 1792. Translated and edited by Iris Higbie Wilson. Seattle, University of Washington Press, 1970. 54, 142 p. (American Ethnological Society, Monograph, 50)

> Waddell, Jack O., ed. The American Indian in urban society. Edited by Jack O. Waddell and O. Michael Watson. Boston, Little, Brown, 1971. 14, 414 p.

> Harkins, Arthur M., et al., comps. Modern Native Americans: a selective bibliography. Minneapolis, University of Minnesota, Training Center for Community Programs, 1971. 131 p. ERIC ED054890.

Note that in this last citation, three or more individuals were responsible for the compilation of the bibliography. Only the name of the first compiler (or author) is given, however, together with the phrase "et al." The example previous to this one shows the format for a case where there are two authors, editors, or compilers. Note that the name of the second individual is given, along with the first individual, in a statement following the title. The note ERIC ED054890 in the third citation indicates that the bibliography is also available from the Educational Resources Information Center (ERIC). This organization is discussed later in the introduction.

Citation format for journal articles.

> Oswalt, Wendell H. The future of the Caribou Eskimo. By Wendell H. Oswalt and James W. VanStone. Anthropologica, n.s., 2 (1960): 154-176.

The author and title sections here are similar to those in the book citation format. However, in this example there are two authors. This is indicated by the statement following the title. Following this author statement is the journal citation. It includes the name of the journal; the abbreviation "n.s.," which indicates that it is the new series of the journal which is being referred to; the volume number; the year, enclosed within parentheses, to which the volume number refers (1960), followed by a colon; and the inclusive pagination of the article in full (154-176), followed by a period. Another example of the format is:

> Amoss, Pamela Thorsen. The persistence of aboriginal beliefs and practices among the Nooksack Coast Salish. Dissertation Abstracts International, 32 (1971/1972): 6174B. UM 72-15, 064.

The latter citation shows two variations. When the date to which a journal volume refers extends over two or more years, that fact is indicated by listing the beginning year and the ending year and placing a slash (/) between the two years. The note UM 72-15,064 indicates that this citation refers to a dissertation which is available from Xerox University Microfilms. These dissertations are discussed later in the introduction.

Citation format for chapters in books.

> Stanton, Max E. A remnant Indian community: the Houma of southern Louisiana. In J. Kenneth Morland, ed. The Not So Solid South. Athens, Ga., Southern Anthropological Society, 1971: 82-92.

The author and title sections here are as in previous examples. Following the title is the name of the book in which the chapter may be found. This section begins with the word "In," underlined, followed by the name of the author(s) or editor(s) of the book, and the title of the book. Then comes the imprint information for the book (place of publication, publisher, and date of publication), followed by a colon, and then the inclusive pagination for the article within the book.

Citation format for articles in the proceedings of conferences or congresses.

> Spicer, Edward H. Apuntes sobre el tipo de religión de los Yuto-Aztecas centrales. In Congreso Internacional de Americanistas, 35th. 1962, México. Actas y Memorias, 2. México, D. F., 1964: 27-38.

> Rose, A. P. Can religion be treated as a branch of anthropology? In Pacific Science Congress of the Pacific Science Association, 9th. 1957, Bangkok. Proceedings, 3, Anthropology and Social Sciences. Bangkok, The Secretariat, Ninth Pacific Science Congress, 1963: 230-232.

Again, the author and the title are handled like those in the book citation format. Following the title here is the underlined word "In." After this comes the name of the conference or congress as it appears on the title page, and the number of the conference, if it occur regularly. Then comes the date on which the conference was held and the place where it was held. This is followed by the particular title of the volume (if it have one) and the volume number if applicable. Then comes the imprint for that volume, including the place of publication (which may be different from the place where the conference was held), the publisher (if different from the conference), and the date of publication. The date of publication is followed by a colon and then by the inclusive pagination of the article, and is closed by a period.

The preceding examples cover the basic types of the citation formats for the items included in this bibliography. There may be minor additions to the format which include further information, but these will not change the basic form. We believe that these formats are clear and easy to use. The major variation from the bibliographic style with which most researchers are probably familiar lies in the duplication of the author's name in a case where there are two authors. This is done in order to accord with the usual procedure librarians follow in making catalog cards. The book citation format closely follows that of the Library of Congress catalog cards, in order that users may quickly locate books in library catalogs.

Government Publications

As mentioned previously, no specific effort was made to locate and cite government publications. While it had been hoped at the beginning of the compilation process that we would be able to make a thorough search for materials of this type, it proved to be impossible to accomplish with the limited amount of time and other resources we had available. We certainly did not realize at the time the magnitude of the task, the general inaccessibility of these materials, and the great amount of specialized knowledge necessary to locate the materials. However, such publications have been included whenever we encountered them during the course of the compilation. We did, of course, include the standard publications and series relevant to the study of Native American peoples, such as the publications of the Bureau of American Ethnology. Because of their importance, however, we do want to indicate to the user of this bibliography at least how to start doing a bibliographic search for government materials on the Native Americans. Accordingly, we have prepared a brief listing and explanation of the major

reference tools for locating these publications. We will discuss the United States federal, state, and municipal publications first, and then the Canadian. We do not know enough about Mexican government publications to be able to include a discussion of them in this introduction.

The major reference tools for locating United States federal government publications are government publications themselves. They cover the period from 1774 to the present. Until the establishment of the Government Printing Office in 1861, government publications were printed by private contractors. There is still no complete listing of these publications. The closest one can get to such a complete listing is Poore's catalog, referenced as follows:

Poore, Benjamin Perley
1885 *A descriptive catalogue of the government publications of the United States, September 5, 1775—March 4, 1881, compiled by order of Congress.* Washington, D.C., Government Printing Office. (U.S., 48th Congress, 2d Session, Senate, Miscellaneous Document, 67) [reprint edition available]

The citations in Poore are arranged chronologically by Congress (covering the 1st through the 46th Congresses), and within each Congress by title of the publication (not in any discernible order). There is a large index, with publications on Indians being listed on pages 1302-1304, and individual Indian tribes being listed alphabetically on pages 1303-1304. However, there is no listing on the Eskimo. References in the index are to pages in the body of the bibliography, and not to a specific citation. The approximately fifty items on each page must be scanned until the particular item wanted is found.

John G. Ames compiled an index to United States Government publications for the period 1881-1893, thereby taking up the task where Poore left off. The full citation is:

U.S. Superintendent of Documents
1905 *Comprehensive index to the publications of the United States Government, 1881-1893.* By John G. Ames. Washington, D.C., Government Printing Office. 2v. (U.S., 58th Congress, 2d Session, House of Representatives, Document, 754) [reprint edition available]

This tool is a combined catalog and index. The index is a list of the documents arranged alphabetically by the key word in the title, e.g. "Indian women marrying white men, legislation prescribing citizenship in U.S. as effect of, recommended"/vol. 1, p. 677/. Eskimos are indexed on page 445 of vol. 1. Indians are indexed on pages 665-677 of vol. 1. An alphabetical list of tribal names appears on page 673 of vol. 1.

For most of the period from 1893 to the present, there are two reference tools that can be used. The first is the permanent and complete catalog of all United States government publications, usually known as the *Document Catalog*, from the binder's title on the spine of each volume. The full citation is:

U.S. Superintendent of Documents
   1896- *Catalogue of the public documents of*
   1945 *Congress and of all departments of the*
        Government of the United States for the
        period March 4, 1893-[Dec. 31, 1940].
        Washington, D.C., Government Printing
        Office. 25 v. (SuDocs no. GP3.6:) [reprint
        edition available]

This catalog provides approximately one volume for each Congress, from the 53d Congress to the 76th Congress, inclusive. It is a dictionary catalog, with the same document appearing under the author, the subject, and the title when necessary. The serial numbers for the documents themselves are usually included only with the main (author) entry. Superintendent of Documents classification numbers are sometimes given. An explanation of these numbers is given later in this section. The major key terms to be checked in each volume are Eskimo, Indian, Indians, and the names of individual tribes.

The second tool to be used for this period is the *Monthly Catalog of United States Government Publications*, which covers the period from 1895 to the present. The full citation is:

U.S. Superintendent of Documents
   1895- *Monthly catalog of United States Gov-*
        ernment publications. Washington, D.C.,
        Government Printing Office. (SuDocs no.
        GP3.8:)

This catalog is supposed to be a current bibliography of all publications issued by all branches of the federal government. However, in practice it is essentially a list of all publications printed by the Government Printing Office, in addition to whatever materials the various government agencies send to the Superintendent of Documents. Since most agencies are not compelled to send their publications to the Superintendent of Documents (although they are supposed to), there are large gaps in the listing—one of the reasons why working with government publications can be so difficult. Publications are listed in each monthly issue, alphabetically by the name of the issuing office. Since 1945, there has been a monthly index, and there is an annual index. In 1974 a three-part index, consisting of author, title, and subject indexes, was begun. Again the

most used key terms are Eskimo, Indian, Indians, and the names of individual tribes. A major problem for most users of the index is that the indexing has been very erratic, and it is easy to miss key items. There is now available a cumulated subject index to the *Monthly Catalog* for the period 1900-1971. This is a great time-saver in making retrospective searches through the *Catalog.* The full citation is:

U.S. Superintendent of Documents
   1974- *Cumulative subject index to the monthly*
   1975 *catalog of United States Government*
        publications, 1900-1971. Compiled by
        William W. Buchanan and Edna M.
        Kanely. Washington, D.C., Carrollton
        Press. 14 v.

By using the above tools, one can get at least an idea of what has been issued on the Native Peoples in United States government publications. However, the hardest part of the search is actually locating copies of the needed publications. Since, so far as we know, there is no complete set of United States government publications existing anywhere, locating a needed publication can be a very long job for the individual researcher and for the government publications librarian who will have to assist him. A recent directory is certain to be of great assistance in this type of search since it lists more than 1,900 libraries in the United States with government document collections. The citation is:

American Library Association. Government Documents Round Table
   1974 *Directory of government document col-*
        lections & librarians. Washington, D.C.,
        Congressional Information Service.

For general information concerning the publications of the United States federal government, a good guide is:

Schmeckebier, Laurence F., and Roy B. Eastin
   1969 *Government publications and their use.*
        2d rev. ed. Washington, D.C., Brookings
        Institution.

While this is a very useful volume, it can only begin to give the researcher an idea of the complexity and volume of federal government publications. As noted above, most researchers in this field will become highly dependent on their local government publications librarian.

We mentioned Superintendent of Documents classification numbers previously. These refer to the codes of the Superintendent of Documents classification system, which is used in the Public Documents Library of the Government Printing Office. It is an unusual classification, in that its basis is the issuing agency for the individual publications, and not the subjects of the individual publications. An individual code consists of a combination of letters and numbers, which, taken together, are unique to a specific document. The letters, which precede the numbers, designate the issuing agency of the document. The numbers indicate the issuing office within the agency, the particular series of documents issued by that office, and the particular number of the document within that series. Thus GS stands for General Services Administration; HE for the Department of Health, Education, and Welfare; LC for Library of Congress; and Y for the publications of Congress. The SuDocs (the usual abbreviation for Superintendent of Documents) number S12.3:78, for example, is the number for *Bureau of American Ethnology Bulletin* 78 (Kroeber's *Handbook of the Indians of California*). The SI stands for Smithsonian Institution, and the 2 stands for the Bureau of American Ethnology within the Smithsonian Institution, or, alternatively, SI2 stands for Bureau of American Ethnology. The .3 indicates the third type of publication issued by the Bureau of American Ethnology, in this case the *Bulletin* (.1 would indicate the series *Annual Reports*). The colon indicates that the document represented by the number (or sometimes by a combination of letters and numbers) following is issued as part of the preceding series. In the SuDocs numbers given in this bibliography, where a reference is given to a complete series of publications, we have not indicated any number or code after the colon. since by including such a number or code we would be specifying a particular volume in the series. Thus, in the citation in the next paragraph, the SuDocs no. LC30.9: refers to the complete series titled *Monthly checklist of state publications.* If we do include a number or code after the colon, we are specifying a single publication; thus, SuDocs no. CR1.10:33 refers to the *American Indian civil rights handbook,* published in 1972. This is the general form that SuDocs numbers follow, with variations. Many collections of government publications are arranged according to this classification, and the numbers must be used when ordering publications from the Government Printing Office.

Moving from the federal level to the state and municipal levels, the situation immediately becomes much more difficult. There is only one general listing of state publications, which is issued by the Library of Congress. The full citation is:

U.S. Library of Congress. Exchange and Gift Division
    1910- *Monthly checklist of state publications.* Washington, D.C., Government Printing Office. (SuDocs no. LC 30.9:)

This listing is limited to publications received by

the Library of Congress. While the Library makes every effort to ensure that they receive everything, in the course of events this does not happen. Each monthly checklist is arranged alphabetically by states, territories, and insular possessions, with individual publications listed under each category. Each title is accompanied by the necessary cataloging information. The table of contents of an individual publication is sometimes listed, if it is a composite report. There is no monthly index, but there is an annual index published separately. The key terms again are Eskimo, Indian, Indians of North America, and the names of individual tribes.

This is the only recurrent general listing of state publications, and it is incomplete. There is also one general guide to state publications, which is now quite out of date. It may be of some use in the search of the earlier literature, however. The citation is:

Wilcox, Jerome Kear
    1940 *Manual on the use of state publications.* Chicago, American Library Association.

When we turn to municipal publications, the situation is almost hopeless so far as having any bibliographical control is concerned. There is only one recent general index or listing available, and it is, comparatively, quite limited in scope. The citation is:

Index to current Urban Documents
    1972- Westport, Conn., Greewood Press.

This index tries to make available complete and detailed descriptions of the majority of the known official documents issued annually by the largest cities and counties in the United States and Canada. In the 1974 volume, the publications of 173 cities and 26 counties of one million or more inhabitants in the United States (as determined from the 1970 Census), and 23 Canadian cities were surveyed. The two headings to be checked are Indians and Minority Groups. So far, very little has been indexed on the Native Americans.

Aside from the above, there is no general index or listing. Therefore, for each municipality one would have to check with the local library and the city or town hall and go through their holdings. Such a procedure could be very profitable in particular municipalities. Here, the individual researcher is completely on his own so far as this bibliography is concerned. concerned.

When we turn to Canada, we find most of the same problems as with United States government publications. The general bibliographical control of earlier publications is probably not quite as good. The one general guide that discusses publications issued between 1668 and 1935 contains a good index. The citation is:

Higgins, Marion Villiers
1935 *Canadian government publications; a manual for librarians.* Chicago, American Library Association.

There is one official catalog series, which covers the period 1928 to the present. The citation is:

Canada. Department of Public Printing and Stationery
1928- *Canadian Government publications: catalogue.* Ottawa. (formerly titled: *Catalogue of official publications of the Parliament and Government of Canada*)

The series is bilingual in English and French, and is now a monthly. It covers parliamentary publications and publications of federal agencies and departments. Key terms to check in the index are Eskimo, Esquimau, Indians, Indiens, and the names of various tribes.

Two other series also cover government publications and offer somewhat better indexing for our purposes. These are:

The Canadian Catalogue of Books Published in Canada, Books about Canada, as Well as Those Written by Canadians
1921- Toronto, Department of Education of
1951 Ontario, Public Libraries Branch.

Canadiana. Publications of Canadian Interest Received by the National Library of Canada.
1950- Ottawa, Information Canada.

These are also bilingual publications, in French and English, and do a somewhat better job of indexing than the *Canadian Government Publications: Catalogue. Canadiana* has two sections which index federal and provincial publications. Part VII indexes publications of the government of Canada, and Part VIII indexes publications of the provincial governments of Canada. However, it indexes only those publications received by the National Library and is therefore incomplete.

There are a few catalogs which cover the publications of some of the Canadian provinces. These are:

Bishop, Olga Bernice
1957 *Publications of the governments of Nova Scotia, Prince Edward Island, New Brunswick, 1758-1852.* Ottawa, National Library of Canada.

Holmes, Marjorie C.
1950 *Publications of the government of British Columbia, 1871-1947.* Victoria, Provincial Library.

MacDonald, Christine
1952 *Publications of the governments of the Northwest Territories, 1876-1905 and of the Province of Saskatchewan, 1905-1952.* Regina, Legislative Library.

Unfortunately, however, none of these guides is very helpful for obtaining citations about the Native Peoples of Canada. Beyond these listings, both on the provincial and on the municipal level, there is very little to consult, aside from the *Index to Current Urban Documents*, noted previously.

From the preceding discussion, it can be seen that a great need in the field of Native American studies is a comprehensive, well-indexed bibliography and guide to the government publications of the United States, Canada, and Mexico. To compile such a guide and bibliography would take a great deal in time, money, personnel, and dedication, but the result would well repay the effort involved. We do not see any possibility of such a guide's being published in the near future, however.

Finally, a recent publication provides an extensive sampling of various types of U.S. federal government documents relating to the North American Indian, including Reports of the U.S. Commissioner of Indian Affairs, congressional debates on Indian affairs, treaties, etc. This should give the researcher a good idea of the kind of information contained in these various types of publication. The citation is:

Washburn, Wilcomb E., comp.
1973 *The American Indian and the United States; a documentary history.* New York, Random House. 4 v.

Indian Claims

Closely related to the preceding is a group of publications partly governmental and partly nongovernmental in origin. These relate to the United States Indian Claims Commission and comprise its decisions, the reports of expert testimony before it, and the General Accounting Office reports on its awards. The Indian Claims Commission hears and determines claims against the United States on behalf of any Indian tribe, band, or other identifiable group of American Indians residing within the United States. The Commission was established by Act of Congress of August 13, 1946, and is independent of all other agencies of the U.S. government. A large number of claims has been adjudicated by the Commission since that time. In the course of adjudication, claims have been brought, the testimony of Indians and academic experts (e.g. anthropologists, historians, lawyers) heard, and decisions rendered. Naturally, since these claims involve American Indian groups, all of the information contained in these cases is properly the subject of this bibliography. Unfortunately, until very recently, this information has not been generally available. However, two private companies, both based in New York City, are now in the process of publishing most, if not all, of these data.

Garland Publishing, Inc. has organized reports of expert testimony and findings by tribe into 118 volumes, with the series entitled "American Indian Ethnohistory," being edited by David Agee Horr of Brandeis University. The Clearwater Publishing Company is making available on microfiche the decisions of the Commission and also the reports of expert testimony. Index volumes to each of the series are available in hard copy or on microfiche. The publishers also plan to make available on microfiche the General Accounting Office reports on awards. In additon, individual reports of expert testimony on hard copy (i.e. paper, not microfiche) are available on demand. In general, for information on the availability of all these material, it is a good idea to check the current *Subject Guide to Books in Print* under the heading Indians of North American—Indian Claims, or write the publishers. It might be noted that the total number of pages involved in these cases will probably exceed 150,000 (the equivalent of approximately 500 volumes containing 300 pages each). Having this vast amount of data available should have a great effect on studies of the North American Indian.

ERIC

ERIC (Educational Resources Information Center) is a nationwide, comprehensive information system under the jurisdiction of the Department of Health, Education, and Welfare, which is concerned with the transmittal of the results of research in education and related fields to the government, the public, the education profession, and to commercial and industrial organizations. A network of clearinghouses in different parts of the country under the general supervision of central ERIC in Washington gathers, organizes, indexes, and disseminates the most significant educational research or research-related documents that fall within their specialized subject areas. As part of its function, ERIC publishes the abstract journal *Resources in Education* (formerly *Research in Education*). This journal catalogs, abstracts, and indexes a large number of reports, both published and unpublished, every year. Many of these reports relate directly or indirectly to Native American studies. A very valuable feature of this journal is that nearly all of the items abstracted are available in a reproduced form on microfiche and/or paper copy. For the user, this means that many papers and fugitive documents, which would otherwise be extremely difficult to locate and ac-

quire, are now easily available. In the following bibliography, where it is known that ERIC has made the document available, we have included the ERIC accession number—which is needed for ordering the document—as part of the citation. This accession number appears at the end of the citation as a six-digit number, preceded by the acronym ERIC and the letters ED, e.g. ERIC ED045687. To order an ERIC document, follow the directions given below, which are taken from the May 1975 issue of *Resources in Education*. Since ERIC prices have changed in the past, it is best to check the most recent issue of *Resources in Education* to be certain of the price schedule, but the essentials are listed here. We have tried to be as accurate as possible in transferring the ERIC accession numbers in *Resources in Education* to the citations in this bibliography. However, it is probable that some errors in transcription have crept in during the process. Therefore, it would probably be safest if the user were to check the original abstracts in *Resources in Education* before ordering. The abstracts are listed in accession number order in the journal from 1966 on.

ORDERING ERIC DOCUMENTS

Mail orders to:
ERIC Document Reproduction Service
P.O. Box 190,
Arlington, Virginia 22210

Order by accession number (ED Number)
Specify microfiche (MF) or paper copy (HC)
Use the price schedule below.
Enclose check or money order PAYABLE TO EDRS
Official institution, State, Federal government purchase orders accepted.

MICROFICHE (MF)

Number of microfiche	Price
1 to 5	$ .75
6	.90
7	1.05
8	1.20
Each additional microfiche	.15

Postage: $.18 for up to 60 microfiche
$.08 for each additional 60 fiche

PAPER COPY (HC)

Number of pages	Price
1 to 25	$1.50
26 to 50	1.85
51 to 75	3.15
76 to 100	4.20
Each additional	
25 pages	1.20

Postage: $.18 for first 100 pages
$.08 for each additional 100 pages

Note
1. Postage for first class airmail or foreign is extra.
2. Paper copy (HC) will be full page reproductions with heavy paper covers.

Theses and Dissertations

This bibliography classifies and lists published print-ed materials on Native American studies, but does not attempt to do the same for the many unpublished documents that are available. This is not to say, however, that such materials do not form an important adjunct to Native American studies — in fact, in the case of theses and dissertations, a vitally important one. Fortunately, we have two very useful aids for locating and making available theses and dissertations relating to our subject field. These are the two-volume bibliography compiled by the Dockstaders and the publications of Xerox University Microfilms.

The full citations for the Dockstader volumes are:

Dockstader, Frederick J., comp.
    1973 *The American Indian in graduate studies; a bibliography of theses and dissertations.* 2d ed. New York, Museum of the American Indian, Heye Foundation. (Museum of the American Indian, Heye Foundation, Contributions, v. 25, pt. 1)

Dockstader, Frederick J., and Alice W. Dockstader, comps.
    1974 *The American Indian in graduate studies; a bibliography of theses and dissertations.* New York, Museum of the American Indian, Heye Foundation. (Museum of the American Indian, Heye Foundation, Contributions, v. 25, pt. 2)

In spite of the title, theses and dissertations on the Eskimos are also included in this bibliography. The two volumes list 7,446 items, covering the period between 1890 and 1970, inclusive. It is well indexed (in part 2) and easy to use, and includes the addresses of the relevant institutions for borrowing purposes. This is the only reference tool that contains a comprehensive listing of master's theses relating to our subject. The listing of dissertations overlaps considerably that in the tools discussed immediately below, but it has the advantages of being specific to our subject and of being available in an easily usable, compact form.

Xerox University Microfilms (XUM) publishes two important aids, which together control the vast number of dissertations issued in the United States and Canada and several other countries as well. These are:

Dissertation Abstracts International
    1935- Ann Arbor, Mich., Xerox University Microfilms. (formerly called *Microfilm Abstracts* and *Dissertation Abstracts*)

Comprehensive Dissertation Index, 1861-1972
    1973- Ann Arbor, Mich., Xerox University Microfilms. 37 v. (annual cumulations are also issued)

Dissertation Abstracts International is a monthly compilation of abstracts of the doctoral dissertations that have been submitted to XUM by cooperating educational institutions, principally in the United States and Canada. It is, therefore, an incomplete listing, since some institutions do not require that dissertations be sent to XUM, and some institutions make copies of the dissertations available on their own. However, a tremendous number are abstracted and indexed. The journal is issued in two sections: Humanities (A) and Sciences (B), which are paginated separately. Key-word title indexes and author indexes are published in each issue. These monthly indexes are cumulated annually. Each of the sections (A) and (B) is divided into subsections by major academic discipline. Most of the dissertations relevant to Native American studies will be found in the subsections devoted to Anthropology, Education, Geography, and History. However, they are also found scattered through a range of other subsections as disparate as Home Economics and Geology.

A major problem in using *Dissertation Abstracts International* is that what must be used as a subject index is the key-word title index, in which the bibliographic entries are classified and arranged alphabetically by key words contained in the title only. In other words, if a title does not contain the key words Indian, Eskimo, Native American, or the name of a tribal group, the dissertation will not be found under any of these headings in the index. Thus it could be very easy to miss what might be a very important dissertation relating to a particular research subject. The same caution applies to the *Comprehensive Dissertation Index*, which will be discussed below. Because of this problem, the compilers of this edition of the bibliography, in addition to using the various indexes, also checked the abstracts on every page of the most relevant discipline subsections (Anthropology, History, Education, Geography, Geology, Home Economics, Psychology, Social Psychology, Sociology) for the years 1955 to 1972 inclusive in *Dissertation Abstracts International*. Through this procedure, we hope that we have been able to list most of the dissertations relevant to Native American studies. We have been so thorough because we believe that such dissertations contain much of the most important recent work in this field. The citations listed in our bibliography refer to the abstracts in the journal only, and not to the original dissertations. Our citations also include the XUM publication number, which will be found at the end of the citation, e.g. UM 61-23, 609. We have included the publication number, because each dissertation so designated is available from XUM either on microfilm or in Xerographic paper copy. The ordering information for such copies is as follows (information taken from the April 1975 issue of *Dissertation Abstracts International*):

1. Order by publication number and author's name and specify whether a positive microfilm copy or a bound Xerographic paper copy is wanted.

2. Send the order to Xerox University Microfilms, Dissertation Copies, Post Office Box 1764, Ann Arbor, Michigan 48106. The standard charge for any microfilmed dissertation is $5.00; for a Xerographic paper copy, $11.00. Shipping and handling charges and any applicable taxes are additional. Individuals must send checks or money orders with their orders.

While we have made every effort in the compilation of this bibliography to make sure that we have copied the XUM publication numbers correctly, ordinary caution dictates that the abstract itself be rechecked before ordering from XUM.

The *Comprehensive Dissertation Index 1861-1972* covers about 417,000 doctoral dissertations accepted by United States educational institutions and by some foreign universities. It is based both on entries from *Dissertation Abstracts International* and on local school handlists. The indexing system is similar to that in *Dissertation Abstracts International* and has the same inherent problem of the title key-word index. Under each key word, the titles are listed first by the date of the dissertation, with the most recent first, followed alphabetically by the name of the school, and then by the name of the author. This is the most comprehensive listing of dissertations available and is quite useful for that reason. The *Index* is supplemented by annual cumulations.

Manuscripts and Archives

Research with manuscripts and archives is a very special and complicated field, which is outside the scope of this bibliography. However, there is a great fund of information available in these resources, which can be very useful in some specialized studies. Since these types of materials cannot be discussed adequately in the space available here, we will simply list first a general work discussing research in archives, and then a few publications relating to archives and manuscript collections which contain material relevant to Native American studies.

Brooks, Philip Coolidge
> 1969 *Research in archives; the use of unpublished primary sources*. Chicago, University of Chicago Press.

This is an introduction for the beginner, which concentrates on research procedures, with emphasis on American archives.

Beers, Henry Putney
> 1957 *The French in North America; a bibliographical guide to French archives, reproductions, and research missions*. Baton Rouge, Louisiana State University Press.

> 1964 *The French & British in the Old Northwest; a bibliographical guide to archive and manuscript sources*. Detroit, Wayne State University Press.

California. University. Bancroft Library
> 1963 *A guide to the manuscript collections*. Edited by Dale L. Morgan and George P. Hammond. Berkeley, Published for the Bancroft Library by the University of California Press. v. 1.

Carnegie Institution, Washington
> 1906- [*Guides to manuscript materials for the*
> 1943 *history of the United States.*] Washington, D.C., The Institution. 23 v. (Reprinted in 1965. The title is a collective one, with individual titles varying considerably.)

Canada. Public Archives
> 1968 *Union list of manuscripts in Canadian repositories*. Ottawa, Public Archives of Canada.

Fenton, William N., et al.
> 1957 *American Indian and White relations to 1830: needs and opportunities for study*. Chapel Hill, University of North Carolina Press.

Fliegel, Carl John
  1970 *Index to the records of the Moravian Mission among the Indians of North America.* New Haven, Research Publications.

Freeman, John Frederick
  1966 *A guide to the manuscripts relating to the American Indian in the library of the American Philosophical Society.* Philadelphia, The Society. (American Philosophical Society, Memoir, 65)

National Union Catalog of Manuscript Collections
  1959- Hamden, Conn., Shoe String Press; Washington, D.C., Library of Congress. (SuDocs no. LC9.8:) (Still in progress; lists a very large number of collections, many relevant to Native American studies.)

Newberry Library, Chicago. Edward E. Ayer Collection
  1937 *A check list of manuscripts in the Edward E. Ayer collection.* Compiled by Ruth Lapham Butler. Chicago, The Library.

U.S. National Archives
  1972 *The American Indian. Select catalog of National Archives microfilm publications.* Washington, D.C., National Archives and Records Service. (U.S. National Archives, Publication 72-27) (SuDocs no. GS4. 2: In 2)

  1974 *Guide to the National Archives of the United States.* Washington, D.C., National Archives and Records Service. (SuDocs no. GS4.6/2:N21)

U.S National Historical Publications Commission
  1961 *A guide to archives and manuscripts in the United States.* Philip M. Hamer, ed. New Haven, Yale University Press. (A basic listing. Look under Indians, American.)

Yale University. Library. Yale University Collection of Western Americana
  1952 *A catalogue of the manuscripts in the Collection of Western Americana founded by William Robertson Coe, Yale University Library.* Compiled by Mary C. Withington. New Haven, Yale University Press.

In addition to the above, the archives catalog of numbered manuscripts of the National Anthropo-

logical Archives at the Smithsonian Institution in Washington is scheduled for publication by G. K. Hall in Boston in 1975. The catalog will cover about a quarter of the total collection and will obviously be of great importance to researchers on the Native Americans.

Nonprint Materials and Maps

As noted previously, nonprint materials and maps have not been included in this bibliography. Because of their growing importance and widespread use, however, we will try to indicate in the following section the principal resources to use in locating relevant materials of these types. A general introductory work on reference tools in the audiovisual field is that by Limbacher, which annotates a number of the basic sources. Also basic is the Brigham Young University bibliography, which lists about 1,400 items, covering all types of nonprint instructional materials. The citations are:

Limbacher, James
  1972 *A reference guide to audiovisual information.* New York, R. R. Bowker.

Brigham Young University, Provo, Utah. Instructional Development Program
  1972 *Bibliography of nonprint instructional materials on the American Indian.* Provo, Institute of Indian Services and Research. ERIC ED070310.

The most complete general tools in this field are the *Library of Congress Catalog* and its continuation, the *National Union Catalog,* cited as:

U.S. Library of Congress
  1947- *Library of Congress catalog; a cumu-*
  1955 *lative list of works represented by Library of Congress printed cards. Books: authors.* Washington, D.C., The Library. (SuDocs no. LC30.8:)

National Union Catalog: A Cumulative Author List Representing Library of Congress Printed Cards and Some Titles Reported by Other American Libraries.
  1956- Washington, D.C., The Library. (SuDocs no. LC30.8:)

These two publications list a large number of sound recordings, films, and maps. Beginning in 1953, entries for *Maps and Atlases, Films and Filmstrips,* and *Music and Phonorecords* formed separate parts of the *Library of Congress Catalog.* In the *National Union Catalog, Films and Other Materials for Projection* (formerly *Motion Pictures and Filmstrips*) and *Music and Phonorecords* form separate parts of the catalog, but the section on maps and atlases does not. The *National Union Catalog* is issued monthly, with nine monthly issues and three quarterly cumulations each year, four annual cumulations, and a general cumulation every five years. These latter quinquennial cumulations have been issued for the years 1953-1957, 1958-1962, 1963-1967, and 1968-1972. The sections cited within these cumulations, with their individual subject indexes, form a great bibliographical resource for nonprint materials. The Library of Congress publishes a listing of the subject headings used in its dictionary catalogs and publications. Users of these publications should become familiar with these headings, since they facilitate use of the catalogs and indexes. These headings are discussed more fully on p. xxviii.

Since the above catalogs list only those materials received *and* cataloged by the Library of Congress and the cooperating libraries, the researcher must necessarily use other tools as well, if he wants his search to be as complete as possible. Therefore, we will go on to discuss other reference tools for locating relevant information on sound recordings, films, and maps, in that order.

Sound Recordings

As a brief introduction to the field, the user might want to consult the article by Highwater, which mentions some of the problems involved and the general types of recordings available:

Highwater, Jamake Mamake (J. Marks)
1973 American Indian music; a brief guide to the (recorded) real thing. *Stereo Review*, 30, no. 3: 134-135.

Two major reference tools may be used to keep up with sound recordings generally. The first is:

U.S. Library of Congress
1973- *Music, books on music and sound recordings*. Washington, D.C., The Library. (SuDocs no. LC30.8/6:)

This is a continuing and cumulative list of works that have been cataloged by the Library of Congress and by several North American libraries selected by the Music Library Association as representing a broad spectrum of music collections. It appears semiannually and is cumulated annually, and in the quinquennial cumulations of the *National Union Catalog* (noted above). Check the subject index under the usual Library of Congress subject headings.

The journal *Ethnomusicology*, published by the Society for Ethnomusicology, includes in each issue a current bibliography and discography of ethnic music, as well as reviews of selected sound recordings. Native American materials are listed in the

bibliography under "Americas-recordings."

The National Information Center for Educational Media (NICEM) publishes irregularly two indexes which indicate the availability of a number of specialized sound recordings. These are the *Index to Educational Audio Tapes* and the *Index to Educational Records*. The subject index in each should be checked under the headings Social Science-Indians of North America, Sociology-Anthropology, and History-U.S. The index entries refer back to the main listings, which include information on availability and contents.

For current information on commercially available phonograph recordings, check the semiannual *Schwann-2 Guide* under the heading Indian, American, in the section headed International Popular & Folk Music. The full citation is:

Schwann-2 Record & Tape Guide
1965- Boston, W. Schwann.

Three sources taken together list many of the earlier sound recordings relating to the Native Americans. These are:

International Folk Music Council
1954 *International catalogue of recorded folk music*. Edited by Norman Fraser. London, Published for UNESCO by Oxford University Press. (Archives de la Musique Enregistrée, Série C: Musique Ethnographique et Folklorique, 4)

Kunst, Jaap
1959, *Ethnomusicology, a study of its na-*
1960 *ture, its problems, methods and representative personalities to which is added a bibliography*. 3d enlarged edition, and supplement. The Hague, Martinus Nijhoff.

U.S. Library of Congress. Music Division
1964 *Folk music; a catalog of folk songs, ballads, dances, instrumental pieces, and folk tales of United States and Latin America on phonograph records*. Washington, D.C., The Library (SuDocs no. LC12.2:F71/3/964)

While the above tools will help the researcher locate information on particular recordings, he still has to find the recordings themselves. The Archive of Folk Song at the Library of Congress has quite a large collection of recordings of Native American music. In addition, the researcher should turn to the following publication, which lists 124 collections in the United States and Canada, most of which have holdings in the music of the Native Americans:

Society for Ethnomusicology
    1971 *Directory of ethnomusicological and sound recording collections in the U.S. and Canada.* Edited by Ann Briegleb. Ann Arbor, Mich., Society for Ethnomusicology. (Society for Ethnomusicology, Special Series, 2)

Films

A basic source of information on films is the Library of Congress publication, *Films and Other Materials for Projection*, whose subject index should be consulted under the usual Library of Congress subject headings. This continuing list of works cataloged by the Library of Congress appears quarterly and is cumulated annually and quinquennially, the latter as part of the *National Union Catalog*. The full citation is:

U.S. Library of Congress
    1953- *Films and other materials for projection.* Washington, D.C., The Library. (SuDocs no. LC30.8/4:) formerly titled *Motion Pictures and Filmstrips*)

There is quite a good listing of 251 "Educational films on the American Indian" compiled by George Hunt and Frank Lobo, on pages 718-744 of Owen et al.'s source book. This title list with annotations presents films available in 1965-1966 and is a good place to begin a search. The full citation is:

Owen, Roger C., et al.
    1967 *The North American Indians: a source book.* New York, Macmillan.

The National Information Center for Educational Media at the University of Southern California in Pasadena has published since 1969 a series of educational film indexes, which include much material relating to the Native Americans. These NICEM Media Indexes, which are revised at irregular intervals, are:

Index to 16mm. educational films;
Index to 35mm. educational filmstrips;
Index to 8mm. motion cartridges;
Index to educational overhead transparencies;
Index to educational video tapes.

In the subject indexes, the primary heading to investigate is Social Sciences-Indians of North America. Other headings which should be checked are History-U.S. and Sociology-Anthropology.

In addition to the above, the American Anthropological Association publishes a selected catalog of ethnographic films for teaching purposes. The films are listed alphabetically by title. The listings include technical data, rental and purchase fees, a directory of distributors, a brief description of each film, and bibliographical and review data. Relevant films can be located under North America in the geographical index. The citation is:

Heider, Karl G.
    1972 *Films for anthropological teaching.* 5th ed. Washington, D.C., American Anthropological Association.

Maps

It is not easy to locate relevant maps for research purposes. Maps are included in the printed catalog of the Library of Congress, but except for a few years in the 1950s, they are not listed separately from books. As a result, trying to locate a map in the various card catalogs issued by the Library is a long and tedious process, and is not recommended. Among the many reference tools available, the following would probably be the more helpful to users of this bibliography.

The American Geographical Society has two publications, a retrospective catalog and a current list, which are good places to check for maps in this field. These are:

American Geographical Society of New York
    1938- *Current geographical publications; additions to the research catalogue of the American Geographical Society.* New York, The Society.

    1968, *Index to maps in books and period-*
    1971 *icals.* Boston, G. K. Hall. 10 v. plus one supplement.

The first lists selected maps received by the Society in a separate section in each issue, and is arranged by region and then by subject. Look under the human (cultural) geography numbers (5-57). The second is a bibliography of maps that have appeared in books or articles, not as separate publications. Check under Eskimos, Ethnography, Ethnology, Indians, and the names of various tribes.

Another general retrospective source is the card catalog of the Map Division of the New York Public Library, which has a very large collection. Check under Eskimos, Ethnology (with the names of tribes), and Indians. The citation is:

New York (City) Public Library. Research Libraries
    1971 *Dictionary catalog of the Map Division.* Boston, G. K. Hall. 10 v.

In additon to these American publications, there are two foreign-language current and comprehensive indexes available. These are the *Bibliographie Cartographique Internationale* (French) and *Referativnyi Zhurnal: Geografiia* (Russian), with the former probably being more accessible to American users. The citations are:

Bibliographie Cartographique Internationale
  1938- Paris, Armand Colin.

Referativnyi Zhurnal: Geografiia
  1954- Moskva, Akademiia Nauk SSSR, Institut Nauchnoi Informatsii.

In addition to the above, two other bibliographies may be useful for special purposes. These are:

Wheat, Carl Irving
  1957- *Mapping the Transmississippi West,*
  1963 *1540-1861.* San Francisco, Institute of Historical Cartography. 5 v. in 6.

Wheat, James Clements, and Christian F. Brun
  1969 *Maps and charts published in America before 1800; a bibliography.* New Haven, Yale University Press.

Beyond these, there are several lists and catalogs of individual collections which can be very helpful in locating individual maps. Especially to be noted are those in the National Archives, which contain basic data on Native American groups over a 200-year period.

California. University. Bancroft Library
  1964 *Index to printed maps.* Boston, G. K. Hall.

Newberry Library, Chicago. Edward E. Ayer Collection
  1927 *List of manuscript maps in the Edward E. Ayer collection.* Compiled by Clara A. Smith. Chicago, The Library.

U.S. Library of Congress. Map Division
  1909- *A list of geographical atlases in the*
  1973 *Library of Congress with bibliographical notes.* Compiled by Philip Lee Phillips and Clara Egli LeGear. Washington, D.C., Government Printing Office. 7 v. (in progress) (SuDocs no. LC5.2:G291/)

  1950- *United States atlases; a catalog of*
  1953 *national, state, county, city, and regional atlases in the Library of Congress and cooperating libraries.* Compiled by Clara Egli LeGear. Washington, D.C., Government Printing Office. 2 v. (SuDocs no. LC5.2:Un351/)

U.S. National Archives
  1954 *List of cartographic records of the Bureau of Indian Affairs (Record group 75).* Compiled by Laura E. Kelsay. Washington, D.C., National Archives. (U.S., National Archives, Publications, 55-1; Special Lists, 13) (SuDocs no. GS4.7:13)
  1971 *Guide to cartographic records in the National Archives.* Washington, D.C., National Archives and Records Service. (U.S., National Archives, Publications, 71-16) (SuDocs no. GS4.6/2:C24)
  1974 *Cartographic records in the National Archives of the United States relating to American Indians.* Washington, D.C., National Archives and Records Service. (SuDocs no. GS4.15:71)

In addition to the publications listed above, the reference tools listed in the section on government publications should also be checked, since the United States and Canadian governments publish many maps.

Going Beyond This Bibliography

While this bibliography is certainly a large one, it is still a *selected* bibliography, and it does not pretend to approach completeness on its subject, particularly for the earlier materials. Therefore, if completeness on a particular group or subject is desired, recourse must be made to a large variety of bibliographical reference tools, those used depending upon whether the researcher intend to make a complete retrospective search for all relevant published materials, or whether he/she be interested only in recently published items. If it be the latter, he/she will use recent issues of recurrent periodical and book indexes. If he/she be interested in a complete search, he/she will use these as well as numerous retrospective bibliographies and catalogs. The general approach to library research and use of these bibliographical tools is examined in a number of works. Reference can be made to those listed immediately below, and to the volumes by Freides and Katz listed later in this section.

Cook, Margaret G.
  1963 *The new library key.* 2d ed. New York, H. W. Wilson.

Downs, Robert B.
  1966 *How to do library research.* Urbana, University of Illinois Press.

Frantz, Charles
  1972 *The student anthropologist's handbook; a guide to research, training, and career.* Cambridge, Mass., Schenkman Publishing Company.

Fried, Morton H.
> 1972 *The study of anthropology.* New York, Thomas Y. Crowell Company.

Hook, Lucyle, and Mary V. Gaver
> 1969 *The research paper; gathering library material, organizing and preparing the manuscript.* 4th ed. Englewood Cliffs, N.J., Prentice-Hall.

Current Bibliographical Tools

Because this is a retrospective bibliography through the year 1972, and because a new edition is not scheduled to be compiled for several years, we have decided that a brief commentary on what we have found to be the more useful of the recurrent bibliographical tools for obtaining information about the Native Americans might be of benefit to the researcher. The following list of bibliographies and indexes is only a small part of the large number of reference tools that can be used for this type of search. All of those listed, except for the *Current Index to Journals on Education*, the *Social Sciences Index*, the *National Indian Law Library Catalogue*, and the *Internationale Bibliographie des Zeitschriftenliteratur aus allen Gebieten des Wissens*, were utilized in the preparation of the present bibliography. Perhaps the basic tools for anyone doing a bibliographic search of current materials on the Native Americans would be, in order of currentness: *American Book Publishing Record; Public Affairs Information Service Bulletin; Anthropological Index to Current Periodicals Received in the Library of the Royal Anthropological Institute; America: History and Life; Library of Congress Catalog. Books: Subjects; Subject Guide to Books in Print; Index to Literature on the American Indian; International Bibliography of Social and Cultural Anthropology;* and the *Bibliographie Américaniste*. Many of the indexes and bibliographies listed below are discussed in the general reference works, particularly those by Freides and Katz, to be mentioned later.

The indexes and bibliographies discussed below are subject indexed or classified in some way. The most commonly used subject headings are based on the system used by the Library of Congress. However, many indexes follow an arrangement based on the Dewey Decimal Classification. *Resources in Education* and *Current Index to Journals in Education* use a special set of descriptors listed in the *Thesaurus of ERIC Descriptors*. Those not using any of the above usually have their own special classifications and headings, with which the researcher should become familiar before using the indexes and bibliographies. The numerous indexes published by the

H. W. Wilson Company and the R. R. Bowker Company use subject headings based primarily on the Library of Congress list and on the Sears list (see below).

We list below the most relevant headings in each of the three major systems for ease in using the reference tools based on these systems.

Library of Congress Subject Headings:

Aleut
Beadwork
Eskimos
Folk-lore, Eskimo
Folk-lore, Indian
Hymns, [plus tribal name]
Indian Ponies
Indian Warfare
Indians
Indians of North America
Indians of North America as Soldiers
Indians, Civilization of
Moccasins
Numeration, Indian
Picture-writing, Indian
Wampum, Indian
Yuit Language

Dewey Decimal Classification:

016.9701 (bibliography on the American Indian)
497 (American aboriginal languages)
722.91 (architecture, ancient American)
784.751 (songs of Amerindians)
789.91364751 (recordings of Amerindian songs)
897 (literatures in American aboriginal languages)
917.1-917.98 (geography of North America)
970.1 (Indians of North America)
970.3 (specific Indian tribes)
970.4 (Indians in specific places in North America)
970.5 (government relations with Indians)

The terms "Amerindian" and "Indian" used here also include Eskimo.

ERIC Descriptors:
American Indian
American Indians
Bureau of Indian Affairs
Canadian Indians
Canadian Eskimos
Eskimo
Eskimos

The citations for the base documents for these headings are:

Dewey, Melvil
   1971 *Decimal classification and relative index.* 18th ed. Lake Placid Club, N.Y., Forest Press, Inc., of Lake Placid Club Education Foundation. 3 v.

Sears, Minnie E.
   1972 *Sears list of subject headings.* 10th ed. Edited by Barbara M. Westby. New York, H. W. Wilson.

U.S. Educational Resources Information Center
   1974 *Thesaurus of ERIC descriptors.* 5th ed. New York, Macmillan Information.

U.S. Library of Congress. Subject Cataloging Division
   1966 *Subject headings used in the dictionary catalogs of the Library of Congress.* 7th ed. Edited by Marguerite V. Quattlebaum. Washington, D.C., The Library. (SuDocs no. LC26.7:7)

The following list of recurrent indexes and bibliographies is divided into several sections, with comments on general reference tools being followed by comments on reference tools in several subject fields. We have indicated in these listings whether the reference tool uses the Library of Congress subject headings (alone or in conjunction with the Sears headings), the Dewey Decimal Classification, or the ERIC Descriptors, by placing the label [LC], [DDC], or [ERIC], respectively, after the title.

Books.

American Book Publishing Record [DDC]
   1961- New York, R. R. Bowker.

Canadiana [DDC]
   1951- Ottawa, Information Canada.

Bibliografía Mexicana
   1967- México, D. F., Biblioteca Nacional de México, Instituto de Investgaciones Bibliográficas.

U.S. Library of Congress [LC]
   1950- *Library of Congress catalog. Books: subjects. A cumulated list of works represented by Library of Congress printed cards.* Washington, D.C., The Library. (SuDocs no. LC30.8/3:)

Cumulative Book Index [LC]
   1898- New York, H. W. Wilson.

Subject Guide to Forthcoming Books
   1967- New York, R. R. Bowker.

These six tools are grouped together because they appear a varying number of times each year. The *American Book Publishing Record* appears monthly, and is cumulated annually and quinquennially in *BPR Cumulative* (not discussed here). It lists books by United States publishers only, but includes some foreign works handled by these publishers. Book titles are classified by subject, with an author and title index. *Canadiana* appears monthly, with annual cumulations. It is concerned with books, pamphlets, and periodicals (but not articles) of Canadian interest. It is a classified list of catalog cards, and has French- and English-language indexes. *Bibliografía Mexicana* appears bimonthly in a classified arrangement with an author-title subject index in the individual issues. It is not cumulated, and refers only to Mexican book publications. Basic headings to check are etnología, costumbres, folclore, and arqueología. The *Library of Congress Catalog. Books: Subjects* appears in three quarterly issues, with annual and quinquennial cumulations. It is international in scope and covers books cataloged during a specified period. Thus it is a retrospective tool as well. The *Cumulative Book Index* is a monthly, with quarterly and annual cumulations. It includes most books published in the English language and is not limited to American publications. The *Subject Guide to Forthcoming Books* appears bimonthly and lists books by American publishers due to appear in the near future. Headings to check are History-U.S. and Sociology, Anthropology, and Archeology-Anthropology.

Subject Guide to Books in Print [LC]
   1957- New York, R. R. Bowker.

Subject Guide to Microforms in Print
   1962/63- Washington, D.C., Microcard Editions.

These two annual guides provide subject approaches for determining the availability for purchase of in-print books and microforms, respectively. The first is based on *Books in Print*, which provides an author-title approach to currently available United States publications. The *Books in Print Supplement*, an annual that was first issued in 1973, provides an author-title-subject approach to the books published since the last annual issue of *Books in Print*. Thus it also supplements the *Subject Guide to Books in Print*. The *Subject Guide to Microforms in Print* is a classified list of available microfilm, microcards, and microfiche books. Relevant items can be located under 440 (America-General) and 970 (Languages and Literatures-Non-European). These guides are restricted to publications available in the United States.

Articles.

> *Reader's Guide to Periodical Literature* [LC]
> 1905-   New York, H. W. Wilson.

> *Canadian Periodical Index*
> 1948-   Ottawa, Canadian Library Association.

> *Essay and General Literature Index* [LC]
> 1900-   New York, H. W. Wilson.

> *Internationale Bibliographie des Zeitschriften-*
> *literatur aus allen Gebieten des Wissens*
> 1965-   Osnabrück, Felix Dietrich.

These four tools are concerned with indexing journal articles, together with essays and book chapters forming parts of collected works. The *Reader's Guide to Periodical Literature* appears semimonthly, with quarterly, annual, and biennial cumulations. It covers about 160 magazines of broad, general, and popular interest published in the United States. The *Canadian Periodical Index* is a monthly subject index to about 90 general magazines published in Canada and is approximately equivalent in aims and type of coverage to the *Reader's Guide to Periodical Literature*. The *Essay and General Literature Index* analyzes essays and articles in volumes of English-language collections of essays and miscellaneous works written by individual authors in all fields of the humanities and the social sciences. Individual chapters are listed by author and subject. Since very few indexes cover the contents of such collections, this is the only relatively easy way to get at this type of material. The *Internationale Bibliographie . . .* is an attempt at a world periodical index, with more than 7,500 periodicals being consulted. Headings to check in the "Schlagwort" index are Eskimo, Eskimoische, Indianer, and Indianische.

Books and articles combined.

> Arctic Institute of North America
> 1953-   *Arctic bibliography.* Washington, D.C.,
> and Montreal. (SuDocs no. D1.22:)

> *Bibliographie Américaniste*
> 1914/19-   Paris, Société des Américanistes.

> *Vertical File Index* [LC]
> 1932/34-   New York, H. W. Wilson.

> *Index to Literature on the American Indian*
> 1972-   San Francisco, Indian Historian Press.
> (Covers the literature from 1970 on.)

These four tools index a combination of materials. The *Arctic Bibliography* appears irregularly and apparently will cease publication in the near future. It covers and abstracts published materials in all lan-

guages relating to the Arctic, and thus contains citations relating to Alaska, Greenland, and most of Canada and eastern Siberia. It is one of the best available bibliographies in terms of completeness, coverage, and indexing. The index should be consulted under Aleuts, Eskimos, and Indians. The *Bibliographie Américaniste* appeared annually as part of the *Journal de la Société des Américanistes* through vol. 53 (1964), and as a separate publication thereafter. It is classified by major subjects (archéologie, ethnologie, etc.) and within the major subjects by major areas (Amérique du Nord, etc.). It is very good for non-English-language materials, but lags greatly in publication. The *Vertical File Index* covers separate publications that are fewer that 49 pages in length and not usually picked up by the book and article indexes. It occasionally includes publications of much greater length. It appears monthly, with annual cumulations. The *Index to Literature on the American Indian* is an annual compilation by a group of Native American scholars which covers both Eskimo and Indian English-language materials. About 150 periodicals are searched and relevant books listed, usually under a variety of subject categories. This index, while not pretending to completeness, is a good place to begin a bibliographic search, because of its indexing and the completeness of its citations. Special features of its 1970 and 1971 volumes were long lists of Native American periodicals, with ordering information. This is a good place to see what was happening in this special field at that time.

Social Sciences.

> Public Affairs Information Service
> 1915-   *Bulletin.* New York, The Service.

> *Social Sciences Index* [LC]
> 1974-   New York, H. W. Wilson.

Both of these items are general social science indexes, with the first probably being the more useful at present. The *Public Affairs Information Service Bulletin*, usually known as *PAIS*, is a weekly index which is cumulated five times a year and annually. It is a selected subject index to more than 1,000 periodicals, as well as to some of the books and U.S. government publications that fall within this very broad field. Limited to works written in the English language, its coverage is international. Headings to check are Eskimos, Indians, and United States-Indian Affairs Bureau. The Service also publishes a bulletin surveying foreign-language materials, but it rarely includes any material on Native Americans in it. The *Social Sciences Index* replaced the *Social Sciences and Humanities Index* in 1974. A quarterly, with annual cumulations, it indexes 263 of the more scholarly English and American journals in the social sciences.

Anthropology.

Royal Anthropological Institute of Great Britain and Ireland. Library

1963- *Anthropological index to current periodicals received in the library of the Royal Anthropological Institute.* London, The Institute.

International Bibliography of Social and Cultural Anthropology

1955- London, Tavistock; Chicago, Aldine.

These tools cover the general anthropological literature. The *Anthropological Index* appears quarterly, has a worldwide coverage, and indexes about 500 periodicals in all fields of anthropology. Each issue classifies the articles listed by major world areas, and then by broad subject categories (archeology, cultural anthropology, etc.). The key section to check is America. The *International Bibliography of Social and Cultural Anthropology* appears annually and covers the anthropological publications issued during the listed year. Each volume appears two to three years after the listed date, which is understandable, considering its extensive coverage of books and articles in all languages. The citations are arranged in a unique classification scheme, with an author index and subject indexes in English and in French. Subject entry is therefore possible, and at times necessary, in three ways, through the classification and through both indexes, since the latter do not always jibe with each other.

History.

America: History and Life

1964- Santa Barbara, Calif., American Bibliographic Center-Clio Press.

Writings on American History

1906- New York, etc.

Revue d'Histoire de l'Amérique Française

1947- *Bibliographie d'histoire de l'Amérique française.* Montréal, Institut d'Histoire de l'Amérique Française.

Each of these tools contains numerous citations on the Native Peoples. *America: History and Life* is a quarterly abstract journal of United States and Canadian publications. Originally indexing only periodical literature, it began in 1974 to appear in three parts, A — article abstracts and citations; B — Index to book reviews; and C — American history index (books, articles, and dissertations). Subject headings to check are Eskimos, Indians, and the names of tribes. A cumulation of annotated entries on the

American Indian for the period 1954-1972, totaling 1,687 items, was issued in 1974. The citation is:

Smith, Dwight L., ed.

1974 *Indians of the United States and Canada; a bibliography.* Santa Barbara, Calif., ABC-Clio.

Writings on American History is an annual that has appeared irregularly and has ceased publication at various times in the past. The time lag between date of coverage and publication is now about fifteen years, but efforts are being made to catch up. Attempting a complete listing, it has a very thorough coverage of American publications. Check under Indians in the index. The *Bibliographie d'Histoire de l'Amérique Française* appears quarterly in the *Revue. . . .* Publications on Native America are covered in Section A. 1 ("Les civilisations amérindiennes et les premières découvertes"). The area coverage is limited to French America, but includes many books, articles, and theses that are hard to locate elsewhere.

Other Subjects.

Ethnomusicology

1953- *Current bibliography and discography.* Ann Arbor, Mich., Society for Ethnomusicology.

Music Index

1949- Detroit, Information Coordinators.

These list publications on Native American music. The *Current Bibliography . . .* appears three times a year in the journal *Ethnomusicology.* See the section labeled "Americas." The *Music Index* is a monthly, cumulated annually, giving subject and author entry to about 180 periodicals on music. Check the headings Eskimo Music; Indian, American; Indian Music, American; and Indian Music, North American.

American Geographical Society of New York

1938- *Current geographical publications.* New York, The Society.

This monthly is a classified listing of books, periodical articles, and maps received in the library of the Society. It is arranged by region, then by the Society's subject classification. Check North America and then the codes 5-57 for human (cultural) geography.

Art Index [LC]

1929- New York, H. W. Wilson.

This is a quarterly, with annual cumulations. It has a dictionary catalog arrangement and lists materials on many subjects related to the field of art, including, among others, archeology, arts and crafts, art history, and fine arts.

Current Index to Journals in Education [ERIC]
    1969- New York, Macmillan Information.

Education Index [LC]
    1929- New York, H. W. Wilson.

Resources in Education [ERIC]
    1966- Washington, D.C., U.S. Office of Education. (SuDocs no. HE18.10:)

The *Current Index to Journals in Education* (known also as *CIJE*) is a monthly index, cumulated annually, of about 700 United States and foreign education journals, which are scanned, briefly abstracted, and indexed by ERIC descriptors. The *Education Index* is a monthly, cumulated annually, subject index to 200 English-language education journals. There is some, but not a great deal of, overlap with *CIJE*. *Resources in Education* (formerly *Research in Education*) is a monthly listing of abstracts of research reports selected by ERIC clearinghouses and is indexed by ERIC descriptors.

Index Medicus
    1960- Washington, D.C., National Library of Medicine. (SuDocs no. HE20.3612:)

Biological Abstracts
    1926- Philadelphia.

Psychological Abstracts
    1927- Washington, D.C., American Psychological Association.

The *Index Medicus* (cumulated annually by the *Cumulated Index Medicus*, which is not discussed here) is a monthly subject index to the world's medical and medical-related periodical literature. It surveys several thousand periodicals in all languages, with over 200,000 articles being indexed each year. It is a basic index for human biology. It has its own list of subject headings, which is printed as part of each January issue. The two headings to check are Eskimos and Indians, North American. *Biological Abstracts* is a semimonthly abstract journal, covering more than 5,000 periodicals, which has a computer-produced index based on all significant words in the titles and the abstracts. It complements *Index Medicus* for human biology and related fields. *Psychological Abstracts* is a monthly abstract journal of periodical articles and books, with semiannual and annual subject indexes. Relevant citations will generally be found under Ethnology in the index, although this has varied in the past.

Business Periodicals Index [LC]
    1958- New York, H. W. Wilson.

Index to Legal Periodicals [LC]
    1909- New York, H. W. Wilson.

National Indian Law Library
    1973/74- *Catalogue*. Boulder, Colo.

Modern Language Association of America
    1921- *MLA international bibliography of books and articles on the modern languages and literatures.* New York, The Association.

Bibliographie Linguistique de l'Année . . .
    1949- Utrecht, Spectrum, for Comité International Permanent de Linguistique.

Business Periodicals Index is a monthly, cumulated annually, subject index to about 120 business periodicals, most of them not covered by other indexes. The *Index to Legal Periodicals* is a quarterly subject index to about 300 English-language legal periodicals, mainly university law reviews and bar association journals. Many articles are listed on Indian claims and general government relations. The *National Indian Law Library Catalogue* is a new annual index to Indian legal materials and resources. It has not yet been seen by the compilers. The *MLA International Bibliography . . .* is an annual bibliography in four volumes, which are bound together in the library edition. Volume 1 covers folklore, and Volume 3, linguistics. Each contains materials relating to the Native Americans in a classified arrangement, but the indexes are difficult to use. The *Bibliographie Linguistique . . .* is an annual bibliography containing a section on American languages [Langues américaines], with an author index. In spite of the publication lag of about three years, it is probably the first choice for information on Native American languages.

Retrospective Bibliographical Tools

Since this bibliography itself is a retrospective bibliography, and since the major tools for making retrospective searches are to be discussed comprehensively in the forthcoming introductory volume of the *Handbook of North American Indians*, the use of these tools will not be further dicussed here. However, we will list some references which will enable the researcher to make a beginning in this direction. In addition, the bibliographies listed in the area and ethnic bibliographies in the present set of volumes should be perused for additional materials, since not all of the citations contained in them have been utilized in the present bibliography.

Freides, Thelma K.
    1973 *Literature and bibliography of the social sciences.* Los Angeles, Melville Publishing Company.

Katz, William A.
    1974 *Introduction to reference work.* 2d ed. New York, McGraw-Hill Book Company. 2 v.

McInnis, Raymond G., and James W. Scott
1975   *Social science research handbook.* New York, Harper and Row, Barnes and Noble Books.

Walford, Arthur J., ed.
1973   *Guide to reference materials.* 3d ed. London, Library Association. 3 v.

White, Carl M., and associates
1973   *Sources of information in the social sciences; a guide to the literature.* 2d ed. Chicago, American Library Association.

Winchell, Constance M., ed.
1967   *Guide to reference books.* 8th ed. Chicago, American Library Association. (Three supplements compiled by Eugene P. Sheehy covering the years 1965 through 1970 have also been issued.)

Winchell and Walford are standard general guides to the reference literature, Winchell with an American and Walford with a European slant. The annotations of reference works in Winchell are more descriptive, while those in Walford are more critical. White and associates discuss social science materials in general and include separate chapters on history, geography, economics and business administration, sociology, anthropology, psychology, education, and political science. Each chapter contains two sections, one a bibliographical essay concentrating on the history of the subject, trends, areas of concern, and important works; the other a guide to the literature, annotating various types of information sources, such as abstracts and summaries, current and retrospective bibliographies, directories and biographical information, and sources of current information. The McInnis and Scott handbook is a bibliographical guide for students and others engaged in social science research. It is in two parts, one devoted to studies by discipline (anthropology, sociology, etc.), the other to area studies. Its orientation is toward the immediate assistance of students engaged in research, while that of White and associates is toward the scrutiny of the general social science information system and the evaluation of its major products. These four works together provide a general characterization of the tools available for bibliographical research, from which the researcher wishing to proceed further in his search for materials on the Native Americans may select the particular tools relevant to his needs. The remaining two works, by Katz and Freides, contain assessments of the general reference and social science literature and information from the librarian's point of view on how to proceed in library research. They form quite a useful adjunct to the detailed guides listed previously.

There remains the problem of actually locating copies of the chosen books and articles, once citations to them have been found. Procedures for doing this at the local library level are given in the guides cited at the beginning of this section (e.g. Cook 1963, Hook and Gaver 1969). If the materials not be in the local library, recourse may be made to the interlibrary loan system, the use of which can be arranged for by the librarian. Locations of library holdings of individual books in the United States and Canada are given in the *National Union Catalog*, while the locations of libraries that contain holdings of particular periodicals are given in the *Union List of Serials* and in *New Serial Titles*, cited below. A good aid for locating libraries with substantial holdings in the field is Ash's guide to subject collections, which lists numerous collections under the two headings: Eskimos and Indians of North America.

Ash, Lee, with the assistance of William Miller and Alfred Waltermire, Jr.
1974   *Subject collections; a guide to special book collections and subject emphases as reported by university, college, public, and special libraries and museums in the United States and Canada.* 4th ed. New York, R. R. Bowker.

New Serial Titles
1950-   Washington, D.C., Library of Congress. (8 issues a year, cumulated quarterly and annually) (SuDocs no. LC1.23/5:)

New Serial Titles 1950-1970
1972   New York, R. R. Bowker. 5 v. (cumulates the preceding)

Union List of Serials in Libraries of the United States and Canada
1965   3d ed. Edited by Edna Brown Titus. New York, H. W. Wilson. 5 v.

Handbook of North American Indians

Mention has been made a number of times in this introduction of the forthcoming *Handbook of North American Indians*. The *Handbook*, which is under the general editorship of William C. Sturtevant, is scheduled to be issued in 20 large volumes by the Smithsonian Institution Press beginning in 1976. This mammoth enterprise will summarize what is known of the anthropology and history of the Native Americans north of Mesoamerica. It should remain the standard reference work in the field for many years. As of this date, there has been only one generally available published description concerning the *Handbook*, its structure and contents. This is:

Sturtevant, William C.
1971   Smithsonian plans new Native American handbook. *Indian Historian 4, no. 4*: 5-8.

As noted previously, this edition of the bibliography has been enlarged and generally organized to cover as much as possible the same groups as are discussed in the *Handbook*. However, the fit between them is not particularly close at times, because of the different classificatory systems and emphases of the two works. We should point out that the articles in the *Handbook* will complement this bibliography very directly, in that much of the literature is given a critical discussion in these articles. In addition, the articles themselves will provide extensive bibliographies on the ethnic groups and subject fields discussed. Since the individual bibliographies will have been prepared by experts on these groups and fields, it is inevitable that there will be much in them which is not to be found in this bibliography. Of course, the converse will also be the case. Therefore, it will behoove the conscientious investigator to peruse both the present bibliography and those in the *Handbook* articles, in order to be certain that he/she has defined the general bibliographical parameters of the ethnic groups and subjects that he/she is studying.

Timothy J. O'Leary
June 1975

REFERENCES

Hodge, Frederick Webb, ed.
1910   *Handbook of American Indians north of Mexico. Pt. 2.* Washington, D.C., Government Printing Office. (U.S., Bureau of American Ethnology, Bulletin, 30, pt. 2) (SuDocs no. SI2.3:30/pt.2)

Swanton, John R.
1952   *The Indian tribes of North America.* Washington, D.C., Government Printing Office. (U.S., Bureau of American Ethnology, Bulletin, 145) (SuDocs no. SI2.3:145)

Abbreviations

A.D.	Anno Domini	n.p.	no place of publication
Alta.	Alberta	n.s.	new series
app.	appendix	N.Y.	New York
Apr.	April	no.	number
assoc.	association	Nov.	November
B.C.	British Columbia; Before Christ	Nr.	Nummer (number, in German)
Bd.	Band (volume in German)	o.s.	old series
ca.	circum, circa	Oct.	October
Calif.	California	Ont.	Ontario
Co.	Company	Or.	Oregon
col.	column(s)	p.	page, pages
Colo.	Colorado	pt.	part
comp.	compiler(s)	rev.	revised
Conn.	Connecticut	S.D.	South Dakota
D.C.	District of Columbia	Sask.	Saskatchewan
D.F.	Distrito Federal	sec.	section
Dec.	December	Sept.	September
dept.	department	SSSR	Soiuz Sovetskikh Sotsialisticheskikh Respublik (Union of Soviet Socialist Republics)
ed.	editor; edited; edition		
enl.	enlarged	SuDocs	Superintendent of Documents (see discussion on pp. xii-xix)
ERIC	Educational Resources Information Center (see discussion on pp. xxi-xxii)	suppl.	supplement
et al.	et alii (and others)	t.	tome (volume, in French)
fasc.	fascicle	tr.	translator; translated; translations
Feb.	February	UM	University Microfilms (see discussion on p. xxii-xxiii)
illus.	illustration(s); illustrated		
Jan.	January	U.S.	United States
Jr.	Junior	v.	volume, volumes
jt.	joint	Vt.	Vermont
Ky.	Kentucky	1st	first
l.	leaves (i.e. pages printed on one side only)	2d	second
		3d	third
Mar.	March	4th	fourth
Mass.	Massachusetts		
Me.	Maine		
mimeo.	mimeographed		
ms., mss.	manuscript, manuscripts		
n.d.	no date of publication		
n.F.	neue Folge (new series, in German)		

It should also be noted that underlining has been used in the citations to indicate that letters or numbers are superscript letters or numbers. Thus, "blood group antigen Di^a" is given as "blood group antigen Di<u>a</u>" in the listing.

01   Arctic Coast

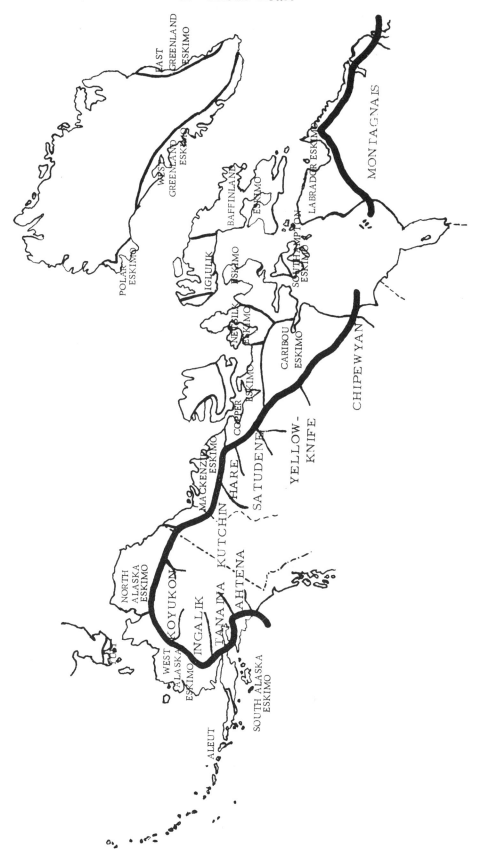

01   Arctic Coast

This vast area, stretching from Eastern Siberia to Greenland, includes a number of ethnic groups who speak languages of the Eskimo-Aleut language family and have a general cultural adaptation to the rigors of life in Arctic coastal conditions. The primary subsistence pattern of these groups varies from dependency on sea mammal hunting to fishing to caribou hunting, depending upon local ecological conditions. The Western Eskimo, including the Aleut, the Alaskan Eskimo, and the Siberian Yuit, have been much influenced by the cultures of Siberia to the west and those of the Northwest Coast to the southeast, in contradistinction to the Central and Eastern Eskimo, who have lived for a long period in relative isolation and who are assumed to have preserved more of the traditional Eskimo cultural patterns.

A major linguistic division occurs at Norton Sound in western Alaska, with the Siberian Eskimo and the Alaskan Eskimo living south of this area speaking a language (Yupik, Alaskan Eskimo) which is quite different from that of the Eskimo living to the north and east, who speak a language called Inupik, Inuit, or Central-Greenlandic. Linguistic defferences occuring in the vast geographical spread of the latter language are comparatively insignificant. In addition to the above, there are two Aleut languages, Eastern Aleut (Unalaskan) and Western Aleut (Atkan, Attuan). It has been estimated that there are more than 80,000 speakers of these four languages.

Arora, Ved Parkash. Eskimos; a bibliography. Regina, Sask., Provincial Library, Bibliographic Services Division, 1972. 4, 50 p.

Fisher, John. Bibliography for the study of Eskimo religion. Anthropologica, n.s., 15 (1973): 231-271.

Hirschfelder, Arlene B. American Indian and Eskimo authors; a comprehensive bibliography. New York, Association on American Indian Affairs, 1973. 99 p.

Kjellström, Rolf. Eskimo marriage; an account of traditional Eskimo courtship and marriage. Stockholm, Nordiska, 1973. 267 p. illus., maps.

Malaurie, Jean, ed. The Eskimo people today and tomorrow. Paris, Mouton, 1973. 14, 696 p. map. (Bibliothèque Arctique et Antarctique, 4)

01-01.   Aleut.   There are approximately 2,300 Aleut, who live principally on the Alaska Peninsula and the Aleutian Islands, as well as a small group living in the Commander (Komandorskii) Islands of the Soviet Union.

01-02.   Baffinland Eskimo.   The Central-Greenlandic-speaking Baffinland Eskimo live in the southern and central parts of Baffin Island and include the Eskimo living at Cape Dorset, Cumberland Sound, and Frobisher Bay, among others.

01-03.   Caribou Eskimo.   The Central-Greenlandic-speaking Caribou Eskimo live primarily in Keewatin District on the western shores of Hudson's Bay in Canada and include the Eskimo living at the settlements of Baker Lake, Eskimo Point, Chesterfield Inlet, and Rankin Inlet, among others.

01-04.   Copper Eskimo.   The Copper Eskimo live in the northern Northwest Territories of Canada, principally on the mainland shores of Coronation Gulf, Bathurst Inlet, and on Victoria and Banks Islands. They speak Central-Greenlandic, and in 1963 they numbered about 1,100.

01-05.   East Greenland Eskimo.   The Central-Greenlandic-speaking East Greenland Eskimo live in southeastern Greenland, principally at the settlements of Angmagssalik and Scoresbysund.

01-06.   Iglulik Eskimo.   The Central-Greenlandic-speaking Iglulik Eskimo live in the central Canadian Arctic on northwestern Baffin Island, the Melville Peninsula, and the northern part of Southampton Island, including the modern settlements of Repulse Bay, Pond Inlet, and Arctic Bay.

01-07.   Labrador Eskimo.   The Central-Greenlandic-speaking Labrador Eskimo live on the shores of the Labrador Peninsula and on the Belcher Islands in eastern Hudson's Bay, particularly in the modern settlements of Makkovik, Port Harrison, Port Burwell, Sugluk, and Povungnituk.

Graburn, Nelson H. H. Eskimos of northern Canada. New Haven, Human Relations Area Files, 1972. 2 v. [6, 466 l.] (HRAFlex Books ND2-001 and ND2-002)

01-08.   Mackenzie Eskimo.   The Central-Greenlandic-speaking Mackenzie Eskimo lived in the Mackenzie River delta area in northwestern Canada. They are apparently no longer viable as a group, and numerous North Alaskan Eskimos have moved into the area. Since it is difficult to distinguish between the original inhabitants and the newcomers in the literature, this division of the bibliography contains materials on both.

Jones, Mary Jane. Mackenzie Delta bibliography. Ottawa, 1969. 119 p. (Canada, Department of Indian Affairs and Northern Development, Mackenzie Delta Research Project, 6)

McGhee, Robert. Beluga hunters; an archaeological reconstruction of the history and culture of the Mackenzie Delta Kittegaryumiut. Toronto, University of Toronto Press, 1974. 12, 124 p. illus., maps. (Memorial University of Newfoundland, Newfoundland Social and Economic Studies, 13)

01-09. Netsilik Eskimo. The Central-Greenlandic-speaking Netsilik Eskimo live in the northeastern Northwest Territories of Canada on the Boothia Peninsula, King William Island, and the Adelaide Peninsula, including the Back River hinterland and the settlement of Pelly Bay.

Taylor, J. Garth. Netsilik Eskimo material culture; the Roald Amundsen Collection from King William Island. Oslo, Universitetsforlaget, 1974. 173 p. illus. map.

01-10. North Alaska Eskimo. The Central-Greenlandic-speaking North Alaska Eskimo live in northern Alaska, between Kotzebue Sound on the west and the Canadian border and inland to Anaktuvuk Pass, including communities at Barter Island, Point Barrow, Wainwright, Point Hope, Kivalina, and Noatak.

01-11. Polar Eskimo. The Central-Greenlandic-speaking Polar Eskimo (Arctic Highlanders, Cape York Eskimo, Smith Sound Eskimo) live in the extreme northwest of Greenland and include those living at Etah and Thule.

01-12. South Alaska Eskimo. The South Alaska Eskimo live in southwestern Alaska, between Bristol Bay and Prince William Sound, and include the Chugach and Koniag, as well as other groups. They speak Alaskan Eskimo (Yupik) and number about 10,000.

01-13. Southampton Eskimo. The Central-Greenlandic-speaking Southampton Eskimo live on Southampton Island in the northern part of Hudson's Bay in Canada and include the recently extinct Sagdlirmiut and recent immigrants to the island, particularly of Aggomiut and Aivilik Eskimo.

01-14. West Alaska Eskimo. The West Alaska Eskimo live in western Alaska, between Kotzebue Sound and Bristol Bay, including those living in settlements at Unalakleet, Shishmareff, Wales, St. Michael, and Bethel, among others. Since the division between Yupik- and Inupik-speakers occurs in the center of this area, this bibliographic division includes materials on both. They number about 4,000.

01-15. West Greenland Eskimo. The Central-Greenlandic-speaking West Greenland Eskimo live in western and southwestern Greenland, between Melville Bugt and Kap Farvell.

01-16. Yuit. The Yuit (Siberian Eskimo) include those Eskimo living on the shores of the Chukchi Peninsula in Siberia, as well as those living on St. Lawrence Island and the Diomede Islands in the Bering Sea. They speak Alaskan Eskimo (Yupik). The Siberian group numbered 1,292 persons in the Soviet census of 1926-1927, while the St. Lawrence Island and Diomede groups numbered about 430 in 1970.

Hughes, Charles C. Eskimo boyhood; autobiography in psychosocial perspective. Lexington, University of Kentucky Press, 1974. 6, 429 p.

01-00   Arctic Coast Area Bibliography

Arora, Ved P.   Eskimos: a bibliography.
Regina, Saskatchewan Provincial Library,
Bibliographical Services Division, 1972.
50 p.

Balle, Povl.   Avîsit atuagagssiatdlo
kalâtdlisût agdlagsimavfiat 1861-1968.
Fortegnelse over grønlandske aviser og
periodica 1861-1968. Index of
Greenlandic newspapers and periodica
1861-1968. By Povl Balle and Helge
Tønnesen. København, Minerva Mikrofilm
A/S, 1969.   19 p.

Carney, R. J.   A selected and annotated
bibliography on the sociology of Eskimo
education. By R. J. Carney and W. O.
Ferguson. Edmonton, 1965.   5, 59 l.
(Alberta, University, Boreal Institute,
Occasional Publication, 2) ERIC
ED037280.

Carrière, Gaston.   Catalogue des
manuscrits en langues indiennes
conservés aux archives oblates, Ottawa.
Anthropologica, n.s., 12 (1970): 151-
179.

Cavanagh, Beverley.   Annotated
bibliography: Eskimo music.
Ethnomusicology, 16 (1972): 479-487.

Fortuine, Robert, comp.   The health of the
Eskimos; a bibliography 1857-1967.
Hanover, Dartmouth College Libraries,
Stefansson Collection, 1968.   87 p.

Hippler, Arthur E.   Eskimo acculturation:
a selected annotated bibliography of
Alaskan and other Eskimo acculturation
studies. College, 1970.   6, 209 p.
(Alaska, University, Institute of
Social, Economic, and Government
Research, ISEGR Report, 28) ERIC
ED048983.

Loriot, James.   A selected bibliography of
comparative American Indian linguistics.
International Journal of American
Linguistics, 30 (1964): 62-80.

Lotz, James R.   Yukon bibliography,
preliminary edition. Ottawa, 1964.   7,
155 p. (Canada, Department of Northern
Affairs and National Resources, Northern
Co-ordination and Research Centre, Yukon
Research Project Series, 1)

Meiklejohn, Christopher.   Annotated
bibliography of the physical
anthropology and human biology of
Canadian Eskimos and Indians. Toronto,
University of Toronto, Department of
Anthropology, 1971.   169, 16 l.

Meiklejohn, Christopher.   Bibliography of
the physical anthropology and human
biology of Canadian Eskimos and Indians.
Toronto, University of Toronto,
Department of Anthropology, 1970.   2,
102, 11 l.

Ontario, Education Department.   Multi-
media resource list: Eskimos and
Indians. Toronto, 1969.   50 p.

Pilling, J. C.   Bibliography of the Eskimo
language. U.S. Bureau of American
Ethnology, Bulletin, 1 (1887): 1-112.

U.S., Indian Arts and Crafts Board.
Bibliography of contemporary American
Indian and Eskimo arts and crafts.
Washington, D.C., 1964.   4 p.

Ackerknecht, E. H.   Medicine and disease
among Eskimos. Ciba Symposia, 10 (1948):
916-921.

Ackerknecht, E. H.   The Eskimo's fight
against hunger and cold. Ciba Symposia,
10 (1948): 894-902.

Adams, Colin.   Flexibility in Canadian
Eskimo social forms and behavior: a
situational and transactional appraisal.
In D. Lee Guemple, ed. Alliance in
Eskimo Society. Seattle, American
Ethnological Society, 1972: 9-16.

Adamson, J. D.   Poliomyelitis in the
Arctic. Canadian Medical Association
Journal, 61 (1949): 339-348.

Agranat, G. A.   Polozhenie korennogo
naseleniia krainego Severa Ameriki.
Sovetskaia Etnografiia, no. 4 (1961):
100-113.

Alaska Publications.   Eskimo life in
Alaska; a photo story of these arctic
people. Anchorage, M. Roberts, 1964.
52 p. illus.

Alaska, Rural Development Board.   The
Beaver report. Juneau, 1959.   71 l.
illus., maps.

Alaska, University.   Alaska native arts
and crafts: potential for expansion.
College, 1964.   162 p.   illus.

Alaska, University, Alaskan Native
Education Project.   Alaskan native
secondary school dropouts: a research
report. By Charles K. Ray, Joan Ryan,
and Seymour Parker. College, University
of Alaska, 1962.   411 p.   illus.

Allen, F. H.   Summary of blood group
phenotypes in some aboriginal Americans.

American Journal of Physical
Anthropology, n.s., 17 (1959): 86.

Allen, W. Sidney. Transitivity and
possession. Language, 40 (1964): 337-
343.

Allison, A. C. and B. S. Blumberg.
Ability to taste phenylthiocarbamide
among Alaskan Eskimos and other
populations. Human Biology, 31 (1959):
352-359.

Allison, A. C., et al. Urinary B-
aminoisobutyric acid excretion in Eskimo
and Indian populations of Alaska.
Nature, 183 (1959): 118-119.

Andree, K. T. Die Skulpturen der Eskimos.
Globus, 59 (1891): 348.

Anonymous. Canadian Eskimo art. Ottawa,
1955. 40 p.

Anonymous. El desarrollo de los grupos
nativos de Alaska. Anuario Indigenista,
23 (1963): 89-92.

Anonymous. Eskimo art of the Canadian
Eastern Arctic. Ann Arbor [n.d.].
10 p.

Anonymous. Eskimo masks. World Theatre,
10, no. 1 (1961): 46-48.

Anonymous. Eskimo origins. Archaeology,
11 (1958): 217-218.

Anonymous. On the rights of the Eskimo.
Eskimo, 39 (1956): 3-5.

Anonymous. Repertoire géographique des
missions indiennes et esquimaudes des
Pères Oblats au Canada. Gazetteer of
Indian and Eskimo stations of the Oblate
Fathers in Canada. Ottawa, Services
Oblates, 1960. 10, 119 p.

Anonymous. The Eskimo and the principle
of conserving hot air. Eskimo, 42
(1956): 18-21.

Anonymous. To civilize the Eskimo.
Eskimo, 42 (1956): 3-9.

Arnold, Winton C. Native land claims in
Alaska. Anchorage, 1967. 18, 78, 42 p.

Aronson, J. D. The history of disease
among the natives of Alaska. Alaska's
Health, 5, no. 3 (1947): 1-2; 5, no. 4
(1947): 3-4; 5, no. 5 (1947): 5-6; 5,
no. 6 (1947): 4-5; 5, no. 7 (1947): 3-4.

Arron, W. J. Aspects of the epic in
Eskimo folklore. Alaska, University,
Anthropological Papers, 5 (1957): 119-
141.

Arthaud, J. Bradley. Anaplastic parotid
carcinoma ("malignant lymphoepithelial
lesion") in seven Alaskan natives.
American Journal of Clinical Pathology,
57 (1972): 275-286.

Auer, J. Fingerprints in Eskimos of the
Northwest Territories. American Journal
of Physical Anthropology, n.s., 8
(1950): 485-488.

Baird, I. Summer school north of sixty.
Canadian Geographical Journal, 50
(1955): 18-23.

Balikci, Asen. "Ethnic relations and the
marginal man in Canada": a comment.
Human Organization, 19 (1960/1961): 170-
171.

Balikci, Asen. The Central Eskimo: a
marginal case? By Asen Balikci, David
Damas, Fred Eggan, June Helm, and
Sherwood L. Washburn. In Richard B. Lee
and Irven DeVore, eds. Man the Hunter.
Chicago, Aldine, 1968: 83-85.

Bandi, Hans Georg. Eskimo prehistory.
London, Methuen, 1969. 12, 226 p.
illus., maps.

Bandi, Hans Georg. Urgeschichte der
Eskimo. Stuttgart, G. Fischer, 1965.
171 p. illus., maps.

Bandi, Hans Georg. Eskimo prehistory.
Translated by Ann E. Keep. College,
University of Alaska Press, 1972. 12,
226 p. illus., maps.

Bang, Gisle. Morphologic characteristics
of the Alaskan Eskimo dentition. II.
Carabelli's cusp. By Gisle Bang and
Asbjörn Hasund. American Journal of
Physical Anthropology, 37 (1972/1973):
35-39.

Barclay, Isabel. Art of the Canadian
Indians and Eskimos. Ottawa, National
Galley of Canada, 1969. 18 p. illus.

Barüske, Heinz, comp. Eskimo-Märchen.
Düsseldorf, E. Diederichs, 1969.
369 p. map.

Bayliss, C. K. A treasury of Eskimo
tales. New York, 1923. 135 p.

Beard, Edmund. Warfare among Eskimos. In
Andrew W. Cordier, ed. Columbia Essays
in International Affairs: the Dean's
Papers, 1969. Vol. 5. New York,
Columbia University Press, 1971: 28-50.

Beaudry, Pierre H. Pulmonary function
survey of the Canadian Eastern Arctic
Eskimo. Archives of Environmental
Health, 17 (1968): 524-528.

Belcher, E. On the manufacture of works of art by the Esquimaux. Ethnological Society (London), Transactions, n.s., 1 (1861): 129-146.

Belousov, Vladimir Germanovich. Sergeĭ Esenin. Lit. khonika. Moskva, "Sov. Rossiĭa", 1969.

Benveniste, É. The "Eskimo" name. International Journal of American Linguistics, 19 (1953): 242-245.

Berghuis, Hans. Im Lande des weissen Bären. Freiburg, Herder, 1963. 305 p. map.

Berghuis, Hans. Kamakto, het wordt dag! Voorhout, Forcholte, 1960. 192 p. illus.

Bergsland, Knut. Morphological analysis and syntactical reconstruction in Eskimo-Aleut. In International Congress of Linguists, 9th. 1962, Cambridge, Mass. Proceedings. The Hague, Mouton, 1964: 1009-1015. (Janua Linguarum, Series Maior, 12)

Bergsland, Knut. The Eskimo shibboleth inuk/yuk. In To Honor Roman Jakobson; Essays on the Occasion of His Seventieth Birthday, 11 October 1966. The Hague, Mouton, 1967: 203-221. (Janua Linguarum, Series Maior, 31)

Bergsøe, P. Where did the Eskimo get their copper? Nationalmuseets Skrifter, Etnografisk Raekke, 1 (1941): 107-120.

Biasutti, R. Le razzi e i popoli della Terra. 2d ed. Vol. 4. Torino, 1957. 352-373.

Bird, Peter M. Studies of fallout 137Cs in the Canadian North. Archives of Environmental Health, 17 (1968): 631-638.

Birket-Smith, K. Anthropological observations on the Central Eskimos. Fifth Thule Expedition, Report, 3, no. 2 (1940): 1-123.

Birket-Smith, K. Danish activities in Eskimo research since 1940. International Congress of Americanists, Proceedings, 28 (1948): 231-236.

Birket-Smith, K. Danish activities in Eskimo research 1949-1954. International Congress of Americanists, Proceedings, 31, no. 2 (1955): 1119-1128.

Birket-Smith, K. Det eskimoiske slaegtskabssystem. Geografisk Tidsskrift, 30 (1927): 96-111.

Birket-Smith, K. Die Eskimos. Zürich, 1948.

Birket-Smith, K. Eskimo cultures and their bearing upon the prehistoric cultures of North America and Eurasia. In G. G. MacCurdy, ed. Early Man. Philadelphia, 1937: 293-302.

Birket-Smith, K. Eskimo prehistory. Scientia, sér. 6 (Avril 1959): 1-4.

Birket-Smith, K. Ethnographical collections from the Northwest Passage. Fifth Thule Expedition, Report, 6, no. 2 (1945).

Birket-Smith, K. Five hundred Eskimo words. Fifth Thule Expedition, Report, 3, no. 2 (1928): 5-64.

Birket-Smith, K. Folk wanderings and culture drifts in northern North America. Société des Américanistes, Journal, 22 (1930): 1-32.

Birket-Smith, K. Moeurs et coutumes des Eskimos. New ed. Paris, 1955. 292 p.

Birket-Smith, K. Nye fremskridt inden for Eskimoforskningen. København, Fra Nationalmuseets Arbejdsmark (1950): 81-100.

Birket-Smith, K. On the origin of Eskimo culture. International Congress of Americanists, Proceedings, 23 (1930): 470-476.

Birket-Smith, K. Preliminary report of the Fifth Thule Expedition. International Congress of Americanists, Proceedings, 21, no. 2 (1924): 190-205.

Birket-Smith, K. Recent achievements in Eskimo research. Royal Anthropological Institute of Great Britain and Ireland, Journal, 77 (1951): 145-157.

Birket-Smith, K. Spørgsmaalet om Eskimo-kulturens oprindelse. Geografisk Tidsskrift, 32 (1929): 222-239; 33 (1930): 161-168.

Birket-Smith, K. The Eskimos. New York, 1936. 250 p.

Birket-Smith, K. The present status of the Eskimo problem. International Congress of Americanists, Proceedings, 29, no. 3 (1952): 8-21.

Birket-Smith, K. The question of the origin of Eskimo culture. American Anthropologist, n.s., 32 (1930): 608-624.

Birket-Smith, K. Über die Herkunft der Eskimos und ihre Stellung in der

zirkumpolaren Kulturentwicklung.
Anthropos, 25 (1930): 1-23.

Birket-Smith, Kaj. Eskimoerne. 3d ed.
København, Rhodos, 1971. 295 p. illus.

Birket-Smith, Kaj. Eskimos. New York,
Crown, 1971. 271 p. illus.

Birket-Smith, Kaj. Moeurs et coutumes des
Eskimo. Paris, Payot, 1955. 290 p.
illus.

Birket-Smith, Kaj. The Eskimos. New ed.
London, Methuen, 1959. 262 p. illus.

Black, L. Morbidity, mortality and
medical care in the Keewatin area of the
Central Arctic--1967. Canadian Medical
Association Journal, 101 (1969): 577-
581.

Blanchet, Guy Houghton. Search in the
North. New York, St. Martin's Press,
1960. 197 p. illus.

Bland, Laurel L. Perception and visual
memory of school-age Eskimos and
Athabascan Indians in Alaskan villages.
Anchorage, 1970. 1, 25 l. illus.
(Human Environmental Resources Systems,
Monograph, 1)

Blomkvist, E. E. Amerikanskie eskimosy.
By E. E. Blomkvist, E. P. Orlova, and L.
A. Faĭnberg. In A. V. Efimov and S. A.
Tokarev, eds. Narody Ameriki. Vol. 1.
Izdatel'stvo Akademiĭa Nauk SSSR, 1959:
105-131.

Bloom, Joseph D. Psychiatric problems and
cultural transitions in Alaska. Arctic,
25 (1972): 203-215.

Blue, Arthur William. Prediction of
learning ability across cultures.
Dissertation Abstracts International, 30
(1969/1970): 5220B. UM 70-7677.

Boag, Thomas J. Mental health of native
peoples of the Arctic. Canadian
Psychiatric Association Journal, 15
(1970): 115-120.

Boas, F. The Eskimo. Annual
Archaeological Report, being Part of
Appendix to the Report of the Minister
of Education, Ontario (1905): 107-116.

Boas, F. The Folk-lore of the Eskimo.
Journal of American Folklore, 17 (1904):
1-13.

Boas, F. Über die ehemalige Verbreitung
der Eskimos. Gesellschaft für Erdkunde
(Berlin), Zeitschrift, 18 (1883): 118-
136.

Bogoraz, V. G. Elements in the culture of
the circumpolar zone. American
Anthropologist, n.s., 31 (1929): 579-
601.

Bogoraz, V. G. Le mythe de l'animal-dieux
mourant et ressuscitant. International
Congress of Americanists, Proceedings,
22, no. 2 (1928): 35-52.

Bogoraz, V. G. New problems of
ethnographical research in polar
countries. International Congress of
Americanists, Proceedings, 21, no. 1
(1924): 226-246.

Bogoraz, V. G. O tak nazyvaemom ĭazykie
dukhov (shamanskom). Akademiĭa Nauk
SSSR, Izvestiĭa, ser. 6, 8/11 (1919):
489-495.

Bogoraz, V. G. Osnovnye tipy fol'klora
Severnoi Evrazi-i Severnoi Ameriki.
Sovetskii Fol'klor, no. 4/5 (1936): 29-
50.

Bogoraz, V. G. The folklore of
Northeastern Asia, as compared with that
of Northwestern America. American
Anthropologist, n.s., 4 (1902): 577-683.

Bohlen, Joseph Glenn. Circumpolar
chronobiology. Dissertation Abstracts
International, 32 (1971/1972): 6795B.
UM 72-15,340.

Bolles, T. D. A preliminary catalogue of
the Eskimo collection in the U.S.
National Museum. United States National
Museum, Reports, vol. 2 (1887): 335-365.

Breuil, H. L'art des populations
arctiques américaines. Paris, Collège de
France, Annuaire, 39 (1939): 138-144.

Brody, Jacob A. Lower respiratory illness
among Alaskan Eskimo children. Archives
of Environmental Health, 11 (1965): 620-
623.

Brown, G. M. Cold acclimatization in
Eskimo. Arctic, 7 (1954): 343-353.

Brown, Greeta Elaine Knight. An
adaptation in music listening: a program
designed for Eskimo children in grade
one. Dissertation Abstracts
International, 33 (1972/1973): 345A-
346A. UM 72-20,908.

Brown, R. The origin of the Eskimo.
Archaeological Review, 1 (1888): 237-
253.

Brown, R. N. R. Some problems of polar
geography. Smithsonian Institution,
Annual Reports of the Board of Regents
(1928): 349-375.

Bruemmer, F.   George Wetaltuk, Eskimo.
Canadian Geographical Journal, 50
(1955): 157-159.

Bruemmer, Fred.   Seasons of the Eskimo: a
vanishing way of life.   Greenwich, New
York Graphic Society, 1971.   131 p.
illus.

Bruet, E.   L'Alaska.   Paris, 1945.   451 p.

Brun de Neergaard, H.   Grønlaenderindernes
klaededragt.   Grønlandske Selskab,
Arsskrift (1951): 61-66.

Bugge, A.   Grønlandsk religiøsitet.
Grønland, no. 2 (1954): 59-64.

Buliard, R. P.   Inuk.   London, 1956.
320 p.

Bunger, Marianna.   Teaching Alaskan native
youth.   Anchorage, Alaska Methodist
University, 1970.   166 p.   ERIC
ED045588.

Burch, Ernest S., Jr.   The nonempirical
environment of the Arctic Alaskan
Eskimos.   Southwestern Journal of
Anthropology, 27 (1971): 148-165.

Burr, Christina.   Eskimo ivory carvings in
the Rochester Museum.   Rochester,
Rochester Museum and Science Center,
1972.   88 p.   illus.

Bushnell, G. H. S.   Some old Western
Eskimo spearthrowers.   Man, 49 (1949):
121.

Byhan, A.   Die Polarvölker.   Leipzig,
1909.   148 p.

Calder, R.   The changing Arctic.
Montreal, 1956.   4 p.

Callebaut, Ruth.   The Indian and Eskimo
cultural influences on the practice of
occupational therapy.   Canadian Journal
of Occupational Therapy, 37 (1970): 145-
148.

Cameron, J.   Correlations between cranial
capacity and cranial length, breadth,
and height.   American Journal of Physical
Anthropology, 11 (1928): 259-299.

Canada, Department of Indian Affairs and
Northern Development.   People of light
and dark.   Edited by Maja van Steensel.
Ottawa, Queen's Printer, 1966.   20,
156 p.   illus., maps.

Canada, Department of National Health and
Welfare.   Health services for small
population groups in outlying areas of
northern Canada.   Ottawa, 1963.   10 p.
map.

Canada, Department of Northern Affairs and
National Resources.   Canadian Eskimo
fine crafts.   Text by W. T. Larmour.
Ottawa, Queen's Printer, 1965.   68 p.
illus., map.

Canadian Arctic Producers.   Canadian
Arctic Producers; a new framework.
Ottawa, Mortimer, 1971.   31 p.   illus.

Canadian Corrections Association.   Indians
and the law.   Journal of Canadian
Studies, 3, no. 2 (1968): 31-55.

Canadian Eskimo Arts Council.
Sculpture/Inuit.   Toronto, Published for
the Canadian Eskimo Arts Council by the
University of Toronto Press, 1971.
493 p.   illus., map.

Carpenter, Edmund S.   Artists of the
North.   Natural History, 71, no. 2
(1962): 8-13.

Carpenter, Edmund S.   Eskimo.   Toronto,
University of Toronto Press, 1964.
illus., maps.

Carpenter, Edmund S.   Image making in
Arctic art.   In Gyorgy Kepes, ed. Sign,
Image, Symbol.   New York, George
Braziller, 1966: 206-225.

Carpenter, Edmund S.   The Eskimo artist.
In Charlotte M. Otten, ed. Anthropology
and Art.   Garden City, Natural History
Press, 1971: 163-171.

Carpenter, Edmund S., ed.   Anerca.
Toronto, J. M. Dent, 1959.   48 p.
illus.

Caswell, Helen R.   Shadows from the
singing house; Eskimo folk tales.
Rutland, Vt., Tuttle, 1968.   108 p.
illus.

Caswell, J. E.   The utilization of the
scientific reports of the United States
Arctic Expeditions 1850-1909.   Stanford,
1951.   304 p.

Chafe, Wallace L.   Estimates regarding the
present speakers of North American
Indian languages.   International Journal
of American Linguistics, 28 (1962): 162-
171.

Chamberlain, A. F.   The Eskimo race and
language.   Canadian Institute,
Proceedings, ser. 3, 6 (1887/1888): 261-
337.

Chambers, John R.   Arctic bush mission;
the experiences of a missionary bush
pilot in the Far North.   Seattle,
Superior, 1970.   174 p.   illus.

Chard, Chester S. Arctic anthropology in
America. In Jacob W. Gruber, ed. The
Philadelphia Anthropological Society;
Papers Presented on Its Golden
Anniversary. New York, distributed by
Columbia University Press for Temple
University Publications, 1967: 77-106.

Chard, Chester S. The western roots of
Eskimo culture. In Congreso
Internacional de Americanistas, 33d.
1958, San José. Actas. Tomo 2. San
José, Lehmann, 1959: 81-87.

Chart, I. E. Sentinels in mukluks. Flying
Safety, 11, no. 10 (1955): 20-21.

Chipman, P. The living stone. Beaver, 286
(Spring 1956): 12-19.

Choque, C. Comment Paul vendit sa fille
pour une longue-vue. Eskimo, 31 (1954):
9, 12-13.

Christiansen, Niels Otto. Certain
socioeconomic conditions in Greenland: a
brief survey. Archives of Environmental
Health, 17 (1968): 464-473.

Clairmont, Donald H. J. Deviance among
Indians and Eskimos in Aklavik, N.W.T.
Ottawa, 1963. 11, 84 p. illus., maps.
(Canada, Department of Northern Affairs
and National Resources, Northern Co-
ordination and Research Centre, NCRC-63-
9)

Clairmont, Donald H. J. Notes on the
drinking behavior of the Eskimos and
Indians in the Aklavik area; a
preliminary report. Ottawa, 1962. 1,
13 p. illus. (Canada, Department of
Northern Affairs and National Resources,
Northern Co-ordination and Research
Centre, NCRC-62-4)

Clark, E. M. and A. J. Rhodes.
Poliomyelitis in Canadian Eskimos.
Canadian Journal of Medical Sciences, 29
(1951): 216-235; 30 (1952): 290-402.

Clifton, Rodney A. The social adjustment
of native students in a northern
Canadian hostel. Canadian Review of
Anthropology and Sociology, 9 (1972):
163-166.

Coffey, M. F. A comparative study of
young Eskimo and Indian males with
acclimatized white males. Conference on
Cold Injury, 3 (1955): 100-116.

Colby, Benjamin N. The analysis of
culture content and the patterning of
narrative concern in texts. American
Anthropologist, 68 (1966): 374-388.

Collins, H. B. Arctic Area. Instituto
Panamericano de Geografía e Historia,
Publicación, 170 (1954): 1-152.

Collins, H. B. Eskimo archaeology and its
bearing on the problem of man's
antiquity in America. American
Philosophical Society, Proceedings, 86
(1943): 220-235.

Collins, H. B. Eskimo archaeology and
somatology. American Anthropologist,
n.s., 36 (1934): 309-313.

Collins, H. B. Outline of Eskimo
prehistory. Smithsonian Miscellaneous
Collections, 100 (1940): 533-592.

Collins, H. B. The origin and antiquity
of the Eskimo. Smithsonian Institution,
Annual Report of the Board of Regents
(1950): 423-467.

Collins, Henry B. Prehistoric cultural
relations between Japan and the American
Arctic: Eskimo and pre-Eskimo. In
International Congress of
Anthropological and Ethnological
Sciences, 8th. 1968, Tokyo and Kyoto.
Proceedings. Vol. 3. Tokyo, Science
Council of Japan, 1970: 358-359.

Collis, Dermot Ronan F. On the
establishment of visual parameters for
the formalization of Eskimo semantics.
Folk, 11/12 (1969/1970): 309-328.

Collis, Dermot Ronan F. Pour une
sémiologie de l'esquimau. Paris, Dunod,
1971. 159 p. illus., map. (Documents
de Linguistique Quantitative, 14)

Coon, Carleton S. The hunting peoples.
Boston, Little, Brown, 1971. 21,
413 p. illus., maps.

Copenhagen, Nationalmuseet, Etnografiske
samling. Polarfolk og indianere.
København, 1960. 112 p. illus.

Correll, Thomas Clifton. Ungalaqlingmiut:
a study in language and society.
Dissertation Abstracts International, 33
(1972/1973): 5103B-5104B. UM 73-10,684.

Crawe, Keith L. A cultural geography of
the northern Foxe Basin, NWT. Ottawa,
Department of Indian Affairs and
Northern Development, Northern Science
Research Group, 1969.

Curzon, M. E. J. Dental caries in Eskimo
children of the Keewatin District in the
Northwest Territories. By M. E. J.
Curzon and Jennifer A. Curzon. Canadian
Dental Association, Journal, 36 (1970):
342-345.

Curzon, M. E. J.   Three-rooted mandibular molars in the Keewatin Eskimo. By M. E. J. Curzon and Jennifer A. Curzon. Canadian Dental Association, Journal, 37 (1971): 71-72.

Dadisman, A. J.   Eastern Arctic Eskimo land. West Virginia Archaeological Society, Proceedings, 27 (1956): 91-94.

Damas, David.   Characteristics of Central Eskimo band structure. In Contributions to Anthropology: Band Societies. Ottawa, Queen's Printer, 1969: 116-141. (Canada, National Museums, Bulletin, 228)

Damas, David.   Environment, history, and Central Eskimo society. In Contributions to Anthropology: Ecological Essays. Ottawa, Queen's Printer, 1969: 40-64. (Canada, National Museums, Bulletin, 230)

Damas, David.   Social anthropology in the Eskimo area. In Congreso Internacional de Americanistas, 36th. 1964, España. Actas y Memorias. Tomo 3. Sevilla, 1966: 289-301.

Damas, David.   The diversity of Eskimo societies. In Richard B. Lee and Irven DeVore, eds. Man the Hunter. Chicago, Aldine, 1968: 111-117.

Damas, David.   The structure of Central Eskimo associations. In D. Lee Guemple, ed. Alliance in Eskimo Society. Seattle, American Ethnological Society, 1972: 40-55.

Danielo, E.   Bapteme de Misère. Eskimo, 42 (1956): 13-17.

Danielo, E.   Une histoire de sorcier. Eskimo, 36 (1955): 3-6.

Dannevig, K.   Ingeniør i Polarstrøkene. Polarboken (1956): 39-55.

Darbois, Dominique.   Indian and Eskimo art of Canada. Text: Ian Christie Clark. Toronto, Ryerson Press, 1971.   11-23 p. illus.

Dawson, John L. M.   Theoretical and research bases of bio-social psychology; an inaugural lecture from the chair of psychology. Hong Kong, University of Hong Kong, 1969.   10 p.   illus., tables. (Hong Kong, University, Supplement to the Gazette, 16, no. 3)

Debets, G. F.   Antropologicheskie issledovaniia v Kamchatskoi Oblasti. Akademiia Nauk SSSR, Institut Etnografii, Trudy, n.s., 17 (1951): 262 p.

Dolgikh, B. O.   Problems in the ethnography and physical anthropology of the Arctic. Translated by Gerald H. Clark. Arctic Anthropology, 3, no. 1 (1965): 1-9.

Dolgikh, B. O.   Some parallel features in the culture of Samoyeds and Eskimos. By B. O. Dolgikh and L. A. Fainberg. In Congreso Internacional de Americanistas, 33d. 1958, San José. Actas. Tomo 2. San José, Lehmann, 1959: 88-97.

Donaghue, L. and C. Lucier.   The University of Alaska Eskimo Music and Folklore Project. Alaskan Science Conference, Proceedings (1952): 121-125.

Dumond, Don E.   Eskimos and Aleuts. In International Congress of Anthropological and Ethnological Sciences, 8th. 1968, Tokyo and Kyoto. Proceedings. Vol. 3.   Tokyo, Science Council of Japan, 1970: 102-107.

Dumond, Don E.   On Eskaleutian linguistics, archaeology, and prehistory. American Anthropologist, 67 (1965): 1231-1257.

Dumond, Don E.   Toward a prehistory of Alaska. Alaska Review, 3, no. 1 (1967/1969): 31-50.

Edmonson, Munro S.   A measurement of relative racial difference. Current Anthropology, 6 (1965): 167-198.   [With comments].

Edwards, Clinton R.   Aboriginal sail in the New World. Southwestern Journal of Anthropology, 21 (1965): 351-358.

Edwards, Newton.   Economic development of Indian reserves. Human Organization, 20 (1961/1962): 197-202.

Eisenman, Russell.   Scapegoating the deviant in two cultures. International Journal of Psychology, 2 (1967): 133-138.

Elliott, Jean Leonard, ed.   Minority Canadians. Scarborough, Prentice-Hall of Canada, 1971.   2 v.

Emel'ianova, N. M.   O sootnoshenii ergativnoi i nominativnoi konstrukcii v eskimosskom iazyke. In V. M. Zhirmunskii. Ergativnaia Konstrukcia Predlozhenia v Iazykach Razlichnych Tipov. Leningrad, Izdatel'stvo "Nauka", 1967: 269-276.

Emel'ianova, N. M.   Ob aggliutinacii v eskimosskom iazyke. In B. A. Serebrennikov and O. P. Sunik, eds. Morfologicheskaia Tipologia i Problema

Klassifikacii I͡Azykov. Moskva,
Izdatel'stvo "Nauka", 1965: 205-216.

Emerson, W. C. The land of the midnight
sun. Philadelphia, 1956. 179 p.

Erichsen, M. Désinences casuelles et
personnelles en Eskimo. Acta
Linguistica, 4 (1944): 67-88.

Estreicher, Z. Die Musik der Eskimos.
Anthropos, 45 (1950): 659-720.

Estreicher, Zygmunt. Eskimo-Musik. In
Friedrich Blume, ed. Die Musik in
Geschichte und Gegenwart. Bd. 3.
Kassel, Bärenreiter-Verlag, 1954: 1526-
1533.

Faĭnberg, C. Ocherki etnicheskiĭ istorii
zarubezhnogo Severa. Moskva, Nauka,
1971. 279 p.

Faĭnberg, L. A. K voprosu o rodovom stroe
u Eskimosov. Sovetskai͡a Etnografii͡a,
no. 2 (1955): 82-99.

Faĭnberg, L. A. Obshchestvennyĭ stroĭ
eskimosov i aleutov; ot materialskogo
roda k sosedskoĭ obshchine. Moskva,
Nauka, 1964. 257 p. illus., maps.

Faĭnberg, L. A. Ocherki etnicheskoĭ
istorii zarubezhnogo severa. (Ali͡aska,
Kanadskai͡a Arktika, Labrador,
Grelandii͡a). Moskva, Nauka, 1971.
279 p.

Faĭnberg, L. A. On the question of the
Eskimo kinship system. Translated by
Charles C. Hughes. Arctic Anthropology,
4 (1967): 244-256.

Faĭnberg, L. A. The contemporary
situation of the Eskimos (1940-1960) and
the problem of their future in the works
of American and Canadian ethnographers.
Soviet Anthropology and Archaeology, 4,
no. 1 (1965): 27-45.

Faĭnberg, L. A. Vklad amerikanskikh
eskimosov v osvoenie arktiki. In
Akademii͡a Nauk SSSR, Institut
Etnografii. Kul'tura Indeĭt͡sev. Moskva,
Izdatel'stvo Akademii Nauk SSSR, 1963:
271-287.

Falck, Étienne. Les portes de glace.
Paris, Éditions France Empire, 1955.
318 p. illus.

Faustini, A. Gli Eschimesi. Torino,
1912. 204 p.

Fellows, F. S. Mortality in the native
races of the Territory of Alaska. United
States Public Health Service, Public
Health Reports, 49 (1934): 289-298.

Fenna, D., et al. Ethanol metabolism in
various racial groups. Canadian Medical
Association, Journal, 105 (1971): 472-
475.

Field, Edward, tr. Some Eskimo songs
about people and animals. Translated by
Edward Field and Armand Schwerner.
Alcheringa, 1 (1970): 34-36.

Findeisen, H. Der Adler als
Kulturbringer. Zeitschrift für
Ethnologie, 81 (1956): 70-82.

Finnegan, Michael John. Population
definition on the Northwest Coast by
analysis of discrete character
variation. Dissertation Abstracts
International, 33 (1972/1973): 3433B.
UM 73-1769.

Fleshman, J. Kenneth. Bronchiectasis in
Alaska native children. By J. Kenneth
Fleshman, Joseph F. Wilson, and J.
Jerome Cohen. Archives of Environmental
Health, 17 (1968): 517-523.

Foote, Don Charles. American whalemen in
northwestern Arctic Alaska. Arctic
Anthropology, 2, no. 2 (1964): 16-20.

Foote, Don Charles. Remarks on Eskimo
sealing and the harp seal controversy.
Arctic, 20 (1967): 267-268.

Forbin, V. Industrie et commerce chez les
Eskimaux. Nature (Paris), 54 (1926): 97-
100.

Fortuine, Robert. Characteristics of
cancer in the Eskimos of southwestern
Alaska. Cancer, 23 (1969): 468-474.

Fortuine, Robert. Current status of
animal-borne diseases among the Eskimos.
Canadian Journal of Comparative Medicine
and Veterinary Science, 25 (1961): 185-
189.

Frederick, Saradell Ard. Alaskan Eskimo
art today. Alaska Journal, 2, no. 4
(1972): 30-41.

Frederick, Saradell Ard. An analysis of
two-dimensional Eskimo pictorial
representation with relevance for art
teaching in Alaska. Dissertation
Abstracts International, 32 (1971/1972):
3889A. UM 72-4167.

Frederiksen, Svend. The "primitive"
Eskimo conception of souls. In
International Congress of
Anthropological and Ethnological
Sciences, 6th. 1960, Paris. Tome II,
v. 2. Paris, Musée de l'Homme, 1964:
383-387.

Frederiksen, Svend. The structure and function of the soul in Eskimo shamanism. In Congreso Internacional de Americanistas, 36th. 1964, España. Actas y Memorias. Tomo 3. Sevilla, 1966: 455-464.

Freeman, Milton M. R. The significance of demographic changes occurring in the Canadian East Arctic. Anthropologica, n.s., 13 (1971): 215-236.

Freuchen, P. Out of the stone age. Beaver, 282, no. 2 (1951): 3-9.

Freuchen, Peter. Book of the Eskimos. Edited by Dagmar Freuchen. Cleveland, World, 1961. 441 p. illus.

Freuchen, Peter. The Arctic year. By Peter Freuchen and Finn Salomonsen. New York, G. P. Putnam's Sons, 1958.

Fried, Jacob. Urbanization and ecology in the Canadian Northwest Territories. Arctic Anthropology, 2, no. 2 (1964): 56-60.

Fritz, M. H. and P. Thygeson. Phlyctenular kerato-conjunctivitis among Alaskan Indians and Eskimos. United States Public Health Service, Public Health Reports, 66 (1951): 934-939.

Frost, Orcutt W., ed. Tales of Eskimo Alaska. Anchorage, Alaska Methodist University Press, 1971. 91 p. (Alaska Review, 15)

Furesz, J. Vaccination against measles in the Canadian Arctic. By J. Furesz and Mary Habgood. Canadian Journal of Public Health, 57 (1966): 36.

Gad, F. The language situation in Greenland. American-Scandinavian Review, 45 (1957): 377-383.

Gagné, Raymond C. In defence of a standard phonemic spelling in Roman letters for the Canadian Eskimo language. Arctic, 12 (1959): 203-213.

Gagné, Raymond C. Towards a Canadian Eskimo orthography and literature. Canadian Journal of Linguistics, 7 (1961/1962): 95-107; 8 (1962/1963): 33-39.

Gahs, A. Kopf-, Schädel- und Langknochenopfer bei Rentiervölkern. In Festschrift P. W. Schmidt. Wien, 1928: 231-268.

Garber, C. M. Eskimo infanticide. Scientific Monthly, 64 (1947): 98-102.

Gates, R. R. Eskimo blood groups and physiognomy. Man, 35 (1935): 33-34.

Gessain, R. Deux journées d'un chasseur esquimau. Connaissance du Monde, 2 (1955): 179-186.

Gessain, R. Figurine androgyne eskimo. Société des Américanistes, Journal, n.s., 43 (1954): 207-217.

Gessain, R. L'Ajagaq, bilboquet eskimo. Société des Américanistes, Journal, n.s., 41 (1952): 238-293.

Gessain, R. Le motif vagina dentata. International Congress of Americanists, Proceedings, 32 (1958): 583-586.

Gessain, R. Les Esquimaux aiment à s'amuser. Neuf, 3 (1951): 66-71.

Gessain, R. Les Esquimaux du Groenland à l'Alaska. Paris, 1947. 121 p.

Gibson, James R. Russian America in 1833: the survey of Kirill Khlebnikov. Pacific Northwest Quarterly, 63 (1972): 1-13.

Giddings, J. L. Observations on the "Eskimo type" of kinship and social structure. Alaska, University, Anthropological Papers, 1 (1952): 5-10.

Giffen, N. M. The roles of men and women in Eskimo culture. Chicago, 1930. 114 p.

Gilbertson, A. N. Some ethical phases of Eskimo culture. Journal of Religious Psychology, 6 (1913): 321-374; 7 (1914): 45-74.

Gilíarevskiĭ, R. S. Opredelitel' íazykov mira po pis'mennostíam. By R. S. Gilíarevskiĭ and V. S. Grivnin. Moskva, Izdatel'stvo Nauka, 1965. 375 p.

Godsell, P. H. Is there time to save the Eskimo. Natural History, 61 (1952): 56-62.

Goldschmidt, V. Samfundsforskning: Grønland. Grønland, no. 3 (1959): 112-120.

Goldstein, M. S. Caries and attrition in the molar teeth of the Eskimo mandible. American Journal of Physical Anthropology, 16 (1932): 421-431.

Goldstein, M. S. Congenital absence and impaction of the third molar in the Eskimo mandible. American Journal of Physical Anthropology, 16 (1932): 381-388.

Goldstein, M. S. The cusps in the mandibular molar teeth of the Eskimo. American Journal of Physical Anthropology, 16 (1931): 215-236.

Gottman, Arthur W. A report of one hundred three autopsies on Alaskan natives. Archives of Pathology, 70 (1960): 117-124.

Graham, Andrew. Andrew Graham's observations on Hudson's Bay, 1767-91. Edited by Glyndwr Williams. London, 1969. 72, 423 p. illus., maps. (Hudson's Bay Record Society, Publications, 27)

Grantham, E. N. Education goes North. Canadian Geographical Journal, 42 (1951): 44-49.

Graves, Theodore D. Culture change and psychological adjustment: the case of the American Indian and Eskimo. By Theodore D. Graves and Norman A. Chance. In International Congress of Anthropological and Ethnological Sciences, 8th. 1968, Tokyo and Kyoto. Proceedings. Vol. 3. Tokyo, Science Council of Japan, 1970: 395.

Gravesen, P. B. Tuberkulosen i Grønland. Ugeskrift for Laeger, 114 (1952): 801-805.

Gray, C. G. Some orthopaedic problems in Indians and Eskimos. Canadian Journal of Occupational Therapy, 27 (1960): 45-50.

Green, Paul. I am Eskimo, Aknik my name. Juneau, Alaska-Northwest Publishing, 1959. 85 p. illus.

Greenberg, Joseph H. A quantitative approach to the morphological typology of language. International Journal of American Linguistics, 26 (1960): 178-194.

Greenman, Emerson F. The Upper Palaeolithic and the New World. Current Anthropology, 4 (1963): 41-91.

Gsovski, V. Russian administration of Alaska and the status of the Alaskan natives. Washington, 1950. 104 p.

Gudmand-Høyer, E. Lactose malabsorption in Greenland Eskimos. By E. Gudmand-Høyer and Stig Jarnum. Acta Medica Scandinavica, 186 (1969): 235-237.

Guemple, D. Lee, ed. Alliance in Eskimo society. Seattle, American Ethnological Society, 1972. 5, 131 p. diagrs., map. (American Ethnological Society, Proceedings of the Annual Spring Meeting, 1971, Supplement)

Gunn, Sisvan W. A. Medicine in primitive Indian and Eskimo art. Canadian Medical Association Journal, 102 (1970): 513-514.

Gurunanjappa, Bale S. Life tables for Alaska natives. U.S., Public Health Service, Public Health Reports, 84 (1969): 65-69.

Gutsche, Brett B. Hereditary deficiency of pseudo cholinesterase in Eskimos. By Brett B. Gutsche, Edward M. Scott, and Rita C. Wright. Nature, 215 (1967): 322-323.

Haldeman, J. C. Problems of Alaskan Eskimos, Indians, Aleuts. United States Public Health Service, Public Health Reports, 66 (1951): 912-917.

Hallock, C. The Eskimo and their written language. American Anthropologist, 9 (1896): 369-370.

Halpern, J. M. Arctic jade. Rocks and Minerals, 28 (1953): 237-242.

Hamilton, T. M. The Eskimo bow and the Asiatic composite. Arctic Anthropology, 6, no. 2 (1970): 43-52.

Hammerich, L. L. The cases of Eskimo. International Journal of American Linguistics, 17 (1951): 18-22.

Hammerich, L. L. The origin of the Eskimo. International Congress of Americanists, Proceedings, 32 (1958): 640-644.

Hammerich, Louis L. An Arctic hunting method mentioned in the Bible? Folk, 5 (1963): 133-142.

Hammerich, Louis L. The Eskimo language. Oslo, Universitetsforlaget, 1970. 42 p. (Det Norske Videnskaps-Akademi i Oslo, Fridtjof Nansen Minneforelesninger, 6)

Hanna, Gerald S. WAIS performance of Alaskan native university freshmen. By Gerald S. Hanna, Betty House, and Lee H. Salisbury. Journal of Genetic Psychology, 112 (1968): 57-61.

Hanna, R. E. and S. L. Washburn. The determination of the sex of skeletons. Human Biology, 25 (1953): 21-27.

Hansen, H. H. Eskimo clothing. American-Scandinavian Review, 46 (1958): 342-351.

Harcourt, R. d'. Arts de l'Amérique: 21-26. Paris, 1948.

Harkey, Ira B., Jr. Wolfes, Kuspuks and 70 below. Indian Historian, 5, no. 3 (1972): 13-17.

Harrington, L. People who live in snow houses. Forest and Outdoors, 45, no. 3 (1949): 24-25.

Harrington, M. R. A hunter outfit from the Central Eskimo. Masterkey, 25 (1951): 66-68.

Harrington, R. Eskimos I have known. Geographical Magazine, 28 (1955): 387-389.

Harrington, R. Northern exposures. New York, 1953. 119 p.

Harrison, Gordon Scott. Electoral behavior of Alaska native villages. Fairbanks, 1970. 19 p. (Alaska, University, Institute of Social, Economic and Government Research, Research Note, G1)

Harrison, Gordon Scott. Flow of communication between government agencies and Eskimo villages. Human Organization, 31 (1972): 1-9.

Harrison, Gordon Scott. Native voting in village Alaska. Arctic, 24 (1971): 62-63.

Hart, J. S., et al. Thermal and metabolic responses of coastal Eskimos during a cold night. Journal of Applied Physiology, 17 (1962): 953-960.

Harvey, James B. Scouting amongst the Eskimos and Northern Indians. North, 12, no. 3 (1965): 18-23.

Hassert, K. Die Völkerwanderung der Eskimos. Geographische Zeitschrift, 1 (1895): 302-322.

Hatt, G. Arktiske skinddragter i Eurasien og Amerika. Kjøbenhavn, 1914. 255 p.

Hatt, G. Early instrusion of agriculture in the North Atlantic subarctic region. Alaska, University, Anthropological Papers, 2 (1953): 51-100.

Hatt, G. Kyst- og indlandskultur i det arktiske. Geografisk Tidsskrift, 23 (1916): 284-290.

Hatt, G. North American and Eurasian culture connections. Pacific Science Congress, Proceedings, 5, vol. 4 (1934): 2755-2765.

Hatt, Gudmund. Arctic skin clothing in Eurasia and America, an ethnographic study. Translated by Kirsten Taylor. Arctic Anthropology, 5, no. 2 (1968): 3-132.

Haugaard, E. Five Eskimo poems. American-Scandinavian Review, 44 (1956): 163-167.

Heinrich, Albert. Divorce as an alliance mechanism among Eskimos. In D. Lee Guemple, ed. Alliance in Eskimo Society. Seattle, American Ethnological Society, 1972: 79-88.

Heinrich, Albert. Some formal aspects of a kinship system. By Albert Heinrich and Russell L. Anderson. Current Anthropology, 12 (1971): 541-557.

Heinrich, Albert. Structural features of northwestern Alaskan Eskimo kinship. Southwestern Journal of Anthropology, 16 (1960): 110-126.

Heinrich, Albert Carl. Eskimo type kinship and Eskimo kinship: an evaluation and a provisional model for presenting data pertaining to Inupiaq kinship systems. Dissertation Abstracts, 24 (1963/1964): 4345. UM 64-4507.

Heller, C. A. Alaska nutrition survey report: dietary study. Alaska's Health, 6, no. 10 (1948): 7-9.

Heller, C. A. Food and dental health. Alaska's Health, 4, no. 12 (1946): 4-5.

Heller, Christine A. The Alaska dietary survey, 1956-1961. By Christine A. Heller and Edward M. Scott. Anchorage, Arctic Health Research Center, 1967. 281 p. illus., map.

Henry, V. Grammaire comparée de trois langues hyperboréennes. International Congress of Americanists, Proceedings, 3, vol. 2 (1880): 405-509.

Henshaw, H. W. and J. R. Swanton. Eskimo. U.S. Bureau of American Ethnology, Annual Reports, 30 vol. 1 (1907): 433-437.

Herbert, F. A., et al. Pneumonia in Indian and Eskimo infants and children: Part I. A clinical study. Canadian Medical Association Journal, 96 (1967): 257-265.

Hermant, P. Evolution économique et sociale de certaines peuplades de l'Amérique du Nord. Société Royale Belge de Géographie, Bulletin, 28 (1904): 321-341.

Herreid, Clyde F., II. Differences in MMPI scores in native and nonnative Alaskans. By Clyde F. Herreid, II, and Janet R. Herreid. Journal of Social Psychology, 70 (1966): 191-198.

Hinckley, Ted C. The Presbyterian leadership in pioneer Alaska. Journal of American History, 52 (1965/1966): 742-756.

Hippler, Arthur E. Additional perspective on Eskimo female infanticide. American Anthropologist, 74 (1972): 1318-1319.

Hirsch, D. I. Glottochronology and Eskimo and Eskimo-Aleut prehistory. American Anthropologist, 56 (1954): 825-838.

Hobart, Charles W. Report on Canadian Arctic Eskimos: some consequences of residential schooling. Journal of American Indian Education, 7, no. 2 (1967/1968): 7-17.

Hobart, Charles W. Some consequences of residential schooling of Eskimos in the Canadian Arctic. Arctic Anthropology, 6, no. 2 (1970): 123-135.

Hoebel, E. A. Eskimo infanticide and polyandry. Scientific Monthly, 64 (1947): 535.

Hoffman, W. J. The graphic art of the Eskimos. United States National Museum, Reports (1895): 739-968.

Holcomb, R. C. Syphilis of the skull among Aleuts and the Asian and North-American Eskimo about Bering and Arctic Seas. U.S. Naval Medical Bulletin, 38 (1940): 177-192.

Holmer, Nils M. On the Amerindian character of Aleut and Eskimo. In Studi Linguistici in Onore di Vittore Pisani. Vol. 2. Brescia, Paideia, 1969: 545-567.

Holmer, Nils M. The native place names of arctic America. Names, 15 (1967): 182-196; 17 (1969): 138-148.

Holtved, E. Blandt sagnfortaellere i Grønland og Alaska. Det Grønlandske Selskabs Aarsskrift, København (1950): 69-80.

Holtved, E. Eskimo. I. Religionsgeschichtlich. In Religion in Geschichte und Gegenwart. [n.p., n.d.]: 690-691.

Holtved, E. Eskimokunst. Alverdens Kunst, 4 (1942): 64 p.

Holtved, E. Remarks on Eskimo semantics. International Congress of Americanists, Proceedings, 32 (1958): 617-623.

Holtved, E. The Eskimo legend of Navaranaq. Acta Arctica, 1 (1943): 1-42.

Holtved, Erik. The Eskimo myth about the Sea-Woman: a folkloristic sketch. Folk, 8/9 (1966/1967): 145-153.

Holtved, Erik. Tôrnârssuk, an Eskimo deity. Folk, 5 (1963): 157-171.

Honigmann, John J. Community organization and patterns of change among North Canadian and Alaskan Indians and Eskimos. Anthropologica, n.s., 5 (1963): 3-8.

Honigmann, John J. Understanding culture. New York, Harper and Row, 1963. 8, 468 p. illus., maps.

Hough, W. The lamp of the Eskimo. United States National Museum, Reports (1896): 1025-1057.

Hough, W. The origin and range of the Eskimo lamp. American Anthropologist, 11 (1898): 116-122.

Houston, J. A. Eskimo handicrafts. Montreal, 1951. 32 p.

Houston, J. A. In search of contemporary Eskimo art. Canadian Art, 9, no. 3 (1952): 99-104.

Houston, J. A. The creation of Anoutoaloak. Beaver, 286 (Winter 1955/1956): 50-53.

Houston, James A. The white archer; an Eskimo legend. Don Mills, Longmans Canada, 1967. 95 p. illus.

Houston, Tex., Museum of Fine Arts. The Eskimo. Houston, 1969. 29 p. illus., map.

Howerd, Gareth. DEW line doctor. London, Robert Hale, 1960. 191 p. illus.

Howerd, Gareth. DEW line doctor. London, Adventurers Club, 1962. 191 p. illus.

Hrdlička, A. Catalogue of human crania in the United States National Museum collections. United States National Museum, Proceedings, 91 (1942): 169-429.

Huber, Albert. Alaskan Native Industries Co-operative Association. Boletín Indigenista, 19 (1959): 221, 223, 225.

Hughes, Charles C. Observations on community change in the North: an attempt at summary. Anthropologica, n.s., 5 (1963): 69-79.

Hughes, Charles C. The changing Eskimo world. In Eleanor Burke Leacock and Nancy Oestreich Lurie, eds. North American Indians in Historical Perspective. New York, Random House, 1971: 375-417.

Hughes, Charles Campbell. Under four flags: recent culture change among the Eskimos. Current Anthropology, 6 (1965): 3-69. [With comments].

Hultkrantz, Åke. Die Religion der amerikanischen Arktis. In Ivar Paulson, et al. Die Religionen Nordeurasiens und der amerikanischen Arktis. Stuttgart, Kohlhammer, 1962: 357-415.

Hunns, Derek John. A reconstruction of Proto-Yupik phonology. Dissertation Abstracts International, 31 (1970/1971): 6581A. UM 71-7365.

Iglauer, Edith. The new people; the Eskimo's journey into our time. Garden City, Doubleday, 1966. 205 p. maps.

Indian-Eskimo Association of Canada. Concerns of Indians in British Columbia. Theme: "Equal Opportunity in Our Land". Toronto, 1966. 33 p. ERIC ED041659.

Irving, Laurence. Adaptations of native populations to cold. Archives of Environmental Health, 17 (1968): 592-594.

Ivanov, S. V. Chukotsko-eskimosskaia graviura na kosti. Sovetskaia Etnografiia, no. 4 (1949): 107-124.

Ivanov, S. V. O znachenii dvukh unikal'nykh zhenskikh statuetok Amerikanskikh Eskimosoi. Akademiia Nauk SSSR, Muzei Antropologii i Etnografii, Sbornik, 11 (1949): 162-170.

Jacobsen, N. K. and P. P. Sveistrup. Erhverb og kultur langs polarkredsen. Copenhagen, 1950. 140 p.

Jannasch, Hans-Windekilde. Unter Hottentotten und Eskimos. Lüneburg, Heliand-Verlag, 1950. 125 p.

Jansen, J. V. The life of the Eskimos. Antiquity and Survival, 1 (1955): 83-92.

Jeanes, C. W. L. Inactivation of isoniazid by Canadian Eskimos and Indians. By C. W. L. Jeanes, O. Shaefer, and L. Eidus. Canadian Medical Association Journal, 106 (1972): 331-335.

Jenness, D. Ethnological problems of Arctic America. American Geographical Society, Special Publications, 7 (1928): 167-175.

Jenness, D. Indians of Canada. Canada, Department of Mines, National Museum of Canada, Bulletin, 65 (1932): 405-423.

Jenness, D. Prehistoric culture waves from Asia to America. Smithsonian Institution, Annual Reports of the Board of Regents (1940): 383-396.

Jenness, D. Prehistoric culture waves from Asia to America. Washington Academy of Sciences, Journal, 30 (1940): 1-15.

Jenness, D. The problem of the Eskimo. In his The American Aborigines. Toronto, 1933: 373-396.

Jenness, Diamond. Eskimo administration. Montreal, 1962-1968. 5 v. illus., maps. (Arctic Institute of North America, Technical Paper, 10, 14, 16, 19, 21)

Jensen, Bent. Eskimoisk festlighed; et essay om menneskelig overlevelsesteknik. København, Gad, 1965. 114 p.

Jensen, L. A. Grønlandsk husflid. Grønlandske Selskab, Arsskrift (1950): 81-93.

Jochelson, W. Past and present subterranean dwellings of the tribes of North Eastern Asia and North Western America. International Congress of Americanists, Proceedings, 15, vol. 2 (1906): 115-123.

Jochelson, W. The ethnological problems of Bering Sea. Natural History, 26 (1926): 90-95.

Jonkel, C. J. Some comments on polar bear management. Biological Conservation, 2 (1970): 115-119.

Jordan, D. Survey of blood grouping and Rh factor in Eskimos of the Eastern Arctic. Canadian Medical Association Journal, 56 (1946): 429-434.

Jørgensen, J. B. The Eskimo skeleton. Meddelelser om Gronland, 146, no. 2 (1953): 1-158.

Jouvancourt, Hugues de. Eros eskimo. Montréal, Éditions La Frégate, 1969. 24 p. illus.

Juel, E. Notes on seal-hunting ceremonialism in the Arctic. Ethnos, 10 (1945): 143-164.

Katz, Solomon H. Change on "Top of the world". Expedition, 15, no. 1 (1972): 15-21.

Keithahn, E. L. Igloo tales. Lawrence, 1950. 142 p.

Kennedy, Michael. Festival: reviving native arts. Alaska Review, 4, no. 2 (1970): 11-39.

Kidd, K. E. Trading into Hudson's Bay. Beaver, 288, no. 3 (1957): 12-17.

King, B. Eskimo art of the Canadian Eastern Arctic. El Palacio, 61 (1954): 74-76.

King, R. On the physical characters of
   the Esquimaux. Ethnological Society
   (London), Journal, 1 (1848): 45-59.

Kleivan, Inge. Why is the raven black? An
   analysis of an Eskimo myth. København,
   Munksgaard, 1971. 52 p. illus. (Acta
   Arctica, 17)

Knowles, F. H. S. The glenoid fossa in
   the skull of the Eskimo. Canada,
   Department of Mines, Geological Survey,
   Museum Bulletin, 9, no. 4 (1915): 1-25.

König, H. Das Recht der Polarvölker.
   Anthropos, 22 (1927): 689-746; 24
   (1929): 87-143, 621-664.

König, H. Das Rechtsbruch und sein
   Ausgleich bei den Eskimo. Anthropos,
   18/19 (1923/1924): 484-515, 771-792; 20
   (1925): 276-315.

König, H. Gedanken zur Frage nach der
   Urheimat der Eskimo. International
   Congress of Americanists, Proceedings,
   21 (1924): 256-262.

König, H. Präanimistische Vorstellungen
   im Weltbilde der Eskimos. International
   Congress of the Anthropological and
   Ethnological Sciences, Acts, 1 (1934):
   232-233.

König, H. Waren die Eskimos die ersten
   Besiedler des hohen Nordens? Forschungen
   und Fortschritte, 10 (1934): 426-427.

Konitzky, Gustav A. Arktische Jäger.
   Stuttgart, Kosmos, 1961. 72 p. illus.
   (Kosmos-Bibliothek, 231)

Koo, Jang H. The copulative 'u' in Yupik
   Eskimo and crossover convention.
   International Journal of American
   Linguistics, 37 (1971): 215-218.

Koolage, William W., Jr. Adaptation of
   Chipewyan Indians and other persons of
   native background in Churchill,
   Manitoba. Dissertation Abstracts
   International, 32 (1971/1972): 681B. UM
   71-20,978.

Koranda, Lorraine D. Eskimo music: the
   songs and the instruments. Alaska
   Review, 4, no. 2 (1970): 73-80.

Krenov, J. Legends from Alaska. Société
   des Américanistes, Journal, n.s., 40
   (1951): 173-195.

Kroeber, A. L. Animal tales of the
   Eskimo. Journal of American Folklore, 12
   (1899): 17-23.

Kroeber, Alfred L. On typological
   indices, I: ranking of languages.

International Journal of American
   Linguistics, 26 (1960): 171-177.

Krupa, Viktor. On quantification of
   typology. Linguistics, 12 (1965): 31-36.

Krupa, Viktor. Relations between
   typological indices. By Viktor Krupa and
   Gabriel Altman. Linguistics, 24 (1966):
   29-37.

Laguna, F. de. A comparison of Eskimo and
   palaeolithic art. American Journal of
   Archaeology, 36 (1932): 477-508; 37
   (1933): 77-107.

Laguna, F. de. Eskimo lamps and pots.
   Royal Anthropological Institute of Great
   Britain and Ireland, Journal, 70 (1940):
   53-76.

Laguna, F. de. The importance of the
   Eskimo in Northeastern archaeology.
   Robert S. Peabody Foundation for
   Archaeology, Papers, 3 (1946): 106-142.

Lantis, M. Eskimo herdsmen. In Edward H.
   Spicer, ed. Human Problems in
   Technological Change. New York, 1952:
   127-148.

Lantis, M. Note on the Alaskan whale cult
   and its affinities. American
   Anthropologist, n.s., 42 (1940): 366-
   368.

Lantis, M. Present status of the Alaskan
   Eskimos. Alaskan Science Conference,
   Proceedings (1950): 38-51.

Lantis, M. Problems of human ecology in
   the North American Arctic. Arctic, 7
   (1954): 307-320.

Lantis, M. Security for Alaskan Eskimos.
   American Indian, 4 (1950): 32-40.

Lantis, M. The Alaskan whale cult and its
   affinities. American Anthropologist,
   n.s., 40 (1938): 438-464.

Lantis, M. The reindeer industry in
   Alaska. Arctic, 3 (1950): 27-44.

Lantis, Margaret. The religion of the
   Eskimos. In Vergilius Ferm, ed.
   Forgotten Religions. New York,
   Philosophical Library, 1950: 311-339.

Larmour, W. T. The art of the Canadian
   Eskimo. Ottawa, Queen's Printer, 1967.
   103 p. illus., map.

Larsen, E. L., ed. The Eskimos, an
   American people. Alaska, University,
   Anthropological Papers, 5 (1957): 83-90.

Larsen, H. Recent developments in Eskimo
   archaeology. International Congress of

the Anthropological and Ethnological
Sciences, Acts, 4, vol. 2 (1952): 315-
319.

Larsen, H. E. Grønlaenderne. In K.
Birket-Smith. Grønlands Bogen, I. 1950:
205-252.

Larsen, Helge. Some examples of bear cult
among the Eskimo and other northern
peoples. Folk, 11/12 (1969/1970): 27-42.

Larsen, Helge. The Eskimo culture and its
relationship to northern Eurasia. In
International Congress of
Anthropological and and Ethnological
Sciences, 8th. 1968, Tokyo and Kyoto.
Proceedings. Vol. 3. Tokyo, Science
Council of Japan, 1970: 338-340.

Larsen, Helge F. Eskimokulturen. 2. opl.
København, Munksgaard, 1962. 81 p.
illus.

Larsen, Henry A. Henry med det store
skipet. Oslo, E. G. Mortensen, 1964.
276 p. illus., map.

Larsen, Henry A. The North-West Passage,
1940-1942 and 1944. Ottawa, Queen's
Printer, 1969. 51 p. illus., maps.

Laufer, B. The Eskimo screw as a culture-
historical problem. American
Anthropologist, n.s., 17 (1915): 396-
406.

Laughlin, W. S. Blood groups, morphology,
and population size of the Eskimos. Cold
Spring Harbor Symposia on Quantitative
Biology, 15 (1950): 165-173.

Laughlin, W. S. Contemporary problems in
the anthropology of southern Alaska.
Alaskan Science Conference, Proceedings
(1950): 66-84.

Laughlin, W. S. The Alaska gateway viewed
from the Aleutian Islands. In Papers on
the Physical Anthropology of the
American Indian. New York, 1951: 98-
126.

Laughlin, W. S. The Aleut-Eskimo
Community. Alaska, University,
Anthropological Papers, 1 (1952): 24-48.

Laughlin, William S. Eskimos and Aleuts:
their origins and evolution. Science,
142 (1963): 633-645.

Laughlin, William S. Genetical and
anthropological characteristics of
Arctic populations. In P. T. Baker and
J. S. Weiner, eds. The Biology of Human
Adaptability. Oxford, at the Clarendon
Press, 1966: 469-495.

Laughlin, William S. The demography of
hunters: an Eskimo example. In Richard
B. Lee and Irven DeVore, eds. Man the
Hunter. Chicago, Aldine, 1968: 241-243.

Laughlin, William S. The purpose of
studying Eskimos and their population
systems. Arctic, 23 (1970): 3-13.

LaVallee, Mary Anne, ed. National
conference on Indian and northern
education (Saskatoon, Canada, 1967).
Saskatoon, Saskatchewan University,
Extension Division, 1967. 130 p. ERIC
ED028861.

Laviolette, G. Atlas des missions
indiennes et esquimaudes confiées au
Oblats de Marie Immaculée du Canada.
Ottawa, Commission Oblate des Oeuvres
Indiennes et Esquimaudes, 1953. 48 p.
maps.

Laviolette, G. Notes on the aborigines of
the prairie provinces. Anthropologica, 2
(1956): 107-130.

Leechman, D. Aboriginal paints and dyes
in Canada. Royal Society of Canada,
Proceedings and Transactions, ser. 3,
26, no. 2 (1932): 37-42.

Leechman, D. Beauty's only skin deep.
Beaver, 282, no. 2 (1951): 38-40.

Leechman, D. Eskimo sculpture in stone.
Canadian Geographical Journal, 48
(1954): 126-127.

Leechman, D. Igloo and tupik. Beaver,
275, no. 3 (1945): 36-39.

Lefebvre, Gilles R. A draft orthography
for the Canadian Eskimos; towards a
future unification with Greenland.
Ottawa, 1957. 17 p. (Canada,
Department of Northern Affairs and
National Resources, Northern Co-
ordination and Research Centre, NCRC-57-
1)

Lehmann, Henri. A propos de l'Exposition
"Chefs-d'oeuvre des arts indiens et
esquimaux du Canada". Objets et Mondes,
9 (1969): 193-214.

Lehmann-Filhés, M. Die letzten Isländer
in Grönland. Verein für Volkskunde,
Zeitschrift, 19 (1909): 170-173.

Lergh, R. W. Dental pathology of the
Eskimo. Dental Cosmos, 67 (1925): 884-
898.

Leroi-Gourhan, A. Esquisse d'une
classification craniologique des Eskimo.
International Congress of Americanists,
Proceedings, 28 (1948): 19-42.

Leroi-Gourhan, A. La civilisation du renne. 2d ed. Paris, 1936. 178 p.

Leroi-Gourhan, A. Le mammouth dans la zoologie des Eskimos. La Terre et la Vie, 5, no. 2 (July 1935): 3-12.

Lestrange, M. de. À propos d'empreintes d'Eskimo. International Congress of Americanists, Proceedings, 28 (1948): 43-53.

Levin, M. G. K antropologii Eskimosov. Sovetskaia Etnografiia, no. 6/7 (1947): 216-223.

Levin, M. G. Kraniologicheskie tipy Chukchei i Eskimosov. Akademiia Nauk SSSR, Muzei Antropologii i Etnografii, Sbornik, 10 (1949): 293-302.

Levin, M. G. Novye materialy po gruppam krovi y eskimosov i lamutov. Sovetskaia Etnografiia, no. 3 (1959): 98-99.

Lewis, H. W. and G. J. Wherrett. An X-ray survey of Eskimos. Canadian Medical Association Journal, 57 (1947): 357-359.

Lewis, Marion. Inheritance of blood group antigens in a largely Eskimo population sample. By Marion Lewis, Bruce Chown, and Hiroko Kaita. American Journal of Human Genetics, 15 (1963): 203-208; 16 (1964): 261; 18 (1966): 231.

Lewis, Richard, comp. I breathe a new song; poems of the Eskimo. New York, Simon and Schuster, 1971. 128 p. illus.

Lidegaard, M. Grønlands historie. København, J. H. Schultz, 1961. 166 p. illus., maps.

Lindig, Wolfgang H. Die Kulturen der Eskimo und Indianer Nordamerikas. Frankfurt am Main, Athenaion, 1972. 378 p. illus.

Linnik, E. Eskimosy. Vokrug Sveta, no. 8 (1956): 22-23.

Little, Arthur D., Inc. An evaluation of the feasibility of native industry in northwestern Alaska. Report to U.S. Bureau of Indian Affairs C-64870. Cambridge, Mass., 1963. 99 p. map.

Lloyd, Trevor. Map of the distribution of Eskimos and Greenlanders in North America. Canadian Geographer, 13 (1959): 41-42.

Lot-Falck, E. Les masques eskimo et aléoutes de la collection Pinart. Société des Américanistes, Journal, n.s., 46 (1957): 5-44.

Lotz, James R. Human rights of Indians and Eskimos. Canadian Labour, 12, no. 12 (1967): 12-15.

Lotz, Jim. Closing the gap: the Eskimo as educator. Alaska Review, 3, no. 3 (1967/1969): 229-239.

Lundman, Bertil. Ein paar kleine Bemerkungen über die Anthropologie der Beringvölker. Folk, 5 (1963): 233-234.

Lyon, George F. The private journal of Captain G. F. Lyon of H.M.S. Hecla, during the recent voyage of discovery under Captain Parry, 1821-1823. Barre, Mass., Imprint Society, 1970. 17, 297 p. illus.

MacArthur, Russell. Sex differences in field dependence for the Eskimo: replication of Berry's findings. International Journal of Psychology, 2, no. 2 (1967): 139-140.

Machetanz, Sara. The howl of the malemute; the story of an Alaskan winter. New York, William Sloane Associates, 1961. 204 p. illus.

MacNeish, R. S. A speculative framework of northern North American prehistory as of April 1959. Anthropologica, n.s., 1 (1959): 7-23.

Madsen, C. and J. S. Douglas. Arctic trader. New York, 1957. 283 p.

Magnus, Preben von. Influenza in isolated communities. Archives of Environmental Health, 17 (1968): 537-542.

Maher, Ramona. The blind boy and the loon, and other Eskimo myths. New York, John Day, 1969. 158 p. illus.

Mahon, W. A., et al. Pneumonia in Indian and Eskimo infants and children: Part II. A controlled clinical trial of antibiotics. Canadian Medical Association Journal, 96 (1967): 265-268.

Maksimov, A. Eskimosy. Bol'shaia Sovetskaia Entsiklopediia, 64 (1947): 632-634.

Mallet, T. Glimpses of the barren lands. New York, 1930. 146 p.

Mallet, T. Plain tales of the North. New York, 1926. 136 p.

Malvesin-Fabre, G. Un redresseur de flèches orné en ivoire. Anthropologie (Paris), 53 (1949): 74-80.

Mann, George V., et al. The health and nutritional status of Alaskan Eskimos. A survey of the Interdepartmental

Committee on Nutrition for National Defense--1958. American Journal of Clinical Nutrition, 11 (1962): 31-76.

Marcussen, P. V. and J. Rendal. Udryddelse af gonorrhoe i et grønlandsk laegedistrikt. Ugeskrift for Laeger, 114 (1952): 819-821.

Marderner, J. Das Gemeinschaftsleben der Eskimo. Anthropologischen Gesellschaft in Wien, Mitteilungen, 69 (1940): 273-348.

Markham, C. H. On the origin and migrations of the Greenland Esquimaux. Royal Geographical Society, Journal, 35 (1865): 87-99.

Markham, C. H. The voyages and works of John Davis the navigator. London, 1880. 373 p.

Markov, S. Letopis' Aliaski. Moscow, 1948. 220 p.

Marriott, R. S. Canada's Eastern Arctic patrol. Canadian Geographical Journal, 20 (1940): 156-161.

Marsh, D. B. Life in a snowhouse. Natural History, 60 (1951): 64-66.

Martijn, Charles A. Canadian Eskimo carving in historical perspective. Anthropos, 59 (1964): 546-596.

Mary-Rousselière, G. Longévité Esquimaude. Eskimo, 43 (1957): 13-15.

Mason, O. T. Aboriginal American harpoons. United States National Museum, Reports, vol. 2 (1900): 193-304.

Mason, O. T. The ulu or woman's knife of the Eskimo. United States National Museum, Reports, vol. 2 (1890): 411-416.

Mason, O. T. Throwing-sticks in the National Museum. United States National Museum, Reports (1884): 279-289.

Mathiassen, T. Det vingede naalehus. Geografisk Tidsskrift, 32 (1929): 15-22.

Mathiassen, T. Foreløbig beretning om femte Thule-ekspedition. Geografisk Tidsskrift, 30 (1927): 39-56, 72-88.

Mathiassen, T. Notes on Knud Rasmussen's archaeological collections from the Western Eskimo. International Congress of Americanists, Proceedings, 23 (1928): 395-399.

Mathiassen, T. Preliminary report of the Fifth Thule Expedition. International Congress of Americanists, Proceedings, 21 (1924): 206-215.

Mathiassen, T. The present stage of Eskimo archaeology. Acta Archaeologica, 2 (1931): 185-199.

Mathiassen, T. The question of the origin of Eskimo culture. American Anthropologist, n.s., 32 (1930): 591-607.

Matis, John A. Odontognathic discrimination of United States Indian and Eskimo groups. By John A. Matis and Thomas J. Zwemer. Journal of Dental Research, 50 (1971): 1245-1248.

Mauss, M. and M. H. Beuchat. Essai sur les variations saisonnières des sociétés eskimos. L'Année Sociologique, 9 (1906): 39-130.

Mayhall, John T. Torus mandibularis in an Alaskan Eskimo population. By John T. Mayhall, A. A. Dahlberg, and David G. Owen. American Journal of Physical Anthropology, n.s., 33 (1970): 57-60.

Maynard, James E. Mortality due to heart disease among Alaskan natives, 1955-65. By James E. Maynard, Laurel M. Hammes, and Francis E. Kester. U.S., Public Health Service, Public Health Reports, 82 (1967): 714-720.

McClellan, Catharine. Culture contacts in the early historic period in northwestern North America. Arctic Anthropology, 2, no. 2 (1964): 3-15.

McLean, Charles M. Phlyctenulosis in the Eskimos of the Canadian Eastern Arctic. Canadian Medical Association Journal, 89 (1963): 1212-1213.

McMinimy, D. J. Preliminary report on tuberculosis incidence in Alaska. Alaska's Health, 5, no. 10 (1947): 4-5.

Meier, Ernst. Zeitungen auf Grönland. Berlin, Duncker und Humblot, 1961. 109 p. illus. (Erlangen--Nürnberg, Universität, Institut für Publizistik, Schriften, 1)

Meier, Robert J. Fingerprint patterns from Karluk Village, Kodiak Island. Arctic Anthropology, 3, no. 2 (1965): 206-210.

Meissner, H. O. Bezaubernde Wildnis: Wandern, Jagen, Fliegen in Alaska. Stuttgart, J. G. Cotta'sche Buchhandlung, 1963. 400 p. illus., maps.

Meldgaard, J. Eskimo skulptur. København, 1959. 87 p.

Meldgaard, J. Eskimo-arkaeologien i
etnografiens tjeneste. In Menneskets
Mangfoldighed. København [n.d.]: 25-39.

Meldgaard, Jørgen. Eskimo sculpture.
London, Methuen, 1960. 48 p. illus.

Meldgaard, Jørgen. Eskimo skulptur.
København, J. H. Schulz, 1959. 46 p.
illus.

Melzack, Ronald. Raven, creator of the
world. Eskimo legends retold. Boston,
Little, Brown, 1970. 91 p. illus.

Ménager, Francis M. The kingdom of the
seal. Chicago, Loyola University Press,
1962. 203 p. illus.

Menovshchikov, G. A. Eskimossko-aleutskie
paralleli. Leningrad, Gosudarstvennyĭ
Pedagogicheskiĭ Institut, Uchenye
Zapiski, 167 (1960): 171-192.

Menovshchikov, G. A. I͡Azyk eskimosov
Beringova proliva. In Akademii͡a Nauk
SSSR. Sibirskoe Otdelenie, I͡Azyki i
Fol'klor Narodov Sibirskogo Severa.
Moskva, Nauka, 1966: 69-83.

Menovshchikov, G. A. Kauzativnye glagoly
i kauzativnye konstrukcii v eskimosskom
i͡azyke. By G. A. Menovshchikov and V. S.
Chrakovskii. Voprosy I͡Azykoznanii͡a,
no. 4 (1970): 102-110.

Menovshchikov, G. A. Les constructions
fondamentales de la proposition simple
dans les langues eskimo-aléoutes (en
liaison avec la construction ergative).
Langages, 15 (1969): 127-133.

Menovshchikov, G. A. Ob ustoichivosti
grammaticheskogo stroi͡a. Akademii͡a Nauk
SSSR, Institut I͡Azykoznanii͡a, Voprosy
Teorii i Istorii I͡Azyka v Svete Taudov
I. V. Stalina po I͡Azykoznanii͡u (1952):
430-460.

Merbs, Charles F. Anterior tooth loss in
Arctic populations. Southwestern Journal
of Anthropology, 24 (1968): 20-32.

Mey, Jacob. Possessive and transitive in
Eskimo. Journal of Linguistics, 6
(1969): 47-56.

Mey, Jacob. Reflexives in Eskimo.
International Journal of American
Linguistics, 37 (1971): 1-5.

Mey, Jacob. The analysis of reference in
Eskimo and the computer. In Tilegnet
Carl Hj. Borgstrøm. Oslo,
Universitetsforlaget, 1969: 97-110.

Meyers, Walter E. Eskimo village. New
York, Vantage Press, 1957. 125 p.
illus.

Michaud, Rollande. L'adaptation des
Esquimaux au froid. Québec, 1969.
48 l. illus. (Laval, Universite Centre
d'Études Nordiques, Travaux Divers, 26)

Michéa, J. P. La Baie d'Hudson.
Géographia, 8 (1952): 21-26; 9 (1952):
27-34.

Michéa, Jean. Esquimaux et Indiens du
Grand Nord. Paris, Société Continentale
d'Éditions Modernes Illustrées, 1967.
351 p. illus.

Michie, G. H. and E. M. Neil. Cultural
conflict in the Canadian Arctic.
Canadian Geographer, 5 (1955): 33-41.

Milan, Frederick A. A study of the
maintenance of the thermal balance in
the Eskimo. Ladd Air Force Base, 1960.
20 p. (U.S., Arctic Aeronautical
Laboratory, Ladd Air Force Base, Alaska,
Technical Report, 60-40)

Milan, Frederick A. An experimental study
of thermoregulation in two Arctic races.
Dissertation Abstracts, 24 (1963/1964):
2216-2217. UM 64-587.

Miles, Charles. Indian and Eskimo
artifacts of North America. Chicago,
Regnery, 1963. 12, 244 p. illus.

Miyaoka, Osahito. On syllable
modification and quantity in Yuk
phonology. International Journal of
American Linguistics, 37 (1971): 219-
226.

Moore, P. E. Health for Indians and
Eskimos. Canadian Geographical Journal,
48 (1954): 216-221.

Moore, P. E. Medical care of Canada's
Indians and Eskimos. Canadian Journal of
Public Health, 47 (1956): 227-233.

Morant, G. M. A contribution to Eskimo
craniology. Biometrika, 29 (1937): 1-20.

Morgan, Lael. Eskimo Olympics. New York,
Alicia Patterson Fund, 1972. 8 p.
illus. (Alicia Patterson Fund, LM-9)

Morgan, Lael. Tundra Times; a survival
story. New York, Alicia Patterson Fund,
1972. 12 p. illus. (Alicia Patterson
Fund, LM-7)

Moss, Melvin L. Morphological variations
of the crista galli and medial orbital
margin. American Journal of Physical
Anthropology, n.s., 21 (1963): 159-164.

Mouat, W. Ivan. Education in the Arctic
District. Musk-Ox, 7 (1969): 1-9.

Mouratoff, George J. Diabetes mellitus in Athabaskan Indians in Alaska. By George J. Mouratoff, Nicholas V. Carroll, and Edward M. Scott. Diabetes, 18 (1969): 29-32.

Mouratoff, George J. Diabetes mellitus in Eskimos. By George J. Mouratoff, Nicholas V. Carroll, and Edward M. Scott. American Medical Association, Journal, 199 (1967): 961-966.

Munn, H. T. Tales of the Eskimo. London, 1925. 196 p.

Murdoch, J. A study of the Eskimo bows in the U.S. National Museum. United States National Museum, Reports, vol. 2 (1884): 207-216.

Murdoch, J. Dr. Rink's "Eskimo Tribes". American Anthropologist, 1 (1888): 125-133.

Murdoch, J. On the Siberian origin of some customs of the Western Eskimo. American Anthropologist, 1 (1888): 325-335.

Murdoch, J. Sinew-backed bow of the Eskimo. Smithsonian Miscellaneous Collections, 34, no. 2 (1893): 168-171.

New Brunswick Museum, St. John. Arctic values '65. St. John, 1965. 62 p. illus.

Newell, Edythe W. The rescue of the sun, and other tales from the far North. Chicago, A. Whitman, 1970. 142 p. illus.

Newman, M. T. Adaptation of man to cold climates. Evolution, 10 (1956): 101-105.

Nippgen, J. Les résultats ethnographiques de l'Expedition Danoise dans l'Amérique arctique. Revue Anthropologique, 36 (1926): 411-426.

Noyes, J. R. The Alaska National Guard. Military Engineer, 48 (1956): 96-98.

Oetteking, B. Ein Beitrag zur Kräniologie der Eskimo. Dresden, Königliches Zoologisches und Anthropologisch-Ethnographisches Museum, Abhandlungen und Berichte, 12, no. 3 (1908): 1-58.

Oleson, Tryggvi J. Early voyages and northern approaches 1000-1632. Toronto, McClelland and Stewart, 1963. 12, 211 p. illus., maps.

Oman, Lela K., comp. The ghost of Kingikty (ee-ahk-meute), and other Eskimo legends. Anchorage, K. Wray's Print Shop, 1967. 56 p. illus.

Ortner, Donald J. Description and classification of degenerative bone changes in the distal joint surfaces of the humerus. American Journal of Physical Anthropology, n.s., 28 (1968): 139-155.

Oschinsky, L. and R. Smithurst. On certain dental characters of the Eskimo of the Canadian Arctic. Anthropologica, n.s., 2 (1960): 105-112.

Oschinsky, Lawrence. Facial flatness and cheekbone morphology in Arctic Mongoloids. Anthropologica, n.s., 4 (1962): 349-377.

Oschinsky, Lawrence. On certain dental characters of the Eskimo of the eastern Canadian Arctic. Anthropologica, n.s., 2 (1960): 105-112.

Oswalt, W. H. The saucer-shaped Eskimo lamp. Alaska, University, Anthropological Papers, 1, no. 2 (1953): 15-23.

Oswalt, Wendell H. Alaskan Eskimos. San Francisco, Chandler, 1967. 15, 297 p. illus., maps.

Oswalt, Wendell H. The future of the Caribou Eskimos. By Wendell H. Oswalt and James W. VanStone. Anthropologica, n.s., 2 (1960): 154-176.

Päivänsalo, P. Sosiologinen tutkimus eskimoiden lastenhoito ja kasvatustavoista. Suomen Mastavus-Sosiologisen Yhdistyksen Julkaisuja, 1 (1947): 1-158.

Pales, L. Les perforations posthumes naturelles des crânes Eskimo du Groenland. Société d'Anthropologie (Paris), Bulletin, sér. 10, 3 (1952): 229-237.

Palmer, Harvey E., et al. Cs-137 in Alaskan Eskimos. Health Physics, 9 (1963): 875.

Paris, Musée de l'Homme. Catalogue analytique et descriptif des têtes de harpons eskimo du Musée de l'Homme. By R. and E. Falck. Paris, 1963. 52 p. illus. (Paris, Musée de l'Homme, Catalogues, Série G: Arctiques, 1)

Parker, Seymour. Eskimo psychopathology in the context of Eskimo personality and culture. American Anthropologist, 64 (1962): 76-96.

Parran, T., et al. Alaska's health. Pittsburgh, 1954.

Parry, William Edward. Journal of a second voyage for the discovery of a northwest passage from the Atlantic to the Pacific. New York, Greenwood Press, 1969. 30, 571 p. illus., maps.

Paulson, I. The "Seat of Honor" in aboriginal dwellings in the circumpolar zone. International Congress of Americanists, Proceedings, 29, vol. 3 (1952): 63-65.

Peck, E. J. Eskimo grammar. Ottawa, 1919. 92 p.

Peck, E. J. Revised Eskimo grammar book. Toronto, 1954. 79 p.

Pedersen, P. O. Anatomical studies of the East Greenland Eskimo dentition. International Congress of Americanists, Proceedings, 29, vol. 3 (1952): 46-49.

Pedersen, P. O. Some dental aspects of anthropology. Dental Record, Copenhagen (July/August 1952): 170-178.

Persson, Ib. The Gc-system in Greenland Eskimos. Acta Genetica et Statistica Medica, 13 (1963): 84-87.

Persson, Ib. The main haptoglobin types in Greenland Eskimos. Acta Genetica et Statistica Medica, 12 (1962): 292-295.

Persson, Ib. Transferrins in Greenland Eskimos. Acta Genetica et Statistica Medica, 12 (1962): 41-44.

Petersen, Robert. Burial-forms and death cult among the Eskimos. Folk, 8-9 (1966/1967): 260-280.

Petersen, Robert. On phonological length in the eastern Eskimo dialects. Folk, 11/12 (1969/1970): 329-344.

Petitot, E. Étude des Esquimaux. International Congress of Americanists, Proceedings, 1, vol. 1 (1875): 329-339.

Petitot, E. Origine asiatique des Esquimaux. International Congress of Americanists, Proceedings, 8 (1892): 296-297.

Phebus, George. Alaskan Eskimo life in the 1890s as sketched by native artists. Washington, D.C., Smithsonian Institution Press, 1972. 168 p. illus.

Pinart, A. La chasse aux animaux marins et les pecheries chez les indigènes de la cote nord-ouest d'Amérique. Boulogne-sur-Mer, 1875. 15 p.

Poncins, G. de M. Eskimos. New York, 1949. 112 p.

Pool, Beekman H. The Chauncey C. Nash Collection: contemporary Canadian Eskimo art. Boston, Club of Odd Volumes, 1964. 14 p. illus.

Porsild, A. E. Edible plants of the arctic. Arctic, 6 (1953): 15-34.

Porsild, A. E. Land use in the arctic. Canadian Geographical Journal, 48 (1954): 232-243; 49 (1954): 20-31.

Porsild, M. P. The principle of the screw in the technique of the Eskimo. American Anthropologist, n.s., 17 (1915): 1-16.

Porter, Merilys E. Ambulatory chemotherapy in Alaska. By Merilys E. Porter and George W. Comstock. U.S., Public Health Service, Public Health Reports, 77 (1962): 1021-1032.

Prague, Narodní Galerie. Grafika kanadských Eskymáku. Praha, 1972. 15 p. illus. (Edice Grafika, 15)

Price, Ray. The howling Arctic; the remarkable people who made Canada sovereign in the farthest North. Toronto, P. Martin, 1970. 7, 284 p. illus., map.

Pritchard, G. B. New town in the far North. Geographical Magazine, 37 (1964): 344-357.

Rabeau, E. S. Programa para mejorar el status de salud de los residentes comunales de aldeas en Alaska. Anuario Indigenista, 28 (1968): 163-168.

Rabeau, E. S. Proyección de una actividad sanitaria del medio ambiente para un pueblo menesteroso. Anuario Indigenista, 28 (1968): 169-174.

Rabinowitch, I. M. Clinical and other observations on Canadian Eskimos in the eastern arctic. Canadian Medical Association Journal, 34 (1936): 487-501.

Radin, P. and L. H. Gray. Eskimos. In J. Hastings, ed. Encyclopaedia of Religion and Ethics. Vol. 5. New York, 1912: 391-395.

Rae, J. Correspondence with the Hudson's Bay Company on arctic exploration 1844-1855. Hudson's Bay Record Society, 16 (1953): 1-509.

Raine, David F. The Eskimo bosses. Beaver, 302, no. 1 (1971/1972): 30-35.

Rainey, F. The vanishing art of the Arctic. Expedition, 1, no. 2 (1959): 3-13.

Rainey, Froelich. Return to the Arctic. Expedition, 8, no. 3 (1966): 2-8.

Rainey, Froelich G.   The vanishing art of
the Arctic. In Charlotte M. Otten, ed.
Anthropology and Art.   Garden City,
Natural History Press, 1971: 341-353.

Rasmussen, K.   Across Arctic America.   New
York, 1927.

Rasmussen, K.   Adjustment of the Eskimos
to European civilization. Pacific
Science Congress, Proceedings, 5, vol. 4
(1934): 2889-2896.

Rasmussen, K.   Alaskan Eskimo words.   Fifth
Thule Expedition, Report, 3, no. 4
(1941): 1-83.

Rasmussen, K.   Du Groenland au Pacifique.
Paris, 1929.

Rasmussen, K.   Eskimos and stone age
peoples. Pacific Science Congress,
Proceedings, 5, vol. 4 (1934): 2767-
2772.

Rasmussen, K.   Eskimos and stone-age
peoples. Geografisk Tidsskrift, 32
(1929): 201-216.

Rasmussen, K.   Tasks for future research
in Eskimo culture. American Geographical
Society, Special Publications, 7 (1928):
177-187.

Rasmussen, Knud J. V.   Across Arctic
America; narrative of the Fifth Thule
Expedition.   New York, Greenwood Press,
1969.   20, 388 p.   illus.

Rasmussen, Knud J. V., comp.   Beyond the
high hills; a book of Eskimo poems.
Cleveland, World, 1961.   32 p.   illus.

Rausch, R.   On the status of some arctic
mammals. Arctic, 6 (1953): 91-148.

Rausch, Robert L.   Zoonotic diseases in
the changing Arctic. Archives of
Environmental Health, 17 (1968): 627-
630.

Ray, Dorothy Jean.   Artists of the tundra
and the sea.   Seattle, University of
Washington Press, 1961.   170 p.   illus.

Ray, Dorothy Jean.   Eskimo masks; art and
ceremony.   Seattle, University of
Washington Press, 1967.   7, 246 p.
illus., map.

Ray, Dorothy Jean.   Graphic arts of the
Alaskan Eskimo.   Washington, D.C.,
Government Printing Office, 1969.
87 p.   illus.   (U.S., Indian Arts and
Crafts Board, Native American Arts, 2)

Richardson, J.   The polar regions.
Edinburgh, 1861.

Riddell, F. A.   Climate and the aboriginal
occupation of the Pacific coast of
Alaska. Kroeber Anthropological Society,
Publications, 11 (1954): 60-123.

Riedel, F.   Die Polarvölker.   Halle, 1902.
71 p.

Riesman, P.   The Eskimo discovery of man's
place in the universe. In Gyorgy Kepes,
ed. Sign, Image, Symbol.   New York,
George Braziller, 1966: 226-235.

Rink, H.   Om de eskimoiske dialekter.
Aarboger for Nordisk Oldkyndighed og
Historie, 20 (1885): 219-260.

Rink, H.   Om eskimoernes herkomst.
Aarboger for Nordisk Oldkyndighed og
Historie, n.s., 5 (1890): 185-208.

Rink, H.   On a safe conclusion concerning
the origin of the Eskimo. Royal
Anthropological Institute of Great
Britain and Ireland, Journal, 19 (1890):
452-458.

Rink, H.   The Eskimo dialects. Royal
Anthropological Institute of Great
Britain and Ireland, Journal, 15 (1886):
239-245.

Rink, H.   The Eskimo tribes. Meddelelser
om Grønland, 11 (1887): 1-163.

Rink, H.   The migrations of the Eskimo.
Royal Anthropological Institute of Great
Britain and Ireland, Journal, 17 (1887):
68-74.

Rink, S.   The girl and the dogs--an Eskimo
folk-tale with comments. American
Anthropologist, 11 (1898): 181-187, 209-
215.

Ristvedt, P.   Minner fra "Gjoa"-ferden.
Polarboken (1956): 137-146.

Ritter, A.   A doctor among the Eskimos.
American Indian, 6, no. 1 (1951): 33-36.

Robertson, E. C.   Family allowances in the
Canadian Arctic. Polar Record, 16,
no. 43 (1952): 345-347.

Roche, Aimé.   Le secret des iglous; recit
historique. Lyon, Éditions du Chalet,
1962.   206 p.   illus., maps.

Rochester Museum and Science Center.
Eskimos ivory carvings in the Rochester
Museum. By Christina Burr.   Rochester,
1972.   2, 88 p.   illus.

Rodahl, K.   Basal metabolism of the
Eskimo. Federation Proceedings, 11
(1952): 130.

Rodahl, K. Eskimo metabolism. Norsk
Polarinstitutt, Skrifter, 99 (1954): 1-
83.

Rodahl, K. The body surface area of
Eskimos. American Journal of Physical
Anthropology, n.s., 10 (1952): 419-426.

Rodahl, K. The body surface area of the
Eskimo. Journal of Applied Physiology, 5
(1952): 242-246.

Rodahl, Kåre. The last of the few. New
York, Harper and Row, 1963. 10, 208 p.
illus., map.

Roessel, Robert A., Jr., ed. Indian
education workshops. Edited by Robert A.
Roessel and Nicholas Lee. Tempe,
Arizona State University, Indian
Education Center, 1962. 329 p. ERIC
ED017855.

Roheim, G. Die Sedna Sage. Imago, 10
(1924): 159-177.

Rosing, J. Renjakt i det gamle Grønland.
Polarboken (1956): 99-112.

Rousseau, J. J. L'Origine et l'evolution
du mot Esquimau. Cahiers des Dix, 20
(1955): 179-198.

Rowley, G. W. What are Eskimos? North,
10, no. 5 (1963): 12-18.

Rubel, Arthur J. Partnership and wife-
exchange among the Eskimo and Aleut of
northern North America. Alaska,
University, Anthropological Papers, 10
(1961/1963): 59-72.

Rubtsova, Ekaterina S. Eskimossko-russkiĭ
slovar'. Moskva, "Sov. Entsiklopediîa",
1971. 644 p.

Rudenko, S. I. Drevnîaîa Kul'tura
Beringova Moria i Eskimosskaîa Problema.
Moscow, 1947. 131 p.

Rudenko, Sergeĭ Ivanovich. The ancient
culture of the Bering Sea and the Eskimo
problem. Translated by Paul Tolstoy.
Toronto, University of Toronto Press,
1961. 186 p. illus., maps.

Rymer, Sheila. New approaches to health
problems of the Indian and Eskimo
people. Canadian Medical Association
Journal, 101 (1969): 614-615.

Salisbury, Lee H. College orientation
program for Alaskan natives, COPAN--
education for survival. College, 1971.
8, 186 p. (Alaska, University,
Institute of Social, Economic, and
Government Research, ISEGR Report, 27)

Salisbury, Lee H. Cross-cultural
communication and dramatic ritual.
Washington, D.C., Spartan Press, 1967.
(ERIC ED017358)

Sargent, M. Folk and primitive music in
Canada. National Museum of Canada,
Bulletin, 123 (1951): 75-79.

Sauvageot, A. Caractère ouraloide du
verbe Eskimo. Société Linguistique de
Paris, Bulletin, 49 (1953): 107-121.

Schaefer, Otto. Carbohydrate metabolism
in Eskimos. Archives of Environmental
Health, 18 (1969): 144-147.

Schaefer, Otto. Otitis media and bottle-
feeding: an epidemiological study of
infant feeding habits and incidence of
recurrent and chronic middle ear disease
in Canadian Eskimos. Canadian Journal of
Public Health, 62 (1971): 478-489.

Schaefer-Simmern, Henry. Eskimo-Plastik
aus Kanada. 2d ed. Kassel, F. Lometsch,
1968. 71 p. illus.

Schmeiser, Douglas A. Indians, Eskimos
and the law. Musk-Ox, 3 (1968): 1-23.

Schmitt, A. Die Alaska-Schrift. Marburg,
1951. 200 p.

Schmitt, Alfred. Die Alaska-Schrift.
Studium Generale, 20 (1967): 565-574.

Schuster, C. A survival of the Eurasiatic
animal style in modern Alaskan Eskimo
art. International Congress of
Americanists, Proceedings, 29, vol. 3
(1952): 35-45.

Scott, E. M. Nutrition of Alaskan
Eskimos. Nutrition Reviews, 14 (1956):
1-3.

Scott, E. M., et al. Anemia in Alaskan
Eskimos. Journal of Nutrition, 55
(1955): 137-149.

Scott, Edward M. Diabetes mellitus in
Eskimos. By E. M. Scott and Isabelle V.
Griffith. Metabolism, 6 (1957): 320-325.

Scott, Edward M. Nutrition in the Arctic.
By Edward M. Scott and Christine A.
Heller. Archives of Environmental
Health, 17 (1968): 603-608.

Scott, Edward M., et al. The absence of
close linkage of methemoglobinemia and
blood group loci. American Journal of
Human Genetics, 15 (1963): 493-494.

Sellers, F. J. The incidence of anaemia
in infancy and early childhood among
Central Arctic Eskimos. By F. J.
Sellers, W. J. Wood, and J. A. Hildes.

Canadian Medical Association Journal, 81 (1959): 656-657.

Senungetuk, Ronald. The artist speaks. Alaska Review, 4, no. 2 (1970): 41-54.

Sergeev, M. A. Skazni Narodov Severa. Moscow, 1951. 685 p.

Shapiro, H. L. Some observations on the origin of the Eskimos. Pacific Science Congress, Proceedings, 5, vol. 4 (1933): 2723-2732.

Shapiro, H. L. The Alaskan Eskimo. American Museum of Natural History, Anthropological Papers, 31 (1931): 347-384.

Shepard, B. Current study of six Alaskan edible plants. Alaska's Health, 9 (June 1952): 4-5.

Simmons, H. G. Eskimaernas forna och nutida utbredning samt deras vandringsvägar. Ymer, 25 (1905): 173-192.

Small, G. W. The usefulness of Canadian Army selection tests in a culturally restricted population. Canadian Psychologist, 10 (1969): 9-19.

Smith, Glenn. Education for the natives of Alaska: the work of the United States Bureau of Education, 1884-1931. Journal of the West, 6 (1967): 440-450.

Smith, I. N., ed. The unbelievable land. Ottawa, Queen's Printer, 1964. 140 p. illus., map.

Snowden, Donald S. Eskimo fine crafts, another Arctic find. North, 9, no. 1 (1962): 1-11, 26-27.

Søby, Regitze Margrethe. The Eskimo animal cult. Folk, 10/11 (1969/1970): 43-78.

Société des Amis du Musée de l'Homme. Chefs-d'oeuvre des arts indiens et esquimaux du Canada. Paris, 1969. illus., maps.

Soper, J. D. Eskimo dogs of the Canadian Arctic. Canadian Geographical Journal, 20 (1940): 96-108.

Spalding, A. E. SALLIQ: an Eskimo grammar. Ottawa, Department of Indian Affairs and Northern Development, Education Branch, 1969. 5, 128 p.

Speck, F. G. Central Eskimo and Indian dot ornamentation. Indian Notes, 2 (1925): 151-172.

Spencer, R. F. Eskimo polyandry and social organization. International Congress of Americanists, Proceedings, 32 (1958): 539-544.

Spink, John. Historic Eskimo awareness of past changes in sea level. Musk-Ox, 5 (1969): 37-40.

Steensby, H. P. An anthropogeographical study of the origin of Eskimo culture. Meddelelser om Grønland, 53 (1917): 39-228.

Steensby, H. P. Om eskimokulturens oprindelse. København, 1905. 219 p.

Stefansson, V. A word common to the natives of Alaska, Canada, Greenland and Brazil. Nature, 178 (1956): 1008.

Stefansson, V. Causes of Eskimo birthrate increase. Nature, 178 (1956): 1132.

Stefansson, V. Clothes make the Eskimo. Natural History, 64 (1955): 32-41.

Stefansson, V. Eskimos. In Encyclopaedia Britannica. 14th ed. Vol. 8. 1937: 708-710.

Stefansson, V. Prehistoric and present commerce among the Arctic Coast Eskimo. Canada, Department of Mines, Geological Survey, Museum Bulletin, 6 (1914): 1-29.

Stefansson, V. The Eskimo and civilization. American Museum Journal, 12 (1912): 195-204.

Stefansson, V. The fat of the land. New York, 1956. 381 p.

Stefánsson, Vilhjálmur. Discovery. New York, MacGraw-Hill, 1964. 8, 411 p. illus.

Stefánsson, Vilhjálmur. Doing as the Eskimos do. In Frederica de Laguna, ed. Selected Papers from the American Anthropologist 1888-1920. Evanston, Row, Peterson, 1960: 946-958.

Stefánsson, Vilhjálmur. My life with the Eskimo. New York, Collier Books, 1962. 447 p.

Stefánsson, Vilhjálmur. The friendly Arctic. New ed. New York, Greenwood Press, 1969. 37, 812 p. illus., maps.

Stein, K. P. S., et al. Tuberculosis in Greenland. Archives of Environmental Health, 17 (1968): 501-506.

Steinert, W. Die Wirkung des Landschaftszwanges auf die materielle Kultur des Eskimo. Hamburg, 1935. 58 p.

Steinmetz, N. Some aspects of health care in northern Canada. 2. Medical care of Eskimo children. Nova Scotia Medical Bulletin, 49 (1970): 163-164.

Steinmetz, Nicolas. Pediatric needs in the Arctic: a challenge and an opportunity. Clinical Pediatrics, 7 (1968): 498-504.

Stevenson, D. S. Problems of Eskimo relocation for industrial employment. A preliminary study. Ottawa, Canada, Department of Indian Affairs and Northern Development, 1968. 30 p. ERIC ED031334.

Stewart, W. D. The definition and evaluation of values and goals in a cross-cultural region. By W. D. Stewart and Doug Schweitzer. Musk-Ox, 7 (1970): 32-52.

Stuart, C. I. J. M. American Indian languages at Haskell Institute. International Journal of American Linguistics, 28 (1962): 151.

Sveistrup, Poul Peter. The economy of Greenland. København, C. A. Reitzels Forlag, 1967. 218 p. (Meddelelser om Grønland, 182, no. 1)

Swadesh, M. Unaaliq and Proto Eskimo. International Journal of American Linguistics, 17 (1951): 66-70; 18 (1952): 25-34, 69-76, 166-171, 241-256.

Swinton, G. Eskimo carving today. Beaver, 288, no. 4 (1958): 40-47.

Swinton, George. Eskimo fantastic art. Winnipeg, University of Manitoba, Gallery 1 1 1, 1972. 34 p. illus.

Swinton, George. Eskimo sculpture. Toronto, McClelland and Stewart, 1965. 224 p. illus., map.

Taylor, J. G. Eskimo answers to an eighteenth century questionnaire. Ethnohistory, 19 (1972): 135-145.

Taylor, J. Garth. The Canadian Eskimos. Toronto, Royal Ontario Museum, 1971. 16 p. illus.

Taylor, Phyllis M. Dog sled and school desk. London, Herbert Jenkins, 1960. 160 p. illus.

Taylor, W. E. Review and assessment of the Dorset problem. Anthropologica, n.s., 1 (1959): 24-46.

Thalbitzer, W. A note on the derivation of the word "Eskimo" (Inuit). American Anthropologist, 52 (1950): 564.

Thalbitzer, W. A phonetical study of the Eskimo language. Meddelelser om Grønland, 31 (1904): 1-406.

Thalbitzer, W. Der ethnographische Zusammenhang der Eskimo Grönlands mit denen der Hudsonbai. Baessler-Archiv, 2 (1912): 32-44.

Thalbitzer, W. Die kultischen Gottheiten der Eskimos. Archiv für Religionswissenschaft, 26 (1928): 364-430.

Thalbitzer, W. Eskimo as a linguistic type. International Congress of Americanists, Proceedings, 23 (1928): 895-904.

Thalbitzer, W. Eskimo dialects and wanderings. International Congress of Americanists, Proceedings, 14 (1904): 107-118.

Thalbitzer, W. Eskimo language. In Encyclopaedia Britannica. 14th ed. Vol. 8. 1937: 707-708.

Thalbitzer, W. Eskimo. U.S. Bureau of American Ethnology, Bulletin, 40, vol. 1 (1911): 967-1069.

Thalbitzer, W. Eskimoiske stednavne fra Alaska og Grønland. Geografisk Tidsskrift, 35 (1932): 137-155.

Thalbitzer, W. Is Eskimo a primitive language? Congrès International de Linguiste, Actes, 4 (1938): 254-262.

Thalbitzer, W. Is there any connection between the Eskimo language and the Uralian? International Congress of Americanists, Proceedings, 22 vol. 2 (1926): 551-567.

Thalbitzer, W. Possible early contacts between Eskimo and Old World languages. International Congress of Americanists, Proceedings, 29 vol. 3 (1952): 50-54.

Thalbitzer, W. The cultic deities of the Innuit. International Congress of Americanists, Proceedings, 22, vol. 2 (1926): 367-393.

Thalbitzer, W. The Eskimo numerals. Société Finno-Ougrienne, Journal, 25, no. 2 (1908): 1-25.

Thalbitzer, W. Uhlenbeck's Eskimo-Indoeuropean hypothesis. Copenhagen, Cercle Linguistique, Travaux, 1 (1945): 66-96.

Thibert, A. Dictionary English-Eskimo--Eskimo-English. Ottawa, 1954. 184 p.

Thibert, A. Dictionnaire Français-
Esquimau--Esquimau-Francais. Ottawa,
1955. 200 p.

Thompson, Charles T. Patterns of
housekeeping in two Eskimo settlements.
Ottawa, 1969. 11, 59 p. illus., map.
(Canada, Department of Indian Affairs
and Northern Development, Northern
Science Research Group, NSRG 69-1)

Tiffany, George E. The church and the
frontier in the Old Northwest, 1699 to
1812. Catholic Records and Studies, 35
(1946): 73-144.

Tolboom, W. N. People of the snow. New
York, 1956. 96 p.

Tompkins, Stuart Ramsay. Another view of
Russian America, a comment. Alaska
Review, 3, no. 1 (1967/1969): 75-88.

Torrey, E. Fuller. Malignant neoplasms
among Alaskan natives: an
epidemiological approach to cancer.
McGill Medical Journal, 31 (1962): 107-
115.

Torrey, E. Fuller. Mental health services
for American Indians and Eskimos.
Community Mental Health Journal, 6
(1970): 455-463.

Toshach, Sheila. Brucellosis in the
Canadian Arctic. Canadian Journal of
Public Health, 54 (1963): 271-275.

Turner, Christy G., II. Dental chipping
in Aleuts, Eskimos and Indians. By
Christy G. Turner, II and James D.
Cadien. American Journal of Physical
Anthropology, n.s., 31 (1969): 303-310.

Turner, Christy G., II. The dentition of
Arctic peoples. Dissertation Abstracts,
28 (1967/1968): 3143B-3144B. UM 67-
12,162.

Turner, E. H. Problems confronting the
Eskimo artist. Canadian Art, 20 (1963):
226-231.

Tweedsmuir, J. Men and beasts in the
Canadian artic islands. Geographical
Magazine, 26 (1953): 182-191.

Uhlenbeck, C. C. Eskimo en Oer-
Indogermaansch. Koninklijke Akademie van
Wetenschappen, Afdeeling Letterkunde,
Mededeelingen, 77, A, no. 6 (1935): 179-
196.

Uhlenbeck, C. C. Ontwerp van eene
vergelijkende vormleer der Eskimo-talen.
Amsterdam, Koninklijke Akademie van
Wetenschappen, Afdeeling Letterkunde,
Verhandelingen, n.s., 8, no. 3 (1907):
1-76.

Uhlenbeck, C. C. Opmerkingen over het
Eskimo-problem. Amsterdam, Koninklijke
Akademie van Wetenschappen, Jaarboek
(1936): 1-14.

Uhlenbeck, C. C. Oude aziatische
Contacten van het Eskimo. Koninklijke
Akademie van Wetenschappen, Afdeeling
Letterkunde, Mededeelingen, n.s., 4
(1941): 201-227.

Uhlenbeck, C. C. Ur- und
altindogermanische Anklänge im
Wortschatz des Eskimo. Anthropos, 37
(1942): 133-148.

Uhlenbeck, C. C. Uralische Anklänge in
den Eskimosprachen. Deutsche
Morgenländische Gesellschaft,
Zeitschrift, 59 (1905): 757-765.

Uhlenbeck, C. C. Zu einzelnen
Eskimowörtern. Anthropos, 45 (1950):
177-182.

Ulving, T. Consonant gradation in Eskimo.
International Journal of American
Linguistics, 19 (1953): 45-52.

Ulving, T. Two Eskimo etymologies. Studia
Linguistica, 8 (1954): 16-33.

Ulving, Tor. Observations on the language
of the Asiatic Eskimo as presented in
Soviet linguistic works. Linguistics, 69
(1971): 87-119.

U.S., Bureau of Indian Affairs. Indians,
Eskimos and Aleuts of Alaska.
Washington, D.C., Government Printing
Office, 1968. 20 p. ERIC ED028870.

U.S., Congress, Senate, Committee on
Interior and Insular Affairs. Alaska
native claims settlement act of 1971;
report together with additional and
supplemental views. Washington, D.C.,
Government Printing Office, 1971.
223 p. (U.S., Congress, Senate, Senate
Report, 92-405)

U.S., Congress, Senate, Committee on
Interior and Insular Affairs. Alaska
native claims settlement act of 1970;
report [to accompany S. 1830].
Washington, D.C., 1970. 219 p. (U.S.,
Congress, Senate, Senate Report, 91-925)

U.S., Federal Field Committee for
Development Planning in Alaska.
Estimates of native population in
villages, towns, and boroughs of Alaska,
1969. Anchorage, 1969. 4, 30 l. maps.

U.S., Interdepartmental Committee on
Nutrition for National Development.
Alaska, an appraisal of the health and
nutritional status of the Eskimo; a

report. Washington, D.C., 1959. 13,
165 p. illus., maps.

U.S., National Park Service. Alaska
history, 1741-1910. Washington, D.C.,
Government Printing Office, 1961.
222 p. illus., map.

U.S., Public Health Service. Eskimos,
Indians and Aleuts of Alaska, a digest;
Anchorage area. Washington, D.C., 1963.
47 p. (U.S., Public Health Service,
Publication, 615, pt. 7)

Valentine, Victor F., ed. Eskimo of the
Canadian Arctic. Edited by Victor F.
Valentine and Frank G. Vallee. Toronto,
McClelland and Stewart, 1968. 241 p.

Vallee, Frank G. Eskimo theories of
mental illness in the Hudson Bay region.
Anthropologica, n.s., 8 (1966): 53-83.

Vallee, Frank G. Notes on the cooperative
movement and community organization in
the Canadian Arctic. Arctic
Anthropology, 2, no. 2 (1964): 45-49.

Vallee, Frank G. Sociological research in
the Arctic. Ottawa, 1962. 2, 21 p.
(Canada, Department of Northern Affairs
and National Resources, Northern Co-
ordination and Research Centre, NCRC-62-
8)

Vallee, Frank G. Stresses of change and
mental health among the Canadian
Eskimos. Archives of Environmental
Health, 17 (1968): 565-570.

Vallee, Frank G. The co-operative
movement in the Arctic. North, 13, no. 3
(1966): 45-49.

VanStone, James W. An introduction to
Baron F. P. von Wrangell's observations
on the Eskimos and Indians of Alaska.
Arctic Anthropology, 6, no. 2 (1970): 1-
4.

VanStone, James W. Ethnohistorical
research in Alaska. Alaska Review, 3,
no. 1 (1967/1969): 51-59.

Vastokas, Joan M. The relation of form to
iconography in Eskimo masks. Beaver,
298, no. 2 (1967/1968): 26-31.

Velde, F. L'Infanticide chez les
Esquimaux. Eskimo, 34 (1954): 6-8.

Veniaminov, Innokentii. The condition of
the Orthodox Church in Russian America:
Innokentii Veniaminov's history of the
Russian church in Alaska. Translated and
edited by Robert Nichols and Robert
Croskey. Pacific Northwest Quarterly, 63
(1972): 41-54.

Victor, Paul-Émile. Eskimos, nomades des
glaces. Paris, Hachette, 1972. 176 p.
illus., map.

Vienna, Museum für Völkerkunde. Eskimo.
Sonderaustellung 1969. Wien, 1969.
14 p. illus.

Voegelin, Carl F. Typological
classification of systems with included,
excluded and self-sufficient alphabets.
By C. F. Voegelin and F. M. Voegelin.
Anthropological Linguistics, 3, no. 1
(1961): 55-96.

Vogeler, E. Lieder der Eskimos.
Copenhagen, 1930. 62 p.

Volkov, T. and S. I. Rudenko.
Etnograficheskaia kollektsii iz byvshikh
rossiisko-amerikanskikh vladienii. St.
Petersburg, 1910. 47 p.

Vrangel', Ferdinand Petrovich von.
Statistische und ethnographische
Nachrichten über die russische
Besitzungen an der Nordwestküste von
Amerika. Osnabrück, Biblio-Verlag,
1968. 32, 332 p. map.

Wachtmeister, A. Naming and reincarnation
among the Eskimos. Ethnos, 21 (1956):
130-142.

Walker, Harley Jesse. The changing nature
of man's quest for food and water as
related to snow, ice, and permafrost in
the American Arctic. Dissertation
Abstracts, 21 (1960/1961): 589-590. UM
60-2985.

Wallace, Anthony F. C. An
interdisciplinary approach to mental
disorder among the Polar Eskimos of
Northwest Greenland. By Anthony F. C.
Wallace and Robert E. Ackerman.
Anthropologica, n.s., 2 (1960): 249-260.

Walton, W. G., ed. Eskimo-English
Dictionary. Toronto, 1925. 310 p.

Wardle, H. N. The Sedna cycle. American
Anthropologist, n.s., 2 (1900): 568-580.

Wasescha, Blaine Eugene. Comparison of
American-Indian, Eskimo, Spanish-
American, and Anglo youthful offenders
on the Minnesota Counseling Inventory.
Dissertation Abstracts International, 32
(1971/1972): 1929A-1930A. UM 71-25,658.

Webster, Donald H. Iñupiat Eskimo
dictionary. By Donald H. Webster and
Wilfried Zibell. Fairbanks, 1970. 12,
211 p. illus., map.

Webster, Donald H. Let's learn Eskimo. 2d
ed. Fairbanks, Summer Institute of
Linguistics, 1968. 66 p. illus.

Webster, J. H. Eskimos glaze their sled runners. Natural History, 59 (1950): 36-37.

Webster, J. H. Fishing under the ice. Natural History, 59 (1950): 140-141.

Wells, R. and J. Kelly. English-Eskimo and Eskimo-English vocabularies. U.S. Bureau of Education, Circular of Information, no. 2 (1890): 1-72.

Weyer, E. M. The Eskimos. New Haven, 1932.

Weyer, Edward M. Eskimo ingenuity. In Walter R. Goldschmidt, ed. Exploring the Ways of Mankind. New York, Holt, 1960: 148-151.

Weyer, Edward M., Jr. Art of the Eskimo. Natural History, 69, no. 2 (1960): 34-45.

*Weyer, Edward M., Jr. The Eskimos, their environment and folk ways. Hamden, Conn., Archon Books, 1969. 17, 491 p. illus., maps.

Weyer, Edward M., Jr. The structure of social organization among the Eskimo. In Ronald Cohen and John Middleton, eds. Comparative Political Systems. Garden City, Natural History Press, 1967: 1-13.

Wheeler, Mary E. Empires in conflict and cooperation: the "Bostonians" and the Russian-American Company. Pacific Historical Review, 40 (1971): 419-441.

White, G. Canadian apartheid. Canadian Forum, 31 (August 1951): 102-103.

White, Leslie A. The ethnography and ethnology of Franz Boas. Austin, 1963. 76 p. illus. (Texas Memorial Museum, Bulletin, 6)

Whiteford, L. Jean. In-service education: its application in the health service for Eskimos and Indians. Canadian Nurse, 58 (1962): 427-429.

Whitmore, Dorothy Gates. A study of attitudes and achievement of disadvantaged adolescents in Alaska. 4239A-4240A. Dissertation Abstracts International, 30 (1969/1970): UM 70-5906.

Wik, Dennis R. Studies on housing for Alaska natives. By Dennis R. Wik, William B. Page, and Michael L. Shank. Anchorage, Arctic Health Research Center, 1965. 12, 127 p. illus., maps. (U.S., Public Health Service, Publication, 99-AH-1)

Wilkinson, Paul F. Oomingmak: a model for man-animal relationships in prehistory. [With comments by Helmuth Fuchs and Gary A. Wright.] Current Anthropology, 13 (1972): 23-44.

Williams, C. H. M. An investigation concerning the dentition of the Eskimos of Canada's Eastern Arctic. Canadian Dental Association, Journal, 6 (1940): 169-172.

Williamson, Robert G. The Arctic Research and Training Centre, Rankin Inlet, N.W.T. Musk-Ox, 1 (1967): 26-37.

Williamson, Robert G. The Canadian Arctic, sociocultural change. Archives of Environmental Health, 17 (1968): 484-491.

Willmott, W. E. The flexibility of Eskimo social organization. Anthropologica, n.s., 2 (1960): 48-59.

Wilson, C. The new North in pictures. Toronto, 1947. 223 p.

Winnipeg Art Gallery. Eskimo sculpture. Winnipeg, Winnipeg Art Gallery, 1967. 60 p. illus., maps.

Winter, Gordon. The art of the Inuit. Country Life, 152 (1972): 880-881.

Winters, R. H. The Eskimos. Canadian Weekly Bulletin, 8, no. 12 (1953): 6.

Wissler, C., ed. Notes concerning new collections. American Museum of Natural History, Anthropological Papers, 2 (1909): 314-320.

Witthoft, John. Metallurgy of the Tlingit, Dene, and Eskimo. By John Witthoft and Frances Eyman. Expedition, 11, no. 3 (1969): 12-23.

Wolfgang, Robert W. Indian and Eskimo diphyllobothriasis. Canadian Medical Association Journal, 70 (1954): 536-539.

Wolforth, John Raymond. "Dual allegiance" in the Mackenzie Delta, NWT--aspects of the evolution and contemporary spacial structure of a northern community. Dissertation Abstracts International, 32 (1971/1972): 2791B.

Woodbury, Robert L. Clothing, its evolution and development by the inhabitants of the Arctic. Archives of Environmental Health, 17 (1968): 586-591.

Young, H. A. Care of Indians, Eskimos. Canadian Weekly Bulletin, 8, no. 6 (1952): 5-6.

Zagoskin, L. A. Puteshestviia i
   issledovaniia Leitenanta Lavrentiia
   Zagoskina v Russkoi Amerike v 1842-1844
   gg. Moscow, 1956. 453 p.

Zegura, Stephen Luke. A multivariate
   analysis of the inter- and intra-
   population variation exhibited by Eskimo
   crania. Dissertation Abstracts
   International, 32 (1971/1972): 4377B-
   4378B. UM 72-1064.

Zolotarevskaia, I. A. Sovremennoe
   polozhenie indeitsev i eskimosov
   Severnoi Ameriki. By I. A.
   Zolotarevskaia and IU. P. Averkieva. In
   A. V. Efimov and S. A. Tokarev, eds.
   Narody Ameriki. Vol. 1. Moskva,
   Izdatel'stvo Akademiia Nauk SSSR, 1959:
   306-350.

                    01-01 Aleut

Alexander, F. A medical survey of the
   Aleutian Islands (1948). New England
   Journal of Medicine, 240 (1949): 1035-
   1040.

Anderson, H. D. and W. C. Eells. Alaska
   natives. Stanford, 1935. 472 p.

Anonymous. Aleut. U.S. Bureau of American
   Ethnology, Bulletin, 30, vol. 1 (1907):
   36-67.

Anonymous. Aleuty. Bol'shaia Sovetskaia
   Entsiklopediia, 2 (1950): 96-97.

Anonymous. El desarrollo de los grupos
   nativos de Alaska. Anuario Indigenista,
   23 (1963): 89-92.

Avdeev, A. D. Aleutskie maski v
   sobraniiakh Muzeia antropologii i
   etnografii Akademiia Nauk SSSR.
   Akademiia Nauk SSSR, Muzei Antropologii
   i Etnografii, Sbornik, 18 (1958): 279-
   304.

Babikov, S. S. Komandorskie Ostrova.
   Sovetskaia Aziia, 2, no. 2 (1926): 66-
   74.

Bancroft, H. H. The native races of the
   Pacific states, 1. New York, 1875. 87-
   94 p.

Bank, T. P. Aleut vegetation and Aleut
   culture. Michigan Academy of Science,
   Arts and Letters, Papers, 37 (1951): 13-
   30.

Bank, T. P. Birthplace of the winds. New
   York, 1956. 286 p.

Bank, T. P. Health and medical lore of
   the Aleuts. Michigan Academy of Science,

Arts and Letters, Papers, 38 (1953):
   415-431.

Bank, Theodore P., II. People of the
   Bering Sea. New York, MSS Educational
   Publishing, 1971. 101 p.

Bank, Theodore P., II. The Aleuts.
   Scientific American, 199, no. 5 (1958):
   112-120.

Berg, L. On the origin of the Aleut.
   Pacific Science Congress, Proceedings,
   5, vol. 4 (1934): 2773-2775.

Bergsland, K. Aleut and proto-Eskimo.
   International Congress of Americanists,
   Proceedings, 32 (1958): 624-631.

Bergsland, K. Aleut demonstratives and
   the Aleut-Esquimo relationship.
   International Journal of American
   Linguistics, 17 (1951): 167-179.

Bergsland, K. Aleut dialects of Atka and
   Attu. American Philosophical Society,
   Transactions, n.s., 49, no. 3 (1959):
   128 p.

Bergsland, Knut. A problem of
   transformation in Aleut. Word, 25
   (1969): 24-38.

Bergsland, Knut. An aspect of
   subordination in Aleut. In Roman
   Jakobson and Shigeo Kawamoto, eds.
   Studies in General and Oriental
   Linguistics. Tokyo, TEC Co., 1970: 10-
   20.

Bergsland, Knut. Morphological analysis
   and syntactical reconstruction in
   Eskimo-Aleut. In International Congress
   of Linguists, 9th. 1962, Cambridge,
   Mass. Proceedings. The Hague, Mouton,
   1964: 1009-1015. (Janua Linguarum,
   Series Maior, 12)

Bergsland, Knut. The Eskimo shibboleth
   inuk/yuk. In To Honor Roman Jakobson;
   Essays on the Occasion of His Seventieth
   Birthday, 11 October 1966. The Hague,
   Mouton, 1967: 203-221. (Janua
   Linguarum, Series Maior, 31)

Berreman, G. D. Effects of a
   technological change in an Aleutian
   village. Arctic, 7 (1952): 102-107.

Berreman, G. D. Inquiry into community
   integration in an Aleutian village.
   American Anthropologist, 57 (1955): 49-
   59.

Berreman, Gerald D. Aleut reference group
   alienation, mobility, and acculturation.
   In Deward E. Walker, Jr., ed. The
   Emergent Native Americans. Boston,
   Little, Brown, 1972: 532-549.

Berreman, Gerald D. Aleut reference group alienation, mobility, and acculturation. American Anthropologist, 66 (1964): 231-250.

Berreman, Gerald D. Effects of technological change in an Aleutian village. In Deward E. Walker, Jr., ed. The Emergent Native Americans. Boston, Little, Brown, 1972: 322-326.

Birket-Smith, Kaj. An analysis of the potlatch institution of North America. Folk, 6, pt. 2 (1964): 5-13.

Blomkvist, E. E. A Russian scientific expedition to California and Alaska, 1839-1849; the drawings of I. G. Voznesenskii. Translated by Basil Dmytryshyn and E. A. Crownhart-Vaughan. Oregon Historical Quarterly, 73 (1972): 100-170.

Brody, Jacob A. Rubella epidemic on St. Paul Island in the Pribilofs, 1963. I. Epidemiologic, clinical, and serologic findings. American Medical Association, Journal, 191 (1965): 619-623.

Bushnell, D. I. Drawings by John Webber of natives of the northwest coast. Smithsonian Miscellaneous Collections, 80, no. 10 (1928): 1-12.

Buynitzky, S. N. English-Aleutian dictionary. San Francisco, 1871. 13 p.

Candela, P. B. Blood-group determinations upon the bones of thirty Aleutian mummies. American Journal of Physical Anthropology, 24 (1939): 361-383.

Chamberlain, A. F. Aleuts. In J. Hastings, ed. Encyclopaedia of Religion and Ethics. Vol. 1. New York, 1908: 303-305.

Chard, Chester S. Arctic anthropology in America. In Jacob W. Gruber, ed. The Philadelphia Anthropological Society; Papers Presented on Its Golden Anniversary. New York, distributed by Columbia University Press for Temple University Publications, 1967: 77-106.

Chisum, Gary Lee. Systematic phonology of the simple intransitive verb phrase in Central Sierra Miwok. Dissertation Abstracts International, 32 (1971/1972): 4368B. UM 72-7327.

Choris, Louis. An early nineteenth-century artist in Alaska; Louis Choris and the First Kotzebue Expedition. Edited by James W. VanStone. Pacific Northwest Quarterly, 51 (1960): 145-158.

Collins, H. B., A. H. Clark, and E. H. Walker. The Aleutian Islands.

Smithsonian Institution War Background Series, 21 (1945): 1-131.

Coppock, Henry Aaron. Interactions between Russians and Native Americans in Alaska, 1741-1840. Dissertation Abstracts International, 31 (1970/1971): 4767B. UM 71-2049.

Coxe, W. Account of the Russian discoveries between Asia and America. 4th ed. London, 1804.

Czaplicka, M. A. Aboriginal Siberia. Oxford, 1914. 388 p.

Dall, W. H. Alaska and its resources. Boston, 1870. 385-400 p.

Dall, W. H. Alaskan mummies. American Naturalist, 9 (1875): 433-440.

Dall, W. H. Masks, labrets and certain aboriginal customs. U.S. Bureau of American Ethnology, Annual Reports, 3 (1882): 137-143.

Dall, W. H. On succession in the shell-heaps of the Aleutian Islands. Contributions to North American Ethnology, 1 (1877): 41-91.

Dall, W. H. On the distribution and nomenclature of the native tribes of Alaska. Contributions to North American Ethnology, 1 (1877): 7-40.

Dall, W. H. On the distribution of the native tribes of Alaska. American Association for the Advancement of Science, Proceedings, 18 (1869): 263-273.

Dall, W. H. On the remains of later pre-historic man obtained from caves in the Catherina Archipelago. Smithsonian Contributions to Knowledge, 22, no. 6 (1878): 1-35.

Denniston, Glenda Boyd. Ashishik Point: an economic analysis of a prehistoric Aleutian community. Dissertation Abstracts International, 34 (1973/1974): 33B. UM 73-9265.

Dumond, Don E. Eskimos and Aleuts. In International Congress of Anthropological and Ethnological Sciences, 8th. 1968, Tokyo and Kyoto. Proceedings. Vol. 3. Tokyo, Science Council of Japan, 1970: 102-107.

Dumond, Don E. On Eskaleutian linguistics, archaeology, and prehistory. American Anthropologist, 67 (1965): 1231-1257.

Dunn, Ethel. Educating the small peoples of the Soviet North: the limits of culture change. Arctic Anthropology, 5, no. 1 (1968): 1-31.

Edwards, Newton. Economic development of Indian reserves. Human Organization, 20 (1961/1962): 197-202.

Eells, W. C. Mechanical, physical, and musical ability of the native races of Alaska. Journal of Applied Psychology, 17 (1933): 493-506.

Eells, W. C. Mental ability of the native races of Alaska. Journal of Applied Psychology, 17 (1933): 417-438.

Eklund, Carl M. Outbreak of Type 3 poliomyelitis on St. Paul Island, Alaska. By Carl M. Eklund and Carl L. Larson. American Journal of Hygiene, 63 (1956): 115-126.

Elliott, C. P. Salmon fishing grounds and canneries. In Compilation of Narratives of Explorations in Alaska. Washington, D.C., 1900: 738-741.

Erman, A. Ethnographische Wahrnehmungen und Erfahrungen an den Küsten des Berings-Meeres. Zeitschrift für Ethnologie, 2 (1870): 295-327, 369-393; 3 (1871): 149-175, 205-219.

Faĭnberg, L. A. K voprosu o rodovom Stroe Aleutov. Akademiĭa Nauk SSSR, Institut Etnografiĭ, Kratkie Soobshcheniĭa, 23 (1955): 68-77.

Faĭnberg, L. A. Obshchestvennyĭ stroĭ eskimosov i aleutov; ot materialskogo roda k sosedskoĭ obshchine. Moskva, Nauka, 1964. 257 p. illus., maps.

Faĭnberg, L. A. The contemporary situation of the Eskimos (1940-1960) and the problem of their future in the works of American and Canadian ethnographers. Soviet Anthropology and Archaeology, 4, no. 1 (1965): 27-45.

Fassett, H. C. Sea otter hunting; how the Aleuts conduct the chase. Edited by Robert F. Heizer. Alaska, University, Anthropological Papers, 8 (1959/1960): 131-135.

Feltz, Elmer T., et al. California encephalitis virus: serological evidence of human infections in Alaska. Canadian Journal of Microbiology, 18 (1972): 757-762.

Field, H. Contributions to the anthropology of the Soviet Union. Smithsonian Miscellaneous Collections, 110, no. 13 (1948): 230-234.

Finnegan, Michael John. Population definition on the Northwest Coast by analysis of discrete character variation. Dissertation Abstracts International, 33 (1972/1973): 3433B. UM 73-1769.

Fleshman, J. Kenneth. Bronchiectasis in Alaska native children. By J. Kenneth Fleshman, Joseph F. Wilson, and J. Jerome Cohen. Archives of Environmental Health, 17 (1968): 517-523.

Gapanovich, I. I. Rossiĩa v Severovostochnoi Azii. Peking, 1933-1934. 2 v. (402 p.).

Garn, S. M. and C. F. A. Moorrees. Stature, bodybuild, and tooth emergence in Aleutian Aleut children. Yearbook of Physical Anthropology, 7 (1953): 45-54.

Garn, S. M. and C. F. A. Moorrees. Stature, bodybuild, and tooth emergence in Aleutian Aleut children. Child Development, 22 (1951): 261-270.

Garn, S. M. and M. M. Gertler. Age and sex differences in serum cholesterol of Aleut. Canadian Medical Association Journal, 64 (1951): 338-340.

Gebhard, P. and K. P. Kent. Some textile specimens from the Aleutian Islands. American Antiquity, 7 (1941): 171-178.

Geoghegan, R. H. The Aleut language. Washington, D.C., 1944. 169 p.

Georgi, J. G. Beschreibung aller Nationen des Russischen Reichs. St. Petersburg, 1776-1780. 357-374 p.

Gibson, James R. Russian America in 1833: the survey of Kirill Khlebnikov. Pacific Northwest Quarterly, 63 (1972): 1-13.

Golder, F. A. Aleutian stories. Journal of American Folklore, 18 (1905): 215-222.

Golder, F. A. Eskimo and Aleut stories. Journal of American Folklore, 22 (1909): 10-24.

Golder, F. A. The songs and stories of the Aleuts. Journal of American Folklore, 20 (1907): 132-142.

Guggenheim, P. An anthropological campaign on Amchitka. Scientific Monthly, 61 (1945): 21-32.

Gurunanjappa, Bale S. Life tables for Alaska natives. U.S., Public Health Service, Public Health Reports, 84 (1969): 65-69.

Gutsche, Brett B. Hereditary deficiency of pseudo cholinesterase in Eskimos. By Brett B. Gutsche, Edward M. Scott, and

Rita C. Wright. Nature, 215 (1967): 322-323.

Haldeman, J. C. Problems of Alaskan Eskimos, Indians, Aleuts. United States Public Health Service, Public Health Reports, 66 (1951): 912-917.

Hammerich, L. L. Russian loan-words in Alaska. International Congress of Americanists, Proceedings, 30 (1955): 114-126.

Hammerich, L. L. The Russian stratum in Alaskan Eskimo. Slavic Word, 10 (1954): 401-428.

Hammerich, L. L. The Western Eskimo dialects. International Congress of Americanists, Proceedings, 32 (1958): 632-639.

Hanna, Gerald S. WAIS performance of Alaskan native university freshmen. By Gerald S. Hanna, Betty House, and Lee H. Salisbury. Journal of Genetic Psychology, 112 (1968): 57-61.

Harrison, Gordon Scott. Native voting in village Alaska. Arctic, 24 (1971): 62-63.

Hatt, Gudmund. Arctic skin clothing in Eurasia and America, an ethnographic study. Translated by Kirsten Taylor. Arctic Anthropology, 5, no. 2 (1968): 3-132.

Heizer, R. F. A Pacific Eskimo invention in whale hunting in historic times. American Anthropologist, n.s., 45 (1943): 120-122.

Heizer, R. F. Aconite poison whaling in Asia and America. U.S. Bureau of American Ethnology, Bulletin, 133 (1943): 415-468.

Heizer, R. F. Archaeology of the Uyak Site, Kodiak Island, Alaska. Anthropological Records, 17, no. 1 (1956): 1-205.

Hellwald, F. von. Das Volk der Aleuten. Ausland, 54 (1881): 789-793.

Henry, V. Esquisse d'une grammaire raisonneé de la langue aléoute. Paris, 1879. 73 p.

Henry, V. Grammaire comparée de trois langues hyperboréennes. International Congress of Americanists, Proceedings, 3, vol. 2 (1880): 405-509.

Herreid, Clyde F., II. Differences in MMPI scores in native and nonnative Alaskans. By Clyde F. Herreid, II, and

Janet R. Herreid. Journal of Social Psychology, 70 (1966): 191-198.

Hinckley, Ted C. The Presbyterian leadership in pioneer Alaska. Journal of American History, 52 (1965/1966): 742-756.

Holmer, Nils M. On the Amerindian character of Aleut and Eskimo. In Studi Linguistici in Onore di Vittore Pisani. Vol. 2. Brescia, Paideia, 1969: 545-567.

Hrdlička, A. Anthropological explorations on the Aleutian and Commander Islands. Smithsonian Institution, Explorations and Field-Work, (1937): 87-94.

Hrdlička, A. Catalogue of human crania in the United States National Museum Collections. United States National Museum, Proceedings, 94 (1944): 1-172.

Hrdlička, A. Exploration in the Aleutian and the Commander Islands. Smithsonian Institution, Explorations and Field-Work, (1938): 79-86.

Hrdlička, A. Exploration of mummy caves in the Aleutian Islands. Scientific Monthly, 52 (1941): 5-23, 113-130.

Hrdlička, A. Ritual ablation of front teeth in Siberia and America. Smithsonian Miscellaneous Collections, 99, no. 3 (1940): 1-32.

*Hrdlička, A. The Aleutian and Commander Islands and their inhabitants. Philadelphia, 1945. 630 p.

Huber, Albert. Alaskan Native Industries Co-operative Association. Boletín Indigenista, 19 (1959): 221, 223, 225.

Īokel'son, Vladīmīr Il'ich. History, ethnology, and anthropology of the Aleut. By Waldemar Jochelson. Oosterhout N.B., Anthropological Publications, 1966. 3, 91 p. illus.

Ivanov, S. V. Aleut hunting headgear and its ornamentation. International Congress of Americanists, Proceedings, 23 (1928): 477-504.

Ivanov, S. V. Sidīachie chelovecheskie figurki. Akademiīa Nauk SSSR, Muzeĭ Antropologiĭ i Etnografiĭ, Sbornik, 12 (1949): 194-212.

Jacobi, A. Carl Heinrich Mercks ethnographische Beobachtungen über die Völker des Beringsmeers in 1791. Baessler-Archiv, 20 (1937): 113-137.

Jochelson, W. Archaeological investigations in the Aleutian Islands. New York, 1925.

*Jochelson, W. History, ethnology and anthropology of the Aleut. Washington, D.C., 1933. 91 p.

Jochelson, W. Past and present subterranean dwellings of the tribes of North Eastern Asia and North Western America. International Congress of Americanists, Proceedings, 15, vol. 2 (1906): 115-123.

Jochelson, W. People of the foggy seas. Natural History, 28 (1928): 413-424.

Jochelson, W. Scientific results of the ethnological section of the Riabouschinsky Expedition. International Congress of Americanists, Proceedings, 18 (1912): 334-343.

Jochelson, W. The Aleut language and its relation to the Eskimo dialects. International Congress of Americanists, Proceedings, 18 (1912): 96-104.

Jones, Dorothy Miriam. A study of social and economic problems in Unalaska, an Aleut village. Dissertation Abstracts International, 30 (1969/1970): 4554A. UM 70-6048.

Kissell, M. An Aleutian basket. American Museum Journal, 7 (1907): 133-136.

Kleinfeld, J. S. Regionalism in Indian community control. Journal of American Indian Education, 11, no. 3 (1971/1972): 7-14.

Kleinfeld, J. S. Sources of parental ambivalence toward education in an Aleut community. Journal of American Indian Education, 10, no. 2 (1970/1971): 8-14.

Langsdorff, G. H. von. Voyages and travels in various parts of the World. Carlisle, 1817. 331-347 p.

Laughlin, W. S. The Aleut-Eskimo community. Alaska, University, Anthropological Papers, 1 (1952): 24-48.

Laughlin, W. S. and G. H. Marsh. A new view of the history of the Aleutians. Arctic, 4 (1951): 75-88.

Laughlin, William S. Eskimos and Aleuts: their origins and evolution. Science, 142 (1963): 633-645.

Laughlin, William S. The earliest Aleuts. In Early Man in the Western American Arctic: A Symposium. College, University of Alaska, 1963: 73-91.

(Alaska, University, Anthropological Papers, 10, no. 2)

Lavrischeff, T. I. Two Aleut tales. American Anthropologist, n.s., 30 (1928): 121-124.

Lazarev, A. P. Zapiski o Plavanii Voennogo Shliupa Blagonamerennogo. Moscow, 1950. 475 p.

Lee, C. A. Aleutian Indian and English dictonary. Seattle, 1896. 23 p.

Leroi-Gourhan, A. Archéologie du Pacifique-Nord. Paris, Institut d'Ethnologie, Travaux et Mémoires, 47 (1946): 1-542.

Lewis, Marion. Inheritance of blood group antigens in a largely Eskimo population sample. By Marion Lewis, Bruce Chown, and Hiroko Kaita. American Journal of Human Genetics, 15 (1963): 203-208; 16 (1964): 261; 18 (1966): 231.

Liapunova, R. G. Aleutskie baĭdarki. Akademiia Nauk SSSR, Muzeĭ Antropologii i Etnografii, Sbornik, 22 (1964): 223-242.

Liapunova, R. G. Ekspeditsiia I. G. Voznesenskogo i ee znachenie dlia etnografii Russkoĭ Ameriki. Akademiia Nauk SSSR, Muzeĭ Antropologii i Etnografii, Sbornik, 24 (1967): 5-33.

Liapunova, R. G. Muzeĭnye materialy po Aleutam orudiia Aleutov (po materialam MAE). Akademiia Nauk SSSR, Muzeĭ Antropologii i Etnografii, Sbornik, 21 (1963): 149-171.

Liapunova, R. G. Zoomorfnaia skul'ptura Aleutov. Akademiia Nauk SSSR, Muzeĭ Antropologii i Etnografii, Sbornik, 24 (1967): 38-54.

Lot-Falck, E. Les masques eskimo et aléoutes de la collection Pinart. Société des Américanistes, Journal, n.s., 46 (1957): 5-44.

Löwe, F. Wenjaminow über die aleutischen Inseln und deren Bewohner. Archiv für Wissenschaftliche Kunde von Russland, 2 (1842): 459-495.

Lundman, Bertil. Ein paar kleine Bemerkungen über die Anthropologie der Beringvölker. Folk, 5 (1963): 233-234.

Lütke, F. Voyage autour du monde. Paris, 1835. 3 v.

Marsh, G. H. A comparative study of Eskimo-Aleut religion. Alaska, University, Anthropological Papers, 3 (1954): 21-36.

Marsh, G. H. and W. S. Laughlin. Human anatomical knowledge among the Aleutian Islanders. Southwestern Journal of Anthropology, 12 (1956): 38-78.

Martin, F. I. The hunting of the silver fleece. New York, 1946. 328 p.

Martin, F. I. Three years of Pribilof progress. American Indian, 5, no. 3 (1950): 17-26.

Martin, F. I. Wanted, a Pribilof bill of rights. American Indian, 3, no. 4 (1946): 15-25.

Martin, Fredericka I. Sea bears; the story of the fur seal. Philadelphia, Chilton, 1960. 201 p. illus.

Martinson, Charles Richard. Aleut settlements of the Makushin Bay area, Alaska. Dissertation Abstracts International, 34 (1973/1974): 2695B-2696B. UM 73-28,614.

Masterson, J. R. and H. Brower. Bering's successors, 1745-1780. Pacific Northwest Quarterly, 38 (1947): 35-83, 109-155.

May, A. G. Attu. Natural History, 50 (1942): 132-137.

Mayhall, John T. Torus mandibularis in an Alaskan Eskimo population. By John T. Mayhall, A. A. Dahlberg, and David G. Owen. American Journal of Physical Anthropology, n.s., 33 (1970): 57-60.

Maynard, James E. Mortality due to heart disease among Alaskan natives, 1955-65. By James E. Maynard, Laurel M. Hammes, and Francis E. Kester. U.S., Public Health Service, Public Health Reports, 82 (1967): 714-720.

McCracken, H. God's frozen children. New York, 1930. 291 p.

Meissner, H. O. Bezaubernde Wildnis: Wandern, Jagen, Fliegen in Alaska. Stuttgart, J. G. Cotta'sche Buchhandlung, 1963. 400 p. illus., maps.

Melartin, Liisa. Albumin polymorphism (albumin Naskapi) in Eskimos and Navajos. By Liisa Melartin, Baruch S. Blumberg, and John R. Martin. Nature, 218 (1968): 787-789.

Menovshchikov, G. A. Aleutskiĭ ͡iazyk. In Akademi͡ia Nauk SSSR. Institut ͡iazykoznani͡ia. ͡iazyki Narodov SSSR. Vol. 5. Moskva, Nauka, 1968: 386-406.

Menovshchikov, G. A. Eskimossko-Aleutska͡ia gruppa. In Akademi͡ia Nauk SSSR. Institut ͡iazykoznani͡ia. ͡iazyki

Narodov SSSR. Vol. 5. Moskva, Nauka, 1968: 352-365.

Menovshchikov, G. A. K voprosu o proni͡tsaemosti grammaticheskogo stro͡ia ͡iazyka. Voprosy ͡iazykoznani͡ia, 13, no. 5 (1964): 100-106.

Menovshchikov, G. A. Les constructions fondamentales de la proposition simple dans les langues eskimo-aléoutes (en liaison avec la construction ergative). Langages, 15 (1969): 127-133.

Menovshchikov, G. A. Novye dannye o ͡iazyke aleutov Komandorskikh ostrovov. Akademi͡ia Nauk SSSR, Sibirskoe Otdelenie, Izvesti͡ia, no. 1 (1965): 84-92.

Merrill, Ralph G. Occlusal anomalous tubercles on premolars of Alaskan Eskimos and Indians. Oral Surgery, Oral Medicine, Oral Pathology, 17 (1964): 484-496.

Miller, Polly. Lost heritage of Alaska: the adventure and art of the Alaskan Coastal Indian. Cleveland, World, 1967. 15, 289 p. illus., maps.

Moorrees, C. F. A. Dentition as a criterion of race with special reference to the Aleut. Journal of Dental Research, 30 (1951): 815-821.

Moorrees, C. F. A. The Aleut dentition. Cambridge, 1957. 206 p.

Moorrees, C. F. A., et al. Torus mandibularis. American Journal of Physical Anthropology, 10 (1952): 319-329.

Morgan, Lael. Atka--the place the Tsar, the U.S. government and even God forgot. New York, Alicia Patterson Foundation, 1972. 12 p. illus. (Alicia Patterson Foundation, LM-13)

Muir, J. The cruise of the Corwin. Boston, 1917.

Muller, T. P. Analysis of contingency table data on torus mandibularis using a log linear model. By T. P. Muller and John T. Mayhall. American Journal of Physical Anthropology, n.s., 34 (1971): 149-153.

Naert, Pierre. Un emprunt chinois archaïque en aléoute? Anthropos, 57 (1962): 192-193.

Orlova, E. P. Chukotska͡ia, kor͡iakska͡ia, eskimosska͡ia, aleutska͡ia rezna͡ia kost'. Novosibirsk, 1964. 111 p. illus.

Oswalt, Robert L. Russian loanwords in Southwestern Pomo. International Journal of American Linguistics, 24 (1958): 245-247.

Petroff, I. Report on the population, industries and resources of Alaska. U.S. Department of the Interior, Tenth Census, 8 (1881): 146-160.

Petroff, I. The limit of the Innuit tribes on the Alaskan Coast. American Naturalist, 16 (1882): 567-575.

Petroff, I. The population and resources of Alaska. In Compilation of Narratives of Explorations in Alaska. Washington, D.C., 1900: 239-257.

Petroff, Ivan. Ivan Petroff's journal of a trip to Alaska in 1878. Edited by Theodore C. and Caryl Hinckley. Journal of the West, 5 (1966): 25-70.

Pfizmaier, A. Die Sprache der Aleuten und Fuchsinseln. Akademie der Wissenschaften der Wien, Sitzungsberichte, Phil.-hist. Classe, 105 (1883): 801-880; 106 (1884): 237-316.

Philip, R. N., et al. Serologic and skin test evidence of tularemia infection among Alaskan Eskimos, Indians and Aleuts. Journal of Infectious Diseases, 110 (1962): 220-230.

Philip, Robert N., et al. Observations on Asian influenza on two Alaskan islands. U.S., Public Health Service, Public Health Reports, 74 (1959): 737-745.

Pinart, A. Les Aléoutes et leur origine. Société d'Ethnographie, Mémoires, 11 (1872): 155-165.

Porter, Merilys E. Ambulatory chemotherapy in Alaska. By Merilys E. Porter and George W. Comstock. U.S., Public Health Service, Public Health Reports, 77 (1962): 1021-1032.

Preston, W. D. Some methodological suggestions based on Aleut linguistic material. International Journal of American Linguistics, 13 (1947): 171-174.

Quimby, G. I. Aleutian islanders. Field Museum of Natural History, Department of Anthropology, Leaflets, 35 (1944): 1-48.

Quimby, G. I. Periods of prehistoric art in the Aleutian Islands. American Antiquity, 11 (1945): 76-79.

Quimby, G. I. Pottery from the Aleutian Islands. Field Museum, Anthropological Series, 36 (1946): 1-13.

Quimby, G. I. Prehistoric art of the Aleutian Islands. Field Museum, Anthropological Series, 36 (1946): 77-92.

Quimby, G. I. The sadiron lamp of Kamchatka as a clue to the chronology of the Aleut. American Antiquity, 11 (1946): 202-203.

Quimby, G. I. Toggle harpoon heads from the Aleutian Islands. Field Museum, Anthropological Series, 36 (1946): 15-23.

Ransom, J. E. Aleut linguistic perspective. Southwestern Journal of Anthropology, 2 (1946): 48-55.

Ransom, J. E. Aleut natural-food economy. American Anthropologist, n.s., 48 (1946): 607-623.

Ransom, J. E. Aleut religious beliefs: Veniaminov's account. Journal of American Folklore, 58 (1945): 346-349.

Ransom, J. E. Aleut semaphore signals. American Anthropologist, n.s., 43 (1941): 422-427.

Ransom, J. E. Children's games among the Aleut. Journal of American Folklore, 59 (1946): 196-198.

Ransom, J. E. Derivation of the word "Alaska". American Anthropologist, n.s., 42 (1940): 550-551.

Ransom, J. E. Do-it-yourself doctor. Alaska Sportsman, 30, no. 8 (1964): 26-28.

Ransom, J. E. Stories, myths, and superstitions of Fox Island Aleut children. Journal of American Folklore, 60 (1947): 62-72.

Ransom, J. E. Writing as a medium of acculturation among the Aleut. Southwestern Journal of Anthropology, 1 (1945): 333-344.

Reed, Dwayne, et al. A mumps epidemic on St. George Island, Alaska. American Medical Association, Journal, 199 (1967): 967-971.

Rubel, Arthur J. Partnership and wife-exchange among the Eskimo and Aleut of northern North America. Alaska, University, Anthropological Papers, 10 (1961/1963): 59-72.

Rychkov, IU. G. Populiatsionnaia genetika Aleutov Komandorskikh Ostrovov (v sviazi s problemami istorii narodov i adaptatsii drevnei Beringii). By IU. G. Rychkov and V. A. Sheremet'eva. Voprosy

Antropologii, 40 (1972): 45-70; 41 (1972): 3-18; 42 (1972): 3-30.

Santos, A. Jesuitos en el Polo Norte. Madrid, 1943. 546 p.

Scheffer, V. B. Use of fur-seal carcasses by natives of the Pribilof Islands. Pacific Northwest Quarterly, 39 (1948): 131-132.

Schneider, R. G., et al. Hemoglobin G Coushatta: a new variant in an American Indian family. Science, 143 (1964): 697-698.

Schott, W. Ueber die Sprachen des russischen Amerika nach Wenjaminow. Archiv für Wissenschaftliche Kunde von Russland, 7 (1849): 126-143.

Schwatka, F. Report of a military reconnaissance made in Alaska in 1883. Washington, D.C., 1900. 111-118 p.

Scott, Edward M. Diabetes mellitus in Eskimos. By E. M. Scott and Isabelle V. Griffith. Metabolism, 6 (1957): 320-325.

Scott, Edward M., et al. Frequency of polymorphic types of red cell enzymes and serum factors in Alaskan Eskimos and Indians. American Journal of Human Genetics, 18 (1966): 408-411.

Sever, John L., et al. Rubella epidemic on St. Paul Island in the Pribilofs, 1963. American Medical Association, Journal, 191 (1965): 624-626.

Shade, C. I. The girls' puberty ceremony of Umnak, Aleutian Islands. American Anthropologist, n.s., 53 (1951): 145-148.

Sherwood, Morgan B. Science in Russian America, 1741 to 1865. Pacific Northwest Quarterly, 58 (1967): 33-39.

Sh[ternberg], L. I. Aleuty. Novyi Entsiklopedicheskii Slovar, 2 (1916): 40-43.

Spaulding, A. C. The current status of Aleutian archaeology. Society for American Archaeology, Memoirs, 9 (1953): 29-31.

Spaulding, Albert C. Archaeological investigations on Agattu, Aleutian Islands. Ann Arbor, 1962. 79 p. illus. (Michigan, University, Museum of Anthropology, Anthropological Papers, 18)

Tarenetzky, A. Beiträge zur Skelet- und Schädelkunde der Aleuten, Konaegen, Kenai und Koljuschen. Académie Impériale des Sciences de St.-Pétersbourg,

Mémoires, sér. 8, Classe Physico-Mathématique, 9, no. 4 (1900): 1-73.

Thalbitzer, W. Et manuskript of Rasmus Rask om Aleuternes sprog. Oversigt over det Kongelige Danske Videnskabernes Selskabs Forhandlinger (1916): 211-249.

Thalbitzer, W. The Aleutian language compared with Greenlandic. International Journal of American Linguistics, 1 (1921): 40-57.

Torrey, E. Fuller. Malignant neoplasms among Alaskan natives: an epidemiological approach to cancer. McGill Medical Journal, 31 (1962): 107-115.

Traĭnin, G. A. Aleuty. By G. A. Traĭnin, M. V. Stepanova, and R. G. Lîapunova. In A. V. Efimov and S. A. Tokarev, eds. Narody Ameriki. Vol. 1. Moskva, Izdatel'stvo Akademiĭa Nauk SSSR, 1959: 132-150.

Turner, Christy G., II. Dental chipping in Aleuts, Eskimos and Indians. By Christy G. Turner, II and James D. Cadien. American Journal of Physical Anthropology, n.s., 31 (1969): 303-310.

Turner, Christy G., II. Microevolutionary interpretations from the dentition. American Journal of Physical Anthropology, n.s., 30 (1969): 421-426.

Turner, Christy G., II. The dentition of Arctic peoples. Dissertation Abstracts, 28 (1967/1968): 3143B-3144B. UM 67-12,162.

U.S., Bureau of Indian Affairs. Indians, Eskimos and Aleuts of Alaska. Washington, D.C., Government Printing Office, 1968. 20 p. ERIC ED028870.

U.S., Federal Field Committee for Development Planning in Alaska. Estimates of native population in villages, towns, and boroughs of Alaska, 1969. Anchorage, 1969. 4, 30 l. maps.

U.S., Interdepartmental Committee on Nutrition for National Development. Alaska, an appraisal of the health and nutritional status of the Eskimo; a report. Washington, D.C., 1959. 13, 165 p. illus., maps.

U.S., Public Health Service. Eskimos, Indians and Aleuts of Alaska, a digest; Anchorage area. Washington, D.C., 1963. 47 p. (U.S., Public Health Service, Publication, 615, pt. 7)

VanStone, James W., ed. and tr. An early account of the Russian discoveries in the North Pacific. Alaska, University,

Anthropological Papers, 7 (1958/1959): 91-112.

Veniaminov. I. Charakterzüge der Aleuten. Beiträge zur Kenntnis des Russischen Reiches, 1 (1839): 177-225.

Veniaminov, I. Introduction to the study of the Aleutian language. Seattle, 1940. 71 p.

Veniaminov, I. Les Iles Aléoutes et leurs habitants. Nouvelles Annales des Voyages, 124 (1849): 112-148.

Veniaminov, I. Opyt grammatiki aleutsko-lisevskago yazyka. St. Petersburg, 1846. 120 p.

*Veniaminov, I. Zapiski ob Atkhinskikh Aleutakh i Koloskakh. St. Petersburg, 1840. 155 p.

*Veniaminov, I. Zapiski ob ostrovakh unalashkinskago otdela. St. Petersburg, 1840. 3 v.

Veniaminov, Innokentii. The condition of the Orthodox Church in Russian America: Innokentii Veniaminov's history of the Russian church in Alaska. Translated and edited by Robert Nichols and Robert Croskey. Pacific Northwest Quarterly, 63 (1972): 41-54.

Veniaminov, Ioann. A Russian Orthodox priest in a Mexican Catholic parish; Father Ioann Veniaminov's sojourn at Fort Ross and visit to Missions San Rafael, San José, Santa Clara, and San Francisco in 1836. Edited by James R. Gibson. Pacific Historian, 15, no. 2 (1971): 57-66.

Volkov, T. Etnograficheskaîa kollektsii iz byvshikh rossiisko-amerikanskikh vladienii. T. Volkov and S. I. Rudenko. St. Petersburg, 1910. 47 p.

Wardle, H. N. Attu treasure. Pennsylvania, University, Museum Bulletin, 11 (1946): 23-26.

Weyer, E. M. An Aleutian burial. American Museum of Natural History, Anthropological Papers, 31 (1929): 219-238.

Weyer, E. M. Archaeological material from the village site at Hot Springs. American Museum of Natural History, Anthropological Papers, 31 (1930): 239-279.

Wheeler, Mary E. Empires in conflict and cooperation: the "Bostonians" and the Russian-American Company. Pacific Historical Review, 40 (1971): 419-441.

Wik, Dennis R. Studies on housing for Alaska natives. By Dennis R. Wik, William B. Page, and Michael L. Shank. Anchorage, Arctic Health Research Center, 1965. 12, 127 p. illus., maps. (U.S., Public Health Service, Publication, 99-AH-1)

Wilde, E. Health and growth of Aleut children. Journal of Pediatrics, 36 (1950): 149-158.

Winchell, M. E. Home by the Bering Sea. Caldwell, 1951. 226 p.

Worth, Dean Stoddard. Russian kniga, Southwestern Pomo kalikak. International Journal of American Linguistics, 26 (1960): 62-66.

Yarmolinsky, A. Aleutian manuscript collection. New York, 1944. 12 p.

Yeatman, Gentry W. Preservation of chrondrocyte ultrastructure in an Aleutian mummy. New York Academy of Medicine, Bulletin, 47 (1971): 104-108.

Zimmerman, Michael R., et al. Examination of an Aleutian mummy. New York Academy of Medicine, Bulletin, 47 (1971): 80-103.

01-02   Baffinland Eskimo

Abbes, H. Die Eskimos des Cumberlandgolfes. [n.p., n.d.]. 60 p.

Abbes, H. Die Eskimos des Cumberland-Sundes. Globus, 46 (1884): 198-201, 213-218.

Anders, G., ed. Baffin Island--East Coast; area economic survey. Ottawa, 1966. (Canada, Department of Northern Affairs and National Resources, Industrial Division, Area Economic Survey Report, 66-4)

Andersen, Kristian Lange. Aerobic working capacity of Eskimos. By K. Lange Andersen and J. S. Hart. Journal of Applied Physiology, 18 (1963): 764-768.

Andersen, Kristian Lange, et al. Metabolic and thermal response of Eskimos during muscular exertion in the cold. Journal of Applied Physiology, 18 (1963): 613-618.

Anderson, G. A whale is killed. Beaver, 277 (1947): 18-21.

Anderson, James Watt. Fur trader's story. Toronto, Ryerson Press, 1961. 15, 245 p. illus.

Anonymous. Sailors in Eskimoland. Crowsnest, 7, no. 8 (1955): 14-16.

Anonymous. Starvation near Piling, Foxe Basin, N.W.T. Arctic Circular, 3 (1950): 31-32.

Anonymous. Step toward tomorrow. North, 9, no. 2 (1962): 1-5.

Atherton, D. Climbing in Baffin Island. Appalachia, 35 (1964): 316-324.

Baird, Irene. Land of the lively arts. Beaver, 292, no. 2 (1961/1962): 12-21.

Balikci, Asen. Female infanticide on the Arctic Coast. Man, n.s., 2 (1967): 615-625.

Berry, John W. Ecology and socialization as factors in figural assimilation and the resolution of binocular rivalry. International Journal of Psychology, 4 (1969): 271-280.

Berry, John W. Ecology, perceptual development and the Müller-Lyer illusion. British Journal of Psychology, 59 (1968): 205-210.

Bilby, J. W. Among unknown Eskimo. London, 1923. 280 p.

Black, F. L., et al. Intensified reactions to measles vaccine in unexposed populations of American Indians. Journal of Infectious Diseases, 124 (1971): 306-317.

Boas, F. A year among the Eskimo. American Geographical Society, Journal, 19 (1887): 383-402.

Boas, F. An Eskimo winter. In E. C. Parsons, ed. American Indian Life. New York, 1925: 363-378.

Boas, F. Baffin-Land. Petermanns Mitteilungen, Ergänzungshefte, 17, no. 5 (1885): 1-100.

Boas, F. Cumberland Sound and its Eskimos. Popular Science Monthly, 26 (1885): 768-779.

Boas, F. Der Eskimo-Dialekt des Cumberland-Sundes. Anthropologischen Gesellschaft in Wien, Mitteilungen, 24 (1894): 97-114.

Boas, F. Die religiösen Vorstellungen und einige Gebräuche der zentralen Eskimos. Petermanns Mitteilungen, 33 (1887): 302-316.

Boas, F. Die Sagen der Baffin-Land Eskimos. Berliner Gesellschaft für Anthropologie, Ethnologie und Urgeschichte, Verhandlungen (1885): 161-166.

Boas, F. Eskimo tales and songs. Journal of American Folklore, 7 (1894): 45-50; 10 (1897): 109-115.

Boas, F. Religious beliefs of the Central Eskimo. Popular Science Monthly, 57 (1900): 624-631.

*Boas, F. The Central Eskimo. U.S. Bureau of American Ethnology, Annual Reports, 6 (1888): 390-669.

*Boas, F. The Eskimo of Baffin Land and Hudson Bay. American Museum of Natural History, Bulletin, 15 (1901-1907): 1-570.

Boas, F. The Eskimo of Baffin Land. Smithsonian Miscellaneous Collections, 34, no. 2 (1893): 95-102.

Boas, F. and H. Rink. Eskimo tales and songs. Journal of American Folklore, 2 (1889): 123-131.

Boas, Franz. The Central Eskimo. Lincoln, University of Nebraska Press, 1964. 11, 261 p. illus., maps.

Brack, D. M. Southampton Island area economic survey; with notes on Repulse Bay and Wager Bay. Ottawa, Department of Northern Affairs and Natural Resources, Area and Commumity Planning Section, Industrial Division, 1962. 5, 96 p. illus., map.

Bruemmer, Fred. Summer camp. Beaver, 297, no. 4 (1966/1967): 40-49.

Chown, Bruce. The blood group and secretor genes of the Eskimo on Southampton Island. By Bruce Chown and Marion Lewis. In Contributions to Anthropology 1960. Part I. Ottawa, Queen's Printer, 1962: 181-190. (Canada, National Museum, Bulletin, 180)

Clark, E. M. and A. J. Rhodes. Poliomyelitis in Canadian Eskimos. Canadian Journal of Medical Sciences, 29 (1951): 216-235; 30 (1952): 390-402.

Corrigan, C. and S. Hanson. Brucellosis and miliary tuberculosis in an Eskimo woman. Canadian Medical Association Journal, 72 (1955): 217-218.

Danielo, E. Baptism by misery. Eskimo, 42 (1956): 13-17.

DeNevi, Don. Essays in musical retribalization: Hudson Bay. Music Educators Journal, 56, no. 1 (1969/1970): 66-68.

Dorais, Louis-Jacques. Some notes on the semantics of Eastern Eskimo localizers. Anthropological Linguistics, 13 (1971): 91-95.

Fairfield, Robert C. New towns in the far North. Journal of Canadian Studies, 2, no. 2 (1967): 18-26.

Flint, M. S. The Arctic, land of snowmen. London, 1948. 39 p.

Foote, Don Charles. An Eskimo sea-mammal and caribou hunting economy: human ecology in terms of energy. In International Congress of Anthropological and Ethnological Sciences, 8th. 1968, Tokyo and Kyoto. Proceedings. Vol. 3. Tokyo, Science Council of Japan, 1970: 262-267.

Frison-Roche, Roger. Hunters of the Arctic. Translated by Len Ortzen. London, Souvenir, 1969. 8, 260 p. illus., maps.

Frison-Roche, Roger. Peuples chasseurs de l'Arctique. Paris, Arthand, 1966. 283 p. illus., maps.

Fryer, A. C. Eskimo rehabilitation program at Craig Harbour. Royal Canadian Mounted Police Quarterly, 20 (1954): 139-142.

Gagné, Raymond C. Towards a Canadian Eskimo orthography and literature. Canadian Journal of Linguistics, 7 (1961/1962): 95-107; 8 (1962/1963): 33-39.

Gillis, E. M. North Pole boarding house. Toronto, 1951. 214 p.

Gimpel, Charles. Cape Dorset. Beaver, 292, no. 4 (1961/1962): 28-31.

Godt, P. The Canadian Eskimo co-operative movement. Polar Record, 12, no. 77 (1964): 157-160.

Graburn, Nelson H. H. Lake Harbour, Baffin Island. Ottawa, 1963. 2, 34 l. (Canada, Department of Northern Affairs and National Resources, Northern Co-ordination and Research Centre, NCRC-63-2)

Hall, C. F. Life with the Esquimaux. London, 1864. 2 v.

Hall, Charles F. Life with the Esquimaux. Edmonton, M. G. Hurtig, 1970. 26, 547 p. illus., map.

Hall, Charles F. Life with the Esquimaux. Rutland, Vt., Tuttle, 1970. 26, 547 p. illus., maps.

Harrington, R. The cheerful Eskimo. Beaver, 282, no. 4 (1952): 7-15.

Hart, J. S., et al. Thermal and metabolic responses of coastal Eskimos during a cold night. Journal of Applied Physiology, 17 (1962): 953-960.

Heinbecker, P. and R. H. Pauli. Blood grouping of Baffin Island Eskimos. Journal of Immunology, 15 (1928): 407-409.

Hildes, J. A. Comparison of coastal Eskimos and Kalahari Bushmen. Federation Proceedings, 22 (1963): 843-845.

Holm, Gustav Frederik, ed. Grønlandske sagn. København, Foreningen Fremtiden, 1959. 57 p. illus.

Honigmann, John J. Arctic townsmen: ethnic backgrounds and modernization. By John J. and Irma Honigmann. Ottawa, Canadian Research Centre for Anthropology, 1970. 20, 303 p. illus., maps.

Honigmann, John J. [Comment on] "Alcohol and culture, by David G. Mandelbaum". Current Anthropology, 6 (1965): 290-291.

Honigmann, John J. Eskimo under tutelage in an Eastern Arctic urban setting. In Congreso Internacional de Americanistas, 36th. 1964, España. Actas y Memorias. Tomo 3. Sevilla, 1966: 557-561.

Honigmann, John J. Field work in two northern Canadian communities. In Morris Freilich, ed. Marginal Natives: Anthropologists at Work. New York, Harper and Row, 1970: 39-72.

Honigmann, John J. Five Canadian Arctic and Subarctic towns: their native populations. In Internationale Amerikanistenkongress, 38th. 1968, Stuttgart-München. Verhandlungen. Band 3. München, Klaus Renner, 1971: 125-132.

Honigmann, John J. Frobisher Bay Eskimo leadership. North, 12, no. 3 (1965): 38-47.

Honigmann, John J. How Baffin Island Eskimo have learned to use alcohol. By John J. Honigmann and Irma Honigmann. Social Forces, 44 (1965/1966): 73-83.

Honigmann, John J. Patterns of Eskimo deviance in a new eastern Arctic town. Research Previews, 12, no. 1 (1965): 5-15.

Houston, James A. Eskimo prints. Barre, Mass., Barre Publishers, 1967. 110 p. illus., map.

Irving, Laurence. Stability in Eskimo naming of birds on Cumberland Sound, Baffin Island. Alaska, University, Anthropological Papers, 10 (1961/1963): 1-12.

Jenness, D. A new Eskimo culture in Hudson Bay. Geographical Review, 15 (1925): 428-437.

Kemp, William B. The flow of energy in a hunting society. Scientific American, 225, no. 3 (1971): 104-115.

Kumlien, L. Fragmentary notes on the Eskimo of Cumberland Sound. United States National Museum, Bulletin, 15 (1879): 11-46.

Lewis, Arthur. Life and work of the Rev. E. J. Peck among the Eskimos. New York, A. C. Armstrong and Son, 1904. 16, 349 p. illus.

Ling, Daniel. The incidence of middle ear disease and its educational implications among Baffin Island Eskimo children. By Daniel Ling, R. Hall McCoy, and Edward D. Levinson. Canadian Journal of Public Health, 60 (1969): 385-390.

Mackey, William F. Concept categories as measures of cultural distance. In Samir K. Ghosh, ed. Man, Language and Society; Contributions to the Sociology of Language. The Hague, Mouton, 1972: 134-168. (Janua Linguarum, Series Minor, 109)

Markham, C. R., ed. The voyages of William Baffin. London, 1881. 192 p.

Marsh, D. B. An Eskimo girl builds a snowhouse. Natural History, 51 (1943): 46-47.

Mary-Rousselière, G. Issingut. Eskimo, 34 (1954): 9-13.

McElroy, Ann Pulver. Modernization and cultural identity: Baffin Island Inuit strategies of adaptation. Dissertation Abstracts International, 34 (1973/1974): 1848B. UM 73-26,210.

Meldgaard, J. Eskimoiske stenalderkulturer i Arktisk Canada. Polarboken (1955): 113-127.

Morgan, L. H. Systems of consanguinity and affinity. Smithsonian Contributions to Knowledge, 17 (1871): 291-382.

Munn, H. T. The economic life of the Baffin Island Eskimo. Geographical Journal, 59 (1922): 269-273.

Nag, Moni. Factors affecting human fertility in nonindustrial societies: a cross-cultural study. New Haven, Yale University, Department of Anthropology, 1962. 227 p. (Yale University Publications in Anthropology, 66)

Nag, Moni. Factors affecting human fertility in nonindustrial societies: a cross-cultural study. New Haven, Human Relations Area Files Press, 1968. 227 p. (Yale University Publications in Anthropology, 66)

Nichols, P. A. C. Boat-building Eskimos. Beaver, 285, no. 1 (1955): 52-55.

Nielsen, F. Besøg hos Eskimoiske Stammefraender pa Baffinland. Grønland, no. 12 (1956): 441-450.

Nielsen, T. W. Hos canadiske eskimoer. Grønland, no. 7 (1964): 241-251.

Oetteking, B. A contribution to the physical anthropology of Baffin Land. American Journal of Physical Anthropology, 15 (1931): 421-468.

Ottawa, National Gallery of Canada. Cape Dorset; a decade of Eskimo prints and recent sculpture. Ottawa, 1967. illus.

Parry, W. Journal of a voyage for the discovery of a north-west passage. London, 1821. 202-203, 276-288 p.

Pitseolak. Pictures out of my life. Edited by Dorothy Eber. Montreal, Design Collaborative Books in association with Oxford University Press, Toronto, 1971. illus.

Pitseolak. Pictures out of my life. Edited by Dorothy Eber. Seattle, University of Washington Press, 1972. 95 p. illus.

Rabinowitch, I. M. and F. C. Smith. Metabolic studies of Eskimos in the Canadian Eastern Arctic. Journal of Nutrition, 12 (1936): 337-356.

Radwanski, P. Anthropological structure of 101 Eskimo. Anthropologica, 1 (1955): 72-83.

Robinson, J. L. Eskimo population in the Canadian Eastern Arctic. Canadian Geographical Journal, 29 (1944): 128-142.

Rousseau, Jérôme. L'adoption chez les Esquimaux Tununermiut. Québec, 1970. 173 p. map. (Laval, Université, Centre d'Études Nordiques, Travaux Divers, 28)

Ryan, T. Eskimo pencil drawings, a neglected art. Canadian Art, 22, no. 1 (1965): 30-35.

Schaefer, Otto. Familial occurrence of
abnormal placentation and fetal
malformations, observed in Baffin Island
Eskimos. Canadian Medical Association
Journal, 83 (1960): 437-438.

Schaefer, Otto. Pre- and post-natal
growth acceleration and increased sugar
consumption in Canadian Eskimos.
Canadian Medical Association Journal,
103 (1970): 1059-1068.

Service, E. R. The Candian Eskimo. In his
A Profile of Primitive Culture. New
York, 1958: 64-85.

Sewall, K. W. Blood, taste, digital hair,
and color of eyes in Eastern Eskimo.
American Journal of Physical
Anthropology, 25 (1939): 93-99.

Soper, Carolyn K. A nurse goes to Baffin
Island. Beaver, 295, no. 3 (1964/1965):
30-39.

Speck, F. G. Eskimo collection from
Baffin Land and Ellesmere Land. Indian
Notes, 1 (1924): 143-149.

Stefansson, V. Eskimos. Encyclopaedia
Britannica, 14th ed., 8 (1929): 708-710.

Stefansson, V., ed. The three voyages of
Martin Frobisher. London, 1938. 2 v.

Stevenson, David. The social organization
of the Clyde Inlet Eskimos. Dissertation
Abstracts International, 33 (1972/1973):
2912B.

Stewart, S. J. White whale drive. Beaver,
270, no. 2 (1940): 23-25.

Stuart, Donald. Weaving in the Arctic.
Beaver, 303, no. 1 (1972/1973): 60-62.

Stuart, P. F., et al. Botulism among Cape
Dorset Eskimos and suspected botulism at
Frobisher Bay and Wakeham Bay. Canadian
Journal of Public Health, 61 (1970):
509-517.

Tweedsmuir, J. N. S. B. Men and beasts in
the Canadian Arctic islands.
Geographical Magazine, 26 (1953): 182-
191.

Van Norman, R. D. Life at an eastern
arctic detachment. Royal Canadian
Mounted Police Quarterly, 17 (1951):
110-117.

VanStone, James W. Notes on the economy
and population shifts of the Eskimos of
Southampton Island. Alaska, University,
Anthropological Papers, 8 (1959/1960):
80-87.

Wallace, A. C., et al. Salivary gland
tumors in Canadian Eskimos. Cancer, 16
(1963): 1338-1353.

Washburne, H. C. and A. Blackmore. Land
of the good shadows. New York, 1940.
329 p.

Wells, J. R. The origin of immunity to
diphtheria in Central ard Polar Eskimos.
American Journal of Hygiene, 18 (1933):
629-673.

Wells, J. R. and P. Heinbecker. Further
studies on immunity to diphtheria among
Central and Polar Eskimos. Society for
Experimental Biology and Medicine,
Proceedings, 29 (1932): 1028-1030.

West-Baffin Eskimo Co-operative. Eskimo
graphic art. Ottawa, 1966. 44 p.
illus.

Wherrett, G. J. A study of tuberculosis
in the Eastern Arctic. Canadian Journal
of Public Health, 60 (1969): 7-14.

Wherrett, G. J. An epidemiological study
of non-tuberculous respiratory diseases
in the Eastern Arctic. Canadian Journal
of Public Health, 61 (1970): 137-140.

Wilkinson, D. How I became an Eskimo.
Maclean's Magazine, 67, no. 22 (1954):
28-30, 103-109.

Wilkinson, D. Land of the long day.
Toronto, 1955. 261 p.

Wilkinson, Douglas. Land of the long day.
New York, Holt, 1956. 261 p. illus.

Wilkinson, Douglas. Land of the long day.
Toronto, Clarke, Irwin, 1966. 271 p.

Wilson, C. White whale roundup. Forest
and Outdoors, 41 (1945): 187-188.

Yatsushiro, Tashio. Frobisher Bay 1958.
Ottawa, 1963. (Canada, Department of
Northern Affairs and National Resources,
Northern Co-ordination and Research
Centre, NCRC-63-6)

Yatsushiro, Toshio. The changing Eskimo.
Beaver, 293, no. 1 (1962/1963): 19-26.

01-03   Caribou Eskimo

Carrière, Gaston. Catalogue des
manuscrits en langues indiennes
conservés aux archives oblates, Ottawa.
Anthropologica, n.s., 12 (1970): 151-
179.

Anderson, G. Pagan Eskimos. Beaver, 274, no. 2 (1943): 38-40.

Banfield, A. W. F. The Barren-Ground caribou. Ottawa, 1951. 58 p.

Bird, John B. Bathurst Inlet, Northwest Territories. By John B. Bird and M. B. Bird. Ottawa, 1961. 66 p. illus., maps. (Canada, Department of Mines and Technical Surveys, Geographical Branch, Memoir, 7)

Birket-Smith, K. Anthropological observations on the Central Eskimos. Fifth Thule Expedition, Report, 3, no. 2 (1940): 1-123.

Birket-Smith, K. Geographical notes on the Barren Ground. Fifth Thule Expedition, Report, 1, no. 4 (1933): 1-129.

*Birket-Smith, K. The Caribou Eskimos. Fifth Thule Expedition, Report, 5 (1929): 1-725.

Boas, F. The Eskimo of Baffin Land and Hudson Bay. American Museum of Natural History, Bulletin, 15 (1901-1907): 1-570.

Bourget, Clermont. Douze ans chez les sauvages au Grand-Lac des Esclaves, comme médecin et agent des Indiens (1923-1935). Ste.-Anne-de-Beaupré, Québec, en vente chez l'auteur, 1938. 249 p.

Brack, D. M. Keewatin Mainland; area economic survey and regional appraisal. By D. M. Brack and D. McIntosh. Ottawa, 1963. (Canada, Department of Northern Affairs and National Resources, Industrial Division, Area Economic Survey Report, 63-2)

Burch, Ernest S., Jr. The caribou/wild reindeer as a human resource. American Antiquity, 37 (1972): 339-368.

Burgess, Helen. A talent to carve. North, 12, no. 2 (1965): 19-27.

Butler, Sheila. Wall hangings from Baker Lake. Beaver, 303, no. 2 (1972/1973): 26-31.

Crile, G. W. and D. P. Quiring. Indian and Eskimo metabolisms. Journal of Nutrition, 18 (1939): 361-368.

Curzon, M. E. J. Dental caries in Eskimo children of the Keewatin District in the Northwest Territories. By M. E. J. Curzon and Jennifer A. Curzon. Canadian Dental Association, Journal, 36 (1970): 342-345.

Curzon, M. E. J. Evaginated odontomes in the Keewatin Eskimo. By M. E. J. Curzon, Jennifer A. Curzon, and H. G. Poyton. British Dental Journal, 129 (1970): 324-328.

Curzon, M. E. J. Three-rooted mandibular molars in the Keewatin Eskimo. By M. E. J. Curzon and Jennifer A. Curzon. Canadian Dental Association, Journal, 37 (1971): 71-72.

Dailey, Robert G. The Eskimo of Rankin Inlet; a preliminary report. By Robert G. Dailey and Lois A. Dailey. Ottawa, 1961. 106 p. illus., maps. (Canada, Department of Northern Affairs and National Resources, Northern Co-ordination and Research Centre, NCRC-61-7)

Douglas, W. O. Last resort. Beaver, 303, no. 1 (1972/1973): 52-55.

Estreicher, Z. La musique des Esquimaux-caribous. Société Neuchâteloise de Géographie, Bulletin, 54 (1948): 1-53.

Estreicher, Z. Polyrhythmik in der Musik der Eskimos. Schweizerische Musikzeitung, 87 (1947): 411-415.

Fisher, Doug. Neighbours. North, 13, no. 1 (1966): 10-15.

Foster, Terrence W. Rankin Inlet: a lesson in survival. Musk-Ox, 10 (1972): 32-41.

Gabus, J. Iglous. Neuchâtel, 1944. 259 p.

Gabus, J. La construction des iglous chez les Padleirmiut. Société Neuchâteloise de Géographie, Bulletin, 47 (1940): 43-51.

Gabus, J. Les mouvements migratoires chez les Esquimaux-caribous. Anthropos, 35 (1940): 221-238.

Gabus, J. Préparation des peaux chez les Esquimaux-caribous. Anthropos, 35 (1940): 355-356.

Gabus, J. Touctou. Neuchâtel, 1943. 205 p.

Gabus, J. Vie et coutumes des Esquimaux caribous. Paris, 1944. 224 p.

Giddings, J. L., Jr. A holiday with the Padlimiut. Philadelphia Anthropological Society, Bulletin, 7 (1953): 3-5.

Gilder, W. H.   Schwatka's search. New
    York, 1881.

Gottschalk, C. W. and D. W. Riggs.
    Protein-bound iodine in the serum of
    soldiers and of Eskimos in the Arctic.
    Journal of Clinical Endocrinology, 12
    (1952): 235-243.

Graham, Andrew. Andrew Graham's
    observations on Hudson's Bay, 1767-91.
    Edited by Glyndwr Williams. London,
    1969. 72, 423 p. illus., maps.
    (Hudson's Bay Record Society,
    Publications, 27)

Hanbury, D. T.   Sport and travel in the
    northland of Canada. New York, 1904.

Harper, Francis. Caribou Eskimos of the
    upper Kazan River, Keewatin. Lawrence,
    1964. 74 p. illus. (Kansas,
    University, Museum of Natural History,
    Miscellaneous Publications, 36)

Harrington, R.   The face of the Arctic.
    New York, 1952. 369 p.

Harrington, R.   The Padleimiuts. Canadian
    Geographical Journal, 44 (1952): 2-15.

Heinrich, Albert C.   Co-affinal
    siblingship as a structural feature
    among some northern North American
    peoples. By Albert C. Heinrich and
    Russell Anderson. Ethnology, 7 (1968):
    290-295.

Hewitt, Michael J.   A Kabloona hunts with
    the inlanders. Beaver, 298, no. 4
    (1967/1968): 27-29, 32-33.

Höhn, E. O.   Eskimo bird names at
    Chesterfield Inlet and Baker Lake,
    Keewatin, Northwest Territories. Arctic,
    22 (1969): 72-76.

Iglauer, Edith.   A change of taste. New
    Yorker, 41, no. 10 (Apr. 24, 1965): 121-
    162.

Iglauer, Edith.   The new people; the
    Eskimo's journey into our time. Garden
    City, Doubleday, 1966. 205 p. maps.

Kilvert, Barbara.   Rankin Inlet. Beaver,
    296, no. 1 (1965/1966): 14-17.

Larmour, W. T.   She sits and sings. North,
    15, no. 6 (1968): 1-7.

Lathrop, Thomas.   Eskimo games and the
    measurement of cultural change. Musk-Ox,
    5 (1969): 1-15.

Leden, C. Eine Schlittenfahrt mit den
    kanadischen Eskimos. Erdball, 1 (1926):
    183-187.

Leden, C. Über Kiwatins Eisfelder.
    Leipzig, 1927. 285 p.

Lubart, Joseph M.   A study of basic
    personality traits of the Caribou
    Eskimos: a preliminary report. In George
    S. Goldman and Daniel Shapiro, eds.
    Developments in Psycnoanalysis at
    Columbia University. New York, Hafner,
    1966: 301-332.

Lubart, Joseph M.   A study of basic
    personality traits of the Caribou
    Eskimos: a preliminary report. Ottawa,
    Department of Indian Affairs and
    Northern Development, 1965.

Manning, T. H.   Pipestems of the Caribou
    Eskimos. American Anthropologist, n.s.,
    50 (1948): 162-163.

Marsh, D. B.   Canada's Caribou Eskimos.
    National Geographic Magazine, 41 (1947):
    87-104.

Marsh, D. B.   Life in a snowhouse. Natural
    History, 60 (1951): 64-67.

Marsh, D. B.   Padlemiut drum dance.
    Beaver, 276 (1945): 20-21.

Mathiassen, T.   Spørgsmaalet om
    Eskimokulturens oprindelse. Geografisk
    Tidsskrift, 32 (1929): 116-126; 33
    (1930): 65-74.

McConnell, J. G.   Seal-hunting in
    Keewatin. Musk-Ox, 8 (1971): 23-26.

McConnell, John G.   The economics of seal
    hunting in three Keewatin settlements.
    Musk-Ox, 5 (1969): 49-50.

Michéa, J. P.   La civilisation du caribou.
    Géographia, 17 (1953): 31-35.

Michéa, J. P.   Some Eskimos of
    Chesterfield Inlet. Canadian
    Geographical Journal, 42 (1951): 222-
    225.

Michéa, J. P.   Uomini e caribou. Vie del
    Mondo, 15 (1953): 847-856.

Montgomery, Maurice.   The murder of
    missionary Thornton. Pacific Northwest
    Quarterly, 54 (1963): 167-173.

Moore, P. E.   Puvalluttuq. An epidemic of
    tuberculosis at Eskimo Point, Northwest
    Territories. Canadian Medical
    Association Journal, 90 (1964): 1193-
    1202.

Morgan, L. H.   Systems of consanguinity
    and affinity. Smithsonian Contributions
    to Knowledge, 17 (1871): 291-382.

Mowat, F. People of the deer. Boston, 1952. 352 p.

Mowat, Farley. The desperate people. Toronto, Little, Brown, 1959. 305 p. illus.

Nagy, Hendrika G. Pottery in Keewatin. Beaver, 298, no. 2 (1967/1968): 60-66.

Oswalt, Wendell H. Caribou Eskimo without caribou. Beaver, 291, no. 4 (1960/1961): 12-17.

Oswalt, Wendell H. Other peoples, other customs; world ethnography and its history. New York, Holt, Rinehart and Winston, 1972. 15, 430 p. illus., maps.

Oswalt, Wendell H. The future of the Caribou Eskimos. By Wendell H. Oswalt and James W. VanStone. Anthropologica, n.s., 2 (1960): 154-176.

Philippe, J. Eskimo psychology. Eskimo, 5 (1947): 5-7; 8 (1948): 8-15; 9 (1948): 2-7; 10 (1948): 2-7; 11 (1948): 5-7; 12 (1949): 7-10.

Pryde, Duncan. Nunaga: ten years of Eskimo life. London, MacGibbon and Kee, 1972. 285 p. illus., maps.

Pryde, Duncan. Nunaga; ten years of Eskimo life. New York, Walker, 1972. 285 p. illus.

Rasmussen, K. Iglulik and Caribou Eskimo texts. Fifth Thule Expedition, Report, 7, no. 3 (1930): 1-160.

*Rasmussen, K. Observations on the intellectual culture of the Caribou Eskimos. Fifth Thule Expedition, Report, 7, no. 2 (1930): 1-114.

Ross, W. Gillies. On the Barrens 1934. Beaver, 299, no. 2 (1968/1969): 48-53.

Sachot, J. Jusqu'au dernier "mangeur-decru'" Paris, 1944. 291 p.

Scott, P. M. Wild geese and Eskimos. New York, 1951. 254 p.

Sellers, F. J. The incidence of anaemia in infancy and early childhood among Central Arctic Eskimos. By F. J. Sellers, W. J. Wood, and J. A. Hildes. Canadian Medical Association Journal, 81 (1959): 656-657.

Service, E. R. The Canadian Eskimo. In his A Profile of Primitive Culture. New York, 1958: 64-85.

Smith, Lorne. Story time at Rankin Inlet. Beaver, 303, no. 2 (1972/1973): 18-19.

Spalding, A. E. A grammar of the east and west coasts of Hudson Bay. Ottawa, Queen's Printer, 1960. 178 p.

Steenhoven, G. van den. Caribou Eskimo legal concepts. International Congress of Americanists, Proceedings, 32 (1958): 531-538.

Steenhoven, G. van den. Legal concepts among the Caribou Eskimo. Arctic Circular, 9, no. 1 (1956): 7-9.

Steenhoven, G. van den. Report to the Department of Northern Affairs on a field-research journey for the study of legal concepts among the Eskimos in some parts of the Keewatin District. Den Haag, 1956. 74 p.

Swinton, George. Artists from the Keewatin. Canadian Art, 23 (Apr. 1966): 32-34.

Troels-Smith, J. Nulevende rensdyrjaegere. Kobenhavn, Fra Nationalmuseets Arbejdsmark (1956): 23-40.

Turquetil, A. Have the Eskimo the concept of a supreme being? Primitive Man, 9 (1936): 33-38.

Turquetil, A. Le mariage chez les Esquimaux. Université d'Ottawa, Revue, Section Spéciale, 4 (1935): 125-137, 197-237.

Turquetil, A. Notes sur les Eskimaux de Baie Hudson. Anthropos, 21 (1926): 419-434.

Turquetil, A. The religion of the Central Eskimo. Primitive Man, 2 (1929): 57-64.

Tyrrell, J. W. Across the sub-arctics of Canada. Toronto, 1897.

*Vallee, Frank G. Kabloona and Eskimo in the Central Keewatin. Ottawa, 1962. 7, 218 p. illus., maps. (Canada, Department of Northern Affairs and National Resources, Northern Co-ordination and Research Centre, NCRC-62-2)

Vallee, Frank G. Sociological research in the Arctic. Ottawa, 1962. 2, 21 p. (Canada, Department of Northern Affairs and National Resources, Northern Co-ordination and Research Centre, NCRC-62-8)

Van Den Steenhoven, Geert. Leadership and law among the Eskimos of the Keewatin District, Northwest Territories. Rijswijk, Excelsior, 1962. 155 p. maps.

Van Deu Steenhoven, Geert. Ennadai Lake people 1955. Beaver, 298, no. 4 (1967/1968): 12-18.

VanStone, James W. The Caribou Eskimos of Eskimo Point. By James W. VanStone and Wendell Oswalt. Ottawa, 1959. 38 p. (Canada, Department of Northern Affairs and National Resources, Northern Co-ordination and Research Centre, NCRC-59-2)

VanStone, James W. Three Eskimo communities. By J. W. VanStone and W. H. Oswalt. Alaska, University, Anthropological Papers, 9 (1960/1961): 17-56.

Various. Baker Lake prints estampes 1971. Baker Lake, Government of the Northwest Territories, 1971. 52 p. illus.

Wallace, A. C., et al. Salivary gland tumors in Canadian Eskimos. Cancer, 16 (1963): 1338-1353.

Williamson, Robert G. The Keewatin settlements. Musk-Ox, 8 (1971): 14-23.

Zavatti, Silvio. Giochi di cordicelle a Rankin Inlet; contributo all'etnografia degli Eschimesi della baia di Hudson. Archivio per l'Antropologia et la Etnografia, 98 (1968): 36-39.

Zavatti, Silvio. Le dimore umane ad Angmagssallik. Società Geografica Italiana, Bollettino, ser. 9, 5 (1964): 336-343.

01-04 Copper Eskimo

Carrière, Gaston. Catalogue des manuscrits en langues indiennes conservés aux archives oblates, Ottawa. Anthropologica, n.s., 12 (1970): 151-179.

Abrahamson, G. The Copper Eskimo; an area economic survey, 1963. Ottawa, 1964. 4, 194 p. illus. (Canada, Department of Northern Affairs and National Resources, Industrial Division, Area Economic Survey Report, 63-1)

Adam, C. I. The Bathurst Inlet patrol. Royal Canadian Mounted Police Quarterly, 16, no. 1 (July 1950): 12-25.

Amundsen, Roald. Mitt liv som polarforsker. Oslo, Gyldendal, Norsk Forlag, 1927. 3, [9]-256 p. illus.

Amundsen, Roald. My life as an explorer. Garden City, Doubleday, Page, 1927. 4, 282 p. illus., maps.

Anaveluk, Etienne. Eskimo week. Beaver, 285, no. 2 (Autumn 1954): 42.

Anderson, Ian Stuart. Bathurst Inlet patrol. Beaver, 302, no. 4 (1971/1972): 20-25.

Anderson, Rudolph Martin. Recent explorations on the Canadian arctic coast. Geographical Review, 4 (Oct. 1917): 241-266.

Anonymous. L'Evangile est annoncé chez les Esquimaux du cuivre. Pôle et Tropiques, 2 (1950): 1-32.

Balikci, Asen. Female infanticide on the Arctic Coast. Man, n.s., 2 (1967): 615-625.

Béclard-d'Harcourt, Marguerite. Le système pentaphone dans les chants des Copper-Eskimos. In International Congress of Americanists, 22nd. 1926, Rome. Vol. 2. Roma, 1928: 15-22.

Bird, John Brian. Bathurst Inlet, Northwest Territories. By John Brian Bird and M. B. Bird. Ottawa, Queen's Printer, 1961. 66 p. illus., maps. (Canada, Dept. of Mines and Technical Surveys, Geographical Branch, Memoir, 7)

Birket-Smith, Kaj. Ethnographical collections from the Northwest Passage. Copenhagen, Gyldendal, 1945. 298 p. illus. (Thule Expedition, 5th, 1921-1924, Report, 6, no. 2)

Birket-Smith, Kaj. Five hundred Eskimo words; a comparative vocabulary from Greenland and Central Eskimo dialects. Copenhagen, Gyldendal, 1928. 64 p. map. (Thule Expedition, 5th, 1921-1924, Report, 3, no. 3)

Birket-Smith, Kaj. Preliminary report of the Fifth Thule Expedition: physical anthropology, linguistics, and material culture. In International Congress of Americanists, 21st. 1924, Göteborg. Proceedings. Pt. 2. Göteborg, 1925: 190-205.

Breynat, Gabriel Joseph Elie. Bishop of the winds: fifty years in the arctic regions. Translated by Alan Gordon Smith. New York, P. J. Kenedy, 1955. 266 p. map.

Breynat, Gabriel Joseph Elie. Evêque volant: cinquante ans au Grand Nord canadien. Paris, Amiot-Dumont, 1953. 254 p. (Bibliothèque catholique, 2)

Breynat, Gabriel Joseph Elie. The flying
bishop: fifty years in the Canadian Far
North. London, Burns and Oates, 1955.
12, 288 p. illus., maps.

Buliard, Roger. Inuk. With an
introduction by Fulton J. Sheen. New
York, Farrar, Straus and Young, 1951.
9, 322 p. illus., map.

Burgess, Helen. Eskimo art from Holman.
North, 13, no. 3 (1966): 12-16.

Cadzow, Donald A. Eskimo lamps and
cooking vessels. Indian Notes, 1 (1924):
26-28.

Cadzow, Donald A. Native copper objects
of the Copper Eskimo. New York, 1920.
22 p. illus. (Museum of the American
Indian, Heye Foundation, Indian Notes
and Monographs, ser. 2, 8)

Cadzow, Donald A. Unusual Eskimo snow-
shovel. Indian Notes, 1 (1924): 150-152.

Cameron, John. Osteology of the Western
and Central Eskimos. In his Osteology of
the Western and Central Eskimos.
Ottawa, F. A. Acland, King's Printer,
1923: 3-58. (Canadian Arctic
Expedition, 1913-1918, Report, 12,
pt. C)

Cameron, John. Researches in Craniometry.
No. 2--Correlations between cranial
capacity and cranial length, breadth and
height, as studies in the Eskimo crania
of the Canadian Arctic Expedition, 1913-
1918. Royal Society of Canada,
Proceedings and Transactions, 3d. ser.,
20, section 5 (1926): 261-267.

Canada, Dept. of the Interior, Northwest
Territories and Yukon Branch. Canada's
Western Arctic. Report on investigations
in 1925-26, 1928-29, and 1930. Major L.
T. Burwash investigator. Ottawa, King's
Printer, 1931. 116 p. illus., maps.

Chown, Bruce. Blood groups in
anthropology: with special reference to
Canadian Indians and Eskimos. By Bruce
Chown and Marion Lewis. In Contributions
to Anthropology 1958. Ottawa, Queen's
Printer, 1960: 66-79. (Canada, National
Museum, Bulletin, 167. Anthropological
Series, 48)

Chown, Bruce. The blood group genes of
the Copper Eskimo. By Bruce Chown and
Marion Lewis. American Journal of
Physical Anthropology, n.s., 17 (1959):
13-18.

Coccola, Raymond de. Ayorama. By Raymond
de Coccola and P. King. New York,
Oxford University Press, 1956. 9,
316 p. illus., map.

Collins, Henry B. Eskimo archaeology and
somatology. American Anthropologist,
n.s., 36 (1934): 309-313.

Collinson, Richard. Account of the
proceedings of H.M.S. Enterprise from
Behring Strait to Cambridge Bay. Royal
Geographical Society, Journal, 25
(1855): 194-206.

Collinson, Richard. Journal of H.M.S.
Enterprise, on the expedition in search
of Sir John Franklin's ships by Behring
Strait. London, Sampson Low, Marston,
Searle, and Rivington, 1889. 11,
531 p. illus., maps.

Crisp, W. G. The casual Kogmoliks.
Beaver, 294 (1963): 50-53.

Damas, David. Central Eskimo systems of
food sharing. Ethnology, 11 (1972): 220-
240.

Damas, David. Characteristics of Central
Eskimo band structure. In Contributions
to Anthropology: Band Societies.
Ottawa, Queen's Printer, 1969: 116-141.
(Canada, National Museums, Bulletin,
228)

Damas, David. Diversity in White-Eskimo
leadership interaction. Anthropologica,
n.s., 8 (1966): 45-52.

Damas, David. Domestic group structure
among Eastern Canadian Eskimo. Man,
n.s., 2 (1967): 304-305.

Damas, David. Environment, history, and
Central Eskimo society. In Contributions
to Anthropology: Ecological Essays.
Ottawa, Queen's Printer, 1969: 40-64.
(Canada, National Museums, Bulletin,
230)

Damas, David. Social anthropology in the
Eskimo area. In Congreso Internacional
de Americanistas, 36th. 1964, España.
Actas y Memorias. Tomo 3. Sevilla,
1966: 289-301.

Damas, David. The Copper Eskimo. In Mario
G. Bicchieri, ed. Hunters and Gatherers
Today. New York, Holt, Rinehart, and
Winston, 1972: 3-50.

Damas, David. The diversity of Eskimo
societies. In Richard B. Lee and Irven
DeVore, eds. Man the Hunter. Chicago,
Aldine, 1968: 111-117.

Damas, David. The structure of Central
Eskimo associations. In D. Lee Guemple,
ed. Alliance in Eskimo Society.
Seattle, American Ethnological Society,
1972: 40-55.

Davies, L. E. C. The Eskimos of the
Northwest Passage: a survey of dietary
composition and various blood and
metabolic measurements. By L. E. C.
Davies and S. Hanson. Canadian Medical
Association Journal, 92 (1965): 205-216.

Dodwell, C. H. The Copper Eskimos of
Coronation Gulf. Canadian Geographical
Journal, 13 (June 1936): 60-81.

Douglas, George Mellis. Lands forlorn: a
story of an expedition to Hearne's
Coppermine River. New York, G. P.
Putnam's Sons, 1914. 15, 285 p.
illus., maps.

Dunning, Robert W. Domestic group
structure among Eastern Canadian Eskimo.
Man, n.s., 2 (1967): 303-304.

Edwards, Allan M. Observations on
juvenile hypothyroidism in native races
of Northern Canada. By Allan M. Edwards
and Gordon C. Gray. Canadian Medical
Association Journal, 84 (1961): 1116-
1124.

Fehlinger, Hans. Die "blonden Eskimo".
Naturwissenschaftliche Wochenschrift,
26, no. 26 (June 1914): 409-411.

Finnie, Richard. Lure of the North.
Philadelphia, David McKay, 1940. 19,
227 p. illus., maps.

Forbin, Victor. La psychologie d'un race
primitive: les esquimaux. Nature
(Paris), 54, no. 2719 (May 1926): 305-
308.

Forbin, Victor. L'organization sociale
des esquimaux. Nature (Paris), 54,
no. 2704 (Jan. 30, 1926): 65-68.

Franklin, John. Narrative of a journey to
the shores of the polar sea, in the
years 1819, 20, 21, and 22; with a brief
account of the second journey in 1825-
26-27. London, John Murray, 1829. 4 v.

Franklin, John. Narrative of a journey to
the shores of the polar sea, in the
years 1819, 20, 21, and 22.
Philadelphia, H. C. Carey and I. Lea,
1824.

Franklin, John. Narrative of a journey to
the shores of the polar sea, in the
years 1819, 20, 21, and 22. London, J.
M. Dent and Sons; New York, E. P.
Dutton, 1924. 10, 434 p. (Everymans
Library, 447)

Franklin, John. Narrative of a journey to
the shores of the polar sea, in the
years 1819, 20, 21, and 22. London, J.
Murray, 1823. [2, 10, 768] p. illus.,
maps.

Gavin, Angus. Notes on mammals observed
in the Perry River district, Queen Maud
Sea. Journal of Mammalogy, 26 (Aug.
1945): 226-230.

Godsell, Philip Henry. Arctic trader: the
account of twenty years with the
Hudson's Bay Company. New York, Putnam,
1932. 12, 2, 19-322 p. illus.

Godsell, Philip Henry. Is there time to
save the Eskimo? Natural History, 61,
no. 2 (Feb. 1952): 56-62.

Godsell, Philip Henry. Red hunters of the
snows; an account of thirty years'
experience with primitive Indian and
Eskimo tribes of the Canadian North-West
and arctic coast, with a brief history
of the early contact between white fur
traders and the aborigines. Toronto,
Ryerson Press, 1938. 3, 11-324 p.
illus., map.

Godsell, Philip Henry. The "blond Eskimo"
and the created want. Forest and
Outdoors, 34 (Aug. 1938): 231-234, 254.

Godsell, Philip Henry. The passing of
Herschel Island. Royal Canadian Mounted
Police Quarterly, 9 (Apr. 1942): 380-
392.

Great Britain. Papers relative to the
recent arctic expeditions in search of
Sir John Franklin and the crews of HMS.
Erebus and Terror. Presented to both
Houses of Parliament by command of Her
Majesty. London, Eyre and Spottiswoode,
1854. 225 p. illus., maps. (Great
Britain, Parliament, House of Commons,
Sessional Papers, Accounts and Papers,
1854, 42, no. 1725)

Greely, Adolphus Washington. The origin
of Stefansson's blond Eskimo. National
Geographic Magazine, 23 (Dec. 1912):
1225-1238.

Halpern, Joel Martin. Use of minerals by
the Copper Eskimo. Rocks and Minerals,
27, no. 1/2 (Jan./Feb. 1952): 21-24.

Hanbury, David T. Sport and travel in the
northland of Canada. New York,
Macmillan, 1904. 32, 319 p. illus.,
maps.

Harcourt, Raoul d'. Epidémies chez les
Eskimo. Société des Américanistes
(Paris), Journal, n.s., 38 (1949): 184-
185.

Harrington, Richard. Coppermine patrol:
story and pictures. Canadian
Geographical Journal, 41 (Dec. 1950):
256-269.

Hearne, Samuel. A journey from Prince of Wales's Fort in Hudson's Bay to the Northern Ocean. Rutland, Vt., C. E. Tuttle, 1971. 56, 458 p. illus., maps.

Hearne, Samuel. Journey from Fort Prince of Wales, in Hudson's Bay, to the northern ocean. In William Mavor, ed. Historical Account of the Most Celebrated Voyages, Travels, and Discoveries, from the Time of Columbus to the Present Period. Vol. 17. London, E. Newbury, 1797: 241-312.

Hewes, Gordon W. The Ainu double foreshaft toggle harpoon and western North America. Washington Academy of Sciences, Journal, 32 (1942): 93-104.

Hoare, William H. B. Report of investigations affecting Eskimo and wildlife, District of Mackenzie 1924-1925-1926. Ottawa, Canadian Dept. of the Interior, Northwest Territories and Yukon Branch [1926?]. 3, 16, 44 p. illus., maps.

Iokhel'son, Vladimir Il'ich. Belokurye eskimosy i novaia ekspeditsiia na poliarnyi sever kanadskikh vladenii. Ėtnograficheskoe Obozrienie, 25, no. 1/2 (1912): 236-241.

Jenness, Diamond. Comparative vocabulary of the Western Eskimo dialects. Ottawa, King's Printer, 1928. 134 p. (Canadian Arctic Expedition, 1913-1918, Report, 15, pt. A)

Jenness, Diamond. Copper objects of the Copper Eskimos--a reply to Mr. Cadzow. American Anthropologist, n.s., 24 (1922): 89-92.

Jenness, Diamond. Eskimo string figures. Ottawa, F. A. Acland, King's Printer, 1924. 192 p. illus., map. (Canadian Arctic Expedition, 1913-1918, Report, 13, pt. B)

Jenness, Diamond. Grammatical notes on some Western Eskimo dialects. Ottawa, King's Printer, 1944. 34 p. (Canadian Arctic Expedition, 1913-1918, Report, 15, pt. B)

*Jenness, Diamond. Material culture of the Copper Eskimo. Ottawa, King's Printer, 1946. 148 p. illus. (Canadian Arctic Expedition, 1913-1918, Report, 16)

Jenness, Diamond. Notes on the phonology of the Eskimo dialect of Cape Prince of Wales, Alaska. International Journal of American Linguistics, 4 (1927): 168-180.

Jenness, Diamond. Origin of the Copper Eskimos and their Copper culture. Geographical Review, 13 (1923): 540-551.

Jenness, Diamond. Physical characteristics of the Copper Eskimos. Ottawa, F. A. Acland, King's Printer, 1923. 65 p. illus. (Canadian Arctic Expedition, 1913-1918, Report, 12, pt. B)

Jenness, Diamond. Schneehütten-Völkchen, ein Reisebericht aus der Arktis. Wiesbaden, H. Hartmanshenn [1947]. 139 p.

Jenness, Diamond. The "blond" Eskimos. American Anthropologist, n.s., 23 (1921): 257-267.

Jenness, Diamond. The Copper Eskimos. Geographical Review, 4 (1917): 81-91.

Jenness, Diamond. The cultural transformation of the Copper Eskimo. Geographical Review, 11 (1921): 541-550.

*Jenness, Diamond. The life of the Copper Eskimos. Ottawa, F. A. Acland, King's Printer, 1922. 277 p. illus., maps. (Canadian Arctic Expedition, 1913-1918, Report, 12, pt. A)

*Jenness, Diamond. The life of the Copper Eskimos. New York, Johnson Reprint, 1970. 277 p. illus., map.

Jenness, Diamond. The people of the twilight. New York, Macmillan, 1928. [3, 2, 3, 247] p. illus., maps.

Jenness, Diamond. The people of the twilight. Chicago, University of Chicago Press, 1959. 251 p. illus.

Jenness, Dimamond. Myths and traditions from northern Alaska, the Mackenzie Delta and Coronation Gulf. Ottawa, F. A. Acland, King's Printer, 1924. 90 p. (Canadian Arctic Expedition, 1913-1918, Report, 13, pt. A)

Joss, William F. Sealing, new style. Beaver, 280, no. 4 (Mar. 1950): 43-45.

Kemp, V. A. M. Without fear, favour or affection. Toronto, Longmans, Green, 1958. 264 p.

Kidd, G. E. The skull of a Copper Eskimo. Man, 46 (1946): 1-2.

La Nauze, C. D. A police patrol in the North-West Territories of Canada. Geographical Journal, 51 (May 1918): 316-323.

Le Mer, L. Deep in Eskimo country. Eskimo, 64 (1963): 9-11.

Lewis, Marion. Inheritance of blood group antigens in a largely Eskimo population sample. By Marion Lewis, Bruce Chown,

and Hiroko Kaita. American Journal of
Human Genetics, 15 (1963): 203-208; 16
(1964): 261; 18 (1966): 231.

MacBrien, James Howden. Some patrols made
by members of the Royal Canadian Mounted
Police in the Canadian Arctic, 1935.
Polar Record, 12 (July 1936): 149-155.

Marsh, D. B. The North changes. Beaver,
271, no. 1 (1940/1941): 46-50.

Matas, M. Brucellosis in an Eskimo boy.
By M. Matas and C. Corrigan. Canadian
Medical Association Journal, 69 (1953):
531.

McGhee, Robert. An archaeological survey
of western Victoria Island, N.W.T.,
Canada. In Contributions to Anthropology
VII: Archaeology and Physical
Anthropology. Ottawa, Queen's Printer,
1971: 157-191. (Canada, National
Museums, Bulletin, 232)

McGhee, Robert. Copper Eskimo prehistory.
Ottawa, National Museum of Man, 1972.
142 p. illus.

Merwin, B. W. The Copper Eskimo.
(Pennsylvania, University, Museum,
Museum Journal, 6, no. 4 (1915): 163-
168)

Metayer, Maurice, ed. Tales from the
igloo. Edmonton, Hurtig, 1972. 127 p.
illus.

Miertsching, Johann August. Frozen ships:
the arctic diary of Johann Miertsching,
1850-1854. Translated and with an
introduction by L. H. Neatby. Toronto,
Macmillan of Canada, 1967. 13, 254 p.
illus., maps.

Miertsching, Johann August. Journal de M.
Miertsching, interprète du Capitaine
MacClure dan son voyage au pole nord.
Genève, Imprimerie Ramboz et Schuchardt,
1857. 2, 79 p. map.

Miertsching, Johann August. Reise-
Tagebuch des Missionars Johann August
Miertsching, welcher als Dolmetscher die
Nordpol-Expedition zur Aufsuchung Sir
John Franklins auf dem Schiff
Investigator begleitete. In den Jahren
1850 bis 1854. 2d ed. Gnadau, Im Verlag
der Unitäts-Buchhandlung bei H. L. Menz
und in Commission bei E. Kummer in
Leipzig, 1856. 15, [1] 206 p.

Monestier, Marianne. Avec les rois du
Nord. Paris, La Table Ronde, 1953.
348 p.

Noice, H. H. Further discussion of the
"blond" Eskimo. American Anthropologist,
n.s., 24 (1922): 228-232.

Nuttall, G. H. F. Report on Pediculus
collected from Eskimos. In Mallophaga
and Anoplura. Ottawa, King's Printer,
1918: 11. (Canadian Arctic Expedition,
1913-1918, Report, 3, pt. D)

Parker, Seymour. Motives in Eskimo and
Ojibwa mythology. Ethnology, 1, no. 4
(Oct. 1962): 516-523.

Polar Record. Influenza virus epidemic at
Victoria Island, Northwest Territories,
1949. Polar Record, 6, no. 45 (Jan.
1953): 680-681.

Pryde, Duncan. Nunaga: ten years of
Eskimo life. London, MacGibbon and Kee,
1972. 285 p. illus., maps.

Pryde, Duncan. Nunaga; ten years of
Eskimo life. New York, Walker, 1972.
285 p. illus.

Quimby, George Irving. The Old Copper
culture and the Copper Eskimo. In
Alaskan Science Conference . . . 1958.
Proceedings. Washington, D.C., 1960: 7-
14.

Quimby, George Irving. The Old Copper
culture and the Copper Eskimos, an
hypothesis. In John Martin Campbell, ed.
Prehistoric Cultural Relations between
the Arctic and Temperate Zones of North
America. Montréal, Arctic Institute of
North America, 1962: 76-79. (Arctic
Institute of North America, Technical
Paper, 11)

Rae, John. On the condition and
characteristics of some of the native
tribes of the Hudson's Bay Company's
territories. Society of Arts (London),
Journal, 30, no. 1,531 (Mar. 24, 1882):
483-499.

Rae, John. Rae on the Eskimo. Beaver,
284, no. 4 (Mar. 1954): 38-41.

Rasmussen, Knud J. V. Across arctic
America; narrative of the Fifth Thule
Expedition. New York, London, G. P.
Putnam's Sons, 1927. 20, 388 p.
illus., maps.

Rasmussen, Knud J. V. Fra Grønland til
Stillehavet, rejser og mennesker: fra 5.
Thule-ekspedition 1921-1924. København,
Gyldendal, 1925. 2 v. (1) 464 p. (2)
415 p. illus., maps.

*Rasmussen, Knud J. V. Intellectual
culture of the Copper Eskimos.
Copenhagen, Gyldendal, 1932. 350 p.
illus., maps. (Thule Expedition, 5th,
1921-1924, Report, 9)

Rasmussen, Knud J. V. Rasmussens
Thulefahrt: zwei Jahre im Schlitten

durch unerforschtes Eskimoland. Edited
with a preface by Friedrich Sieburg.
Frankfurt a.M., Societäts-verlag
[c1934]. 346, [2] p. illus., maps.

Rasmussen, Knud J. V. The MacKenzie
Eskimos after Knud Rasmussen's
posthumous notes. Edited by H.
Ostermann. Copenhagen, Gyldendal, 1942.
164, [2] p. illus. (Thule Expedition,
5th, 1921-1924, Report, 10, no. 2)

Rasmussen, Knud J. V., comp. Beyond the
high hills; a book of Eskimo poems.
Cleveland, World, 1961. 32 p. illus.

Reynolds, Vernon. Kinship and the family
in monkeys, apes and man. Man, n.s., 3
(1968): 209-223.

Richardson, John. Arctic searching
expedition. London, Longman, Brown,
Green, and Longmans, 1851. 2 v.

Rickard, T. A. The chalcolithic Eskimos.
Man, 38 (1938): 191-192.

Ritchie, S. G. The dentition of the
Western and Central Eskimos. By S. G.
Ritchie and J. Stanley Bagnall. In John
Cameron. Osteology of the Western and
Central Eskimos. Ottawa, F. A. Acland,
King's Printer, 1923: 59-66. (Canadian
Arctic Expedition, 1913-1918, Report,
12, pt. C)

Roberts, Helen H. Songs of the Copper
Eskimos. By Helen H. Roberts and Diamond
Jenness. Ottawa, F. A. Acland, King's
Printer, 1925. 506 p. illus.
(Canadian Arctic Expedition, 1913-1918,
Report, 14)

Robinson, John Lewis. Canada's western
Arctic. Canadian Geographical Journal,
37 (Dec. 1948): 242-260.

Royal Canadian Mounted Police. Report of
the Bathurst Inlet patrol, Royal
Northwest Mounted Police, 1917-18.
Ottawa, King's Printer, 1919. 43 p.
map.

Schaefer, Otto. Pre- and post-natal
growth acceleration and increased sugar
consumption in Canadian Eskimos.
Canadian Medical Association Journal,
103 (1970): 1059-1068.

Schiller, E. A. A pride of Umingmaktung-
niks. North, 12, no. 5 (1965): 18-23.

Seltzer, Carl C. The anthropometry of the
Western and Copper Eskimos, based on
data of Vilhjálmur Stefánsson. Human
Biology, 5 (1933): 313-370.

Service, Elman R. The Canadian Eskimo. In
his A Profile of Primitive Culture. New
York, Harper and Brothers, 1958: 64-85.

Shapiro, Harry Lionel. The Alaskan
Eskimo: a study of the relationship
between the Eskimo and the Chipewyan
Indians of central Canada. New York,
1931. 347-384 p. illus., maps.
(American Museum of Natural History,
Anthropological Papers, 31, pt. 6)

Simpson, Thomas. Narrative of the
discoveries on the north coast of
America; effected by the officers of the
Hudson's Bay Company during the years
1836-39. London, R. Bentley, 1843. 19,
419, [1] p. maps.

Stefánsson, Vilhjálmur. Corrections and
comments. In his The Stefánsson-Anderson
Arctic Expedition of the American
Museum. New York, 1919: 445-457.
(American Museum of Natural History,
Anthropological Papers, 14, pt. 3)

Stefánsson, Vilhjálmur. Gostepriimnaîa
Arktika. Leningrad, Izdatel'stvo
Glavsevmorputi, 1935. 512, [2] p.
illus., maps.

Stefánsson, Vilhjálmur. Länder der
Zukunft: fünf Jahre Reisen im höchsten
Norden. Leipzig, F. A. Brockhaus, 1923.
2 v. map.

Stefánsson, Vilhjálmur. Lessons in living
from the stone age. Harper's Magazine,
179 (July 1939): 158-164.

Stefánsson, Vilhjálmur. My life with the
Eskimo. New York, Macmillan, 1913. 9,
538 p. illus., maps.

Stefánsson, Vilhjálmur. My life with the
Eskimos. Abridged edition. New York,
Macmillan, 1927. 17, 2, 382 p. illus.

Stefánsson, Vilhjálmur. My quest in the
Arctic. Harper's Magazine, 126 (Dec.
1912-May 1913): 3-13, 176-187, 348-359,
512-522, 671-684, 888-900.

Stefánsson, Vilhjálmur. On Eskimo work,
1908-12. Canada, Department of Mines,
Geological Survey, Summary Report
(1912): 488-496.

Stefánsson, Vilhjálmur. Prehistoric and
present commerce among the arctic coast
Eskimo. Ottawa, Government Printing
Bureau, 1914. 29 p. map. (Canada,
National Museum, Bulletin, 6.
Anthropological Series, 3)

Stefánsson, Vilhjálmur. The "blond"
Eskimos. Harper's Magazine, 156 (Jan.
1928): 191-198.

Stefánsson, Vilhjálmur. The friendly Arctic, the story of five years in polar regions. New York, Macmillan, 1921. 31, 784 p. illus., maps.

Stefánsson, Vilhjálmur. The friendly Arctic, the story of five years in polar regions. New ed. New York, Macmillan, 1943. 27, 812 p. illus., maps.

*Stefánsson, Vilhjálmur. The Stefánsson-Anderson Arctic Expedition of the American Museum: preliminary ethnological report. New York, 1914. 1-395 p. illus., maps. (American Museum of Natural History, Anthropological Papers, 14, pt. 1)

Stefánsson, Vilhjálmur. The story of the blond Eskimos. Recreation, n.s., 48 (Dec. 1912): 10-14.

Sullivan, Louis R. The "blond" Eskimo--a question of method. American Anthropologist, n.s., 24 (1922): 225-228.

Urquhart, J. A. Eskimos of the Canadian Western Arctic. In C. A. Dawson, ed. The New North-West. Toronto, University of Toronto Press, 1947: 271-282.

Urquhart, J. A. Present day Eskimos of the Canadian Western Arctic. In William C. Bethune, ed. Canada's Western Northland: Its History, Resources, Population and Administration. Ottawa, J. O. Patenaude, I.S.O., Printer to the King's Most Excellent Majesty, 1937: 60-69.

Usher, Peter J. Economic basis and resource use of the Coppermine-Holman region, N.W.T. Ottawa, 1965. 21, 290 p. illus., maps. (Canada, Department of Northern Affairs and National Resources, Northern Co-ordination and Research Centre, NCRC-65-2)

*Usher, Peter J. The Bankslanders: economy and ecology of a frontier trapping community. Ottawa, Department of Indian Affairs and Northern Development, Northern Science Research Group, 1970. 3 v. (422 p.) illus., maps.

Usher, Peter Joseph, Jr. The Bankslanders: economy and ecology of a frontier trapping community. Dissertation Abstracts International, 31 (1970/1971): 7366B-7367B.

Van Rooyen, Clennel Evelyn. Influenza in Canada during 1949, including studies on Eskimos. By Clennel Evelyn Van Rooyen, L. McClelland, and E. K. Campbell. Canadian Journal of Public Health, 40 (Nov. 1949): 447-456.

Velde, F. V. de. Les règles du portage des phoques pris par la chasse aux aglus. Anthropologica, 3 (1956): 5-14.

Wallace, A. C., et al. Salivary gland tumors in Canadian Eskimos. Cancer, 16 (1963): 1338-1353.

Webster, J. H. Deerskin clothing. Beaver, 280, no. 3 (Dec. 1949): 44-47.

Webster, J. H. Fishing under the ice. Natural History, 59 (Mar. 1950): 140-141.

Whittaker, C. E. Arctic Eskimo, a record of fifty years' experience and observation among the Eskimo. London, Seeley, Service [1937]. 5, 17-259, [1] p. illus., map.

Wilson, David S. Processing of arctic char at Coppermine. Northern Affairs Bulletin, 3, no. 3 (Apr./May 1956): 7-9.

Wissler, Clark. Harpoons and darts in the Stefánsson collection. New York, 1916. 397-443 p. illus. (American Museum of Natural History, Anthropological Papers, 14, pt. 2)

01-05   East Greenland Eskimo

Abel, W. Finger und Handlinienmuster ostgrönländischer Eskimos. Deutsche Grönland-Expedition, Wissenschaftliche Ergebnisse, 6, no. 6 (1934).

Amdrup, G. The former Eskimo settlements on the east coast of Greenland. Meddelelser om Grønland, 28 (1909): 285-328.

Andersen, Soren. Audiologie et otologie a Angmassalik. By Soren Andersen and Jorgen Hähr. Société d'Anthropologie de Paris, Bulletins et Mémoires, Série 12, 5 (1969): 231-250.

Bandi, H. G. and J. Meldgaard. Archaeological investigations on Clavering Ø, Northeast Greenland. Meddelelser om Grønland, 126, no. 4 (1952): 85 p.

Barfod, H. P. Dansk-grønlandsk ordliste til skolebrug. 2d ed. Godthaab, 1952. 34 p.

Bergsland, Knut. On the validity of glottochronology. By Knut Bergsland and Hans Vogt. [With comment by Morris Swadesh.] Current Anthropology, 3 (1962): 115-153.

Bertelsen, A. Grønlandsk medicinsk statistik og nosografi. Meddelelser om

Grønland, 117, no. 3 (1940): 1-234; 117, no. 4 (1943): 1-246.

Birket-Smith, K. Etnografiske problemer i Grønland. Geografisk Tidsskrift, 25 (1920): 179-197.

Birket-Smith, K. The Greenland bow. Meddelelser om Grønland, 56 (1918): 1-28.

Birket-Smith, K. The Greenlanders of the present day. Greenland, 2 (1928): 1-207.

Boas, F. The relationships of the Eskimos of East Greenland. Science, n.s., 30 (1909): 535-536.

Bojlén, K. The influence of climate and nutrition on age at menarche: a historical review and a modern hypothesis. By K. Bojlén and M. W. Bentzon. Human Biology, 40 (1968): 69-85.

Carles-Trochain, Elisabeth. Étude cytogénétique d'un isolat: le groupe eskimo d'Angmassalik. Anthropologie, 75 (1971): 263-268.

Clavering, D. C. Journal of a voyage to Spitzbergen and the east coast of Greenland. Edinburgh New Philosophical Journal, 9 (1830): 1-30.

Digby, P. S. B. and V. Digby. Beyond the pack ice. London, 1954. 186 p.

Ducros, Albert. Adiposité et densité corporelle d'une population arctique (Eskimo Ammassalimiut). Anthropologie, 75 (1971): 605-620.

Dumbrava, C. Une année au milieu des Esquimaux. La Géographie, 51 (1929): 14-23.

Faïnberg, L. A. Grenlandiia i ee naselenie. Sovetskaia Etnografiia, no. 6 (1966): 47-56.

Faure, J. L. Au Groënland avec Charcot. Paris, 1933. 249 p.

Fischer-Möller, K. Skeletons from ancient Greenland graves. Meddelelser om Grønland, 119, no. 4 (1938): 1-30.

Frederiksen, S. Stylistic forms in Greenland Eskimo literature. Copenhagen, 1954. 40 p.

Fürst, C. M. and F. C. C. Hansen. Crania groenlandica. Copenhagen, 1915. 234 p.

Gessain, R. La tache pigmentaire congénitale chez les Eskimo d'Angmassalik. Société des

Américanistes, Journal, n.s., 42 (1953): 301-332.

Gessain, R. Statuettes eskimo composites à trois personnages. Société des Américanistes, Journal, n.s., 44 (1956): 199-204.

*Gessain, Robert. Ammassalik; ou, La civilisation obligatoire. Paris, Flammarion, 1969. 251 p. illus., maps.

Gessain, Robert. Angmassalik, trente ans après. Evolution d'une tribu eskimo dans le monde moderne. Objets et Mondes, 7 (1967): 133-156.

Gessain, Robert. Contribution à l'anthropologie des Eskimo d'Angmagssalik. København, C. A. Reitzel, 1960. 167 p. illus., maps. (Meddelelser om Grønland, 161, nr. 4)

Gessain, Robert. De franske antropologiske undersøgelser på Grønland 1970. Nordisk Medicin, 86 (1971): 1194.

Gessain, Robert. Dermatoglyphes digitaux et palmaires des Eskimo d'Angmassalik. Société d'Anthropologie de Paris, Bulletins et Mémoires, Série 10, 10 (1959): 233-250.

Gessain, Robert. La dentition des Eskimo d'Angmassalik; génétique, croissance et pathologie. Société d'Anthropologie de Paris, Bulletins et Mémoires, Série 10, 10 (1959): 364-396.

Gessain, Robert. La methode généalogique appliquée aux Eskimo d'Angmassalik. Premiers résultats, le coefficient moyen de consanguinité. In International Congress of Anthropological and Ethnological Sciences, 6th. 1960, Paris. Tome II, v. 1. Paris, Musée de l'Homme, 1963: 107-109.

Gessain, Robert. La vie et la mort chez les Eskimo. Ethno-Psychologie, 27 (1972): 125-136.

Gessain, Robert. L'adaptation des Ammassalimiut à leur nouvel environment biologique et culturel. In International Congress of Anthropological and Ethnological Sciences, 8th. 1968, Tokyo and Kyoto. Proceedings. Vol. 3. Tokyo, Science Council of Japan, 1970: 267-269.

Gessain, Robert. L'art eskimo. Société Suisse des Américanistes, Bulletin, 18 (1959): 46-47.

Gessain, Robert. L'art squelettique des Eskimo. Société des Américanistes (Paris), Journal, n.s., 48 (1959): 237-244.

Gessain, Robert. Le kayak des
  Ammassalimiut. Evolution demographique.
  Objets et Mondes, 8 (1968): 247-264.

Gessain, Robert. Le kayak des
  Ammassalimiut. Évolution technique. By
  R. Gessain and P.-E. Victor. Cbjets et
  Mondes, 9 (1969): 145-166, 225-244.

Gessain, Robert. Les Eskimo
  d'Angmassalik. Principaux caractères
  anthropologiques. Anthropologie, 62
  (1958): 452-484.

Gessain, Robert. Un jeu des Ammassalimiut
  et d'ailleurs. Jeu eskimo? Diffusion?
  Convergence? Objets et Mondes, 11
  (1971): 263-272.

Glarborg, K. Child-rearing in West
  Greenland. In G. Nielsen, ed.
  Proceedings of the XIV International
  Congress of Applied Psychology. Vol. 3.
  Child and Education. Copenhagen,
  Munksgaard, 1962: 106-120.

Glob, P. V. Eskimo settlements in Kempe
  Fjord and King Oscar Fjord. Meddelelser
  om Grønland, 102, no. 2 (1935): 1-97.

Glob, P. V. Eskimo settlements in
  Northeast Greenland. Meddelelser om
  Grønland, 144, no. 6 (1946): 1-40.

Graah, W. A. Narrative of an expedition
  to the east coast of Greenland. London,
  1837.

Graah, W. A. Undersøgelses-reise til
  østkysten af Grønland. Kjøbenhavn,
  1832.

Hansen, J. Dagbog om de hedenske
  östgrönländere. Kjöbenhavn, 1900.

Hansen, J. List of the inhabitants of the
  east coast of Greenland. Meddelelser om
  Grønland, 39 (1911): 181-202.

Hansen, J. Liste over beboerne of
  Grønlands østkyst. Meddelelser om
  Grønland, 10 (1888): 183-206.

Hansen, S. Bidrag til Østgrønlaendernes
  anthropologi. Meddelelser om Grønland,
  10 (1886): 1-41.

Hansen, S. Contributions to the
  anthropology of the East Greenlanders.
  Meddelelser om Grønland, 39 (1911): 149-
  179.

Helms, P. Investigations into
  tuberculosis at Angmagssalik.
  Meddelelser om Grønland, 160, no. 1
  (1957): 1-140.

Henshaw, H. W. East Greenlanders. U.S.
  Bureau of American Ethnology, Bulletin,
  30, vol. 1 (1907): 411-412.

Hoessly, H. Kraniologische Studien an
  einer Schädelserie aus Ost-Grönland.
  Neue Denkschriften der Schweizerischen
  Naturforschenden Gesellschaft, 53
  (1916): 1-54.

*Holm, G. Ethnological sketch of the
  Angmagsalik Eskimo. Meddelelser om
  Grønland, 39 (1911): 1-147.

*Holm, G. Ethnologisk skizze af Angmagsal-
  ikerne. Meddelelser om Grønland, 10
  (1887): 43-132.

Holm, G. Konebaads-Expeditionen til
  Grønlands østkyst. Geografisk
  Tidsskrift, 8 (1886): 79-98.

Holm, G. Legends and tales from
  Angmagsalik. Meddelelser om Grønland, 29
  (1912): 225-305.

Holm, G. Sagn og fortaellinger fra
  Angmagsalik. Meddelelser om Grønland, 10
  (1888): 235-334.

Holm, G. and V. Garde. Den Danske
  Konebaads-expedition til Grönlands
  oestkyst. Kjöbenhavn, 1887.

Holtved, Erik. Tôrnârssuk, an Eskimo
  deity. Folk, 5 (1963): 157-171.

Høygaard, A. Im Treibeisgürtel.
  Braunschweig, 1940. 127 p.

Høygaard, A. Tuberculosis in Eskimos.
  Lancet, 235 (1938): 758-759.

Hughes, C. C. Anomie, the Ammassalik, and
  the standardization of error.
  Southwestern Journal of Anthropology, 14
  (1958): 352-377.

Hughes, Charles Campbell. Under four
  flags: recent culture change among the
  Eskimos. Current Anthropology, 6 (1965):
  3-69. [With comments].

Hymes, Dell H. Validity of
  glottochronology. Current Anthropology,
  5 (1964): 324-326.

Ingstad, H. East of the great glacier.
  New York, 1937. 286 p.

Johansen, A. Gitz. Characters of
  Greenland mythology. Copenhagen, 1949.
  58 p.

Johansen, J. P. Den østgrønlandske
  angakoqkult og dens Sorudsaetninger.
  Geografisk Tidsskrift, 43 (1940): 31-55.

Johnson, D. M. Observations on the Eskimo remains on the east coast of Greenland. Meddelelser om Grønland, 92, no. 6 (1933): 1-69.

Jørgensen, J. B. The Eskimo skeleton. Meddelelser om Grønland, 146, no. 2 (1953): 1-154.

Kleivan, Helge. Culture and ethnic identity; on modernization and ethnicity in Greenland. Folk, 11/12 (1969/1970): 209-234.

Kleivan, Inge. Language and ethnic identity: language policy and debate in Greenland. Folk, 11/12 (1969/1970): 235-285.

Knudsen, E. H. Konebadsrejser i Angmagssalikdistriktet. Grønland (1956): 341-350.

Krabbe, T. N. Greenland. Copenhagen, 1930. 145 p.

Kruuse, C. Angmagsalikerne. Geografisk Tidsskrift, 16 (1902): 211-217.

Larsen, H. Dødemandsbugten: an Eskimo settlement on Clavering Island. Meddelelser om Grønland, 102, no. 1 (1934): 1-185.

Laughlin, W. S. and J. B. Jørgenson. Isolate variation in Greenlandic Eskimo crania. Acta Genetica et Statistica Medica, 6 (1956): 3-12.

Laughlin, William S. Races of mankind: continental and local. Alaska, University, Anthropological Papers, 8 (1959/1960): 89-99.

Le Méhauté, P. J. Un hivernage au Groenland. Archives de Médecine et Pharmacie Navales, 125 (1935): 5-39.

Le Méhauté, P. J. and P. Tcherniakofsky. Quelques considérations sur la nosologie des Esquimaux du Groenland Oriental. Presse Médicale, 42 (1934): 491-492.

Leden, C. Über die Musik der Ostgrönländer. Meddelelser om Grønland, 152, no. 4 (1954): 1-112.

Lorm, A. J. Kunstzin der Eskimo's. 1945. 21 p.

Markham, C. R. Papers on the Greenland Eskimos. In Royal Geographical Society. Arctic Geography and Ethnology. London, 1875: 163-229.

Mathiassen, T. Bidrag til Angmagssalik-Eskimoernes for-historie. Geografisk Tidsskrift, 35 (1932): 129-136.

Mathiassen, T. Eskimo migrations in Greenland. Geographical Review, 25 (1935): 408-422.

Mathiassen, T. The archaeological collection of the Cambridge East Greenland Expedition. Meddelelser om Grønland, 74 (1929): 137-166.

Mathiassen, T. The Eskimo archeology of Greenland. Smithsonian Institution, Annual Reports of the Board of Regents (1936): 397-404.

Mathiassen, T. The former Eskimo settlements on Frederik VI's Coast. Meddelelser om Grønland, 109, no. 2 (1936): 1-55.

Mathiassen, T. The prehistory of the Angmagssalik Eskimos. Meddelelser om Grønland, 92 (1933): 1-158.

Mathiassen, T. The Sermermiut excavations 1955. Meddelelser om Grønland, 156, no. 3 (1958).

Meldgaard, J. Grønlaendere i tre tusinde aar. Grønland, no. 45 (1958): 121-129, 170-178.

Meldgaard, Jørgen. Traditional sculpture in Greenland. Beaver, 298, no. 2 (1967/1968): 54-59.

Mikkelsen, E. Scoresbysund kolonien. Grønland (1965): 369-378, 409-428.

Mikkelsen, E. and P. P. Sueistrup. The East Greenlanders' possibilities of existence. Meddelelser om Grønland, 134, no. 2 (1944): 1-244.

Mikkelsen, R. Øst-Grønland. Grønlands Bogen, 2 (1950): 251-268.

Mikkelsen, R. The Eskimo of East Greenland. Man, 38 (1938), 188-189.

Mikkelsen, R. The Eskimo of East Greenland. Scottish Geographical Magazine, 64, no. 1 (1948): 16-24.

Mikkelsen, R. The Eskimos of East Greenland. Canadian Geographical Journal, 43 (1951): 88-98.

Mirsky, J. The Eskimo of Greenland. In M. Mead, ed. Cooperation and Competition among Primitive Peoples. New York, 1937: 51-86.

Murdoch, J. The East Greenlanders. American Naturalist, 21 (1887): 133-138.

Nellemann, George. Hinrich Rink and applied anthropology in Greenland in the 1830's. Human Organization, 28 (1969): 166-174.

Nielsen, F. Grønlands kultur.
Turistforeningen for Danmark, Arbog
(1952/1953): 65-88.

Nielsen, J. C., et al. Gm types of
Greenland Eskimos. Human Heredity, 21
(1971): 405-419.

Nippgen, J. Le folklore des Eskimos.
Revue d'Ethnographie et des Traditions
Populaires, 4 (1923): 118-192.

Nippgen, J. Le folklore des Eskimos.
Revue d'Ethnographie et des Traditions
Populaires, 4 (1923): 189-192.

Nippgen, J. Les pretres payens du
Groenland oriental. Ethnographie, n.s.,
3 (1914): 55-65.

Normann, C. En rejse langs Grønlands
ostkyst i aaret 1777. Geografisk
Tidsskrift, 2 (1878): 49-63.

Orlova, E. P. Naselenie Grenlandii. In A.
V. Efimov and S. A. Tokarev, eds. Narody
Ameriki. Vol. 1. Moskva, Izdatel'stvo
Akademiia Nauk SSSR, 1959: 594-608.

*Ostermann, H. Knud Rasmussen's posthumous
notes on the life and doings of the East
Greenlanders. Meddelelser om Grønland,
109, no. 1 (1938): 1-212.

Paterson, T. T. Anthropogeographical
studies in Greenland. Royal
Anthropological Institute of Great
Britain and Ireland, Journal, 69 (1939):
45-76.

Pedersen, A. Auf Jagd in Grönland. Wien,
1953. 158 p.

Pedersen, A. Der Scoresbysund. Berlin,
1930. 156 p.

Pedersen, P. O. Anatomical studies of the
East Greenland Eskimo dentition.
International Congress of Americanists,
Proceedings, 29, vol. 3 (1951): 46-49.

Pedersen, P. O. Dental investigations of
Greenland Eskimos. Royal Society of
Medicine (London), Proceedings, 40
(1947): 726-732.

Pedersen, P. O. Investigations into
dental conditions of about 3,000 ancient
and modern Greenlanders. Dental Record,
58 (1938): 191-198.

Pedersen, P. O. The East Greenland Eskimo
dentition. Meddelelser om Grønland, 142,
no. 3 (1949): 1-244.

Pedersen, P. O. and E. Hinsch. Numerical
variations in Greenland Eskimo
dentition. Acta Odontologica
Scandinavica, 1 (1939): 93-134.

Persson, Ib. A deviating Gc type. By I.
Persson and P. Tingsgaard. Acta Genetica
et Statistica Medica, 15 (1965): 51-56.

Persson, Ib. Serum protein types in East
Greenland Eskimos. By I. Persson and P.
Tingsgård. Acta Genetica et Statistica
Medica, 18 (1968): 61-69.

Persson, Ib. Serum types in East
Greenland Eskimos. By I. Persson and P.
Tingsgård. Acta Genetica et Statistica
Medica, 16 (1966): 84-88.

Persson, Ib, et al. Ten Gm factors and
the Inv system in Eskimos in Greenland.
Human Heredity, 22 (1972): 519-528.

Peters, H. B. Biologische und
Anthropologische Ergebnisse. Deutsche
Grönland-Expedition, Wissenschafliche
Ergebnisse, 1 (1933): 175-198.

Petersen, Robert. Overtryk i
Angmagssalik. Jordens Folk, 6, no. 2
(1970): 241-247.

Petersen, Robert. The Greenland tupilak.
Folk, 6, pt. 2 (1964): 73-101.

Poulsen, K. Contributions to the
anthropology and nosology of the East
Greenlanders. Meddelelser om Grønland,
28 (1909): 131-150.

Rasmussen, K. Eskimo folk-tales. Edited
by W. Worster. London, 1921. 156 p.

Rasmussen, K. Myter og sagn fra Grønland.
Vol. 1. Kjøbenhavn, 1921. 1-382.

Rasmussen, K. South East Greenland.
Geografisk Tidsskrift, 35 (1932): 169-
197.

Richter, S. A contribution to the
archaeology of North-East Greenland.
Skrifter om Svalbard og Ishavet (Oslo),
63 (1934): 1-149.

Rink, H. Bemaerkninger til G. Holms
samling of sagn og fortaellinger fra
Angmagsalik. Meddelelser om Grønland, 10
(1887): 335-345.

Rink, H. Den østgrønlandske dialekt.
Meddelelser om Grønland, 10 (1887): 207-
234.

Rink, H. Die Ostgrönlander. Deutsche
Geographische Blätter, 9, no. 3 (1886):
228-239.

Rink, H. Notes to G. Holm's Collection of
legends and tales from Angmagsalik.
Meddelelser om Grønland, 39 (1912): 307-
317.

Rink, H. Østgrønlaenderne i deres forhold
til Vestgrønlaenderne og de ørrige
Eskimostammer. Geografisk Tidsskrift, 8
(1886): 139-145.

Rink, H. The East Greenland dialect.
Meddelelser om Grønland, 39 (1911): 203-
223.

Robert, J. Démographie et acculturation:
une nouvelle phase dans l'histoire des
Ammassalimiut émigrés au Scoresbysund.
Société des Américanistes (Paris),
Journal, n.s., 59 (1970): 147-154.

Robert, Joëlle. Enquête sociologique au
Scoresbysund (côte orientale du
Groënland--1968). Société des
Américanistes (Paris), Journal, n.s., 57
(1968): 101-125.

Roberts, B. The Cambridge Expedition to
Scoresby Sound. Geographical Journal, 85
(1935): 234-251.

Roch, A. and G. Piderman. Quer durchs
"Schweizerland". Zürich, 1941. 251 p.

Roland, K. Folket ved elven. Grønland
(1964): 174-184, 349-360, 456-460.

*Rosing, C. Østgrønlaendere; Tunuamiut.
Det Grønlandske Selskabs Skrifter, 15
(1945): 1-150.

Rosing, J. Den østgrønlandske
"maskekultur". Grønland, no. 7 (1957):
241-251.

Rosing, J. Renjakt i det gamle Grønland.
Polarboken (1956): 99-112.

Rosing, Jens. Îsímardik, den store
dræbsmand. København, Grønlandske
Selskab, 1960. 89 p. illus.
(Grønlandske Selskabs Skrifter, 20)

Rosing, Jens. Kimilik. Digte fra
Angmagssalik. København, Gyldendal,
1970. 146 p. illus.

Rosing, Jens. Sagn og saga fra
Angmagssalik. København, Rhodos, 1963.
303 p. illus.

Rosing, Jens. Snehuset. København,
Bikuben, 1969. 15 p. illus.

Rosing, Jens. The ajagaq game from
Angmagssalik. Folk, 5 (1963): 287-293.

Rosing, Jens. Two ethnological survivals
in Greenland. Folk, 3 (1961): 13-22.

Røvsing Olsen, Poul. Dessins mélodiques
dans les chants esquimaux du Groenland
de l'est. Dansk Aarbog for
Musikforskning (1963): 101-110.

Røvsing Olsen, Poul. Intervals and rhythm
in the music of the Eskimos of East
Greenland. Copenhagen, 1969. 6 p.
(Dansk Folkemindesamling, Studier, 6)

Røvsing Olsen, Poul. Intervals and rhythm
in the music of the Eskimos of East
Greenland. In Peter Crossley-Holland,
ed. Centennial Workshop in
Ethnomusicology. June 19-23, 1967,
University of British Columbia,
Vancouver. Proceedings. Victoria,
Government of the Province of British
Columbia, 1968: 54-59.

Ryder, C. H. Om den tidligere eskimoiske
bebyggelse af Scoresby Sund. Meddelelser
om Grønland, 17 (1895): 281-343.

Sagild, Uffe, et al. Epidemiological
studies in Greenland 1962-1964. I.
Diabetes mellitus in Eskimos. Acta
Medica Scandinavica, 179 (1966): 29-39.

Schell, O. Die Ostgrönlander. Globus, 94
(1908): 85-88.

Schultz-Lorentzen, C. W. Eskimoernes
indvandring i Gronland. Meddelelser om
Grønland, 26 (1904): 289-330.

Schultz-Lorentzen, C. W. Intellectual
culture of the Greenlanders. Greenland,
2 (1928): 209-270.

Skeller, E. Anthropological and
ophthalmological studies on the
Angmagssalik Eskimos. Meddelelser cm
Grønland, 107, no. 4 (1954): 1-231.

Solberg, O. Beiträge zur Vorgeschichte
der Osteskimo. Norske Videnskaps-
Akademi, Oslo, Historisk-filosofisk
Klasse, Skrifter, no. 2 (1907): 1-92.

Sollas, W. J. On some Eskimos' bone
implements from the east coast of
Greenland. Royal Anthropological
Institute of Great Britain and Ireland,
Journal, 9 (1880): 329-336.

Sølver, C. V. Eskimoisk kartografi.
Grønland, no. 5 (1954): 187-192.

Stolpe, H. Über die Forschungsergebnisse
der schwedischen Grönland-Expedition.
International Congress of Americanists,
Proceedings, 14 (1904): 101-105.

Tchernia, M. P. Considérations
d'anthropologie physiologique sur les
Esquimaux. Société d'Anthropologie
(Paris), Bulletin, sér. 9, 3 (1942): 44-
55.

Thalbitzer, W. Cultic games and festivals
in Greenland. International Congress of
Americanists, Proceedings, 21, vol. 2
(1924): 236-255.

Thalbitzer, W.   Eskimoiske digte fra
   Östgrönland.   Kjöbenhavn, 1920.

Thalbitzer, W.   Eskimokulturen ved
   Angmagssalik. Geografisk Tidsskrift, 19
   (1907): 56-69.

*Thalbitzer, W.   Ethnographical collections
   from East Greenland. Meddelelser om
   Gronland, 39 (1912): 319-755.

Thalbitzer, W.   Ethnological description
   of the Amdrup Collection from East
   Greenland. Meddelelser om Grønland, 28
   (1909): 329-542.

Thalbitzer, W.   Grønlandske sagn om
   Eskimoernes fortid.   Stockholm, 1913.

Thalbitzer, W.   Hos östgrönlaenderne i
   Grönlands sydfjorde. Ymer, 37 (1917): 1-
   35.

Thalbitzer, W.   Legendes et chants
   esquimaux du Groenland. Paris, 1929.
   188 p.

Thalbitzer, W.   Les magiciens esquimaux,
   leurs conceptions du monde, de l'âme et
   de la vie. Société des Américanistes,
   Journal, n.s., 22 (1930): 73-106.

*Thalbitzer, W.   The Ammassalik Eskimo.
   Meddelelser om Grønland, 40 (1917/1921):
   113-564, 569-739; 53 (1941): 435-481.

Thalbitzer, W.   The heathen priests of
   East Greenland. International Congress
   of Americanists, Proceedings, 16 (1908):
   447-464.

Thalbitzer, W. and H. Thuren.   Dans i
   Grønland. In Fästskrift till F. H.
   Feilberg. Stockholm, 1911: 77-97.

Thalbitzer, W. and H. Thuren.   Melodies
   from East Greenland. Meddelelser om
   Grønland, 40 (1914): 47-112.

Thalbitzer, William C.   Hedensk digt.
   Eskimodigte fra det sydlige Østgrønland.
   Esbjerg, BHM-Tryk, 1967. 27 p. illus.

Thomsen, T.   Eskimo archaeology.
   Greenland, 2 (1928): 271-329.

Thomsen, T.   Implements and artefacts of
   the North-East Greenlanders. Meddelelser
   om Grønland, 44 (1917): 357-492.

Thomsen, T.   The Angmagsalik Eskimo.
   Meddelelser om Grønland, 53 (1917): 379-
   434.

Thostrup, C. B.   Ethnographic description
   of the Eskimo settlements and stone
   remains in North-East Greenland.
   Meddelelser om Grønland, 44 (1917): 177-
   355.

Thuren, H.   On the Eskimo music of
   Greenland. Meddelelser om Grønland, 40
   (1911): 1-45.

Vebaek, Mâliârak.   Umiarîssat, a boat of
   ill omen. Folk, 11/12 (1969/1970): 79-
   81.

Vibaek, P.   Contributions to the study of
   the Eskimo language in Greenland.
   Meddelelser om Grønland, 33 (1907): 9-
   60.

Victor, P. E.   Apoutsiak. Paris, 1948.
   32 p.

*Victor, P. E.   Contributions à
   l'ethnographie des Eskimo
   d'Angmagssalik. Meddelelser om Grønland,
   125, no. 8 (1940): 1-213.

Victor, P. E.   Le bilboquet chez les
   Eskimo d'Angmagssalik. Société des
   Américanistes, Journal, n.s., 30 (1938):
   299-331.

Victor, P. E.   Les jeux de ficelle chez
   les Eskimo d'Angmagssalik. Société des
   Américanistes, Journal, n.s., 29 (1937):
   387-395.

Victor, P. E.   My Eskimo life. London,
   1938. 349 p.

Wyss-Dunant, E.   Sur les hauts plateaux
   groenlandais.   Paris, 1939.   207 p.

Zavatti, Silvio.   La poesia degli
   Eschimesi. Nuova Antologia, 486 (1962):
   99-106.

Zavatti, Silvio.   Le dimore umane ad
   Angmagssallik. Società Geografica
   Italiana, Bollettino, ser. 9, 5 (1964):
   336-343.

Zavatti, Silvio.   Note di etnografia
   groenlandese. Rivista di Etnografia, 19
   (1965): 92-96.

Zavatti, Silvio.   Una spedizione in
   Groenlandia. Nuova Antologia, 490
   (1964): 95-104.

01-06   Iglulik Eskimo

Carrière, Gaston.   Catalogue des
   manuscrits en langues indiennes
   conservés aux archives oblates, Ottawa.
   Anthropologica, n.s., 12 (1970): 151-
   179.

Anders, G.   Northern Foxe Basin; an area
   economic survey, 1965. Ottawa,
   Department of Northern Affairs and

National Resources, Industrial Division,
1965. 4, 139 p. illus., map.

Anonymous. Artists of Arctic Bay. Beaver,
298, no. 2 (1967/1968): 20-25.

Anonymous. Study of genetics, physiology,
pathology and ecology of the Eskimo.
Canadian Medical Association Journal,
101 (Oct. 18, 1969): 16.

Bentham, R. and D. Jenness. Eskimo
remains in S.E. Ellesmere Island. Royal
Society of Canada, Proceedings and
Transactions, ser. 3, 35, pt. 2 (1941):
41-55.

Berry, John W. Ecology, perceptual
development and the Müller-Lyer
illusion. British Journal of Psychology,
59 (1968): 205-210.

Bird, J. B. Southampton Island. Canada,
Geographical Branch, Memoir, 5. Ottawa,
1953. 84 p.

Birket-Smith, K. Anthropological
observations on the Central Eskimos.
Fifth Thule Expedition, Report, 3, no. 2
(1940): 1-123.

Bisset, D. Recent changes in the life of
the Iglulik Eskimos. Albertan
Geographer, 1 (1964/1965): 12-16.

*Boas, F. The Eskimo of Baffin Land and
Hudson Bay. American Museum of Natural
History, Bulletin, 15 (1901-1907): 1-
570.

Brack, D. M. Southampton Island area
economic survey; with notes on Repulse
Bay and Wager Bay. Ottawa, Department
of Northern Affairs and Natural
Resources, Area and Community Planning
Section, Industrial Division, 1962. 5,
96 p. illus., map.

Brown, M. Progress report on clinical and
biochemical studies of the Eskimo.
Ottawa, 1951. 20 p.

Brown, M. The occurrence of cancer in an
Eskimo. Cancer, 5 (1952): 142-143.

Brown, M. and J. Page. The effect of
chronic exposure to cold on temperature
and blood flow of the hand. Journal of
Applied Physiology, 5 (1952): 221-227

Brown, M., et al. Blood volume and basal
metabolic rate of Eskimos. Metabolism, 3
(1954): 246-254.

Brown, M., et al. Cold acclimatization.
Canadian Medical Association Journal, 70
(1954): 258-261.

Brown, M., et al. Some remarks on
premature ageing in the Eskimos.
Canadian Physiological Society,
Proceedings, 11 (1947): 5.

Brown, M., et al. Temperature and blood
flow in the forearm of the Eskimo.
Journal of Applied Physiology, 5 (1953):
410-420.

Brown, Malcolm, et al. Parasitic
infections in the Eskimos at Igloolik,
N.W.T. Canadian Journal of Public
Health, 41 (1950): 508-512.

Bruemmer, Fred. The long hunt. Toronto,
Ryerson Press, 1969. 152 p. illus.

Carpenter, E. S. Changes in the Sedna
myth among the Aivilik. Alaska,
University, Anthropological Papers, 3,
no. 2 (1955): 69-73.

Carpenter, E. S. Eskimo poetry.
Explorations, 4 (1955): 101-111.

Carpenter, E. S. Eternal life.
Explorations, 2 (1954): 59-65.

Carpenter, E. S. Ivory carvings of the
Hudson Bay Eskimo. Canadian Art, 15
(1958): 212-215.

Carpenter, E. S. Space concepts of the
Aivilik Eskimos. Explorations, 5 (1955):
131-145.

Carpenter, E. S. The timeless present in
the mythology of the Aivilik Eskimos.
Anthropologica, 3 (1956): 1-4.

Carpenter, E. S. Witch-fear among the
Aivilik Eskimos. American Journal of
Psychiatry, 110 (1953): 194-199.

Carpenter, E. S., et al. Eskimo.
Explorations, 9 (1959): 1-64.

Chown, Bruce. The blood group and
secretor genes of the Eskimo on
Southampton Island. By Bruce Chown and
Marion Lewis. In Contributions to
Anthropology 1960. Part I. Ottawa,
Queen's Printer, 1962: 181-190.
(Canada, National Museum, Bulletin, 180)

Comer, G. Notes on the natives of the
northwestern shores of Hudson Bay.
American Anthropologist, n.s., 23
(1921): 243-244.

Curzon, M. E. J. Evaginated odontomes in
the Keewatin Eskimo. By M. E. J. Curzon,
Jennifer A. Curzon, and H. G. Poyton.
British Dental Journal, 129 (1970): 324-
328.

Dall, W. H. On some peculiarities of the
Eskimo dialect. American Association for

the Advancement of Science, Proceedings, 19 (1870): 332-349.

Damas, David. Central Eskimo systems of food sharing. Ethnology, 11 (1972): 220-240.

Damas, David. Characteristics of Central Eskimo band structure. In Contributions to Anthropology: Band Societies. Ottawa, Queen's Printer, 1969: 116-141. (Canada, National Museums, Bulletin, 228)

Damas, David. Diversity in White-Eskimo leadership interaction. Anthropologica, n.s., 8 (1966): 45-52.

Damas, David. Domestic group structure among Eastern Canadian Eskimo. Man, n.s., 2 (1967): 304-305.

Damas, David. Environment, history, and Central Eskimo society. In Contributions to Anthropology: Ecological Essays. Ottawa, Queen's Printer, 1969: 40-64. (Canada, National Museums, Bulletin, 230)

*Damas, David. Igluligmiut kinship and local groupings: a structural approach. Ottawa, 1963. 7, 216 p. maps. (Canada, National Museum, Bulletin, 196)

Damas, David. Social anthropology in the Eskimo area. In Congreso Internacional de Americanistas, 36th. 1964, España. Actas y Memorias. Tomo 3. Sevilla, 1966: 289-301.

Damas, David. The diversity of Eskimo societies. In Richard B. Lee and Irven DeVore, eds. Man the Hunter. Chicago, Aldine, 1968: 111-117.

Damas, David. The structure of Central Eskimo associations. In D. Lee Guemple, ed. Alliance in Eskimo Society. Seattle, American Ethnological Society, 1972: 40-55.

Daniel, R. Cytogenetic investigation of chromosomes from Eskimos in Igloolik, N.W.T., Canada. By R. Daniel and B. Chiarelli. Rivista di Antropologia, 57 (1970/1971): 259-262.

DeNevi, Don. Essays in musical retribalization: Hudson Bay. Music Educators Journal, 56, no. 1 (1969/1970): 66-68.

Dunning, Robert W. An aspect of recent Eskimo polygyny and wife-lending in the Eastern Arctic. Human Organization, 21 (1962/1963): 17-20.

Dunning, Robert W. Domestic group structure among Eastern Canadian Eskimo. Man, n.s., 2 (1967): 303-304.

Foote, Don Charles. An Eskimo sea-mammal and caribou hunting economy: human ecology in terms of energy. In International Congress of Anthropological and Ethnological Sciences, 8th. 1968, Tokyo and Kyoto. Proceedings. Vol. 3. Tokyo, Science Council of Japan, 1970: 262-267.

Freeman, Milton. Tolerance and rejection of roles in an Eskimo settlement. In Robert Paine, ed. Patrons and Brokers in the East Arctic. St. John's, Memorial University of Newfoundland, 1971: 34-54. (Newfoundland Social and Economic Studies, 2)

Freeman, Milton M. R. Eskimo thanking-acts in the eastern Canadian Arctic. Folk, 10 (1968): 25-28.

Freeman, Milton M. R. Patrons, leaders and values in an Eskimo settlement. In Internationale Amerikanistenkongress, 38th. 1968, Stuttgart-München. Verhandlungen. Band 3. München, Klaus Renner, 1971: 113-124.

Freeman, Milton M. R. Studies in maritime hunting. I. Ecologic and technologic restraints on walrus hunting, Southampton Island N.W.T. Folk, 11/12 (1969/1970): 155-171.

Gilder, W. H. Schwatka's search. New York, 1881.

Godsell, P. H. The trail of Tamowenuk. Alberta Folklore Quarterly, 1 (1945): 74-78.

Hague, E. Eskimo songs. Journal of American Folklore, 28 (1915): 96-98.

Hall, C. F. Narrative of the Second Arctic Expedition. Washington, D.C., 1879.

Harrington, R. Walrus at Igloolik. Beaver, 284 (Dec. 1953): 28-34.

Harrington, R. and E. Weyer. Walrus hunt. Natural History, 65, no. 1 (1956): 28-32.

Helm, June. The contact-traditional all-native community of the Canadian North: the Upper MacKenzie "Bush" Athapaskans and the Igluligmiut. By June Helm and David Damas. Anthropologica, n.s., 5 (1963): 9-21.

Hinds, Margery. High Arctic adventure. Toronto, Ryerson Press, 1968. 212 p. illus.

Hinds, Margery. School in the high Arctic. Beaver, 290, no. 3 (1959/1960): 12-17.

Hippler, Arthur E. Shaman curers and personality. Suggestions toward a theoretical model. Transcultural Psychiatric Research, 8 (1971): 190-193.

Hippler, Arthur E. Some observations on witchcraft: the case of the Aivilik Eskimos. Transcultural Psychiatric Research, 8 (1971): 181-189.

Klutschak, H. W. Als Eskimo unter den Eskimos. Wien, 1881.

Lewis, Brian W. Etuk makes a drum. Beaver, 299, no. 3 (1968/1969): 26-29.

Lyon, G. F. The private journal of Captain G. F. Lyon of H.M.S. Hecla. London, 1824.

Manning, T. H. Eskimo Stone Houses in Foxe Basin. Arctic, 3 (1950): 108-112.

Manning, T. H. Notes on the coastal district of the Eastern Barren Grounds and Melville Peninsula from Igloolik to Cape Fullerton. Canadian Geographical Journal, 26 (1943): 84-105.

Mary-Rousselière, G. Ainsi parlait la "reine" d'Iglulik. Eskimo, 37 (1955): 7-12.

Mary-Rousselière, G. Dans le folklore des Arviligjuarmiut. Eskimo, 42 (1956): 10-12.

Mary-Rousselière, G. Les "tunit" d'après les traditions d'Iglulik. Eskimo, 35 (1955): 14-20.

Mary-Rousselière, G. Mythical and prehistoric animals in Arviligjuarmiut folklore. Eskimo, 42 (1956): 10-12.

Mary-Rousselière, G. Trois légendes d'Iglulik. Eskimo (Dec. 1955): 18-25.

Mary-Rousselière, Guy. Reconnaissance archéologique dans la region de Pond Inlet; territoires du Nord-Ouest. Québec, 1968. 83 p. illus., maps. (Laval, Université, Centre d'Études Nordiques, Travaux Divers, 21)

Mathiassen, T. Archaeology of the Central Eskimos. Fifth Thule Expedition, Report, 4, nos. 1-2 (1927): 1-533.

*Mathiassen, T. Material culture of the Iglulik Eskimos. Fifth Thule Expedition, Report, 6, no. 1 (1928): 1-242.

Mathiassen, T. Traek af Iglulik-Eskimoernes materielle kultur. Geografisk Tidsskrift, 30 (1927): 72-88.

Matthiasson, John Stephen. Eskimo legal acculturation: the adjustment of Baffin Island Eskimos to Canadian law. Dissertation Abstracts, 28 (1967/1968): 1324B. UM 67-11,344.

Mayhall, John T. The effect of culture change upon the Eskimo dentition. Arctic Anthropology, 7, no. 1 (1970): 117-121.

Mayhall, John T. Torus mandibularis in two Northwest Territories villages. By John T. Mayhall and Melinda F. Mayhall. American Journal of Physical Anthropology, n.s., 34 (1971): 143-148.

Mitchell, E. H. Stones of mystery. Beaver, 284 (Dec. 1953): 26-27.

Muller, T. P. Analysis of contingency table data on torus mandibularis using a log linear model. By T. P. Muller and John T. Mayhall. American Journal of Physical Anthropology, n.s., 34 (1971): 149-153.

Papion, R. Le hibou des neiges. Eskimo, 36 (1955): 16-17.

Parry, W. E. Journal of a second voyage for the discovery of a north west passage. London, 1824. 492-569 p.

Petersen, Robert. Den sidste Eskimo-indvandring til Grønland. Folk, 4 (1962): 186-188.

Petersen, Robert. The last Eskimo immigration into Greenland. Folk, 4 (1962): 95-110.

Rabinowitch, I. M. and F. C. Smith. Metabolic studies of Eskimos in the Canadian Eastern Arctic. Journal of Nutrition, 12 (1936): 337-356.

Rae, J. On the Esquimaux. Ethnological Society (London), Transactions, n.s., 4 (1866): 138-153.

Rasmussen, K. Iglulik and Caribou Eskimo texts. Fifth Thule Expedition, Report, 7, no. 3 (1930): 1-160.

*Rasmussen, K. Intellectual culture of the Iglulik Eskimos. Fifth Thule Expedition, Report, 7, no. 1 (1929): 1-304.

Rawson, N. R. Medical practice in the Eastern Arctic. Manitoba Medical Association Review, 31 (1951): 587-595.

Reynolds, Vernon. Kinship and the family in monkeys, apes and man. Man, n.s., 3 (1968): 209-223.

Robinson, J. L. Eskimo population in the Canadian Eastern Arctic. Canadian Geographical Journal, 29 (1944): 128-142.

Robitaille, B. L'Agglomération Esquimaude de Resolute, Ile de Cornwallis. Cahiers de Géographie de Québec, 2 (1957): 206-207.

Rode, A. Cardiorespiratory fitness of an Arctic community. By A. Rode and R. J. Shephard. Journal of Applied Physiology, 31 (1971): 519-526.

Ross, W. Gillies. The Igloolik Eskimos. Scottish Geographical Magazine, 76 (1960): 156-163.

Rousseau, Jérôme. L'adoption chez les Esquimaux Tununermiut. Québec, 1970. 173 p. map. (Laval, Université, Centre d'Études Nordiques, Travaux Divers, 28)

Schaefer, Otto. Pre- and post-natal growth acceleration and increased sugar consumption in Canadian Eskimos. Canadian Medical Association Journal, 103 (1970): 1059-1068.

Service, E. R. The Canadian Eskimo. In his A Profile of Primitive Culture. New York, 1958: 64-85.

Simpson, Nancy E. Polyacrylamide electrophoresis used for the detection of C5+ cholinesterase in Canadian Caucasians, Indians, and Eskimos. American Journal of Human Genetics, 24 (1972): 317-320.

Skovbo, Bob. From the world of Tomasik Nutarareak. Natural History, 80, no. 1 (1971): 28-35.

Smith, Lorne. Stone fox trap. Beaver, 296, no. 4 (1965/1966): 46-47.

Smith, Lorne. The seal hunt. North, 13, no. 6 (1966): 9-13.

Speck, F. G. Eskimo collection from Baffin Land and Ellesmere Land. Indian Notes, 1 (1924): 143-149.

Stevenson, Alex. Arctic Christmas--thirty years ago. North, 12, no. 6 (1965): 28-31.

Sutton, G. M. Eskimo year. New York, 1934.

VanStone, James W. Notes on the economy and population shifts of the Eskimos of Southampton Island. Alaska, University, Anthropological Papers, 8 (1959/1960): 80-87.

Velde, F. Religion et morale chez les Esquimaux de Pelly Bay. Eskimo, 39 (1956): 6-8, 14-16.

Wallace, A. C., et al. Salivary gland tumors in Canadian Eskimos. Cancer, 16 (1963): 1338-1353.

Waterman, T. T. Hudson Bay Eskimo. American Museum of Natural History, Anthropological Papers, 4 (1910): 299-307.

Wherrett, G. J. A study of tuberculosis in the Eastern Arctic. Canadian Journal of Public Health, 60 (1969): 7-14.

Wherrett, G. J. An epidemiological study of non-tuberculous respiratory diseases in the Eastern Arctic. Canadian Journal of Public Health, 61 (1970): 137-140.

01-07　　Labrador Eskimo

Cooke, Alan, comp. Bibliographie de la peninsule du Québec-Labrador. Compiled by Alan Cooke and Fabien Caron. Boston, G. K. Hall, 1968. 2 v.

Anderson, James Watt. Fur trader's story. Toronto, Ryerson Press, 1961. 15, 245 p. illus.

Anonymous. Suhinimiut. U.S. Bureau of American Ethnology, Bulletin, 30, vol. 2 (1910): 647.

Anonymous. Supplementary materials on location, numbers and socio-economic conditions of Indians and Eskimos. Eastern Canadian Anthropological Series, 1 (1955): 103-116.

Anonymous. Tuberculosis survey: James and Hudson Bays. Arctic Circular, 4 (1951): 45-47.

Appleton, V. B. Observations on deficiency diseases in Labrador. American Journal of Public Health, 11 (1921): 617-621.

Arbess, Saul. Economic realities and political development: the George River case. Anthropologica, n.s., 9 (1967): 65-76.

Arbess, Saul E. Social change and the Eskimo co-operative at George River, Quebec. Ottawa, 1966. 8, 79 p. illus. (Canada, Department of Northern Affairs and National Resources, Northern Co-ordination and Research Centre, NCRC-66-1)

Arima, E. Y. Report on a Eskimo umiak built at Ivuyivik, P.Q., in the summer of 1960. Ottawa, Queen's Printer, 1963. 6, 88 p. illus. (Canada, National Museum, Bulletin, 189)

Arima, Eugene Y. Itivimiut sled construction. In Contributions to Ethnology V. Ottawa, Queen's Printer, 1967: 100-123. (Canada, National Museum, Bulletin, 204)

Arima, Eugene Y. Notes on the kayak and its equipment at Ivuyivik, P.Q. In Contributions to Anthropology 1961-62. Part II. Ottawa, Queen's Printer, 1964: 221-261. (Canada, National Museum, Bulletin, 194)

Balikci, A. Two attempts at community organization among the Eastern Hudson Bay Eskimos. Anthropologica, n.s., 1 (1959): 122-135.

Balikci, Asen. Anthropological field work at Great Whale River and Povungnituk. Arctic Circular, 11, no. 4 (1958): 68-71.

Balikci, Asen. Community patterning in two northern trading posts. By Asen Balikci and Ronald Cohen. Anthropologica, n.s., 5 (1963): 33-45.

Balikci, Asen. Development of basic socio-economic units in two Eskimo communities. Ottawa, 1964. 10, 114 p. maps. (Canada, National Museum, Bulletin, 202)

Balikci, Asen. Development of basic socio-economic units in two Eskimo communities. Dissertation Abstracts, 24 (1963/1964): 462. UM 63-5771.

Balikci, Asen. Female infanticide on the Arctic Coast. Man, n.s., 2 (1967): 615-625.

Balikci, Asen. Some acculturative trends among the Eastern Canadian Eskimos. In Internationale Amerikanistenkongress, 34th. 1960, Wien. Akten. Horn-Wien, Berger, 1962: 504-513.

Balikci, Asen. Some acculturative trends among the eastern Canadian Eskimos. Anthropologica, n.s., 2 (1960): 139-153.

Barger, Kenneth. Differential adaptation to northern town life by the Eskimos and Indians of Great Whale River. By Kenneth Barger and Daphne Earl. Human Organization, 30 (1971): 25-30.

Bauer, George W. Seals today, maybe. Beaver, 300, no. 3 (1969/1970): 34-39.

Bell, Robert. The Labrador Peninsula. Scottish Geographical Magazine, 11 (1895): 335-361.

Ben-Dor, Shmuel. Eskimos and settlers in a Labrador community. Dissertation Abstracts, 27 (1966/1967): 4220B. UM 67-8068.

Ben-Dor, Shmuel. Makkovik: Eskimos and settlers in a Labrador community; a contrastive study in adaptation. St. John's, Memorial University of Newfoundland, Institute of Social and Economic Research, 1966. 5, 208 p. illus., maps. (Newfoundland Social and Economic Studies, 4)

Biays, P. Conditions et genres de vie au Labrador Septentrionale. Quebec, 1955. 33 p.

Biays, Pierre. Les marges de l'oekoumène dans l'est du Canada. Québec, Presses de l'Université Laval, 1964. 29, 760 p. illus. (Laval, Université, Centre d'Études Nordiques, Travaux et Documents, 2)

Bird, J. B. Archaeology of the Hopedale Area, Labrador. American Museum of Natural History, Anthropological Papers, 39 (1945): 121-186.

Boas, F. The Eskimo of Baffin Land and Hudson Bay. American Museum of Natural History, Bulletin, 15 (1901-1907): 1-570.

Boas, F. Two Eskimo riddles from Labrador. Journal of American Folklore, 39 (1926): 486.

Bolus, Malvina. Lucy of Povungnetuk. Beaver, 290, no. 1 (1959/1960): 22-29.

Bonenfant, M. Fort-Chimo. Québec, 1964. 24 p. (Laval, Université, Centre d'Études Nordiques, Travaux Divers, 1)

Bourquin, T. Grammatik der Eskimo-Sprache. London, 1891.

British and Foreign Bible Society, ed. Testamentetokak hiobib aglangit salomoblo imgerusersoanga tikkilugit. Stolpen, 1871. 274 p.

British and Foreign Bible Society, ed. Testamentitak tamaedsa nalegapta piulijipta Jesusib Kristusib apostelingitalo piniaringit ajokertusingillo. London, 1876. 282 p.

Brochu, Michel. A preliminary study of the establishment of equalization prices for the pelts of fur-bearing animals in New-Quebec. Musk-Ox, 9 (1971): 42-52.

Brochu, Michel. Étude préliminaire sur
l'établissement d'un prix de péréquation
des peaux d'animaux à fourrure au
Nouveau-Québec. Actualité Économique, 46
(1970/1971): 287-315.

Brochu, Michel. Le défi du Nouveau-
Québec. Montréal, Éditions du Jour,
1962. 156 p. map.

Bruemmer, F. George Wetaltuk-Eskimo.
Canadian Geographical Journal, 50
(1955): 157-159.

Bruet, E. Le Labrador et le Nouveau-
Quebec. Paris, 1949. 346 p.

Burgesse, J. A. Esquimaux in the
Saguenay. Primitive Man, 22 (1949): 23-
32.

Cadzow, D. A. Archeological work with the
Putnam Baffin Island Expedition. Indian
Notes, 5 (1928): 98-106.

Campbell, B. D. Where the high winds
blow. New York, 1946. 230 p.

Cartwright, G. A journal of transactions
and events during a residence of nearly
sixteen years on the coast of Labrador.
London, 1792. 3 v.

Chown, B. and M. Lewis. The blood group
genes of the Eskimos of the Ungava
District of Canada. American Journal of
Physical Anthropology, n.s., 14 (1956):
215-224.

Cloutier, F. Réflexions médicales à
propos des Esquimaux de l'Ungava. Laval
Médical, 14 (1949): 532-538.

Coffey, J. E. and F. W. Wiglesworth.
Trichinosis in Canadian Eskimos.
Canadian Medical Association Journal, 75
(1956): 295-299.

Cotter, J. L. The Eskimos of Eastmain.
Beaver (Dec. 1929).

Courval, Michel de. Les nouvelles
sculptures de Povungnitak. North, 15,
no. 6 (1968): 14-17.

Curtis, H. Fragments sur les Eskimaux.
Nouvelles Annales des Voyages, no. 4
(1838): 329-339.

Davenport, C. B. The dietaries of
primitive peoples. American
Anthropologist, n.s., 47 (1945): 60-82.

Davies, Kenneth G., ed. Letters from
Hudson Bay 1703-40. Edited by K. G.
Davies, assisted by A. M. Johnson.
London, 1965. 68, 455 p. (Hudson's Bay
Record Society, Publications, 25)

Davies, Kenneth G., ed. Northern Quebec
and Labrador journals and correspondence
1819-35. Edited by K. G. Davies,
assisted by A. M. Johnson. London,
1963. 79, 415 p. maps. (Hudson's Bay
Record Society, Publications, 24)

Davies, W. H. A. Notes on Esquimaux Bay
and the surrounding country. Literary
and Historical Society of Québec,
Transactions, 4, pt. 1 (1843): 70-94.

Davies, W. H. A. Notes on Ungava Bay and
its vicinity. Literary and Historical
Society (Quebec), Transactions, 4
(1854): 119-137.

Desgoffe, C. Contact culturel: le cas des
Esquimaux des Iles Belcher.
Anthropologica, 1 (1955): 45-71.

Dorais, Louis-Jacques. L'acculturation
lexicale chez les Esquimaux du Labrador.
Langages, 18 (1970): 65-77.

Dorais, Louis-Jacques. Some notes on the
semantics of Eastern Eskimo localizers.
Anthropological Linguistics, 13 (1971):
91-95.

Dryfoos, Robert J., Jr. The Belcher
Island murders: an "anti-nativistic"
movement. Man in the Northeast, 2
(1971): 82-87.

Duckworth, W. L. H. and B. H. Pain. A
contribution to Eskimo craniology. Royal
Anthropological Institute of Great
Britain and Ireland, Journal, 30 (1900):
125-140.

Duckworth, W. L. H. and B. H. Pain. An
account of some Eskimo from Labrador.
Cambridge Philosophical Society,
Proceedings, 10 (1900): 286-291.

Dunbar, M. J. Common cause in the North.
International Journal, 1 (1946): 358-
364.

Dunbar, M. J. The caribou of Northeastern
Ungava. Quebec (Province) Association
for the Protection of Fish and Game,
Annual Report, 91 (1950): 10-14.

Dunbar, M. J. The Ungava Bay problem.
Arctic, 5 (1952): 4-16.

Duncan, Kenneth. The Angnasheotik: an
account of the invention of a spiritual
entity among the Ungava Eskimos. Arctic,
15 (1962): 289-294.

Erdmann, F. Eskimoisches Wörterbuch.
Budissin, 1864.

Findlay, M. The Eskimo population.
Eastern Canadian Anthropological Series,
1 (1955): 97-100.

Flaherty, R. J.   My Eskimo friends.
London, 1924.

Flaherty, Robert.   Nanook of the North.
Edited, from the film, by Robert Kraus.
New York, Windmill Books, 1971.   32 p.
illus.

Frajkor, G.   Tentative d'intégration de
300 Esquimaux au Labrador. North, 11,
no. 1 (1964): 40-41.

Freeman, Milton.   Tolerance and rejection
of roles in an Eskimo settlement.   In
Robert Paine, ed. Patrons and Brokers in
the East Arctic.   St. John's, Memorial
University of Newfoundland, 1971: 34-54.
(Newfoundland Social and Economic
Studies, 2)

Freeman, Milton M. R.   An ecological study
of mobility and settlement patterns
among the Belcher Island Eskimo. Arctic,
20 (1967): 154-175.

Freeman, Milton M. R.   Eskimo thanking-
acts in the eastern Canadian Arctic.
Folk, 10 (1968): 25-28.

Freeman, Milton M. R.   Observations on the
kayak-complex, Belcher Islands, N.W.T.
In Contributions to Anthropology 1961-
62. Part II.   Ottawa, Queen's Printer,
1964: 56-91.   (Canada, National Museum,
Bulletin, 194)

Freeman, Milton M. R.   Patrons, leaders
and values in an Eskimo settlement.   In
Internationale Amerikanistenkongress,
38th. 1968, Stuttgart-München.
Verhandlungen. Band 3.   München, Klaus
Renner, 1971: 113-124.

Gathorne-Hardy, G. M.   A recent journey to
Northern Labrador. Geographical Journal,
59 (1922): 153-169.

Gilliat, Rosemary.   The shaggy toys of
Port Burwell. Beaver, 292, no. 3
(1961/1962): 28-33.

Gosling, W. G.   Labrador.   London, 1910.

*Graburn, Nelson H. H.   Eskimos without
igloos; social and economic development
in Sugluk.   Boston, Little, Brown, 1967.
10, 244 p.   illus., map.

Graburn, Nelson H. H.   Some aspects of
linguistic acculturation in Northern
Ungava Eskimo. Kroeber Anthropological
Society Papers, 32 (1965): 11-46.

*Graburn, Nelson H. H.   Taqagmiut Eskimo
kinship terminology.   Ottawa, 1964.   6,
222 p.   illus., maps.   (Canada, Dept. of
Northern Affairs and National Resources,
Northern Co-ordination and Research
Centre, NCRC-64-1)

Grenfell, W. T.   Labrador.   New York,
1909.

Grenfell, W. T.   Medicine in the subarctic. College of Physicians of
Philadelphia, Transactions, 52 (1930):
73-95.

Guemple, D. L.   The Eskimo ritual sponsor:
a problem in the fusion of semantic
domains. Ethnology, 8 (1969): 468-483.

Guemple, D. Lee.   Kinship and alliance in
Belcher Island Eskimo society. In his
Alliance in Eskimo Society.   Seattle,
American Ethnological Society, 1972: 56-
78.

Guemple, D. Lee.   Saunik: name sharing as
a factor governing Eskimo kinship terms.
Ethnology, 4 (1965): 323-335.

Guemple, D. Lee.   The pacalik kayak of the
Belcher Islands. In Contributions to
Ethnology V.   Ottawa, Queen's Printer,
1967: 124-190.   (Canada, National
Museum, Bulletin, 204)

Guilbeault, Albert.   Étude de la
croissance chez quelques enfants
esquimaux. By Albert Guilbeault and
Louis Morazain. Union Médicale du
Canada, 94 (1965): 620-625.

Hanzsch, B.   Beiträge zur Kenntnis des
nordöstlichen Labradors. Dresden, Verein
für Erdkunde, Mitteilungen, 1, no. 9
(1909): 245-320.

Hanzsch, B.   Eskimo stone graves in northeastern Labrador. Canadian Field-
Naturalist, 44 (1930): 180-182.

Harp, E.   An archaeological survey in the
Strait of Belle Isle area. American
Antiquity, 16 (1951): 203-220.

Harrington, R.   Eskimos carve soapstone.
Popular Mechanics, 114, no. 3 (1960):
134-136.

Harrington, R.   Journey in arctic Quebec.
Canadian Geographical Journal, 41
(1950): 90-104.

Harrington, R.   People of the snows.
Beaver, 280, no. 4 (1950): 16-21.

Hartweg, Raoul.   La dentition des
Esquimaux de l'Ungava et des Indiens
Wabemakustewatsh de la côte orientale de
la Baie d'Hudson.   Québec, 1966.
156 l.   illus., map.   (Laval,
Université, Centre d'Études Nordiques,
Travaux Divers, 13)

Hartweg, Raoul.   Les malpositions
dentaires des Indiens Wabemakustewatsh
de la cote orientale de la Baie

d'Hudson. Société des Américanistes
(Paris), Journal, n.s., 54 (1965): 123-
126.

Hartweg, Raoul. L'implantation dentaire
chez les Esquimaux de l'Ungava. Société
des Américanistes (Paris), Journal,
n.s., 54 (1965): 117-122.

*Hawkes, E. W. The Labrador Eskimo.
Canada, Department of Mines, Geological
Survey, Memoirs, 91 (1916): 1-165.

*Hawkes, Ernest W. The Labrador Eskimo.
New York, Johnson Reprint, 1970. 10,
235 p. illus., map.

Heinrich, Albert. Some borrowings from
German into Eskimo. Anthropological
Linguistics, 13 (1971): 96-99.

Hiller, James. Early patrons of the
Labrador Eskimos: the Moravian Mission
in Labrador, 1764-1805. In Robert Paine,
ed. Patrons and Brokers in the East
Arctic. St. John's, Memorial University
of Newfoundland, 1971: 74-97.
(Newfoundland Social and Economic
Papers, 2)

Hind, Henry Youle. Explorations in the
interior of the Labrador Peninsula, the
country of the Montagnais and Nasquapee
Indians. London, Longman, Roberts and
Green, 1863. 2 v.

Hoebel, E. A. Law-ways of the primitive
Eskimos. Journal of Criminal Law and
Criminology, 31 (1941): 663-683.

Holtved, Erik. Tôrnârssuk, an Eskimo
deity. Folk, 5 (1963): 157-171.

Honigmann, I. and J. J. Honigmann. Child
rearing patterns among the Great Whale
River Eskimo. Alaska, University,
Anthropological Papers, 2 (1953): 31-50.

Honigmann, J. J. An episode in the
administration of the Great Whale River
Eskimo. Human Organization, 10, no. 2
(1951): 5-14.

Honigmann, J. J. Intercultural relations
at Great Whale River. American
Anthropologist, 54 (1952): 510-522.

Honigmann, J J. and I. Honigmann. Notes
on Great Whale River Ethos.
Anthropologica, n.s., 1 (1959): 106-121.

Honigmann, J. J. and R. N. Carrera.
Cross-cultural use or Machover's Figure
Drawing Test. American Anthropologist,
59 (1957): 650-654.

Honigmann, John J. Five Canadian Arctic
and Subarctic towns: their native
populations. In Internationale

Amerikanistenkongress, 38th. 1968,
Stuttgart-München. Verhandlungen. Band
3. München, Klaus Renner, 1971: 125-
132.

Honigmann, John J. Social networks in
Great Whale River: notes on an Eskimo,
Montagnais-Naskapi, and Euro-Canadian
community. Ottawa, Queen's Printer,
1962. 6, 110 p. illus., map. (Canada,
National Museum, Bulletin, 178)

Honigmann, John J. The Great Whale River
Eskimo: a focussed social system.
Alaska, University, Anthropological
Papers, 9 (1960/1961): 11-16.

Honigmann, John J. The pre-radar period
of the Great Whale River Eskimo. In
Internationale Amerikanistenkongress,
34th. 1960, Wien. Akten. Horn-Wien,
Berger, 1962: 499-503.

Houston, J. A. Eskimo sculptors. Beaver,
282, no. 1 (1951): 34-39.

Hutton, M. W. Among the Eskimos of
Labrador. Philadelphia, 1912.

Hutton, M. W. An Eskimo village. London,
1929.

Hutton, M. W. By Eskimo dog-sled and
kayak. London, 1919. 219 p.

Iglauer, Edith. Return to George River.
New Yorker, 41, no.38 (Nov. 6, 1965):
174-205.

Jaeger, Jiří. Šest let mez Eskymáky. 2
vyd. Praha, Orbis, 1971. 185 p.
illus., map.

Johnson, William D. An exploratory study
of ethnic relations at Great Whale
River. Ottawa, 1962. 21 p. (Canada,
Department of Northern Affairs and
National Resources, Northern Co-
ordination and Research Centre, NCRC-62-
7)

Kleinschmidt, Samuel P. Grammatik der
grönländischen Sprache, mit teilweisem
Einschluss des Labradordialects.
Berlin, G. Reimer, 1851. 10, 182 p.

Kleinschmidt, Samuel P. Grammatik der
grönländischen Sprache, mit teilweisem
Einschluss des Labradordialekts.
Hildesheim, Olms, 1968. 12, 182 p.

Kleivan, H. Labrador i Støpeskjeen.
Polarboken (1956): 65-98.

Kleivan, Helge. Acculturation, ecology
and human choice: case studies from
Labrador and South Greenland. Folk, 6,
pt. 1 (1964): 63-74.

Kleivan, Helge. The Eskimos of Northeast Labrador. A history of Eskimo-White relations. Oslo, 1966. 195 p. maps. (Oslo, Norsk Polarinstitutt, Skrifter, 139)

Klimek, S. Przyczynek do kranjologji Indjan Amerykanskich. Société des Naturalistes "Kopernik", Bulletin, sér. A, Mémoires, 53 (1928): 809-829.

Knight, Frederica. The new kayak. Beaver, 290, no. 4 (1959/1960): 30-37.

Kohlmeister, B. and G. Kmoch. Journal of a voyage from Okkak on the Coast of Labrador to Ungava Bay. London, 1814. 83 p.

König, H. Die Eskimo-Mundarten von Nord- und Nordost-Labrador. Anthropos, 32 (1937): 595-632.

König, H. Die Eskimos von Labrador. Erdball, 5 (1931): 465-469.

Koon, Levi. The hunter and the giant. Beaver, 292, no. 4 (1961/1962): 16-19.

Kranck, Ernst Håkan. Med motor och hammare längs Labradorküsten. Helsingfors, Söderström, 1940. 170 p. illus., map.

La Trobe, C. I. Narrative of the remarkable preservation experienced by the Brn. Samuel Liebisch and W. Turner. Moravian Church Miscellany, 1 (1850): 297-304.

Laguna, F. de. The prehistory of northern North America as seen from the Yukon. Society for American Archaeology, Memoirs, 3 (1947): 1-360.

Laird, Marshall. Parasites from northern Canada. I. Entozoa of Fort Chimo Eskimos. By Marshall Laird and Eugene Meerovitch. Canadian Journal of Zoology, 39 (1961): 63-67.

Le Mehauté, P. J. and P. Tcherniskofsky. L'alimentation des Esquimaux. Société Scientifique d'Hygiène Alimentaire, Bulletin, 22 (1934): 8.

Leechman, D. A new type of adze head. American Anthropologist, n.s., 45 (1943): 153-155.

Leechman, D. Eskimo summer. Toronto, 1945. 247 p.

Leechman, D. Two new Cape Dorset sites. American Antiquity, 8 (1943): 363-375.

Lefebvre, G. R. A comparative and annotated glossary of the East Hudson Bay Eskimo Dialect. Ottawa, 1955. 100 p.

Lefebvre, G. R. Remarques phonologiques pour une orthographie du dialecte eskimau de l'Est de la Baie d'Hudson. Anthropologica, 2 (1956): 39-60.

Leitch, A. Village with a mission. Canadian Geographical Journal, 40 (1950): 102-113.

Leith, Charles K. A summer and winter on Hudson Bay. By Charles K. Leith and A. T. Leith. Madison, Cartwell, 1912. 203 p. illus., map.

Lewis, Arthur. Life and work of the Rev. E. J. Peck among the Eskimos. New York, A. C. Armstrong and Son, 1904. 16, 349 p. illus.

Lindow, H. Labrador och dess Eskimaer. Terra, 35 (1923): 4-19.

Low, A. P. Report on explorations in the Labrador Peninsula. Canada, Geological Survey, Annual Reports, n.s., 8 (1896): 1-387.

MacKeevor, Thomas. A voyage to Hudson's Bay, during the summer of 1812. London, printed for Sir R. Phillips and Co., 1819. 2, 76 p. (New Voyages and Travels, 3d Series, 2, no. 2)

MacMillan, M. Far North with "Captain Mac". National Geographic Magazine, 100 (1951): 465-513.

Magnan, Hormidas. Notes historiques sur le nord de la province de Québec, le baie d'Hudson, l'Ungava. Bulletin des Recherches Historiques, 25, no. 4 (1919): 105-119.

Malaurie, Jean, ed. Le Nouveau-Québec. Contribution à l'étude de l'occupation humaine. Edited by Jean Malaurie and Jacques Rousseau. Paris, Mouton, 1964. 466 p. illus.

Manning, T. H. Eskimo stone house ruins on the east side of Hudson Bay. American Antiquity, 13 (1948): 250-251.

Manning, T. H. Ruins of Eskimo stone houses on the east side of Hudson Bay. American Antiquity, 11 (1946): 201-202.

Manning, T. H. and E. W. Manning. The preparation of skins and clothing in the eastern Canadian Arctic. Polar Record, 28 (1944): 156-169.

Markham, C. R., ed. The voyages of William Baffin. London, 1881. 192 p.

McLean, J. Notes of a twenty-five years' service in the Hudson's Bay Territory. Edited by W. S. Wallace. Champlain Society, Publications, 19 (1932): 1-402.

McLean, John. Notes of a twenty-five years' service in the Hudson's Bay territory. New York, Greenwood Press, 1968. 36, 402 p. map. (Champlain Society, Publication, 19)

Melartin, Liisa. Albumin polymorphism (albumin Naskapi) in Eskimos and Navajos. By Liisa Melartin, Baruch S. Blumberg, and John R. Martin. Nature, 218 (1968): 787-789.

Michéa, J. P. Exploration in Ungava Peninsula. National Museum of Canada, Bulletin, 118 (1950): 54-58.

Miller, E. C. Aksunai. Canadian Geographical Journal, 51 (1955): 256-263.

Mills, C. A. Eskimo sexual functions. Science, 89 (1939): 11-12.

Morrissette, Hugues, ed. Problèmes nordiques des façades de la Baie de James. Edited by Hugues Morrissette and Louis-Edmond Hamelin. Québec, 1967. 179 l. illus., maps. (Laval, Université, Centre d'Études Nordiques, Travaux Divers, 18)

Murdock, P. Seeguapik. Beaver, 287 (Winter 1956): 24-31.

Nungak, Zebedee. Unikkaatuat sanuagarngnik atyingualiit Puvirngniturnmit. Eskimo stories from Povungnituk, Quebec. By Zebedee Nungak and Eugene Arima. Ottawa, 1969. 10, 137 p. illus. (Canada, National Museums, Bulletin, 235)

Oetteking, B. Ein Beitrag zur Kräniologie der Eskimo. Dresden, Königliches Zoologisches und Anthropologisch-Ethnographisches Museum, Abhandlungen und Berichte, 12, no. 3 (1908): 1-58.

Packard, A. S. Notes on the Labrador Eskimo. American Naturalist, 19 (1885): 471-481, 553-560.

Packard, A. S. The Esquimaux of Labrador. In W. W. Beach, ed. Indian Miscellany. Albany, 1877: 65-73.

Packard, A. S. The Labrador Coast. New York, 1891.

Payne, F. F. A few notes upon the Eskimo of Cape Prince of Wales. American Association for the Advancement of Science, Proceedings, 38 (1890): 358-360.

Payne, F. F. Eskimo of Hudson's Strait. California Academy of Sciences, Proceedings, ser. 3, 6 (1899): 213-230.

Payne, F. F. Some customs and habits of the Eskimo at Stupart Bay. Royal Canadian Institute, Proceedings, ser. 3, 6 (1887/1888): 10.

Peacock, F. W. Some Eskimo remedies. Canadian Medical Association Journal, 56 (1947): 328-330.

Peacock, F. W. Some psychological aspects of the impact of the White man upon the Labrador Eskimo. Nain, Labrador, 1947.

Pittard, E. Contribution à l'étude anthropologique des Esquimaux du Labrador et de la Baie d'Hudson. Société Neuchâteloise de Géographie, Bulletin, 13 (1901): 158-176.

Postel, A. W. Dolls of the Netcetu'mint. Ethnos, 2 (1937): 338-339.

Povungnituk Cooperative Society. Povungnituk. Québec, 1965. 60 p. illus.

Proulx, Jean Baptiste. À la baie d'Hudson, où récit de la première visite pastorale de Mgr. N. Z. Lorrain. Montréal, Librairie Saint-Joseph, Cadieux and Derome, 1886. 284 p.

Quimby, G. I. The Manitunik Eskimo culture of East Hudson's Bay. American Antiquity, 6 (1940): 148-165.

Radwanski, P. Anthropological structure of 101 Eskimo. Anthropologica, 1 (1955): 72-83.

Raine, David F. The miniatures of Bobby Takrik. Beaver, 302, no. 3 (1971/1972): 16-17.

Ribbach, C. A. Labrador. Tijdschrift van het Aardrijkskundig Genootschap, 1 (1876): 281-290.

Robinson, J. L. Eskimo population in the Canadian Eastern Arctic. Canadian Geographical Journal, 29 (1944): 128-142.

Rousseau, J. J. Attroverso il Quebec Artico. Le Vie del Mondo, 14 (1952): 143-154.

Rousseau, J. J. Le caribou et le renne dans la Québec Arctique et Hémiarctique. Revue Canadienne de Géographie, 4 (1950): 60-89.

Rousseau, J. J. Le nom du caribou chez les Montagnais-Naskapi et les Esquimaux de l'Ungava. Anthropologica, 1 (1955): 212-214.

Rousseau, J. J. Les voyages du Pere Albanel au Lac Mistassini et à la Baie James. Revue d'Histoire de l'Amérique Française, 3 (1950): 556-586.

Rousseau, J. J. On human and animal adaptation. Canadian Geographer, 6 (1955): 17-20.

Russell, F. and H. M. Huxley. A comparative study of the physical structure of the Labrador Eskimos and the New England Indians. American Association for the Advancement of Science, Proceedings, 48 (1899): 365-379.

Saladin d'Anglure, Bernard. L'organisation sociale traditionnelle des Esquimaux de Kangirsujuaaq (Nouveau-Québec). Québec, 1967. 213 l. illus., maps. (Laval, Université, Centre d'Études Nordiques, Travaux Divers, 17)

Saladin d'Anglure, Bernard. Mission chez les Esquimaux Tarramiut du Nouveau-Québec (Canada). Homme, 7, no. 4 (1967): 92-100.

Sapper, K. T. Nachrichten über Zukunfts-aussichten der Eskimobevölkerung von Grönland und Labrador. Petermanns Mitteilungen, 64 (1918): 210-218.

Savoie, Donat. Two Eskimo games at Port Nouveau-Quebec, P.Q. Musk-Ox, 7 (1970): 70-74.

Schenk, A. Note sur deux crânes d'Esquimaux du Labrador. Société Neuchâteloise de Géographie, Bulletin, 11 (1899): 166-175.

Schneider, Lucien. Dictionnaire alphabético-syllabique du langage esquiman de l'Ungava et contrées limitrophes. Québec, 1966. 380 p. (Laval, Université, Centre d'Études Nordiques, Travaux et Documents, 3)

Schneider, Lucien. Dictionnaire alphabético-syllabique du langage esquimau de l'Ungava et contrées limitrophes. Québec, 1966. 380 p. (Laval, Université, Centre d'Études Nordiques, Travaux et Documents, 3)

Service, E. R. The Canadian Eskimo. In his A Profile of Primitive Culture. New York, 1958: 64-85.

Sewall, K. W. Blood, taste, digital hair and color of eyes in Eastern Eskimo. American Journal of Physical Anthropology, 25 (1939): 93-99.

Silvy, A. Relation par lettres de l'Amérique septentrionale. Edited by C. de Rochemonteix. Paris, 1904. 42-60 p.

Smith, H. I. Notes on Eskimo traditions. Journal of American Folklore, 7 (1894): 209-216.

Spalding, A. E. A grammar of the east and west coasts of Hudson Bay. Ottawa, Queen's Printer, 1960. 178 p.

Speck, F. G. Analysis of Eskimo and Indian skin-dressing methods in Labrador. Ethnos, 2 (1937): 345-353.

Speck, F. G. Collections from Labrador Eskimo. Indian Notes, 1 (1924): 211-217.

Speck, F. G. Eskimo carved ivories from northern Labrador. Indian Notes, 4 (1927): 309-314.

Speck, F. G. Eskimo jacket ornaments of ivory. American Antiquity, 5 (1940): 225-228.

Speck, F. G. Indian and Eskimo backgrounds in southern Labrador. General Magazine and Historical Chronicle, University of Pennsylvania, 38 (1935): 1-17, 143-163.

Speck, F. G. Inland Eskimo bands of Labrador. In Essays in Anthropology presented to A. L. Kroeber. Berkeley, 1936: 313-330.

Speck, F. G. Labrador Eskimo mask and clown. General Magazine and Historical Chronicle, University of Pennsylvania, 37 (1935): 159-173.

Speck, F. G. Montagnais-Naskapi bands and early Eskimo distribution in the Labrador Peninsula. American Anthropologist, n.s., 33 (1931): 557-600.

Stefansson, V. Eskimos. Encyclopaedia Britannica, 14th ed., 8 (1929): 708-710.

Steinert, W. Die Wirkung des Landschaftzwanges auf die materielle Kultur des Eskimos. Hamburg, 1935. 58 p.

Stewart, T. D. Anthropometric observations on the Eskimos and Indians of Labrador. Field Museum, Anthropological Series, 31 (1939): 1-163.

Stewart, T. D. Change in physical type of the Eskimos of Labrador since the eighteenth century. American Journal of Physical Anthropology, 23 (1937): 493-494.

Stewart, T. D. New measurements on the
Eskimos and Indians of Labrador.
American Journal of Physical
Anthropology, 21 (1935): 10.

Stuart, P. F., et al. Botulism among Cape
Dorset Eskimos and suspected botulism at
Frobisher Bay and Wakeham Bay. Canadian
Journal of Public Health, 61 (1970):
509-517.

Stupart, R. F. The Eskimo of Stupart Bay.
Canadian Institute, Proceedings, ser. 3,
4 (1887): 95-114.

Suk, V. Congenital pigment spots in
Eskimo children. Anthropologie (Prague),
6 (1928): 1-34.

Suk, V. On the occurrence of syphilis and
tuberculosis amongst Eskimos and mixed
breeds of the north coast of Labrador.
Université Masaryk, Faculté des
Sciences, Publications, 84 (1927): 1-18.

Tanner, V. Folk och kulturer pa Labrador.
Acta Societatis Scientiarum Fennicae,
17, pt. 2 (1939).

Tanner, V. Outline of the geography, life
and customs of Newfoundland-Labrador.
Acta Geographica, 8, no. 1, pt. 2
(1944): 1-470.

Tanner, V. Ruinerna pa Sculpin Island
(Kanayoktok) i Nain's Skärgard.
Geografisk Tidsskrift, 44 (1941): 129-
155.

Tanner, Vaïnö. Folk och kulturer på
Labrador. Helsinki, 1939. 54 p.
illus., maps. (Finska Vetenskaps-
societeten, Årsbok-Vuosikirja, 17B,
no. 2)

Taylor, James Garth. An analysis of the
size of Eskimo settlements on the coast
of Labrador during the early contact
period. Dissertation Abstracts
International, 31 (1970/1971): 1034B.

Thomas, Gordon W. Carcinoma among
Labrador Eskimos and Indians. Canadian
Journal of Surgery, 4 (1960/1961): 465-
468.

Tolboom, W. N. Arctic bride. Toronto,
1956. 256 p.

Trafford, Diana. Takushurnaituk. North,
15, no. 2 (1968): 52-55.

Treude, Erhard. Die gegenwärtige
Siedlungs- und Wirtschaftsstruktur
Nordlabradors. In Internationale
Amerikanistenkongress, 38th. 1968,
Stuttgart-München. Verhandlungen. Band
3. München, Klaus Renner, 1971: 151-
162.

Trinel, Ernest. Atii, parlez esquimau.
Ottawa, Canadian Research Centre for
Anthropology, 1970. 12, 206 p.

*Turner, L. M. Ethnology of the Ungava
District. U.S. Bureau of American
Ethnology, Annual Reports, 11 (1894):
159-267.

Turner, L. M. On the Indians and Eskimos
of the Ungava District. Royal Society of
Canada, Proceedings and Transactions, 5,
no. 2 (1887): 99-119.

Turner, William. William Turner's
journeys to the caribou country with the
Labrador Eskimos in 1780. Edited by J.
G. Taylor. Ethnohistory, 16 (1969): 141-
164.

Turquetil, A. Notes sur les Esquimaux de
Baie Hudson. Anthropos, 21 (1926): 419-
434.

Twomey, Arthur C. Needle to the North,
the story of an expedition to Ungava and
the Belcher Islands. By Arthur C. Twomey
and Nigel Herrick. Boston, Houghton
Mifflin, 1942. 8, 360 p. illus., map.

Uhlenbeck, R. L. Eskimo children. Beaver,
271 (1940): 18-19.

Vallee, Frank G. Eskimo theories of
mental illness in the Hudson Bay region.
Anthropologica, n.s., 8 (1966): 53-83.

Vallee, Frank G. Povungnetuk and its
cooperative: a case study in community
change. Ottawa, 1967. 5, 57 p.
illus., map. (Canada, Department of
Indian Affairs and Northern Development,
Northern Co-ordination and Research
Centre, NCRC-67-2)

Virchow, R. Eskimos von Labrador.
Berliner Gesellschaft für Anthropologie,
Ethnologie und Urgeschichte,
Verhandlungen (1880): 253-274.

Waldmann, S. Les Esquimaux du Nord du
Labrador. Société Neuchâteloise de
Géographie, Bulletin, 19 (1908): 430-
441.

Wallace, D. The long Labrador trail. New
York, 1907.

Washburne, H. C. and Anauta. Land of the
good shadows. New York, 1940. 329 p.

Waugh, L. M. A study of the influences of
diet and of racial admixture on the
development of the jaw and face of the
American Eskimo. Journal of Dental
Research, 12 (1932): 426-429.

Waugh, L. M. Influences of diet on the
development of the jaws and face of the

American Eskimo. Journal of Dental Research, 13 (1933): 149-151.

Waugh, L. M. Nutrition and health of the Labrador Eskimo, with special reference to the mouth and teeth. Journal of Dental Research, 8 (1928): 428-429.

Weyer, Edward M., Jr. Art of the Eskimo. Natural History, 69, no. 2 (1960): 34-45.

Wheeler, E. P. Journeys about Nain. Geographical Review, 20 (1930): 454-468.

Wheeler, E. P. List of Labrador Eskimo place names. National Museum of Canada, Bulletin, 131 (1953): 1-109.

Wherrett, G. J. A study of tuberculosis in the Eastern Arctic. Canadian Journal of Public Health, 60 (1969): 7-14.

Williamson, H. Anthony. The Moravian mission and its impact on the Labrador Eskimo. Arctic Anthropology, 2, no. 2 (1964): 32-36.

Willmott, W. E. The Eskimo community at Port Harrison, P.Q. Ottawa, 1961. (Canada, Department of Northern Affairs and National Resources, Northern Co-ordination and Research Centre, NCRC-61-1)

Willmott, W. E. The flexibility of Eskimo social organization. Anthropologica, n.s., 2 (1960): 48-59.

Wintemberg, W. J. Eskimo sites of the Dorset culture in Newfoundland. American Antiquity, 5 (1939-1940): 83-102, 309-333.

01-08   Mackenzie Eskimo

Abrahamson, G. Tuktoyaktuk--Cape Parry area economic survey. Ottawa, Department of Northern Affairs and National Resources, Industrial Division, 1963. 109 p. illus., maps.

Boas, F. A. J. Stone's measurements of natives of the Northwest Territories. American Museum of Natural History, Bulletin, 14 (1901): 53-68.

Bompas, W. C. Diocese of Mackenzie River. London, 1888. 108 p.

Cameron, A. D. The new North. New York, 1910.

Cameron, J. Osteology of the Western and Central Eskimos. Canadian Arctic Expedition, Report, 13, pt. C (1923): 1-79.

Carrothiers, A. W. R. Canada: reluctant imperialist. Journal of Canadian Studies, 2, no. 1 (1967): 11-23.

Ferguson, J. D. The human ecology and social and economic change in the community of Tuktoyaktuk, N.W.T. Ottawa, 1961. 90 p. illus., maps. (Canada, Department of Northern Affairs and National Resources, Northern Co-ordination and Research Centre, NCRC-61-2)

Flyger, Vagn. Hunters of white whales. Beaver, 296, no. 3 (1965/1966): 32-37.

Franklin, J. Narrative of a second expedition to the shores of the Polar Sea. London, 1828.

Gagné, Raymond C. Towards a Canadian Eskimo orthography and literature. Canadian Journal of Linguistics, 7 (1961/1962): 95-107; 8 (1962/1963): 33-39.

Gates, R. R. Blood groups of Canadian Indians and Eskimos. American Journal of Physical Anthropology, 12 (1929): 475-485.

Godsell, P. H. Is there time to save the Eskimo? Natural History, 61 (1952): 56-62.

Heinrich, Albert C. Co-affinal siblingship as a structural feature among some northern North American peoples. By Albert C. Heinrich and Russell Anderson. Ethnology, 7 (1968): 290-295.

Hourde, R. N. Sophisticated Eskimos. Beaver, 283 (Sept. 1952): 36-37.

Jenness, D. Comparative vocabulary of the Western Eskimo dialects. Canadian Arctic Expedition, Report, 15, pt. A (1928): 1-134.

Jenness, D. Eskimo string figures. Canadian Arctic Expedition, Report, 13, pt. B (1924): 1-192.

Jenness, D. Myths and traditions from northern Alaska, the Mackenzie Delta and Coronation Gulf. Canadian Arctic Expedition, Report, 13, pt. A (1924): 1-90.

Lubart, Joseph M. Field study of the problems of adaptation of Mackenzie Delta Eskimos to social and economic change. Psychiatry, 32 (1969): 447-458.

Lubart, Joseph M. Psychodynamic problems of adaptation--Mackenzie Delta Eskimos; a preliminary study. Ottawa, 1969. 12, 49 p. illus. (Canada, Department of

Indian Affairs and Northern Development,
Northern Science Research Group,
Mackenzie Delta Research Project, 7)

Mackenzie, A. Voyages from Montreal
through the continent of North America
to the frozen and Pacific Oceans.
London, 1801.

Marsh, D. B. White whales in the Arctic.
Canadian Geographical Journal, 41
(1950): 34-40.

Mathiassen, T. Archaeological collections
from the Western Eskimos. Fifth Thule
Expedition, Report, 10 (1930): 1-98.

McClure, R. J. L. The discovery of the
north-west passage. London, 1856.

McGhee, Robert. Excavation at
Kittigazuit. Beaver, 302, no. 2
(1971/1972): 34-39.

Monestier, Marianne. Avec les rois du
Nord. Paris, La Table Ronde, 1953.
348 p.

Nash, D. W. Arctic farmer. Country Guide,
68 (1949): 13, 34-35.

Nuligak. I, Nuligak. Translated from the
Eskimo by Maurice Metayer. Toronto, P.
Martin Associates, 1966. 208 p.
illus., map.

Osborne, D. Late Eskimo archaeology in
the western Mackenzie Delta area.
American Antiquity, 18 (1952): 30-39.

Oschinsky, Lawrence. Facial flatness and
cheekbone morphology in Arctic
Mongoloids. Anthropologica, n.s., 4
(1962): 349-377.

*Ostermann, H., ed. The MacKenzie Eskimos,
after K. Rasmussen's posthumous notes.
Fifth Thule Expedition, Report, 10,
no. 2 (1942): 1-166.

Petitot, E. F. S. Die Eskimos am
Mackenzie und Anderson. Globus, 31
(1877): 103-105.

Petitot, E. F. S. Les grands Esquimaux.
Paris, 1887.

*Petitot, E. F. S. Monographie des
Esquimaux Tchiglit du Mackenzie et de
l'Anderson. Paris, 1876.

Petitot, E. F. S. Quinze ans sous le
cercle polaire. Vol. 2. Paris, 1889.

Petitot, E. F. S. Traditions indiennes du
Canada nord-ouest. Paris, 1886.

Petitot, E. F. S. Vocabulaire français-
esquimaux. Paris, 1876.

Petitot, Émile F. Les Amérindiens du
Nord-Ouest canadien au 19e siècle selon
Émile Petitot. Edited by Donat Savcie.
Ottawa, 1970. 2 v. illus. (Canada,
Ministry of Indian Affairs and of the
Canadian North, MacKenzie Delta Research
Project, MDRP, 9-10)

Richardson, J. Arctic searching
expedition. London, 1851. 2 v.

Rogers, Edward S. An Athapaskan type of
knife. Ottawa, Queen's Printer, 1965.
16 p. illus. (Canada, National Museum,
Anthropology Papers, 9)

Russell, F. Explorations in the Far
North. Iowa City, 1898.

Schwartz, Herbert T. Elik, and other
stories of the Mackenzie Eskimos.
Toronto, McClelland and Stewart, 1970.
79 p. illus.

Seltzer, C. C. The anthropometry of the
Western and Copper Eskimos. Human
Biology, 5 (1933): 313-370.

Service, E. R. The Canadian Eskimo. In
his A Profile of Primitive Culture. New
York, 1958: 64-85.

Simpson, T. Narrative of the discoveries
on the north coast of America. London,
1843. 419 p.

Smith, Derek G. The implications of
pluralism for social change programs in
a Canadian Eskimo community.
Anthropologica, n.s., 13 (1971): 193-
214.

Stefansson, V. Hunters of the great
north. New York, 1922.

Stefansson, V. My life with the Eskimo.
New York, 1913.

Stefansson, V. Notes on the theory and
treatment of disease among the Mackenzie
River Eskimo. Journal of American
Folklore, 21 (1908): 43-45.

Stefansson, V. Religious beliefs of the
Eskimo. Harper's Monthly Magazine, 127
(1913): 869-878.

Stefansson, V. The friendly Arctic. New
York, 1921.

Stefansson, V. The Stefansson-Anderson
Arctic Expedition. American Museum of
Natural History, Anthropological Papers,
14 (1914): 1-395.

Taylor, P. Tales from the delta. Beaver,
284 (June 1953): 22-25.

Urquhart, J. A.   Eskimos of the Canadian Western Arctic.   In C. A. Dawson, ed. The New North-West.   Toronto, 1947: 271-282.

Urquhart, J. A.   The most northerly practice in Canada. Canadian Medical Association Journal, 33 (1935): 193-196.

Usher, Peter J.   The Canadian Western Arctic: a century of change. Anthropologica, n.s., 13 (1971): 169-183.

01-09   Netsilik Eskimo

Carrière, Gaston.   Catalogue des manuscrits en langues indiennes conservés aux archives oblates, Ottawa. Anthropologica, n.s., 12 (1970): 151-179.

Amundsen, R.   Nordvestpassagen. Christiania, 1908.

Amundsen, R.   The north west passage. London, 1908.   2 v.

Balikci, Asen.   A comparative study on subsistence ecology and social systems: the !Kung Bushmen and Netsilik Eskimos. In International Congress of Anthropological and Ethnological Sciences, 8th. 1968, Tokyo and Kyoto. Proceedings. Vol. 3.   Tokyo, Science Council of Japan, 1970: 261-262.

Balikci, Asen.   Development of basic socio-economic units in two Eskimo communities. Dissertation Abstracts, 24 (1963/1964): 462.   UM 63-5771.

Balikci, Asen.   Development of basic socio-economic units in two Eskimo communities. Ottawa, 1964.   10, 114 p. maps.   (Canada, National Museum, Bulletin, 202)

Balikci, Asen.   Female infanticide on the Arctic Coast. Man, n.s., 2 (1967): 615-625.

Balikci, Asen.   Le régime matrimonial des Esquimaux Netsilik. Homme, 3, no. 3 (1963): 88-101.

Balikci, Asen.   Quelques cas de suicide parmi les Esquimaux Netsilik.   In International Congress of Anthropological and Ethnological Sciences, 6th. 1960, Paris. Tome II, v. 2.   Paris, Musée de l'Homme, 1964: 511-516.

Balikci, Asen.   Shamanistic behavior among the Netsilik Eskimos. In John Middleton, ed. Magic, Witchcraft, and Curing. Garden City, Natural History Press, 1967: 191-209.

Balikci, Asen.   Shamanistic behavior among the Netsilik Eskimos. Southwestern Journal of Anthropology, 19 (1963): 380-396.

Balikci, Asen.   Some acculturative trends among the Eastern Canadian Eskimos. In Internationale Amerikanistenkongress, 34th. 1960, Wien. Akten.   Horn-Wien, Berger, 1962: 504-513.

Balikci, Asen.   Some acculturative trends among the eastern Canadian Eskimos. Anthropologica, n.s., 2 (1960): 139-153.

Balikci, Asen.   Suicidal behaviour among the Netsilik Eskimos.   Ottawa, 1960. (Canada, Department of Northern Affairs and National Resources, Northern Co-ordination and Research Centre, NCRC-60-2)

Balikci, Asen.   The Central Eskimo: a marginal case? By Asen Balikci, David Damas, Fred Eggan, June Helm, and Sherwood L. Washburn. In Richard B. Lee and Irven DeVore, eds. Man the Hunter. Chicago, Aldine, 1968: 83-85.

*Balikci, Asen.   The Netsilik Eskimo. Garden City, Natural History Press, 1970.   24, 264 p.   illus., map.

Balikci, Asen.   The Netsilik Eskimos: adaptive processes. In Richard B. Lee and Irven DeVore, eds. Man the Hunter. Chicago, Aldine, 1968: 78-82.

Birket-Smith, K.   Anthropological observations on the Central Eskimos. Fifth Thule Expedition, Report, 3, no. 2 (1940): 1-123.

Boas, F.   Über die Wohnsitze der Neitchillik Eskimos. Gesellschaft für Erdkunde (Berlin), Zeitschrift, 18 (1883): 222-233.

Briggs, Jean.   Kapluna daughter. In Peggy Golde, ed. Women in the Field.   Chicago, Aldine, 1970: 17-44.

Briggs, Jean.   Strategies of perception: the management of ethnic identity. In Robert Paine, ed. Patrons and Brokers in the East Arctic.   St. John's, Memorial University of Newfoundland, 1971: 55-73. (Newfoundland Social and Economic Papers, 2)

*Briggs, Jean L.   Never in anger; portrait of an Eskimo family.   Cambridge, Harvard University Press, 1970.   21, 379 p. illus., maps.

Damas, David.   Central Eskimo systems of
   food sharing. Ethnology, 11 (1972): 220-
   240.

Damas, David.   Characteristics of Central
   Eskimo band structure. In Contributions
   to Anthropology: Band Societies.
   Ottawa, Queen's Printer, 1969: 116-141.
   (Canada, National Museums, Bulletin,
   228)

Damas, David.   Domestic group structure
   among Eastern Canadian Eskimo. Man,
   n.s., 2 (1967): 304-305.

Damas, David.   Environment, history, and
   Central Eskimo society. In Contributions
   to Anthropology: Ecological Essays.
   Ottawa, Queen's Printer, 1969: 40-64.
   (Canada, National Museums, Bulletin,
   230)

Damas, David.   The diversity of Eskimo
   societies. In Richard B. Lee and Irven
   DeVore, eds. Man the Hunter.   Chicago,
   Aldine, 1968: 111-117.

Damas, David.   The structure of Central
   Eskimo associations. In D. Lee Guemple,
   ed. Alliance in Eskimo Society.
   Seattle, American Ethnological Society,
   1972: 40-55.

Danielo, E.   The story of a medicine man.
   Eskimo, 36 (1955): 3-6.

Davies, L. E. C.   The Eskimos of the
   Northwest Passage: a survey of dietary
   composition and various blood and
   metabolic measurements. By L. E. C.
   Davies and S. Hanson. Canadian Medical
   Association Journal, 92 (1965): 205-216.

Dunning, Robert W.   Domestic group
   structure among Eastern Canadian Eskimo.
   Man, n.s., 2 (1967): 303-304.

Freeman, Milton M. R.   A social and
   ecologic analysis of systematic female
   infanticide among the Netsilik Eskimo.
   American Anthropologist, 73 (1971):
   1011-1018.

Gilder, W. H.   Schwatka's search.   New
   York, 1881.

Hall, C. F.   Narrative of the Second
   Arctic Expedition. Washington, D.C.,
   1879.

Hanbury, D. T.   Sport and travel in the
   northland of Canada.   London, 1904.

Harrington, R.   Spring break-up at
   Boothia. Canadian Geographical Journal,
   46 (1953): 150-162.

Harrington, R.   The cheerful Eskimo.
   Beaver, 282, no. 4 (1952): 7-15.

Hyenaes, T.   Noen Glimt fra Primitive
   Eskimostammer. Polarboken (1954): 44-52.

Klutschak, H. W.   Als Eskimo unter den
   Eskimos.   Wien, 1881.

Learmonth, L. A.   Interrupted journey.
   Beaver, 282, no. 2 (1951): 20-25.

Lentz, J. W.   Through the Barrens by
   canoe. Explorers Journal, 43 (1965): 39-
   45.

Mary-Rousselière, G.   Christmas igloo.
   Beaver, 287 (Winter 1956): 4-5.

Mary-Rousselière, Guy.   Les jeux de
   ficelle des Arviligjuarmiut.   Ottawa,
   Imprimeur de la Reine, 1969.   17,
   182 p.   illus., map.   (Canada, National
   Museums, Bulletin, 233)

Petersen, C.   Den sidste Franklin
   ekspedition.   Kjøbenhaven, 1860.

Poncins, G. de.   Kabloona.   New York,
   1941.   339 p.

Rae, J.   Narrative of an expedition to the
   shores of the arctic sea.   London, 1850.

*Rasmussen, K.   The Netsilik Eskimos. Fifth
   Thule Expedition, Report, 8 (1931): 1-
   542.

Reynolds, Vernon.   Kinship and the family
   in monkeys, apes and man. Man, n.s., 3
   (1968): 209-223.

Ross, J.   Narrative of a second voyage in
   search of a north-west passage.   London,
   1835.

Schwatka, F.   The implements of the igloo.
   Science, 4 (1884): 81-85.

Schwatka, F.   The Netschilluk Innuits.
   Science, 4 (1884): 543-545.

Service, E. R.   The Canadian Eskimo.   In
   his A Profile of Primitive Culture.   New
   York, 1958: 64-85.

Urquhart, J. A.   Eskimos of the Canadian
   Western Arctic. In C. A. Dawson, ed. The
   New North-West.   Toronto, 1947: 271-282.

Van de Velde, Frans.   Principes de
   religion et de morale chez les Esquimaux
   de Pelly Bay (Vicariat de la Baie
   d'Hudson). By Frans Vandevelde.
   Catéchèse et Missions (1955): 225-233.

Van de Velde, Frans.   Religion et morale
   chez les Esquimaux de Pelly Bay.
   Bannière de Marie Immaculée, 67 (1959):
   54-67.

Van Den Steenhoven, Geert. Legal concepts among the Netsilik Eskimos of Pelly Bay, N.W.T. Ottawa, 1959. (Canada, Department of Northern Affairs and National Resources, Northern Co-ordination and Research Centre, NCRC-59-3)

VanStone, James W. An archaeological collection from Somerset Island and Boothia Peninsula, N.W.T. Toronto, 1962. 1-63 p. (Royal Ontario Museum, Art and Archaeology Division, Occasional Paper, 4)

Velde, F. Religion and morals among the Pelly Bay Eskimos. Eskimo, 39 (1956): 6-16.

Velde, F. Rules governing the sharing of seal after the "aglus" hunt. Eskimo, 41 (1956): 3-7.

Velde, F. van de. Infanticide among the Eskimo. Eskimo, 34 (1954): 6-8.

01-10   North Alaska Eskimo

Alexander, Herbert L. Alaska: archaeology in the Atigun Valley. Expedition, 11, no. 1 (1968): 35-37.

Alexander, Herbert L. Alaskan survey. Expedition, 9, no. 3 (1967): 20-29.

Allison, A. C. Ability to taste phenylthiocarbamide among Alaskan Eskimos and other populations. By A. C. Allison and B. S. Blumberg. Human Biology, 31 (1959): 352-359.

Anderson, H. D. and W. C. Eells. Alaska natives. Stanford, 1935. 472 p.

Andrews, C. L. The Eskimo and his reindeer in Alaska. Caldwell, 1939. 253 p.

Balikci, Asen. Female infanticide on the Arctic Coast. Man, n.s., 2 (1967): 615-625.

Bang, Gisle. Morphologic characteristics of the Alaskan Eskimo dentition. I. Shovel-shaped incisors. By Gisle Bang and Asbjörn Hasund. American Journal of Physical Anthropology, n.s., 35 (1971): 43-47.

Blumberg, Baruch S., et al. A study of the prevalence of arthritis in Alaskan Eskimos. Arthritis and Rheumatism, 4 (1961): 325-341.

Boas, F. Property marks of the Alaskan Eskimo. American Anthropologist, n.s., 1 (1899): 601-613.

Bohlen, Joseph G. Circadian and circannual rhythms in Wainwright Eskimos. Arctic Anthropology, 7, no. 1 (1970): 95-100.

Bohlen, Joseph Glenn. Circumpolar chronobiology. Dissertation Abstracts International, 32 (1971/1972): 6785B. UM 72-15,340.

Brevig, T. L. Apauruk in Alaska. Philadelphia, 1944. 325 p.

Brown, Pamela K. Respiratory virus antibodies in sera of persons living in isolated communities. By Pamela K. Brown and D. Taylor-Robinson. World Health Organization, Bulletin, 34 (1966): 895-900.

Burch, Ernest S., Jr. Alliance and conflict: inter-regional relations in North Alaska. By Ernest S. Burch, Jr. and Thomas C. Correll. In D. Lee Guemple, ed. Alliance in Eskimo Society. Seattle, American Ethnological Society, 1972: 17-39.

Burch, Ernest S., Jr. Marriage and divorce among the North Alaskan Eskimos. In Paul Bohannan, ed. Divorce and After. Garden City, Doubleday, 1970: 152-181.

Burch, Ernest S., Jr. The caribou/wild reindeer as a human resource. American Antiquity, 37 (1972): 339-368.

Burg, A. North Star cruises Alaska's Wild West. National Geographic Magazine, 102 (1952): 57-86.

Cameron, J. Osteology of the Western and Central Eskimos. Canadian Arctic Expedition, Report, 12, pt. C (1923): 1-79.

Campbell, John M. The hungry summer. In Philip K. Bock, ed. Culture Shock. New York, Knopf, 1970: 165-170.

Campbell, John Martin. Anaktuvuk prehistory: a study in environmental adaptation. Dissertation Abstracts International, 32 (1971/1972): 3754B-3755B. UM 72-1157.

Cash, A. Anaktuvuk Pass. Alaska Sportsman, 30, no. 4 (1964): 19-21.

Chance, Norman A. Acculturation, self-identification, and personality adjustment. American Anthropologist, 67 (1965): 372-393.

Chance, Norman A. Acculturation, self-identification, and personality adjustment. In Deward E. Walker, Jr., ed. The Emergent Native Americans. Boston, Little, Brown, 1972: 513-532.

Chance, Norman A.   Community adjustment to rapid change among the Eskimo and Cree. By Norman A. Chance and John Trudeau. North, 11, no. 1 (1964): 34-39.

Chance, Norman A.   Culture change and integration: an Eskimo example. American Anthropologist, 62 (1960): 1028-1044.

Chance, Norman A.   Investigation of the adjustment of the Eskimos at Barter Island, Alaska to rapid cultural changes. Arctic, 13 (1960): 205.

Chance, Norman A.   Modernization, value identification, and mental health: a cross-cultural study. By Norman A. Chance, Hsien Rin, and Hung-ming Chu. Anthropologica, n.s., 8 (1966): 197-216.

Chance, Norman A.   Notes on culture change and personality adjustment among the North Alaska Eskimos. Arctic, 16 (1963): 264-270.

Chance, Norman A.   Social organization, acculturation, and integration among the Eskimo and the Cree: a comparative study. By Norman A. Chance and John Trudeau. Anthropologica, n.s., 5 (1963): 47-56.

Chance, Norman A.   Symptom formation and patterns of psychopathology in a rapidly changing Alaskan Eskimo society. By Norman A. Chance and Dorothy A. Foster. Alaska, University, Anthropological Papers, 11, no. 1 (1962): 32-42.

Chance, Norman A.   The changing role of government among the North Alaskan Eskimo. Arctic Anthropology, 2, no. 2 (1964): 41-44.

Chance, Norman A.   The Eskimo of North Alaska. New York, Holt, Rinehart and Winston, 1966. 12, 107 p. illus., map.

Chandler, Robert P.   Radionuclides in the northwestern Alaska food chain, 1959-1961--a review. By Robert P. Chandler and Samuel Wieder. Radiological Health Data, 4 (1963): 317-324.

Chard, Chester S.   Arctic anthropology in America. In Jacob W. Gruber, ed. The Philadelphia Anthropological Society; Papers Presented on Its Golden Anniversary.   New York, distributed by Columbia University Press for Temple University Publications, 1967: 77-106.

Cline, Michael Slater.   The impact of formal education upon the Nunamiut Eskimos of Anaktuvuk Pass, Alaska: a case study. Dissertation Abstracts International, 33 (1972/1973): 25B-26B. UM 72-20,911.

Coleman, James R.   Projected values of cesium-137 body burdens in Anaktuvuk Pass Eskimos for the summer of 1965, based on findings in caribou muscle. Radiological Health Data, 6 (1965): 578-582.

Collins, H. B.   Archeological investigations at Point Barrow. Smithsonian Institution, Explorations and Field-Work (1932): 45-48.

Collins, H. B.   Caries and crowding in the teeth of the living Alaska Eskimo. American Journal of Physical Anthropology, 16 (1932): 451-463.

Coon, Carleton S.   The hunting peoples. Boston, Little, Brown, 1971.   21, 413 p.   illus., maps.

Corbett, Thomas H.   An epidemic in an Eskimo village due to group-B meningococcus. II. Clinical features. By Thomas H. Corbett and Jacob A. Brody. American Medical Association, Journal, 196 (1966): 388-390.

Corcoran, P. A., et al.   Blood groups of Alaskan Eskimos and Indians. American Journal of Physical Anthropology, n.s., 17 (1959): 187-194.

Cumming, J. R.   Metaphysical implications of the folktales of the Eskimos of Alaska. Alaska, University, Anthropological Papers, 3, no. 1 (1954): 37-63.

Cummins, H.   Dermatoglyphics in Eskimos from Point Barrow. American Journal of Physical Anthropology, 20 (1935): 13-18.

Dale, G. A.   Northwest Alaska and the Bering Sea Coast. In I. T. Sanders, ed. Societies Around the World. Vol. 1. 1952: 111-130.

Eagan, C. J.   The responses of finger cooling of Alaskan Eskimos after nine months of urban life in a temperate climate. Biometeorology, 2, pt. 2 (1967): 822-830.

Fejes, Claire.   People of the Noatak. New York, Knopf, 1966.   12, 368 p.   illus.

Feldman, Carol F.   Cognitive studies among residents of Wainwright Village, Alaska. By Carol F. Feldman and R. Darrell Bock. Arctic Anthropology, 7, no. 1 (1970): 101-108.

Feldman, Sheldon A., et al.   Lipid and cholesterol metabolism in Alaskan Arctic Eskimos. Archives of Pathology, 94 (1972): 42-58.

Feltz, Elmer T., et al. California encephalitis virus: serological evidence of human infections in Alaska. Canadian Journal of Microbiology, 18 (1972): 757-762.

Foote, Don C. A human geographical study. In N. J. Wilimovsky and J. N. Wolfe, eds. Environment of the Cape Thompson Region, Alaska. Oak Ridge, U.S. Atomic Energy Commission, Committee on Environmental Studies for Project Chariot, 1966: 1041-1107.

Foote, Don Charles. American whalemen in northwestern Arctic Alaska. In Deward E. Walker, Jr., ed. The Emergent Native Americans. Boston, Little, Brown, 1972: 301-308.

Foote, Don Charles. An Eskimo sea-mammal and caribou hunting economy: human ecology in terms of energy. In International Congress of Anthropological and Ethnological Sciences, 8th. 1968, Tokyo and Kyoto. Proceedings. Vol. 3. Tokyo, Science Council of Japan, 1970: 262-267.

Ford, J. A. Eskimo burial customs. El Palacio, 33 (1932): 198-199.

Foulks, Edward Francis. The Arctic Hysterias of the North Alaskan Eskimo. Dissertation Abstracts International, 33 (1972/1973): 2905B. UM 73-1387.

Gamō, Masao. Arasuka esukimo ni okeru bando no kōzō genri (Structural principles of Alaskan Eskimo bands). Minzokugaku-Kenkyu, 28, no. 2 (1964): 149-180.

Giddings, J. L. Dated Eskimo ruins of an inland zone. American Antiquity, 10 (1944): 113-134.

Giddings, J. L. Ethnographic notes: Kobuk River region. Kiva, 6 (1941): 25-28.

*Giddings, J. L. Forest Eskimos. Pennsylvania, University, Museum Bulletin, 20, no. 2 (1956): 1-55.

Giddings, J. L. The Arctic woodland culture of the Kobuk River. Philadelphia, 1952. 154 p.

Giddings, James L., Jr. Kobuk River people. College, Alaska, 1961. 166 p. illus., map. (Alaska, University, Department of Anthropology and Geography, Studies of Northern Peoples, 1)

Gillham, C. E. Beyond the clapping mountains. New York, 1943. 134 p.

Godsell, P. H. The Eskimo goes modern. Natural History, 45 (1940): 38-39, 56.

*Gubser, Nicholas J. The Nunamiut Eskimos; hunters of caribou. New Haven, Yale University Press, 1965. 15, 384 p. maps.

Hall, Edwin S., Jr. An addition to Eskimo material culture? Alaska, University, Anthropological Papers, 14, no. 1 (1968): 23-26.

Hall, Edwin S., Jr. Kangiguksuk: a cultural reconstruction of a 16th century Eskimo site in northern Alaska. Dissertation Abstracts, 27 (1966/1967): 4223B. UM 67-7018.

Hall, Edwin S., Jr. Kangiguksuk: a cultural reconstruction of a sixteenth century site in northern Alaska. Arctic Anthropology, 8, no. 1 (1971): 1-101.

Hall, Edwin S., Jr. Speculations on the late prehistory of the Kutchin Athapaskans. Ethnohistory, 16 (1969): 317-333.

Hall, Edwin S., Jr. The "iron dog" in northern Alaska. Anthropologica, n.s., 13 (1971): 237-254.

Hammerich, L. L. Russian loan-words in Alaska. International Congress of Americanists, Proceedings, 30 (1955): 114-126.

Hammerich, L. L. The Russian stratum in Alaskan Eskimo. Slavic Word, 10 (1954): 401-428.

Hammerich, L. L. The Western Eskimo dialects. International Congress of Americanists, Proceedings, 32 (1958): 632-639.

Hanson, W. C. Radioactivity in Northern Alaskan Eskimos and their foods, summer 1962. In N. J. Wilimovsky and J. N. Wolfe, eds. Environment of the Cape Thompson Region, Alaska. Oak Ridge, U.S. Atomic Energy Commission, Committee on Environmental Studies for Project Chariot, 1966: 1151-1164.

Hanson, Wayne C. Cesium-137 body burdens in Alaskan Eskimos during the summer of 1965. Science, 153 (1966): 525-526.

Hanson, Wayne C. Cesium-137 in Alaskan lichens, caribou, and Eskimos. Health Physics, 13 (1967): 383-389.

Hanson, Wayne C. Fallout radionuclides in northern Alaskan ecosystems. Archives of Environmental Health, 17 (1968): 639-648.

Hanson, Wayne C. Radioactivity in
Northern Alaskan Eskimos and their
foods, summer 1962. By W. C. Hanson, H.
E. Palmer, and B. I. Griffin. Health
Physics, 10 (1964): 421-429.

Harmeling, P. C. Therapeutic theater of
Alaska Eskimos. Group Psychotherapy, 3
(1950): 74-76.

Harrington, M. R. The Huntley Eskimo
Collection. Masterkey, 23 (1949): 165-
173.

Hawkes, E. W. Skeletal measurements and
observations of the Point Barrow Eskimo.
American Anthropologist, n.s., 18
(1916): 203-244.

Heinrich, Albert. Structural features of
northwestern Alaskan Eskimo kinship.
Southwestern Journal of Anthropology, 16
(1960): 110-126.

Heller, C. A. The Alaskan Eskimo and the
white man's diet. Journal of Home
Economics, 44 (1949): 177-178.

Heller, Christine A. Meat consumption at
three Northern Eskimo villages. In N. J.
Wilimovsky and J. N. Wolfe, eds.
Environment of the Cape Thompson Region,
Alaska. Oak Ridge, U.S. Atomic Energy
Commission, Committee on Environmental
Studies for Project Chariot, 1966: 1109-
1111.

Helmericks, C. and M. Helmericks. Our
summer with the Eskimos. London, 1952.
255 p.

Helms, Mary W. The purchase society:
adaptation to economic frontiers.
Anthropological Quarterly, 42 (1969):
325-342.

Hennigh, Lawrence. Functions and
limitations of Alaskan Eskimo wife
trading. Arctic, 23 (1970): 24-34.

Hennigh, Lawrence. You have to be a good
lawyer to be an Eskimo. In D. Lee
Guemple, ed. Alliance in Eskimo Society.
Seattle, American Ethnological Society,
1972: 89-109.

Hinnant, John. The possibility of
genotypic adaptation to cold in man.
Anthropology Tomorrow, 9, no. 3 (1964):
38-52.

Hippler, Arthur E. Barrow and Kotzebue:
an exploratory comparison of
acculturation and education in two large
northwestern Alaska villages.
Minneapolis, University of Minnesota,
Training Center for Community Programs,
1969. 64 p.

Hippler, Arthur E. From village to town:
an intermediate step in the
acculturation of Alaska Eskimos.
Minneapolis, University of Minnesota,
Training Center for Community Programs,
1970. 68 p. ERIC ED045247.

Holland, D. The trophy is still there.
Elks Magazine, 31, no. 7 (1952): 6-7,
39-42.

Hooper, W. H. Ten months among the tents
of the Tuski. London, 1853.

Hrdlička, A. Anthropological survey of
Alaska. U.S. Bureau of American
Ethnology, Annual Reports, 46 (1930):
19-374.

Hrdlička, A. Anthropological work in
Alaska. Smithsonian Miscellaneous
Collections, 78, no. 7 (1927): 137-158.

Hrdlička, A. Ritual ablation of front
teeth in Siberia and America.
Smithsonian Miscellaneous Collections,
99, no. 3 (1940): 1-32.

Hurst, Edgar E., Jr. Malignant tumors in
Alaskan Eskimos: unique predominance of
carcinoma of the esophagus in Alaskan
Eskimo women. Cancer, 17 (1964): 1187-
1196.

*Ingstad, H. Nunamiut. London, 1954.
254 p.

Irving, L. On the naming of birds by
Eskimos. Alaska, University,
Anthropological Papers, 6 (1958): 61-78.

Irving, L. The naming of birds by
Nunamiut Eskimo. Arctic, 6 (1953): 35-
43.

Irving, Laurence. Adaptations of native
populations to cold. Archives of
Environmental Health, 17 (1968): 592-
594.

Irving, W. Archaeology in the Brooks
Range of Alaska. American Antiquity, 17
(1951): 52-53.

Jamison, Paul L. An anthropometric study
of the Eskimos of Wainwright, Alaska. By
Paul L. Jamison and Stephen L. Zegura.
Arctic Anthropology, 7, no. 1 (1970):
125-143.

Jamison, Paul L. Growth of Wainwright
Eskimos: stature and weight. Arctic
Anthropology, 7, no. 1 (1970): 86-94.

Jamison, Paul Lytle. The Eskimos of
northwestern Alaska: their univariate
and multivariate anthropometric
variation. Dissertation Abstracts

International, 33 (1972/1973): 4629B-4630B. UM 72-33,858.

Jenness, D. Comparative vocabulary of the Western Eskimo Dialects. Canadian Arctic Expedition, Report, 15, pt. A (1928): 1-134.

Jenness, D. Dawn in Arctic Alaska. Minneapolis, 1957. 222 p.

Jenness, D. Eskimo music in northern Alaska. Musical Quarterly, 8 (1922): 377-383.

Jenness, D. Eskimo string figures. Canadian Arctic Expedition, Report, 13, pt. B (1924): 1-192.

Jenness, D. Myths and traditions from northern Alaska. Canadian Arctic Expedition, Report, 13, pt. A (1924): 1-91.

Jenness, D. Stray notes on the Eskimo of arctic Alaska. Alaska, University, Anthropological Papers, 1, no. 2 (1953): 5-13.

Jenness, D. The Eskimos of northern Alaska. Geographical Review, 5 (1918): 89-101.

Kaplan, Gary J., et al. Echovirus type 30 meningitis and related febrile illness: epidemiologic study of an outbreak in an Eskimo community. American Journal of Epidemiology, 92 (1970): 257-265.

Kennedy, J. R. Walrus at twenty-five yards. Alaska Sportsman, 31, no. 2 (1965): 8-11.

Kettelkamp, Donald B. Spondylolysis in the Alaskan Eskimo. By Donald B. Kettelkamp and D. Gilbert Wright. Journal of Bone and Joint Surgery, 53-A (1971): 563-566.

Kleinfeld, Judith. Visual memory in village Eskimo and urban Caucasian children. Arctic, 24 (1971): 132-138.

Koertvelyessy, Tibor. Relationships between the frontal sinus and climatic conditions: a skeletal approach to cold adaptation. American Journal of Physical Anthropology, 37 (1972/1973): 161-172.

Koranda, Lorraine D. Music of the Alaskan Eskimo. Music Journal, 24, no. 1 (1966): 89, 94.

Koranda, Lorraine D. Some traditional songs of the Alaskan Eskimos. Alaska, University, Anthropological Papers, 12 (1964): 17-32.

Laguna, F. de. The prehistory of northern North America as seen from the Yukon. Society for American Archaeology, Memoirs, 3 (1947): 1-360.

Lantis, M. Alaskan Eskimo ceremonialism. American Ethnological Society, Monographs, 11 (1947): 1-127.

Larsen, H. Archaeological investigations in Alaska since 1939. Polar Record, 6 (1953): 593-607.

Larsen, H. Ipiutak kulturen. København, Fra Nationalmuseets Arbejdsmark (1948): 5-20.

Larsen, H. The Ipiutak culture and its position within the Eskimo culture. International Congress of Americanists, Proceedings, 28 (1948): 419-421.

Larsen, H. The Ipiutak culture. International Congress of Americanists, Proceedings, 29, vol. 3 (1951): 22-34.

Larsen, H. The material culture of the Nunamiut. International Congress of Americanists, Proceedings, 32 (1958): 574-582.

Larsen, H. The position of Ipiutak in Eskimo culture. American Antiquity, 20 (1954): 74-79.

Larsen, H. and F. Rainey. Ipiutak and the arctic whale hunting culture. American Museum of Natural History, Anthropological Papers, 42 (1948): 1-276.

Laughlin, W. S. Blood groups of the Anaktuvuk Eskimos, Alaska. Alaska, University, Anthropological Papers, 6 (1957): 5-16.

Laughlin, W. S. Blood groups of the Anaqtuavik Eskimos, Alaska. International Congress of Americanists, Proceedings, 32 (1958): 594.

Levine, V. E. Ascorbic acid content of the blood of the Eskimo. Journal of Biological Chemistry, 133 (1940): lxi.

Levine, V. E. The basal metabolic rate of the Eskimo. Journal of Biological Chemistry, 128 (1939): lix.

Levine, V. E. and M. N. Jorgensen. Urinary chlorides and blood chlorides in the Eskimo. Journal of Biological Chemistry, 140 (1941): lxxvii-lxxviii.

Lindsay, George E. The Eskimo whalers of Point Barrow. Pacific Discovery, 21, no. 2 (1968): 11-15.

Lucier, Charles. Wolf kill observances, Northwest Alaska. Alaska, University, Anthropological Papers, 7 (1958/1959): 39.

Lucier, Charles V. Medical practices and human anatomical knowledge among the Noatak Eskimos. By Charles V. Lucier, James W. VanStone, and Della Keats. Ethnology, 10 (1971): 251-264.

MacCurdy, G. G. An example of Eskimo art. American Anthropologist, n.s., 23 (1921): 384-385.

Mann, George V., et al. The health and nutritional status of Alaskan Eskimos. A survey of the Interdepartmental Committee on Nutrition for National Defense--1958. American Journal of Clinical Nutrition, 11 (1962): 31-76.

Mason, J. A. Eskimo pictorial art. Museum Journal, 18 (1927): 248-283.

Mason, J. A. Excavations of Eskimo Thule sites at Point Barrow. International Congress of Americanists, Proceedings, 23 (1930): 383-394.

Mathiassen, T. Archaeological collections from the Western Eskimos. Fifth Thule Expedition, Report, 10 (1930): 1-98.

Mathiassen, T. Notes on Knud Rasmussen's archaeological collections. International Congress of Americanists, Proceedings, 13 (1928): 395-399.

Mayhall, John T. Torus mandibularis in an Alaskan Eskimo population. By John T. Mayhall, A. A. Dahlberg, and David G. Owen. American Journal of Physical Anthropology, n.s., 33 (1970): 57-60.

Mazess, Richard B. Bone mineral content in Wainwright Eskimos: preliminary report. Arctic Anthropology, 7, no. 1 (1970): 114-116.

McVay, Scott. Stalking the Arctic whale. American Scientist, 61 (1973): 24-37.

Melartin, Liisa. Albumin polymorphism (albumin Naskapi) in Eskimos and Navajos. By Liisa Melartin, Baruch S. Blumberg, and John R. Martin. Nature, 218 (1968): 787-789.

Merrill, Ralph G. Occlusal anomalous tubercles on premolars of Alaskan Eskimos and Indians. Oral Surgery, Oral Medicine, Oral Pathology, 17 (1964): 484-496.

Milan, Frederick A. A demographic study of an Eskimo village on the north slope of Alaska. Arctic, 23 (1970): 82-99.

Milan, Frederick A. Maintenance of thermal balance in Arctic Eskimos and Antarctic sojourners. Actualités Scientifiques et Industrielles, 1312 (1964): 529-534.

Milan, Frederick A. Oxygen consumption and body temperatures of Eskimos during sleep. By Frederick A. Milan and Eugene Evonuk. Journal of Applied Physiology, 22 (1967): 565-567.

Milan, Frederick A. Preliminary estimates of inbreeding levels in Wainwright Eskimos. Arctic Anthropology, 7, no. 1 (1970): 70-72.

Milan, Frederick A. Temperature regulation of Eskimos, Indians and Caucasians in a bath calorimeter. By Frederick A. Milan, John P. Hannon, and Eugene Evonuk. Journal of Applied Physiology, 18 (1963): 378-382.

Milan, Frederick A. The acculturation of the contemporary Eskimo of Wainwright, Alaska. Alaska, University, Anthropological Papers, 11, no. 2 (1964): 1-95.

Milan, Frederick A. The demography of an Alaskan Eskimo village. Arctic Anthropology, 7, no. 1 (1970): 26-43.

Miller, L. Keith. Local reactions to air cooling in an Eskimo population. By L. Keith Miller and Laurence Irving. Journal of Applied Physiology, 17 (1962): 449-455.

Miller, Lawrence G. Possible origin of Clostridium botulinum contamination of Eskimo foods in northwestern Alaska. By Lawrence G. Miller, Paul S. Clark, and George A. Kunkle. Applied Microbiology, 23 (1972): 427-428.

Morden, I. We liked the Eskimos. Alaska Sportsman, 17, no. 7 (1951): 18-23, 35-36.

Morgan, Lael. Caribou versus pipeline: can they take it in stride? New York, Alicia Patterson Fund, 1972. 8 p. illus. (Alicia Patterson Fund, LM-3)

Morgan, Lael. The last of the independents. New York, Alicia Patterson Fund, 1972. 12 p. illus. (Alicia Patterson Fund, LM-4)

Morris, I. G. Arctic trap line. Alaska Sportsman, 16, no. 12 (1950): 6-9, 25-26.

Murdoch, J. A few legendary fragments from Point Barrow Eskimos. American Naturalist, 20 (1886): 593-599.

Murdoch, J.   Dress and physique of the Point-Barrow Eskimos. Popular Science Monthly, 38 (1890-1891): 222-229.

*Murdoch, J.   Ethnological results of the Point Barrow Expedition. U.S. Bureau of American Ethnology, Annual Reports, 9 (1892): 3-441.

Murdoch, J.   Fish and fishing at Point Barrow, Arctic Alaska. American Fisheries Society, Transactions, 13 (1884): 111-115.

Murdoch, J.   Notes on the counting and measuring among the Eskimo of Point Barrow. American Anthropologist, 3 (1890): 37-43.

Murdoch, J.   Notes on the names of the heavenly bodies and the points of the compass among the Point Barrow Eskimo. American Anthropologist, 3 (1890): 136.

Murdoch, J.   Seal catching at Point Barrow. Smithsonian Miscellaneous Collections, 34, no. 2 (1893): 102-108.

Murdoch, J.   The animals known to the Eskimos of northwestern Alaska. American Naturalist, 32 (1898): 719-734.

Murdoch, J.   The retrieving harpoon. American Naturalist, 19 (1885): 423-425.

Murie, Olaus.   Winter adventures on the Alaskan trail. American West, 10, no. 1 (1973): 10-15, 59-60.

*Nelson, Richard K.   Hunters of the northern ice. Chicago, University of Chicago Press, 1969. 24, 429 p. illus.

Ostermann, H.   The Alaskan Eskimos. Fifth Thule Expedition, Report, 10, no. 3 (1952): 1-291.

Palmer, Harvey E.   Cesium-134 in Alaskan Eskimos and in fallout. By Harvey E. Palmer and Richard W. Perkins. Science, 142 (1963): 66-67.

Palmer, Harvey E.   Radioactivity measured in Alaskan natives, 1962-1964. By Harvey E. Palmer, Wayne C. Hanson, Bobby I. Griffin, and Leslie A. Braby. Science, 147 (1965): 620-621.

Palmer, Harvey E., et al.   Cesium-137 in Alaskan Eskimos. Science, 142 (1963): 64-66.

Palmer, Harvey E., et al.   Cs-137 in Alaskan Eskimos. Health Physics, 9 (1963): 875.

Palmer, Harvey E., et al.   Radioactivity measurements in Alaskan Eskimos in 1963. Science, 144 (1964): 859-860.

Paneak, S.   We hunt to live. Alaska Sportsman, 26, no. 3 (1960): 12-13.

Parker, Seymour.   Ethnic identity and acculturation in two Eskimo villages. American Anthropologist, 66 (1964): 325-340.

Paul, J. R. and J. T. Riordan.   Observations on serological epidemiology. American Journal of Hygiene, 52 (1950): 202-212.

Paul, J. R., et al.   Antibodies to three different antigenic types of poliomyelitis virus in sera from North Alaskan Eskimos. American Journal of Hygiene, 54 (1951): 275-285.

Paul, J. R., et al.   Serological epidemiology. Journal of Immunology, 66 (1951): 695-713.

Pedersen, P. O. and D. B. Scott.   Replica studies of the surfaces of teeth from Alaskan Eskimo, West Greenland Natives, and American Whites. Acta Odontologica Scandinavica, 9 (1951): 261-292.

Philip, R. N., et al.   Serologic and skin test evidence of tularemia infection among Alaskan Eskimos, Indians and Aleuts. Journal of Infectious Diseases, 110 (1962): 220-230.

Plato, Chris C.   Polymorphism of the C line of palmar dermatoglyphics with a new classification of the C line terminations. American Journal of Physical Anthropology, n.s., 33 (1970): 413-419.

Pospisil, Leopold.   Kinship terminology and kindred among the Nunamiut Eskimo. By Leopold Pospisil and William S. Laughlin. Ethnology, 2 (1963): 180-189.

Preston, Caroline E.   Psychological testing with northwest coast Alaskan Eskimos. Genetic Psychology Monographs, 69 (1964): 323-419.

Rainey, F. G.   A new form of culture on the Arctic Coast. National Academy of Sciences, Proceedings, 27 (1941): 141-144.

Rainey, F. G.   Culture changes on the Arctic Coast. New York Academy of Sciences, Transactions, n.s., 3 (1941): 122-126.

Rainey, F. G.   Eskimo prehistory. American Museum of Natural History, Anthropological Papers, 37 (1941): 453-569.

Rainey, F. G. Mystery people of the
Arctic. Natural History, 47 (1941): 148-
155, 170-171.

Rainey, F. G. Native economy and survival
in Alaska. Human Organization, 1, no. 1
(1941): 9-14.

Rainey, F. G. The Ipiutak culture at
Point Hope Alaska. American
Anthropologist, n.s., 43 (1941): 364-
375.

*Rainey, F. G. The whale hunters of
Tigara. American Museum of Natural
History, Anthropological Papers, 41
(1947): 231-283.

Rausch, R. L. Notes on the Nunamiut
Eskimo. Arctic, 4 (1951): 147-195.

Ray, D. J. Birch bark baskets of the
Kobuk Eskimos. Alaska Sportsman, 31,
no. 3 (1965): 15-17.

Ray, Dorothy Jean. Land tenure and polity
of the Bering Strait Eskimos. Journal of
the West, 6 (1967): 371-394.

Ray, Dorothy Jean. The Bible in picture
writing. Beaver, 302, no. 2 (1971/1972):
20-24.

Ray, P. H. Ethnographic sketch of the
natives of Point Barrow. In Report of
the International Polar Expedition to
Point Barrow. Washington, D.C., 1885:
35-87.

Reed, Dwayne, et al. An epidemic in an
Eskimo village due to group-B
meningococcus. I. Epidemiology. American
Medical Association, Journal, 196
(1966): 383-387.

Reid, D. Meningococcus outbreak at Point
Barrow. Alaska Medicine, 7, no. 3
(1965): 49-52.

Rennie, D. W. Comparison of
nonacclimatized Americans and Alaskan
Eskimos. Federation Proceedings, 22
(1963): 828-830.

Rennie, D. W. Physical fitness and
respiratory function of Eskimos of
Wainwright, Alaska. By D. W. Rennie, P.
di Prampero, R. W. Fitts, and L.
Sinclair. Arctic Anthropology, 7, no. 1
(1970): 73-82.

Rennie, Donald W., et al. Physical
regulation of temperature in Eskimos.
Journal of Applied Physiology, 17
(1962): 326-332.

Roberts, P. W. Employment of Eskimos by
the Navy at Point Barrow, Alaska.
Alaskan Science Conference, Proceedings,
3 (1954): 40-43.

Robinhold, D. Cardiovascular health of
Wainwright Eskimos. By D. Robinhold and
D. Rice. Arctic Anthropology, 7, no. 1
(1970): 83-85.

Rooth, Anna B. The Alaska expedition
1966. Myths, customs and beliefs among
the Athabascan Indians and the Eskimos
of northern Alaska. Lund, Gleerup,
1971. 16, 392 p. illus. (Acta
Universitatis Lundensis, Sectio I:
Theologica, Juridica, Humaniora, 14)

Rosenthal, Hank. New skills for Nanook.
Alaska Journal, 2, no. 4 (1972): 25-29.

Saario, D. Human ecological
investigations at Kivalina. By D. Saario
and B. Kessel. In N. J. Wilimovsky and
J. N. Wolfe, eds. Environment of the
Cape Thompson Region, Alaska. Oak
Ridge, U.S. Atomic Energy Commission,
Committee on Environmental Studies for
Project Chariot, 1966: 969-1039.

Sauberlich, H. E., et al. Biochemical
assessment of the nutritional status of
the Eskimos of Wainwright, Alaska.
American Journal of Clinical Nutrition,
25 (1972): 437-445.

Sauberlich, H. E., et al. Preliminary
report on the nutrition survey conducted
among the Eskimos of Wainwright, Alaska,
21-27 January 1969. Arctic Anthropology,
7, no. 1 (1970): 122-124.

Schulert, Arthur R. Strontium-90 in
Alaska. Alaskan Eskimos for whom the
caribou is a dietary staple have a high
strontium-90 concentration. Science, 136
(1962): 146-148.

Scott, Edward M. Anemia in Alaskan
Eskimos. By E. M. Scott, Rita C. Wright,
and Barbara T. Hanan. Journal of
Nutrition, 55 (1955): 137-149.

Scott, Edward M., et al. Frequency of
polymorphic types of red cell enzymes
and serum factors in Alaskan Eskimos and
Indians. American Journal of Human
Genetics, 18 (1966): 408-411.

Seltzer, C. C. The anthropometry of the
Western and Copper Eskimos. Human
Biology, 5 (1933): 313-370.

Shade, C. I. and H. T. Cain. An
anthropology survey of the Pt. Barrow,
Alaska, region. Alaskan Science
Conference, Proceedings (1951): 248-251.

Simpson, J. Observations on the Western
Eskimo and the country they inhabit. In
Royal Geographical Society. Arctic

Geography and Ethnology. London, 1875: 233-275.

Simpson, T. Narrative of the discoveries on the north coast of America. London, 1843. 419 p.

Smith, Derek G. Las implicaciones del pluralismo para los programas de cambio social en una comunidad del ártico canadiense. Anuario Indigenista, 29 (1969): 73-96.

Smith, M. Superstitions of the Eskimo. In R. Kersting, ed. The White World. New York, 1902: 113-130.

Smith, Valene Lucy. Kotzebue: a modern Alaskan Eskimo community. Dissertation Abstracts, 28 (1967/1968): 35B. UM 66-9398.

Solecki, R. S. Archeology and ecology of the arctic slope of Alaska. Smithsonian Institution, Annual Reports of the Board of Regents (1950): 469-495.

Solecki, R. S. New data on the inland Eskimo of northern Alaska. Washington Academy of Sciences, Journal, 40 (1950): 137-157.

Sonnenfeld, J. Changes in an Eskimo hunting technology, an introduction to implement geography. Association of American Geographers, Annals, 50 (1960): 172-186.

Spencer, M. Forms of cooperation in the culture of the Barrow Eskimo. Alaskan Science Conference, Proceedings, 3 (1954): 128-130.

Spencer, M. The child in the contemporary culture of the Barrow Eskimo. Alaskan Science Conference, Proceedings, 3 (1954): 130-132.

Spencer, R. F. The hunted and the hunters. Pacific Discovery, 6, no. 3 (1953): 22-27.

*Spencer, R. F. The North Alaska Eskimo. U.S. Bureau of American Ethnology, Bulletin, 171 (1959): 1-496.

Spencer, R. F. and W. K. Carter. The blind man and the loon. Journal of American Folklore, 67 (1954): 65-72.

Spencer, Robert F. Die Organisation der Ehe unter den Eskimo Nordalaskas. Wiener Völkerkundliche Mitteilungen, 14/15 (1967/1968): 13-31.

*Spencer, Robert F. The North Alaska Eskimo; a study in ecology and society. Washington, D.C., Smithsonian

Institution Press, 1969. 8, 490 p. illus., maps.

Spencer, Robert F. The social composition of the North Alaskan whaling crew. In D. Lee Guemple, ed. Alliance in Eskimo Society. Seattle, American Ethnological Society, 1972: 110-120.

Stefansson, V. F. Eskimo longevity in northern Alaska. Science, 127 (1958): 16-19.

Stefansson, V. F. My life with the Eskimo. New York, 1913.

Steinberg, Arthur G., et al. Gm phenotypes and genotypes in U.S. Whites and Negroes; in American Indians and Eskimos; in Africans; and in Micronesians. American Journal of Human Genetics, 13 (1961): 205-213.

Stockton, C. H. The arctic cruise of the U.S.S. Thetis. National Geographic Magazine, 2 (1890): 171-198.

Taber, Richard D. Eskimo hunters. Pacific Discovery, 11, no. 3 (1958): 18-20; 11, no. 4 (1958): 7-10; 11, no. 5 (1958): 10-12.

Thompson, D. T. Two Eskimo geographers. Journal of Geography, 50 (1951): 342-347.

Totter, J. R. and C. F. Shukers. Nutrition surveys of Eskimos. Alaska's Health, 6, no. 10 (1948): 4-6.

Ulving, Tor. Observations on the language of the Asiatic Eskimo as presented in Soviet linguistic works. Linguistics, 69 (1971): 87-119.

U.S., Committee on Environmental Studies for Project Chariot. Environment of the Cape Thompson region, Alaska. Oak Ridge, Tenn., U.S. Atomic Energy Commission, Division of Technical Information, 1966. 16, 1,250 p. illus., maps.

Usher, Peter J. The Canadian Western Arctic: a century of change. Anthropologica, n.s., 13 (1971): 169-183.

VanStone, James W. An Eskimo community and the outside world. Alaska, University, Anthropological Papers, 7 (1958/1959): 27-38.

VanStone, James W. Masks of the Point Hope Eskimo. Anthropos, 63/64 (1968/1969): 828-840.

*VanStone, James W. Point Hope; an Eskimo village in transition. Seattle,

University of Washington Press, 1962. 10, 177 p. illus., maps. (American Ethnological Society, Monograph, 36)

VanStone, James W. Some aspects of religious change among native inhabitants in West Alaska and the Northwest Territories. Arctic Anthropology, 2, no. 2 (1964): 21-24.

VanStone, James W. Three Eskimo communities. By J. W. VanStone and W. H. Oswalt. Alaska, University, Anthropological Papers, 9 (1960/1961): 17-56.

Walker, E. F. An Eskimo harpoon-thrower. Masterkey, 20 (1946): 193-194.

Watkins, J. A. The Alaskan Eskimo. American Journal of Public Health, 4 (1914): 643-648.

Waugh, L. M. A study of the nutrition and teeth of the Eskimo of North Bering Sea and Arctic Alaska. Journal of Dental Research, 10 (1930): 387-393.

Way, Anthony B. A method of measuring general health and its relationship to effective fertility in Wainwright Eskimos. Arctic Anthropology, 7, no. 1 (1970): 109-113.

Wells, R. and J. W. Kelly. English-Eskimo and Eskimo-English Vocabularies. U.S. Bureau of Education, Circulars of Information, no. 2 (1890): 1-72.

Whitten, Norman E., Jr. Towards a classification of West Alaskan social structure. Alaska, University, Anthropological Papers, 12 (1964): 79-91.

Wiggins, I. L. North of Anaktuvuk. Pacific Discovery, 6 (1953): 8-15.

Wilber, C. G. and V. E. Levine. Fat metabolism in Alaskan Eskimos. Experimental Medicine and Surgery, 8 (1950): 422-425.

Wilson, G. S. Barrow Day School nutrition program. Alaska's Health, 7, no. 5 (1949): 1-3.

Wissler, C. Harpoons and darts in the Stefansson Collection. American Museum of Natural History, Anthropological Papers, 14 (1916): 397-443.

Witthoft, John. Flint arrowpoints from the Eskimo of northwestern Alaska. Expedition, 10, no. 2 (1968): 30-37.

Young, Francis A., et al. The transmission of refractive errors within Eskimo families. American Journal of Optometry, 46 (1969): 676-685.

Young, Francis, et al. Comparison of cycloplegic and non-cycloplegic refractions of Eskimos. American Journal of Optometry, 48 (1971): 814-825.

01-11   Polar Eskimo

Anonymous. Greenland's Harley Street. Geographical Magazine, 12 (1940): 36-41.

Astrup, E. Blandt nordpolens naboer. Christiania, 1895.

Astrup, E. With Peary near the Pole. London, 1898.

Bessels, E. Die amerikanische Nordpol-Expedition. Leipzig, 1879. 350-373 p.

Bessels, E. Einige Worte über die Innuit (Eskimo) des Smith-Sundes. Archiv für Anthropologie, 8 (1873): 107-122.

Bessels, E. The northernmost inhabitants of the Earth. American Naturalist, 18 (1884): 861-882.

Birket-Smith, K. Etnografiske problemer i Grønland. Geografisk Tidsskrift, 25 (1920): 179-197.

Birket-Smith, K. The Greenland bow. Meddelelser om Grønland, 56, no. 1 (1918): 1-28.

Birket-Smith, K. The Greenlanders of the present day. Greenland, 2 (1928): 1-207.

Black, F. L., et al. Intensified reactions to measles vaccine in unexposed populations of American Indians. Journal of Infectious Diseases, 124 (1971): 306-317.

Bruemmer, Fred. Dovekies. Beaver, 303, no. 2 (1972/1973): 40-47.

Bryant, H. G. Notes on the most northern Eskimos. International Geographical Congress, Report (1895): 677-683.

Bugge, A. Kallihirua, polareskimoen i Canterbury. Grønland, no. 5 (1965): 161-175.

Dege, Wilhelm. Die Westküste Grönlands: Bevölkerung, Wirtschaft und Siedlung im Strukturwandel. Deutsche Geographische Blätter, 50, nr. 1/2 (1965): 5-212.

Dege, Wilhelm. Die Westküste Grönlands im Strukturwandel. Polarforschung, 6, nr. 35 (1965): 12-19.

Ekblaw, W. E.   Distribution of settlement among the Polar Eskimo. Massachusetts Archaeological Society, Bulletin, 8 (1947): 39-44.

Ekblaw, W. E.   Eskimo dogs. Natural History, 37 (1936): 173-184.

Ekblaw, W. E.   Significance of movement among the Polar Eskimo. Massachusetts Archaeological Society, Bulletin, 10 (1948): 1-4.

Ekblaw, W. E.   The food birds of the Smith Sound Eskimos. Wilson Bulletin, 31 (1919): 1-5.

Ekblaw, W. E.   The material response of the Polar Eskimo to their far arctic environment. Association of American Geographers, Annals, 17 (1927): 147-198; 18 (1928): 1-24.

Faĭnberg, L. A.   Grenlandiĭa i ee naselenie. Sovetskaĭa Etnografiĭa, no. 6 (1966): 47-56.

Frederiksen, S.   Stylistic forms in Greenland Eskimo literature. Copenhagen, 1954.   40 p.

Freeman, Milton M. R.   Eskimo thanking-acts in the eastern Canadian Arctic. Folk, 10 (1968): 25-28.

Freuchen, P.   Arctic adventure. New York, 1935.   467 p.

Freuchen, P.   Ice floes and flaming water. New York, 1954.   242 p.

Freuchen, P.   Ivalu, the Eskimo wife. New York, 1935.   332 p.

Freuchen, P.   Om plantekost hos Smith-Sund Eskimoerne. Geografisk Tidsskrift, 24 (1918): 306-310.

Freuchen, P.   Vagrant Viking. New York, 1953.   422 p.

Fürst, C. M. and F. C. C. Hansen. Crania groenlandica. Copenhagen, 1915.   234 p.

Gilberg, Aa. Serum protein types in Polar Eskimos. By Aa. Gilberg and I. Persson. Acta Genetica et Statistica Medica, 17 (1967): 422-432.

Gilberg, Aa. Thule 25 år efter. Grønland, no. 6 (1964): 201-216.

Gilberg, Rolf. Uisâkavsak, "The big liar". Folk, 11/12 (1969/1970): 83-95.

Haig-Thomas, D.   Tracks in the snow. London, 1939.   292 p.

Hansen, Keld.   The people of the Far North. Folk, 11/12 (1969/1970): 97-108.

Hansen, P. M.   Jagt og fiskeri. Grønlands Bogen, 2 (1950): 59-82.

Hayes, I. I.   The open polar sea.   New York, 1867.

Heinbecker, P. and R. H. Pauli. Blood grouping of the Polar Eskimo. Journal of Immunology, 13 (1927): 279-283.

Holtved, E.   Archaeological investigations in the Thule District III. Nûgdlît and Comer's Midden. Meddelelser om Grønland, 146, no. 3 (1954): 1-135.

Holtved, E.   Foreløbig beretning om den arkaeologisk-etnografiske expedition til Thule Distriktet. Geografisk Tidsskrift, 41 (1938): 1-24.

Holtved, E.   Har Nordboerne Vaeret i Thule Distriktet? København, Fra Nationalmuseets Arbejdsmark (1945): 79-84.

Holtved, E.   Nugdlit, en Forhistorisk Boplads i Thule Distriktet. Grønland, no. 3 (1954): 89-94.

Holtved, E.   Remarks on the Polar Eskimo dialect. International Journal of American Linguistics, 18 (1952): 20-24.

*Holtved, E.   The Polar Eskimos: language and folklore. 2 vol. Meddelelser om Grønland, 152, no. 1-2 (1951): 1-520.

Holtved, E.   Thule District. Grønlands Bogen, 2 (1950): 269-290.

*Holtved, Erik.   Contributions to Polar Eskimo ethnography. København, C. A. Reitzels Forlag, 1967.   180 p.   illus., map. (Meddelelser om Grønland, 182, no. 2)

Hovey, E. O.   Child-life among the Smith Sound Eskimo. American Museum Journal, 18 (1918): 361-371.

Høyrup, F.   By dog sled in Thule. Danish Foreign Office Journal, 39 (1961): 11-14.

Hrdlička, A.   An Eskimo brain. American Anthropologist, n.s., 3 (1901): 454-500.

Hrdlička, A.   Contribution to the anthropology of Central and Smith Sound Eskimo. American Museum of Natural History, Anthropological Papers, 5 (1910): 177-280.

Hughes, Charles Campbell. Under four flags: recent culture change among the

Eskimos. Current Anthropology, 6 (1965):
3-69. [With comments].

Jørgensen, J. B. The Eskimo skeleton.
Meddelelser om Grønland, 146, no. 2
(1953): 1-154.

Kane, E. K. Arctic explorations.
Philadelphia, 1856. 2 v.

Kleivan, Helge. Culture and ethnic
identity; on modernization and ethnicity
in Greenland. Folk, 11/12 (1969/1970):
209-234.

Kleivan, Inge. Language and ethnic
identity: language policy and debate in
Greenland. Folk, 11/12 (1969/1970): 235-
285.

Knuth, E. An outline of the archaeology
of Peary Land. Arctic, 5 (1952): 17-33.

Knuth, E. Archaeology in the farthest
North. International Congress of
Americanists, Proceedings, 32 (1958):
561-573.

Knuth, E. Danmark Fjord. København, Fra
Nationalmuseets Arbejdsmark (1956): 71-
78.

Knuth, E. Det Mystiske X i Danmark Fjord.
København, 1958. 40 p.

Knuth, E. Pearyland-Eskimoerne.
København, Fra Nationalmuseets
Arbejdsmark (1948): 29-36.

Knuth, E. The Paleo-Eskimo cultures of
Northeast Greenland. American Antiquity,
19 (1954): 367-381.

Koch, L. Ethnographical observations from
the southern coast of Washington Land.
American Anthropologist, n.s., 24
(1922): 484-487.

Krabbe, T. N. Greenland. Copenhagen,
1930. 145 p.

Kroeber, A. L. Tales of the Smith Sound
Eskimo. Journal of American Folklore, 12
(1899): 166-182.

*Kroeber, A. L. The Eskimo of Smith Sound.
American Museum of Natural History,
Bulletin, 12 (1899): 265-327.

Laughlin, W. S. and J. B. Jørgenson.
Isolate variation in Greenlandic Eskimo
crania. Acta Genetica et Statistica
Medica, 6 (1956): 3-12.

Laughlin, William S. Races of mankind:
continental and local. Alaska,
University, Anthropological Papers, 8
(1959/1960): 89-99.

Laursen, Dan. The place names of North
Greenland. København, C. A. Reitzels
Forlag, 1972. 443 p. illus., maps.
(Meddelelser om Grønland, 180, no. 2)

Leden, C. Musik und Tänze der
grönländischen Eskimos. Zeitschrift für
Ethnologie, 43 (1911): 260-270.

Leden, C. Über die Musik der Smith Sund
Eskimos. Meddelelser om Grønland, 152,
no. 3 (1952): 1-92.

Luzzio, A. J. Comparison of serum
proteins in Americans and Eskimos.
Journal of Applied Physiology, 21
(1966): 685-688.

Lynge, H. Inegpait. Copenhagen, 1955.
187 p.

MacMillan, D. B. Food supply of the Smith
Sound Eskimo. American Museum Journal,
18 (1918): 161-192.

Malaurie, J. Amours et jeux dans le nuit
polaire. Marco Polo, 8 (1955): 18-29.

Malaurie, J. Destin des rois de Thulé.
Société Royale de Géographie d'Anvers,
Bulletin, 68 (1956): 6-13.

Malaurie, J. Perspectives offertes par
l'evolution économique et sociale des
Eskimos de Thulé. Bulletin International
des Sciences Sociales, 6 (1954): 513-
519.

Malaurie, J. The Last Kings of Thule.
New York, 1956. 295 p.

Malaurie, J., et al. L'Isolat Esquimau de
Thulé (Groenland). Population, 7 (1952):
675-692.

Malaurie, Jean. Les hommes du pôle.
Paris Éditions du Temps, 1958. 141 p.
illus., maps.

Markham, C. R. Papers on the Greenland
Eskimos. In Royal Geographical Society.
Arctic Geography and Ethnology. London,
1875: 163-229.

Markham, C. R. The arctic highlanders.
Ethnological Society (London),
Transactions, n.s., 4 (1866): 125-137.

Mathiassen, T. Eskimo migrations in
Greenland. Geographical Review, 25
(1935): 408-422.

Mathiassen, T. Eskimo relics from
Washington Land and Hall Land.
Meddelelser om Grønland, 71 (1928): 183-
216.

Mathiassen, T. Eskimoernes Sammentraef
med Nordboerne i Grønland. Grønland
(1953): 139-142.

Mathiassen, T. and E. Holtved. The
archaeology of the Thule District.
Geografisk Tidsskrift, 47 (1945): 43-57.

Meldgaard, J. Grønlaendere i tre tusinde
Aar. Grønland, nos. 4-5 (1958): 121-129,
170-178.

Murdock, G. P. The Polar Eskimo. In his
Our Primitive Contemporaries. New York,
1934: 192-218.

Mylius-Erichsen, L. and H. Moltke.
Grønland. Kjøbenhavn, 1906.

Nares, G. S. Narrative of a voyage to the
Polar Sea. London, 1878. 2 v.

Nielsen, F. Grønlands Kultur.
Turistforeningen for Danmark, Arbog
(1952/1953): 65-88.

Nielsen, J. C., et al. Gm types of
Greenland Eskimos. Human Heredity, 21
(1971): 405-419.

Orlova, E. P. Naselenie Grenlandii. In A.
V. Efimov and S. A. Tokarev, eds. Narody
Ameriki. Vol. 1. Moskva, Izdatel'stvo
Akademiia Nauk SSSR, 1959: 594-608.

Osborn, S. Stray leaves from an arctic
journal. London, 1852.

Paterson, T. T. Anthropogeographical
studies in Greenland. Royal
Anthropological Institute of Great
Britain and Ireland, Journal, 69 (1939):
45-76.

Paterson, T. T. Eskimo "cats' cradles".
Geographical Magazine, 9 (1939): 85-91.

Peary, J. D. My Arctic journal. New
York, 1893.

Peary, R. E. Nearest the Pole. New York,
1907.

Peary, R. E. Northward over the "great
ice". New York, 1898. 2 v.

Peary, Robert E. Correspondence between
Lieutenant R. E. Peary and Professor F.
W. Putnam on Arctic ethnology. By R. E.
Peary and F. W. Putnam. Edited by Ralph
W. Dexter. Ethnohistory, 16 (1969): 177-
189.

Persson, Ib. Alloalbuminemia: a search
for albumin variants in Greenland
Eskimos. By I. Persson, Liisa Melartin,
and A. Gilberg. Human Heredity, 21
(1971): 57-59.

Persson, Ib, et al. Ten Gm factors and
the Inv system in Eskimos in Greenland.
Human Heredity, 22 (1972): 519-528.

Petersen, C. Erindringer fra
polarlandene. Kjøbenhavn, 1857.

Petersen, Robert. Den sidste Eskimo-
indvandring til Grønland. Folk, 4
(1962): 186-188.

Petersen, Robert. The last Eskimo
immigration into Greenland. Folk, 4
(1962): 95-110.

Powers, W. E. Polar Eskimos of Greenland
and their environment. Journal of
Geography, 49 (1950): 186-193.

Preuss, K. T. Die ethnographische
Veränderung der Eskimo des Smith-Sundes.
Ethnologisches Notizblatt, 2, no. 1
(1899): 38-43.

Rasmussen, K. Greenland by the Polar Sea.
London, 1921.

Rasmussen, K. Grønland langs Polhavet.
Kjøbenhavn, 1919.

Rasmussen, K. Myter og sagn fra Grønland,
3. Kjøbenhavn, 1925. 1-340 p.

*Rasmussen, K. Nye mennesker. Kjøbenhavn,
1905.

*Rasmussen, K. The people of the Polar
North. London, 1908.

*Rasmussen, K. Under nordenvindens svøbe.
Kjøbenhavn, 1906. 202 p.

Ross, J. A voyage of discovery. London,
1819.

Savard, Rémi. Mythologie esquimaude;
analyse de textes nord-groenlandais.
Québec, 1966. 242 l. illus., maps.
(Laval, Université, Centre d'Études
Nordiques, Travaux Divers, 14)

Schultz-Lorentzen, C. W. Eskimoernes
invandring i Grønland. Meddelelser om
Grønland, 26 (1904): 289-330.

Schultz-Lorentzen, C. W. Intellectual
culture of the Greenlanders. Greenland,
2 (1928): 209-270.

Skeller, E. Øjensgdomme i Grønland.
Ugeskrift for Laeger, 111 (1949): 529-
532.

Spitzka, E. A. Three Eskimo brains from
Smith's Sound. American Journal of
Anatomy, 2 (1902): 25-71.

*Steensby, H. P. Contributions to the
ethnology and anthropogeography of the

Polar Eskimos. Meddelelser cm Grønland,
34 (1910): 253-405.

Stein, R. Eskimo music. In R. Kersting,
ed. The White World. New York, 1902:
337-356.

Stein, R. Geographische Nomenklatur bei
den Eskimos des Smith-Sundes. Petermanns
Mitteilungen, 48 (1902): 195-201.

Steinhoff, I. Dreizehn Monate bei den
Polareskimos von Thule. Atlantis, 25,
no 2 (1953): 75-80.

Taubert, H. Die Eskimo-Siedlungsinsel
Thule in Grönland. Petermanns
Mitteilungen, 97 (1953): 295-296.

Thalbitzer, W. Nordboerne ved Uparnavik.
København, Det Grønlandske Selskabs
Aarsskrift (1945): 28-37.

Thomsen, T. Eskimo archaeology.
Greenland, 2 (1928): 271-329.

VanStone, James W. New evidence
concerning Polar Eskimo isolation.
American Anthropologist, 74 (1972):
1062-1065.

Vibe, C. The marine mammals and the
marine fauna in the Thule District.
Meddelelser om Grønland, 150, no. 6
(1950): 1-115.

Wallace, Anthony F. C. An
interdisciplinary approach to mental
disorder among the Polar Eskimos of
Northwest Greenland. By Anthony F. C.
Wallace and Robert E. Ackerman.
Anthropologica, n.s., 2 (1960): 249-260.

Wells, J. R. The origin of immunity to
diphtheria in Central and Polar Eskimos.
American Journal of Hygiene, 18 (1933):
629-673.

Wells, J. R. and E. Dixon. Hemophilus
influenzae from the throats of Polar
Eskimos. Journal of Infectious Diseases,
51 (1932): 412-415.

Wells, J. R. and P. Heinbecker. Further
studies on immunity to diphtheria among
Central and Polar Eskimos. Society for
Experimental Biology and Medicine,
Proceedings, 29 (1932): 1028-1030.

Whitaker, W. L. The question of season
sterility among the Eskimos. Science, 88
(1938): 214-215.

Wissler, C. Archaeology of the Polar
Eskimo. American Museum of Natural
History, Anthropological Papers, 22
(1918): 105-166.

01-12   South Alaska Eskimo

Anderson, H. D. and W. C. Eells. Alaska
natives. Stanford, 1935. 472 p.

Bancroft, H. H. The native races of the
Pacific States, 1. New York, 1875. 37-
94.

Befu, Harumi. An ethnographic sketch of
Old Harbor, Kodiak: an Eskimo village.
Arctic Anthropology, 6, no. 2 (1970):
29-42.

Birket-Smith, K. Foreløbig beretning om
den Dansk-Amerikanske Ekspedition til
Alaska. Geografisk Tidsskrift, 37
(1934): 187-227.

*Birket-Smith, K. The Chugach Eskimo.
Nationalmuseets Skrifter, Etnografisk
Raekke, 6 (1953): 1-270.

Blumberg, Baruch S., et al. A study of
the prevalence of arthritis in Alaskan
Eskimos. Arthritis and Rheumatism, 4
(1961): 325-341.

Burg, A. North Star cruises Alaska's Wild
West. National Geographic Magazine, 102
(1952): 57-86.

Chown, Bruce. The blood groups and
secretor status of three small
communities in Alaska. By Bruce Chown
and Marion Lewis. Oceania, 32
(1961/1962): 211-218.

Clark, Donald W. Perspectives in the
prehistory of Kodiak Island, Alaska.
American Antiquity, 31 (1965/1966): 358-
371.

Clark, Donald W. Two late prehistoric
pottery-bearing sites on Kodiak Island,
Alaska. Arctic Anthropology, 3, no. 2
(1965): 157-184.

Clark, Donald Woodforde. Koniag
prehistory. Dissertation Abstracts, 29
(1968/1969): 4489B-4490B. UM 68-17,886.

Collins, H. B. Archaeology of the Bering
Sea region. Pacific Science Congress,
Proceedings, 5, vol. 4 (1934): 2825-
2839.

Cook, J. A voyage to the Pacific Ocean.
2d ed. London, 1785. 3 v.

Coxe, W. Account of the Russian
discoveries between Asia and America.
4th ed. London, 1804.

Cressman, Luther S. Research on Northwest
prehistory, prehistory in the Naknek
drainage, southeastern Alaska. By L. S.
Cressman and D. E. Dumond. Eugene,

University of Oregon, Department of Anthropology, 1962. 3, 54 p. illus., maps.

Cumming, J. R. Metaphysical implications of the folktales of the Eskimos of Alaska. Alaska, University, Anthropological Papers, 3, no. 1 (1954): 37-63.

Dall, W. H. Alaskan mummies. American Naturalist, 9 (1875): 433-440.

Dall, W. H. On the distribution and nomenclature of the native tribes of Alaska. Contributions to North American Ethnology, 1 (1877): 7-40.

Dall, W. H. On the distribution of the native tribes of Alaska. American Association for the Advancement of Science, Proceedings, 18 (1869): 263-273.

Dall, W. H. The native tribes of Alaska. American Association for the Advancement of Science, Proceedings, 34 (1885): 363-379.

Davis, Nancy Yaw. The effects of the 1964 Alaska earthquake, tsunami, and resettlement on two Koniag Eskimo villages. Dissertation Abstracts International, 32 (1971/1972): 1332B. UM 71-24,028.

Denniston, Carter. The blood groups of three Konyag isloates. Arctic Anthropology, 3, no. 2 (1965): 195-205.

Disselhoff, H. Bemerkungen zu einigen Eskimo-Masken. Baessler-Archiv, 18 (1935): 130-137.

Eells, W. C. Mechanical, physical, and musical ability of the native races of Alaska. Journal of Applied Psychology, 17 (1933): 493-506.

Eells, W. C. Mental ability of the native races of Alaska. Journal of Applied Psychology, 17 (1933): 417-438.

Elliott, C. P. Salmon fishing grounds and canneries. In Compilation of Narratives of Explorations in Alaska. Washington, D.C., 1900: 738-741.

Emmons, G. T. Jade in British Columbia and Alaska. Indian Notes and Monographs, 35 (1923): 11-53.

Erman, A. Ueber die Reise und Entdeckungen des Lieutenant L. Sagoskin. Archiv für Wissenschaftliche Kunde von Russland, 6 (1848): 499-522, 613-672; 7 (1849): 429-512.

Gibbs, G. Vocabulary of the Kaniag'mut. Contributions to North American Ethnology, 1 (1877): 136-142.

Gillham, C. E. Beyond the clapping mountains. New York, 1943. 134 p.

Golder, F. A. A Kadiak Island story. Journal of American Folklore, 20 (1907): 296-299.

Golder, F. A. Eskimo and Aleut stories from Alaska. Journal of American Folklore, 12 (1909): 10-24.

Golder, F. A. Tales from Kodiak Island. Journal of American Folklore, 16 (1903): 16-31, 85-103.

Gordon, G. B. The double axe and some other symbols. Museum Journal, 7 (1916): 46-68.

Hammerich, L. L. Russian loan-words in Alaska. International Congress of Americanists, Proceedings, 30 (1955): 114-126.

Hammerich, L. L. The Russian stratum in Alaskan Eskimo. Slavic Word, 10 (1954): 401-428.

Hammerich, L. L. The Western Eskimo dialects. International Congress of Americanists, Proceedings, 32 (1958): 632-639.

Heizer, R. F. Aconite poison whaling in Asia and America. U.S. Bureau of American Ethnology, Bulletin, 133 (1943): 415-468.

Heizer, R. F. Incised slate figurines from Kodiak Island. American Antiquity, 17 (1952): 266.

Heizer, R. F. Notes on Koniag material culture. Alaska, University, Anthropological Papers, 1 (1952): 11-19.

Heizer, R. F. Petroglyphs from southwestern Kodiak Island, Alaska. American Philosophical Society, Proceedings, 91 (1947): 284-293.

Heizer, R. F. Pottery from the Southern Eskimo region. American Philosophical Society, Proceedings, 93 (1949): 48-56.

Heizer, R. F. The sickle in aboriginal Western North America. American Antiquity, 16 (1951): 247-252.

Himmelheber, H. Eskimokünstler. Stuttgart, 1938. 111 p.

Holmberg, H. J. Ethnographische Skizzen über die Völker des russischen Amerika.

Acta Societatis Scientiarum Fennicae, 4 (1856): 355-421.

Hrdlička, A. Anthropological explorations on Kodiak Island. Smithsonian Institution, Explorations and Field-Work (1932): 41-44.

Hrdlička, A. Anthropological work in Alaska. Smithsonian Institution, Explorations and Field-Work (1931): 91-102.

Hrdlička, A. Archeological excavations on Kodiak Island. Smithsonian Institution, Explorations and Field-Work (1934): 47-52.

Hrdlička, A. Artifacts on human and seal skulls from Kodiak Island. American Journal of Physical Anthropology, 28 (1941): 411-421.

Hrdlička, A. Catalogue of human crania in the United States National Museum collections. United States National Museum, Proceedings, 94 (1944): 1-172.

Hrdlička, A. Diseases of and artifacts on skulls and bones from Kodiak Island. Smithsonian Miscellaneous Collections, 101, no. 4 (1941): 1-14.

Hrdlička, A. Ritual ablation of front teeth in Siberia and America. Smithsonian Miscellaneous Collections, 99, no. 3 (1940): 1-32.

*Hrdlička, A. The anthropology of Kodiak Island. Philadelphia, 1944. 486 p.

Hurst, Edgar E., Jr. Malignant tumors in Alaskan Eskimos: unique predominance of carcinoma of the esophagus in Alaskan Eskimo women. Cancer, 17 (1964): 1187-1196.

Jacobi, A. Carl Heinrich Mercks ethnographische Beobachtungen über die Völker des Beringsmeers in 1791. Baessler-Archiv, 20 (1937): 113-137.

Johannsen, Uwe. Versuch einer Analyse dokumentarischen Materials über die Identitätsfrage und die kulturelle Position der Eyak-Indianer Alaskas. Anthropos, 58 (1963): 868-896.

Jørgensen, J. Balslev. Growth studies on a hybrid population of Eskimo-White origin in southwestern Alaska. By J. Balslev Jørgensen and William S. Laughlin. Folk, 5 (1963): 199-208.

Laguna, F. de. A pottery vessel from Kodiak Island. American Antiquity, 4 (1939): 334-343.

Laguna, F. de. Chugach prehistory. Washington, University, Publications in Anthropology, 13, (1956): 1-308.

Laguna, F. de. Peintures rupestres eskimo. Société des Américanistes, Journal, n.s., 25 (1933): 17-30.

Laguna, F. de. The archaeology of Cook Inlet. Philadelphia, 1934.

Langsdorff, G. H. von. Voyages and travels in various parts of the world. London, 1813.

Lantis, M. Alaskan Eskimo ceremonialism. American Ethnological Society, Monographs, 11 (1947): 1-127.

Lantis, M. The mythology of Kodiak Island. Journal of American Folklore, 51 (1938): 123-172.

Larsen, H. Archaeological investigations in Alaska since 1939. Polar Record, 6 (1953): 593-607.

Lewis, Marion. Inheritance of blood group antigens in a largely Eskimo population sample. By Marion Lewis, Bruce Chown, and Hiroko Kaita. American Journal of Human Genetics, 15 (1963): 203-208; 16 (1964): 261; 18 (1966): 231.

Liapunova, R. G. Ekspeditsiia I. G. Voznesenskogo i ee znachenie dlia etnografii Russkoĭ Ameriki. Akademiia Nauk SSSR, Muzeĭ Antropologii i Etnografii, Sbornik, 24 (1967): 5-33.

Lisiansky, U. A voyage round the world. London, 1814. 190-215 p.

Mann, George V., et al. The health and nutritional status of Alaskan Eskimos. A survey of the Interdepartmental Committee on Nutrition for National Defense--1958. American Journal of Clinical Nutrition, 11 (1962): 31-76.

Mason, J. A. A remarkable stone lamp from Alaska. Museum Journal, 19 (1928): 170-194.

Mason, J. A. Eskimo pictorial art. Museum Journal, 18 (1927): 248-283.

Meier, Robert J. Fingerprint patterns from Karluk Village, Kodiak Island. Arctic Anthropology, 3, no. 2 (1965): 206-210.

Norick, Frank A. Acculturation and drinking in Alaska. Rehabilitation Record, 11, no. 5 (1970): 13-17.

Oswalt, Wendell H. Guiding culture change among Alaskan Eskimos. América Indígena, 21 (1961): 65-83, 151-170.

Petroff, I. Report on the population, industries and resources of Alaska. U.S. Census Office, 10th Census, 8 (1881): 124-146.

Petroff, I. The limit of the Innuit tribes on the Alaskan coast. American Naturalist, 16 (1882): 567-575.

Petroff, I. The population and resources of Alaska. In Compilation of Narratives of Explorations in Alaska. Washington, D.C., 1900: 210-239.

Philip, R. N., et al. Serologic and skin test evidence of tularemia infection among Alaskan Eskimos, Indians and Aleuts. Journal of Infectious Diseases, 110 (1962): 220-230.

Philip, Robert N. Phlyctenular keratoconjunctivitis among Eskimos in southwestern Alaska. II. Isoniazid prophylaxis. By Robert N. Philip and George W. Comstock. American Review of Respiratory Diseases, 91 (1965): 188-196.

Philip, Robert N. Phlyctenular keratoconjunctivitis among Eskimos in southwestern Alaska. I. Epidemiologic characteristics. By Robert N. Philip, George W. Comstock, and Joseph H. Shelton. American Review of Respiratory Diseases, 91 (1965): 171-187.

Pinart, A. L. Eskimaux et Koloches. Revue d'Anthropologie, 2 (1873): 673-680.

Portlock, N. A voyage round the world. London, 1789.

Radloff, L. Ueber die Sprache der Ugalachmut. Académie Impériale des Sciences de St.-Pétersbourg, Classe Historico-philologique, Bulletin, 15 (1858): 26-38, 48-63, 126-139.

Riddell, F. Climate and the aboriginal occupation of the Pacific Coast of Alaska. Kroeber Anthropological Society, Publications, 11 (1954): 60-123.

Schott, W. Ueber ethnographische Ergebnisse der Sagoskinschen Reise. Archiv für Wissenschaftliche Kunde von Russland, 7 (1849): 480-512.

Schulert, Arthur R. Strontium-90 in Alaska. Alaskan Eskimos for whom the caribou is a dietary staple have a high strontium-90 concentration. Science, 136 (1962): 146-148.

Tarenetzky, A. Beiträge zur Skelet- und Schädelkunde der Aleuten, Konaegen, Kenai und Koljuschen. Académie Impériale des Sciences de St.-Pétersbourg,

Mémoires, sér. 8, Classe Physico-Mathématique, 9, no. 4 (1900): 1-73.

Taylor, Kenneth I. A demographic study of Karluk, Kodiak Island, Alaska, 1962-1964. Arctic Anthropology, 3, no. 2 (1965): 211-243.

Totter, J. R. and C. F. Shukers. Nutrition surveys of Eskimos. Alaska's Health, 6, no. 10 (1948): 4-6.

Townsend, Joan B. Archaeological investigations at Pedro Bay, Alaska. By Joan B. Townsend and Sam-Joe Townsend. Alaska, University, Anthropological Papers, 10 (1961/1963): 25-58.

Turner, Christy G., II. Dental genetics and microevolution in prehistoric and living Koniag Eskimo. Journal of Dental Research, 46 (1967): 911-917.

Turner, Christy G., II. Microevolutionary interpretations from the dentition. American Journal of Physical Anthropology, n.s., 30 (1969): 421-426.

VanStone, James W. Some aspects of religious change among native inhabitants in West Alaska and the Northwest Territories. Arctic Anthropology, 2, no. 2 (1964): 21-24.

Veniaminov, I. Remarks on the Koloshian and Kadiak Languages (in Russian). St. Petersburg, 1846. 83 p.

Veniaminov, Innokentii. The condition of the Orthodox Church in Russian America: Innokentii Veniaminov's history of the Russian church in Alaska. Translated and edited by Robert Nichols and Robert Croskey. Pacific Northwest Quarterly, 63 (1972): 41-54.

Vrangel', Ferdinand Petrovich von. The inhabitants of the Northwest Coast of America. Translated and edited by James W. VanStone. By Ferdinand Petrovich von Wrangell. Arctic Anthropology, 6, no. 2 (1970): 5-20.

Woldt, A., ed. Capitain Jacobsen's Reise an der Nordwestküste Amerikas. Leipzig, 1884.

Workman, William B. Archaeological reconnaissance on Chirikof Island, Kodiak group; a preliminary report. Arctic Anthropology, 3, no. 2 (1965): 185-192.

Wrangell, F. P. Statistische und ethnographische Nachrichten über die russischen Besitzungen an der Nordwestküste von Amerika. Beiträge zur Kenntnis des Russischen Reiches, 1 (1839): 1-332.

Zagoskin, Lavrentiĭ Alekseevich.
Lieutenant Zagoskin's travels in Russian
America, 1842-1844. Edited by Henry N.
Michael. Toronto, Published for the
Arctic Institute of North America by
University of Toronto Press, 1967. 14,
358 p. illus., maps. (Anthropology of
the North: Translations from Russian
Sources, 7)

01-13 Southampton Eskimo

Anderson, James Watt. Fur trader's story.
Toronto, Ryerson Press, 1961. 15,
245 p. illus.

Bird, J. B. Southampton Island. Canada,
Geographical Branch, Memoir, 5 (1953):
1-84.

Boas, F. The Eskimo of Baffin Land and
Hudson Bay. American Museum of Natural
History, Bulletin, 15 (1901-1907): 1-
570.

Brack, D. M. Southampton Island area
economic survey; with notes on Repulse
Bay and Wager Bay. Ottawa, Department
of Northern Affairs and Natural
Resources, Area and Community Planning
Section, Industrial Division, 1962. 5,
96 p. illus., map.

Brown, G. Malcolm, et al. Response to
cold of Eskimos of the eastern Canadian
Arctic. Journal of Applied Physiology,
18 (1963): 970-974.

Brown, M. Queen's University Expedition
to Southampton Island, 1948. Arctic
Circular, 1, no. 7 (1948): 81-82.

Brown, Malcolm, et al. Intestinal
parasites of Eskimos on Southampton
Island, Northwest Territories: a
preliminary survey. Canadian Journal of
Public Health, 39 (1948): 451-454.

Bruemmer, Fred. Sealskin thong. Beaver,
299, no. 1 (1968/1969): 45-50.

Bruemmer, Fred. The caribou hunt. North,
15, no. 3 (1968): 1-9.

Chown, Bruce. The blood group and
secretor genes of the Eskimo on
Southampton Island. By Bruce Chown and
Marion Lewis. In Contributions to
Anthropology 1960. Part I. Ottawa,
Queen's Printer, 1962: 181-190.
(Canada, National Museum, Bulletin, 180)

Comer, G. A geographical description of
Southampton Island and notes upon the
Eskimo. American Geographical Society,
Bulletin, 42 (1910): 84-90.

Comer, G. Notes on the natives of the
northern shores of Hudson Bay. American
Anthropologist, n.s., 23 (1921): 243-
244.

Cooch, G. Techniques for mass capture of
flightless blue and lesser snow geese.
Journal of Wildlife Management, 17
(1953): 460-465.

Copeland, Donalda McKillop. Remember,
nurse. Toronto, Ryerson Press, 1960.
250 p. illus.

Danning, Robert W. A note on adoption
among the Southampton Island Eskimo.
Man, 62 (1962): 163-167.

DeNevi, Don. Hudson Bay. Music Educators
Journal, 56, no. 1 (1969): 66-68.

Ferguson, R. Arctic Harpooner.
Philadelphia, 1938. 216 p.

Freeman, Milton M. R. Studies in maritime
hunting. I. Ecologic and technologic
restraints on walrus hunting,
Southampton Island N.W.T. Folk, 11/12
(1969/1970): 155-171.

Graham, Andrew. Andrew Graham's
observations on Hudson's Bay, 1767-91.
Edited by Glyndwr Williams. London,
1969. 72, 423 p. illus., maps.
(Hudson's Bay Record Society,
Publications, 27)

Hamelin, L. E. Genre de vie à l'Ile de
Southhampton d'après le journal d'un
Esquimau. Cahiers de Géographie de
Québec, n.s., 1 (1956): 49-54.

Hrdlička, A. Contribution to the
anthropology of Central and Smith Sound
Eskimo. American Museum of Natural
History, Anthropological Papers, 5
(1910): 177-280.

Lewis, Marion. Inheritance of blood group
antigens in a largely Eskimo population
sample. By Marion Lewis, Bruce Chown,
and Hiroko Kaita. American Journal of
Human Genetics, 15 (1963): 203-208; 16
(1964): 261; 18 (1966): 231.

Lyon, G. F. A brief narrative of an
unsuccessful attempt to reach Repulse
Bay. London, 1825.

Manning, T. H. Remarks on the
physiography, Eskimo, and mammals of
Southampton Island. Canadian
Geographical Journal, 24 (1942): 16-33.

Mathiassen, T. Archaeology of the Central
Eskimos. Fifth Thule Expedition, Report,
4 (1927): 1-533.

Mathiassen, T. Southampton Island og dens oprindelige beboere. Geografisk Tidsskrift, 30 (1927): 39-56.

Mazess, Richard B. Bone density in Sadlermiut Eskimo. Human Biology, 38 (1966): 42-49.

Mazess, Richard B. Weight and density of Sadlermiut Eskimo long bones. By Richard B. Mazess and Robert Jones. Human Biology, 44 (1972): 537-548.

Merbs, Charles F. Anomalies and pathologies of the Sadlermiut Eskimo vertebral column. By Charles F. Merbs and William H. Wilson. In Contributions to Anthropology 1960. Part I. Ottawa, Queen's Printer, 1962: 154-180. (Canada, National Museum, Bulletin, 180)

Merbs, Charles Francis. Patterns of activity-induced pathology in a Canadian Eskimo isolate. Dissertation Abstracts International, 31 (1970/1971): 490B. UM 70-3624.

Moyer, David S. The social context of economic change: a study of Eskimo boat management. Human Organization, 30 (1971): 11-24.

Popham, R. E. A comparative analysis of the digital patterns of Eskimo from Southampton Island. American Journal of Physical Anthropology, n.s., 11 (1953): 203-213.

Radwanski, P. Anthropological structure of 101 Eskimo. Anthropologica, 1 (1955): 72-83.

Rasmussen, Knud J. V. The Tunits of Hudson Bay. In Leo Deuel, ed. Conquistadors without Swords. New York, St. Martins Press, 1967: 547-555.

Robinson, J. L. Eskimo population in the Canadian Eastern Arctic. Canadian Geographical Journal, 29 (1944): 128-142.

Service, E. R. The Canadian Eskimo. In his A Profile of Primitive Culture. New York, 1958: 64-85.

Taylor, William E. The mysterious Sadlermiut. Beaver, 290, no. 3 (1959/1960): 26-33.

Teicher, M. I. Adoption practices among the Eskimos on Southampton Island. Canadian Welfare, 29, no. 2 (1953): 32-37.

Teicher, M. I. Three cases of psychosis among the Eskimos. Journal of Mental Science, 100 (1954): 527-535.

Thibert, A. Le journal quotidien d'un Esquimau de Southampton. Anthropologica, 1 (1955): 144-197.

Tocher, J. F. Note on some measurements of Eskimo of Southampton Island. Man, 2 (1902): 165-167.

Tweedsmuir, J. N. S. B. Hudson's Bay Trade. New York, 1951. 195 p.

VanStone, James W. Notes on the economy and population shifts of the Eskimos of Southampton Island. Alaska, University, Anthropological Papers, 8 (1959/1960): 80-87.

VanStone, James W. The economy and population shifts of the Eskimos of Southampton Island. Ottawa, 1959. (Canada, Department of Northern Affairs and National Resources, Northern Coordination and Research Centre, NCRC-59-1)

Waterman, T. T. Hudson Bay Eskimo. American Museum of Natural History, Anthropological Papers, 4 (1910): 299-307.

01-14   West Alaska Eskimo

Oswalt, Wendell H. The Kuskokwim River drainage, Alaska: an annotated bibliography. College, 1965. 73 p. (Alaska, University, Anthropological Papers, 13, no. 1)

VanStone, James W. An annotated ethnohistorical bibliography of the Nushagak River region, Alaska. Chicago, Field Museum of Natural History, 1968. 149-189 p. (Fieldiana: Anthropology, 54, no. 2)

Albee, W. Kangut: a boy of Bering Strait. Boston, 1939. 116 p.

Anderson, H. D. and W. C. Eells. Alaska natives. Stanford, 1935. 472 p.

Andrews, C. L. The Eskimo and his reindeer in Alaska. Caldwell, 1939. 253 p.

Baker, George L. Nutritional survey of northern Eskimo infants and children. American Journal of Clinical Nutrition, 22 (1969): 612-616.

Bancroft, H. H. The native races of the Pacific States. Vol. 1. New York, 1875. 37-94 p.

Barnum, F. Grammatical fundamentals of
the Innuit language. Boston, 1901.

Barnum, Francis. Grammatical fundamentals
of the Innuit language as spoken by the
Eskimo of the western coast of Alaska.
Hildesheim, G. Olms, 1970. 25, 384 p.

Bartels, P. Kasuistische Mitteilung über
den Mongolenfleck bei Eskimo.
Zeitschrift für Ethnologie, 41 (1909):
721-725.

Beechey, F. W. Narrative of a voyage to
the Pacific and Beering's Strait.
London, 1831. 2 v.

Benson, Barrett E. Reduction of high
nitrate content from well water in a
remote Eskimo village. Journal of
Environmental Health, 30 (1967): 164-
170.

Bergsland, Knut. On the validity of
glottochronology. By Knut Bergsland and
Hans Vogt. [With comment by Morris
Swadesh.] Current Anthropology, 3
(1962): 115-153.

Birchard, Bruce A. The validity of rating
scales and interviews for evaluating
Indian education; perceptions of Indian
education. Chicago, University of
Chicago, 1970. 10 p. (National Study
of American Indian Education, Series 4,
8) ERIC ED047873.

Birket-Smith, K. Early collections from
the Pacific Eskimo. Nationalmuseets
Skrifter, Etnografisk Raekke, 1 (1941):
121-163.

Blomkvist, E. E. A Russian scientific
expedition to California and Alaska,
1839-1849; the drawings of I. G.
Voznesenskii. Translated by Basil
Dmytryshyn and E. A. Crownhart-Vaughan.
Oregon Historical Quarterly, 73 (1972):
100-170.

Blumberg, Baruch S., et al. A study of
the prevalence of arthritis in Alaskan
Eskimos. Arthritis and Rheumatism, 4
(1961): 325-341.

Boas, F. A. J. Stone's measurements of
natives of the Northwest Territories.
American Museum of Natural History,
Bulletin, 14 (1901): 53-68.

Boas, F. Decorative designs of Alaskan
needlecases. United States National
Museum, Proceedings, 34 (1908): 321-344.

Boas, F. Notes on the Eskimo of Port
Clarence. Journal of American Folklore,
7 (1894): 205-208.

Boas, F. Property marks of the Alaskan
Eskimo. American Anthropologist, n.s., 1
(1899): 601-613.

Burch, Ernest S., Jr. Alliance and
conflict: inter-regional relations in
North Alaska. By Ernest S. Burch, Jr.
and Thomas C. Correll. In D. Lee
Guemple, ed. Alliance in Eskimo Society.
Seattle, American Ethnological Society,
1972: 17-39.

Burg, A. North Star cruises Alaska's Wild
West. National Geographic Magazine, 102
(1952): 57-86.

Carrighar, S. Unalakleet, Alaska.
Saturday Evening Post, 223 (Jan. 12,
1952): 32, 42-43, 45-46.

Chandler, Robert P. Radionuclides in the
northwestern Alaska food chain, 1959-
1961--a review. By Robert P. Chandler
and Samuel Wieder. Radiological Health
Data, 4 (1963): 317-324.

Collins, H. B. Archeological excavations
at Bering Strait. Smithsonian
Institution, Explorations and Field-Work
(1936): 63-68.

Collins, H. B. Check-stamped pottery from
Alaska. Washington Academy of Sciences,
Journal, 18 (1928): 254-256.

Collins, H. B. Culture migrations and
contacts in the Bering Sea region.
American Anthropologist, n.s., 39
(1937): 375-384.

Coon, Carleton S. The hunting peoples.
Boston, Little, Brown, 1971. 21,
413 p. illus., maps.

Correll, Thomas Clifton. Ungalaqlingmiut:
a study in language and society.
Dissertation Abstracts International, 33
(1972/1973): 5103B-5104B. UM 73-10,684.

Coxe, W. Account of the Russian
discoveries between Asia and America.
4th ed. London, 1804.

Cross, J. F. Eskimo children. Southern
Workman, 37 (1908): 433-437.

Cumming, J. R. Metaphysical implications
of the folktales of the Eskimos of
Alaska. Alaska, University,
Anthropological Papers, 3, no. 1 (1954):
37-63.

*Curtis, E. S. The North American Indian.
Vol. 20. Norwood, 1930. 1-320 p.

Dale, G. A. Northwest Alaska and the
Bering Sea coast. In I. T. Sanders, ed.
Societies Around the World, I.
Lexington, Ky., 1952: 111-130.

Dall, W. H. Alaska and its resources. Boston, 1870. 627 p.

Dall, W. H. On the distribution and nomenclature of the native tribes of Alaska. Contributions to North American Ethnology, 1 (1877): 7-40.

Dall, W. H. On the distribution of the native tribes of Alaska. American Association for the Advancement of Science, Proceedings, 18 (1869): 263-273.

Dall, W. H. Social life among our aborigines. American Naturalist, 12 (1878): 1-10.

Dall, W. H. The native tribes of Alaska. American Association for the Advancement of Science, Proceedings, 34 (1885): 363-379.

Dall, W. H., G. M. Dawson, and W. Ogilvie. The Yukon Territory. London, 1898. 438 p.

Disselhoff, H. D. Bemerkungen zu einigen Eskimo-Masken. Baessler-Archiv, 18 (1935): 130-137.

Drebert, Ferdinand. Alaska missionary. Bethlehem, Pa., Moravian Book Shop, 1959. 165 p. illus.

Edmonds, H. M. W. The Eskimo of St. Michael and vicinity. As related by H. M. W. Edmonds. Edited by Dorothy Jean Ray. College, 1961. 2, 143 p. illus., map. (Alaska, University, Anthropological Papers, 13, no. 2)

Eells, W. C. Mechanical, physical, and musical ability of the native races of Alaska. Journal of Applied Psychology, 17 (1933): 493-506.

Eells, W. C. Mental ability of the native races of Alaska. Journal of Applied Psychology, 17 (1933): 417-438.

Eide, A. H. Drums of Diomede. Hollywood, 1952. 242 p.

Erman, A. Ueber die Reise und Entdeckungen des Lieutenant L. Sagoskin im russischen Amerika. Archiv für Wissenschaftliche Kunde von Russland, 6 (1848): 499-522, 613-672; 7 (1849): 429-512.

Foote, Don Charles. American whalemen in northwestern Arctic Alaska. In Deward E. Walker, Jr., ed. The Emergent Native Americans. Boston, Little, Brown, 1972: 301-308.

Fortuine, Robert. Hemophilus aprophilus endocarditis, with cerebral embolism, in an Alaskan Eskimo. By Robert Fortuine and Fred W. Bell, Jr. Annals of Internal Medicine, 64 (1966): 873-875.

Frederick, Saradell Ard. Teaching art: Paul Forrer and children of Eek. Alaska Review, 4, no. 2 (1970): 55-63.

Fritz, M. H. Corneal opacities among Alaska natives. Alaska's Health, 5, no. 12 (1947): 3-7.

Fritz, Milo H. A clinic to St. Mary's. Northwest Medicine, 60 (1961): 589-591.

Fulcomer, A. An Eskimo "Kashim". Natural History, 11 (1898): 55-58.

Gagné, Raymond C. Towards a Canadian Eskimo orthography and literature. Canadian Journal of Linguistics, 7 (1961/1962): 95-107; 8 (1962/1963): 33-39.

Garber, C. M. Eating with Eskimos. Hygeia, 16 (1938): 242-245, 272, 278-279.

Garber, C. M. Marriage and sex customs of the Western Eskimos. Scientific Monthly, 41 (1935): 215-227.

Garber, C. M. Some mortuary customs of the Western Alaska Eskimos. Scientific Monthly, 39 (1934): 203-220.

Garber, C. M. Stories and legends of the Bering Strait Eskimos. Boston, 1940. 260 p.

Gillham, C. E. Beyond the clapping mountains. New York, 1943. 134 p.

Gillham, Charles E. Medicine men of Hooper Bay. New York, Macmillan, 1955. 10, 134 p. illus.

Giraux, L. Gravures coloriées sur dents de morse des Esquimaux de l'Alaska. Société des Américanistes, Journal, n.s., 18 (1926): 91-102.

Glazunov, Andrei. Russian exploration in interior Alaska; an extract from the journal of Andrei Glazunov. Edited by James W. VanStone. Pacific Northwest Quarterly, 50 (1959): 37-47.

Gordon, G. B. In the Alaskan wilderness. Philadelphia, 1917. 247 p.

Gordon, G. B. Notes on the Western Eskimo. Pennsylvania, University, Free Museum of Science and Art, Transactions, 2 (1906): 69-101.

Gordon, G. B. The double axe and some other symbols. Museum Journal, 7 (1916): 46-68.

Hammerich, L. L. Russian loan-words in
Alaska. International Congress of
Americanists, Proceedings, 30 (1955):
114-126.

Hammerich, L. L. The dialect of Nunivak.
International Congress of Americanists,
Proceedings, 30 (1955): 110-113.

Hammerich, L. L. The Russian stratum in
Alaskan Eskimo. Slavic Word, 10 (1954):
401-428.

Hammerich, L. L. The Western Eskimo
dialects. International Congress of
Americanists, Proceedings, 32 (1958):
632-639.

Hammes, L. M. Characteristics of housing
for the Yukon-Kuskokwim delta of
southwestern Alaska. Alaska Medicine, 7,
no. 1 (1965): 7-10.

Hanson, Mary L. Community isoniazid
prophylaxis program in an underdeveloped
area of Alaska. By Mary L. Hanson, G. W.
Comstock, and C. E. Haley. U.S., Public
Health Service, Public Health Reports,
82 (1967): 1045-1056.

Hanson, Wayne C. Fallout radionuclides in
northern Alaskan ecosystems. Archives of
Environmental Health, 17 (1968): 639-
648.

Hanson, Wayne C. Radioactivity in
Northern Alaskan Eskimos and their
foods, summer 1962. By W. C. Hanson, H.
E. Palmer, and B. I. Griffin. Health
Physics, 10 (1964): 421-429.

Hawkes, E. W. The dance festivals of the
Alaskan Eskimo. Pennsylvania,
University, Free Museum of Science and
Art, Transactions, 6, no. 2 (1914): 1-
41.

Hawkes, E. W. The "inviting-in" feast of
the Alaskan Eskimo. Canada, Department
of Mines, Geological Survey, Memoirs, 45
(1913): 1-20.

Healy, M. A. Report of the cruise of the
revenue marine steamer Corwin in the
Arctic Ocean. Washington, D.C., 1887.

Healy, M. A. The Eskimo trade ninety
years ago. Museum of the Fur Trade
Quarterly, 6, no. 4 (1970): 6-11.

Heinrich, A. Some present-day
acculturative innovations in a
nonliterate society. American
Anthropologist, 52 (1950): 235-242.

Heinrich, Albert. Some formal aspects of
a kinship system. By Albert Heinrich and
Russell L. Anderson. Current
Anthropology, 12 (1971): 541-557.

Heinrich, Albert. Structural features of
northwestern Alaskan Eskimo kinship.
Southwestern Journal of Anthropology, 16
(1960): 110-126.

Heizer, R. F. Aconite poison whaling in
Asia and America. U.S. Bureau of
American Ethnology, Bulletin, 133
(1943): 415-468.

Heller, Christine A. Height, weight, and
growth of Alaskan Eskimos. By Christine
A. Heller, Edward M. Scott, and Laurel
M. Hammes. American Journal of Diseases
of Children, 113 (1967): 338-344.

Himmelheber, H. Der gefrorene Pfad.
Eisenach, 1951. 135 p.

Himmelheber, H. Eskimokünstler.
Stuttgart, 1938. 111 p.

Himmelheber, Hans. Nasenblut als
Bindemittel für Mal-Farbe bei den
Eskimos. HNO: Wegweiser für die
Facharztliche Praxis, 16 (1968): 29-30.

Hinz, J. Grammar and vocabulary of the
Eskimo language. Bethlehem, 1944.
194 p.

Hipszer, Hermine. Les masques de chamans
du Musee Ethnographique de Berlin.
Baessler-Archiv, n.F., 19 (1971): 421-
450.

Hirschfeld, A. James. An unusually high
incidence of salt-losing congenital
adrenal hyperplasia in the Alaskan
Eskimo. By A. James Hirschfeld and J.
Kenneth Fleshman. Journal of Pediatrics,
75 (1969): 492-494.

Hitchcock, D. J. Parasitological study on
the Eskimos in the Bethel area of
Alaska. Journal of Parasitology, 36
(1950): 232-234.

Hitchcock, D. J. Parasitological study on
the Eskimos in the Kotzebue area of
Alaska. Journal of Parasitology, 37
(1951): 309-311.

Hitchcock, Dorothy J. Parasitological
study on the Eskimos in the Bethel area
of Alaska. Journal of Parasitology, 36
(1950): 232-234.

Hrdlička, A. Anthropological survey of
Alaska. U.S. Bureau of American
Ethnology, Annual Reports, 46 (1930):
19-374.

Hrdlička, A. Anthropological work in
Alaska. Smithsonian Miscellaneous
Collections, 78, no. 7 (1927): 137-158.

Hrdlička, A. Anthropological work on the
Kuskokwim River. Smithsonian

Institution, Explorations and Field-Work (1930): 123-134.

Hrdlička, A. Fecundity of Eskimo women. American Journal of Physical Anthropology, 22 (1936): 91-95.

Hrdlička, A. Height and weight of Eskimo children. American Journal of Physical Anthropology, 28 (1941): 331-341.

Hrdlička, A. Puberty in Eskimo girls. National Academy of Sciences, Proceedings, 22 (1936): 355-357.

Hrdlička, A. Ritual ablation of front teeth in Siberia and America. Smithsonian Miscellaneous Collections, 99, no. 3 (1940): 1-32.

Hrdlička, A. The ancient and modern inhabitants of the Yukon. Smithsonian Institution, Explorations and Field-Work (1929): 137-146.

Hrdlička, A. The Eskimo of the Kuskokwim. American Journal of Physical Anthropology, 18 (1933): 93-145.

Hurst, Edgar E., Jr. Malignant tumors in Alaskan Eskimos: unique predominance of carcinoma of the esophagus in Alaskan Eskimo women. Cancer, 17 (1964): 1187-1196.

Ivanov, S. V. O Znachenii Dvukh. Akademiia Nauk SSSR, Muzei Antropologii i Etnografii, Sbornik, 11 (1949): 162-170.

Jacobsen, J. A. Leben und Treiben der Eskimo. Ausland, 64 (1891): 593-598, 636-639, 656-658.

Jenness, D. Archaeological investigations in Bering Strait. Canada, Department of Mines, National Museum of Canada, Bulletin, 50 (1926): 71-80.

Jenness, D. Little Diomede Island. Geographical Review, 19 (1929): 78-86.

Jenness, D. Notes on the phonology of the Eskimo dialect of Cape Prince of Wales. International Journal of American Linguistics, 4 (1927): 168-180.

Kamerling, Leonard. Kassigeluremiut; the people of Kasigluk in pictures and poems. College, University of Alaska, Alaska Rural School Project, 1970. 42 p. illus.

Keithahn, Edward L. Eskimo adventure; another journey into the primitive. Seattle, Superior, 1963. 170 p. illus.

Kettelkamp, Donald B. Spondylolysis in the Alaskan Eskimo. By Donald B.

Kettelkamp and D. Gilbert Wright. Journal of Bone and Joint Surgery, 53-A (1971): 563-566.

Klein, David R. Waterfowl in the economy of the Eskimos on the Yukon-Kuskokwim Delta, Alaska. Arctic, 19 (1966): 319-336.

Koertvelyessy, Tibor. Relationships between the frontal sinus and climatic conditions: a skeletal approach to cold adaptation. American Journal of Physical Anthropology, 37 (1972/1973): 161-172.

Koo, Jang H. The copulative 'u' in Yupik Eskimo and crossover convention. International Journal of American Linguistics, 37 (1971): 215-218.

Koranda, Lorraine D. Music of the Alaskan Eskimo. Music Journal, 24, no. 1 (1966): 89, 94.

Koranda, Lorraine D. Some traditional songs of the Alaskan Eskimos. Alaska, University, Anthropological Papers, 12 (1964): 17-32.

Koranda, Lorraine D. Three songs for the Bladder Festival, Hooper Bay. Alaska, University, Anthropological Papers, 14, no. 1 (1968): 27-31.

Kowta, Makoto. Old Togiak in prehistory. Dissertation Abstracts, 24 (1963/1964): 1793. UM 63-7710.

Krause, E. Die Schraube, eine Eskimo-Erfindung? Globus, 79 (1901): 8-9.

Kunce, Joseph. Maze performance and personal, social, and economic adjustment of Alaskan natives. By Joseph Kunce, L. S. Rankin, and Elaine Clement. Journal of Social Psychology, 73 (1967): 37-45.

Laguna, F. de. The prehistory of northern North America as seen from the Yukon. Society for American Archaeology, Memoirs, 3 (1947): 1-360.

Lantis, M. Alaskan Eskimo ceremonialism. American Ethnological Society, Monographs, 11 (1947): 1-127.

Lantis, M. Mme. Eskimo proves herself an artist. Natural History, 59 (1950): 68-71.

Lantis, M. No wonder they worship the seal. Natural History, 48 (1941): 166-172.

Lantis, M. Nunivak Eskimo personality as revealed in the mythology. Alaska, University, Anthropological Papers, 2, no. 1 (1953): 109-174.

*Lantis, M. The social culture of the
Nunivak Eskimo. American Philosophical
Society, Transactions, n.s., 35 (1946):
153-323.

Lantis, Margaret. Alaskan Eskimo cultural
values. Polar Notes, 1 (1959): 35-48.

Lantis, Margaret. Eskimo childhood and
interpersonal relationships; Nunivak
biographies and genealogies. Seattle,
University of Washington Press, 1960.
15, 215 p. illus., map. (American
Ethnological Society, Monograph, 33)

Lantis, Margaret. Folk medicine and
hygiene; Lower Kuskokwim and Nunivak-
Nelson Island areas. College, 1959. 4,
75 p. map. (Alaska, University,
Anthropological Papers, 8, no. 1)

Lantis, Margaret. The religion of the
Eskimos. In Vergilius Ferm, ed.
Forgotten Religions. New York,
Philosophical Library, 1950: 311-339.

Larsen, H. Archaeological investigations
in Alaska since 1939. Polar Record, 6
(1953): 593-607.

Larsen, H. Archaeological investigations
in southwestern Alaska. American
Antiquity, 15 (1949): 177-186.

Larsen, H. De Dansk-amerikanske Alaska-
ekspeditioner 1949-50. Geografisk
Tidsskrift, 51 (1951): 63-93.

Larsen, H. Et Naturfolk Fortaeller. Vor
Viden, 36 (1951): 183-188.

Levine, V. E. Dental caries, attrition
and crowding in the Eskimos of the
coasts of the Bering Sea and Arctic
Ocean. Journal of Dental Research, 18
(1939): 255-256.

Liapunova, R. G. Ekspeditsiia I. G.
Voznesenskogo i ee znachenie dlia
etnografii Russkoi Ameriki. Akademiia
Nauk SSSR, Muzei Antropologii i
Etnografii, Sbornik, 24 (1967): 5-33.

Lucier, C. Buckland Eskimo myths. Alaska,
University, Anthropological Papers, 2
(1954): 215-233.

Lucier, C. Noatagmiut Eskimo Myths.
Alaska, University, Anthropological
Papers, 6 (1958): 89-118.

Mann, George V., et al. The health and
nutritional status of Alaskan Eskimos. A
survey of the Interdepartmental
Committee on Nutrition for National
Defense--1958. American Journal of
Clinical Nutrition, 11 (1962): 31-76.

Mason, J. A. Eskimo pictorial art. Museum
Journal, 18 (1927): 248-283.

Mason, Lynn D. Disease, ecology, and
economy among Eskimos in southwestern
Alaska. Anthropology UCLA, 3, no. 1
(1971): 26-35.

Mason, Lynn Douglas. Disabled fishermen:
disease and livelihood among the
Kuskowagamiut Eskimos of Lower Kalskag,
Alaska. Dissertation Abstracts
International, 33 (1972/1973): 2910B-
2911B. UM 72-23,953.

Mathiassen, T. Some specimens from the
Bering Sea culture. Indian Notes, 6
(1929): 33-56.

Matson, G. A. and H. J. Roberts.
Distribution of the blood groups, M-N
and Rh Types among Eskimos of the
Kuskokwim Basin in Western Alaska.
American Journal of Physical
Anthropology, 7 (1949): 109-122.

Mattina, Anthony. Phonology of Alaskan
Eskimo, Kuskokwim dialect. International
Journal of American Linguistics, 36
(1970): 38-45.

Maynard, James E. A study of growth,
morbity and mortality among Eskimo
infants of Western Alaska. By James E.
Maynard and Laurel M. Hammes. World
Health Organization, Bulletin, 42
(1970): 613-622.

Maynard, James E. Otitis media in Alaskan
Eskimo children. Prospective evaluation
of chemoprophylaxis. By James E.
Maynard, J. Kenneth Fleshman, and
Charles F. Tschopp. American Medical
Association, Journal, 219 (1972): 597-
599.

Maynard, James E., et al. Surveillance of
respiratory virus infections among
Alaskan Eskimo children. American
Medical Association, Journal, 200
(1967): 927-931.

Mayokok, R. I was a failure as a polar
bear hunter. Alaska Sportsman, 16, no. 2
(1950): 6-9.

Mayokok, R. Seals. Alaska Sportsman, 16,
no. 4 (1950): 20-21, 29-31.

Mayokok, R. We caught a whale. Alaska
Sportsman, 16, no. 7 (1950): 10-13.

Merrill, Ralph G. Occlusal anomalous
tubercles on premolars of Alaskan
Eskimos and Indians. Oral Surgery, Oral
Medicine, Oral Pathology, 17 (1964):
484-496.

Mickey, B. H. The family among the Western Eskimo. Alaska, University, Anthropological Papers, 4, no. 1 (1955): 13-22.

Minner, J. L. Old man of the ice floes. Alaska Sportsman, 19, no. 3 (1953): 18-21, 38-39.

Miyaoka, Osahito. On syllable modification and quantity in Yuk phonology. International Journal of American Linguistics, 37 (1971): 219-226.

Montgomery, Maurice. The murder of missionary Thornton. Pacific Northwest Quarterly, 54 (1963): 167-173.

Mouratoff, George J. Diabetes mellitus in Eskimos. By George J. Mouratoff, Nicholas V. Carroll, and Edward M. Scott. American Medical Association, Journal, 199 (1967): 961-966.

Muir, J. The cruise of the Corwin. Boston, 1917.

Muñoz, J. Cliff dwellers of the Bering Sea. National Geographic Magazine, 105 (1954): 129-146.

Murdoch, J. On the Siberian origin of some customs of the Western Eskimo. American Anthropologist, 1 (1888): 325-336.

Murie, M. E. Modern Eskimo art. Natural History, 44 (1939): 49-52.

*Nelson, E. W. The Eskimo about Bering Strait. U.S. Bureau of American Ethnology, Annual Reports, 18, vol. 1 (1899): 3-518.

*Nelson, Edward W. The Eskimo about Bering Strait. New York, Johnson Reprint, 1971. 518, 965-997 p. illus., map.

Nordenskiöld, A. E. The voyage of the Vega. New York, 1882.

Norick, Frank A. Acculturation and drinking in Alaska. Rehabilitation Record, 11, no. 5 (1970): 13-17.

Olson, Dean F. Cooperative ownership experiences of Alaskan Eskimo reindeer herders. Human Organization, 29 (1970): 57-62.

Orchard, W. C. Present-day pictography. Indian Notes, 1 (1924): 70-73.

Ostermann, H. The Alaskan Eskimos. Fifth Thule Expedition, Report, 10, no. 3 (1952): 291 p.

Oswalt, W. H. Pottery from Hooper Bay Village, Alaska. American Antiquity, 18 (1952): 18-29.

Oswalt, W. H. Recent pottery from the Bering Strait region. Alaska, University, Anthropological Papers, 2 (1953): 5-18.

Oswalt, W. H. The archaeology of Hooper Bay Village, Alaska. Alaska, University, Anthropological Papers, 1 (1952): 47-91.

Oswalt, Wendell H. A Western Eskimo ethnobotany. Alaska, University, Anthropological Papers, 6, no. 1 (1957): 17-36.

Oswalt, Wendell H. Guiding culture change among Alaskan Eskimos. América Indígena, 21 (1961): 65-83, 151-170.

Oswalt, Wendell H. Historical populations in western Alaska and migration theory. Alaska, University, Anthropological Papers, 11 (1962/1964): 1-14.

Oswalt, Wendell H. Mission of change in Alaska: Eskimos and Moravians on the Kuskokwim. San Marino, Calif., Huntington Library, 1963. 10, 170 p. maps.

Oswalt, Wendell H. Partially acculturated communities: Canadian Athapaskans and West Alaskan Eskimos. By Wendell H. Oswalt and James W. VanStone. Anthropologica, n.s., 5 (1963): 23-31.

Oswalt, Wendell H. The ethnoarcheology of Crow Village, Alaska. By Wendell H. Oswalt and James W. VanStone. Washington, D.C., Government Printing Office, 1967. 8, 136 p. illus., map. (U.S., Bureau of American Ethnology, Bulletin, 199)

Oswalt, Wendell H., ed. Eskimos and Indians of western Alaska 1861-1868: extracts from the diary of Father Illarion. Alaska, University, Anthropological Papers, 8 (1959/1960): 100-118.

Oswalt, Wendell Hillman. Napaskiak: an Eskimo village in western Alaska. Dissertation Abstracts, 20 (1959/1960): 848. UM 59-3029.

Packard, Robert C. Demographic discrimination of American Indian and Alaskan Eskimo groups by means of Bjork analysis. By Robert C. Packard and Thomas J. Zwemer. Journal of Dental Research, 50 (1971): 364-370.

Palmer, Harvey E. Cesium-134 in Alaskan Eskimos and in fallout. By Harvey E.

Palmer and Richard W. Perkins. Science, 142 (1963): 66-67.

Parker, Seymour. Ethnic identity and acculturation in two Eskimo villages. American Anthropologist, 66 (1964): 325-340.

Pedersen, P. O. Eine besondere Form der Abnutzung von Eskimozähnen aus Alaska. Deutsche Zahnärztliche Zeitschrift, 10 (1955): 41-46.

Petroff, I. Report on the population, industries, and resources of Alaska. U.S. Census Office, Tenth Census, 8 (1881): 124-146.

Petroff, I. The population and resources of Alaska. In Compilation of Narratives of Explorations in Alaska. Washington, D.C., 1900: 210-239.

Philip, R. N., et al. Serologic and skin test evidence of tularemia infection among Alaskan Eskimos, Indians and Aleuts. Journal of Infectious Diseases, 110 (1962): 220-230.

Philip, Robert N. Phlyctenular keratoconjunctivitis among Eskimos in southwestern Alaska. II. Isoniazid prophylaxis. By Robert N. Philip and George W. Comstock. American Review of Respiratory Diseases, 91 (1965): 188-196.

Philip, Robert N. Phlyctenular keratoconjunctivitis among Eskimos in southwestern Alaska. I. Epidemiologic characteristics. By Robert N. Philip, George W. Comstock, and Joseph H. Shelton. American Review of Respiratory Diseases, 91 (1965): 171-187.

Preston, Caroline E. Psychological testing with northwest coast Alaskan Eskimos. Genetic Psychology Monographs, 69 (1964): 323-419.

Price, W. A. New light on the etiology of facial deformity and dental irregularities from field studies among Eskimos and Indians in various stages of modernization. Journal of Dental Research, 14 (1934): 229-230.

Price, W. A. Relation of nutrition to dental caries among Eskimos and Indians in Alaska and northern Canada. Journal of Dental Research, 14 (1934): 227-229.

Price, W. A. Some causes for change in susceptibility of Eskimos and Indians to acute and chronic infections upon contact with modern civilization. Journal of Dental Research, 14 (1934): 230-231.

Rainey, F. G. Native economy and survival in Arctic Alaska. Human Organization, 1, no. 1 (1941): 9-14.

Rausch, R. L. Helminths in Eskimos in Western Alaska, with particular reference to Diphyllobothrium infection and anaemia. By R. L. Rausch, E. M. Scott, and V. R. Rausch. Royal Society of Tropical Medicine and Hygiene, Transactions, 61 (1967): 351-357.

Ray, Dorothy Jean. Land tenure and polity of the Bering Strait Eskimos. Journal of the West, 6 (1967): 371-394.

Ray, Dorothy Jean. Nineteenth century settlement and subsistence patterns in Bering Strait. Arctic Anthropology, 2, no. 2 (1964): 61-94.

Reed, Dwayne. Epidemiologic studies of otitis media among Eskimo children. By Dwayne Reed and Wallace Dunn. U.S., Public Health Service, Public Health Reports, 85 (1970): 699-706.

Reed, Dwayne. Seasonal response to oral poliovirus vaccine among Eskimo children. By Dwayne Reed, Jacob Brody, and Joan Lunsford. Archives of Environmental Health, 13 (1966): 429-432.

Richet, E. Les Esquimaux de l'Alaska. Société Royale de Géographie d'Anvers, Bulletin, 41 (1921): 5-51, 103-153, 197-245; 42 (1922): 5-50, 185-231.

Rosebury, T. Dental caries and related mouth conditions among Eskimos of the Kuskokwim Region. Journal of Dental Research, 16 (1936): 305-306.

Rosenthal, Hank. New skills for Nanook. Alaska Journal, 2, no. 4 (1972): 25-29.

Rychkov, IŪ. G. Populiatsionnaia genetika Aleutov Komandorskikh Ostrovov (v sviazi s problemami istorii narodov i adaptatsii drevneĭ Beringii). By IŪ. G. Rychkov and V. A. Sheremet'eva. Voprosy Antropologii, 40 (1972): 45-70; 41 (1972): 3-18; 42 (1972): 3-30.

Santos, A. Jesuitos en el Polo Norte. Madrid, 1943. 546 p.

Schott, W. Ueber ethnographische Ergebnisse der Sagoskinschen Reise. Archiv für Wissenschaftliche Kunde von Russland, 7 (1849): 480-512.

Schulert, Arthur R. Strontium-90 in Alaska. Alaskan Eskimos for whom the caribou is a dietary staple have a high strontium-90 concentration. Science, 136 (1962): 146-148.

Schultze, A. Grammar and vocabulary of the Eskimo language. Bethlehem, 1894. 21 p.

Schwatka, F. Report of a military reconnaissance made in Alaska in 1883. Washington, D.C., 1900. 104-111 p.

Scott, Edward M. Anemia in Alaskan Eskimos. By E. M. Scott, Rita C. Wright, and Barbara T. Hanan. Journal of Nutrition, 55 (1955): 137-149.

Scott, Edward M. Discrimination of phenotypes in human serum cholinesterase deficiency. By Edward M. Scott, David D. Weaver, and Rita C. Wright. American Journal of Human Genetics, 22 (1970): 363-369.

Scott, Edward M. Iron deficiency in Alaska Eskimos. By E. M. Scott and Christine A. Heller. American Journal of Clinical Nutrition, 15 (1964): 282-286.

Scott, Edward M., et al. Frequency of polymorphic types of red cell enzymes and serum factors in Alaskan Eskimos and Indians. American Journal of Human Genetics, 18 (1966): 408-411.

Senungetuk, Joseph. Nome Eskimo youth show unique talent. Indian Historian, 3, no. 1 (1970): 55-57.

Senungetuk, Joseph E. Give or take a century; an Eskimo chronicle. San Francisco, Indian Historian Press, 1971. 10, 206 p. illus.

Senungetuk, Joseph E. The Eskimo seal hunt. Indian Historian, 4, no. 2 (1971): 4-7.

Shapiro, H. A. The Alaskan Eskimo. American Museum of Natural History, Anthropological Papers, 31 (1931): 347-384.

Simpson, R. de E. Eskimo art in ivory. Masterkey, 22 (1948): 183-188.

Smith, Valene L. Intercontinental aboriginal trade in the Bering Straits area. In International Congress of Anthropological and Ethnological Sciences, 8th. 1968, Tokyo and Kyoto. Proceedings. Vol. 2. Tokyo, Science Council of Japan, 1969: 236-238.

Stegink, Lewis D. Serum amino acid levels of northern Alaskan Eskimo infants and children. By Lewis D. Stegink and George L. Baker. American Journal of Clinical Nutrition, 23 (1970): 1642-1648.

Steinen, K. von den. Die Schraube, keine Eskimo-Erfindung. Globus, 79 (1901): 125-127.

Stepanova, M. V. Dva Eskimosskikh Poiasa iz Sobraniia MAE. Akademiia Nauk SSSR, Muzeĭ Antropologiĭ i Etnografiĭ, Sbornik, 11 (1949): 62-72.

Thompson, D. J. The Eskimo woman of Nome, Alaska. Alaskan Science Conference, Proceedings (1951): 251-255.

*Thornton, H. R. Among the Eskimos of Wales, Alaska. Baltimore, 1931.

Totter, J. R. and C. F. Shukers. Nutrition surveys of Eskimos. Alaska's Health, 6, no. 10 (1948): 4-6.

Turner, J. Henry, comp. St. Michael Eskimo myths and tales. Collected by J. Henry Turner and H. M. W. Edmonds. Edited by Dorothy Jean Ray. Alaska, University, Anthropological Papers, 14, no. 1 (1968): 43-83.

Van Valin, W. B. Eskimoland speaks. Caldwell, 1941. 242 p.

VanStone, James W. Eskimos of the Nushagak River; an ethnographic history. Seattle, University of Washington Press, 1967. 24, 192 p. maps.

VanStone, James W. Ethnohistorical research in Alaska. Alaska Review, 3, no. 1 (1967/1969): 51-59.

VanStone, James W. Historic settlement patterns in the Nushagak River region, Alaska. Chicago, Field Museum of Natural History, 1971. 149 p. illus., maps. (Fieldiana: Anthropology, 61)

VanStone, James W. Nushagak. Alaska Journal, 2, no. 3 (1972): 49-53.

VanStone, James W. Nushagak: an historic trading center in southeastern Alaska. Chicago, Field Museum of Natural History, 1972. 5, 93 p. (Fieldiana: Anthropology, 62)

VanStone, James W. Three Eskimo communities. By J. W. VanStone and W. H. Oswalt. Alaska, University, Anthropological Papers, 9 (1960/1961): 17-56.

VanStone, James W. Tikchik Village: a nineteenth century riverine community in southwestern Alaska. Chicago, Field Museum of Natural History, 1968. 215-368 p. illus., maps. (Fieldiana: Anthropology, 56, no. 3)

Veniaminov, Innokentii. The condition of the Orthodox Church in Russian America: Innokentii Veniaminov's history of the Russian church in Alaska. Translated and edited by Robert Nichols and Robert

Croskey. Pacific Northwest Quarterly, 63 (1972): 41-54.

Vrangel', Ferdinand Petrovich von. The inhabitants of the Northwest Coast of America. Translated and edited by James W. VanStone. By Ferdinand Petrovich von Wrangell. Arctic Anthropology, 6, no. 2 (1970): 5-20.

Walton, W. B. Eskimo or Innuit dictionary. Seattle, 1901. 32 p.

Waugh, L. M. Influences of diet on the development of the jaw and face of the American Eskimo. Journal of Dental Research, 13 (1933): 149-151.

Waugh, L. M. Survey of mouth conditions, nutritional study and gnathodynamometer data in most primitive and populous native villages in Alaska. Journal of Dental Research, 16 (1936): 355-356.

Whitten, Norman E., Jr. Towards a classification of West Alaskan social structure. Alaska, University, Anthropological Papers, 12 (1964): 79-91.

Whymper, F. Russian America. Ethnological Society (London), Transactions, n.s., 7 (1869): 167-185.

Wiedemann, T. Cheechako into sourdough. Portland, 1942. 266 p.

Woldt, A., ed. Capitain Jacobsen's Reise an der Nordwestküste Amerikas. Leipzig, 1884.

Young, Steven B. Contributions to the ethnobotany of the St. Lawrence Island Eskimo. By Steven B. Young and Edwin S. Hall, Jr. Alaska, University, Anthropological Papers, 14, no. 2 (1969): 43-53.

*Zagoskin, L. A. Peshexodnaa opic chasti russkix vladenii v Amerike. St.-Petersburg, 1847-1848. 2 v.

Zagoskin, L. A. Puteshestvie i otkrytia v russkoi Amerike. St.-Petersburg, 1847.

Zagoskin, Lavrentiĭ Alekseevich. Lieutenant Zagoskin's travels in Russian America, 1842-1844. Edited by Henry N. Michael. Toronto, Published for the Arctic Institute of North America by University of Toronto Press, 1967. 14, 358 p. illus., maps. (Anthropology of the North: Translations from Russian Sources, 7)

01-15   West Greenland Eskimo

Ahrengot, V. and K. Eldon. Distribution of ABO-MN and Rh types among Eskimos in Southwest Greenland. Nature, 169 (1952): 1065.

Alsbirk, K. E. PTC taste sensitivity in Greenland Eskimos from Umanaq: distribution and correlation to ocular anterior chamber depth. By K. E. Alsbirk and P. H. Alsbirk. Human Heredity, 22 (1972): 445-452.

Anderson, J. Nachrichten von Island, Grönland und der Strasse Davis. Hamburg, 1746.

Anonymous. Kaladlit okalluktualliait. Godthaab, 1859-1963. 4 v.

Anonymous. New Herrnhut. Moravian Church Miscellany, 1 (1850): 81-90.

Bang, H. O. Plasma lipid and lipoprotein pattern in Greenlandic west-coast Eskimos. By H. O. Bang, J. Dyerberg, and Aase Brøndum Nielsen. Lancet, 1 (1971): 1143-1146.

Barfod, H. P. Dansk-grønlandsk ordliste til skolebrug. 2d ed. Godthaab, 1952. 34 p.

Bartels, M. C. A. Ein Eismesser der Eskimo in Groenland. Zeitschrift für Ethnologie, 31 (1899): 747-748.

Bartels, M. C. A. Geräthe der Eskimo aus Neu-Herrnhut bei Godhaab. Berliner Gesellschaft für Anthropologie, Ethnologie und Urgeschichte, Verhandlungen (1900): 542-543.

Bay-Schmith, E. Versuche über die schicksche Reaction bei Eskimos in Grönland. Klinische Wochenschrift, 8 (1929): 974-976.

Behrens, W. Ethnografisk beskrivelse over Nord Grønland. Kjøbenhavn, 1860. 46 p.

Berg, K. Genetic marker systems in Arctic populations. I. Lp and Ag data on the Greenland Eskimos. By K. Berg and A. W. Eriksson. Human Heredity, 21 (1971): 129-133.

Bergsland, Knut. On the validity of glottochronology. By Knut Bergsland and Hans Vogt. [With comment by Morris Swadesh.] Current Anthropology, 3 (1962): 115-153.

Bertelsen, A. Folkemedicinen i Grønland i aeldre og nyere tid. Copenhagen, Grønlandske Selskabs Aarsskrift, 1914.

Bertelsen, A. Grønlandsk medicinsk
Statistik og Nosografi. Meddelelser om
Grønland, 117, no. 3 (1940): 1-234; 117,
no. 4 (1943): 1-246.

Bertelsen, A. Navnegivning i Grønland.
Meddelelser om Grønland, 56 (1918): 221-
287.

Birket-Smith, K. Det eskimoiske
slaegtskabs-system. Geografisk
Tidsskrift, 30 (1927): 96-111.

*Birket-Smith, K. Ethnography of the
Egedesminde District. Meddelelser om
Grønland, 66 (1924): 1-484.

Birket-Smith, K. Etnografiske problemer i
Grønland. Geografisk Tidsskrift, 25
(1920): 179-197.

Birket-Smith, K. Foreløbigt bidrag til
Kap Farvel-Distrikternes kulturhistorie.
Meddelelser om Grønland, 53 (1917): 1-
38.

Birket-Smith, K. Opdagelse og
Udforskning. In Grønlandsbogen.
København, 1950: 15-40.

Birket-Smith, K. The Greenland bow.
Meddelelser om Grønland, 56, no. 1
(1918): 1-28.

Birket-Smith, K. The Greenlanders of the
present day. Greenland, 2 (1928): 1-207.

Bistrup, A. Eskimo women in Greenland.
Century Magazine, 82 (1911): 667-674.

Black, F. L., et al. Intensified
reactions to measles vaccine in
unexposed populations of American
Indians. Journal of Infectious Diseases,
124 (1971): 306-317.

Bohlen, Joseph Glenn. Circumpolar
chronobiology. Dissertation Abstracts
International, 32 (1971/1972): 6795B.
UM 72-15,340.

Bojlén, K. The influence of climate and
nutrition on age at menarche: a
historical review and a modern
hypothesis. By K. Bojlén and M. W.
Bentzon. Human Biology, 40 (1968): 69-
85.

Borreby, K., et al. [Nutrition Studies].
Denmark, Grønlands Styrelse, Beretninger
Verdrørende Grønland, nr. 3-I (1955): 7-
117.

Brierley, J. and F. Parsons. Notes on a
collection of ancient Eskimo skulls.
Royal Anthropological Institute of Great
Britain and Ireland, Journal, 36 (1906):
104-120.

Brun, E. Grønland after Krigen. Grønlands
Bogen, 2 (1950): 5-16.

Brun, E. Vor Opgave i Grønland. Grønland,
no. 1 (1952): 8-12.

Bruun, D. Arkaeologiske undersøgelser i
Julianehaabs Distrikt. Meddelelser om
Grønland, 16 (1896): 171-461.

Bugge, A. Mødet mellem gammelt og nyt i
grønlandsk tankegang. Grønlandske
Selskab, Arsskrift (1950): 136-144.

Bugge, A. The native Greenlander. Arctic,
5 (1952): 45-53.

Carmichael, D. M. Psychology and
ethnology. The Cambridge Expedition to
West Greenland, by H. I. Drever.
Geographical Journal, 94 (1939): 398-
401.

Cranz, D. Historie von Grönland. 2d ed.
Barby, 1770. 3 v.

Cranz, D. The history of Greenland.
London, 1767. 2 v.

Cummins, H. and V. Fabricus-Hansen.
Dermatoglyphics in Eskimos of West
Greenland. American Journal of Physical
Anthropology, n.s., 4 (1946): 395-402.

Dalager, L. Grønlandske relationer.
Kiebenhavn, 1752.

Dege, Wilhelm. Die Westküste Grönlands:
Bevölkerung, Wirtschaft und Siedlung im
Strukturwandel. Deutsche Geographische
Blätter, 50, nr. 1/2 (1965): 5-212.

Dege, Wilhelm. Die Westküste Grönlands im
Strukturwandel. Polarforschung, 6,
nr. 35 (1965): 12-19.

Dege, Wilhelm. Grönland ohne Eskimos.
Wiesbaden, Brockhaus, 1964. 284 p.
illus., map.

Denmark, Udvalget for Samfundsforskning i
Grønland. Samarbejdsproblemer mellem
grønlaendere og danskere i Vestgrønland.
København, 1963. 142 p. illus.
(Denmark, Udvalget for Samfundsforskning
i Grønland, Rapport, 9)

Edmonson, Munro S. A measurement of
relative racial difference. Current
Anthropology, 6 (1965): 167-198. [With
comments].

Egede, H. P. A description of Greenland.
London, 1745.

Egede, H. P. Ausführliche und wahrhafte
Nachricht vom Anfange und Fortgange der
grönländischen Mission. Hamburg, 1740.

Egede, H. P. Continuation af relationerne betreffende den grønlandske missions tilstand og beskaffenhed. Kjøbenhavn, 1741. 184 p.

Egede, H. P. Description et histoire naturelle du Groenland. Copenhague, 1763.

Egede, H. P. Det gamle Grønlands nye perlustration eller naturel-historie. Meddelelser om Grønland, 54 (1925): 305-431.

Egede, H. P. Nachrichten von Grönland. Kopenhagen, 1790.

Egede, H. P. Omstaendelig og udførlig relation angaaende den grønlandske missions begyndelse og fortsaettelse. Kjøbenhavn, 1738.

Egede, H. P. Relationer fra Grønland. Meddelelser om Grønland, 64 (1925): 1-304.

Egede, P. H. Dictionarium Groenlandico-Danico-Latinum. Hafniae, 1750.

Egede, P. H. Efterretninger om Grønland. Kjøbenhavn, 1788.

Egede, P. H. Grammatica grönlandico-danico-latina. Havniae, 1760.

Ehström, M. C. Inre Medicinska Undersökningar pa Nord-Grönland 1948-1949. Finska Läkaresallskapet, Handlingar, 93 (1950): 3-24.

Ehström, M. C. Internmedicenska Undersokningar pa Nord-Grönland 1948-1949. Nordisk Medicin, 44 (1950): 1668-1673, 1707-1710, 1750, 1787-1789, 1823-1825.

Elgström, C. Moderna Eskimaer. Stockholm, 1916.

Eriksson, A. W., et al. Adenylate kinase polymorphism in populations in Finland (Swedes, Finns, Lapps), in Maris, and in Greenland Eskimos. Humangenetik, 12 (1971): 123-130.

Eriksson, A. W., et al. Red cell phosphoglucomutase polymorphism in Finland-Swedes, Finns, Finnish Lapps, Maris (Cheremisses) and Greenland Eskimos, and segregation studies of PGM1 types in Lapp families. Human Heredity, 21 (1971): 140-153.

Eriksson, Aldur W. Population genetic characteristics of a Greenland Eskimo population. By Aldur W. Eriksson, Mikko Kirjarinta, and Hans Gürtler. Arctic Anthropology, 7, no. 1 (1970): 3-5.

Eriksson, Aldur W., et al. Adenosine deaminase polymorphism in Finland (Swedes, Finns, and Lapps), the Mari Republic (Cheremisses), and Greenland (Eskimos). American Journal of Human Genetics, 23 (1971): 568-577.

Fabricius, O. Den grønlandske ordbog. Kjøbenhavn, 1804.

Fabricius, O. Nöiagtig beskrivelse over alle Grönlaendernes fange-redskaber ved saelhundefangsten. Kongelige Danske Videnskabernes-Selskabs Skrivter, 5, no. 1 (1810): 125-178.

Fabricius, O. Nöiagtig beskrivelse over Grönlaendernes landdyr-, figle-, og fiskefangst med dertil hörende redskaber. Kongelige Danske Videnskabernes-Selskabs Skrivter, 6, no. 1 (1818): 231-272.

Fabricius, O. Udförlig beskrivelse over de grønlandske saele. Skrivter af Naturhistorie-Selskabet, 1, no. 1 (1790): 79-157.

Fabricius, Otto. Ethnographical works. Edited by Erik Holtved. København, C. A. Reitzel, 1962. 137 p. illus. (Meddelelser om Grønland, 140, no. 2)

Fabricus-Hansen, V. Blood groups and MN types of Eskimos. Journal of Immunology, 38 (1940): 405-411.

Faĭnberg, L. A. Grenlandiĭa i ee naselenie. Sovetskaĭa Etnografiĭa, no. 6 (1966): 47-56.

Finck, F. N. Die Grundbedeutung des grönländischen Subjektivs. Berliner Akademie, Sitzungsberichte, no. 1 (1905): 280-287.

Findlay, M. C. Impressions in Greenland. Contemporary Review, 1051 (1953): 32-36.

Findlay, M. C. Miss M. C. Findlay's investigations of sheep farming in West Greenland, 1951. Polar Record, 6 (1952): 528-529.

Findlay, M. C. Sheep farming in Greenland. Arctic, 6 (1952): 166-167.

Fischer-Möller, K. Skeletons from ancient Greenland graves. Meddelelser om Grønland, 119, no. 4 (1938): 1-30.

Forsius, Henrik. Opthalmological characteristics of Eskimos in Augpilagtok. By Henrik Forsius, A. W. Eriksson, and H. Luukka. Arctic Anthropology, 7, no. 1 (1970): 9-16.

Frederiksen, S. Aspects of European
influence in West Greenlandic poetry.
Midwest Folklore, 2 (1952): 251-261.

Frederiksen, S. European influences in
the poetry of Greenland. Georgetown
College Journal, 79, no. 6 (1951): 3-12.

Frederiksen, S. Henrik Lund. American
Philosophical Society, Proceedings, 96
(1952): 653-659.

Frederiksen, S. Stylistic forms in
Greenland Eskimo literature.
Copenhagen, 1954. 40 p.

Fries, T. M. Grönland, dess natur och
innevanare. Upsala, 1872.

Funch, J. C. W. Syv aar i Nordgrønland.
Viborg, 1840.

Fürst, C. M. and F. C. C. Hansen. Crania
groenlandica. Copenhagen, 1915. 234 p.

Gad, F. Samisk og Grønlandsk. Grønland,
11 (1956): 401-413.

Giesecke, K. L. Mineralogisches
Reisejournal über Grönland. Meddelelser
om Grønland, 35 (1910): 1-478.

Glahn, H. C. Anmaerkninger over de tre
første bøger af Hr. David Crantzes
Historie om Grønland. Kjøbenhavn, 1771.

Glahn, H. C. Dagbøger. København, 1921.
247 p.

Glahn, H. C. Forsøg til en afhandling om
Grønlaendernes skikke ved hvalfiskeriet.
Norske Videnskabers Selskab, Trondheim,
Skrifter, Nye Samling, 1 (1784): 273-
296.

Glahn, H. C. Om den grønlandske hund.
Norske Videnskabers Selskab, Trondheim,
Skrifter, Nye Samling, 1 (1784): 485-
496.

Goldschmidt, Verner. Problems in changing
criminal law in West Greenland. Archives
of Environmental Health, 18 (1969): 122-
126.

Gosch, C. C. A., ed. Danish Arctic
Expeditions, 1605 to 1620. London,
1897. 2 v.

Gudmand-Høyer, E. Hyppigheden og den
praktiske betydning af
laktosemalabsorption i Vestgrønland. By
E. Gudmand-Høyer, S. Jarnum, and A.
McNair. Nordisk Medicin, 86 (1971):
1195.

Gussow, Zachary. A preliminary report of
kayak-angst among the Eskimo of West
Greenland: a study in sensory

deprivation. International Journal of
Social Psychiatry, 9 (1963): 18-26.

Gysin, Alfred. Mission im Heimatland der
Eskimos. Hamburg, Appel, 1966. 67 p.
illus.

Haan, L. F. Beschryving van de Straat
Davids. Amsterdam, 1720.

Hansen, Keld. The people of the Far
North. Folk, 11/12 (1969/1970): 97-108.

Hansen, P. M. Jagt og fiskeri. Grønlands
Bogen, 2 (1950): 59-82.

Hansen, S. Bidrag til Eskimoernes
kraniologi. Meddelelser om Grønland, 17
(1895): 347-356.

Hansen, S. Bidrag til Vestgrønlaendernes
anthropologi. Meddelelser om Grønland, 7
(1893): 163-248.

Harrington, Richard. Greenland's new era.
Beaver, 299, no. 4 (1968/1969): 44-53.

Harris, Z. S. Structural restatements.
International Journal of American
Linguistics, 13 (1947): 47-55.

Harvald, Bent. The incidence of cardiac
malformations in Greenlandic Eskimos. By
Bent Harvald and Jørgen Hels. Acta
Medica Scandinavica, 185 (1969): 41-44.

Hertz, Ole. Plant utilization in a West
Greenland hunting community. Folk, 10
(1968): 37-44.

Hirschsprung, G. Lerslettemanden.
Grønland, no. 8 (1964): 300-306.

Holm, G. Beskrivelse af ruiner i
Julianehaabs Distrikt. Meddelelser om
Grønland, 6 (1894): 57-145.

Holtved, E. Archaeological investigations
in the Thule District. Meddelelser om
Grønland, 141, no. 1 (1944): 1-492.

Holtved, Erik. Samuel Kleinschmidt i
anleding af 150-året for hans fødsel.
Grønland, no. 6 (1964): 217-230.

Holtved, Erik. Tôrnârssuk, an Eskimo
deity. Folk, 5 (1963): 157-171.

Hymes, Dell H. Validity of
glottochronology. Current Anthropology,
5 (1964): 324-326.

Isâk, of Igdlorpait. Îsâp assilialiai.
Isaks bildebog. Text by G. N. Bugge.
Lyngby, Det Grønlandske Landsbibliotek,
Stadsbiblioteket i Lyngby, 1969. 76 p.
illus.

Israel, H. Alte eskimoische Wertzeuge mit eisernen Klingen. Dresden, Staatliches Museum für Völkerkunde, Abhandlungen und Berichte, 24 (1965): 5-30.

Israel, Heinz. Kulturwandel grönlandischer Eskimo im 18. Jahrhundert. Wandlungen in Gesellschaft und Wirtschaft unter dem Einfluss der Herrnhüter Brüdermission. Berlin, Akademie-Verlag, 1969. 6, 203 p. illus., map. (Dresden, Staatliche Museum für Völkerkunde, Abhandlungen und Berichte, 29)

Jackson, N. With the "doctor boat" along the Greenland coast. Geographical Review, 33 (1943): 545-568.

Jensen, B. Lilleputsamfundet. Grønland, no. 5 (1959): 181-192.

Jensen, B. Lilleputsamfundet og de Fremmede. Grønland, no. 8 (1959): 281-290.

Jensen, Bent. Development policy and Greenland man; field studies, impressions, and points of view. Folk, 11/12 (1969/1970): 287-307.

Jensen, Bent. Folkways of Greenland dog-keeping. Folk, 3 (1961): 43-66.

Jensen, Bent. Notes on an Eskimo 'thanking act'. Folk, 5 (1963): 188-198.

Jørgensen, J. B. De Første Eskimoes pa Grønland. Grønland, no. 7 (1954): 265-271.

Jørgensen, J. B. Hvad Skeletfund Kan Berette om Sygdonsme Hos de Første Eskimoer pa Grønland. Grønland, no. 8 (1954): 306-311.

Jørgensen, J. B. The Eskimo skeleton. Meddelelser om Grønland, 146, no. 2 (1953): 1-154.

Kane, E. K. Walrus hunting a century ago. Beaver, 284 (Dec. 1953): 35.

Kjer, J. and C. Rasmussen. Dansk-Grønlandsk ordbog. Kjøbenhavn, 1893.

Klausen, L. A. Greenlandic dictionary of useful phrases. Washington, D.C., 1942. 58 p.

Kleinschmidt, S. Den grønlandske ordbog. Kjøbenhavn, 1871.

Kleinschmidt, Samuel P. Grammatik der grönländischen Sprache, mit teilweisem Einschluss des Labradordialekts. Hildesheim, Olms, 1968. 12, 182 p.

Kleinschmidt, Samuel P. Grammatik der grönländischen Sprache, mit teilweisem Einschluss des Labradordialects. Berlin, G. Reimer, 1851. 10, 182 p.

Kleinschmidt, Samuel P. Kleinschmidts Briefe an Theodor Bourquin. Edited by Erik Holtved. København, C. A. Reitzel, 1964. 124 p. (Meddelelser om Grønland, 140, no. 3)

Kleivan, Helge. Acculturation, ecology and human choice: case studies from Labrador and South Greenland. Folk, 6, pt. 1 (1964): 63-74.

Kleivan, Helge. Culture and ethnic identity; on modernization and ethnicity in Greenland. Folk, 11/12 (1969/1970): 209-234.

Kleivan, Inge. Language and ethnic identity: language policy and debate in Greenland. Folk, 11/12 (1969/1970): 235-285.

Kleivan, Inge. Mitârtut; vestiges of the Eskimo sea-woman cult in West Greenland. København, C. A. Reitzels Forlag, 1960. 30 p. (Meddelelser om Grønland, 161, no. 5)

Kleivan, Inge. Song duels in West Greenland--joking relationship and avoidance. Folk, 13 (1970): 9-36.

Knudsen, A. Status for flytningerne fra Upernavik. Grønland, no. 4 (1964): 121-134.

Knuth, Eigil. Âlut Kangermio. Aron fra Kangek'--Aron of Kangek'. Godthåb, Det Grønlandske Forlag, 1968. 111 p. illus.

Knuth, Eigil. Singajuk's family saga. Folk, 5 (1963): 209-218.

Koegels, J. Letters. Moravian Church Miscellany, 1 (1850): 249-250, 356-359; 2 (1851): 191-192.

Krabbe, T. N. Greenland. Copenhagen, 1930. 145 p.

Kragh, P. Udtog af missionair P. Kraghs dagbog. Haderslev, 1875. 2 v.

Kreutzmann, J. De to Venner. Grønlandske Selskab, Arsskrift (1951): 132-136.

Kreutzmann, J. En Fortaelling om Blodhaevn. Grønlandske Selskab, Arsskrift (1950): 145-147.

Larsen, H. Paleo-Eskimo in Disko Bay, West Greenland. International Congress of the Anthropological and Ethnological Sciences, Acts, 5 (1960): 574-579.

Larsen, H. and J. Meldgaard.   Paleo-Eskimo cultures in Disko Bugt, West Greenland. Meddelelser om Grønland, 161, no. 2 (1958): 1-75.

Laughlin, W. S. and J. B. Jørgenson. Isolate variation in Greenlandic Eskimo crania. Acta Genetica et Statistica Medica, 6 (1956): 3-12.

Laughlin, William S.   Races of mankind: continental and local. Alaska, University, Anthropological Papers, 8 (1959/1960): 89-99.

Lauridsen, P.   Bibliographia groenlandica. Meddelelser om Grønland, 12 (1890): 137-161, 199-217.

Laursen, Dan.   The place names of North Greenland. København, C. A. Reitzels Forlag, 1972.   443 p.   illus., maps. (Meddelelser om Grønland, 180, no. 2)

Le Mouel, J. F.   Connaissance et utilisation des végétaux chez les Eskimo Naujamiut (Groenland occidental). Journal de l'Agriculture Tropicale et de Botanique Appliqué, 16 (1971): 469-494.

Lund-Larsen, Kari.   Circulatory responses of the hand of Greenlanders to local cold stimulation. By Kari Lund-Larsen, Marie Wika, and John Krog. Arcitc Anthropology, 7, no. 1 (1970): 21-25.

Lyngby Kunstforening.   Kâgssagssuk. Sagnet om den foraeldreløse. Kâgssagssuk. The legend of the orphan boy.   København, Spektrum, 1967.   65 p.   illus.

MacMillan, M.   Far North with "Captain Mac". National Geographic Magazine, 100 (1951): 465-513.

Marcussen, P. V. and J. Rendal.   En Studie over Syphilis i en Grønlandsk Boplads. Ugeskrift for Laeger, 111 (1949): 1-4.

Markham, A. H., ed.   The voyages and works of John Davis the Navigator. London, 1880.   373 p.

Mathiassen, T.   Ancient Eskimo settlements in the Kangamiut Area. Meddelelser om Grønland, 91 (1931): 1-150.

Mathiassen, T.   Arkaeologiske undersøgelser i Sukkertoppens Distrikt. Geografisk Tidsskrift, 33 (1930): 189-197.

Mathiassen, T.   Arkaeologiske undersøgelser i Uperniviks Distrikt. Geografisk Tidsskrift, 33 (1930): 2-17.

Mathiassen, T.   Contributions to the archaeology of Disko Bay. Meddelelser om Grønland, 93, no. 2 (1934): 1-192.

Mathiassen, T.   Eskimo finds from the Kangerdlugssuaq region. Meddelelser om Grønland, 104, no. 9 (1934): 1-25.

Mathiassen, T.   Eskimo migrations in Greenland. Geographical Review, 25 (1935): 408-422.

Mathiassen, T.   Inugsuk, a mediaeval Eskimo settlement. Meddelelser om Grønland, 77 (1930): 145-340.

Mathiassen, T.   Sermermiut. Grønland, no. 5 (1964): 161-173.

Mathiassen, T.   The Eskimo archeology of Greenland. Smithsonian Institution, Annual Reports of the Board of Regents (1936): 397-404.

Mathiassen, T. and E. Holtved.   The Eskimo archaeology of Julianhaab District. Meddelelser om Grønland, 118, no. 1 (1936): 1-141.

Mattox, William Gurney.   Fishing in Greenland 1910-1966: the development of a new native industry. Dissertation Abstracts International, 33 (1972/1973): 265B.

McCracken, Robert D.   Lactase deficiency: an example of dietary evolution. Current Anthropology, 12 (1971): 479-517.

Meldgaard, J.   A Paleo-Eskimo culture in West Greenland. American Antiquity, 17 (1952): 222-230.

Meldgaard, J.   Fra en Grønlandsk Mumiehule. København, Fra Nationalmuseets Arbejdsmark (1953): 14-20.

Meldgaard, J.   Grønlaendere i tre tusinde Aar. Grønland, nos. 4-5 (1958): 121-129, 170-178.

Meldgaard, Jørgen.   Traditional sculpture in Greenland. Beaver, 298, no. 2 (1967/1968): 54-59.

Mey, Jacob.   On the notion 'to be' in Eskimo. In John W. M. Verhaar, ed. The Verb 'Be' and Its Synonyms. Part 2. Dordrecht, Reidel, 1968: 1-34. (Foundations of Language, Supplementary Series, 6)

Mørch, Morten.   Tupilangmik pissaussumik ukiume 1864-ne (concerning the tupilak that was caught in 1864). Folk, 6, pt. 2 (1964): 91-101.

Morgan, L. H.   Systems of consanguinity
and affinity. Smithsonian Contributions
to Knowledge, 17 (1871): 291-382.

*Nansen, F.   Eskimo life.   London, 1893.

*Nansen, F.   Eskimoliv.   Christiania, 1891.

Neergaard, Helga Bruun de.   Avigtat;
Grønlandske skindmønstre.   København,
Høst, 1962.   28 p.   illus.

Nellemann, George.   Applied anthropology
in Greenland in the 1860's. H. J. Rink's
administration and view of culture.
Folk, 8/9 (1966/1967): 222-241.

Nellemann, George.   Caribou hunting in
West Greenland. Folk, 11/12 (1969/1970):
133-153.

Nellemann, George.   Hinrich Rink and
applied anthropology in Greenland in the
1830's. Human Organization, 28 (1969):
166-174.

Nellemann, George.   Mitârneq: a West
Greenland winter ceremony. Folk, 2
(1960): 99-113.

Nellemann, George.   The gelding of dogs in
Greenland. Folk, 5 (1963): 245-248.

Nielsen, Isak.   Qarsorsat
oqalugtuagssartât (the story about
Qarsorsat). Folk, 6, pt. 2 (1964): 89-
90.

Nielsen, J. C., et al.   Gm types of
Greenland Eskimos. Human Heredity, 21
(1971): 405-419.

Nielson, F.   Grønlands Kultur.
Turistforeningen for Danmark, Arbog
(1952/1953): 65-88.

Nilsson, L.-O.   Screening for haemoglobin
and lactate dehydrogenase variants in
the Icelandic, Swedish, Finnish,
Lappish, Mari and Greenland Eskimo
populations. By L.-O. Nilsson and A. W.
Eriksson. Human Heredity, 22 (1972):
372-379.

Nooter, Gert.   Tiderida, van Eskimo tot
Groenlander.   's-Gravenhage,
Staatsdrukkerij- en Uitgeverijbedrijf,
1971.   47 p.   illus.

Olsen, P. R.   Acculturation in the Eskimo
songs of the Greenlanders. International
Folk Music Council, Yearbook, 4 (1972):
32-37.

Orlova, E. P.   Naselenie Grenlandii. In A.
V. Efimov and S. A. Tokarev, eds. Narody
Ameriki. Vol. 1.   Moskva, Izdatel'stvo
Akademiia Nauk SSSR, 1959: 594-608.

Paine, Robert.   Animals as capital:
comparisôns among northern nomadic
herders and hunters. Anthropological
Quarterly, 44 (1971): 157-172.

Parbøl, I.   Qivitut. Grønland, no. 12
(1955): 452-463.

Paterson, T. T.   Anthropological studies
in Greenland. Royal Anthropological
Institute of Great Britain and Ireland,
Journal, 69 (1939): 45-76.

Peary, Robert E.   Correspondence between
Lieutenant R. E. Peary and Professor F.
W. Putnam on Arctic ethnology. By R. E.
Peary and F. W. Putnam. Edited by Ralph
W. Dexter. Ethnohistory, 16 (1969): 177-
189.

Pedersen, A.   Auf Jagd in Grönland.   Wien,
1953.   158 p.

Pedersen, P. O.   Dental investigations of
Greenland Eskimos. Royal Society of
Medicine (London), Proceedings, 40
(1947): 726-732.

Pedersen, P. O.   Investigations into
dental conditions of about 3,000 ancient
and modern Greenlanders. Dental Record,
58 (1938): 191-198.

Pedersen, P. O. and D. B. Scott.   Replica
studies of the surfaces of teeth from
Alaskan Eskimo, West Greenland natives,
and American Whites. Acta Odontologica
Scandinavica, 9 (1951): 261-292.

Pedersen, P. O. and E. Hinsch.   Numerical
variations in Greenland Eskimo
dentition. Acta Odontologica
Scandinavica, 1 (1939): 93-134.

Persson, Ib.   Alloalbuminemia: a search
for albumin variants in Greenland
Eskimos. By I. Persson, Liisa Melartin,
and A. Gilberg. Human Heredity, 21
(1971): 57-59.

Persson, Ib.   Anthropological
investigations of the population of
Greenland. København, 1970.   78 p.
illus., map.   (Meddelelser om Grønland,
180, nr. 1)

Persson, Ib.   The distribution of serum
types in West Greenland Eskimos. Acta
Genetica et Statistica Medica, 18
(1968): 261-270.

Persson, Ib, et al.   Ten Gm factors and
the Inv system in Eskimos in Greenland.
Human Heredity, 22 (1972): 519-528.

Petersen, Robert.   Family ownership and
right of disposition in Sukkertoppen
District, West Greenland. Folk, 5
(1963): 269-281.

Petersen, Robert. Some regulating factors in the hunting life of Greenlanders. Folk, 7 (1965): 107-124.

Petersen, Robert. The Greenland tupilak. Folk, 6, pt. 2 (1964): 73-101.

Pleiner, R. Bericht über die metallkundliche Untersuchung zweier Eskimo-Werkzeuge. Dresden, Staatliches Museum für Völkerkunde, Abhandlungen und Berichte, 24 (1965): 31-36.

Poincy, L. de. The Eskimos of Davis Straits in 1656. Scottish Geographical Magazine, 28 (1912): 281-294.

Porsild, M. P. On Eskimo stone rows in Greenland. Geographical Review, 6 (1918): 297-309.

*Porsild, M. P. Studies on the material culture of the Eskimo in West Greenland. Meddelelser om Grønland, 51 (1915): 113-250.

Porsild, M. P. Über einige Geräte der Eskimo. Zeitschrift für Ethnologie, 44 (1912): 600-623.

Porsild, Morten. På sygebesøg hos Lôqe, rejseskitse fra omkring århundredskiftet fundet blandt efterladte papirer. Grønland, no. 12 (1965): 429-434.

Rasmussen, C. Grønlandsk sproglaere. Kjøbenhavn, 1888. 201 p.

Rasmussen, Christian. Grønlandsk sproglaere. [Nyt. opl.] Århus, 1971. 11, 201 p.

Rasmussen, K. Myter og sagn fra Grønland, 2. Kjøbenhavn, 1924. 1-356.

Rasmussen, K. The people of the Polar North. London, 1908.

Rink, H. Danish Greenland. London, 1877.

Rink, H. Eskimoiske eventyr og sagn. Kjøbenhavn, 1866-1871. 2 v.

Rink, H. Grønland geografisk og statistisk beskrevet. Kjøbenhavn, 1857. 2 v.

Rink, H. Om Grønlaendernes gamle tro og hvad der af samme er bevaret under Kristendommen. Aarbøger for Nordisk Oldkyndighed og Historie, 3 (1868): 192-256.

Rink, H. Tales and traditions of the Eskimo. Edinburgh, 1875. 472 p.

Ryberg, C. Dansk-Grønlandsk tolk. Kjøbenhavn, 1891.

Ryberg, C. Om erhvervs- og befolkningsforholdene i Grønland. Geografisk Tidsskrift, 17 (1904): 69-92.

Saabye, H. E. Brudstykker af en dagbog holden i Grønland. Odense, 1816.

Saabye, H. E. Fragmenter af en dagbok. Stockholm, 1817.

Saabye, H. E. Greenland. London, 1818.

Sagild, Uffe, et al. Epidemiological studies in Greenland 1962-1964. I. Diabetes mellitus in Eskimos. Acta Medica Scandinavica, 179 (1966): 29-39.

Sandström, Lennart. Leva på Grönland. Stockholm, LT, 1971. 161 p. illus.

Schultz-Lorentzen, C. W. Den grønlandske ordbog. Kjøbenhavn, 1926.

Schultz-Lorentzen, C. W. Dictionary of the West Greenland Eskimo language. Meddelelser om Grønland, 69 (1927): 1-303.

Schultz-Lorentzen, C. W. Eskimoernes indvandring i Grønland. Meddelelser om Grønland, 26 (1904): 289-330.

Schultz-Lorentzen, C. W. Intellectual culture of the Greenlanders. Greenland, 2 (1928): 209-270.

Schultz-Lorentzen, Christian W. Den grønlandske ordbog. Grønlandsk-dansk. New ed. Godthåb, Det Grønlandske Forlag, 1967. 7, 360 p.

Schultz-Lorentzen, D. L. A grammar of the West Greenland language. Meddelelser om Grønland, 129, no. 3 (1945): 1-103.

Skeller, E. Øjensgdomme i Grønland. Ugeskrift for Laeger, 111 (1949): 529-532.

Solberg, O. Beiträge zur Vorgeschichte der Osteskimo. Norske Videnskaps-Akademi, Oslo, Historisk-filosofisk Klasse, Skrifter, no. 2 (1907): 1-92.

Steensby, H. P. Ethnografiske og antropogeografiske rejsestudier i Nord-Grønland. Meddelelser om Grønland, 50 (1912): 133-173.

Steenstrup, K. J. V. Beretning om undersøgelsesrejserne i Nord-Grønland. Meddelelser om Grønland, 5 (1893): 1-41.

Stefansson, V., ed. The three voyages of Martin Frobisher. London, 1938. 2 v.

Stiasny, G. Volkslieder und Sagen der westgrönländischen Eskimo. Wien, Kaiserlich-Königlichen Geographischen

Gesellschaft, Mitteilungen, 51 (1908):
327-335.

Swadesh, M.   South Greenlandic paradigms.
International Journal of American
Linguistics, 14 (1948): 29-36.

Swadesh, M.   South Greenlandic. Viking
Fund Publications in Anthropology, 6
(1946): 30-54.

Swenander, G.   Harpun-, kastpil- och
lansspetsar fran Väst-Grönland. Kungliga
Svenska Vetenskapsakademiens Handlingar,
40, no. 3 (1906): 1-45.

Thalbitzer, W. C.   A phonetical study of
the Eskimo language. Meddelelser om
Grønland, 31 (1904): 1-405.

Thalbitzer, W. C.   Cultic games and
festivals in Greenland. International
Congress of Americanists, Proceedings,
21, vol. 2 (1924): 236-255.

Thalbitzer, W. C.   Folklore from West
Greenland. Meddelelser om Grønland, 40
(1921): 496-564.

Thalbitzer, W. C.   Grønlandsk
Litteraturhistorie. Grønlands Bogen, 2
(1950): 225-250.

Thalbitzer, W. C.   Inuit sange og danse
fra Grönland. Kjøbenhavn, 1939.   75 p.

Thalbitzer, W. C.   The Aleutian language
compared with Greenlandic. International
Journal of American Linguistics, 2
(1921): 40-57.

Thomsen, T.   Eskimo archaeology.
Greenland, 2 (1928): 271-329.

Thorborg, N. B., et al.   Trikinose paa
Grønland. Ugeskrift for Laeger, 110
(1948): 595-602.

Thorhallesen, E.   Beskrivelse over
missionerne i Grønlands søndre distrikt.
København, 1914.   116 p.

Thuren, H.   On the Eskimo music of
Greenland. Meddelelser om Grønland, 40
(1911): 1-45.

Trebitsch, R.   Bei den Eskimos in
Westgrönland.   Berlin, 1909.

Trebitsch, R.   Die "blauen Geburtsflecke"
bei den Eskimos in Westgrönland. Archiv
für Anthropologie, 34 (1907): 237-242.

Tylor, E. B.   Old Scandinavian
civilisation among the modern Esquimaux.
Royal Anthropological Institute of Great
Britain and Ireland, Journal, 13 (1884):
348-357.

Vebaek, M.   De sma bopladser. Grønland,
no. 5 (1959): 193-199.

Vebaek, M.   Sagnet om Kagssagssuk.
Grønland, no. 11 (1959): 425-435.

Vebaek, M.   Tuneq-en indlandsbo. Grønland,
no. 6 (1959): 230-232.

Vebaek, Mâliârak.   Umiaríssat, a boat of
ill omen. Folk, 11/12 (1969/1970): 79-
81.

Waagstein, P.   Ilulisane nakorsak.
København, Nyt Nordisk Forlag, 1959.
131 p.   illus., map.

Whitaker, W. L.   The question of season
sterility among the Eskimos. Science, 88
(1938): 214-215.

Worster, W. W.   Eskimo folklore and myths.
Edinburgh Review, 242 (1925): 94-107.

Zavatti, Silvio.   La poesia degli
Eschimesi. Nuova Antologia, 486 (1962):
99-106.

Zorgdrager, C. G.   Bloeyende opkomst der
aloude en hedendaagsche groenlandsche
visschery.   Amsterdam, 1728.

Zorgdrager, C. G.   Histoire des peches,
des découvertes et des établissemens des
Hollandois dans les mers du nord.
Paris, 1801.   3 v.

01-16   Yuit

Ackerman, R.   Siberians of the New World.
Expedition, 1, no. 4 (1959): 24-35.

Antropova, V. V.   Sovremennaîa Chukotskaîa
i Eskimosskaîa Reznaîa Kost'. Akademiîa
Nauk SSSR, Muzeî Antropologiî i
Etnografiî, Sbornik, 15 (1953): 5-96.

APN Novosti Press Agency.   The bone
carvers of Uelen. North, 15, no. 4
(1968): 29-33.

Arutîunov, Sergeî Aleksandrovich.   Drevnie
kul'tury aziafskikh eskimosov.   Moskva,
Nauka, 1969.   206 p.   illus.

Bergsland, Knut.   The Eskimo shibboleth
inuk/yuk. In To Honor Roman Jakobson;
Essays on the Occasion of His Seventieth
Birthday, 11 October 1966.   The Hague,
Mouton, 1967: 203-221.   (Janua
Linguarum, Series Maior, 31)

Bogdanovich, K. I.   Ocherki Chukotskogo
Poluostrova.   St. Petersburg, 1901.
254 p.

Bogoras, W. G. Early migrations of the Eskimo between Asia and America. International Congress of Americanists, Proceedings, 21, vol. 2 (1924): 216-235.

Bogoras, W. G. Igry Malykh Narodnostei Severa. Akademiía Nauk SSSR, Muzeĭ Antropologiĭ i Etnografiĭ, Sbornik, 11 (1949): 237-254.

*Bogoras, W. G. Materialy po ĭAzyku Aziatskikh Eskimosov. Leningrad, 1949. 255 p.

Bogoras, W. G. Osnovnye Tipy Fol'klora Severnoi Evrazu-i Severnoi Ameriki. Sovetskii Fol'klor, no. 4-5 (1936): 29-50.

*Bogoras, W. G. The Chukchee. New York, 1904-1909. 2 v.

*Bogoras, W. G. The Eskimo of Siberia. American Museum of Natural History, Memoirs, 12 (1910): 417-456.

Bogoraz, V. G. Einshtein i Religiĭa. Moscow, 1923. 120 p.

Burnham, J B. Siwashing in Siberia. American Wildlife, 11, no. 3 (1922): 6-9, 15.

Buturlin, S. A. Polozhenie tuzemtsev Chukotsko-Anadyrskogo Kraĭa. Sovetskaĭa Aziĭa, 2, no. 2 (1926): 90-92.

Cadzow, D. A. Objects from St. Lawrence Island. Indian Notes, 2 (1925): 122-125.

Cameron, J. Correlations between cranial capacity and cranial length, breadth, and height. American Journal of Physical Anthropology, 11 (1928): 259-299.

Carlson, Gerald F. Two on the rocks. New York, McKay, 1966. 12, 193 p. illus.

Chard, C. S. Eskimo archaeology in Siberia. Southwestern Journal of Anthropology, 11 (1955): 150-177.

Choris, Louis. An early nineteenth-century artist in Alaska; Louis Choris and the First Kotzebue Expedition. Edited by James W. VanStone. Pacific Northwest Quarterly, 51 (1960): 145-158.

Christensen, L. A. Besøg pa Diomede-øen. Grønlandske Selskab, Arsskrift (1951): 124-131.

Collins, H. B. Ancient culture of St. Lawrence Island. Smithsonian Institution, Explorations and Field-Work (1930): 135-144.

Collins, H. B. Archaeological investigations in northern Alaska.

Smithsonian Institution, Explorations and Field-Work (1932): 103-112.

Collins, H. B. Archaeology of St. Lawrence Island. Smithsonian Miscellaneous Collections, 96, no. 1 (1937): 1-424.

Collins, H. B. Archaeology of the Bering Sea region. Pacific Science Congress, Proceedings, 5, vol. 4 (1934): 2825-2839.

Collins, H. B. Prehistoric art of the Alaskan Eskimo. Smithsonian Miscellaneous Collections, 81, no. 14 (1929): 1-52.

Collins, H. B. Prehistoric Eskimo culture of Alaska. Smithsonian Institution, Explorations and Field-Work (1929): 147-156.

Collins, H. B. The ancient Eskimo culture of northwestern Alaska. Smithsonian Institution, Explorations and Field-Work (1928): 141-150.

Connelly, Dolly. Walrus skin boat. Beaver, 296, no. 2 (1965/1966): 12-21.

Coxe, W. Account of the Russian discoveries between Asia and America. 4th ed. London, 1804.

Dall, W. H. Alaska and its resources. Boston, 1870. 378-385 p.

Dall, W. H. The native tribes of Alaska. American Association for the Advancement of Science, Proceedings, 34 (1885): 363-379.

Dunn, Ethel. Educating the small peoples of the Soviet North: the limits of culture change. Arctic Anthropology, 5, no. 1 (1968): 1-31.

Emel'ĭanova, N. M. K voprosu o konversii v eskimosskom ĭazyke. Akademiĭa Nauk SSSR, Otdelenie Literatury i ĭAzyka, Izvestiĭa, 23 (1964): 36-43.

Faĭnberg, L. K Voprosu o Rodovom Stroe y Eskimosov. Sovetskaĭa Etnografiĭa, no. 2 (1955): 82-99.

Faĭnberg, L. A. Obshchestvennyĭ stroĭ eskimosov i aleutov; ot materialskogo roda k sosedskoĭ obshchine. Moskva, Nauka, 1964. 257 p. illus., maps.

Friedman, H. Bird bones from Eskimo ruins on St. Lawrence Island. Washington Academy of Sciences, Journal, 24 (1934): 83-96.

Geist, O. W. and F. G. Rainey. Archaeological excavations at Kukulik.

Alaska, University, Miscellaneous
Publications, 2 (1936): 1-391.

Gerland, G. Zur Ethnographie des
äussersten Nordostens von Asien.
Gesellschaft für Erdkunde (Berlin),
Zeitschrift, 18 (1883): 194-222.

Gillsäter, S. Die grausame Jagd oder das
Walross und der Eskimo. Atlantis, 35,
no. 1 (1963): 1-10.

Grinnell, G. B. The natives of the Alaska
coast region. Harriman Alaska
Expedition, 1 (1901): 171-178.

Hammerich, Louis L. An Arctic hunting
method mentioned in the Bible? Folk, 5
(1963): 133-142.

Hanson, Wayne C. Radioactivity in
Northern Alaskan Eskimos and their
foods, summer 1962. By W. C. Hanson, H.
E. Palmer, and B. I. Griffin. Health
Physics, 10 (1964): 421-429.

Heinrich, A. Some present-day
acculturative innovations in a
nonliterate Society. American
Anthropologist, 52 (1950): 235-242.

Heinrich, Albert. Some formal aspects of
a kinship system. By Albert Heinrich and
Russell L. Anderson. Current
Anthropology, 12 (1971): 541-557.

Heinrich, Albert C. A non-European system
of color classification. Anthropological
Linguistics, 14 (1972): 220-227.

Heizer, R. F. Aconite poison whaling in
Asia and America. U.S. Bureau of
American Ethnology, Bulletin, 133
(1943): 415-468.

Hippler, Arthur E. From village to town:
an intermediate step in the
acculturation of Alaska Eskimos.
Minneapolis, University of Minnesota,
Training Center for Community Programs,
1970. 68 p. ERIC ED045247.

Hodge, F. W. An Eskimo toboggan.
Masterkey, 24 (1950): 193.

Hooper, W. H. Ten months among the tents
of the Tuski. London, 1853.

Hrdlička, A. Catalogue of human crania in
the United States National Museum
collections. United States National
Museum, Proceedings, 94 (1944): 1-172.

Hrdlička, A. Ritual ablation of front
teeth in Siberia and America.
Smithsonian Miscellaneous Collections,
99, no. 3 (1940): 1-32.

Hughes, C. C. An Eskimo deviant from the
"Eskimo" type of social organization.
American Anthropologist, 60 (1958):
1140-1147.

Hughes, Charles C. "The Eskimos" from The
Peoples of Siberia. Alaska, University,
Anthropological Papers, 12 (1964): 1-13.

*Hughes, Charles Campbell. An Eskimo
village in the modern world. With the
collaboration of Jane M. Hughes.
Ithaca, Cornell University Press, 1960.
14, 419 p. illus., maps.

Hughes, Charles Campbell. Translation of
I. K. Voblov's "Eskimo ceremonies".
Alaska, University, Anthropological
Papers, 7 (1958/1959): 71-90.

Hughes, Charles Campbell. Under four
flags: recent culture change among the
Eskimos. Current Anthropology, 6 (1965):
3-69. [With comments].

Hughes, Jane Murphy. An epidemiological
study of psychopathology in an Eskimo
village. Dissertation Abstracts, 21
(1960/1961): 2073. UM 60-6457.

Ivanov, S. V. Chukotsko-Eskimosskaîa
Gravîura na Kosti. Sovetskaîa
Etnografiîa, no. 4 (1949): 107-124.

Ivanov, S. V. Materialy po
Izobrazitel'nomu Iskusstvu Narodov
Sibiri. Akademiîa Nauk SSSR, Institut
Etnografiĭ, Trudy, n.s., 22, (1954): 1-
838.

Jochelson, W. Past and present
subterranean dwellings of the tribes of
North Eastern Asia and North Western
America. International Congress of
Americanists, Proceedings, 1º, vol. 2
(1906): 115-123.

Kalinov, I. Tam, gde nachinaetsîa utro
strany. Na Rubezhe, 17, no. 2 (1956):
140-149.

Keithahn, Edward L. Eskimo adventure;
another journey into the primitive.
Seattle, Superior, 1963. 170 p. illus.

Kirillov, N. V. Sanitarnaîa Obstanovka.
Vestnik Obshchestoennoi Gigieny,
Sudebnoi i Prakticheskoi Meditsiny, 44
(1908): 1769-1799.

Kivagmé. Skazochnik Kivagme. Magadan,
Magadanskoe Knizhnoe Izdatel'stvo, 1962.
134 p.

Kuftin, B. A. Spisok Naibolee
Malochislennykh Narodnostei SSSR.
Antropologicheskii Zhurnal, 14, no. 3/4
(1926): 91-93.

Kuznetsov, M. A. K voprosu o proiskhozhdenii snezhnykh iglu. Letopis' Severa, 4 (1964): 239-244.

Laguna, F. de. The prehistory of northern North America as seen from the Yukon. Society for American Archaeology, Memoirs, 3 (1947): 1-360.

Leighton, A. H. and C. C. Hughes. Notes on Eskimo patterns of suicide. Southwestern Journal of Anthropology, 11 (1955): 327-338.

Levin, M. G. Antropologicheskie tipy Sibiri i ikh genezis. Moscow, 1956. 27 p.

Levin, M. G. Antropologicheskie Tipy Sibiri. In Narody Sibiri. Moscow, 1956: 108-114.

Levin, M. G. Drevnie pereseleniîa cheloveka v severnoi Azii po dannym antropologii. Akademiîa Nauk SSSR, Institut Etnografiĭ, Trudy, n.s., 16 (1951): 469-496.

Levin, M. G. Materialy po kraniologii severovostochnoi Azii. Moskva Universitet, Nauchno-issledovatel'skii Institut i Muzei Antropologii, Kratkie Soobshcheniîa o Nauchnykh Rabotakh, 1938-39. Moskva, 1941.

Lîapunova, R. G. Ekspeditsiîa I. G. Voznesenskogo i ee znachenie dlîa etnografii Russkoĭ Ameriki. Akademiîa Nauk SSSR, Muzeĭ Antropologii i Etnografii, Sbornik, 24 (1967): 5-33.

Lundman, Bertil. Ein paar kleine Bemerkungen über die Anthropologie der Beringvölker. Folk, 5 (1963): 233-234.

Lütke, F. Die Tschuktschen. Archiv für Wissenschaftliche Kunde von Russland, 3 (1843): 446-464.

Malygin, V. M. Dalekie berega. Moscow, 1940. 76 p.

Mathiassen, T. Archaeological collections from the Western Eskimos. Fifth Thule Expedition, Report, 10 (1930): 1-98.

McCutcheon, S. D. Walrus hunters. Alaska Sportsman, 31, no. 11 (1965): 16-22.

Melartin, Liisa. Albumin polymorphism (albumin Naskapi) in Eskimos and Navajos. By Liisa Melartin, Baruch S. Blumberg, and John R. Martin. Nature, 218 (1968): 787-789.

Menovshchikov, G. A. Agglîutinatsiîa i osnovye Konstruktsii prostogo predlozheniîa v eskimosskom îazyke. Akademiîa Nauk SSSR, Izvestiîa, otdel Literatury i îazyka, 8, no. 4 (1949): 355-368.

Menovshchikov, G. A. Eskimosskiĭ îazyk. In Akademiîa Nauk SSSR. Institut îazykoznaniîa. îazyki Narodov SSSR. Vol. 5. Moskva, Nauka, 1968: 366-385.

Menovshchikov, G. A. Eskimossko-Aleutskaîa gruppa. In Akademiîa Nauk SSSR. Institut îazykoznaniîa. îazyki Narodov SSSR. Vol. 5. Moskva, Nauka, 1968: 352-365.

Menovshchikov, G. A. Eskimossko-aleutskie paralleli. Leningrad, Gosudarstvennyĭ Pedagogicheskiĭ Institut, Uchenye Zapiski, 167 (1960): 171-192.

Menovshchikov, G. A. Eskimosy; nauchno-populîarinyĭ istoriko-etnograficheskiĭ ocherk ob aziatskikh eskimosakh. Magadan, Magadanskoe Knizhnoe Izdatel'tsvo, 1959. 141 p. illus.

Menovshchikov, G. A. Grammatika îazyka aziatskikh eskimosov. Leningrad, Izdatel'stvo Akademii Nauk SSSR, 1962-1967. 2 v.

Menovshchikov, G. A. Grammatika îazyka aziatskikh eskimosov, chast' 2: glagol, prichastie, narechiîa, sluzhebnye slova. Leningrad, Izdatel'tsvo Nauka, 1967. 288 p.

Menovshchikov, G. A. îazyk eskimosov Beringova proliva. In Akademiîa Nauk SSSR. Sibirskoe Otdelenie, îazyki i Fol'klor Narodov Sibirskogo Severa. Moskva, Nauka, 1966: 69-83.

Menovshchikov, G. A. îazyk sirenikskich eskimosov. Fonetika, ocherk morfologii, teksty i slovar'. Moskva, Nauka, 1964. 291 p.

Menovshchikov, G. A. Monosemiîa suffiksov aziatskikh eskimosov. In Akademiîa Nauk SSSR. Institut îazykoznaniîa. Morfologicheskaîa Tipologiîa i Problema Klassifikatsii îazykov. Moskva, Nauka, 1965: 198-204.

Menovshchikov, G. A. O perezhitochnykh îavleniîakh rodovoĭ organizatsii u aziatskikh eskimosov. Sovetskaîa Etnografiîa, no. 6 (1962): 29-34.

Menovshchikov, G. A. Un'-ipag'atyt. Leningrad, 1939. 83 p.

Milewski, Krakow. Similarities between the Asiatic and American Indian languages. International Journal of American Linguistics, 26 (1960): 265-274.

Moore, R. D. Social life of the Eskimo of St. Lawrence Island. American Anthropologist, n.s., 25 (1923): 339-375.

Muir, J. The cruise of the Corwin. Boston, 1917.

Murphy, Jane M. Psychotherapeutic aspects of shamanism on St. Lawrence Island, Alaska. In Ari Kiev, ed. Magic, Faith, and Healing. New York, Free Press, 1964: 53-83.

Nechiporenko, G. P. Morzhovyi Promysel na Chokotke. Ekonomicheskaïa Zhizn' Dal'nego Vostoka, 5, no. 6/7 (1927): 169-177.

Nelson, E. W. The Eskimo about Bering Strait. U.S. Bureau of American Ethnology, Annual Reports, 18, vol. 1 (1899): 3-518.

Nelson, Edward W. The Eskimo about Bering Strait. New York, Johnson Reprint, 1971. 518, 965-997 p. illus., map.

Nordenskiöld, A. E. The voyage of the Vega round Asia and Europe. New York, 1882.

Nordenskiöld, A. E. Vega's färd kring Asien og Europa. Stockholm, 1880-1881. 2 v.

Orlova, E. P. Chukotskaïa, korïakskaïa, eskimosskaïa, aleutskaïa reznaïa kost'. Novosibirsk, 1964. 111 p. illus.

Palmer, Harvey E., et al. Cesium-137 in Alaskan Eskimos. Science, 142 (1963): 64-66.

Paulson, I. New Eskimo archaeology from the Soviet Union. Ethnos, 16 (1951): 136-140.

Philip, R. N. Observations on a mumps epidemic in a "virgin" population. By R. N. Philip, K. R. Reinhard, and D. B. Lackman. American Journal of Hygiene, 69 (1959): 91-111.

Philip, R. N., et al. Serologic and skin test evidence of tularemia infection among Alaskan Eskimos, Indians and Aleuts. Journal of Infectious Diseases, 110 (1962): 220-230.

Philip, Robert N., et al. Observations on Asian influenza on two Alaskan islands. U.S., Public Health Service, Public Health Reports, 74 (1959): 737-745.

Potosky, N. and R. L. Potosky. A unique specimen of pressure-flaked pyrite from St. Lawrence Island. American Antiquity, 13 (1947): 181-182.

Rainey, F. G. Eskimo chronology. National Academy of Sciences, Proceedings, 22 (1936): 357-362.

Ray, Dorothy Jean. Land tenure and polity of the Bering Strait Eskimos. Journal of the West, 6 (1967): 371-394.

Reinhard, Karl R. The serologic sequelae of an influenza A-2 epidemic modified by intercurrent vaccination in an insular Eskimo population group. Journal of Immunology, 88 (1962): 551-555.

Ruban, I. P. Vdali of Bol'shoi Zemli. Khudozhnik, no. 6 (1964): 58-60.

Rubcova, E. S. K voprosu o narechijach v eskimosskom ïazyke. In V. A. Avrorin, ed. ïAzyki i Fol'klor Narodov Sibirskogo Severa. Moskva, Nauka, 1966: 116-127.

*Rubcova, E. S. Materialy po ïAzyku i Fol'kloru Eskimosov. Čast 1. Moscow, 1954. 556 p.

*Rubtsova, Ekaterina S. Materialy po ïazyku i fol'kloru eskimosov (chailinskiï dialekt). Moskva, Izdatel'stvo Akademii Nauk SSSR, 1954. illus.

Rudenko, S. I. Tatuirovka Aziatskikh Eskimosov. Sovetskaïa Etnografiïa, no. 1 (1949): 149-154.

Rudenko, S. I., ed. Ob''ïasnitel'naïa zapiska k etnograficheskoi karte Sibiri. Akademiïa Nauk SSSR, Kommissiïa po Izucheniïu Plemennogo Sostava Naseleniïa SSSR i Sopredel'nykh Stran, Trudy, 17 (1929): 1-104.

Sanford, M. H. Sevoonga-Eskimo Village. American Indian, 6, no. 2 (1951): 37-40.

Schulert, Arthur R. Strontium-90 in Alaska. Alaskan Eskimos for whom the caribou is a dietary staple have a high strontium-90 concentration. Science, 136 (1962): 146-148.

Sergeev, D. Nykshak. Akademiïa Nauk SSSR, Institut Etnografii imeni N.N. Miklukho-Maklaïa, Kratkie Soobshcheniïa, 33 (1960): 82-83.

Sergeev, D. A. Morzhovyï promysel naseleniïa beringomor'ïa. Akademiïa Nauk SSSR, Institut Etnografii imeni N.N. Miklukho-Maklaïa, Kratkie Soobshcheniïa, 38 (1963): 77-81.

Sergeev, D. A. Perezhitki otʦovskogo poda u aziatskikh eskimosov. Sovetskaïa Etnografiïa, no. 6 (1962): 35-42.

Sergeev, M. A. Literatura Narodov Severa. Sibirskie Ogni, 31 (1952): 155-166.

Sherman, Glen. Tobacco pipes of the
Western Eskimos. Beaver, 303, no. 1
(1972/1973): 49-51.

Shinen, Marilene. Marriage customs of the
St. Lawrence Island Eskimos.
Anthropologica, n.s., 5 (1963): 198-208.

Smith, Valene L. Intercontinental
aboriginal trade in the Bering Straits
area. In International Congress of
Anthropological and Ethnological
Sciences, 8th. 1968, Tokyo and Kyoto.
Proceedings. Vol. 2. Tokyo, Science
Council of Japan, 1969: 236-238.

Timasheva, Larisa Efremovna. Tant͡sy
narodov Severa; sbornik. Magadan,
Magadanskoe Knizhnoe Izdatel'stvo, 1959.
74 p. illus.

Ulving, Tor. Observations on the language
of the Asiatic Eskimo as presented in
Soviet linguistic works. Linguistics, 69
(1971): 87-119.

Vdovin, I. S. Torgovye svi͡azi naselenii͡a
Severo-Vostoka Sibirii Ali͡aski do
nachala xx veka. Letopis' Severa, 4
(1964): 117-127.

Voblov, I. K. Eskimosskie Prazdniki.
Akademii͡a Nauk SSSR, Institut
Etnografii, Trudy, 18 (1952): 320-334.

Watkins, J. A. The Alaskan Eskimo.
American Journal of Public Health, 4
(1914): 643-648.

Weider, Dudley J. A physician visits
Little Diomede. HSMHA Health Reports, 86
(1971): 8-14.

Wells, R. and J. W. Kelly. English-Eskimo
and Eskimo-English Vocabularies. U.S.
Bureau of Education, Circulars of
Information, no. 2 (1890): 1-72.

Whitten, Norman E., Jr. Towards a
classification of West Alaskan social
structure. Alaska, University,
Anthropological Papers, 12 (1964): 79-
91.

Yarmolinsky, A. Kamchadal and Asiatic
Eskimo manuscript collections. New York
(City) Public Library Bulletin, 51
(1947): 659-669.

Zolotareva, I. M. Blood group
distribution of the peoples of northern
Siberia. Edited by Charles F. Merbs.
Arctic Anthropology, 3, no. 1 (1965):
26-33.

02 Mackenzie-Yukon

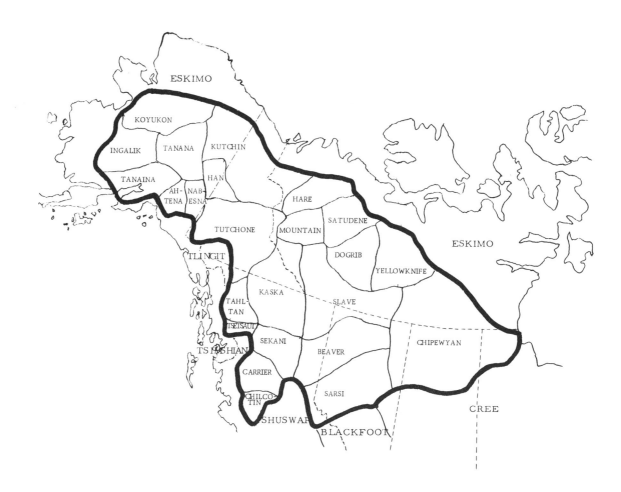

ESKIMO

KOYUKON

INGALIK   TANANA   KUTCHIN

TANAINA

HAN

AH-   NAB-
TENA   ESNA

HARE

TUTCHONE   MOUNTAIN   SATUDENE

ESKIMO

TLINGIT

DOGRIB

YELLOWKNIFE

KASKA   SLAVE

TAHL-
TAN

TSETSAUT

TSIMSHIAN   SEKANI   BEAVER   CHIPEWYAN

CARRIER

CHILCO-
TIN   SARSI

CREE

SHUSWAP

BLACKFOOT

This area includes the western part of the great Boreal coniferous forest stretching across North America from Labrador to Alaska. It is a subarctic region, including patches of tundra as well as the forest. The peoples living in this region were non-agricultural, depending on hunting (particularly of moose and caribou) and fishing for survival. The fur trade, beginning in the eighteenth century, brought about a cultural adaptation to trading post conditions and Western goods in much of the area and a partial breakdown of the aboriginal cultural pattern. This western section of the Boreal forest has two major regions, with the division based on the river drainage (either to the Pacific Ocean or to the Arctic Ocean). These regions are (1) the Yukon Subarctic in Alaska and the Yukon Territory, drained mainly by the Yukon River, and (2) the Mackenzie Subarctic in the Northwest Territories and the northern parts of British Columbia, Alberta, Saskatchewan, and Manitoba, drained principally by the Mackenzie River. All of the Native American groups in this area are speakers of Athapaskan languages. They are culturally quite similar to each other, except that those living in the Pacific Drainage division have a relatively richer ceremonial culture than those of the Arctic Drainage division. (See Osgood 1970 [1936] for general ethnic distributions.) The native population of this area is not large, with population figures for those groups living in Alaska being almost impossible to derive from the listings given in the U.S. census reports. (For additional bibliography on this area, see Helm 1973, 1974.)

Helm, June. Subarctic Athapaskan bibliography: 1973. Iowa City, University of Iowa, Department of Anthropology, 1973. 1, 198 p. (Addenda and corrigenda: 1974. 23 p.)

Hippler, Arthur E. The Subarctic Athabascans; a selected annotated bibliography. By Arthur E. Hippler and John R. Wood. Fairbanks, 1974. (Alaska, University, Institute of Social, Economic, and Government Research, Report Series, 39).

Jones, Mary Jane. Mackenzie Delta bibliography. Ottawa, 1969. 119 p. (Canada, Department of Indian Affairs and Northern Development, Mackenzie Delta Research Project, 6).

Osgood, Cornelius. The distribution of the Northern Athapaskan Indians. New Haven, HRAF Press, 1970. 23 p. map. (Yale University Publications in Anthropology, 7) [reprint of the 1936 edition]

VanStone, James W. Athapaskan adaptations; hunters and fishermen of the subarctic forests. Chicago, Aldine, 1974. 10, 145 p. illus., maps.

02-01. Ahtena. This bibliographic division includes citations on the Ahtena (Atnah, Ahtnakotana) of south-central Alaska and the Eyak of southeastern Alaska, both of the Pacific Drainage division. The Ahtena live in the basin of the Copper River and number about 300. The Eyak live in the delta of the Copper River; their language is nearly extinct.

02-02. Beaver. The Beaver (Tsattine) of the Arctic Drainage division live in the basins of the Peace River and the Athabasca River in northeastern British Columbia and northwestern Alberta. There were 727 Beaver in 1967.

02-03. Carrier. This bibliographic division includes citations on the Carrier (Takulli) and the Babine, both of the Pacific Drainage division. They live on the upper branches of the Fraser River in central British Columbia in the region of Babine and Stuart Lakes. There were 3,862 Carrier in 1967.

02-04. Chilcotin. The Chilcotin (Tsilkotin) of the Pacific Drainage division live in the valley of the Chilcotin River in south-central British Columbia. There were 1,594 Chilcotin in 1967.

02-05. Chipewyan. The Chipewyan of the Arctic Drainage division are the easternmost group in this area, living in the Districts of Mackenzie and Keewatin in the Northwest Territories east of the Great Slave Lake and in the region around Lake Athabasca. There were 643 Chipewyan in 1967.

02-06. Coyukon. The Coyukon (Koyukon), including the Kolchan-Teneyna, both of the Pacific Drainage division, live in the basin of the Yukon River south of the mouth of the Tanana River in central Alaska. There are about 500 Koyukon speakers.

02-07. Dogrib. The Dogrib of the Arctic Drainage division live in the country between Great Bear Lake and Great Slave Lake, in the central part of Mackenzie District of the Northwest Territories. There were 1,068 Dogrib listed in 1967, although Helm counted 1,496 in 1965.

02-08. Han. The Han (Hankutchin) of the Pacific Drainage division live in the western part of the Yukon Territory and the east-central part of Alaska in the upper Yukon River drainage. It has been estimated that there are about 60 speakers of the Han language.

02-09. Hare. The Hare of the Arctic Drainage division live to the northwest of the Great Bear Lake on a section of the lower Mackenzie River and its drainage in the Mackenzie District of the Northwest Territories. There were 679 Hare in 1967.

02-10. Ingalik. The Ingalik of the Pacific Drainage division live in the area between Anvik and Holy Cross on the lower Yukon River (including the drainage of the Anvik River), and in the region southeast of the Kuskokwim River, including the drainage area above Georgetown in west-central Alaska. It has been estimated that there are 500 Ingalik speakers.

02-11. Kaska. The Kaska (also known as the Eastern Nahane or Nahani) of the Arctic Drainage division live in the general area of the drainage of the upper Liard River and its tributaries in the southeastern part of Yukon Territory in Canada. There were 950 Nahani (i.e. Kaska) in 1967.

02-12. Kutchin. The Kutchin (Loucheux), basically of the Pacific Drainage division, live in the region around the great bend of the Yukon River in east-central Alaska and eastward into the valley of the Mackenzie River in Yukon Territory and Mackenzie District of the Northwest Territories. There were 1,138 Kutchin in Canada in 1967.

   Nelson, Richard K. Hunters of the northern forest; designs for survival among the Alaskan Kutchin. Chicago, University of Chicago Press, 1973. 15, 339 p. illus.

02-13. Mountain. The Mountain (Tsethaottine, Chitra-Gottineke) of the Arctic Drainage division live in the basin of the Keele (Gravel) River, the region of Willow Lake, and the country between the Mackenzie River and Lakes La Martre, Grandin, and Tache, in the western part of the Mackenzie District in the Northwest Territories.

02-14. Nabesna. The Nabesna (Nabesnatana, Upper Tanana) of the Pacific Drainage division live in the basins of the Nabesna and Chitana Rivers in southeastern Alaska.

   Guédon, Marie-Francoise. People of Tetlin, why are you singing? Ottawa, National Museum of Man, 1974. 13, 241 p. illus., maps. (Canada, National Museums, Ethnology Division, Mercury Series, Paper, 9)

02-15. Sarsi. The Sarsi (Sarcee) formerly lived in the basin of the Athabasca River and south to the North Saskatchewan River in northern Alberta. They now live on a reserve near Calgary, Alberta.

The Sarsi are not included in the Arctic or Pacific Drainage divisions, since they have taken over Plains culture. There were 404 Sarsi in 1967.

02-16. Satudene. The Satudene (Bear Lake Indians) of the Arctic Drainage division live in the region of the Great Bear Lake in the Mackenzie District of Northwest Territories.

02-17. Sekani. The Sekani (Sikanee) of the Arctic Drainage division live in the basin of the Peace River and its tributaries above Hudson Hope, British Columbia. There were 425 Sekani in 1967.

02-18. Slave. The Slave (Etchareottine) of the Arctic Drainage division live in the region of Slave River and the western end of Great Slave Lake and to the north and west in the northern part of Alberta and southwestern Mackenzie District in the Northwest Territories. There were 3,004 Slave Indians in 1967.

02-19. Tahltan. The Tahltan (Western Nahane) of the Pacific Drainage division live in the upper basin of the Stikine River and in neighboring areas in northern British Columbia. They numbered 656 in 1967.

02-20. Tanaina. The Tanaina (Knaiakutchin) of the Pacific Drainage division live in south-central Alaska in the general drainage area of Cook Inlet.

02-21. Tanana. The Tanana (Tenankutchin) of the Pacific Drainage division live in the basin of the lower Tanana River below Tok River, the region about the confluence of the Tanana and Yukon Rivers, and upstream along the latter river in east-central Alaska.

02-22. Tsetsaut. The Tsetsaut of the Pacific Drainage division lived about the head of Portland Canal on the north coast of British Columbia. They are probably extinct as a culture.

02-23. Tutchone. The Tutchone (Tutchonekutchin) of the Pacific Drainage division live in the general drainage area of the upper Yukon River in Yukon Territory.

02-24. Yellowknife. The Yellowknife (Tatsanottine, Copper Indians) of the Arctic Drainage division live in the country northeast of Great Slave and Great Bear Lakes in Mackenzie District, Northwest Territories. They numbered 466 in 1967.

02-25. Northern Métis. The Northern Métis are racial crosses between Native Americans and other races who live in the general Mackenzie-Yukon area.

They are found in the northern parts of the Prairie Provinces, in the Northwest Territories, and in Yukon Territory, especially in the vicinity of trading posts and urbanized areas. They do not form a corporate group as such, but much has been written on their special problems in recent years.

02-00   Mackenzie-Yukon Area Bibliography

British Columbia, Provincial Museum of
Natural History and Anthropology,
Victoria. A selected list of
publications on the Indians of British
Columbia. Rev. ed. Victoria, 1970.
31 p. map.

Lotz, James R. Yukon bibliography,
preliminary edition. Ottawa, 1964. 7,
155 p. (Canada, Department of Northern
Affairs and National Resources, Northern
Co-ordination and Research Centre, Yukon
Research Project Series, 1)

Pilling, J. C. Bibliography of the
Athapascan languages. U.S. Bureau of
American Ethnology, Bulletin, 14 (1892):
1-125.

Pinnow, Heinz-Jürgen. Einige Züge
indianischen Denkens dargelegt an den
Sprachen der Athapasken. Anthropos, 61
(1966): 9-32.

Agranat, G. A. Polozhenie korennogo
naseleniĭa kraĭnego Severa Ameriki.
Sovetskaĭa Etnografiĭa, no. 4 (1961):
100-113.

Alaska, University. Alaska native arts
and crafts: potential for expansion.
College, 1964. 162 p. illus.

Alaska, University, Alaskan Native
Education Project. Alaskan native
secondary school dropouts: a research
report. By Charles K. Ray, Joan Ryan,
and Seymour Parker. College, University
of Alaska, 1962. 411 p. illus.

Allen, F. H. Summary of blood group
phenotypes in some aboriginal Americans.
American Journal of Physical
Anthropology, n.s., 17 (1959): 86.

Allison, A. C., et al. Urinary B-
aminoisobutyric acid excretion in Eskimo
and Indian populations of Alaska.
Nature, 183 (1959): 118.

Anderson, A. A. Notes on the Indian
tribes of British North America.
Historical Magazine, 7 (1863): 73-81.

Anonymous. El desarrollo de los grupos
nativos de Alaska. Anuario Indigenista,
23 (1963): 89-92.

Arnold, Winton C. Native land claims in
Alaska. Anchorage, 1967. 18, 78, 42 p.

Aronson, J. D. The history of disease
among the natives of Alaska. Alaska's
Health, 5, no. 3 (1947): 1-2; 5, no. 4
(1947): 3-4; 5, no. 5 (1947): 5-6; 5,
no. 6 (1947): 4-5; 5, no. 7 (1947): 3-4.

Arthaud, J. Bradley. Anaplastic parotid
carcinoma ("malignant lymphoepithelial
lesion") in seven Alaskan natives.
American Journal of Clinical Pathology,
57 (1972): 275-286.

Arthur, Donald. "Dena Geleek" song of the
people. Indian Historian, 2, no. 1
(1969): 17-19, 48.

Averkieva, ĬUlia P. Okhotnich'i plemena
Amerikanskogo severa. By ĬU. P.
Averkieva and E. E. Blomkvist. In A. V.
Efimov and S. A. Tokarev, eds. Narody
Ameriki. Vol. 1. Moskva, Izdatel'stvo
Akademiĭa Nauk SSSR, 1959: 171-193.

Bancroft, H. H. The native races of the
Pacific States, Vol. 1: 114-149. New
York, 1875.

Benndorf, Helga, ed. Indianer
Nordamerikas 1760-1860 aus der Sammlung
Speyer. Edited by Helga Benndorf and
Arthur Speyer. Offenbach a.M.,
Deutsches Ledermuseum, Deutsches
Schuhmuseum, 1968. 141 p. illus.

Benveniste, É. Le vocabulaire de la vie
animale chez les Indiens du Haut Yukon
(Alaska). Société Linguistique de Paris,
Bulletin, 49 (1953): 79-106.

Biasutti, R. Le razzi e i popoli della
terra, 2d ed., Vol. 4: 402-424. Torino,
1957.

Bird, Peter M. Studies of fallout 137Cs
in the Canadian North. Archives of
Environmental Health, 17 (1968): 631-
638.

Bland, Laurel L. Perception and visual
memory of school-age Eskimos and
Athabascan Indians in Alaskan villages.
Anchorage, 1970. 1, 25 l. illus.
(Human Environmental Resources Systems,
Monograph, 1)

Bloom, Joseph D. Psychiatric problems and
cultural transitions in Alaska. Arctic,
25 (1972): 203-215.

Boag, Thomas J. Mental health of native
peoples of the Arctic. Canadian
Psychiatric Association Journal, 15
(1970): 115-120.

Boas, F. Die Verbreitung der Indianer-
Sprachen in Britisch-Columbien.
Petermanns Mitteilungen, 42 (1896): 21.

Boas, F. Fifth report on the Indians of
British Columbia. British Association
for the Advancement of Science, Annual
Meeting, Report (1895): 522-592.

Bompas, W. C. Diocese of Mackenzie River.
London, 1888. 108 p.

Bruet, E. L'Alaska. Paris, 1945. 451 p.

Buckham, A. F. Indian engineering.
Canadian Geographical Journal, 40
(1950): 174-181.

Bunger, Marianna. Teaching Alaskan native
youth. Anchorage, Alaska Methodist
University, 1970. 166 p. ERIC
ED045588.

Buschmann, J. C. E. Der athapaskische
Sprachstamm. Berlin, Königliche Akademie
der Wissenschaften, Abhandlungen (1855):
149-319.

Buschmann, J. C. E. Die Verwandtschafts-
Verhältnisse der athapaskischen
Sprachen. Berlin, Königliche Akademie
der Wissenschaften, Abhandlungen, no. 2
(1862): 195-252.

Buschmann, J. C. E. Die Völker und
Sprachen im Innern des britischen
Nordamerika's. Königlichen Preussischen
Akademie der Wissenschaften zu Berlin,
Monatsberichte (1858): 465-486.

Buschmann, J. C. E. Systematische
Worttafel des athapaskischen
Sprachstamms. Berlin, Königliche
Akademie der Wissenschaften,
Abhandlungen, no. 3 (1859): 501-586.

Cameron, J. Correlations between cranial
capacity and cranial length, breadth,
and height. American Journal of Physical
Anthropology, 11 (1928): 259-299.

Canada, Department of Mines and Resources,
Indian Affairs Branch. Census of
Indians in Canada, 1939. Ottawa, 1940.

Canada, Department of Mines and Resources,
Indian Affairs Branch. Census of
Indians in Canada, 1944. Ottawa, 1944.

Canada, Indian Affairs Branch. Indians of
British Columbia (an historical review).
Ottawa, Queen's Printer, 1967. 16 p.
illus.

Cantwell, G. G. Alaskan dead poles. Land
of Sunshine, 8 (1898): 214.

Chalmers, John W., ed. On the edge of the
shield, Fort Chipewyan and its
hinterland. Edmonton, Boreal Institute
for Northern Studies, 1971. 60 p.
illus., map.

Clairmont, Donald H. J. Deviance among
Indians and Eskimos in Aklavik, N.W.T.
Ottawa, 1963. 11, 84 p. illus., maps.
(Canada, Department of Northern Affairs
and National Resources, Northern Co-
ordination and Research Centre, NCRC-63-
9)

Clairmont, Donald H. J. Notes on the
drinking behavior of the Eskimos and
Indians in the Aklavik area; a
preliminary report. Ottawa, 1962. 1,
13 p. illus. (Canada, Department of
Northern Affairs and National Resources,
Northern Co-ordination and Research
Centre, NCRC-62-4)

Clifton, Rodney A. The social adjustment
of native students in a northern
Canadian hostel. Canadian Review of
Anthropology and Sociology, 9 (1972):
163-166.

Cook, Eung-Do. Morphophonemics of two
Sarcee classifiers. International
Journal of American Linguistics, 37
(1971): 152-155.

Cook, Eung-Do. Stress and related rules
in Tahltan. International Journal of
American Linguistics, 38 (1972): 231-
233.

Coon, Carleton S. The hunting peoples.
Boston, Little, Brown, 1971. 21,
413 p. illus., maps.

Cooper, J. M. Land tenure among the
Indians of eastern and northern North
America. Pennsylvania Archaeologist, 8
(1938): 55-59.

Cooper, J. M. Snares, deadfalls, and
other traps of the Northern Algonquians
and Northern Athapaskans. Catholic
University of America, Anthropological
Series, 5 (1938): 1-144.

Crouch, Thomas W. Frederick Funston in
Alaska, 1892-1894: botany above the
forty-ninth parallel. Journal of the
West, 10 (1971): 273-306.

Dall, W. H. On the distribution and
nomenclature of the native tribes of
Alaska. Contributions to North American
Ethnology, 1 (1877): 24-36.

Dall, W. H. On the distribution of the
native tribes of Alaska. American
Association for the Advancement of
Science, Proceedings, 18 (1869): 263-
273.

Dall, W. H. The native tribes of Alaska.
American Association for the Advancement
of Science, Proceedings, 34 (1885): 363-
379.

Dall, W. H. Tribes of the extreme
Northwest. Contributions to North
American Ethnology, 1, no. 1 (1877): 7-
106.

Dawson, G. M. Note on the Indian tribes
of the Yukon district and adjacent
northern portion of British Columbia.
Canada, Geological Survey, Annual
Reports, ser. 2, 3 (1883): 191B-213B.

Dawson, G. M. Sketches of the past and
present condition of the Indians of
Canada. Canadian Naturalist, n.s., 9
(1881): 129-159.

Duchaussois, P. J. B. Mid snow and ice.
London, 1923. 328 p.

Dumond, Don E. Toward a prehistory of
Alaska. Alaska Review, 3, no. 1
(1967/1969): 31-50.

Edwards, Newton. Economic development of
Indian reserves. Human Organization, 20
(1961/1962): 197-202.

Emerson, W. C. The land of the midnight
sun. Philadelphia, 1956. 179 p.

Ervin, A. M. New northern townsmen in
Inuvik. Ottawa, Department of Indian
Affairs and Northern Development, 1968.
30 p. ERIC ED031332.

Fellows, F. S. Mortality in the native
races of the Territory of Alaska. United
States Public Health Service, Public
Health Reports, 49 (1934): 289-298.

Fleshman, J. Kenneth. Bronchiectasis in
Alaska native children. By J. Kenneth
Fleshman, Joseph F. Wilson, and J.
Jerome Cohen. Archives of Environmental
Health, 17 (1968): 517-523.

Flucke, A. F. Introduction to our native
peoples. By A. F. Flucke and A. E.
Pickford. Victoria, Province of British
Columbia, Department of Education, 1966.
41 p. illus., maps. (British Columbia
Heritage Series, Series I, 1)

Franklin, J. Narrative of a journey to
the shores of the Polar Sea. London,
1823.

Fraser, S. Journal of a voyage from the
Rocky Mountains to the Pacific Coast. In
L. F. R. Masson, ed. Les Bourgeois de la
Compagnie du Nord-Ouest. Vol. 1.
Quebec, 1889: 156-221.

Fried, Jacob. Urbanization and ecology in
the Canadian Northwest Territories.
Arctic Anthropology, 2, no. 2 (1964):
56-60.

Fried, Jacob. White-dominant settlements
in the Canadian Northwest Territories.
Anthropologica, n.s., 5 (1963): 57-67.

Fritz, M. H. Corneal opacities among
Alaska natives. Alaska's Health, 5,
no. 12 (1947): 3-7.

Fritz, M. H. and P. Thygeson.
Phlyctenular kerato conjunctivitis among
Alaskan Indians and Eskimos. United
States Public Health Service, Public
Health Reports, 66 (1951): 934-939.

Furesz, J. Vaccination against measles in
the Canadian Arctic. By J. Furesz and
Mary Habgood. Canadian Journal of Public
Health, 57 (1966): 36.

Gates, R. R. Blood groups of Canadian
Indians and Eskimos. American Journal of
Physical Anthropology, 12 (1929): 475-
485.

Gibbs, G. Notes on the Tinneh or
Chepewyan Indians. Smithsonian
Institution, Annual Reports of the Board
of Regents (1866): 303-327.

Glazunov, Andrei. Russian exploration in
interior Alaska; an extract from the
journal of Andrei Glazunov. Edited by
James W. VanStone. Pacific Northwest
Quarterly, 50 (1959): 37-47.

Goddard, P. E. Assimilation to
environment as illustrated by Athapascan
peoples. International Congress of
Americanists, Proceedings, 15, vol. 1
(1906): 337-359.

Goddard, P. E. Similarities and
diversities within Athapascan linguistic
stocks. International Congress of
Americanists, Proceedings, 22, vol. 2
(1926): 489-494.

Goddard, P. E. and J. R. Swanton.
Athapascan family. U.S. Bureau of
American Ethnology, Bulletin, 30, vol. 1
(1907): 108-111.

Godsell, P. H. Red hunters of the snows.
Toronto, 1938. 324 p.

Golla, Victor K. An etymological study of
Hupa noun stems. International Journal
of American Linguistics, 30 (1964): 108-
117.

Gottman, Arthur W. A report of one
hundred three autopsies on Alaskan
natives. Archives of Pathology, 70
(1960): 117-124.

Grantham, E. N. Education goes North.
Canadian Geographical Journal, 42
(1951): 44-49.

Gsovski, V. Russian administration of
Alaska and the status of the Alaskan
natives. Washington, D.C., 1950.
104 p.

Gurunanjappa, Bale S. Life tables for
Alaska natives. U.S., Public Health
Service, Public Health Reports, 84
(1969): 65-69.

Gutsche, Brett B. Hereditary deficiency
of pseudo cholinesterase in Eskimos. By
Brett B. Gutsche, Edward M. Scott, and
Rita C. Wright. Nature, 215 (1967): 322-
323.

Haas, Mary R. Athapaskan, Tlingit, Yuchi,
and Siouan. In Congreso Internacional de
Americanistas, 35th. 1962, Mexico. Actas
y Memorias. Tomo 2. Mexico, 1964: 495-
500.

Haldeman, J. C. Problems of Alaskan
Eskimos, Indians, Aleuts. United States
Public Health Service, Public Health
Reports, 66 (1951): 912-917.

Hanna, Gerald S. WAIS performance of
Alaskan native university freshmen. By
Gerald S. Hanna, Betty House, and Lee H.
Salisbury. Journal of Genetic
Psychology, 112 (1968): 57-61.

Harkey, Ira B., Jr. Wolfes, Kuspuks and
70 below. Indian Historian, 5, no. 3
(1972): 13-17.

Harrington, J. P. Southern peripheral
Athapaskawan origins, divisions and
migrations. Smithsonian Miscellaneous
Collections, 100 (1940): 503-532.

Harrison, Gordon Scott. Electoral
behavior of Alaska native villages.
Fairbanks, 1970. 19 p. (Alaska,
University, Institute of Social,
Economic and Government Research,
Research Note, G1)

Harrison, Gordon Scott. Native voting in
village Alaska. Arctic, 24 (1971): 62-
63.

Harvey, James B. Scouting amongst the
Eskimos and Northern Indians. North, 12,
no. 3 (1965): 18-23.

Heller, C. A. Alaska nutrition survey
report: dietary study. Alaska's Health,
6, no. 10 (1948): 7-9.

Heller, C. A. Food and dental health.
Alaska's Health, 4, no. 12 (1946): 4-5.

Heller, Christine A. The Alaska dietary
survey, 1956-1961. By Christine A.
Heller and Edward M. Scott. Anchorage,
Arctic Health Research Center, 1967.
281 p. illus., map.

Hellon, C. P. Mental illness and
acculturation in the Canadian
aboriginal. Canadian Psychiatric
Association Journal, 15 (1970): 135-139.

Helm, June. A method of statistical
analysis of primary relative bonds in
community composition. In Contributions
to Anthropology: Band Societies.
Ottawa, Queen's Printer, 1969: 218-239.
(Canada, National Museums, Bulletin,
228)

Helm, June. Bilaterality in the socio-
territorial organization of the Arctic
Drainage Dene. Ethnology, 4 (1965): 361-
385.

Helm, June. Patterns of allocation among
the Arctic Drainage Dene. In June Helm,
et al., eds. Essays in Economic
Anthropology. Seattle, University of
Washington Press, 1965: 33-45.
(American Ethnological Society,
Proceedings of the Annual Spring
Meeting, 1965)

Helm, June. Remarks on the methodology of
band composition analysis. In
Contributions to Anthropology: Band
Societies. Ottawa, Queen's Printer,
1969: 212-217. (Canada, National
Museums, Bulletin, 228)

Helm, June. The Dogrib hand game. By June
Helm and Nancy Oestreich Lurie. With
Gertrude Kurath on Dogrib choreography
and music. Ottawa, Queen's Printer,
1966. 8, 101 p. illus., map. (Canada,
National Museum, Bulletin, 205)

Helm, June. The hunting tribes of
subarctic Canada. By June Helm and
Eleanor Burke Leacock. In Eleanor Burke
Leacock and Nancy Oestreich Lurie, eds.
North American Indians in Historical
Perspective. New York, Random House,
1971: 343-374.

Hermant, P. Évolution économique et
sociale de certaines peuplades de
l'Amérique du nord. Société Royale Belge
de Géographie, Bulletin, 28 (1904): 341-
357.

Herreid, Clyde F., II. Differences in
MMPI scores in native and nonnative
Alaskans. By Clyde F. Herreid, II, and
Janet R. Herreid. Journal of Social
Psychology, 70 (1966): 191-198.

Hill-Tout, C. British North America.
London, 1907. 263 p.

Hinckley, Ted C. The Presbyterian
leadership in pioneer Alaska. Journal of
American History, 52 (1965/1966): 742-
756.

Hoijer, Harry. Athapaskan morphology. In
Jesse Sawyer, ed. Studies in American
Indian Languages. Berkeley and Los
Angeles, University of California Press,

1971: 113-147. (California, University, Publications in Linguistics, 65)

Hoijer, Harry. Hare phonology: an historical study. Language, 42 (1966): 499-507.

Hoijer, Harry. Internal reconstruction in Navaho. Word, 25 (1969): 155-159.

Hoijer, Harry. Linguistic sub-groupings by glottochronology and by the comparative method: the Athapaskan languages. Lingua, 11 (1962): 192-198.

Hoijer, Harry. Studies in the Athapaskan languages. By Harry Hoijer, et al. Berkeley and Los Angeles, University of California Press, 1963. 6, 154 p. (California, University, Publications in Linguistics, 29)

Hoijer, Harry. The Athapaskan languages. In Harry Hoijer, et al., eds. Studies in the Athapaskan Languages. Berkeley and Los Angeles, University of California Press, 1963: 1-29. (California, University, Publications in Linguistics, 29)

Honigmann, J. J. and I. Honigmann. Drinking in an Indian-White community. Quarterly Journal of Studies on Alcohol, 5 (1945): 575-619.

Honigmann, John J. Formation of Mackenzie Delta frontier culture. Anthropologica, n.s., 13 (1971): 185-192.

Hrdlička, A. Anthropological survey of Alaska. U.S. Bureau of American Ethnology, Annual Reports, 46 (1930): 19-374.

Hrdlička, A. Catalogue of human crania in the United States National Museum collections. United States National Museum, Proceedings, 94 (1944): 1-172.

Huber, Albert. Alaskan Native Industries Co-operative Association. Boletín Indigenista, 19 (1959): 221, 223, 225.

Ingstad, H. M. Land of feast and famine. New York, 1933. 332 p.

Ingstad, H. M. Pelsjegerliv blandt Nord-Kanadas Indianere. Oslo, 1931. 245 p.

Innis, H. A. The fur trade in Canada. New Haven, 1930. 444 p.

Irving, L. Naming of birds as part of the intellectual culture of Indians at Old Crow, Yukon Territory. Arctic, 11 (1958): 117-122.

Jenkins, Michael R. Trade beads in Alaska. Alaska Journal, 2, no. 3 (1972): 31-39.

Jenness, D. The Indians of Canada. 3d ed. National Museum of Canada, Bulletin, 65 (1955): 1-452.

Kennedy, Michael. Festival: reviving native arts. Alaska Review, 4, no. 2 (1970): 11-39.

Kerr, R. For the Royal Scottish Museum. Beaver, 284 (June 1953): 32-35.

Kidd, K. E. Trading into Hudson's Bay. Beaver, 288, no. 3 (1957): 12-17.

King, Alfred Richard. The school at Mopass; a problem of identity. New York, Holt, Rinehart and Winston, 1967. 12, 96 p. illus., map.

Koch, Walton Boston. The Native Alaskan social movement. Dissertation Abstracts International, 32 (1971/1972): 4371B. UM 72-7655.

Korner, I. N. Notes of a psychologist fieldworker. Anthropologica, n.s., 1 (1959): 91-105.

Krámský, Jiří. The article and the concept of definiteness in language. The Hague, Mouton, 1972. 212 p. (Janua Linguarum, Series Minor, 125)

Krauss, Michael E. Eyak: a preliminary report. Canadian Journal of Linguistics, 10 (1964/1965): 167-187.

Krauss, Michael E. Noun-classification systems in Athapaskan, Eyak, Tlingit, and Haida verbs. International Journal of American Linguistics, 34 (1968): 194-203.

Krauss, Michael E. Proto-Athapaskan-Eyak and the problem of Na-Dene. International Journal of American Linguistics, 30 (1964): 118-131; 31 (1965): 18-28.

Krenov, J. Legends from Alaska. Société des Américanistes, Journal, n.s., 40 (1951): 173-195.

Kroeber, A. L. Athabascan kin term systems. American Anthropologist, n.s., 39 (1937): 602-609.

Kroeber, Alfred L. Semantic contributions of lexicostatistics. International Journal of American Linguistics, 27 (1961): 1-8.

Landar, Herbert J. The language of Friendly Village. International Journal of American Linguistics, 38 (1972): 55-57.

Landar, Herbert J. Two Athapaskan verbs of "being". In John W. M. Verhaar, ed. The Verb 'Be' and Its Synonyms. Part 1. Dordrecht, Reidel, 1967: 40-74. (Foundations of Language, Supplementary Series, 1)

Latham, R. G. On the ethnography of Russian America. Ethnological Society (London), Journal, 1 (1848): 182-191.

Laviolette, G. Notes on the aborigines of the Prairie Provinces. Anthropologica, 2 (1956): 107-130.

Leechman, D. Aboriginal tree-felling. National Museum of Canada, Bulletin, 118 (1950): 44-49.

Leechman, D. Yukon Territory. Canadian Geographical Journal, 40 (1950): 240-267.

Lewis, Marion. Inheritance of blood group antigens in a largely Eskimo population sample. By Marion Lewis, Bruce Chown, and Hiroko Kaita. American Journal of Human Genetics, 15 (1963): 203-208; 16 (1964): 261; 18 (1966): 231.

Lindenkohl, A. Das Gebiet des Jukon-Flusses. Petermanns Mitteilungen, 38 (1892): 134-139.

Lockhart, J. G. Notes on the habits of the moose in the Far North of British America in 1865. United States National Museum, Proceedings, 13 (1890): 305-308.

Loewen, Jacob A. A message for missionaries from Mopass. Practical Anthropology, 17 (1970): 16-27.

Losey, Timothy C. Notes on Athapaskan butchering techniques no. 1. Archaeological Society of Alberta, Newsletter, 26 (1971): 1-6.

Lotz, James R. The Dawson area, a regional monograph. Ottawa, 1965. 209 p. illus., maps. (Canada, Department of Northern Affairs and National Resources, Northern Co-ordination and Research Centre, Yukon Research Project, YRP-2)

Mackenzie, A. Voyage from Montreal through the continent of North America to the Frozen and Pacific Oceans. New ed. New York, 1902. 2 v.

MacNeish, J. H. The Poole Field letters. Anthropologica, 4 (1957): 47-60.

MacNeish, R. S. A speculative framework of northern North American prehistory as

of April 1959. Anthropologica, n.s., 1 (1959): 7-23.

Mallet, T. Glimpses of the Barren Lands. New York, 1930. 146 p.

Mallet, T. Plain tales of the North. New York, 1926. 136 p.

Mason, M. H. The arctic forests. London, 1924.

Maynard, James E. Mortality due to heart disease among Alaskan natives, 1955-65. By James E. Maynard, Laurel M. Hammes, and Francis E. Kester. U.S., Public Health Service, Public Health Reports, 82 (1967): 714-720.

McClellam, Catharine. Introduction: Athabaskan studies. Western Canadian Journal of Anthropology, 2, no. 1 (1970): vi-xix.

McClellan, Catharine. Culture contacts in the early historic period in northwestern North America. Arctic Anthropology, 2, no. 2 (1964): 3-15.

McLean, J. Notes of a twenty-five years' service in the Hudson's Bay Territory. Ed. by W. S. Wallace. Champlain Society, Publications, 19 (1932): 1-402.

McMinimy, D. J. Preliminary report on tuberculosis incidence in Alaska. Alaska's Health, 5, no. 10 (1947): 4-5.

Meigs, Peveril. Capes of human hair from Baja California and outside. Pacific Coast Archaeological Society, Quarterly, 6, no. 1 (1970): 21-28.

Meissner, H. O. Bezaubernde Wildnis: Wandern, Jagen, Fliegen in Alaska. Stuttgart, J. G. Cotta'sche Buchhandlung, 1963. 400 p. illus., maps.

Merrill, Ralph G. Occlusal anomalous tubercles on premolars of Alaskan Eskimos and Indians. Oral Surgery, Oral Medicine, Oral Pathology, 17 (1964): 484-496.

Michéa, Jean. Esquimaux et Indiens du Grand Nord. Paris, Société Continentale d'Éditions Modernes Illustrées, 1967. 351 p. illus.

Michéa, Jean. Moeurs et coutumes des Indiens du Fleuve Mackenzie. Société Suisse des Américanistes, Bulletin, 33 (1969): 62-63.

Milan, Frederick A. An experimental study of thermoregulation in two Arctic races. Dissertation Abstracts, 24 (1963/1964): 2216-2217. UM 64-587.

Milke, Wilhelm. Athapaskische chronologie: versuch einer revision. International Journal of American Linguistics, 25 (1959): 182-188.

Moore, A. Education in the MacKenzie District. In C. A. Dawson, ed. The New North-West. Toronto, 1947: 243-269.

Morgan, Lael. Galena--how to win a flood. New York, Alicia Patterson Fund, 1972. 12 p. illus. (Alicia Patterson Fund, LM-6)

Morgan, Lael. Tundra Times; a survival story. New York, Alicia Patterson Fund, 1972. 12 p. illus. (Alicia Patterson Fund, LM-7)

Morice, A. G. Au pays de l'ours noir. Paris, 1897.

Morice, A. G. Déné roots. Canadian Institute, Transactions, 3 (1891): 145-164.

Morice, A. G. Dénés. In Catholic Encyclopedia. Vol. 4. New York [n.d.]: 717-719.

Morice, A. G. Dénés. In J. Hastings, ed. Encyclopaedia of Religion and Ethics. Vol. 4. New York, 1912: 636-641.

Morice, A. G. La femme chez les Dénés. International Congress of Americanists, Proceedings, 15, vol. 1 (1906): 361-394.

Morice, A. G. Le verbe dans les langues dénées. International Congress of Americanists, Proceedings, 16 (1908): 577-595.

Morice, A. G. Les Dénés du nord. Société de Géographie (Québec), Bulletin, 22 (1928): 146-190.

Morice, A. G. Northwestern Dénés and northeastern Asiatics. Canadian Institute, Transactions, 10 (1914): 131-193.

Morice, A. G. On the classification of the Déné tribes. Canadian Institute, Transactions, 6 (1899): 75-83.

Morice, A. G. Smoking and tobacco among the Northern Dénés. American Anthropologist, n.s., 23 (1921): 482-488.

Morice, A. G. The Canadian Dénés. Annual Archaeological Report, being Part of Appendix to the Report of the Minister of Education, Ontario (1905): 187-219.

Morice, A. G. The Déné languages. Canadian Institute, Transactions, 1 (1889): 170-212.

Morice, A. G. The Great Déné race. Anthropos, 1 (1906): 229-277, 483-508, 695-730; 2 (1907): 1-34, 181-196; 4 (1909): 582-606; 5 (1910): 113-142, 419-443, 643-653, 969-990.

Morice, A. G. The unity of speech among the Northern and the Southern Déné. American Anthropologist, n.s., 9 (1907): 720-737.

Mouratoff, George J. Diabetes mellitus in Athabaskan Indians in Alaska. By George J. Mouratoff, Nicholas V. Carroll, and Edward M. Scott. Diabetes, 18 (1969): 29-32.

Norick, Frank A. Acculturation and drinking in Alaska. Rehabilitation Record, 11, no. 5 (1970): 13-17.

Olson, R. L. Adze, canoe, and house types of the Northwest Coast. Washington, University, Publications in Anthropology, 2 (1927): 1-38.

Osgood, C. The distribution of the Northern Athapaskan Indians. Yale University Publications in Anthropology, 7 (1936): 1-23.

Osgood, C. Winter. New York, 1953. 255 p.

Osgood, Cornelius. The distribution of the Northern Athabaskan Indians. New Haven, Human Relations Area Files Press, 1970. 23 p. map. (Yale University Publications in Anthropology, 7)

Oswalt, Robert L. Towards the construction of a standard lexicostatistic list. Anthropological Linguistics, 13 (1971): 421-434.

Palmer, Harvey E. Radioactivity measured in Alaskan natives, 1962-1964. By Harvey E. Palmer, Wayne C. Hanson, Bobby I. Griffin, and Leslie A. Braby. Science, 147 (1965): 620-621.

Paulson, I. The "seat of honor" in aboriginal dwellings in the circumpolar zone. International Congress of Americanists, Proceedings, 29, vol. 3 (1952): 63-65.

Peake, Frank A. Fur traders and missionaries: some reflections on the attitudes of the Hudson's Bay Company towards missionary work among the Indians. Western Canadian Journal of Anthropology, 3, no. 1 (1972): 72-93.

Pearson, Roger W. Settlement patterns and subarctic development: the South Mackenzie, N.W.T. Anthropologica, n.s., 13 (1971): 255-270.

Pearson, Roger William. Resource
management strategies and regional
viability: a study of the Great Slave
Lake region, Canada. Dissertation
Abstracts International, 31 (1970/1971):
2758B. UM 70-21,034.

Petitot, E. F. S. Accord des mythologies
dans la cosmogonie des Danites
arctiques. Paris, 1890. 493 p.

Petitot, E. F. S. En route pour la mer
glaciale. Paris, 1887.

Petitot, E. F. S. Essai sur l'origine des
Déné-Dindjié. Paris, 1875.

Petitot, E. F. S. Étude sur la nation
montagnaise ou tchippewayne. Missions
Catholiques (Lyon), 1 (1868): 135-136,
144, 151-152, 159-160, 168, 183-184,
199-200, 206-208, 215-216.

Petitot, E. F. S. Exploration de la
région du Grand Lac des Ours. Paris,
1893.

Petitot, E. F. S. Les Déné-Dindjiés.
International Congress of Americanists,
Proceedings, 1, vol. 2 (1875): 13-37,
245-256.

Petitot, E. F. S. Monographie des Dene-
Dindjié. Paris, 1876. 109 p.

Petitot, E. F. S. On the Athabasca
District of the Canadian North-West
Territory. Royal Geographical Society,
Proceedings, n.s., 5 (1883): 633-655.

Petitot, E. F. S. Outils en pierre et en
os du Mackenzie. In Matériaux pour
l'Histoire Primitive et Naturelle de
l'Homme. 1875: 398-405.

Petitot, E. F. S. Quinze ans sous le
cercle polaire. Paris, 1889. 322 p.

Petitot, E. F. S. Traditions indiennes du
Canada nord-ouest. Société Philologique,
Actes, 16/17 (1888): 169-614.

Petitot, Émile F. Traditions indiennes du
Canada nord-ouest. Paris, G.-P.
Maisonneuve et Larose, 1967. 17, 521 p.

Philip, R. N., et al. Serologic and skin
test evidence of tularemia infection
among Alaskan Eskimos, Indians and
Aleuts. Journal of Infectious Diseases,
110 (1962): 220-230.

Pinnow, Heinz-Jürgen. Entlehnungen von
Tiernamen im Tsimshian und Na-Dene sowie
Grundsätzliches zur Entlehnungsfrage bei
Indianersprachen. Zeitschrift für
Ethnologie, 94 (1969): 82-102.

Pinnow, Heinz-Jürgen. Genetic
relationship vs. borrowing in Na-dene.
International Journal of American
Linguistics, 34 (1968): 204-211.

Pinnow, Heinz-Jürgen. Grundzüge einer
historischen Lautlehre des Tlingit. Ein
Versuch. Wiesbaden, Otto Harrassowitz,
1966. 166 p.

Pinnow, Heinz-Jürgen. Notes on the
classifiers in the Na-Dene languages.
International Journal of American
Linguistics, 36 (1970): 63-67.

Pinnow, Heinz-Jürgen. On the historical
position of Tlingit. International
Journal of American Linguistics, 30
(1964): 155-164.

Porter, Merilys E. Ambulatory
chemotherapy in Alaska. By Merilys E.
Porter and George W. Comstock. U.S.,
Public Health Service, Public Health
Reports, 77 (1962): 1021-1032.

Pritchard, G. B. New town in the far
North. Geographical Magazine, 37 (1964):
344-357.

Rabeau, E. S. Programa para mejorar el
status de salud de los residentes
comunales de aldeas en Alaska. Anuario
Indigenista, 28 (1968): 163-168.

Rabeau, E. S. Proyección de una actividad
sanitaria del medio ambiente para un
pueblo menesteroso. Anuario Indigenista,
28 (1968): 169-174.

Rae, George Ramsay. The settlement of the
Great Slave Lake frontier Northwest
Territories, Canada: from the eighteenth
to the twentieth century. Dissertation
Abstracts, 25 (1964/1965): 2438-2439.
UM 64-8203.

Rae, J. Correspondence with the Hudson's
Bay Company on arctic exploration 1844-
1855. Hudson's Bay Record Society, 16
(1953): 1-509.

Rainey, Froelich. Return to the Arctic.
Expedition, 8, no. 3 (1966): 2-8.

Rausch, Robert L. Zoonotic diseases in
the changing Arctic. Archives of
Environmental Health, 17 (1968): 627-
630.

Reynolds, Vernon. Kinship and the family
in monkeys, apes and man. Man, n.s., 3
(1968): 209-223.

Rodli, Agnes Sylvia. North of heaven; a
teaching ministry among the Alaskan
Indians. Chicago, Moody Press, 1963.
189 p.

Rogers, Edward S.   An Athapaskan type of
knife. Ottawa, Queen's Printer, 1965.
16 p. illus. (Canada, National Museum,
Anthropology Papers, 9)

Rogers, Edward S.   Indians of the
Subarctic. Toronto, Royal Ontario
Museum, 1970. 16 p. illus., maps.

Rooth, Anna B.   The Alaska expedition
1966. Myths, customs and beliefs among
the Athabascan Indians and the Eskimos
of northern Alaska. Lund, Gleerup,
1971. 16, 392 p. illus. (Acta
Universitatis Lundensis, Sectio I:
Theologica, Juridica, Humaniora, 14)

Ross, B. R.   An account of the animals
useful in an economic point of view to
the various Chipewyan tribes. Canadian
Naturalist, 6 (1861): 433-444.

Ross, B. R.   An account of the botanical
and mineral products useful to the
Chipewyan tribes of Indians. Canadian
Naturalist, 7 (1862): 133-137.

Ross, B. R.   On the Indian tribes of
McKenzie River District and the Arctic
Coast. Canadian Naturalist, 4 (1859):
190-197.

Salisbury, Lee H.   College orientation
program for Alaskan natives, COPAN--
education for survival. College, 1971.
9, 186 p. (Alaska, University,
Institute of Social, Economic, and
Government Research, ISEGR Report, 27)

Sapir, E.   A type of Athapascan relative.
International Journal of American
Linguistics, 2 (1923): 136-142.

Sapir, E.   The Na-dene languages. American
Anthropologist, n.s., 17 (1915): 535-
538.

Sargent, M.   Folk and primitive music in
Canada. National Museum of Canada,
Bulletin, 123 (1951): 75-79.

Schaefer, Otto.   Alcohol withdrawal
syndrome in a newborn infant of a Yukon
Indian mother. Canadian Medical
Association Journal, 87 (1962): 1333-
1334.

Schulert, Arthur R.   Strontium-90 in
Alaska. Alaskan Eskimos for whom the
caribou is a dietary staple have a high
strontium-90 concentration. Science, 136
(1962): 146-148.

Schwatka, F.   Report of a military
reconnaissance in Alaska. Washington,
D.C., 1885. 121 p.

Scott, Edward M.   Diabetes mellitus in
Eskimos. By E. M. Scott and Isabelle V.
Griffith. Metabolism, 6 (1957): 320-325.

Scott, Edward M.   Nutrition in the Arctic.
By Edward M. Scott and Christine A.
Heller. Archives of Environmental
Health, 17 (1968): 603-608.

Scott, Edward M., et al.   The absence of
close linkage of methemoglobinemia and
blood group loci. American Journal of
Human Genetics, 15 (1963): 493-494.

Sherwood, A.   Some remarks about the
Athapaskan Indians. Anthropologica, 6
(1958): 51-56.

Small, G. W.   The usefulness of Canadian
Army selection tests in a culturally
restricted population. Canadian
Psychologist, 10 (1969): 9-19.

Smith, Derek G.   The implications of
pluralism for social change programs in
a Canadian Eskimo community.
Anthropologica, n.s., 13 (1971): 193-
214.

Swanton, J. R.   The development of the
clan system and of secret societies
among the Northwestern Indians. American
Anthropologist, n.s., 6 (1904): 477-485.

Taché, A. A.   Vingt années de missions
dans le nord-ouest de l'Amérique.
Montreal, 1888. 239 p.

Taché, J. C.   Esquisse sur le nord-ouest
de l'Amérique, 86-91. Montreal, 1869.

Tanner, Adrian.   Trappers, hunters and
fishermen; wildlife utilization in the
Yukon Territory. Ottawa, 1966. 79 p.
illus., maps. (Canada, Department of
Northern Affairs and National Resources,
Northern Co-ordination and Research
Centre, Yukon Research Project, YRP-5)

Teit, J. A.   Indian tribes of the
interior. Canada and Its Provinces
(Toronto), 21 (1914): 283-312.

Teit, J. A., et al.   Coiled basketry in
British Columbia. U.S. Bureau of
American Ethnology, Annual Reports, 41
(1924): 119-484.

Termansen, Paul E.   Health and disease in
a British Columbian Indian community. By
Paul E. Termansen and Joan Ryan.
Canadian Psychiatric Association
Journal, 15 (1970): 121-127.

Tharp, George W.   The position of the
Tsetsaut among Northern Athapaskans.
International Journal of American
Linguistics, 38 (1972): 14-25.

Torrey, E. Fuller. Malignant neoplasms among Alaskan natives: an epidemiological approach to cancer. McGill Medical Journal, 31 (1962): 107-115.

Turner, Christy G., II. Dental chipping in Aleuts, Eskimos and Indians. By Christy G. Turner, II and James D. Cadien. American Journal of Physical Anthropology, n.s., 31 (1969): 303-310.

Turner, Christy G., II. The dentition of Arctic peoples. Dissertation Abstracts, 28 (1967/1968): 3143B-3144B. UM 67-12,162.

Urquhart, J. A. The most northerly practice in Canada. Canadian Medical Association Journal, 33 (1935): 193-196.

U.S., Bureau of Indian Affairs. Indians, Eskimos and Aleuts of Alaska. Washington, D.C., Government Printing Office, 1968. 20 p. ERIC ED028870.

U.S., Congress, Senate, Committee on Interior and Insular Affairs. Alaska native claims settlement act of 1970; report [to accompany S. 1830]. Washington, D.C., 1970. 219 p. (U.S., Congress, Senate, Senate Report, 91-925)

U.S., Congress, Senate, Committee on Interior and Insular Affairs. Alaska native claims settlement act of 1971; report together with additional and supplemental views. Washington, D.C., Government Printing Office, 1971. 223 p. (U.S., Congress, Senate, Senate Report, 92-405)

U.S., Federal Field Committee for Development Planning in Alaska. Estimates of native population in villages, towns, and boroughs of Alaska, 1969. Anchorage, 1969. 4, 30 l. maps.

U.S., National Park Service. Alaska history, 1741-1910. Washington, D.C., Government Printing Office, 1961. 222 p. illus., map.

U.S., Public Health Service. Eskimos, Indians and Aleuts of Alaska, a digest; Anchorage area. Washington, D.C., 1963. 47 p. (U.S., Public Health Service, Publication, 615, pt. 7)

VanStone, James W. An introduction to Baron F. P. von Wrangell's observations on the Eskimos and Indians of Alaska. Arctic Anthropology, 6, no. 2 (1970): 1-4.

VanStone, James W. Ethnohistorical research in Alaska. Alaska Review, 3, no. 1 (1967/1969): 51-59.

Voegelin, C. F. and E. W. Voegelin. Linguistic considerations of northeastern North America. Robert S. Peabody Foundation for Archaeology, Papers, 3 (1946): 178-194.

Waugh, F. W. Canadian aboriginal canoes. Canadian Field-Naturalist, 33 (1919): 23-33.

White, M. C. David Thompson's journals relating to Montana and adjacent regions, 1808-1812. Missoula, 1950. 507 p.

Whitmore, Dorothy Gates. A study of attitudes and achievement of disadvantaged adolescents in Alaska. 4239A-4240A. Dissertation Abstracts International, 30 (1969/1970): UM 70-5906.

Wik, Dennis R. Studies on housing for Alaska natives. By Dennis R. Wik, William B. Page, and Michael L. Shank. Anchorage, Arctic Health Research Center, 1965. 12, 127 p. illus., maps. (U.S., Public Health Service, Publication, 99-AH-1)

Williamson, Robert G. The Canadian Arctic, sociocultural change. Archives of Environmental Health, 17 (1968): 484-491.

Wilmeth, Roscoe. Comments on 'The Language of Friendly Village'. International Journal of American Linguistics, 38 (1972): 208.

Wilson, Amy V. No man stands alone. Sidney, B.C., Gray's, 1965. 138 p. illus., map.

Wilson, C. The new North in pictures. Toronto, 1947. 223 p.

Wissler, C. Culture of the North American Indians occupying the caribou area. National Academy of Sciences, Proceedings, 1 (1915): 51-54.

Witthoft, John. Metallurgy of the Tlingit, Dene, and Eskimo. By John Witthoft and Frances Eyman. Expedition, 11, no. 3 (1969): 12-23.

Wolforth, John Raymond. "Dual allegiance" in the Mackenzie Delta, NWT--aspects of the evolution and contemporary spacial structure of a northern community. Dissertation Abstracts International, 32 (1971/1972): 2791B.

Woodbury, Robert L. Clothing, its evolution and development by the inhabitants of the Arctic. Archives of Environmental Health, 17 (1968): 586-591.

Zbinden, Ernst A. Nördliche und südliche
Elemente im Kulturheroenmythus der
Südathapasken. Anthropos, 55 (1960):
689-733.

Zibert, E. V. Kollektsii pervoĭ poloviny
XIX v. po severnym atapaskam. Akademiĭa
Nauk SSSR, Muzeĭ Antropologii i
Etnografii, Sbornik, 24 (1967): 55-84.

02-01   Ahtena

Abercrombie, W. R. A military
reconnaissance of the Copper River
valley. In Compilation of Narratives of
Explorations in Alaska. Washington,
D.C., 1900: 563-591.

Allen, H. T. Atnatanas. Smithsonian
Institution, Annual Reports of the Board
of Regents (1886): 258-266.

Allen, H. T. Report of an expedition to
the Copper, Tanana, and Koyukuk Rivers,
19-23, 127-136. Washington, D.C., 1887.

*Birket-Smith, K. and F. de Laguna. The
Eyak Indians of the Copper River delta.
København, 1938. 591 p.

Crandall, Faye Elizabeth. A cross-
cultural study of Ahtena Indian and non-
Indian high school students in Alaska on
selected value orientations and measured
intellectual ability. Dissertation
Abstracts International, 31 (1970/1971):
214A-215A. UM 70-11,182.

De Laguna, Frederica. The Atna of the
Copper River, Alaska: the world of men
and animals. Folk, 11/12 (1969/1970):
17-26.

De Laguna, Frederica. Yakutat canoes.
Folk, 5 (1963): 219-229.

Galitzin, E. Observations recueillies par
l'Admiral Wrangell. Nouvelles Annales
des Voyages, 137 (1853): 195-221.

Huntington, F. Ahtena. U.S. Bureau of
American Ethnology, Bulletin, 30, vol. 1
(1907): 30-31.

Johannsen, Uwe. Versuch einer Analyse
dokumentarischen Materials über die
Identitätsfrage und die kulturelle
Position der Eyak-Indianer Alaskas.
Anthropos, 58 (1963): 868-896.

Krauss, Michael E. Eyak: a preliminary
report. Canadian Journal of Linguistics,
10 (1964/1965): 167-187.

Krauss, Michael E. Noun-classification
systems in Athapaskan, Eyak, Tlingit,
and Haida verbs. International Journal

of American Linguistics, 34 (1968): 194-
203.

Krauss, Michael E. Proto-Athapaskan-Eyak
and the problem of Na-Dene.
International Journal of American
Linguistics, 30 (1964): 118-131; 31
(1965): 18-28.

Laguna, F. de. A preliminary sketch of
the Eyak Indians. Philadelphia
Anthropological Society, Publications, 1
(1937): 63-75.

Learnard, H. G. A trip from Portage Bay
to Turnagain Arm and up the Sushitna. In
Compilation of Narratives of
Explorations in Alaska. Washington,
D.C., 1900: 648-677.

Li, F.-K. A type of noun formation in
Athabaskan and Eyak. International
Journal of American Linguistics, 22
(1956): 45-48.

McClellan, Catharine. Avoidance between
siblings of the same sex in Northwestern
North America. Southwestern Journal of
Anthropology, 17 (1961): 103-123.

McClellan, Catharine. Culture contacts in
the early historic period in
northwestern North America. Arctic
Anthropology, 2, no. 2 (1964): 3-15.

Petroff, I. Report on the population,
industries, and resources of Alaska.
U.S. Department of the Interior, Tenth
Census, 8, vol. 2 (1880): 164-165.

Pinart, A. L. A few words on the Alaska
Déné. Anthropos, 1 (1906): 907-913.

Pinart, A. L. Sur les Atnahs. Revue de
Philologie et d'Ethnographie, 2 (1875):
1-8.

Pinnow, Heinz-Jürgen. Notes on the
classifiers in the Na-Dene languages.
International Journal of American
Linguistics, 36 (1970): 63-67.

Richardson, J. Arctic searching
expedition, 238-243. New York, 1852.

Troufanoff, I. P. The Ahtena tomahawks in
the Museum of Anthropology and
Ethnography of the Academy of Sciences
of the U.S.S.R. Current Anthropology, 11
(1970): 155-159.

Veniaminov, Innokentii. The condition of
the Orthodox Church in Russian America:
Innokentii Veniaminov's history of the
Russian church in Alaska. Translated and
edited by Robert Nichols and Robert
Croskey. Pacific Northwest Quarterly, 63
(1972): 41-54.

Vrangel', Ferdinand Petrovich von. The inhabitants of the Northwest Coast of America. Translated and edited by James W. VanStone. By Ferdinand Petrovich von Wrangell. Arctic Anthropology, 6, no. 2 (1970): 5-20.

Zibert, E. V. Kollektsii pervoĭ poloviny XIX v. po severnym atapaskam. Akademiia Nauk SSSR, Muzeĭ Antropologii i Etnografii, Sbornik, 24 (1967): 55-84.

02-02 Beaver

Anonymous. Tsattine. U.S. Bureau of American Ethnology, Bulletin, 30, vol. 2 (1910): 822.

Barbeau, C. Marius. Indian days on the western prairies. Ottawa, Queen's Printer, 1960. 6, 234 p. illus., end maps. (Canada, National Museum, Bulletin, 163)

Bowen, P. Serum protein polymorphisms in Indians of Western Canada: gene frequencies and data on the Gc/albumin linkage. By P. Bowen, F. O'Callaghan and Catherine S. N. Lee. Human Heredity, 21 (1971): 242-253.

Dempsey, Hugh A., ed. David Thompson on the Peace River. Alberta Historical Review, 14, no. 1 (1966): 1-10; 14, no. 2 (1966): 14-21; 14, no. 4 (1966): 14-19.

Edwards, Allan M. Observations on juvenile hypothyroidism in native races of Northern Canada. By Allan M. Edwards and Gordon C. Gray. Canadian Medical Association Journal, 84 (1961): 1116-1124.

Faraud, H. J. Dix-huit ans chez les sauvages. Paris, 1866. 456 p.

Garrioch, A. C. A vocabulary of the Beaver Indian language. London, 1885. 138 p.

Goddard, P. E. Beaver dialect. American Museum of Natural History, Anthropological Papers, 10 (1917): 399-517.

Goddard, P. E. Beaver texts. American Museum of Natural History, Anthropological Papers, 10 (1916): 295-397.

*Goddard, P. E. The Beaver Indians. American Museum of Natural History, Anthropological Papers, 10 (1916): 201-293.

Grant, J. C. B. Anthropometry of the Beaver, Sekani, and Carrier Indians. Canada, Department of Mines, National Museum of Canada, Bulletin, 81 (1936): 1-37.

Grant, J. C. B. Progress in an anthropometric survey of the Canadian aborigines. Pacific Science Congress, Proceedings, 5, vol. 4 (1933): 2715-2721.

Keith, G. Letters to Mr. Roderic McKenzie. In L. F. R. Masson, ed. Les Bourgeois de la Compagnie du Nord-Ouest. Vol. 2. Quebec, 1890: 1-92.

Lawson, Virginia Kathryn. Object categorization and nominal classification in some Northern Athapaskan languages: a generative-semantic analysis. Dissertation Abstracts International, 33 (1972/1973): 1708A. UM 72-26,707.

Loggie, Margaret. Fort Dunvegan. Alberta Historical Review, 7, no. 1 (1959): 18-26.

Paine, Robert. Animals as capital: comparisons among northern nomadic herders and hunters. Anthropological Quarterly, 44 (1971): 157-172.

Richmond, S. Cognitive and structural bases for group identity: the case of the Southern Arctic Drainage Dene. Western Canadian Journal of Anthropology, 2, no. 1 (1970): 140-149.

Ridington, Robin. Beaver dreaming and singing. Anthropologica, n.s., 13 (1971): 115-128.

Ridington, Robin. Inner eye of shamanism and totemism. By Robin Ridington and T. Ridington. History of Religions, 10 (1970): 49-61.

Ridington, Robin. Kin categories versus kin groups: a two-section system without sections. Ethnology, 8 (1969): 460-467.

Ridington, Robin. The medicine fight: an instrument of political process among the Beaver Indians. American Anthropologist, 70 (1968): 1152-1160.

Shapiro, Warren. The ethnography of two-section systems. Ethnology, 9 (1970): 380-388.

02-03 Carrier

Anonymous. Takulli. U.S. Bureau of American Ethnology, Bulletin, 30, vol. 2 (1910): 675-676.

Barbeau, C. M. Indian days in the
Canadian Rockies. Toronto, 1923.
208 p.

Barbeau, C. M. Sons of the Northwest.
Musical Quarterly, 19 (1933): 101-111.

Barbeau, C. Marius. Indian days on the
western prairies. Ottawa, Queen's
Printer, 1960. 6, 234 p. illus., end
maps. (Canada, National Museum,
Bulletin, 163)

Boas, F. Summary of the work of the
Committee in British Columbia. British
Association for the Advancement of
Science, Annual Meeting, Report, 68
(1898): 667-683.

Cox, R. Adventures on the Columbia River.
New York, 1932. 335 p.

Davis, Clark A. The identity of
Nétacā́ut'in. International Journal of
American Linguistics, 36 (1970): 59-60.

Duff, W. Notes on Carrier social
organization. Anthropology in British
Columbia, 2 (1951): 28-34.

Flucke, A. F. Déné. By A. F. Flucke and
A. E. Pickford. Victoria, Province of
British Columbia, Department of
Education, 1953. 59 p. illus., maps.
(British Columbia Heritage Series,
Series I, 9)

Goldman, I. The Alkatcho Carrier:
historical background of crest
prerogatives. American Anthropologist,
n.s., 43 (1941): 396-418.

Goldman, I. The Alkatcho Carrier of
British Columbia. In R. Linton, ed.
Acculturation in Seven American Indian
Tribes. New York, 1940: 333-389.

Grant, J. C. B. Anthropometry of the
Beaver, Sekani, and Carrier Indians.
Canada, Department of Mines, National
Museum of Canada, Bulletin, 81 (1936):
1-37.

Grant, J. C. B. Progress in an
anthropometric survey of the Canadian
aborigines. Pacific Science Congress,
Proceedings, 5, vol. 4 (1933): 2715-
2721.

Grossman, Daniel. The nature of descent
groups of some tribes in the interior of
northwestern North America.
Anthropologica, n.s., 7 (1965): 249-262.

Hall, Roberta L. Multivariate analysis of
anthropometric data and classifications
of British Columbian natives. By Roberta
L. Hall and Peter L. Macnair. American

Journal of Physical Anthropology, 37
(1972/1973): 401-409.

Hamilton, G. Customs of the New
Caledonian women belonging to the
Nancausky Tine or Stuart's Lake Indians,
Natotin Tine or Babine's and Nantley
Tine or Fraser Lake tribes. Royal
Anthropological Institute of Great
Britain and Ireland, Journal, 7 (1878):
206-208.

Harmon, D. W. A journal of voyages and
travels in the interior of North
America, 242-264, 353-364. Ed. by W. L.
Grant. Toronto, 1911.

Harris, Donald A. New Caledonia and the
fur trade, a status report. By Donald A.
Harris and George C. Ingram. Journal of
Anthropology, 3, no. 1 (1972): 179-195.

Hill-Tout, C. British North America.
Toronto, 1907. 263 p.

Howren, Robert. A formalization of the
Athabaskan 'D-effect'. International
Journal of American Linguistics, 37
(1971): 96-113.

Jenness, D. An Indian method of treating
hysteria. Primitive Man, 6 (1933): 13-
20.

Jenness, D. Indians of Canada. Canada,
Department of Mines, National Museum of
Canada, Bulletin, 65 (1932): 363-368.

Jenness, D. Myths of the Carrier Indians.
Journal of American Folklore, 47 (1934):
97-257.

Jenness, D. The ancient education of a
Carrier Indian. Canada, Department of
Mines, National Museum of Canada,
Bulletin, 62 (1929): 22-27.

Jenness, D. The Carrier Indians of the
Bulkley River. U.S. Bureau of American
Ethnology, Bulletin, 133 (1943): 469-
586.

Lawson, Virginia Kathryn. Object
categorization and nominal
classification in some Northern
Athapaskan languages: a generative-
semantic analysis. Dissertation
Abstracts International, 33 (1972/1973):
1708A. UM 72-26,707.

Leichter, Joseph. Lactose intolerance in
Canadian West Coast Indians. By Joseph
Leichter and Melvin Lee. American
Journal of Digestive Diseases, n.s., 16
(1971): 809-813.

MacDonald, Joseph Lorne. A study of
stress in the social structure of the
Moricetown Indians as a factor in

reserve housing development.
Dissertation Abstracts, 28 (1967/1968):
2351A-2352A. UM 67-16,564.

Mackenzie, A. Voyages from Montreal. New
ed. New York, 1902. 2 v.

McLean, J. Notes of a twenty-five years
service in the Hudson's Bay Territory.
Ed. by W. S. Wallace. Champlain Society,
Publications, 19 (1932): 176-184.

McLean, John. Notes of a twenty-five
years' service in the Hudson's Bay
territory. New York, Greenwood Press,
1968. 36, 402 p. map. (Champlain
Society, Publication, 19)

Morice, A. G. Are the Carrier sociology
and mythology indigenous or exotic?
Royal Society of Canada, Proceedings and
Transactions, ser. 1, 10, pt. 2 (1892):
109-126.

Morice, A. G. Carrier Indians. In J.
Hastings, ed. Encyclopaedia of Religion
and Ethics. Vol. 3. New York, 1911:
229-230.

Morice, A. G. Carrier onomatology.
American Anthropologist, n.s., 35
(1933): 632-658.

Morice, A. G. Carriers and Ainos at home.
American Antiquarian and Oriental
Journal, 24 (1902): 88-93.

Morice, A. G. Déné surgery. Canadian
Institute, Transactions, 7 (1901): 15-
27.

Morice, A. G. L'abstraction dans la
langue des Porteurs. International
Congress of Americanists, Proceedings,
21, vol. 1 (1924): 323-335.

*Morice, A. G. Notes archaeological,
industrial, and sociological on the
Western Dénés. Canadian Institute,
Transactions, 4 (1893): 1-222.

Morice, A. G. Smoking and tobacco among
the Northern Dénés. American
Anthropologist, n.s., 23 (1921): 482-
488.

Morice, A. G. The Carrier language.
Wien, 1932. 2 v.

Morice, A. G. The Déné languages.
Canadian Institute, Transactions, 1
(1891): 170-212.

Morice, A. G. The great Déné race.
Anthropos, 1 (1906): 229-277, 483-508,
695-730; 2 (1907): 1-34, 181-196; 4
(1909): 582-606; 5 (1910): 113-142, 416-
443, 643-653, 969-990.

Morice, A. G. The history of the northern
interior of British Columbia. Toronto,
1904. 339 p.

Morice, A. G. The Western Dénés. Canadian
Institute, Proceedings, ser. 3, 7
(1889): 109-174.

Morice, A. G. Three Carrier myths.
Canadian Institute, Transactions, 5
(1895): 1-36.

Morice, A. G. Two points of Western Déné
ethnography. American Anthropologist,
n.s., 27 (1925): 478-482.

Ogden, P. S. Traits of American-Indian
life and character. London, 1853.
219 p.

Ray, Verne F. Culture element
distributions: XXII Plateau. Berkeley,
1942. 99-262 p. illus., map.
(California, University, Publications,
Anthropological Records, 8, no. 2)

Scott, L. and D. Leechman. The Carriers.
Beaver, 283, no. 3 (1953): 26.

Seligmann, K. Le Mat-totem de Gédem
Skanish (Gydaedem Skanees). Société des
Américanistes, Journal, n.s., 31 (1939):
121-128.

Smith, H. I. Entomology among the
Bellacoola and Carrier Indians. American
Anthropologist, n.s., 27 (1925): 436-
440.

Smith, H. I. Materia medica of the Bella
Coola and neighbouring tribes. Canada,
Department of Mines, National Museum of
Canada, Bulletin, 56 (1929): 47-68.

Steward, J. H. Determinism in primitive
society? Scientific Monthly, 53 (1941):
491-501.

Steward, J. H. Investigations among the
Carrier Indians of British Columbia.
Scientific Monthly, 52 (1941): 280-283.

Steward, J. H. Recording culture changes
among the Carrier Indians of British
Columbia. Smithsonian Institution,
Explorations and Field-Work (1940): 83-
90.

Steward, J. H. Variation in ecological
adaptation. In his Theory of Culture
Change. Urbana, 1955: 173-177.

Tolmie, W. F. and G. M. Dawson.
Comparative vocabularies of the Indian
tribes of British Columbia, 63B-77B.
Montreal, 1884.

02-04 Chilcotin

Alfred, Braxton M. Blood groups,
phosphoglucomutase, and cerumen types of
the Anaham (Chilcotin) Indians. By
Braxton M. Alfred, T. D. Stout, Melvin
Lee, John Birkbeck, and Nicholas L.
Petrakis. American Journal of Physical
Anthropology, n.s., 32 (1970): 329-337.

Birkbeck, J. A., et al. Nutritional
status of British Columbia Indians. II.
Anthropometric measurements, physical
and dental examinations at Ahousat and
Anaham. Canadian Journal of Public
Health, 62 (1971): 403-414.

Boas, F. Summary of the work of the
Committee in British America. British
Association for the Advancement of
Science, Annual Meeting, Report, 68
(1898): 667-683.

Boas, F. and L. Farrand. Physical
characteristics of the tribes of British
Columbia. British Association for the
Advancement of Science, Annual Meeting,
Report, 68 (1898): 628-644.

Davis, Clark A. The identity of
Nētacā'ut'in. International Journal of
American Linguistics, 36 (1970): 59-60.

Farrand, L. The Chilcotin. British
Association for the Advancement of
Science, Annual Meeting, Report, 68
(1898): 645-648.

Farrand, L. Traditions of the Chilcotin
Indians. American Museum of Natural
History, Memoirs, 4 (1900): 1-54.

Farrand, L. Tsilkotin. U.S. Bureau of
American Ethnology, Bulletin, 30, vol. 2
(1910): 826.

Flucke, A. F. Déné. By A. F. Flucke and
A. E. Pickford. Victoria, Province of
British Columbia, Department of
Education, 1953. 59 p. illus., maps.
(British Columbia Heritage Series,
Series I, 9)

Grant, J. C. B. Progress in an
anthropometric survey of the Canadian
aborigines. Pacific Science Congress,
Proceedings, 5, vol. 4 (1933): 2715-
2721.

Grossman, Daniel. The nature of descent
groups of some tribes in the interior of
northwestern North America.
Anthropologica, n.s., 7 (1965): 249-262.

Haeberlin, H. K., J. A. Teit, and H. H.
Roberts. Coiled basketry in British
Columbia and surrounding regions. U.S.
Bureau of American Ethnology, Annual
Reports, 41 (1928): 119-484.

Hall, Roberta L. Multivariate analysis of
anthropometric data and classifications
of British Columbian natives. By Roberta
L. Hall and Peter L. Macnair. American
Journal of Physical Anthropology, 37
(1972/1973): 401-409.

Harrington, J. P. Pacific Coast
Athapascan discovered to be Chilcotin.
Washington Academy of Sciences, Journal,
33 (1943): 203-213.

Harris, Donald A. New Caledonia and the
fur trade, a status report. By Donald A.
Harris and George C. Ingram. Journal of
Anthropology, 3, no. 1 (1972): 179-195.

Lawson, Virginia Kathryn. Object
categorization and nominal
classification in some Northern
Athapaskan languages: a generative-
semantic analysis. Dissertation
Abstracts International, 33 (1972/1973):
1708A. UM 72-26,707.

Lee, Melvin. Nutritional status of
British Columbia Indians. I. Dietary
studies at Ahousat and Anaham reserves.
By Melvin Lee, Rejeanne Reyburn, and
Anne Carrow. Canadian Journal of Public
Health, 62 (1971): 285-296.

Leichter, Joseph. Lactose intolerance in
Canadian West Coast Indians. By Joseph
Leichter and Melvin Lee. American
Journal of Digestive Diseases, n.s., 16
(1971): 809-813.

*Morice, A. G. Notes archaeological,
industrial, and sociological on the
Western Dénés. Canadian Institute,
Transactions, 4 (1893): 1-222.

Morice, A. G. The great Déné race.
Anthropos, 1 (1906): 229-277, 483-508,
695-730; 2 (1907): 1-34, 181-196; 4
(1909): 582-606; 5 (1910): 113-142, 419-
443, 643-653, 969-990.

Morice, A. G. The history of the northern
interior of British Columbia. Toronto,
1904. 339 p.

Morice, A. G. The Western Dénés. Canadian
Institute, Proceedings, ser. 3, 7
(1889): 109-174.

Petrakis, Nicholas L. Dry cerumen--a
prevalent genetic trait among American
Indians. Nature, 222 (1969): 1080-1081.

Ray, Verne F. Culture element
distributions: XXII Plateau. Berkeley,
1942. 99-262 p. illus., map.
(California, University, Publications,
Anthropological Records, 8, no. 2)

Teit, J. A. Notes on the Chilcotin Indians. American Museum of Natural History, Memoirs, 4 (1907): 759-789.

Tiesenhausen, H. D. von. Chilko fishing camp. Beaver, 297, no. 2 (1966/1967): 28-31.

Tolmie, W. F. and G. M. Dawson. Comparative vocabularies of the Indian tribes of British Columbia, 62B-77B. Montreal, 1884.

02-05 Chipewyan

Carrière, Gaston. Catalogue des manuscrits en langues indiennes conservés aux archives oblates, Ottawa. Anthropologica, n.s., 12 (1970): 151-179.

Anonymous. Chipewyan. U.S. Bureau of American Ethnology, Bulletin, 30, vol. 1 (1907): 275-276.

Anonymous. Thilanottine. U.S. Bureau of American Ethnology, Bulletin, 30, vol. 2 (1910): 742-743.

Back, G. Narrative of the Arctic land expedition. London, 1836. 663 p.

*Birket-Smith, K. Contributions to Chipewyan ethnology. Fifth Thule Expedition, Report, 6, pt. 3 (1930): 1-114.

Birket-Smith, K. The cultural position of the Chipewyan within the circumpolar culture region. International Congress of Americanists, Proceedings, 24 (1930): 97-101.

Bone, Robert M. The Chipewyan Indians of Dene Village: an editorial note. Musk-Ox, 6 (1969): 1-4.

Bourget, Clermont. Douze ans chez les sauvages au Grand-Lac des Esclaves, comme médecin et agent des Indiens (1923-1935). Ste.-Anne-de-Beaupré, Québec, en vente chez l'auteur, 1938. 249 p.

Cohen, Ronald. Dependency and self-sufficiency in Chipewyan stories. By Ronald Cohen and James VanStone. In Contributions to Anthropology 1961-62. Part II. Ottawa, Queen's Printer, 1964: 29-55. (Canada, National Museum, Bulletin, 194)

Crile, G. W. and D. P. Quiring. Indian and Eskimo metabolisms. Journal of Nutrition, 18 (1939): 361-368.

*Curtis, E. S. The North American Indian, Vol. 18: 3-52, 125-129, 147-151, 201-205. Norwood, 1928.

Davidson, William. A preliminary analysis of active verbs in Dogrib. In Harry Hoijer, et al., eds. Studies in the Athapaskan Languages. Berkeley, Los Angeles, University of California Press, 1963: 48-55. (California, University, Publications in Linguistics, 29)

Davidson, William. Athapaskan classificatory verbs. By William Davidson, L. W. Elford, and Harry Hoijer. In Harry Hoijer, et al., eds. Studies in the Athapaskan Languages. Berkeley and Los Angeles, University of California Press, 1963: 30-41. (California, University, Publications in Linguistics, 29)

Davies, Kenneth G., ed. Letters from Hudson Bay 1703-40. Edited by K. G. Davies, assisted by A. M. Johnson. London, 1965. 68, 455 p. (Hudson's Bay Record Society, Publications, 25)

Dickman, Phil. North Knife Lake. Musk-Ox, 8 (1971): 27-30.

Dickman, Phil. Thoughts on relocation. Musk-Ox, 6 (1969): 21-31.

Dobbs, A. An account of the countries adjoining to Hudson's Bay. London, 1744. 211 p.

Dunn, J. History of the Oregon Territory, 2d ed., 101-111. London, 1846.

Faraud, H. J. Dix-huit ans chez les sauvages. Paris, 1866. 456 p.

Fidler, P. Journal of a journey with the Chepawyans or Northern Indians. Champlain Society, Publications, 21 (1934): 493-556.

Fidler, Vera. A journey with the Chipewyans. North, 15, no. 6 (1968): 38-43.

Franklin, J. Narrative of a journey to the shores of the Polar Sea. London, 1823.

Frison-Roche, Roger. Hunters of the Arctic. Translated by Len Ortzen. London, Souvenir, 1969. 8, 260 p. illus., maps.

Frison-Roche, Roger. Peuples chasseurs de l'Arctique. Paris, Arthand, 1966. 283 p. illus., maps.

Gillespie, Beryl C. Yellowknives: quo iverunt? In Robert F. Spencer, ed. Migration and Anthropology. Seattle,

University of Washington Press, 1970:
61-71. (American Ethnological Society,
Proceedings of the Annual Spring
Meeting, 1970)

Goddard, P. E. Analysis of Cold Lake
Dialect, Chipewyan. American Museum of
Natural History, Anthropological Papers,
10 (1912): 67-168.

Goddard, P. E. Chipewyan texts. American
Museum of Natural History,
Anthropological Papers, 10 (1912): 1-65.

Gold, Dolores. Psychological changes
associated with acculturation of
Saskatchewan Indians. Musk-Ox, 2 (1967):
37-45.

Graham, Andrew. Andrew Graham's
observations on Hudson's Bay, 1767-91.
Edited by Glyndwr Williams. London,
1969. 72, 423 p. illus., maps.
(Hudson's Bay Record Society,
Publications, 27)

Grant, J. C. B. Anthropometry of the
Chipewyan and Cree Indians. Canada,
Department of Mines, National Museum of
Canada, Bulletin, 64 (1930): 1-59.

Grant, J. C. B. Progress in an
anthropometric survey of the Canadian
aborigines. Pacific Science Congress,
Proceedings, 5, vol. 4 (1933): 2715-
2721.

Haas, Mary R. Notes on a Chipewyan
dialect. International Journal of
American Linguistics, 34 (1968): 165-
175.

Haas, Mary R. The Menomini terms for
playing cards. International Journal of
American Linguistics, 34 (1968): 217.

Hady, Walter M. Indian migrations in
Manitoba and the West. Historical and
Scientific Society of Manitoba, Papers,
ser. 3, 17 (1960/1961): 24-53.

Harrington, R. In the land of the
Chipewyans. Beaver, 277 (1947): 25-33.

Harrington, R. Making moccasins. Beaver,
284 (June 1953): 36-37.

Hearne, S. A journey from Prince of
Wale's Fort in Hudson's Bay to the
Northern Ocean. Ed. by J. B. Tyrrell.
Champlain Society, Publications, 6
(1911): 1-437.

Hearne, Samuel. A journey from Prince of
Wales's Fort in Hudson's Bay to the
Northern Ocean. Rutland, Vt., C. E.
Tuttle, 1971. 56, 458 p. illus., maps.

Helms, Mary W. The purchase society:
adaptation to economic frontiers.
Anthropological Quarterly, 42 (1969):
325-342.

Henry, A. Travels and adventures in
Canada. Ed. by M. M. Quaife. Chicago,
1921.

Hlady, Walter M. A community development
project amongst the Churchill Band at
Churchill, Manitoba, September 1959-
March 1960. Saskatoon, University of
Saskatchewan, Center for Community
Studies, 1960. 38 l.

Höhn, E. O. The names of economically
important or conspicuous mammals and
birds in the Indian languages of the
District of Mackenzie, N.W.T. and in
Sarcee. Arctic, 15 (1962): 299-308.

Honigmann, John J. Five Canadian Arctic
and Subarctic towns: their native
populations. In Internationale
Amerikanistenkongress, 38th. 1968,
Stuttgart-München. Verhandlungen. Band
3. München, Klaus Renner, 1971: 125-
132.

Howren, Robert. A formalization of the
Athabaskan 'D-effect'. International
Journal of American Linguistics, 37
(1971): 96-113.

Jeanes, C. W. L. Inactivation of
isoniazid by Canadian Eskimos and
Indians. By C. W. L. Jeanes, O. Shaefer,
and L. Eidus. Canadian Medical
Association Journal, 106 (1972): 331-
335.

Jenness, D., ed. The Chipewyan Indians.
Anthropologica, 3 (1956): 15-34.

Keleher, J. J. The fall domestic fishery
at Snowdrift, Northwest Territories.
Canada, Fisheries Research Board,
Journal, 22 (1965): 1571-1573.

Kenney, J. F., ed. The founding of
Churchill, being the Journal of Captain
James Knight. Toronto, 1932. 213 p.

King, R. Narrative of a journey to the
shores of the Arctic Ocean. London,
1836. 2 v.

Koolage, William W., Jr. Adaptation of
Chipewyan Indians and other persons of
native background in Churchill,
Manitoba. Dissertation Abstracts
International, 32 (1971/1972): 681B. UM
71-20,978.

Lagasse, Jean H. Community development in
Manitoba. Human Organization, 20
(1961/1962): 232-237.

Lal, Ravindra. From Duck Lake to Camp 10: old fashioned relocation. Musk-Ox, 6 (1969): 5-13.

Lal, Ravindra. Some observations on the social life of the Chipewyans of Camp 10, Churchill, and their implications for community development. Musk-Ox, 6 (1969): 14-20.

Landar, Herbert J. A note on the Navaho word for coyote. International Journal of American Linguistics, 27 (1961): 86-88.

Landar, Herbert J. Ten'a classificatory verbs. International Journal of American Linguistics, 33 (1967): 263-268.

Lawson, Virginia Kathryn. Object categorization and nominal classification in some Northern Athapaskan languages: a generative-semantic analysis. Dissertation Abstracts International, 33 (1972/1973): 1708A. UM 72-26,707.

Leechman, D. Caribou for Chipewyans. Beaver, 278 (1948): 12-13.

Leechman, D. The pointed skins. Beaver, 278 (1948): 14-18.

Leechman, D. The Trappers. Beaver, 288, no. 3 (1957): 24-31.

Legoff, L. Grammaire de la langue montagnaise. Montreal, 1889. 351 p.

Li, F. K. A list of Chipewyan stems. International Journal of American Linguistics, 7 (1933): 122-151.

Li, F. K. Chipewyan consonants. In Ts'ai Yuan Pe'i Anniversary Volume. Peiping, 1933: 429-467. (Academia Sinica, Institute of History and Philology, Supplementary Volume, 1)

Li, F. K. Chipewyan. Viking Fund Publications in Anthropology, 6 (1946): 398-423.

Li, Fang-kuei. A Chipewyan ethnological text. International Journal of American Linguistics, 30 (1964): 132-136.

Li, Fang-kuei. How to build a canoe. In Philip K. Bock, ed. Culture Shock. New York, Knopf, 1970: 194-200.

Li, Fang-kuei. Some problems in comparative Athapaskan. Canadian Journal of Linguistics, 10 (1964/1965): 129-134.

Lofthouse, J. Chipewyan stories. Canadian Institute, Transactions, 10 (1913): 43-51.

Lowie, R. H. An ethnological trip to Lake Athabasca. American Museum Journal, 9 (1909): 10-15.

Lowie, R. H. Chipewyan tales. American Museum of Natural History, Anthropological Papers, 10 (1912): 171-200.

Lowie, R. H. The Chipewyans of Canada. Southern Workman, 38 (1909): 278-283.

Lowie, R. H. Windigo, a Chipewyan story. In E. C. Parsons, ed. American Indian Life. New York, 1925: 325-336.

MacNeish, J. H. Kin terms of Arctic drainage Déné. American Anthropologist, 62 (1960): 279-295.

MacNeish, J. H. Leadership among the Northeastern Athabascans. Anthropologica, 2 (1956): 131-163.

MacNeish, June Helm. Kin terms of Arctic Drainage Déné: Hare, Slavey, Chipewyan. American Anthropologist, 62 (1960): 279-295.

Mathers, Charles W. A trip to the Arctic Circle. Alberta Historical Review, 20, no. 4 (1972): 6-15.

Mellor, A. H. L. Origin of the Chipewyan. Beaver, 299, no. 1 (1968/1969): 51.

M'Keevor, T. A voyage to Hudson's Bay, 48-76. London, 1819.

Morgan, L. H. Systems of consanguinity and affinity. Smithsonian Contributions to Knowledge, 17 (1871): 291-382.

Morgan, L. H. The Indian journals, 1859-62, p. 128. Ann Arbor, 1959.

Morton, Desmond, ed. Telegrams of the North-West Campaign 1885. Edited by Desmond Morton and Reginald H. Roy. Toronto, 1972. 103, 431 p. illus., maps. (Champlain Society, Publications, 47)

Munsterhjelm, E. The wind and the caribou. London, 1953. 234 p.

Oswalt, Wendell H. Partially acculturated communities: Canadian Athapaskans and West Alaskan Eskimos. By Wendell H. Oswalt and James W. VanStone. Anthropologica, n.s., 5 (1963): 23-31.

Parker, James. The fur trade and the Chipewyan Indian. Western Canadian Journal of Anthropology, 3, no. 1 (1972): 43-57.

Pénard, J. M. Land ownership and chieftaincy among the Chippewayan and

Caribou-Eaters. Primitive Man, 2 (1929): 20-24.

Petitot, E. F. S. Autour de Grand Lac des Esclaves. Paris, 1891. 369 p.

Petitot, E. F. S. De Carlton-House au Fort Pitt. Société Neuchâteloise de Géographie, Bulletin, 11 (1899): 176-195.

Petitot, E. F. S. Dictionnaire de la langue Déné-Dindjié. Paris, 1876. 367 p.

Petitot, E. F. S. La femme au serpent. Mélusine, 2 (1884): 19-20.

Petitot, E. F. S. On the Athabasca District. Canadian Record of Science, 1 (1884): 27-53.

Petitot, E. F. S. Traditions indiennes du Canada nord-ouest. Littératures Populaires de Toutes les Nations, 23 (1886): 345-442.

Pinnow, Heinz-Jürgen. Genetic relationship vs. borrowing in Na-dene. International Journal of American Linguistics, 34 (1968): 204-211.

Richardson, J. Arctic searching expedition, Vol. 2: 33-60, 387-395. London, 1851.

Richardson, Murray. Paradigmatic prefixes in Chipewyan. In Harry Hoijer, et al., eds. Studies in the Athapaskan Languages. Berkeley, Los Angeles, University of California Press, 1963: 56-61. (California, University, Publications in Linguistics, 29)

Richmond, S. Cognitive and structural bases for group identity: the case of the Southern Arctic Drainage Dene. Western Canadian Journal of Anthropology, 2, no. 1 (1970): 140-149.

Robson, J. An account of six years residence in Hudson's Bay. London, 1752. 84 p.

Rogers, Edward S. The Chipewyan. Beaver, 301, no. 3 (1970/1971): 56-59.

Ross, B. R. The Eastern Tinneh. Smithsonian Institution, Annual Reports of the Board of Regents (1866): 304-311.

Rourke, L. The land of the frozen tide, 90-168. London, 1924.

Saunders, L. G. A survey of helminth and protozoan incidence in man and dogs at Fort Chipewyan, Alberta. Journal of Parasitology, 35 (1949): 31-34.

Seton, E. T. The arctic prairies, 147-158. New York, 1911.

Simpson, G. Journal of occurrences in the Athabasca Department, 1820 and 1821. Champlain Society, Publications, 1 (1938): 1-557.

Smith, James G. E. The Chipewyan hunting group in a village context. (1970): 60-66.

Thompson, David. David Thompson's narrative 1784-1812. Edited by Richard Glover. Toronto, 1962. 102, 410 p. map. (Champlain Society, Publications, 40)

Thompson, H. Paul. Estimating aboriginal American population. 2. A technique using anthropological and biological data. Current Anthropology, 7 (1966): 417-449.

Tyrrell, J. B., ed. David Thompson's narrative of his explorations in western America. Champlain Society, Publications, 12 (1916): 1-582.

VanStone, James W. Changing patterns of Indian trapping in the Canadian Subarctic. Arctic, 16 (1963): 158-174.

VanStone, James W. Changing patterns of Indian trapping in the Canadian Subarctic. In Deward E. Walker, Jr., ed. The Emergent Native Americans. Boston, Little, Brown, 1972: 308-321.

VanStone, James W. Some aspects of religious change among native inhabitants in West Alaska and the Northwest Territories. Arctic Anthropology, 2, no. 2 (1964): 21-24.

VanStone, James W. The changing culture of the Snowdrift Chipewyan. Ottawa, Queen's Printer, 1965. 14, 133 p. illus., maps. (Canada, National Museum, Bulletin, 209)

*VanStone, James W. The economy of a frontier community; a preliminary statement. Ottawa, 1961. 4, 34 p. maps. (Canada, Department of Northern Affairs and National Resources, Northern Co-ordination and Research Centre, NCRC-61-4)

*VanStone, James W. The Snowdrift Chipewyan. Ottawa, 1963. 3, 115 p. maps. (Canada, Department of Northern Affairs and National Resources, Northern Co-ordination and Research Centre, NCRC-63-4)

West, J. The substance of a journal during a residence at the Red River Colony. London, 1824.

Whitney, C. On snow-shoes to the barren
grounds. New York, 1896. 324 p.

02-06 Coyukon

Allen, H. T. Report of an expedition to
the Copper, Tananá, and Kóyukuk Rivers,
140-142. Washington, D.C., 1887.

Anonymous. Kaiyukhotana. U.S. Bureau of
American Ethnology, Bulletin, 30, vol. 1
(1907): 643-644.

Anonymous. Koyukukhotana. U.S. Bureau of
American Ethnology, Bulletin, 30, vol. 1
(1907): 729-730.

Bergsland, Knut. The Eskimo shibboleth
inuk/yuk. In To Honor Roman Jakobson;
Essays on the Occasion of His Seventieth
Birthday, 11 October 1966. The Hague,
Mouton, 1967: 203-221. (Janua
Linguarum, Series Maior, 31)

Burch, Ernest S., Jr. Alliance and
conflict: inter-regional relations in
North Alaska. By Ernest S. Burch, Jr.
and Thomas C. Correll. In D. Lee
Guemple, ed. Alliance in Eskimo Society.
Seattle, American Ethnological Society,
1972: 17-39.

Cantwell, J. C. Report of the operations
of the U.S. Revenue Steamer Nunivak,
209-236, 281-284. Washington, D.C.,
1902.

Carroll, Ginger A. Stick dance. Alaska
Journal, 2, no. 2 (1972): 28-33.

Clark, A. M. Koyukon Athabascan
ceremonialism. Western Candian Journal
of Anthropology, 2, no. 1 (1970): 80-88.

Correll, Thomas Clifton. Ungalaqlingmiut:
a study in language and society.
Dissertation Abstracts International, 33
(1972/1973): 5103B-5104B. UM 73-10,684.

Dall, W. H. Alaska and its resources.
Boston, 1870. 627 p.

Dall, W. H., G. M. Dawson, and W. Ogilvie.
The Yukon Territory. London, 1898.
438 p.

Erman, A. Ueber die Reise und
Entdeckungen des Lieutenant L. Sagoskin
im russischen Amerika. Archiv für
Wissenschaftliche Kunde von Russland, 6
(1848): 499-522, 613-672; 7 (1849): 429-
512.

Henry, David. Dinaahto' dinaayit hanaay.
God talks with us. By David and Kay
Henry. Fairbanks, Alaska, Wycliffe
Bible Translators, 1969. 85 p. illus.

Henry, David. Dinaak'a, our language;
Koyukon dialect of Athapaskan Indian. By
David and Kay Henry. Fairbanks, Alaska,
Summer Institute of Linguistics, 1969.
81 p. illus.

Henry, David. Hadohzil - eeyah; we are
reading. By David and Kay Henry.
Fairbanks, Alaska, Summer Institute of
Linguistics, 1969. 53 p. illus.

Henry, David. Koyukon locationals. By
David and Kay Henry. Anthropological
Linguistics, 11, no. 4 (1969): 136-142.

Hrdlička, A. The ancient and modern
inhabitants of the Yukon. Smithsonian
Institution, Explorations and Field-Work
(1929): 137-146.

Jetté, J. L'organisation sociale des
Ten'as. International Congress of
Americanists, Proceedings, 15, vol. 1
(1906): 395-409.

Jetté, J. On Ten'a folk-lore. Royal
Anthropological Institute of Great
Britain and Ireland, Journal, 38 (1908):
298-367; 39 (1909): 460-505.

Jetté, J. On the language of the Ten'a.
Man, 7 (1907): 51-56; 8 (1908): 72-73; 9
(1909): 21-25.

Jetté, J. On the medicine-men of the
Ten'a. Royal Anthropological Institute
of Great Britain and Ireland, Journal,
37 (1907): 157-188.

Jetté, J. On the superstitions of the
Ten'a Indians. Anthropos, 6 (1911): 95-
108, 241-259, 602-615, 699-723.

Jetté, J. Riddles of the Ten'a Indians.
Anthropos, 8 (1913): 181-201, 630-651.

Kunce, Joseph. Maze performance and
personal, social, and economic
adjustment of Alaskan natives. By Joseph
Kunce, L. S. Rankin, and Elaine Clement.
Journal of Social Psychology, 73 (1967):
37-45.

Laguna, F. de. The prehistory of northern
North America as seen from the Yukon.
Society for American Archaeology,
Memoirs, 3 (1947): 1-360.

Landar, Herbert J. Ten'a classificatory
verbs. International Journal of American
Linguistics, 33 (1967): 263-268.

Loyens, William J. The Koyukon Feast for
the Dead. Arctic Anthropology, 2, no. 2
(1964): 133-148.

Loyens, William John. The changing
culture of the Nulato Koyukon Indians.

Dissertation Abstracts, 28 (1967/1968): 451B. UM 66-9937.

McClellan, Catharine. Avoidance between siblings of the same sex in Northwestern North America. Southwestern Journal of Anthropology, 17 (1961): 103-123.

McClellan, Catharine. Culture contacts in the early historic period in northwestern North America. Arctic Anthropology, 2, no. 2 (1964): 3-15.

McKennan, Robert A. Athapaskan groupings and social organization in central Alaska. In Contributions to Anthropology: Band Societies. Ottawa, Queen's Printer, 1969: 93-115. (Canada, National Museums, Bulletin, 228)

McKennan, Robert A. Athapaskan groups of Central Alaska at the time of White contact. Ethnohistory, 16 (1969): 335-343.

Murie, Olaus. Winter adventures on the Alaskan trail. American West, 10, no. 1 (1973): 10-15, 59-60.

Rainey, F. G. Archeology of Central Alaska. American Museum of Natural History, Anthropological Papers, 36 (1939): 351-404.

Santos, A. Jesuitos en el Polo Norte. Madrid, 1943. 546 p.

Sniffen, M. K. and T. S. Carrington. The Indians of the Yukon and Tanana valleys. Indian Rights Association, Publications, ser. 2, 98 (1914): 3-35.

Sullivan, R. J. Temporal concepts of the Ten'a. Primitive Man, 15 (1942): 57-65.

*Sullivan, R. J. The Ten'a food quest. Catholic University of America, Anthropological Series, 11 (1942): 1-142.

Whymper, F. A journey from Norton Sound, Bering Sea, to Fort Youkon. Royal Geographical Society, Journal, 38 (1868): 219-237.

Whymper, F. Russian America. Ethnological Society (London), Transactions, n.s., 7 (1869): 167-185.

Whymper, F. Travel and adventure in the Territory of Alaska, 204-215, 343-344. New York, 1869.

Zagoskin, L. A. Peshexodnaa opic chasti russkix vladenii v Amerike. St. Petersburg, 1847-1848. 2 v.

Zagoskin, L. A. Puteshestvie i otkrytia v russkoi Amerike. St. Petersburg, 1847.

Zagoskin, L. A. Résumé des journaux de l'expédition exécutée dans l'interieur de l'Amérique russe. Ed. by E. Galitzin. Nouvelles Annales des Voyages, 125 (1850): 5-16, 216-229, 249-284; 126 (1850): 170-186, 241-268.

Zagoskin, Lavrentiĭ Alekseevich. Lieutenant Zagoskin's travels in Russian America, 1842-1844. Edited by Henry N. Michael. Toronto, Published for the Arctic Institute of North America by University of Toronto Press, 1967. 14, 358 p. illus., maps. (Anthropology of the North: Translations from Russian Sources, 7)

Zibert, E. V. Kollekt͡sii pervoĭ poloviny XIX v. po severnym atapaskam. Akademii͡a Nauk SSSR, Muzeĭ Antropologii i Etnografii, Sbornik, 24 (1967): 55-84.

02-07   Dogrib

Anonymous. Thlingchadinne. U.S. Bureau of American Ethnology, Bulletin, 30, vol. 2 (1910): 744-745.

Barbeau, C. M. and G. Melvin. The Indian speaks, 49-50. Caldwell, 1943.

Bell, J. M. Fireside stories of the Chippwyans. Journal of American Folklore, 16 (1903): 73-84.

Bourget, Clermont. Douze ans chez les sauvages au Grand-Lac des Esclaves, comme médecin et agent des Indiens (1923-1935). Ste.-Anne-de-Beaupré, Québec, en vente chez l'auteur, 1938. 249 p.

Davidson, William. A preliminary analysis of active verbs in Dogrib. In Harry Hoijer, et al., eds. Studies in the Athapaskan Languages. Berkeley, Los Angeles, University of California Press, 1963: 48-55. (California, University, Publications in Linguistics, 29)

Davidson, William. Athapaskan classificatory verbs. By William Davidson, L. W. Elford, and Harry Hoijer. In Harry Hoijer, et al., eds. Studies in the Athapaskan Languages. Berkeley and Los Angeles, University of California Press, 1963: 30-41. (California, University, Publications in Linguistics, 29)

Finnie, R. Dogrib treaty. Natural History, 46 (1940): 52-58.

Franklin, J. Narrative of a journey to the shores of the polar sea. London, 1823.

Franklin, J.   Narrative of a second
   expedition to the shores of the polar
   sea.   London, 1828.

Gaillard, R.   Au Canada, présence
   française au-delà du Québec.
   Connaissance du Monde, 69 (1964): 66-78.

Gates, R. R.   Blood groups of Canadian
   Indians and Eskimos. American Journal of
   Physical Anthropology, 12 (1929): 475-
   485.

Gillespie, Beryl C.   Yellowknives: quo
   iverunt?   In Robert F. Spencer, ed.
   Migration and Anthropology.   Seattle,
   University of Washington Press, 1970:
   61-71.   (American Ethnological Society,
   Proceedings of the Annual Spring
   Meeting, 1970)

Helm, June.   A method of statistical
   analysis of primary relative bonds in
   community composition.   In Contributions
   to Anthropology: Band Societies.
   Ottawa, Queen's Printer, 1969: 218-239.
   (Canada, National Museums, Bulletin,
   228)

Helm, June.   Bilaterality in the socio-
   territorial organization of the Arctic
   Drainage Dene. Ethnology, 4 (1965): 361-
   385.

Helm, June.   Patterns of allocation among
   the Arctic Drainage Dene.   In June Helm,
   et al., eds. Essays in Economic
   Anthropology.   Seattle, University of
   Washington Press, 1965: 33-45.
   (American Ethnological Society,
   Proceedings of the Annual Spring
   Meeting, 1965)

Helm, June.   Remarks on the methodology of
   band composition analysis.   In
   Contributions to Anthropology: Band
   Societies.   Ottawa, Queen's Printer,
   1969: 212-217.   (Canada, National
   Museums, Bulletin, 228)

Helm, June.   Tales from the Dogribs. By
   June Helm and Vital Thomas. Beaver, 297,
   no. 2 (1966/1967): 16-20; 297, no. 3
   (1966/1967): 52-54.

Helm, June.   The contact-traditional all-
   native community of the Canadian North:
   the Upper MacKenzie "Bush" Athapaskans
   and the Igluligmiut. By June Helm and
   David Damas. Anthropologica, n.s., 5
   (1963): 9-21.

Helm, June.   The Dogrib hand game. By June
   Helm and Nancy Oestreich Lurie. With
   Gertrude Kurath on Dogrib choreography
   and music.   Ottawa, Queen's Printer,
   1966.   8, 101 p.   illus., map. (Canada,
   National Museum, Bulletin, 205)

Helm, June.   The Dogrib Indians. In Mario
   G. Bicchieri, ed. Hunters and Gatherers
   Today.   New York, Holt, Rinehart, and
   Winston, 1972: 51-89.

Helm, June.   The nature of Dogrib
   socioterritorial groups. In Richard B.
   Lee and Irven DeVore, eds. Man the
   Hunter.   Chicago, Aldine, 1968: 118-125.

*Helm, June.   The subsistence economy of
   the Dogrib Indians of Lac La Martre in
   the Mackenzie District of the N.W.T. By
   June Helm and Nancy O. Lurie. Ottawa,
   1961.   119 p.   illus. (Canada,
   Department of Northern Affairs and
   National Resources, Northern Co-
   ordination and Research Centre, NCRC-61-
   3)

Höhn, E. O.   The names of economically
   important or conspicuous mammals and
   birds in the Indian languages of the
   District of Mackenzie, N.W.T. and in
   Sarcee. Arctic, 15 (1962): 299-308.

Howren, Robert.   A formalization of the
   Athabaskan 'D-effect'. International
   Journal of American Linguistics, 37
   (1971): 96-113.

Howren, Robert.   Stem phonology and affix
   phonology in Dogrib (Northern
   Athapaskan). In Bill J. Darden, et al.,
   eds. Papers from the Fourth Regional
   Meeting, Chicago Linguistic Society.
   Chicago, University of Chicago,
   Department of Linguistics, 1968: 120-
   129.

Jeanes, C. W. L.   Inactivation of
   isoniazid by Canadian Eskimos and
   Indians. By C. W. L. Jeanes, O. Shaefer,
   and L. Eidus. Canadian Medical
   Association Journal, 106 (1972): 331-
   335.

Jérémie, N.   Account of Hudson Strait and
   Bay. Ed. by R. Douglas and J. N.
   Wallace.   Ottawa, 1926.   42 p.

Landar, Herbert J.   Ten'a classificatory
   verbs. International Journal of American
   Linguistics, 33 (1967): 263-268.

Leechman, D.   The trappers. Beaver, 288,
   no. 3 (1957): 24-31.

MacNeish, J. H.   Leadership among the
   Northeastern Athabascans.
   Anthropologica, 2 (1956): 131-163.

Mason, J. A.   Notes on the Indians of the
   Great Slave Lake area. Yale University
   Publications in Anthropology, 34 (1946):
   1-46.

Mathers, Charles W. A trip to the Arctic Circle. Alberta Historical Review, 20, no. 4 (1972): 6-15.

Osgood, C. The ethnography of the Great Bear Lake Indians. Canada, Department of Mines, National Museum of Canada, Bulletin, 70 (1931): 31-92.

Petitot, E. F. S. Autour du Grand Lac des Esclaves. Paris, 1891. 369 p.

Petitot, E. F. S. Traditions indiennes du Canada nordouest. Littératures Populaires de Toutes les Nations, 23 (1886): 307-344.

Petitot, Émile F. S. Indian legends of north-western Canada. Translated by Thelma Habgood. Western Canadian Journal of Anthropology, 2, no. 1 (1970): 94-129.

Richardson, J. Arctic searching expedition, Vol. 2: 1-31, 395-402. London, 1851.

Richmond, S. Cognitive and structural bases for group identity: the case of the Southern Arctic Drainage Dene. Western Canadian Journal of Anthropology, 2, no. 1 (1970): 140-149.

Ross, B. R. The Eastern Tinneh. Smithsonian Institution, Annual Reports of the Board of Regents (1866): 304-311.

Russell, F. Explorations in the Far North, 158-186. Iowa City, 1898.

Ryan, Joan. Storekeeping teachers. Beaver, 290, no. 2 (1959/1960): 25-29.

Schmidt, Richard Conrad. The integration of subsistence life in a broader socio-economic system: a subarctic community. Dissertation Abstracts International, 32 (1971/1972): 6178B-6179B. UM 72-14,204.

Wheeler, D. E. The Dog-Rib Indian and his home. Geographical Society of Philadelphia, Bulletin, 12 (1914): ii.

Whitney, C. On snow-shoes to the barren grounds. New York, 1896. 324 p.

02-08 Han

Adney, T. Moose hunting with the Tro-chu-tin. Harper's Monthly Magazine, 100 (1900): 495-507.

Anonymous. Hankutchin. U.S. Bureau of American Ethnology, Bulletin, 30, vol. 1 (1907): 531.

Anonymous. Vuntakutchin. U.S. Bureau of American Ethnology, Bulletin, 30, vol. 2 (1910): 882-884.

Murray, A. H. Journal of the Yukon. Canadian Archives, Publications, 4 (1910): 1-125.

*Osgood, Cornelius. The Han Indians; a compilation of ethnographic and historical data on the Alaska-Yukon boundary area. New Haven, Yale University, Department of Anthropology, 1971. 173 p. illus., maps. (Yale University Publications in Anthropology, 74)

Schmitter, F. Upper Yukon native customs and folk-lore. Smithsonian Miscellaneous Collections, 56, no. 4 (1910): 1-30.

Schwatka, F. Along Alaska's great river. New York, 1885. 360 p.

02-09 Hare

Anonymous. Kawchodinne. U.S. Bureau of American Ethnology, Bulletin, 30, vol. 1 (1907): 667.

Balikci, Asen. Community patterning in two northern trading posts. By Asen Balikci and Ronald Cohen. Anthropologica, n.s., 5 (1963): 33-45.

Bell, J. M. Fireside stories of the Chippwyans. Journal of American Folklore, 16 (1903): 73-84.

Breton, Paul É. Au pays des Peaux-de-Lièvres. Edmonton, Éditions de l'Ermitage, 1962. 177 p. illus., map.

Brown, Bernard. The end-of-the-earth people. North, 12, no. 6 (1965): 16-21.

Cohen, Ronald. An anthropological survey of communities in the Mackenzie--Slave Lake region of Canada. Ottawa, 1962. 8, 119 p. illus., maps. (Canada, Department of Northern Affairs and National Resources, Northern Co-ordination and Research Centre, NCRC-62-3)

Franklin, J. Narrative of a second expedition to the shores of the polar sea. London, 1828.

Gates, R. R. Blood groups of Canadian Indians and Eskimos. American Journal of Physical Anthropology, 12 (1929): 475-485.

Helm, June. A method of statistical analysis of primary relative bonds in community composition. In Contributions

to Anthropology: Band Societies.
Ottawa, Queen's Printer, 1969: 218-239.
(Canada, National Museums, Bulletin,
228)

Helm, June. Bilaterality in the socio-
territorial organization of the Arctic
Drainage Dene. Ethnology, 4 (1965): 361-
385.

Helm, June. Remarks on the methodology of
band composition analysis. In
Contributions to Anthropology: Band
Societies. Ottawa, Queen's Printer,
1969: 212-217. (Canada, National
Museums, Bulletin, 228)

Höhn, E. O. The names of economically
important or conspicuous mammals and
birds in the Indian languages of the
District of Mackenzie, N.W.T. and in
Sarcee. Arctic, 15 (1962): 299-308.

*Hurlbert, Janice. Age as a factor in the
social organization of the Hare Indian
of Fort Good Hope, N.W.T. Ottawa, 1962.
5, 80 p. illus., maps. (Canada,
Department of Northern Affairs and
National Resources, Northern Co-
ordination and Research Centre, NCRC-62-
5)

MacNeish, J. H. Kin terms of Arctic
Drainage Déné. American Anthropologist,
62 (1960): 279-295.

MacNeish, J. H. Leadership among the
Northeastern Athabascans.
Anthropologica, 2 (1956): 131-163.

MacNeish, June Helm. Kin terms of Arctic
Drainage Déné: Hare, Slavey, Chipewyan.
American Anthropologist, 62 (1960): 279-
295.

Morgan, L. H. Systems of consanguinity
and affinity. Smithsonian Contributions
to Knowledge, 17 (1871): 291-382.

Morice, A. G. Hare Indians. In Catholic
Encyclopedia. Vol. 7. New York, 1910:
136-137.

Osgood, C. The ethnography of the Great
Bear Lake Indians. Canada, Department of
Mines, National Museum of Canada,
Bulletin, 70 (1931): 31-92.

Petitot, E. F. S. Dictionnaire de la
langue dene-dindjié. Paris, 1876.

Petitot, E. F. S. Exploration du Grand
Lac des Ours. Paris, 1893.

Petitot, E. F. S. Quinze ans sous le
cercle polaire. Paris, 1889.

Petitot, E. F. S. Traditions indiennes du
Canada nord-ouest. Littératures

Populaires de Toutes les Nations, 23
(1886): 103-306.

Petitot, Émile F. S. Indian legends of
north-western Canada. Translated by
Thelma Habgood. Western Canadian Journal
of Anthropology, 2, no. 1 (1970): 94-
129.

Richardson, J. Arctic searching
expedition, Vol. 2: 1-31. London, 1851.

Ross, B. R. The Eastern Tinneh.
Smithsonian Institution, Annual Reports
of the Board of Regents (1866): 304-311.

Savishinsky, Joel S. Coping with feuding:
the missionary, the fur trader, and the
ethnographer. Human Organization, 31
(1972): 281-290.

Savishinsky, Joel S. Kinship and the
expression of values in an Athabascan
bush community. Western Canadian Journal
of Anthropology, 2, no. 1 Western
Canadian Journal of Anthropology, 2,
no. 1 (1970): 31-59.

Savishinsky, Joel S. Mobility as an
aspect of stress in an Arctic community.
American Anthropologist, 73 (1971): 604-
618.

Savishinsky, Joel Stephen. Stress and
mobility in an Arctic community: the
Hare Indians of Colville Lake, Northwest
Territories. Dissertation Abstracts
International, 31 (1970/1971): 34B. UM
70-12,648.

Simpson, T. Narrative of the discoveries
on the north coast of America. London,
1843. 419 p.

Sue, Hiroko. Bilateral kinship and action
groups among the Hare Indians of
northern Canada: a cross-section of a
changing society. Minzokugaku-Kenkyu,
28, no. 2 (1964): 181-196.

Sue, Hiroko. Hare Indians and their
world. Dissertation Abstracts, 28
(1967/1968): 1326B. UM 67-12,673.

Sue, Hiroko. Pre-school children of the
Hare Indians. Ottawa, 1965. 50 p.
(Canada, Department of Northern Affairs
and National Resources, Northern
Coordination and Research Centre, NCRC-
65-1)

Voudrach, Paul. Good Hope tales. By Paul
Voudrach, with preparation for
publication and of summaries and
analysis by Ronald Cohen and Helgi
Osterreich. In Contributions to
Ethnology V. Ottawa, Queen's Printer,
1967: 1-58. (Canada, National Museum,
Bulletin, 204)

02-10   Ingalik

Burch, Ernest S., Jr. Alliance and conflict: inter-regional relations in North Alaska. By Ernest S. Burch, Jr. and Thomas C. Correll. In D. Lee Guemple, ed. Alliance in Eskimo Society. Seattle, American Ethnological Society, 1972: 17-39.

Cantwell, J. O. Report of the operations of the U.S. Revenue Steamer Nunivak, 209-236, 281-284. Washington, D.C., 1902.

Chapman, J. W. Athapascan traditions from the Lower Yukon. Journal of American Folklore, 16 (1903): 180-185.

Chapman, J. W. Notes on the Tinneh tribe of Anvik. International Congress of Americanists, Proceedings, 15, vol. 2 (1907): 7-38.

Chapman, J. W. Ten'a texts and tales from Anvik. American Ethnological Society, Publications, 6 (1914): 1-230.

Chapman, J. W. Tinneh animism. American Anthropologist, n.s., 23 (1921): 298-310.

Chapman, M. S. The animistic beliefs of the Ten'a of the Lower Yukon. Hartford, 1939. 15 p.

Dall, W. H. Alaska and its resources. Boston, 1870. 627 p.

Dall, W. H., G. M. Dawson, and W. Ogilvie. The Yukon Territory. London, 1898. 438 p.

Disselhoff, H. D. Bemerkungen zu einigen Eskimo-Masken. Baessler-Archiv, 18 (1935): 130-137.

Erman, A. Ueber die Reise und Entdeckungen des Lieutenant L. Sagoskin im russischen Amerika. Archiv für Wissenschaftliche Kunde von Russland, 6 (1848): 499-522, 613-672; 7 (1849): 429-512.

Galitzin, E. Observations recueillies par l'Admiral Wrangell sur les habitants des côtes nord-ouest de l'Amérique. Nouvelles Annales des Voyages, 137 (1853): 195-221.

Glazunov, Andrei. Russian exploration in interior Alaska; an extract from the journal of Andrei Glazunov. Edited by James W. VanStone. Pacific Northwest Quarterly, 50 (1959): 37-47.

Hipszer, Hermine. Les masques de chamans du Musee Ethnographique de Berlin.

Baessler-Archiv, n.F., 19 (1971): 421-450.

Hosley, Edward H. The Kolchan: delineation of a new Northern Athapaskan Indian group. Arctic, 21 (1968): 6-11.

Hosley, Edward H. The McGrath Ingalik. Alaska, University, Anthropological Papers, 9 (1960/1961): 93-113.

Hosley, Edward Howard. Factionalism and acculturation in an Alaskan Athapaskan community. Dissertation Abstracts, 27 (1966/1967): 25B-26B. UM 66-6805.

Hrdlička, A. Anthropological survey of Alaska. U.S. Bureau of American Ethnology, Annual Reports, 46 (1930): 19-374.

Hrdlička, A. The ancient and modern inhabitants of the Yukon. Smithsonian Institution, Explorations and Field-Work (1929): 137-146.

Krieger, H. W. Tinne Indians of the Lower Yukon River valley. Smithsonian Institution, Explorations and Field-Work (1927): 125-132.

Laguna, F. de. Indian masks from the Lower Yukon. American Anthropologist, n.s., 38 (1936): 569-585.

McClellan, Catharine. Culture contacts in the early historic period in northwestern North America. Arctic Anthropology, 2, no. 2 (1964): 3-15.

McKennan, Robert A. Athapaskan groupings and social organization in central Alaska. In Contributions to Anthropology: Band Societies. Ottawa, Queen's Printer, 1969: 93-115. (Canada, National Museums, Bulletin, 228)

McKennan, Robert A. Athapaskan groups of Central Alaska at the time of White contact. Ethnohistory, 16 (1969): 335-343.

*Osgood, C. Ingalik material culture. Yale University Publications in Anthropology, 22 (1940): 1-500.

*Osgood, C. Ingalik social culture. Yale University Publications in Anthropology, 53 (1958): 1-289.

*Osgood, Cornelius. Ingalik material culture. New Haven, Human Relations Area Files Press, 1970. 500 p. illus., maps. (Yale University Publications in Anthropology, 22)

*Osgood, Cornelius. Ingalik mental culture. New Haven, Yale University, Department of Anthropology, 1959.

195 p. illus., maps. (Yale University Publications in Anthropology, 56)

Oswalt, W. The archaeology of Hooper Bay Village, Alaska. Alaska, University, Anthropological Papers, 1 (1952): 47-91.

Oswalt, Wendell H. Historical populations in western Alaska and migration theory. Alaska, University, Anthropological Papers, 11 (1962/1964): 1-14.

Oswalt, Wendell H. Other peoples, other customs; world ethnography and its history. New York, Holt, Rinehart and Winston, 1972. 15, 430 p. illus., maps.

Oswalt, Wendell H., ed. Eskimos and Indians of western Alaska 1861-1868: extracts from the diary of Father Illarion. Alaska, University, Anthropological Papers, 8 (1959/1960): 100-118.

Parsons, E. C. A narrative of the Ten'a of Anvik. Anthropos, 16/17 (1921): 51-71.

Petroff, I. Report of the population, industries, and resources of Alaska. U.S. Department of the Interior, Tenth Census, 8, vol. 2 (1880): 161-162.

Redd, T. B. and E. C. Parsons. Cries-for-Salmon, a Ten'a woman. In E. C. Parsons, ed. American Indian Life. New York, 1925: 337-361.

Schott, W. Ueber ethnographische Ergebnisse der Sagoskinschen Reise. Archiv für Wissenschaftliche Kunde von Russland, 7 (1849): 480-512.

Schwatka, F. Report of a military reconnaissance made in Alaska in 1883, 96-103. Washington, D.C., 1900.

Vrangel', Ferdinand Petrovich von. The inhabitants of the Northwest Coast of America. Translated and edited by James W. VanStone. By Ferdinand Petrovich von Wrangell. Arctic Anthropology, 6, no. 2 (1970): 5-20.

Whymper, F. A journey from Norton Sound, Bering Sea, to Fort Youkon. Royal Geographical Society, Journal, 38 (1868): 219-237.

Whymper, F. Russian America. Ethnological Society (London), Transactions, n.s., 7 (1869): 167-185.

Whymper, F. Travel and adventure in the Territory of Alaska, 174-180. New York, 1869.

Woldt, A. Capitain Jacobsen's Reise an der Nordwestküste Amerikas. Leipzig, 1884.

Zagoskin, L. A. Peshexodonaa opic chasti russkix vladenii v Amerike. St. Petersburg, 1847-1848. 2 v.

Zagoskin, L. A. Puteshestvie i otkrytia v russkoi Amerike. St. Petersburg, 1847.

Zagoskin, L. A. Résumé des journaux de l'expédition exécutée dans l'intérieur de l'Amérique russe. Ed. by E. Galitzin. Nouvelles Annales des Voyages, 125 (1850): 5-16, 216-229, 249-284; 126 (1850): 170-186, 241-268.

Zagoskin, Lavrentiĭ Alekseevich. Lieutenant Zagoskin's travels in Russian America, 1842-1844. Edited by Henry N. Michael. Toronto, Published for the Arctic Institute of North America by University of Toronto Press, 1967. 14, 358 p. illus., maps. (Anthropology of the North: Translations from Russian Sources, 7)

Zibert, E. V. Kollekt͡sii pervoĭ poloviny XIX v. po severnym atapaskam. Akademii͡a Nauk SSSR, Muzeĭ Antropologii i Etnografii, Sbornik, 24 (1967): 55-84.

02-11 Kaska

Allard, E. Notes on the Kaska and Upper Liard Indians. Primitive Man, 2 (1929): 24-26.

Dawson, G. M. Notes on the Indian tribes of the Yukon District and adjacent northern portion of British Columbia. Canada, Geological Survey, Annual Reports, n.s., 3 (1888): 199B-201B.

Flucke, A. F. Déné. By A. F. Flucke and A. E. Pickford. Victoria, Province of British Columbia, Department of Education, 1953. 59 p. illus., maps. (British Columbia Heritage Series, Series I, 9)

Honigmann, J. J. Are there Nahani Indians? Anthropologica, 3 (1956): 35-38.

Honigmann, J. J. Cultural dynamics of sex. Psychiatry, 10 (1947): 37-47.

*Honigmann, J. J. Culture and ethos of Kaska society. Yale University Publications in Anthropology, 40 (1949): 1-368.

Honigmann, J. J. Culture patterns and human stress. Psychiatry, 13 (1950): 25-34.

*Honigmann, J. J. The Kaska Indians. Yale
   University Publications in Anthropology,
   51 (1954): 1-163.

Honigmann, J. J. Witch-fear in post-
   contact Kaska society. American
   Anthropologist, n.s., 49 (1947): 222-
   243.

Honigmann, J. J. and I. Honigmann. A
   Kaska oracle. Man, 47 (1947): 139-140.

Honigmann, John J. Field work in two
   northern Canadian communities. In Morris
   Freilich, ed. Marginal Natives:
   Anthropologists at Work. New York,
   Harper and Row, 1970: 39-72.

Honigmann, John J. Interpersonal
   relations in atomistic communities.
   Human Organization, 27 (1968): 220-229.

*Honigmann, John J. The Kaska Indians: an
   ethnographic reconstruction. New Haven,
   Human Relations Area Files Press, 1964.
   163 p. illus., maps. .(Yale University
   Publications in Anthropology, 51)

Honigmann, John J. Understanding culture.
   New York, Harper and Row, 1963. 8,
   468 p. illus., maps.

Honigmann, John J. World view and self-
   view of the Kaska Indians. In Robert
   Hunt, ed. Personalities and Cultures.
   Garden City, Natural History Press,
   1967: 33-48.

McClellan, C. Shamanistic syncretism in
   southern Yukon. New York Academy of
   Sciences, Transactions, ser. 2, 19
   (1956): 130-137.

Morice, A. G. The great Déné race.
   Anthropos, 1 (1906): 229-277, 483-508,
   695-730; 2 (1907): 1-34, 181-196; 4
   (1909): 582-606; 5 (1910): 113-142, 419-
   443, 643-653, 969-990.

Morice, A. G. The Nah•ane and their
   language. Canadian Institute,
   Transactions, 7 (1903): 517-534.

Morice, A. G. The Western Dénés. Canadian
   Institute, Proceedings, ser. 3, 7
   (1889): 109-174.

Patterson, R. M. The Nahany lands.
   Beaver, 292, no. 1 (1961/1962): 40-47.

Swanton, J. R. Nahane. U.S. Bureau of
   American Ethnology, Bulletin, 30, vol. 2
   (1910): 10.

*Teit, J. A. Field notes on the Tahltan
   and Kaska Indians, 1912-1915.
   Anthropologica, 3 (1956): 39-171.

Teit, J. A. Kaska tales. Journal of
   American Folklore, 30 (1917): 427-473.

Underwood, F. W. and I. Honigmann. A
   comparison of socialization and
   personality in two simple societies.
   American Anthropologist, n.s., 49
   (1947): 557-577.

02-12 Kutchin

Alford, M. E. Old Crow. Alaska Sportsman,
   30, no. 2 (1964): 22-24.

Andersen, Kristian Lange. Comparison of
   Scandinavian Lapps, Arctic fishermen,
   and Canadian Arctic Indians. Federation
   Proceedings, 22 (1963): 834-839.

Andersen, Kristian Lange, et al. Physical
   fitness of Arctic Indians. Journal of
   Applied Physiology, 15 (1960): 645-648.

Anonymous. Kutchin. U.S. Bureau of
   American Ethnology, Bulletin, 30, vol. 1
   (1907): 739-740.

Balikci, Asen. Bad friends. Human
   Organization, 27 (1968): 191-199.

Balikci, Asen. Family organization of the
   Vunta Kutchin. Arctic Anthropology, 1,
   no. 2 (1963): 62-69.

*Balikci, Asen. Vunta Kutchin social
   change. Ottawa, 1963. 4, 161 p.
   illus., maps. (Canada, Department of
   Northern Affairs and National Resources,
   Northern Co-ordination and Research
   Centre, NCRC-63-3)

Benveniste, É. Le vocabulaire de la vie
   animale chez les Indiens du Haut Yukon.
   Société Linguistique de Paris, Bulletin,
   49 (1953): 79-106.

Boas, F. A. J. Stone's measurements of
   natives of the Northwest Territories.
   American Museum of Natural History,
   Bulletin, 14 (1901): 53-68.

Bompas, W. C. Diocese of Mackenzie River.
   London, 1922. 108 p.

Burch, Ernest S., Jr. Alliance and
   conflict: inter-regional relations in
   North Alaska. By Ernest S. Burch, Jr.
   and Thomas C. Correll. In D. Lee
   Guemple, ed. Alliance in Eskimo Society.
   Seattle, American Ethnological Society,
   1972: 17-39.

Cadzow, D. A. Habitat of Loucheux bands.
   Indian Notes, 2 (1925): 172-177.

Cadzow, D. A. Old Loucheux clothing.
   Indian Notes, 2 (1925): 292-295.

Coffey, M. F. A comparative study of young Eskimo and Indian males with acclimatized White males. Conference on Cold Injury, 3 (1955): 100-116.

Cohen, Ronald. An anthropological survey of communities in the Mackenzie--Slave Lake region of Canada. Ottawa, 1962. 8, 119 p. illus., maps. (Canada, Department of Northern Affairs and National Resources, Northern Co-ordination and Research Centre, NCRC-62-3)

Corcoran, P. A., et al. Blood groups of Alaskan Eskimo and Indians. American Journal of Physical Anthropology, n.s., 17 (1959): 187-194.

Dall, W. H. Alaska and its resources. Boston, 1870. 627 p.

Dawson, G. M. Report on an exploration in the Yukon District. Canada, Geological Survey, Annual Reports, n.s., 3, pt. 1 (1889): 7B-277B.

Edwards, Allan M. Observations on juvenile hypothyroidism in native races of Northern Canada. By Allan M. Edwards and Gordon C. Gray. Canadian Medical Association Journal, 84 (1961): 1116-1124.

Elsner, Robert W. Circulation of heat to the hands of Arctic Indians. By Robert W. Elsner, John D. Nelms, and Laurence Irving. Journal of Applied Physiology, 15 (1960): 662-666.

Elsner, Robert W. Thermal metabolic responses of Arctic Indians to moderate cold exposure at the end of winter. By Robert W. Elsner, K. Lange Andersen, and Lars Hermansen. Journal of Applied Physiology, 15 (1960): 659-661.

Franklin, J. Narrative of a second expedition to the shores of the polar sea. London, 1828.

Gates, R. R. Blood groups of Canadian Indians and Eskimos. American Journal of Physical Anthropology, 12 (1929): 475-485.

Hadleigh-West, Frederick. On the distribution and territories of the Western Kutchin tribes. Alaska, University, Anthropological Papers, 7 (1958/1959): 113-116.

Hadleigh-West, Frederick. The Netsi Kutchin: an essay in human ecology. Dissertation Abstracts, 24 (1963/1964): 4344-4345. UM 64-164.

Hall, Edwin S., Jr. Speculations on the late prehistory of the Kutchin Athapaskans. Ethnohistory, 16 (1969): 317-333.

Hardisty, W. L. The Loucheux Indians. Smithsonian Institution, Annual Reports of the Board of Regents (1866): 311-320.

Harrington, Lyn. Old Crow. Beaver, 292, no. 3 (1961/1962): 4-10.

Hildes, J. A., et al. Surveys of respiratory virus antibodies in an Arctic Indian population. Canadian Medical Association Journal, 93 (1965): 1015-1018.

Höhn, E. O. The names of economically important or conspicuous mammals and birds in the Indian languages of the District of Mackenzie, N.W.T. and in Sarcee. Arctic, 15 (1962): 299-308.

Honigmann, John J. Interpersonal relations in atomistic communities. Human Organization, 27 (1968): 220-229.

Hooper, W. H. Ten months among the tents of the Tuski. London, 1853.

Irving, Laurence, et al. Metabolism and temperature of Arctic Indian men during a cold night. Journal of Applied Physiology, 15 (1960): 635-644.

Isbester, J. A. On a short vocabulary of the Loucheux language. Philological Society, Proceedings, 4 (1850): 184-185.

Jeanes, C. W. L. Inactivation of isoniazid by Canadian Eskimos and Indians. By C. W. L. Jeanes, O. Shaefer, and L. Eidus. Canadian Medical Association Journal, 106 (1972): 331-335.

Jones, S. The Kutchin tribes. Smithsonian Institution, Annual Reports of the Board of Regents (1866): 320-327.

Josie, Edith. Christmas in Old Crow. North, 12, no. 6 (1965): 26-27.

Josie, Edith. Here are the news. Toronto, Clarke, Irwin, 1966. 8, 135 p. illus., map.

Josie, Edith. Old Crow news. Whitehorse, Y.T., 1963. 24 p. illus.

Keim, Charles J., ed. Kutchin legends from Old Crow, Yukon Territory. Alaska, University, Anthropological Papers, 11, no. 2 (1964): 97-108.

Kirby, W. W. A journey to the Youcan. Smithsonian Institution, Annual Reports of the Board of Regents (1864): 416-420.

Leechman, D. Folk-lore of the Vanta-
Kutchin. National Museum of Canada,
Bulletin, 126 (1952): 76-93.

Leechman, D. Loucheux tales. Journal of
American Folklore, 63 (1950): 158-162.

Leechman, D. Old Crow's village. Canadian
Geographical Journal, 37 (1948): 2-16.

Leechman, D. The Old Crow altar cloth.
Canadian Geographical Journal, 43
(1951): 204-205.

Leechman, D. The Vanta Kutchin. National
Museum of Canada, Bulletin, 130 (1954):
1-39.

Lewis, M. The blood groups of the Kutchin
Indians at Old Crow, Yukon Territory. By
M. Lewis, J. A. Hildes, H. Kaita, and B.
Chown. American Journal of Physical
Anthropology, n.s., 19 (1961): 383-389.

Mackenzie, A. Voyage from Montreal
through the continent of North America
to the Frozen and Pacific Oceans. New
ed. New York, 1902. 2 v.

Marshall, H. Problems of a contemporary
Arctic village. Arctic, 23 (1970): 286-
287.

Mason, M. H. The Arctic forests, 21-74.
London, 1924.

McClellan, Catharine. Culture contacts in
the early historic period in
northwestern North America. Arctic
Anthropology, 2, no. 2 (1964): 3-15.

McKennan, R. Anent the Kutchin tribes.
American Anthropologist, n.s., 37
(1935): 369.

McKennan, Robert A. Athapaskan groups of
Central Alaska at the time of White
contact. Ethnohistory, 16 (1969): 335-
343.

*McKennan, Robert A. The Chandalar
Kutchin. Montreal, 1965. 156 p.
illus., maps. (Arctic Institute of
North America, Technical Paper, 17)

McKennan, Robert A. The physical
anthropology of two Alaskan Athapaskan
groups. American Journal of Physical
Anthropology, n.s., 22 (1964): 43-52.

Morgan, L. H. Systems of consanguinity
and affinity. Smithsonian Contributions
to Knowledge, 17 (1871): 291-382.

Morgan, L. H. The Indian journals, 1859-
62, p. 115-116. Ann Arbor, 1959.

Morice, A. G. Loucheux. In Catholic
Encyclopedia. Vol. 9. New York, 1910:
367-368.

Munro, D. A. A preliminary report on the
caribou of the northern Yukon Territory.
Vancouver, University of British
Columbia, 1953. 29 p. maps.

Murray, A. H. Journal of the Yukon.
Canadian Archives, Publications, 4
(1910): 1-125.

*Osgood, C. Contributions to the
ethnography of the Kutchin. Yale
University Publications in Anthropology,
14 (1936): 1-189.

Osgood, C. Kutchin tribal distribution
and synonymy. American Anthropologist,
n.s., 36 (1934): 168-179.

*Osgood, Cornelius. Contributions to the
ethnography of the Kutchin. New Haven,
Human Relations Area Files Press, 1970.
189 p. illus., map. (Yale University
Publications in Anthropology, 14)

Petitot, E. F. S. Dictionnaire de la
langue déné-dindjié. Paris, 1876.

Petitot, E. F. S. Monographie des Déné-
Dindjié. Paris, 1876. 109 p.

Petitot, E. F. S. Quinze ans sous le
cercle polaire. Paris, 1889.

Petitot, E. F. S. Six légendes
américaines. Missions Catholiques
(Lyon), 10 (1878): 605-607, 616-620.

Petitot, E. F. S. Traditions indiennes du
Canada nord-ouest. Littératures
Populaires de Toutes les Nations, 23
(1886): 13-102.

Petitot, Émile F. Les Amérindiens du
Nord-Ouest canadien au 19e siècle selon
Émile Petitot. Edited by Donat Savoie.
Ottawa, 1970. 2 v. illus. (Canada,
Ministry of Indian Affairs and of the
Canadian North, MacKenzie Delta Research
Project, MDRP, 9-10)

Petitot, Émile F. S. Indian legends of
north-western Canada. Translated by
Thelma Habgood. Western Canadian Journal
of Anthropology, 2, no. 1 (1970): 94-
129.

Petroff, I. The population and resources
of Alaska. In Compilation of Narratives
of Explorations in Alaska. Washington,
D.C., 1900: 258-263.

Ransom, J. E. Do-it-yourself doctor.
Alaska Sportsman, 30, no. 8 (1964): 26-
28.

Richardson, J. Arctic searching
  expedition, Vol. 1: 377-401. London,
  1851.

Russell, F. Athabascan myths. Journal of
  American Folklore, 13 (1900): 11-18.

Scott, L. The Loucheux. Beaver, 284 (June
  1953): 26-27.

Shafer, Robert. A few more Athapaskan and
  Sino-Tibetan comparisons. International
  Journal of American Linguistics, 35
  (1969): 67.

Simpson, T. Narrative of the discoveries
  on the north coast of America. London,
  1843. 419 p.

*Slobodin, Richard. Band organization of
  the Peel River Kutchin. Ottawa, 1962.
  4, 97 p. illus. (Canada, National
  Museum, Bulletin, 179)

Slobodin, Richard. Band organization of
  the Peel River Kutchin. Dissertation
  Abstracts, 20 (1959/1960): 453-454. UM
  59-2597.

Slobodin, Richard. Eastern Kutchin
  warfare. Anthropologica, n.s., 2 (1960):
  76-94.

Slobodin, Richard. Kutchin concepts of
  reincarnation. Western Canadian Journal
  of Anthropology, 2, no. 1 (1970): 67-79.

Slobodin, Richard. Leadership and
  participation in a Kutchin trapping
  party. In Contributions to Anthropology:
  Band Societies. Ottawa, Queen's
  Printer, 1969: 56-92. (Canada, National
  Museums, Bulletin, 228)

Slobodin, Richard. Some social functions
  of Kutchin anxiety. American
  Anthropologist, 62 (1960): 122-133.

Slobodin, Richard. The stolen girls.
  North, 10, no. 4 (1963): 34-38.

Smith, Derek G. Las implicaciones del
  pluralismo para los programas de cambio
  social en una comunidad del ártico
  canadiense. Anuario Indigenista, 29
  (1969): 73-96.

Steinberg, Arthur G., et al. Gm
  phenotypes and genotypes in U.S. Whites
  and Negroes; in American Indians and
  Eskimos; in Africans; and in
  Micronesians. American Journal of Human
  Genetics, 13 (1961): 205-213.

Stewart, E. Early days at Fort McPherson.
  Beaver, 285, no. 3 (1954/1955): 39-41.

Stewart, Ethel G. Sah-neu-ti, chief of
  the Yukon Kutchin. Beaver, 290, no. 3
  (1959/1960): 52-54.

Taylor, P. Tales from the delta. Beaver,
  284 (June 1953): 22-25.

Taylor, Phyllis M. Dog sled and school
  desk. London, Herbert Jenkins, 1960.
  160 p. illus.

Welsh, A. Community pattern and
  settlement pattern in the development of
  Old Crow Village, Yukon Territory.
  Western Canadian Journal of
  Anthropology, 2, no. 1 (1970): 17-30.

Whymper, F. A journey from Norton Sound,
  Bering Sea, to Fort Yukon. Royal
  Geographical Society, Journal, 38
  (1868): 219-237.

Whymper, F. Travel and adventure in the
  Territory of Alaska. New York, 1869.
  353 p.

Zibert, E. V. Kollektsii pervoĭ poloviny
  XIX v. po severnym atapaskam. Akademiía
  Nauk SSSR, Muzeĭ Antropologii i
  Etnografii, Sbornik, 24 (1967): 55-84.

02-13   Mountain

Franklin, J. Narrative of a second
  expedition to the shores of the polar
  sea. London, 1828.

MacNeish, J. H. Leadership among the
  Northeastern Athabascans.
  Anthropologica, 2 (1956): 131-163.

MacNeish, J. H. The Poole Field letters.
  Anthropologica, 4 (1957): 47-60.

*Michéa, Jean. Les Chitra-Gottinéké;
  groupe athapascan des Montagnes
  Rocheuses. Société des Américanistes
  (Paris), Journal, n.s., 48 (1959): 197-
  235.

02-14   Nabesna

Allen, H. T. Report of an expedition to
  the Copper, Tananá, and Kóyukuk Rivers,
  136-139. Washington, D.C., 1887.

Feltz, Elmer T., et al. California
  encephalitis virus: serological evidence
  of human infections in Alaska. Canadian
  Journal of Microbiology, 18 (1972): 757-
  762.

Guédon, Marie-Françoise. People of
  Tetlin, why are you singing? A study of
  the social life of the Upper Tanana

Indians. Dissertation Abstracts
International, 32 (1971/1972): 6176B.
UM 72-13,765.

*McKennan, R. A. The Upper Tanana Indians.
Yale University Publications in
Anthropology, 55 (1959): 1-223.

McKennan, Robert A. The physical
anthropology of two Alaskan Athapaskan
groups. American Journal of Physical
Anthropology, n.s., 22 (1964): 43-52.

Milan, Frederick A. Temperature
regulation of Eskimos, Indians and
Caucasians in a bath calorimeter. By
Frederick A. Milan, John P. Hannon, and
Eugene Evonuk. Journal of Applied
Physiology, 18 (1963): 378-382.

Murray, A. H. Journal of the Yukon.
Canadian Archives, Publications, 4
(1910): 1-125.

Rainey, F. G. Archaeology in Central
Alaska. American Museum of Natural
History, Anthropological Papers, 36
(1939): 355-405.

Zibert, E. V. Kollektsii pervoĭ poloviny
XIX v. po severnym atapaskam. Akademiĭa
Nauk SSSR, Muzeĭ Antropologii i
Etnografii, Sbornik, 24 (1967): 55-84.

02-15 Sarsi

Barbeau, C. Marius. Indian days on the
western prairies. Ottawa, Queen's
Printer, 1960. 6, 234 p. illus., end
maps. (Canada, National Museum,
Bulletin, 163)

Chown, B. and M. Lewis. The blood group
and secretor genes of the Stony and
Sarcee Indians of Alberta, Canada.
American Journal of Physical
Anthropology, n.s., 13 (1955): 181-189.

Cook, Eung-Do. Morphophonemics of two
Sarcee classifiers. International
Journal of American Linguistics, 37
(1971): 152-155.

Cook, Eung-Do. Sarcee numerals.
Anthropological Linguistics, 13 (1971):
435-441.

Cook, Eung-do. Sarcee verb paradigms.
Ottawa, 1972. 51 p. (Canada, National
Museum, Ethnology Division, Mercury
Series, 2)

Cronk, H. K. Sarcee miscellany: 1885.
Plains Anthropologist, 7 (1956): 34.

Curtis, E. S. The North American Indian,
Vol. 18: 91-122, 136-144, 158-162, 210-
214. Norwood, 1928.

Dorsey, J. O. and P. E. Goddard. Sarsi.
U.S. Bureau of American Ethnology,
Bulletin, 30, vol. 2 (1910): 467-468.

Friesen, John W. Progress of southern
Alberta native peoples. By John W.
Friesen and Louise C. Lyon. Journal of
American Indian Education, 9, no. 3
(1969/1970): 15-23.

Goddard, P. E. Dancing societies of the
Sarsi Indians. American Museum of
Natural History, Anthropological Papers,
11 (1914): 461-474.

Goddard, P. E. Notes on the sun dance of
the Sarsi. American Museum of Natural
History, Anthropological Papers, 16
(1919): 271-282.

Goddard, P. E. Sarsi texts. California,
University, Publications in American
Archaeology and Ethnology, 11 (1915):
189-277.

Graham, Andrew. Andrew Graham's
observations on Hudson's Bay, 1767-91.
Edited by Glyndwr Williams. London,
1969. 72, 423 p. illus., maps.
(Hudson's Bay Record Society,
Publications, 27)

Hady, Walter M. Indian migrations in
Manitoba and the West. Historical and
Scientific Society of Manitoba, Papers,
ser. 3, 17 (1960/1961): 24-53.

Hainline, Jane. Genetic exchange: model
construction and a practical
application. Human Biology, 35 (1963):
167-191.

Höhn, E. O. The names of economically
important or conspicuous mammals and
birds in the Indian languages of the
District of Mackenzie, N.W.T. and in
Sarcee. Arctic, 15 (1962): 299-308.

Hoijer, Harry. Sarsi nouns. By Harry
Hoijer and Janet Joël. In Harry Hoijer,
et al., eds. Studies in the Athapaskan
Languages. Berkeley, Los Angeles,
University of California Press, 1963:
62-75. (California, University,
Publications in Linguistics, 29)

Honigmann, J. J. Morale in a primitive
society. Character and Personality, 12
(1944): 228-236.

Honigmann, J. J. Northern and Southern
Athapaskan eschatology. American
Anthropologist, n.s., 47 (1945): 467-
469.

Honigmann, J. J. Notes on Sarsi kin behavior. Anthropologica, 2 (1956): 17-38.

Honigmann, J. J. Parallels in the development of shamanism among Northern and Southern Athapaskans. American Anthropologist, n.s., 51 (1949): 512-514.

Howren, Robert. A formalization of the Athabaskan 'D-effect'. International Journal of American Linguistics, 37 (1971): 96-113.

Hudson's Bay Company. Saskatchewan journals and correspondence: Edmonton House 1795-1800; Chesterfield House 1800-1802. Edited by Alice M. Johnson. London, 1967. 102, 368, 14 p. map. (Hudson's Bay Record Society, Publications, 26)

*Jenness, D. The Sarcee Indians of Alberta. Canada, Department of Mines, National Museum of Canada, Bulletin, 90 (1938): 1-98.

Lawson, Virginia Kathryn. Object categorization and nominal classification in some Northern Athapaskan languages: a generative-semantic analysis. Dissertation Abstracts International, 33 (1972/1973): 1708A. UM 72-26,707.

Li, F. K. A study of Sarcee verb stems. International Journal of American Linguistics, 6 (1930): 3-27.

MacEwan, John W. G. Portraits from the Plains. Toronto, McGraw-Hill of Canada, 1971. 287 p. illus., map.

MacGregor, James. Lord Lorne in Alberta. Alberta Historical Review, 12, no. 2 (1964): 1-14.

Matson, G. A. Blood groups and ageusia in Indians of Montana and Alberta. American Journal of Physical Anthropology, 24 (1938): 81-89.

Morgan, L. H. The Indian journals, 1859-62, p. 128. Ann Arbor, 1959.

Palliser, J. Further papers. London, 1860. 325 p.

Petitot, E. F. S. Petit vocabulaire sarcis. Société Philologique, Actes, 14 (1884): 193-198.

Richmond, S. Cognitive and structural bases for group identity: the case of the Southern Arctic Drainage Dene. Western Canadian Journal of Anthropology, 2, no. 1 (1970): 140-149.

Rolland, Walpole. My Alberta notebook. Alberta Historical Review, 18, no. 1 (1970): 21-30.

Rowand, John. A letter from Fort Edmonton. Alberta Historical Review, 11, no. 1 (1963): 1-6.

Sapir, E. A note on Sarcee pottery. American Anthropologist, n.s., 25 (1923): 247-253.

Sapir, E. Personal names among the Sarcee Indians. American Anthropologist, n.s., 26 (1924): 109-119.

Sapir, E. Pitch accent in Sarcee. Société des Américanistes, Journal, n.s., 17 (1925): 185-205.

Schmidt, W. Die Sarsi (Sarcee)-Indianer. In his Die Ursprung der Göttesidee. Bd. 7. Münster i. W., 1940: 764-789.

Simms, S. C. Traditions of the Sarcee Indians. Journal of American Folklore, 17 (1904): 180-182.

Skinner, Mark. The Seafort Burial Site (FcPr100), Rocky Mountain House (1835-1861): life and death during the fur trade. Western Canadian Journal of Anthropology, 3, no. 1 (1972): 126-145.

Thompson, David. David Thompson's narrative 1784-1812. Edited by Richard Glover. Toronto, 1962. 102, 410 p. map. (Champlain Society, Publications, 40)

Wilson, E. F. Report on the Sarcee Indians. British Association for the Advancement of Science, Annual Meeting, Report, 58 (1888): 242-255.

Wilson, E. F. The Sarcee Indians. Our Forest Children, 3 (1889): 97-102.

Wissler, Clark. Population changes among the Northern Plains Indians. New Haven, Yale University Press, 1936. 20 p. (Yale University Publications in Anthropology, 1)

Wissler, Clark. Population changes among the Northern Plains Indians. New Haven, Human Relations Area Files Press, 1970. 20 p. (Yale University Publications in Anthropology, 1)

02-16 Satudene

Franklin, J. Narrative of a second expedition to the shores of the polar sea. London, 1928.

Keith, G. Letters to Mr. Roderic
McKenzie. In L. F. R. Masson, ed. Les
Bourgeois de la Compagnie du Nord-Ouest.
Vol. 2. Quebec, 1890: 111-124.

MacNeish, J. H. Leadership among the
Northeastern Athabascans.
Anthropologica, 2 (1956): 131-163.

Morris, Margaret W. Great Bear Lake
Indians: a historical demography and
human ecology. Part I: The situation
prior to European contact. Musk-Ox, 11
(1972): 3-27.

Nag, Moni. Factors affecting human
fertility in nonindustrial societies: a
cross-cultural study. New Haven, Human
Relations Area Files Press, 1968.
227 p. (Yale University Publications in
Anthropology, 66)

Nag, Moni. Factors affecting human
fertility in nonindustrial societies: a
cross-cultural study. New Haven, Yale
University, Department of Anthropology,
1962. 227 p. (Yale University
Publications in Anthropology, 66)

*Osgood, C. The ethnography of the Great
Bear Lake Indians. Canada, Department of
Mines, National Museum of Canada,
Bulletin, 70 (1931): 31-92.

Schaeffer, C. E. The grasshopper or
children's war--a circumboreal legend?.
Pennsylvania Archaeologist, 12 (1942):
60-61.

                02-17 Sekani

Anonymous. Sekani. U.S. Bureau of
American Ethnology, Bulletin, 30, vol. 2
(1910): 498-499.

Barbeau, C. Marius. Indian days on the
western prairies. Ottawa, Queen's
Printer, 1960. 6, 234 p. illus., end
maps. (Canada, National Museum,
Bulletin, 163)

Flucke, A. F. Déné. By A. F. Flucke and
A. E. Pickford. Victoria, Province of
British Columbia, Department of
Education, 1953. 59 p. illus., maps.
(British Columbia Heritage Series,
Series I, 9)

Grant, J. C. B. Anthropometry of the
Beaver, Sekani, and Carrier Indians.
Canada, Department of Mines, National
Museum of Canada, Bulletin, 81 (1936):
1-37.

Harris, Donald A. New Caledonia and the
fur trade, a status report. By Donald A.

Harris and George C. Ingram. Journal of
Anthropology, 3, no. 1 (1972): 179-195.

Hill-Tout, C. British North America.
Toronto, 1907. 263 p.

Jenness, D. Indians of Canada. Canada,
Department of Mines, National Museum of
Canada, Bulletin, 65 (1932): 377-382.

*Jenness, D. The Sekani Indians of British
Columbia. Canada, Department of Mines,
National Museum of Canada, Bulletin, 84
(1937): 1-82.

Jenness, D. The Sekani Indians of British
Columbia. Royal Society of Canada,
Proceedings and Transactions, ser. 3,
25, pt. 2 (1931): 21-34.

Johnson, Patricia. McLeod Lake Post.
Beaver, 296, no. 2 (1965/1966): 22-29.

Lawson, Virginia Kathryn. Object
categorization and nominal
classification in some Northern
Athapaskan languages: a generative-
semantic analysis. Dissertation
Abstracts International, 33 (1972/1973):
1708A. UM 72-26,707.

Morice, A. G. About cremation. American
Anthropologist, n.s., 27 (1925): 576-
577.

Morice, A. G. Déné surgery. Canadian
Institute, Transactions, 7 (1901): 15-
27.

Morice, A. G. Notes archaeological,
industrial and sociological on the
Western Dénés. Canadian Institute,
Transactions, 4 (1893): 1-222.

Morice, A. G. The great Déné race.
Anthropos, 1 (1906): 229-277, 483-508,
695-730; 2 (1907): 1-34, 181-196; 4
(1909): 582-606; 5 (1910): 113-142, 419-
443, 643-653, 969-990.

Morice, A. G. The history of the northern
interior of British Columbia. Toronto,
1904. 339 p.

Morice, A. G. The Western Dénés. Canadian
Institute, Proceedings, ser. 3, 7
(1889): 109-174.

Weber, Michel. Les Indiens Siccanies
(Nord de la Colombie britannique /
Canada). Société Suisse des
Américanistes, Bulletin, 23 (1962): 17-
18.

02-18 Slave

Anonymous. Etchareottine. U.S. Bureau of American Ethnology, Bulletin, 30, vol. 1 (1907): 439-440.

Asch, Michael Ira. A social behavioral approach to music analysis: the case of the Slavey Drum Dance. Dissertation Abstracts International, 33 (1972/1973): 1898B-1899B. UM 72-28,011.

Bell, R. Legends of the Slavey Indians. Journal of American Folklore, 14 (1901): 26-29.

Bourget, Clermont. Douze ans chez les sauvages au Grand-Lac des Esclaves, comme médecin et agent des Indiens (1923-1935). Ste.-Anne-de-Beaupré, Québec, en vente chez l'auteur, 1938. 249 p.

Bowen, P. Serum protein polymorphisms in Indians of Western Canada: gene frequencies and data on the Gc/albumin linkage. By P. Bowen, F. O'Callaghan and Catherine S. N. Lee. Human Heredity, 21 (1971): 242-253.

Cohen, Ronald. An anthropological survey of communities in the Mackenzie--Slave Lake region of Canada. Ottawa, 1962. 8, 119 p. illus., maps. (Canada, Department of Northern Affairs and National Resources, Northern Co-ordination and Research Centre, NCRC-62-3)

Cox, B. Land rights of the Slavey Indians at Hay River, N.W.T. Western Canadian Journal of Anthropology, 2, no. 1 (1970): 150-155.

Fidler, P. Journal of a journey with the Chepawyans or Northern Indians. Champlain Society, Publications, 21 (1934): 493-556.

Fowler, Henry L. The Great Slave Lake: its potential for the development of co-operatives. By H. L. Fowler and J. T. Phalen. Ottawa, Co-operative Union of Canada, 1963. 20 l.

Gates, R. R. Blood groups of Canadian Indians and Eskimos. American Journal of Physical Anthropology, 12 (1929): 475-485.

Heinrich, Albert C. Co-affinal siblingship as a structural feature among some northern North American peoples. By Albert C. Heinrich and Russell Anderson. Ethnology, 7 (1968): 290-295.

Helm, June. A method of statistical analysis of primary relative bonds in community composition. In Contributions to Anthropology: Band Societies. Ottawa, Queen's Printer, 1969: 218-239. (Canada, National Museums, Bulletin, 228)

Helm, June. Bilaterality in the socio-territorial organization of the Arctic Drainage Dene. Ethnology, 4 (1965): 361-385.

Helm, June. Patterns of allocation among the Arctic Drainage Dene. In June Helm, et al., eds. Essays in Economic Anthropology. Seattle, University of Washington Press, 1965: 33-45. (American Ethnological Society, Proceedings of the Annual Spring Meeting, 1965)

Helm, June. Remarks on the methodology of band composition analysis. In Contributions to Anthropology: Band Societies. Ottawa, Queen's Printer, 1969: 212-217. (Canada, National Museums, Bulletin, 228)

Helm, June. The contact-traditional all-native community of the Canadian North: the Upper MacKenzie "Bush" Athapaskans and the Igluligmiut. By June Helm and David Damas. Anthropologica, n.s., 5 (1963): 9-21.

*Helm, June. The Lynx Point people: the dynamics of a Northern Athapaskan band. Ottawa, 1961. 5, 193 p. illus., maps. (Canada, National Museum, Bulletin, 176)

Helm, June. Variations in personality and ego identification within a Slave Indian kin-community. By June Helm, George A. DeVos, and Teresa Carterette. In Contributions to Anthropology 1960. Part II. Ottawa, Queen's Printer, 1963: 94-138. (Canada, National Museum, Bulletin, 190)

Höhn, E. O. The names of economically important or conspicuous mammals and birds in the Indian languages of the District of Mackenzie, N.W.T. and in Sarcee. Arctic, 15 (1962): 299-308.

*Honigmann, J. J. Ethnography and acculturation of the Fort Nelson Slave. Yale University Publications in Anthropology, 33 (1946): 1-169.

Howard, Phillip G. A preliminary presentation of Slave phonemes. In Harry Hoijer, et al., eds. Studies in the Athapaskan Languages. Berkeley and Los Angeles, University of California Press, 1963: 42-47. (California, University, Publications in Linguistics, 29)

Jeanes, C. W. L. Inactivation of
    isoniazid by Canadian Eskimos and
    Indians. By C. W. L. Jeanes, O. Shaefer,
    and L. Eidus. Canadian Medical
    Association Journal, 106 (1972): 331-
    335.

Jenness, D. Indians of Canada. Canada,
    Department of Mines, National Museum of
    Canada, Bulletin, 65 (1932): 389-392.

MacNeish, J. H. Contemporary folk beliefs
    of a Slave Indian band. Journal of
    American Folklore, 67 (1954): 185-197.

MacNeish, J. H. Folktales of the Slave
    Indians. Anthropologica, 1 (1955): 37-
    44.

MacNeish, J. H. Kin terms of Arctic
    Drainage Déné. American Anthropologist,
    62 (1960): 279-295.

MacNeish, J. H. Leadership among the
    Northeastern Athabascans.
    Anthropologica, 2 (1956): 131-163.

MacNeish, June Helm. Kin terms of Arctic
    Drainage Déné: Hare, Slavey, Chipewyan.
    American Anthropologist, 62 (1960): 279-
    295.

Mason, J. A. Notes on the Indians of the
    Great Slave Lake area. Yale University
    Publications in Anthropology, 34 (1946):
    1-46.

Morgan, L. H. Systems of consanguinity
    and affinity. Smithsonian Contributions
    to Knowledge, 17 (1871): 291-382.

Osgood, C. The ethnography of the Great
    Bear Lake Indians. Canada, Department of
    Mines, National Museum of Canada,
    Bulletin, 70 (1931): 31-92.

Petitot, E. F. S. Autour du Grand Lac des
    Esclaves. Paris, 1891. 369 p.

Petitot, E. F. S. Traditions indiennes du
    Canada nord-ouest. Littératures
    Populaires de Toutes les Nations, 23
    (1886): 307-344.

Petitot, Émile F. S. Indian legends of
    north-western Canada. Translated by
    Thelma Habgood. Western Canadian Journal
    of Anthropology, 2, no. 1 (1970): 94-
    129.

Richmond, S. Cognitive and structural
    bases for group identity: the case of
    the Southern Arctic Drainage Dene.
    Western Canadian Journal of
    Anthropology, 2, no. 1 (1970): 140-149.

Ross, B. R. The Eastern Tinneh.
    Smithsonian Institution, Annual Reports
    of the Board of Regents (1866): 304-311.

Tetso, John. Trapping is my life.
    Toronto, Peter Martin Associates, 1970.
    9, 115 p. illus., maps.

Wentzel, W. F. Letters to the Hon.
    Roderic McKenzie. In L. F. R. Masson,
    ed. Les Bourgeois de la Compagnie du
    Nord-Ouest. Vol. 1. Quebec, 1889: 85-
    105. (The Slave are here called the
    "Beaver").

Williamson, R. G. Slave Indian legends.
    Anthropologica, 1 (1955): 119-143; 2
    (1956): 61-92.

                    02-19   Tahltan

Anonymous. Nahane. U.S. Bureau of
    American Ethnology, Bulletin, 30, vol. 2
    (1910): 10.

Barbeau, M. Songs of the Northwest.
    Musical Quarterly, 19 (1933): 101-111.

Boas, F. A. J. Stone's measurements of
    natives of the Northwest Territories.
    American Museum of Natural History,
    Bulletin, 14 (1901): 53-68.

Callbreath, J. C. Notes on the Tahl-tan
    Indians. Canada, Geological Survey,
    Annual Reports, n.s., 3 (1888): 195B-
    199B.

Cook, Eung-Do. Stress and related rules
    in Tahltan. International Journal of
    American Linguistics, 38 (1972): 231-
    233.

Dennis, A. P. Life on a Yukon trail.
    National Geographic Magazine, 10 (1899):
    384-387.

Emmons, G. T. Tahltan. U.S. Bureau of
    American Ethnology, Bulletin, 30, vol. 2
    (1910): 670-671.

*Emmons, G. T. The Tahltan Indians.
    Pennsylvania, University, University
    Museum, Anthropological Publications, 4
    (1911): 1-120.

Flucke, A. F. Déné. By A. F. Flucke and
    A. E. Pickford. Victoria, Province of
    British Columbia, Department of
    Education, 1953. 59 p. illus., maps.
    (British Columbia Heritage Series,
    Series I, 9)

Jenness, D. Indians of Canada. Canada,
    Department of Mines, National Museum of
    Canada, Bulletin, 65 (1932): 370-376.

MacLachlan, B. B. Notes on some Tahltan
    oral literature. Anthropologica, 4
    (1957): 1-10.

Morice, A. G. Nahanes. In Catholic Encyclopedia. Vol. 10. New York, 1911: 669-670.

Morice, A. G. The great Déné race. Anthropos, 1 (1906): 229-277, 483-508, 695-730; 2 (1907): 1-34, 181-196; 4 (1909): 582-606; 5 (1910): 113-142, 419-443, 643-653, 969-990.

Morice, A. G. The history of the northern interior of British Columbia, 1-32. Toronto, 1904.

Morice, A. G. The Nah•ane and their language. Canadian Institute, Transactions, 7 (1903): 517-534.

Morice, A. G. The Western Dénés. Canadian Institute, Proceedings, ser. 3, 7 (1889): 109-174.

Teit, J. A. Field notes on the Tahltan and Kaska Indians, 1912-1915. Anthropologica, 3 (1956): 39-171.

Teit, J. A. Notes on the Tahltan Indians of British Columbia. In Boas Anniversary Volume. New York, 1906: 337-349.

Teit, J. A. On Tahltan (Athabaskan) work, 1912. Canada, Geological Survey, Summary Reports (1912): 484-487.

Teit, J. A. Tahltan tales. Journal of American Folklore, 32 (1919): 198-250; 34 (1921): 223-253, 335-356.

Teit, J. A. Two Tahltan traditions. Journal of American Folklore, 22 (1909): 314-318.

02-20 Tanaina

Abercrombie, W. R. A military reconnaissance of the Copper River Valley. In Compilation of Narratives of Explorations in Alaska. Washington, D.C., 1900: 563-591.

Alexan, N. How Tyonek people used to eat. Alaska Sportsman, 31, no. 1 (1965): 38-39.

Alexan, N. Stories about how to raise children. Alaska Sportsman, 31, no. 4 (1965): 13-14.

Anonymous. Knaiakhotana. U.S. Bureau of American Ethnology, Bulletin, 30, vol. 1 (1907): 715-717.

Anonymous. Ueber die Kinaivölker im äussersten Nord-westen Amerikas. Globus, 26 (1874): 87-88.

Castner, J. C. A story of hardship and suffering in Alaska. In Compilation of Narratives of Explorations in Alaska. Washington, D.C., 1900: 686-709.

Cook, F. A. To the top of the continent, 269-277. New York, 1908.

Dumond, Don E. An archaeological survey along Knik Arm. By D. E. Dumond and Robert L. A. Mace. Alaska, University, Anthropological Papers, 14, no. 1 (1968): 1-21.

Galitzin, É. Observations recueillies par l'Admiral Wrangell sur les habitants des côtes nord-ouest de l'Amérique. Nouvelles Annales des Voyages, 137 (1853): 195-221.

Gleason, Henry A. A note on some Tanaina subgroups. International Journal of American Linguistics, 26 (1960): 348-351.

Glenn, E. F. Explorations in and about Cooks Inlet. In Compilation of Narratives of Explorations in Alaska. Washington, D.C., 1900: 713-724.

Herron, J. S. Explorations in Alaska, 1899, for an all-American overland route from Cook Inlet, Pacific Ocean, to the Yukon. Washington, D.C., 1901. 77 p.

Kent, Frederick J. An archaeological survey of the portions of the northwestern Kenai Peninsula. By Frederick J. Kent, John V. Matthews, and Frederick Hadleigh-West. Alaska, University, Anthropological Papers, 12 (1964): 101-134.

Krusenstern, A. J. von. Wörter-Sammlungen aus den Sprachen einiger Völker des östlichen Asien und der Nordwest-Küste von Amerika, 59-68. St. Petersburg, 1813.

Laguna, F. de. The archaeology of Cook Inlet. Philadelphia, 1934. 263 p.

Landar, Herbert J. Tanaina subgroups. International Journal of American Linguistics, 26 (1960): 120-122.

Learnard, H. G. A trip from Portage Bay to Turnagain Arm and up the Sushitna. In Compilation of Narratives of Explorations in Alaska. Washington, D.C., 1900: 648-677.

Lisiansky, U. A voyage round the world. London, 1814.

Mason, J. A. A remarkable stone lamp from Alaska. Museum Journal, 19 (1928): 170-194.

Morgan, Lael. The Tyonek Indian tycoons;
learning the hard way. New York, Alicia
Patterson Fund, 1972. 8 p. illus.
(Alicia Patterson Fund, LM-10)

Osgood, C. Tanaina culture. American
Anthropologist, n.s., 35 (1933): 695-
717.

*Osgood, C. The ethnography of the
Tanaina. Yale University Publications in
Anthropology, 16 (1937): 1-229.

*Osgood, Cornelius. The ethnography of the
Tanaina. New Haven, Human Relations
Area Files Press, 1966. 229 p. illus.,
maps. (Yale University Publications in
Anthropology, 16)

Oswalt, Wendell H. Historical populations
in western Alaska and migration theory.
Alaska, University, Anthropological
Papers, 11 (1962/1964): 1-14.

Petroff, I. Report on the population,
industries, and resources of Alaska.
U.S. Department of the Interior, Tenth
Census, 8, vol. 2 (1881): 162-164.

Radloff, L. Einige kritische Bemerkungen
über Hrn. Buschmann's Behandlung der
Kinai-Sprache. Académie Impériale des
Sciences, Mélanges Russes, 3 (1857):
364-399.

Radloff, L. Wörterbuch der Kinaisprache.
Académie Impériale des Sciences de St.-
Pétersbourg, Mémoires, sér. 7, 21, no. 8
(1874): 1-33.

Richardson, J. Arctic searching
expedition. London, 1851.

Scott, Edward M., et al. Frequency of
polymorphic types of red cell enzymes
and serum factors in Alaskan Eskimos and
Indians. American Journal of Human
Genetics, 18 (1966): 408-411.

Sherwood, Morgan B. Science in Russian
America, 1741 to 1865. Pacific Northwest
Quarterly, 58 (1967): 33-39.

Townsend, Joan B. Archaeological
investigations at Pedro Bay, Alaska. By
Joan B. Townsend and Sam-Joe Townsend.
Alaska, University, Anthropological
Papers, 10 (1961/1963): 25-58.

Townsend, Joan B. Ethnographic notes on
the Pedro Bay Tanaina. Anthropologica,
n.s., 5 (1963): 209-223.

Townsend, Joan B. Tanaina Athapaskan
ethnohistory and socio-economic change.
In International Congress of
Anthropological and Ethnological
Sciences, 8th. 1968, Tokyo and Kyoto.

Proceedings. Vol. 2. Tokyo, Science
Council of Japan, 1969: 186-188.

Townsend, Joan B. The Tanaina of
southwestern Alaska: an historical
synopsis. Western Canadian Journal of
Anthropology, 2, no. 1 (1970): 2-16.

Townsend, Joan Broom. Ethnohistory and
culture change of the Iliamna Tanaina.
Dissertation Abstracts, 26 (1965/1966):
6964. UM 66-5522.

Troufanoff, I. P. The Ahtena tomahawks in
the Museum of Anthropology and
Ethnography of the Academy of Sciences
of the U.S.S.R. Current Anthropology, 11
(1970): 155-159.

Trufanov, I. P. Kenaĭskie tomagavki iz
etnograficheskoĭ kollekt͡sii I. G.
Voznesenkogo. Akademii͡a Nauk SSSR, Muzeĭ
Antropologii i Etnografii, Sbornik, 24
(1967): 85-92.

VanStone, James W. Kijik: an historic
Tanaina Indian settlement. By James W.
VanStone and Joan B. Townsend. Chicago,
Field Museum of Natural History, 1970.
202 p. illus., map. (Fieldiana:
Anthropology, 59)

Vaudrin, B. The chickadee. Alaska Review,
1, no. 2 (1964): 26-29.

Vaudrin, Bill. Tanaina tales from Alaska.
Norman, University of Oklahoma Press,
1969. 36, 133 p. illus., map.

Veniaminov, Innokentii. The condition of
the Orthodox Church in Russian America:
Innokentii Veniaminov's history of the
Russian church in Alaska. Translated and
edited by Robert Nichols and Robert
Croskey. Pacific Northwest Quarterly, 63
(1972): 41-54.

Volkov, T. and S. I. Rudenko.
Etnograficheskai͡a kollekt͡sii iz byvshikh
rossiisko-amerikanskikh vladienii. St.
Petersburg, 1910. 47 p.

Vrangel', Ferdinand Petrovich von. The
inhabitants of the Northwest Coast of
America. Translated and edited by James
W. VanStone. By Ferdinand Petrovich von
Wrangell. Arctic Anthropology, 6, no. 2
(1970): 5-20.

Woldt, A. Capitain Jacobsen's Reise an
der Nordwestküste Amerikas. Leipzig,
1884.

Wrangell, F. P. von. Obitateli severo-
zapadyx veregov Ameriki. Syn Otechestva,
7 (1839): 51-82.

Wrangell, F. P. von. Statistische und
ethnographische Nachrichten an der

Nordwestküste von Amerika. Beiträge zur
Kenntnis des Russischen Reiches, 1
(1838): 103-116.

Zibert, E. V. Kollektsii pervoĭ poloviny
XIX v. po severnym atapaskam. Akademiia
Nauk SSSR, Muzeĭ Antropologii i
Etnografii, Sbornik, 24 (1967): 55-84.

02-21   Tanana

Anonymous. Tenankutchin. U.S. Bureau of
American Ethnology, Bulletin, 30, vol. 2
(1910): 727-728.

Cantwell, J. C. Report of the operations
of the U.S. Revenue Steamer Nunivak,
209-236, 281-284. Washington, D.C.,
1902.

Dall, W. H. Alaska and its resources.
Boston, 1870. 627 p.

Feltz, Elmer T., et al. California
encephalitis virus: serological evidence
of human infections in Alaska. Canadian
Journal of Microbiology, 18 (1972): 757-
762.

Gordon, G. B. In the Alaskan wilderness.
Philadelphia, 1917. 247 p.

Heinrich, Albert C. Co-affinal
siblingship as a structural feature
among some northern North American
peoples. By Albert C. Heinrich and
Russell Anderson. Ethnology, 7 (1968):
290-295.

Hrdlička, A. Anthropological survey of
Alaska. U.S. Bureau of American
Ethnology, Annual Reports, 46 (1930):
19-374.

McClellan, Catharine. Avoidance between
siblings of the same sex in Northwestern
North America. Southwestern Journal of
Anthropology, 17 (1961): 103-123.

McClellan, Catharine. Culture contacts in
the early historic period in
northwestern North America. Arctic
Anthropology, 2, no. 2 (1964): 3-15.

McKennan, Robert A. Athapaskan groupings
and social organization in central
Alaska. In Contributions to
Anthropology: Band Societies. Ottawa,
Queen's Printer, 1969: 93-115. (Canada,
National Museums, Bulletin, 228)

McKennan, Robert A. Athapaskan groups of
Central Alaska at the time of White
contact. Ethnohistory, 16 (1969): 335-
343.

Morgan, Lael. Letter from Alaskan United
Crow Bands Indians to the Secretary of
the Interior. New York, Alicia
Patterson Fund, 1972. 8 p. illus.
(Alicia Patterson Fund, LM-11)

Murray, W. H. Journal of the Yukon.
Canadian Archives, Publications, 4
(1910): 1-125.

Olson, Wallace. Tree paintings near Tok,
Alaska. By Wallace Olson and Ramon Vitt.
Alaska, University, Anthropological
Papers, 14 (1968/1969): 76-83.

Oswalt, Wendell H. Historical populations
in western Alaska and migration theory.
Alaska, University, Anthropological
Papers, 11 (1962/1964): 1-14.

Rainey, F. G. Archeology in Central
Alaska. American Museum of Natural
History, Anthropological Papers, 36
(1939): 351-404.

Schwatka, F. Report of a military
reconnaissance made in Alaska, 323-362.
Washington, D.C., 1900.

Sniffen, M. K. and T. S. Carrington. The
Indians of the Yukon and Tanana Valleys.
Indian Rights Association, Publications,
ser. 2, 98 (1914): 3-35.

Vrangel', Ferdinand Petrovich von. The
inhabitants of the Northwest Coast of
America. Translated and edited by James
W. VanStone. By Ferdinand Petrovich von
Wrangell. Arctic Anthropology, 6, no. 2
(1970): 5-20.

Zibert, E. V. Kollektsii pervoĭ poloviny
XIX v. po severnym atapaskam. Akademiia
Nauk SSSR, Muzeĭ Antropologii i
Etnografii, Sbornik, 24 (1967): 55-84.

02-22   Tsetsaut

Anonymous. Tsetsaut. U.S. Bureau of
American Ethnology, Bulletin, 30, vol. 2
(1910): 825.

Boas, F. Physical characteristics of the
tribes of the North Pacific Coast.
British Association for the Advancement
of Science, Annual Meeting, Report, 65
(1895): 524-551.

Boas, F. The Tinneh tribe of Portland
Inlet. British Association for the
Advancement of Science, Annual Meeting,
Report, 65 (1895): 555-569, 587-592.

Boas, F. Traditions of the Ts'ets'aut.
Journal of American Folklore, 9 (1896):
257-268; 10 (1897): 35-48.

Boas, F. and P. E. Goddard. Ts'ets'áut.
International Journal of American
Linguistics, 3 (1924): 1-35.

Krauss, Michael E. Proto-Athapaskan-Eyak
and the problem of Na-Dene.
International Journal of American
Linguistics, 30 (1964): 118-131; 31
(1965): 18-28.

Morice, A. G. The Nah·ane and their
language. Canadian Institute,
Transactions, 7 (1903): 517-534.

Tharp, George W. The position of the
Tsetsaut among Northern Athapaskans.
International Journal of American
Linguistics, 38 (1972): 14-25.

02-23   Tutchone

Anonymous. Tutchonekutchin. U.S. Bureau
of American Ethnology, Bulletin, 30,
vol. 2 (1910): 855.

Campbell, R. Discovery and exploration of
the Youcon River. Winnipeg, 1885.

Dawson, G. M. Notes on the Indian tribes
of the Yukon District and adjacent
northern portion of British Columbia.
Canada, Geological Survey, Annual
Reports, n.s., 3 (1888): 191B-213B.

McClellan, C. Shamanistic syncretism in
southern Yukon. New York Academy of
Sciences, Transactions, ser. 2, 19
(1956): 130-137.

McClellan, C. and D. Rainier.
Ethnological survey of southern Yukon
Territory, 1948. National Museum of
Canada, Bulletin, 118 (1950): 50-53.

McClellan, Catharine. Avoidance between
siblings of the same sex in Northwestern
North America. Southwestern Journal of
Anthropology, 17 (1961): 103-123.

McClellan, Catharine. Culture contacts in
the early historic period in
northwestern North America. Arctic
Anthropology, 2, no. 2 (1964): 3-15.

Schwatka, F. Along Alaska's great river.
New York, 1885. 360 p.

Schwatka, F. Report of a military
reconnaissance made in Alaska in 1883,
323-362. Washington, D.C., 1900.

02-24   Yellowknife

Anonymous. Tatsanottine. U.S. Bureau of
American Ethnology, Bulletin, 30, vol. 2
(1910): 698-699.

Franklin, J. Narrative of a journey to
the shores of the polar sea. London,
1823.

Gillespie, Beryl C. Yellowknives: quo
iverunt? In Robert F. Spencer, ed.
Migration and Anthropology. Seattle,
University of Washington Press, 1970:
61-71. (American Ethnological Society,
Proceedings of the Annual Spring
Meeting, 1970)

Hearne, S. A journey from Prince of
Wale's Fort in Hudson's Bay to the
Northern Ocean. Ed. by J. B. Tyrrell.
Champlain Society, Publications, 6
(1911): 1-437.

Hearne, Samuel. A journey from Prince of
Wales's Fort in Hudson's Bay to the
Northern Ocean. Rutland, Vt., C. E.
Tuttle, 1971. 56, 458 p. illus., maps.

Jeanes, C. W. L. Inactivation of
isoniazid by Canadian Eskimos and
Indians. By C. W. L. Jeanes, O. Shaefer,
and L. Eidus. Canadian Medical
Association Journal, 106 (1972): 331-
335.

King, R. Narrative of a journey to the
shores of the Arctic Ocean. London,
1836. 2 v.

MacNeish, J. H. Leadership among the
Northeastern Athabascans.
Anthropologica, 2 (1956): 131-163.

Mason, J. A. Notes on the Indians of the
Great Slave Lake Area. Yale University
Publications in Anthropology, 34 (1946):
1-46.

Morice, A. G. Yellow-Knives. In Catholic
Encyclopedia. Vol. 15. New York, 1912:
733.

Noble, William C. Archaeological surveys
and sequences in central District of
Mackenzie, N.W.T. Arctic Anthropology,
8, no. 1 (1971): 102-135.

Petitot, E. F. S. De l'origine asiatique
des Indiens de l'Amérique arctique.
Société Philologique, Actes, 12 (1883):
41-58.

Petitot, E. F. S. La femme aux metaux.
Meaux, 1888.

Pike, W. M. The barren ground of northern
Canada. London, 1892. 300 p.

Ross, B. R.   The Eastern Tinneh.
Smithsonian Institution, Annual Reports
of the Board of Regents (1866): 304-311.

Simpson, G.   Journal of occurrences in the
Athabasca Department, 1820 and 1821.
Champlain Society, Publications, 1
(1938): 1-557.

02-25   Northern Métis

Buckley, Helen.   Trapping and fishing in
the economy of northern Saskatchewan.
Saskatoon, Centre for Community Studies,
Research Division, 1962.   3, 189 l.
illus.   (Economic and Social Survey of
Northern Saskatchewan, Report, 3)

Canadian Corrections Association.   Indians
and the law.   Journal of Canadian
Studies, 3, no. 2 (1968): 31-55.

Carrothiers, A. W. R.   Canada: reluctant
imperialist.   Journal of Canadian
Studies, 2, no. 1 (1967): 11-23.

Chalmers, J. W.   Inland journey.   Beaver,
303, no. 2 (1972/1973): 52-59.

Clairmont, Donald H. J.   Deviance among
Indians and Eskimos in Aklavik, N.W.T.
Ottawa, 1963.   11, 84 p.   illus., maps.
(Canada, Department of Northern Affairs
and National Resources, Northern Co-
ordination and Research Centre, NCRC-63-
9)

Clairmont, Donald H. J.   Notes on the
drinking behavior of the Eskimos and
Indians in the Aklavik area; a
preliminary report.   Ottawa, 1962.   1,
13 p.   illus.   (Canada, Department of
Northern Affairs and National Resources,
Northern Co-ordination and Research
Centre, NCRC-62-4)

Clifton, Rodney A.   The social adjustment
of native students in a northern
Canadian hostel.   Canadian Review of
Anthropology and Sociology, 9 (1972):
163-166.

Cohen, Ronald.   An anthropological survey
of communities in the Mackenzie--Slave
Lake region of Canada.   Ottawa, 1962.
8, 119 p.   illus., maps.   (Canada,
Department of Northern Affairs and
National Resources, Northern Co-
ordination and Research Centre, NCRC-62-
3)

Ervin, A. M.   New northern townsmen in
Inuvik.   Ottawa, Department of Indian
Affairs and Northern Development, 1968.
30 p.   ERIC ED031332.

Ervin, Alexander M.   Conflicting styles of
life in a northern Canadian town.
Arctic, 22 (1969): 90-105.

Fried, Jacob.   White-dominant settlements
in the Canadian Northwest Territories.
Anthropologica, n.s., 5 (1963): 57-67.

Genini, Ronald.   The Fraser-Cariboo gold
rushes: comparisons and contrasts with
the California gold rush.   Journal of the
West, 11 (1972): 470-487.

Goucher, A. C.   The dropout problem among
Indian and Metis students.   Calgary,
Dome Petroleum, 1967.   52 p.   ERIC
ED042528.

Hatt, F. K.   The Canadian Métis: recent
interpretations.   Canadian Ethnic
Studies, 3 (1971): 1-16.

Honigmann, John J.   Five Canadian Arctic
and Subarctic towns: their native
populations.   In Internationale
Amerikanistenkongress, 38th.   1968,
Stuttgart-München.   Verhandlungen. Band
3.   München, Klaus Renner, 1971: 125-
132.

LaVallee, Mary Anne, ed.   National
conference on Indian and northern
education (Saskatoon, Canada, 1967).
Saskatoon, Saskatchewan University,
Extension Division, 1967.   130 p.   ERIC
ED028861.

Lotz, James R.   The Dawson area, a
regional monograph.   Ottawa, 1965.
209 p.   illus., maps.   (Canada,
Department of Northern Affairs and
National Resources, Northern Co-
ordination and Research Centre, Yukon
Research Project, YRP-2)

MacArthur, R. S.   Assessing the
intellectual ability of Indian and Metis
pupils at Ft. Simpson, N.W.T.   Ottawa,
Canadian Department of Northern Affairs
and National Resources, 1962.   29 p.
ERIC ED027123.

McEwen, Ernest R.   Community development
services for Canadian Indian and Metis
communities.   Toronto, Indian Eskimo
Association of Canada, 1968.   52 p.
ERIC ED050864.

Morton, Desmond.   Des canadiens errants:
French Canadian troops in the North-West
Campaign of 1885.   Journal of Canadian
Studies, 5, no. 3 (1970): 28-39.

Pritchard, G. B.   New town in the far
North.   Geographical Magazine, 37 (1964):
344-357.

Saunders, L. G.   A survey of helminth and
protozoan incidence in man and dogs at

Fort Chipewyan, Alberta. Journal of
Parasitology, 35 (1949): 31-34.

*Slobodin, Richard. Métis of the Mackenzie
District. Ottawa, Canadian Research
Centre for Anthropology, 1966. 12,
175 p. illus., map.

Slobodin, Richard. The Metis of northern
Canada. In Noel P. Gist and Anthony Gary
Dworkin, eds. The Blending of Races.
New York, Wiley-Interscience, 1972: 143-
166.

Slobodin, Richard. The subarctic Metis as
products and agents of culture contact.
Arctic Anthropology, 2, no. 2 (1964):
50-55.

Small, G. W. The usefulness of Canadian
Army selection tests in a culturally
restricted population. Canadian
Psychologist, 10 (1969): 9-19.

Smith, Derek G. Las implicaciones del
pluralismo para los programas de cambio
social en una comunidad del ártico
canadiense. Anuario Indigenista, 29
(1969): 73-96.

Tanner, Adrian. Trappers, hunters and
fishermen; wildlife utilization in the
Yukon Territory. Ottawa, 1966. 79 p.
illus., maps. (Canada, Department of
Northern Affairs and National Resources,
Northern Co-ordination and Research
Centre, Yukon Research Project, YRP-5)

Williamson, Robert G. The Canadian
Arctic, sociocultural change. Archives
of Environmental Health, 17 (1968): 484-
491.

Wolforth, John Raymond. "Dual allegiance"
in the Mackenzie Delta, NWT--aspects of
the evolution and contemporary spacial
structure of a northern community.
Dissertation Abstracts International, 32
(1971/1972): 2791B.

11   Eastern Canada

11 Eastern Canada

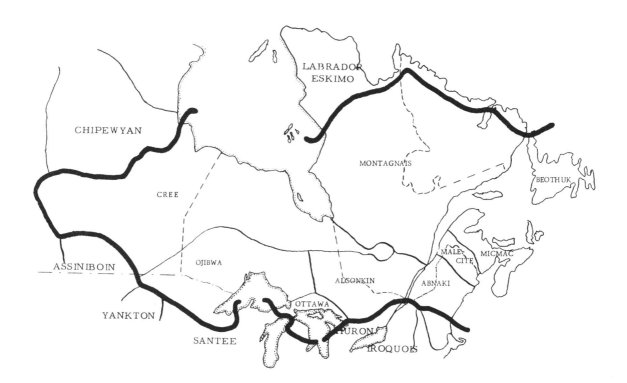

11 Eastern Canada

This area includes the eastern part of the great Boreal coniferous forest stretching across northern North America, as well as portions of other ecological areas. There is a general dependency on game (especially moose and caribou), fish, and wild fruit throughout this area, since most of it lies beyond the northern limits of agriculture. In the southern sections, in the area of the northern Great Lakes and in the North Atlantic Slope region of the Maritime Provinces, there was some agriculture, and cultural influences have come in from the South. The area can be divided into three subareas. The largest is the Eastern Canadian Subarctic, which includes the Hudson's Bay and Atlantic drainages and the area north of the Height of Land, which separates Hudson's Bay from the Great Lakes drainages. This area is ecologically similar to that of the Mackenzie-Yukon area (Area 2 of this bibliography) and includes the Cree, Montagnais-Naskapi, Beothuk, and Northern Ojibwa groups. The second subarea is that of the northern Great Lakes, which had limited agriculture and was exposed to direct contacts with agricultural areas to the south. It includes the Southern Ojibwa, Ottawa, and Algonkin proper. The third subarea is that of the North Atlantic Slope, which lies south of the St. Lawrence River in Maine, Nova Scotia, New Brunswick, and the Gaspé, and is the territory of the Abnaki, Malecite, and Micmac. It had some agriculture, but the subsistence was based upon hunting, fishing, and gathering.

In contrast to the Mackenzie-Yukon Area, which is populated by Athapaskan speakers, all the native peoples of this area were speakers of Algonquian languages of the Eastern and Central types. The Abnaki, Malecite, and Micmac spoke languages of the Eastern type, while the remainder spoke Central Algonquian languages. One branch of the latter is Cree-Montagnais-Naskapi. The area covered by speakers of this branch is immense, stretching from British Columbia to Labrador. Because of dialect similarities, it is difficult at times to assign individual groups to larger units. This is a particular problem along the Cree-Montagnais border in Quebec, with individual groups being called Cree or Montagnais by different reporters. For instance, the publication "Linguistic and cultural affiliations of Canadian Indian bands" includes as Cree the groups at Eastmain, Fort George, Great Whale River, Mistassini, Natashquan, Nemiskari, Rupert House, and Waswanipi. In each of these cases, the present bibliography has assigned them to the Montagnais. Therefore, for this general area of western Quebec, it is a good idea to check both the Cree and the Montagnais bibliographies for pertinent references.

Canada, Department of Indian Affairs and Northern Development, Indian Affairs Branch. Linguistic and cultural affiliations of Canadian Indian bands. Ottawa, 1967. 4, 26 p.

11-01. Abnaki. The Abnaki (Wabanaki, Abenaki), which includes among other divisions the Arosaguntacook, Norridgewock, Penobscot, Sokoki, and Wawenoc, lived mainly in western Maine in the valleys of the Kennebec, Androscoggin, and Saco Rivers, but ranged into Quebec and to the Atlantic Coast. They are now principally living on reserves at Becancour, Odanak, and St. Francis in Quebec. The Canadian Abnaki numbered 616 in 1967.

11-02. Algonkin. The Algonkin, including the Abitibi, Kitcisagi (Grand Lake Victoria), Maniwaki, Nipissing, Temiscaming, and Weskarini, live in the basin of the Ottawa River—particularly its northern tributaries—in southwestern Quebec, and in southeastern Ontario. They numbered 4,514 in 1967.

Gourd, Benoit-Beaudry. Bibliographie de l'Abitibi-Temiscamingue. Rouyn, Universite de Quebec, Direction des Etudes Universitaires dans l'Ouest Quebecois (Nord-ouest), 1973. 10, 270 p.

11-03. Beothuk. The Beothuk, who lived on the island of Newfoundland, probably became extinct in the early nineteenth century.

11-04. Cree. The Cree, a very large group, which includes such divisions as the Maskegon, Plains Cree, Swampy Cree, Tête-de-Boule, Western Wood Cree, and James Bay Cree, inhabit a vast area of the eastern subarctic, stretching from western Quebec to British Columbia and northern Montana (the Cree of Rocky Boys Reservation). They numbered 60,597 in Canada in 1967, which figure includes some groups listed as Montagnais in this bibliography.

11-05. Malecite. The Malecite, including the Etchimin and the Passamaquoddy, lived primarily in the valley of the St. John River in New Brunswick, but extended slightly into the northeastern corner of Maine, and now live principally on reserves in the St. John River and Restigouche Agencies. The Canadian Malecite numbered 1,626 in 1967.

11-06. Micmac. The Micmac (Souriquois) lived in Nova Scotia, Cape Breton Island, Prince Edward Island, the eastern shore of New Brunswick as far north as Restigouche, and at the head of the Bay of Fundy. Today they live on a number of reserves in Quebec (including Restigouche), Prince Edward

Island, Nova Scotia, and New Brunswick. They numbered 8,465 in 1967.

11-07. Montagnais. The Montagnais, including the closely related Naskapi, live in Quebec between the St. Lawrence River and James Bay, as well as in the Labrador interior. As noted earlier, the western boundary with the Cree is not clear. They numbered about 10,350 in 1967.

> Henriksen, Georg. Hunters in the Barrens; the Naskapi on the edge of the White Man's world. St. John's, Memorial University of Newfoundland, Institute of Social and Economic Research, 1973. 11, 130 p. illus., maps. (Newfoundland Social and Economic Studies, 12)

> Rogers, Edward S. The quest for food and furs; the Mistassini Cree, 1953-1954. Ottawa, 1973. 13, 83 p. illus. (Canada, National Museums, National Museum of Man, Publications in Ethnology, 5)

11-08. Ojibwa. The Ojibwa (Chippewa, Anishinabe), including the Bungi (Plains Ojibwa), Saulteaux, Missisauga, and Turtle Mountain Chippewa, inhabit a very large area in the western Northern Great Lakes region, extending from the northern shore of Lake Huron as far west as Montana, southward well into Wisconsin and Minnesota, and northward to Lake Manitoba. The Canadian Ojibwa numbered 43,948 in 1967, while the United States total was 45,986 in 1970, giving a grand total of approximately 89,900 for this general time period.

11-09. Ottawa. The Ottawa lived on the northern shores of Georgian Bay and eastward toward the Ottawa River in southern Ontario, later occupying the northern part of the southern peninsula of Michigan. They now live principally on the Manitoulin Island Agency in Ontario and on the Ottawa Reservation in Oklahoma. The Canadian Ottawa numbered 1,495 in 1967, while the Oklahoma Ottawa numbered 488 in 1970, giving a combined total of 1,983 for this general time period.

11-00   Eastern Canada Area Bibliography

Cooke, Alan, comp.   Bibliographie de la
peninsule du Québec-Labrador. Compiled
by Alan Cooke and Fabien Caron.   Boston,
G. K. Hall, 1968.   2 v.

Feit, H. A., et al.   Bibliographie: native
peoples, James Bay region. Recherches
Amérindiennes, 2, no. 1 (1972): 1-62.

Guthe, Alfred K., ed.   An anthropological
bibliography of the eastern seaboard.
Vol. 2. Edited by Alfred K. Guthe and
Patricia D. Kelly.   Trenton, N.J., The
Federation, 1963.   82 p.   (Eastern
States Archaeological Federation,
Research Publication, 2)

Pilling, J. C.   Bibliography of the
Algonquian languages. U.S. Bureau of
American Ethnology, Bulletin, 13 (1891):
1-614.

Rouse, Irving, ed.   An anthropological
bibliography of the eastern seaboard.
Edited by Irving Rouse and John M.
Goggin.   New Haven, The Federation,
1947.   174 p.   map.   (Eastern States
Archaeological Federation, Research
Publication, 1)

Alberts, R. C.   Trade silver and Indian
silver work in the Great Lakes region.
Wisconsin Archeologist, 34 (1953): 1-
121.

Aller, W. F.   Aboriginal food utilization
of vegetation by the Indians of the
Great Lakes region as recorded in the
Jesuit Relations. West Virginia
Archaeologist, 35, no. 3 (1954): 59-73.

Anonymous.   Supplementary materials on
location, numbers and socio-economic
conditions of Indians and Eskimos.
Eastern Canadian Anthropological Series,
1 (1955): 103-116.

Bailey, A. G.   The conflict of European
and Eastern Algonkian cultures. New
Brunswick Museum, Publications,
Monograph Series, 3 (1937): 1-206.

Bailey, Alfred G.   The conflict of
European and Eastern Algonkian cultures
1504-1700: a study in Canadian
civilization. 2d ed.   Toronto,
University of Toronto Press, 1969.   23,
218 p.

Barbeau, Charles Marius.   Legend and
history in the oldest geographical names
of the St. Lawrence. Inland Seas, 17
(1961): 105-113.

Bauman, Robert F.   The Ottawa trading
system. Northwest Ohio Quarterly, 36
(1964): 60-78, 146-167.

Bauman, Robert F.   The Ottawas of the
Lakes; 1615-1766. Part 2, the heyday of
the Ottawa supremacy over the Great
Lakes fur trade; 1660-1701. Northwest
Ohio Quarterly, 35 (1962/1963): 69-100.

Beers, H. P.   The French in North America.
Baton Rouge, 1957.

Berry, John W.   Psychological research in
the North. Anthropologica, n.s., 13
(1971): 143-157.

Biasutti, R.   Le razzi e i popoli della
terra, 2d ed., Vol. 4: 425-437.   Torino,
1957.

Biggar, H. P., ed.   The works of Samuel de
Champlain.   Toronto, 1922-1936.   6 v.

Birket-Smith, K.   A geographic study of
the early history of the Algonquian
Indians. Internationales Archiv für
Ethnographie, 24 (1918): 174-222.

Black, Albert.   The Pontiac conspiracy in
the novel, 1833-1954. Michigan History,
43 (1959): 115-119.

Blomkvist, E. E.   Indeĭtsy severo-
vostochnogo i prioz ernogo raĭonov SSHA
(irokesy i algonkiny). By E. E.
Blomkvist and IU. P. Averkieva.   In A. V.
Efimov and S. A. Tokarev, eds. Narody
Ameriki. Vol. 1.   Moskva, Izdatel'stvo
Akademiĭa Nauk SSSR, 1959: 194-227.

Bloomfield, L.   Algonquian. Viking Fund
Publications in Anthropology, 6 (1946):
85-129.

Bloomfield, L.   Proto-Algonquian -i·t-
'fellow'. Language, 17 (1941): 292-297.

Boucher, P.   Histoire véritable et
naturelle des moeurs et productions du
pays de la Nouvelle France.   Paris,
1664.

Boucher, Pierre.   Histoire véritable et
naturelle . . . 1644.   Boucherville,
Can., Société Historique de
Boucherville, 1964.   63, 415 p.   illus.,
maps.

Braasch, W. F., et al.   Survey of medical
care among the upper Midwest Indians.
American Medical Association, Journal,
139 (1949): 220-225.

Brasser, T. J. C.   The Coastal Algonkians:
people of the first frontiers. In
Eleanor Burke Leacock and Nancy
Oestreich Lurie, eds. North American

Indians in Historical Perspective. New
York, Random House, 1971: 64-91.

Braunholtz, H. J. The Sloane Collection:
ethnography. British Museum Quarterly,
18, no. 1 (1953): 23-26.

Brose, David S. The direct historic
approach to Michigan archaeology.
Ethnohistory, 18 (1971): 51-61.

Brown, C. E. Winabozho. Madison, 1944.
7 p.

Brown, Jennifer. The cure and feeding of
windigos: a critique. American
Anthropologist, 73 (1971): 20-22.

Brown, L. A. Early maps of the Ohio
Valley. Pittsburgh, 1960.

Burgesse, J. A. Tribal laws of the
woodlands. Beaver, 272, no. 4 (1942):
18-21.

Burgesse, J. Allan. Snowshoes. An outline
of the various types of Eastern Indian
snowshoes and their development with the
aid of steel tools. Beaver, 271, no. 4
(1941): 24-28.

Burrage, Henry S., ed. Early English and
French voyages, chiefly from Hakluyt,
1534-1608. New York, C. Scribner's
Sons, 1906. 22, 451 p. map. (Original
Narratives of Early American History, 3)

Byers, D. S. The environment of the
Northeast. Robert S. Peabody Foundation
for Archaeology, Papers, 3 (1946): 3-32.

Callender, Charles. Social organization
of the Central Algonkian Indians.
Milwaukee, 1962. 13, 140 p. illus.,
maps. (Milwaukee, Public Museum,
Publications in Anthropology, 7)

Canada, Department of Indian Affairs and
Northern Development. Indians of Quebec
and the Maritime Provinces (an
historical review). Ottawa, 1971.
36 p. illus.

Canada, Department of Mines and Resources,
Indian Affairs Branch. Census of
Indians in Canada, 1939. Ottawa, 1940.

Canada, Department of Mines and Resources,
Indian Affairs Branch. Census of
Indians in Canada, 1944. Ottawa, 1944.

Carrière, Gaston. Histoire documentaire
de la Congrégation des Missionaires
Oblats de Marie-Immaculée dans l'Est du
Canada. Ottawa, Éditions de
l'Université d'Ottawa, 1957. 5 v.
(1,709 p.)

Cartier, Jacques. Voyages de découverte
au Canada entre les années 1534 et 1542.
Paris, Éditions Anthropos, 1968. 6,
208 p. illus.

Chamberlain, A. F. Indians of the eastern
provinces of Canada. Annual
Archaeological Report, being Part of
Appendix to the Report of the Minister
of Education, Ontario, 16 (1905): 122-
136.

Chamberlain, A. F. Maple sugar and the
Indians. American Anthropologist, 4
(1891): 381-383.

Chamberlain, A. F. Signification of
certain Algonquian animal-names.
American Anthropologist, n.s., 3 (1901):
669-683.

Chamberlain, A. F. The maple amongst the
Algonkian tribes. American
Anthropologist, 4 (1891): 39-43.

Chamberlain, A. F. The thunder-bird
amongst the Algonkians. American
Anthropologist, 3 (1890): 51-54.

Champlain, Samuel de. Les voyages du
Sieur de Champlain. Ann Arbor,
University Microfilms, 1966. 325,
52 p. illus., maps.

Champlain, Samuel de. Voyages of Samuel
de Champlain. Translated by Charles
Pomeroy Otis. New York, Burt Franklin,
1966. 3 v. illus.

Chaput, Donald. French interest in Lake
Superior copper. Inland Seas, 26 (1970):
20-35.

Chaput, Donald. The semantics of nadowa.
Names, 15 (1967): 228-234.

Charbonneau, A., et al. Le projet de la
baie James: inquiétudes des non-initiés.
Recherches Amérindiennes au Québec, 1,
no. 4/5 (1971): 6-31.

Charency, H. de. Études algiques. Société
des Américanistes, Journal, 4 (1903): 8-
54.

Charlevoix, P. F. X. de. Histoire de la
Nouvelle France. Paris, 1894. 3 v.

Charlevoix, P. F. X. de. History and
general description of New France. Ed.
by J. M. Shea. New York, 1866-1872.
6 v.

Charlevoix, P. F. X. de. Journal of a
voyage to North America. Ed. by L. P.
Kellogg. Chicago, 1923. 2 v.

Charlevoix, Pierre F. X. de. Journal of a voyage to North America. Ann Arbor, University Microfilms, 1966. 2 v.

Cooper, J. M. Is the Algonquian family hunting ground system pre-Columbian? American Anthropologist, n.s., 41 (1939): 66-90.

Cooper, J. M. Land tenure among the Indians of eastern and northern North America. Pennsylvania Archaeologist, 8 (1938): 55-59.

Cooper, J. M. Snares, deadfalls, and other traps of the Northern Algonquians and Northern Athapaskans. Catholic University of America, Anthropological Series, 5 (1938): 1-144.

Cooper, J. M. The culture of the Northeastern Indian hunters. Robert S. Peabody Foundation for Archaeology, Papers, 3 (1946): 272-305.

Covington, J. W. The Indian liquor trade at Peoria, 1824. Illinois State Historical Society, Journal, 46 (1953): 142-150.

Dawson, G. M. Sketches of the past and present condition of the Indians of Canada. Canadian Naturalist, n.s., 9 (1881): 129-159.

Day, Gordon M. A St. Francis Abenaki vocabulary. International Journal of American Linguistics, 30 (1964): 371-392.

Day, Gordon M. English-Indian contacts in New England. Ethnohistory, 9 (1962): 24-40.

Dewdney, Selwyn H. Indian rock paintings of the Great Lakes. 2d ed. By Selwyn Dewdney and Kenneth E. Kidd. Toronto, Published for the Quetico Foundation by University of Toronto Press, 1967. 10, 191 p. illus. (Quetico Foundation Series, 4)

Dixon, R. B. The mythology of the Central and Eastern Algonkins. Journal of American Folklore, 22 (1909): 1-9.

Dobbs, A. An account of the countries adjoining to Hudson's Bay. London, 1744. 211 p.

Dodge, E. S. Ethnology of northern New England and the Maritime Provinces. Massachusetts Archaeological Society, Bulletin, 18 (1957): 68-71.

Douville, Raymond. La vie quotidienne des Indiens au Canada à l'époque de la colonisation française. By R. Douville and J.-D. Casanova. Paris, Hachette, 1967. 319 p.

Dräger, Lothar. Formen der lokalen Organisation bei den Stämmen der Zentral-Algonkin von der Zeit ihrer Entdeckung bis zur Gegenwart. Ethnographisch-Archäologische Zeitschrift, 10 (1969): 387-396.

Du Creux, F. The history of Canada or New France. Champlain Society, Publications, 30/31 (1951/1952): 1-776.

Du Creux, Francois. The history of Canada or New France. New York, Greenwood Press, 1969. 2 v. (27, 775 p.) illus., maps. (Champlain Society, Publications, 30-31)

Eccles, W. J. The history of New France according to Francis Parkman. William and Mary Quarterly, 3d ser., 18 (1961): 163-175.

Eggan, Fred. Northern Woodland ethnology. In Jacob W. Gruber, ed. The Philadelphia Anthropological Society; Papers Presented on Its Golden Anniversary. New York, distributed by Columbia University Press for Temple University Publications, 1967: 107-124.

Eiseley, L. C. Land tenure in the Northeast. American Anthropologist, n.s., 49 (1947): 680-681.

Feest, Christian F. Tomahawk und Keule im östliche Nordamerika. Archiv für Völkerkunde, 19 (1964/1965): 39-84.

Fewkes, V. J. Aboriginal potsherds from Red River, Manitoba. American Antiquity, 3 (1937): 143-155.

Fisher, M. W. The mythology of the Northern and Northeastern Algonkians. Robert S. Peabody Foundation for Archaeology, Papers, 3 (1946): 226-262.

Fitting, James E. Late prehistoric settlement patterns in the Upper Great Lakes. Ethnohistory, 16 (1969): 289-302.

Flannery, R. Algonquian Indian folklore. Journal of American Folklore, 60 (1947): 397-401.

Flannery, R. An analysis of coastal Algonquian culture. Catholic University of America, Anthropological Series, 7 (1939): 1-219.

Flannery, R. The culture of the Northeastern Indian hunters. Robert S. Peabody Foundation for Archaeology, Papers, 3 (1946): 263-271.

Forbes, Allan, Jr. Two and a half centuries of conflict: the Iroquois and the Laurentian wars. Pennsylvania Archaeologist, 40, no. 3/4 (1970): 1-20.

Frémont, D. Les aborigènes du Nord-Ouest Canadien au temps de La Vérendrye. Société Royale du Canada, Mémoires, 43, 3e série, Sect. 1 (1949): 7-21.

Fried, J., ed. A survey of the aboriginal populations of Quebec and Labrador. Eastern Canadian Anthropological Series, 1 (1955): 1-125.

Geary, J. A. Algonquian nasaump and napopi. Language, 21 (1945): 40-45.

Geary, J. A. Proto-Algonquian *čk. Language, 17 (1941): 304-310.

Geary, J. A. The Proto-Algonquian form for "I-thee". Language, 19 (1943): 147-151.

Gerard, W. R. The root kompau, its form and meaning. American Anthropologist, n.s., 14 (1912): 574-576.

Gille, J. Das "Geistertier" als Urbild des Zentralalgonkin "manetoua". Bremen, Museum für Natur- Völker- und Handelskunde, Veröffentlichungen, Reihe B, 1 (1950): 17-23.

Gille, J. Der Manabozho-Flutzyklus der Nord-, Nordost-, and Zentralalgonkin. Göttingen, 1939. 86 p.

Gille, J. Weskarini und Ur-Algonkin. Göttingen, 1939. 16 p.

Gille, J. Zur Lexikologie des Alt-Algonkin. Zeitschrift für Ethnologie, 71 (1939): 71-86.

Goddard, Ives. Algonquian linguistics in the Northeast: 1971. Man in the Northeast, 3 (1972): 55-56.

Goddard, Ives. The Eastern Algonquian intrusive nasal. International Journal of American Linguistics, 31 (1965): 206-220.

Green, Eugene. Generic terms for water and waterways in Algonquian place-names. By Eugene Green and Celia Millward. Anthropological Linguistics, 13 (1971): 33-52.

Greenman, Emerson F. The Indians of Michigan. Michigan History, 45 (1961): 1-33.

Haas, M. R. A new linguistic relationship in North America. Southwestern Journal of Anthropology, 14 (1958): 231-264.

Hadlock, W. S. Warfare among the northeastern Woodland Indians. American Anthropologist, n.s., 49 (1947): 204-221.

Hallowell, A. I. Some psychological characteristics of the Northeastern Indians. Robert S. Peabody Foundation for Archaeology, Papers, 3 (1946): 195-225.

Hallowell, A. I. The size of Algonkian hunting territories: a function of ecological adjustments. American Anthropologist, n.s., 51 (1949): 35-45.

Hallowell, A. Irving. Intelligence of Northeastern Indians. In Robert Hunt, ed. Personalities and Cultures. Garden City, Natural History Press, 1967: 49-55.

Hamilton, J. C. The Algonquian Manabozho and Hiawatha. Journal of American Folklore, 16 (1903): 229-233.

Hamilton, Raphael N. Marquette's explorations: the narratives reexamined. Madison, University of Wisconsin Press, 1970. 15, 275 p.

Hardcastle, David Paul. The defense of Canada under Louis XIV, 1643-1701. Dissertation Abstracts International, 31 (1970/1971): 3470A. UM 70-26,298.

Harris, W. R. Practice of medicine and surgery by the Canadian tribes in Champlain's time. Annual Archaeological Report, being Part of Appendix to the Report of the Minister of Education, Ontario (1915): 35-54.

Herman, M. W. Wampum as a money in northeastern North America. Ethnohistory, 5 (1958): 21-33.

Hickerson, Harold. Notes on the post-contact origin of the Midewiwin. Ethnohistory, 9 (1962): 404-423.

Hockett, C. F. Central Algonquian vocabulary: stems in /k-/. International Journal of American Linguistics, 23 (1957): 247-268.

Hockett, C. F. Implications of Bloomfield's Algonquian studies. Language, 24 (1948): 117-135.

Hoffman, Bernard G. Cabot to Cartier; sources for a historical ethnography of northeastern North America, 1497-1550. Toronto, University of Toronto Press, 1961. 12, 287 p. maps.

Hoffman, Bernard G. The Codex Canadiensis: an important document for

Great Lakes ethnography. Ethnohistory, 8 (1961): 382-400.

Holmer, N. M. Lexical and morphological contacts between Siouan and Algonquian. Lunds Universitets Arsskrift, n.s., 45 (1949): 1-36.

Horsman, Reginald. The British Indian Department and the resistance to General Anthony Wayne, 1793-1795. Mississippi Valley Historical Review, 49 (1962/1963): 269-290.

Howells, W. W. Physical types of the Northeast. Robert S. Peabody Foundation for Archaeology, Papers, 3 (1946): 168-177.

Innis, H. A. The fur trade in Canada. New Haven, 1930. 444 p.

Jeancon, J. A. and F. H. Douglas. Iroquoian and Algonkin wampum. Denver Art Museum, Indian Leaflet Series, 31 (1931): 1-4.

Jenness, D. Indians of Canada. Canada, Department of Mines, National Museum of Canada, Bulletin, 65 (1932): 1-446.

Jesuits, Letters from Missions (North America). Relations des Jésuites. Montréal, Éditions du Jour, 1972. 6 v.

Joblin, E. E. M. The education of the Indians of Western Ontario. Ontario, College of Education, Department of Educational Research, Bulletin, 13 (1948): 1-138.

Johnson, F., ed. Man in Northeastern North America. Robert S. Peabody Foundation for Archaeology, Papers, 3 (1946): 1-347.

Kennedy, J. H. Jesuit and savage in New France. New Haven, 1950. 206 p.

Kennedy, J. H. Jesuit and savage in New France. New Haven, Yale University Press, 1950. 5, 206 p.

Kidd, K. E. Sixty years of Ontario archeology. In J. B. Griffin, ed. Archeology of Eastern United States. Chicago, 1952: 71-82.

Kinietz, V. Notes on the Algonquian family hunting ground system. American Anthropologist, n.s., 42 (1940): 179.

Kinietz, V. Notes on the roached headdress of animal hair among the North American Indians. Michigan Academy of Science, Arts and Letters, Papers, 26 (1940): 463-467.

Knight, Rolf. A re-examination of hunting, trapping, and territoriality among the Northeastern Algonkian Indians. In Anthony Leeds and Andrew P. Vayda, eds. Man, Culture, and Animals. Washington, D.C., 1965: 27-42. (American Association for the Advancement of Science, Publication, 78)

Kurath, G. P. Antiphonal songs of Eastern Woodlands Indians. Musical Quarterly, 42 (1956): 520-526.

Kurath, G. P. Blackrobe and shaman. Michigan Academy of Science, Arts and Letters, Papers, 44 (1959): 209-215.

Kurath, G. P. Ceremonies, songs and dances of Michigan Indians. Michigan History Magazine, 39 (1955): 466-468.

Kurath, G. P. Pan-Indianism in Great Lakes tribal festivals. Journal of American Folklore, 70 (1957): 179-182.

Kurath, Gertrude P. Michigan Indian festivals. Ann Arbor, Ann Arbor Publishers, 1966. 8, 132 p. illus.

Kurtness, J. From nomadism to sedentarism. Recherches Amérindiennes au Quebec, 2, no. 4/5 (1972): 43-48.

Laguna, F. de. The prehistory of northern North America as seen from the Yukon. Society for American Archaeology, Memoirs, 3 (1947): 1-360.

Lahontan, A. L. de D. New voyages to North America. Ed. by R. G. Thwaites. Chicago, 1905. 2 v.

Lahontan, A. L. de D. Nouveaux voyages dans l'Amérique septentrionale. La Haye, 1703. 220 p.

Lahontan, Louis A. New voyages to North America. New York, Burt Franklin, 1970. 2 v. [93, 797 p.] illus., maps.

Larrabee, Charles. Lieutenant Charles Larrabee's account of the Battle of Tippecanoe, 1811. Indiana Magazine of History, 57 (1961): 225-247.

Laverdière, C. H., ed. Oeuvres de Champlain. 2d ed. Québec, 1870. 6 v.

Laviolette, G. Indian bands of the Province of Quebec. Eastern Canadian Anthropological Series, 1 (1955): 90-96.

Laviolette, G. Notes on the aborigines of the Prairie Provinces. Anthropologica, 2 (1956): 107-130.

Laviolette, G. Notes on the aborigines of the Province of Quebec. Anthropologica, 1 (1955): 198-211.

Laviolette, G. Notes on the aborigines of the Province of Ontario. Anthropologica, 4 (1957): 79-106.

Le Clercq, C. First establishment of the faith in New France. Ed. by J. G. Shea. New York, 1881. 2 v.

Leechman, D. Aboriginal paints and dyes in Canada. Royal Society of Canada, Proceedings and Transactions, ser. 3, 26, no. 2 (1932): 37-42.

Léger, Y. Le projet de la baie James: l'enverse de la médaille. Recherches Amérindiennes au Québec, 1, no. 4/5 (1971): 36-42.

Lescarbot, Marc. History of New France. New York, Greenwood Press, 1968. 3 v. (Champlain Society, Publications, 1, 7, 11)

Lowther, G. Archeology in the Province of Quebec. Eastern Canadian Anthropological Series, 1 (1955): 65-73.

MacLean, J. Canadian savage folk. Toronto, 1897. 641 p.

MacNeish, R. S. The archeology of the northeastern United States. In J. B. Griffin, ed. Archeology of Eastern United States. Chicago, 1952: 46-58.

McGee, Harold Franklin, Jr. Windigo psychosis. American Anthropologist, 74 (1972): 244-246.

Michelson, T. Algonquian notes. International Journal of American Linguistics, 9 (1939): 103-112.

Michelson, T. Contributions to Algonquian linguistics. International Journal of American Linguistics, 10 (1939): 75-85.

Michelson, T. Phonetic shifts in Algonquian languages. International Journal of American Linguistics, 8 (1935): 131-171.

Michelson, T. Preliminary report on the linguistic classification of Algonquian tribes. U.S. Bureau of American Ethnology, Annual Reports, 28 (1907): 221-290.

Michelson, T. Some Algonquian kinship terms. American Anthropologist, n.s., 34 (1932): 357-359.

Morris, A. The treaties of Canada with the Indians of Manitoba, the North-West Territories, and Kee-wa-tin. Toronto, 1880.

Morris, J. L. Indians of Ontario. Toronto, 1943. 75 p.

Müller, F. Der grammatische Bau der Algonkin-Sprachen. Wien, Kaiserlichen Akademie der Wissenschaften, Philosophisch-Historische Klasse, Sitzungsberichte, 56 (1867): 132-154.

Mulvaney, C. P. The history of the North-West Rebellion of 1885. Toronto, 1885. 424 p.

Murray, H. Historical and descriptive account of British America, Vol. 1: 73-127. Edinburgh, 1840.

Orr, R. B. North American Indian games-dice. Annual Archaeological Report, being Part of Appendix to the Report of the Minister of Education, Ontario, 27 (1915): 20-34.

Parkman, Francis. The conspiracy of Pontiac and the Indian war after the conquest of Canada. New York, AMS Press, 1969. 2 v. illus.

Pendergast, James F., et al. Cartier's Hochelaga and the Dawson Site. Montreal, McGill-Queen's University Press, 1972. 27, 388 p. illus.

Poirier, Jean. Les êtres supernaturels dans la toponymie amérindienne du Québec. Revue Internationale d'Onomastique, 21 (1969): 287-300.

Quimby, G. I. A subjective interpretation of some design similarities between Hopewell and Northern Algonkian. American Anthropologist, n.s., 45 (1943): 630-633.

Quimby, G. I. The archeology of the Upper Great Lakes area. In J. B. Griffin, ed. Archeology of Eastern United States. Chicago, 1952: 99-107.

Quimby, George I. Indian culture and European trade goods. Madison, University of Wisconsin Press, 1966. 14, 217 p. illus., map.

Quimby, George I. Indian life in the Upper Great Lakes, 11,000 B.C. to A.D. 1800. Chicago, University of Chicago Press, 1960. 182 p. illus.

Radisson, Pierre Esprit. The explorations of Pierre Esprit Radisson. Edited by Arthur T. Adams. Minneapolis, Ross and Haines, 1961. 84, 258 p. illus.

Radisson, Pierre Esprit. Voyages of Peter Esprit Radisson. Edited by Gideon D. Scull. New York, Burt Franklin, 1971. 6, 385 p.

Radwanski, P. Physical anthropological problems in the Province of Quebec.

Eastern Canadian Anthropological Series, 1 (1955): 85-89.

Rogers, Edward S. Algonkians of the Eastern Woodlands. Toronto, Royal Ontario Museum, 1970. 16 p. illus., map.

Rogers, Edward S. Iroquoians of the Eastern Woodlands. Toronto, Royal Ontario Museum, 1970. 16 p. illus., maps.

Rogers, Edward S. The dugout canoe in Ontario. American Antiquity, 30 (1964/1965): 454-459.

Rogers, R. A concise account of North America. London, 1765. 264 p.

Rousseau, J. J. Le couteau croche des Indiens de la forêt boréale. Technique, 21 (1946): 447.

Rousseau, J. J. L'Indien de la forêt boréale. Canada, Royal Society, Studia Varia (1958): 37-51.

Rousseau, J. J. L'origine du motif de la double courbe dans l'art algonkin. Anthropologica, 2 (1956): 218-221.

Rousseau, Jacques J. Chez les Indiens de la forêt et de la toundra québécoises. Les ressources du laïcat missionaire. In Université d'Ottawa. Le Laïcat et les Missions. Ottawa, 1951: 237-251.

Rousseau, M. and J. Rousseau. Le dualisme religieux des peuples de la forêt boréale. International Congress of Americanists, Proceedings, 29, vol. 2 (1952): 118-126.

Sargent, M. Folk and primitive music in Canada. National Museum of Canada, Bulletin, 123 (1951): 75-79.

Savoie, D. Le rapport Dorion et les droits territoriaux des Indiens de la baie de James. Recherches Amérindiennes au Québec, 1, no. 4/5 (1971): 32-35.

Siebert, F. T. Certain Proto-Algonquian consonant clusters. Language, 17 (1941): 298-303.

Siebert, Frank T., Jr. The original home of the Proto-Algonquian people. In Contributions to Anthropology: Linguistics I. Ottawa, Queen's Printer, 1967: 13-47. (Canada. National Museum, Bulletin, 214)

Silvy, A. Relation par lettres de l'Amérique septentrionale. Ed. by C. de Rochemonteix. Paris, 1904. 221 p.

Simonis, Y. Pour une recherche sur l'usage des champignons chez les Indiens du Québec. Recherches Amérindiennes au Québec, 2, no. 2 (1972): 29-36.

Skinner, A. Some aspects of the folk-lore of the Central Algonkin. Journal of American Folklore, 27 (1914): 97-100.

Skinner, A. The Algonkin and the thunderbird. American Museum Journal, 14 (1914): 71-73.

Skinner, A. Traces of the stone age among the eastern and northern tribes. American Anthropologist, 14 (1912): 391-395.

Slotkin, J. S. and K. Schmitt. Studies of wampum. American Anthropologist, n.s., 51 (1949): 223-236.

Smith, James. An account of the remarkable occurrences in the life and travels of Col. James Smith, during his captivity with the Indians in the years 1755, '56, '57, '58, and '59, with an appendix of illustrative notes. Edited by Wm. N. Darlington. Cincinnati, R. Clarke, 1870. 12, 190 p. (Ohio Valley Historical Series, 5)

Speck, F. G. Concerning iconology and the masking complex in eastern North America. Pennsylvania, University, Museum Bulletin, 15 (1950): 6-57.

Speck, F. G. Culture problems in northeastern North America. American Philosophical Society, Proceedings, 65 (1926): 272-311.

Speck, F. G. More Algonkian scapulimancy from the North, and the hunting territory question. Ethnos, 4 (1939): 21-28.

Speck, F. G. Northern elements in Iroquois and New England art. Indian Notes, 2 (1925): 1-12.

Speck, F. G. The family hunting band as the basis of Algonkian social organization. American Anthropologist, n.s., 17 (1915): 289-305.

Speck, F. G. The historical approach to art in archaeology in the northern woodlands. American Antiquity, 8 (1942): 173-175.

Speck, F. G. The social structure of the Northern Algonkian. American Sociological Society, Publications, 12 (1917): 82-100.

Speck, F. G. and L. C. Eiseley. Significance of hunting territory systems of the Algonkian in social theory. American Anthropologist, n.s., 41 (1939): 269-280.

Speck, Frank G. The family hunting band as the basis of Algonkian social organization. In Frederica de Laguna, ed. Selected Papers from the American Anthropologist 1888-1920. Evanston, Row, Peterson, 1960: 607-623.

Stanley, G. F. G. The Indians and the brandy trade during the ancien régime. Revue d'Histoire de l'Amérique Française, 6 (1953): 489-505.

Steeves, T. A. Wild rice. Economic Botany, 6 (1952): 107-142.

Stillfried, I. Studie zu Kosmogonischen und Kultischen Elementen der Algonkonischen und Irokesischen Stämme. Wiener Völkerkundliche Mitteilungen, 4 (1956): 82-85.

Teicher, Morton I. Windigo psychosis; a study of the relationship between belief and behavior among the Indians of northeastern Canada. Seattle, American Ethnological Society, 1960. 14, 129 p. map.

Thomas, C. Historical account. Annual Archaeological Report, being Part of Appendix to the Report of the Minister of Education, Ontario (1905): 71-83.

Thomas, W. J. The art of the Canadian Indians. Annual Archaeological Report, being Part of Appendix to the Report of the Minister of Education, Ontario, 33 (1922): 75-82.

Thwaites, Reuben G., ed. The French regime in Wisconsin [1634-1748]. Madison, 1902, 1906. 2 v. illus. (Wisconsin, State Historical Society, Collections, 16-17)

Thwaites, Reuben G., ed. The French regime in Wisconsin [1743-1760]. Madison, 1908. 25, 1-222 p. (Wisconsin, State Historical Society, Collections, 18)

Trigger, Bruce G. Criteria for identifying the locations of historic Indian sites: a case study from Montreal. Ethnohistory, 16 (1969): 303-316.

Trigger, Bruce G. The French presence in Huronia: the structure of Franco-Huron relations in the first half of the seventeenth century. Canadian Historical Review, 49 (1968): 107-141.

Trigger, Bruce G. Trade and tribal warfare on the St. Lawrence in the sixteenth century. Ethnohistory, 9 (1962): 240-256.

Trumbull, J. H. On the Algonkin verb. American Philological Association, Transactions, 7 (1877): 147-171.

Vinay, J. P. Les manuscrits amérindiens de Québec. Eastern Canadian Anthropological Series, 1 (1955): 74-84.

Voegelin, C. F. and E. W. Voegelin. Linguistic considerations of northeastern North America. Robert S. Peabody Foundation for Archaeology, Papers, 3 (1946): 178-194.

Voegelin, E. W. Mortuary customs of the Shawnee and other eastern tribes. Indiana Historical Society, Prehistory Research Series, 2 (1944): 227-444.

Wade, Robert. Pioneer settlers on the Lake Ontario strand: the Wade letters (1819-67). Edited by Howard Pammett. Journal of Canadian Studies, 2, no. 4 (1967): 16-36.

Waugh, F. W. Canadian aboriginal canoes. Canadian Field-Naturalist, 33 (1919): 23-33.

Waugh, F. W. Notes on Canadian pottery. Annual Archaeological Report, being Part of Appendix to the Report of the Minister of Education, Ontario, 14 (1901): 108-115.

Wells, Robin F. Castoreum and steel traps in eastern North America. American Anthropologist, 74 (1972): 479-483.

Wells, William. William Wells and the Indian Council of 1793. Edited by Dwight L. Smith. Indiana Magazine of History, 56 (1960): 217-226.

White, P. C. T. Lord Selkirk's diary, 1803-04. Champlain Society, Publications, 35 (1958): 1-391.

Wintemberg, W. J. Distinguishing characteristics of Algonkian and Iroquoian cultures. Canada, Department of Mines, National Museum of Canada, Bulletin, 67 (1931): 65-124.

Woehrmann, Paul John. The American invasion of Western Upper Canada in 1813. Northwest Ohio Quarterly, 38 (1965/1966): 74-88; 39, no. 1 (1966/1967): 61-73; 39, no. 4 (1966/1967): 39-48; 40 (1967/1968): 27-44.

Zeisberger, David, et al. Some remarks and annotations concerning the traditions, customs, languages etc. of the Indians in North America, from the

memoirs of the Reverend David
Zeisberger, and other missionaries of
the United Brethren. Edited by Erminie
Wheeler-Voegelin. Ethnohistory, 6
(1959): 42-69.

11-01 Abnaki

Day, Gordon M. A bibliography of the
Saint Francis dialect. International
Journal of American Linguistics, 27
(1961): 80-85.

Ray, Roger B. The Indians of Maine: a
bibliographical guide. Portland, Me.,
Maine Historical Society, 1972. 44 p.

Alger, A. L. In Indian tents. Boston,
1897. 139 p.

Alger, A. L. The creation, a Penobscot
Indian myth. Popular Science Monthly, 44
(1893): 195-196.

Allen, F. H. Summary of blood group
phenotypes in some aboriginal Americans.
American Journal of Physical
Anthropology, n.s., 17 (1959): 86.

Allen, Fred H., Jr. Blood groups of the
Penobscot Indians. By Fred H. Allen, Jr.
and Patricia A. Corcoran. American
Journal of Physical Anthropology, n.s.,
18 (1960): 109-114.

Anonymous. How the Indians learned to
call moose. Smoke Signals, 6, no. 5
(1954): 11-12.

Anonymous. Native America today. Indian
Historian, 4, no. 1 (1971): 55-56, 66.

Baxter, J. P. The Abnakis and their
ethnic relations. Maine Historical
Society, Collections and Proceedings,
ser. 2, 3 (1892): 13-40.

Beck, Horace P. Gluskap the liar, and
other Indian tales. Freeport, Me.,
Wheelwright, 1966. 9, 182 p. illus.

Bibaud, F. M. Biographie des sagamos
illustrés de l'Amérique Septentrionale,
191-194. Montreal, 1848.

Bishop, Charles A. The emergence of
hunting territories among the Northern
Ojibwa. Ethnology, 9 (1970): 1-15.

Boas, F. Zur Anthropologie der
nordamerikanischen Indianer. Berliner
Gesellschaft für Anthropologie,
Ethnologie und Urgeschichte,
Verhandlungen (1895): 367-411.

Bolton, R. P. Indian remains in northern
Vermont. Indian Notes, 7 (1930): 57-69.

Brown, Mrs. W. W. Some indoor and outdoor
games of the Wabanaki Indians. Royal
Society of Canada, Proceedings and
Transactions, 6, pt. 2 (1888): 41-46.

Brown, Mrs. W. W. Wa-ba-ba-nal, or
northern lights. Journal of American
Folklore, 3 (1890): 213-214.

Browne, G. W. Indian legends of Acadia.
Acadiensis, 2 (1902): 54-64.

Burrage, H. S., ed. Early English and
French voyages, 367-381. New York,
1906.

Caldwell, Dorothy J. The Big Neck affair:
tragedy and farce on the Missouri
frontier. Missouri Historical Review, 64
(1969/1970): 391-412.

Chamberlain, A. F. Indians of the eastern
provinces of Canada. Annual
Archaeological Report, being Part of
Appendix to the Report of the Minister
of Education, Ontario (1905): 122-136.

Chamberlain, M. The primitive life of the
Wapanaki women. Acadiensis, 2 (1902):
75-86.

Charland, Thomas M. C'est arrivé le 4
octobre 1759. Revue d'Histoire de
l'Amérique Française, 13 (1959/1960):
328-334.

Charland, Thomas-Marie. Histoire des
Abénakis d'Odanak (1675-1937).
Montréal, Éditions du Lévrier, 1964.
368 p. illus., maps.

Clarke, George F. Someone before us; our
Maritime Indians. Fredericton, N.B.,
Brunswick Press, 1968. 240 p. illus.

Coon, Carleton S. The hunting peoples.
Boston, Little, Brown, 1971. 21,
413 p. illus., maps.

Curtis, N., ed. The Indians' book, 3-27.
New York, 1907.

Day, G. M. Dartmouth and St. Francis.
Dartmouth Alumni Magazine (November
1959): 28-30.

Day, Gordon M. A St. Francis Abenaki
vocabulary. International Journal of
American Linguistics, 30 (1964): 371-
392.

Day, Gordon M. An Agawam fragment.
International Journal of American
Linguistics, 33 (1967): 244-247.

Day, Gordon M. Historical notes on New
England languages. In Contributions to
Anthropology: Linguistics I. Ottawa,
Queen's Printer, 1967: 107-112.
(Canada, National Museum, Bulletin, 214)

Day, Gordon M. Note on St. Francis
nomenclature. International Journal of
American Linguistics, 25 (1959): 272-
273.

Day, Gordon M. The eastern boundary of
Iroquoia: Abenaki evidence. Man in the
Northeast, 1 (1971): 7-13.

Day, Gordon M. The identity of the
Sokokis. Ethnohistory, 12 (1965): 237-
249.

Day, Gordon M. The name Contoocook.
International Journal of American
Linguistics, 27 (1961): 168-171.

Day, Gordon M. The tree nomenclature of
the Saint Francis Indians. In
Contributions to Anthropology 1960. Part
II. Ottawa, Queen's Printer, 1963: 37-
48. (Canada, National Museum, Bulletin,
190)

Deming, E. W. Abenaki witchcraft story.
Journal of American Folklore, 15 (1902):
62-63.

Dexter, H. M. The New England Indians.
Sabbath at Home, 2 (1868): 193-206.

Dixon, R. B. The early migrations of the
Indians of New England and the Maritime
Provinces. American Antiquarian Society,
Proceedings, n.s., 24 (1914): 65-76.

Eckstorm, F. H. Handicrafts of the modern
Indians of Maine. Robert Abbe Museum of
Stone Age Antiquities, Bulletin, 3
(1932): 1-72.

Eckstorm, F. H. Katahdin legends.
Appalachia, n.s., 16 (1924): 39-52.

Eckstorm, F. H. Old John Neptune and
other Maine shamans. Portland, 1945.
209 p.

Eckstorm, F. H. The Indians of Maine. In
L. C. Hatch, ed. Maine, a History.
Vol. 1. New York, 1919: 43-64.

Evans, G. H. Pigwacket. New Hampshire
Historical Society, Publications, 1
(1939): 1-135.

Feest, Christian F. Lukas Vischers
Beiträge zur Ethnographie Nordamerikas.
Archiv für Völkerkunde, 22 (1968): 31-
66.

Fox, John W. Dating kaolin pipes from
Indian Island. Man in the Northeast, 3
(1972): 20-35.

Frisch, Jack A. The Abenakis among the
St. Regis Mohawks. Indian Historian, 4,
no. 1 (1971): 27-29.

Frost, H. K. Two Abnaki legends. Journal
of American Folklore, 25 (1912): 188-
190.

Goddard, Ives. More on the nasalization
of PA *a in Eastern Algonquian.
International Journal of American
Linguistics, 37 (1971): 139-145.

Goddard, Ives. Notes on the genetic
classification of the Algonquian
languages. In Contributions to
Anthropology: Linguistics I. Ottawa,
Queen's Printer, 1967: 7-12. (Canada,
National Museum, Bulletin, 214)

Godfrey, J. E. The ancient Penobscot of
Panawanskek. Maine Historical Society,
Collections and Proceedings, 7 (1876):
1-22.

Godfrey, J. E. The ancient Penobscot of
Panawanskik. Historical Magazine,
ser. 3, 1 (1872): 85-92.

Gravel, Albert. "Suagothel;" ou,
Expédition du major Robert Rogers sur le
village abénakis de Saint-François en
1759. 2. éd. Sherbrooke, 1965. 20 l.
illus., maps. (Page d'Histoire
Régionale, Cahier, 7)

Greenman, Emerson F. The Upper
Palaeolithic and the New World. Current
Anthropology, 4 (1963): 41-91.

Haas, Mary R. Algonkian-Ritwan: the end
of a controversy. International Journal
of American Linguistics, 24 (1958): 159-
173.

Haas, Mary R. Roger William's sound
shift: a study in Algonkian. In To Honor
Roman Jakobson; Essays on the Occasion
of His Seventieth Birthday. Vol. 1. The
Hague, Mouton, 1967: 816-832. (Janua
Linguarum, Series Maior, 31)

Hadlock, W. S. and E. S. Dodge. A canoe
from the Penobscot River. American
Neptune, 8 (1948): 289-301.

Hallowell, A. I. Recent changes in the
kinship terminology of the St. Francis
Abenaki. International Congress of
Americanists, Proceedings, 22, vol. 2
(1926): 97-145.

Hanson, Charles E., Jr. The fur trade
lore of Manly Hardy. Museum of the Fur
Trade Quarterly, 1, no. 4 (1965): 7-10.

Hanson, J. W. History of Gardiner, Pittston and West Gardiner, 13-28. Gardiner, 1852.

Hanson, J. W. History of the old towns Norridgewock and Canaan. Boston, 1849. 373 p.

Hanzeli, Victor E. Missionary linguistics in New France; a study of seventeenth- and eighteenth-century descriptions of American Indian languages. The Hague, Mouton, 1969. 141 p. illus., map. (Janua Linguarum, Series Maior, 29)

Harrington, M. R. An Abanaki "witch-story". Journal of American Folklore, 14 (1901): 160.

Hill, Kay. Glooscap and his magic; legends of the Wabanaki Indians. New York, Dodd, Mead, 1963. 189 p. illus.

Hoffman, B. G. The Souriquois, Etechemin and Wegesh. Ethnohistory, 2 (1955): 65-87.

Hubbard, L. L. Some Indian place-names in northern Maine. Boston, 1884.

Hucksoll, Aurelia C. Primitive versus modern: contrasting attitudes toward environment. Bennington, 1968. 24 p. illus. (Vermont Academy of Arts and Sciences, Occasional Paper, 2)

Jack, D. R. The Indians of Acadia. Acadiensis, 1 (1901): 187-201.

Jack, E. Day with the Abenakis. Acadiensis, 1 (1901): 191-194.

Jack, E. The Abenakis of Saint John River. Canadian Institute, Transactions, 3 (1892): 195-205.

Jackson, E. P. Indian occupation and use of the Champlain lowland. Michigan Academy of Science, Arts and Letters, Papers, 14 (1931): 113-160.

Jennings, Francis. Goals and functions of Puritan missions to the Indians. Ethnohistory, 18 (1971): 197-212.

Johnson, F. Indians of New Hampshire. Appalachia, n.s., 6, no. 7 (1940): 3-15.

Kaplan, Sidney. "The History of New Hampshire"; Jeremy Belknap as literary craftsman. William and Mary Quarterly, 3d ser., 21 (1964): 18-39.

Kawashima, Yasu. Jurisdiction of the colonial courts over the Indians in Massachusetts, 1689-1763. New England Quarterly, 42 (1969): 532-550.

Kenton, E., ed. The Indians of North America, Vol. 2: 364-392, 484-487. New York, 1927.

Kidder, F. The Abenaki Indians. Maine Historical Society, Collections and Proceedings, 6 (1859): 229-263.

Laurent, J. New familiar Abenakis and English dialogues. Quebec, 1884. 230 p.

Laurent, J. The Abenakis. Vermont History, 23 (1955): 286-295.

Le Sueur, J. History of the calumet and of the dance. Museum of the American Indian, Heye Foundation, Contributions, 12, no. 5 (1952): 1-26.

Leger, M. C. The Catholic Indian missions in Maine, 1611-1820. Catholic University of America, Studies in American Church History, 8 (1929): 1-184.

Leland, C. G. The Algonquin legends of New England. Boston, 1884. 379 p.

Leland, C. G. and J. D. Prince. Kulóskap the master and other Algonkin poems. New York, 1902. 370 p.

Leland, Charles G. The Algonquin legends of New England. Detroit, Singing Tree Press, 1968. 15, 379 p. illus.

Lincoln, E. Remarks on the Indian languages. Maine Historical Society, Collections and Proceedings, 1 (1831): 310-323.

Maine, Laws, Statutes, etc. A compilation of laws pertaining to Indians. Rev. Prepared by the Department of Indian Affairs. Augusta, 1969. 30 p.

Maine, State Department of Health and Welfare. Indians of Maine. Augusta, 1964. 14 p. ERIC ED031364.

Mallery, G. The fight with the giant witch: an Abanaki myth. American Anthropologist, 3 (1890): 65-70.

Masta, H. L. Abenaki Indian legends, grammar, and place names. Victoriaville, 1932. 110 p.

Maurault, J. P. A. Histoire des Abenakis. Quebec, 1866. 631 p.

Maurault, Joseph P. A. Histoire des Abenakis depuis 1605 jusqu'à nos jours. New York, Johnson Reprint, 1969. 10, 653 p.

McGuire, J. D. Ethnological and archeological notes on Moosehead Lake.

American Anthropologist, n.s., 10 (1908): 549-557.

Merlet, L. V. C. Histoire des relations des Hurons et des Abnaquis du Canada avec Notre-Dame de Chartres. Chartres, 1858. 78 p.

Mooney, J. Penobscot. U.S. Bureau of American Ethnology, Bulletin, 30, vol. 2 (1910): 226-227.

Mooney, J. and C. Thomas. Abnaki. U.S. Bureau of American Ethnology, Bulletin, 30, vol. 1 (1907): 2-6.

Moorehead, W. K. A report on the archaeology of Maine. Andover, 1922. 272 p.

Nicolar, J. Life and traditions of the Red Man. Bangor, 1893. 147 p.

O'Brien, M. C. Grammatical sketch of the ancient Abnaki. Maine Historical Society, Collections and Proceedings, 9 (1887): 259-294.

Orchard, W. C. Notes on Penobscot houses. American Anthropologist, n.s., 11 (1909): 601-606.

Perkins, G. H. Some relics of the Indians of Vermont. American Naturalist, 5 (1871): 11-17.

Prince, J. D. Notes on Passamaquoddy literature. New York Academy of Sciences, Annals, 13 (1901): 381-386.

Prince, J. D. Notes on the language of the Eastern Algonquin tribes. American Journal of Philology, 9 (1888): 310-316.

Prince, J. D. The differentiation between the Penobscot and the Canadian Abenaki dialects. American Anthropologist, n.s., 4 (1902): 17-32.

Prince, J. D. The modern dialect of the Canadian Abenaki. In Miscellanea Linguistica in Onore di Graziadio Ascoli. Torino, 1901: 343-362.

Prince, J. D. The Penobscot language of Maine. American Anthropologist, n.s., 12 (1910): 183-208.

Provost, H. Les Abénaquis sur la Chaudière. Société Historique de la Chaudière, Publication, 1 (1958): 1-27.

Ralle. Numbers in the Norridgwog language, from Ralle's ms. dictionary of the Norridgwog language, in the library of Harvard College. Massachusetts Historical Society, Collections, 10 (1809): 137-138.

Rasles, S. A dictionary of the Abnaki language. American Academy of Arts and Sciences, Memoirs, n.s., 1 (1833): 375-574.

Reade, J. Some Wabanaki songs. Royal Society of Canada, Proceedings and Transactions, ser. 1, 5, pt. 2 (1887): 1-8.

Rosier, J. Relation of Waymouth's voyage to the coast of Maine. Portland, 1887. 176 p.

Rousseau, J. Ethnobotanique abénakise. Archives de Folklore, 11 (1947): 145-182.

Sabine, L. Indian tribes of New England. Christian Examiner, 62 (1857): 27-54, 210-237.

Schmidt, W. Die Nordost Algonkin. In his Die Ursprung der Göttesidee. Bd. 7. Münster i. W., 1940: 522-530.

Schmidt, W. Die Nordost Algonkin. In his Die Ursprung der Göttesidee. Bd. 2. Münster i. W., 1929: 449-458.

Sewall, R. K. Wawenoc numerals. Historical Magazine, ser. 2, 3 (1868): 179-180.

Sieber, S. A. The Saulteaux, Penobscot-Abenaki, and the concept of totemism. International Congress of the Anthropological and Ethnological Sciences, Acts, 4, vol. 2 (1955): 325-329.

Siebert, F. T. Mammoth or "stiff-legged bear". American Anthropologist, n.s., 39 (1937): 721-725.

Siebert, Frank T., Jr. Discrepant consonant clusters ending in *-k in Proto-Algonquian, a proposed interpretation of saltatory sound changes. In Contributions to Anthropology: Linguistics I. Ottawa, Queen's Printer, 1967: 48-59. (Canada, National Museum, Bulletin, 214)

Silver, Shirley. Natick consonants in reference to Proto-Central Algonquian. International Journal of American Linguistics, 26 (1960): 112-119, 234-241.

Silvy, A. Relation par lettres de l'Amérique septentrionale, 196-201. Ed. by C. de Rochemonteix. Paris, 1904.

Smith, Marion W. Strange tales of Abenaki shamanism. Lewiston, Me., Central Maine Press, 1963. 46 p. illus.

Smith, N. N.   Premonition spirits among the Wabanaki. Massachusetts Archaeological Society, Bulletin, 15 (1954): 52-56.

Smith, N. N.   Smoking habits of the Wabanaki. Massachusetts Archaeological Society, Bulletin, 18 (1957): 76-77.

Smith, N. N.   The survival of the Red Paint complex in Maine. Massachusetts Archaeological Society, Bulletin, 17 (1955): 4-6.

Smith, N. N.   Wabanaki dances. Massachusetts Archaeological Society, Bulletin, 16 (1955): 29-37.

Smith, N. N.   Wabanaki uses of greases and oils. Massachusetts Archaeological Society, Bulletin, 21, no. 2 (1960): 19-21.

Smith, Nicholas N.   St. Francis Indian dances--1960. Ethnomusicology, 6 (1962): 15-18.

Smith, R. V.   New Hampshire remembers the Indians. Historical New Hampshire, 8, no. 2 (1952): 1-36.

Snow, Dean R.   Wabanaki "family hunting territories". American Anthropologist, 70 (1968): 1143-1151.

Sockabasin, Allen J., comp.   Off-reservation Indian survey Me P-74. Compiled by Allen J. Sockabasin and John G. Stone. Augusta, Maine Department of Indian Affairs, 1971.   67 p.

Speck, F. G.   A visit to the Penobscot Indians. Museum Journal, 2 (1911): 21-26.

Speck, F. G.   "Abenaki" clans--never! American Anthropologist, n.s., 37 (1935): 528-530.

Speck, F. G.   Abnaki text. International Journal of American Linguistics, 11 (1945): 45-46.

Speck, F. G.   Bird-lore of the Northern Indians. Pennsylvania, University, University Lectures, 7 (1920): 349-380.

Speck, F. G.   Correction to kinship terms among the Northeastern Algonkian. American Anthropologist, n.s., 22 (1920): 85.

Speck, F. G.   Culture problems in northeastern North America. American Philosophical Society, Proceedings, 65 (1926): 282-287.

Speck, F. G.   European folktales among the Penobscot. Journal of American Folklore, 26 (1913): 81-84.

Speck, F. G.   Game totems among the Northeastern Algonkians. American Anthropologist, n.s., 19 (1917): 9-18.

Speck, F. G.   Kinship terms and the family band among the Northeastern Algonkian. American Anthropologist, n.s., 20 (1918): 143-161.

Speck, F. G.   Mammoth or "stiff-legged bear". American Anthropologist, n.s., 37 (1935): 159-163.

Speck, F. G.   Medicine practices of the Northeastern Algonquians. International Congress of Americanists, Proceedings, 19 (1915): 303-321.

*Speck, F. G.   Penobscot man. Philadelphia, 1940.   325 p.

Speck, F. G.   Penobscot shamanism. American Anthropological Association, Memoirs, 6 (1919): 237-288.

Speck, F. G.   Penobscot tales and religious beliefs. Journal of American Folklore, 48 (1935): 1-107.

Speck, F. G.   Penobscot tales. Journal of American Folklore, 28 (1915): 52-58.

Speck, F. G.   Penobscot transformer tales. International Journal of American Linguistics, 1 (1918): 187-244.

Speck, F. G.   Reptile-lore of the northern Indians. Journal of American Folklore, 36 (1923): 273-280.

Speck, F. G.   Some uses of birch bark by our Eastern Indians. Museum Journal, 1 (1910): 33-36.

Speck, F. G.   Symbolism in Penobscot art. American Museum of Natural History, Anthropological Papers, 29 (1927): 25-80.

Speck, F. G.   The double-curve motive in Northeastern Algonkian art. Canada, Department of Mines, Geological Survey, Memoirs, 42 (1914): 1-17.

Speck, F. G.   The Eastern Algonkian Wabanaki Confederacy. American Anthropologist, n.s., 17 (1915): 492-508.

Speck, F. G.   The family hunting band as the basis of Algonkian social organization. American Anthropologist, n.s., 17 (1915): 289-305.

Speck, F. G. The functions of wampum among the Eastern Algonkian. American Anthropological Association, Memoirs, 6 (1919): 3-71.

Speck, F. G. The Penobscot Indians of Maine. General Magazine and Historical Chronicle, University of Pennsylvania, 39 (1937): 396-405.

Speck, F. G. Wawenock myth texts from Maine. U.S. Bureau of American Ethnology, Annual Reports, 43 (1926): 165-197.

*Speck, Frank G. Penobscot man; the life history of a forest tribe in Maine. New York, Octagon Books, 1970. 20, 325 p. illus., map.

Stamp, H. The water-fairies. Journal of American Folklore, 28 (1915): 310-316.

Sullivan, J. The history of the Penobscott Indians. Massachusetts Historical Society, Collections, 9 (1804): 206-232.

Swadesh, M. Sociologic notes on obsolescent lanugages. International Journal of American Linguistics, 14 (1948): 226-235.

Swanson, Guy E. Rules of descent: studies in the sociology of parentage. Ann Arbor, University of Michigan, 1969. 5, 108 p. (Michigan, University, Museum of Anthropology, Anthropological Papers, 39)

Swauger, James L. Abnaki Indian artifacts in Carnegie Museum. Pittsburgh, Carnegie Museum, Annals, 38 (1965/1966): 117-127.

Thwaites, R. G., ed. The Jesuit Relations and allied documents. Cleveland, 1896-1901. 74 v.

Trumbull, J. H. A mode of counting, said to have been used by the Wawenoc Indians of Maine. American Philological Association, Proceedings, 3 (1871): 13-15.

Vetromile, E. Acadia and its aborigines. Maine Historical Society, Collections and Proceedings, 7 (1876): 337-349.

Vetromile, E. Indian good book. New York, 1856. 449 p.

Vetromile, E. The Abnaki Indians. Maine Historical Society, Collections and Proceedings, 6 (1859): 203-226.

*Vetromile, E. The Abnakis and their history. New York, 1866. 171 p.

Voight, Virginia F. Close to the rising sun; Algonquian Indian legends. Champaign, Ill., Garrard, 1972. 63 p. illus.

Williamson, W. D. The history of the state of Maine, Vol. 1: 453-514. Hallowell, 1832.

Willis, W. The language of the Abnaquies. Maine Historical Society, Collections and Proceedings, 4 (1856): 93-117.

Willoughby, C. C. Antiquities of the New England Indians. Cambridge, 1935. 314 p.

Willoughby, C. C. Dress and ornaments of the New England Indians. American Anthropologist, n.s., 7 (1905): 499-508.

Willoughby, C. C. Houses and gardens of the New England Indians. American Anthropologist, n.s., 8 (1906): 115-132.

Willoughby, C. C. Pottery of the New England Indians. In Putnam Anniversary Volume. New York, 1909: 83-101.

Willoughby, C. C. Textile fabrics of the New England Indians. American Anthropologist, n.s., 7 (1905): 85-93.

Willoughby, C. C. The adze and ungrooved axe of the New England Indians. American Anthropologist, n.s., 9 (1907): 296-306.

Wilson, C. B. Indian relics and encampments in Maine. American Antiquarian and Oriental Journal, 5 (1883): 181-183.

Wilson, G. L. Indian hero tales. New York, 1906. 203 p.

Wzokhilain, P. P. Wawasi lagidamwoganek mdala chowagidamwoganal tabtagil. Boston, 1830. 35 p.

Zoltvany, Yves F. The frontier policy of Philippe de Rigaud de Vaudreuil, 1713-1725. Canadian Historical Review, 48 (1967): 227-250.

11-02 Algonkin

Carrière, Gaston. Catalogue des manuscrits en langues indiennes conservés aux archives oblates, Ottawa. Anthropologica, n.s., 12 (1970): 151-179.

Anonymous. Muggahmaht'adem. Smoke Signals, 4, no. 3 (1952): 5.

Beck, H. P. Algonquin folklore from Maninaki. Journal of American Folklore, 60 (1947): 259-264.

Bibaud, F. M. Biographie des sagamos illustrés de l'Amérique Septentrionale, 115-119. Montreal, 1848.

Black, Meredith Jean. Algonquin ethnobotany: an interpretation of aboriginal adaptation in southwestern Quebec. Dissertation Abstracts International, 34 (1973/1974): 1345B. UM 73-24,526.

Brinton, D. G. The chief god of the Algonkins. American Antiquarian and Oriental Journal, 7 (1885): 137-139.

Brinton, D. G. The hero-god of the Algonkins as a cheat and a liar. In his Essays of an Americanist. Philadelphia, 1890: 130-134.

Carr, L. G. K. Interesting animal foods, medicines, and omens of the Eastern Indians. Washington Academy of Sciences, Journal, 41 (1951): 229-235.

Chamberlain, A. F. The Algonkian Indians of Baptist Lake. Canadian Institute, Annual Report, 4 (1891): 83-89.

Champlain, Samuel de. Les voyages du Sieur de Champlain. Ann Arbor, University Microfilms, 1966. 325, 52 p. illus., maps.

Champlain, Samuel de. Voyages and discoveries made in New France, from the year 1615 to the end of the year 1618. Translated and edited by H. H. Layton and W. F. Ganong. Toronto, The Champlain Society, 1929. illus., maps. (The Works of Samuel de Champlain, 3)

Conard, E. L. M. Les idées des Indiens Algonquins relatives à la vie d'outre-tombe. Revue d'Histoire et Religion, 62 (1900): 9-81, 220-274.

Cooper, J. M. Field notes on Northern Algonkian magic. International Congress of Americanists, Proceedings, 23 (1928): 513-518.

Cooper, J. M. Northern Algonkian scrying and scapulimancy. In Festschrift P. W. Schmidt. Wien, 1928: 205-217.

Cuoq, J. A. Chrestomathie algonquine. Société Philologique, Actes, 3, no. 2 (1873): 39-50.

Cuoq, J. A. Études philologiques sur quelques langues sauvages de l'Amérique. Montreal, 1866. 160 p.

Cuoq, J. A. Grammaire de la langue algonquine. Royal Society of Canada, Proceedings and Transactions, 9, pt. 1 (1891): 85-114; 10, pt. 1 (1892): 41-119.

Cuoq, J. A. Lexique de la langue algonquine. Montreal, 1886. 446 p.

Cuoq, Jean André. Études philologiques sur quelques langues sauvages de l'Amérique. New York, Johnson Reprint, 1966. 160 p.

Davidson, D. S. Folk tales from Grand Lake Victoria. Journal of American Folklore, 41 (1928): 275-282.

Davidson, D. S. The family hunting territories of the Grand Lake Victoria Indians. International Congress of Americanists, Proceedings, 22, vol. 2 (1926): 69-95.

Faillon, Abbé. The Indian tribes on the St. Lawrence at the time of the arrival of the French. Translated by John Squair. Toronto, Ontario Provincial Museum, Annual Archaeological Report, 34 (1923): 82-88.

Goddard, Ives. Notes on the genetic classification of the Algonquian languages. In Contributions to Anthropology: Linguistics I. Ottawa, Queen's Printer, 1967: 7-12. (Canada, National Museum, Bulletin, 214)

Hallowell, A. I. Was cross-cousin marriage practised by the North-Central Algonkian? International Congress of Americanists, Proceedings, 23 (1928): 519-544.

Hamilton, Raphael N. Jesuit mission at Sault Ste. Marie. Michigan History, 52 (1968): 123-132.

Hanzeli, Victor E. Missionary linguistics in New France; a study of seventeenth- and eighteenth-century descriptions of American Indian languages. The Hague, Mouton, 1969. 141 p. illus., map. (Janua Linguarum, Series Maior, 29)

Hanzeli, Victor E. The Algonquin R-dialect in historical records. In International Congress of Linguists, 10th. 1967, Bucarest. Proceedings. Vol. 2. Bucarest, Éditions de l'Académie de la République Socialiste de Roumanie, 1970: 85-89.

Hunter, A. F. Indian village sites in North and South Orillia townships. Annual Archaeological Report, being Part of Appendix to the Report of the Minister of Education, Ontario (1903): 105-125.

Jenkins, W. H. Notes on the hunting economy of the Abitibi Indians. Catholic University of America, Anthropological Series, 9 (1939): 1-31.

Johnson, F. An Algonkian band at Lac Barriere. Indian Notes, 7 (1930): 27-39.

Johnson, F. The Algonquin at Golden Lake. Indian Notes, 5 (1928): 173-178.

Keppler, J. The peace tomahawk Algonkian wampum. Indian Notes, 6 (1929): 130-138.

Lemoine, G. Dictionnaire Français-Algonquin. Quebec, 1911.

Lemoine, G. Le génie de la langue algonquine. International Congress of Americanists, Proceedings, 15, vol. 2 (1906): 225-242.

Long, J. K. Voyages and travels of an Indian interpreter and trader. London, 1791. 295 p.

McGee, J. T. Family hunting grounds in the Kippewa area. Primitive Man, 24 (1951): 47-53.

Mooney, J. Nipissing. U.S. Bureau of American Ethnology, Bulletin, 30, vol. 2 (1910): 73-74.

Mooney, J. and C. Thomas. Algonkin. U.S. Bureau of American Ethnology, Bulletin, 30, vol. 1 (1907): 38.

Nouvel, Henry. A canoe trip to Midland in 1675. Edited and with an introduction by Harold W. Moll. Michigan History, 46 (1962): 255-274.

Orr, R. B. Algonquin subtribes and clans of Ontario. Annual Archaeological Report, being Part of Appendix to the Report of the Minister of Education, Ontario (1921/1922): 24-31.

Orr, R. B. The Nipissings. Annual Archaeological Report, being Part of Appendix to the Report of the Minister of Education, Ontario (1917): 9-23.

Petrullo, V. M. Decorative art on birch-bark from the Algonquin River du Lièvre band. Indian Notes, 6 (1929): 225-242.

Poirier, Jean. Les êtres supernaturels dans la toponymie amérindienne du Québec. Revue Internationale d'Onomastique, 21 (1969): 287-300.

Ridley, Frank. Archaeology of Lake Abitibi, Ontario-Québec. Anthropological Journal of Canada, 4, no. 2 (1966): 2-50.

Speck, F. G. Art processes in birchbark of the River Desert Algonquin. U.S. Bureau of American Ethnology, Bulletin, 128 (1941): 229-274.

Speck, F. G. Boundaries and hunting groups of the River Desert Algonquin. Indian Notes, 6 (1929): 97-120.

Speck, F. G. Divination by scapulimancy among the Algonquin of River Desert. Indian Notes, 5 (1928): 167-173.

Speck, F. G. Family hunting territories and social life of various Algonkian bands of the Ottawa Valley. Canada, Department of Mines, Geological Survey, Memoirs, 70 (1915): 1-10.

Speck, F. G. Myths and folk-lore of the Timiskaming Algonquin and Timiskaming Ojibwa. Canada, Department of Mines, Geological Survey, Memoirs, 71 (1915): 1-27.

Speck, F. G. River Desert Indians of Quebec. Indian Notes, 4 (1927): 240-252.

Speck, F. G. The family hunting band as the basis of Algonkian social organization. American Anthropologist, n.s., 17 (1915): 289-305.

Squair, J. The Indian tribes on the St. Lawrence at the time of the arrival of the French. Annual Archaeological Report, being Part of Appendix to the Report of the Minister of Education, Ontario, 34 (1923): 82-88.

Thwaites, R. G., ed. The Jesuit Relations and allied documents. Cleveland, 1896-1901. 74 v.

Trigger, Bruce G. Champlain judged by his Indian policy: a different view of early Canadian history. Anthropologica, n.s., 13 (1971): 85-114.

Trigger, Bruce G. The Mohawk-Mahican War (1624-28): the establishment of a pattern. Canadian Historical Review, 51 (1971): 276-286.

Wake, C. S. Migrations of the Algonkins. American Antiquarian and Oriental Journal, 16 (1894): 127-139.

11-03 Beothuk

Blake, E. The Beothuks of Newfoundland. Nineteenth Century, 24 (1888): 899-918.

Burrage, H. S., ed. Early English and French voyages, 4-24. New York, 1906.

Busk, G. Description of two Beothuc skulls. Royal Anthropological Institute of Great Britain and Ireland, Journal, 5 (1875): 230-232.

Chamberlain, A. F. The Beothuks of Newfoundland. Annual Archaeological Report, being Part of Appendix to the Report of the Minister of Education, Ontario (1905): 117-122.

Chappell, E. Voyage of His Majesty's Ship Rosamond to Newfoundland, 69-87. London, 1818.

Gatschet, A. S. The Beothuk Indians. American Philosophical Society, Proceedings, 22 (1885): 408-424; 23 (1886): 411-432; 28 (1890): 1-16.

Greenman, Emerson F. The Upper Palaeolithic and the New World. Current Anthropology, 4 (1963): 41-91.

Harp, E. An archaeological survey in the Strait of Belle Isle area. American Antiquity, 16 (1951): 203-220.

Hewitt, J. N. B. and A. S. Gatschet. Beothukan family. U.S. Bureau of American Ethnology, Bulletin, 30, vol. 1 (1907): 141-142.

Hewson, John. Beothuk and Algonkian: evidence old and new. International Journal of American Linguistics, 34 (1968): 85-93.

Hewson, John. Beothuk consonant correspondences. International Journal of American Linguistics, 37 (1971): 244-249.

*Howley, J. P. The Beothucks or Red Indians. Cambridge, 1915. 345 p.

Hughes, David R. Human remains from near Manuels River, Conception Bay, Newfoundland. In Contributions to Anthropology: Archaeology and Physical Anthropology. Ottawa, Queen's Printer, 1969: 195-207. (Canada, National Museum, Bulletin, 224)

Jenness, D. Notes on the Beothuk Indians of Newfoundland. Canada, Department of Mines, National Museum of Canada, Bulletin, 56 (1929): 36-37.

Klittke, M. Die Beothuk-Indianer von Neufundland. Aus Allen Welttheilen, 25 (1894): 235-247.

Lloyd, T. G. B. A further account of the Beothucs of Newfoundland. Royal Anthropological Institute of Great Britain and Ireland, Journal, 5 (1875): 222-230.

Lloyd, T. G. B. On the "Beothucs". Royal Anthropological Institute of Great Britain and Ireland, Journal, 4 (1874): 21-39.

Lloyd, T. G. B. On the stone implements of Newfoundland. Royal Anthropological Institute of Great Britain and Ireland, Journal, 5 (1875): 233-248.

Macdougall, A. The Boeothic Indians. Canadian Institute, Transactions, 2 (1891): 98-102.

Morice, A. G. Disparus et survivants. Société de Géographie (Québec), Bulletin, 20 (1926): 78-94.

Murray, C. A. The Red Indians of Newfoundland. Philadelphia, 1854. 176 p.

Patterson, G. Beothik vocabularies. Royal Society of Canada, Proceedings and Transactions, 10, pt. 2 (1892): 19-32.

Patterson, G. The Beothiks or Red Indians of Newfoundland. Royal Society of Canada, Proceedings and Transactions, 9, pt. 2 (1891): 123-171.

Pilot, W. and L. H. Gray. Beothuks. In J. Hastings, ed. Encyclopaedia of Religion and Ethics. Vol. 2. New York, 1910: 501-503.

Ryan, D. W. S. Relics of a lost race. Atlantic Guardian, 5 (1948): 41-44.

Speck, F. G. Beothuk and Micmac. Indian Notes and Monographs, ser. 2, 22 (1921): 1-187.

Speck, F. G. Eskimo jacket ornaments of ivory suggesting function of bone pendants found in Beothuk sites in Newfoundland. American Antiquity, 5 (1940): 225-228.

Speck, F. G. The Beothuks of Newfoundland. Southern Workman, 41 (1913): 559-563.

Townsend, C. W., ed. Captain Cartwright and his Labrador journal, 16-25. Boston, 1911.

Whitby, Barbara. The Beothucks and other primitive people of Newfoundland: a review. Anthropological Journal of Canada, 5, no. 4 (1967): 2-19.

Willoughby, C. C. Antiquities of the New England Indians, 11-15. Cambridge, 1935.

Wintemberg, W. J. Shell beads of the Beothuk Indians. Royal Society of

Canada, Proceedings and Transactions, ser. 2, 30, pt. 2 (1936): 23-26.

11-04 Cree

Carrière, Gaston. Catalogue des manuscrits en langues indiennes conservés aux archives oblates, Ottawa. Anthropologica, n.s., 12 (1970): 151-179.

Feit, H., et al. Bibliography: native peoples, James Bay region. Recherches Amérindiennes au Québec, 2, no. 1, suppl. (1972): 1-62.

Adam, L. Esquisse d'une grammaire comparée de la langue des Chippeways et de la langue des Crees. International Congress of Americanists, Proceedings, 1, vol. 2 (1875): 88-148.

Adam, L. Examen grammatical comparé de seize langues américaines. International Congress of Americanists, Proceedings, 2, vol. 2 (1877): 161-244.

Adams, J. Sketches of the Tete de Boule Indians. Literary and Historical Society (Quebec), Transactions, 2 (1831): 25-39.

Ahenakew, E. Cree trickster tales. Journal of American Folklore, 42 (1929): 309-353.

Allan, Iris. A Riel Rebellion diary. Alberta Historical Review, 12, no. 3 (1964): 15-25.

Anderson, Frank W. Almighty Voice. Calgary, Frontier Publishers, 1971. 47 p.

Anderson, James Watt. Fur trader's story. Toronto, Ryerson Press, 1961. 15, 245 p. illus.

Anonymous. Anthropological studies among the Attawapiskat Indians. Arctic Circular, 9, no. 1 (1956): 9-10.

Anonymous. Naming of Medicine Hat. Alberta Historical Review, 9, no. 1 (1961): 7.

Anonymous. Smallpox epidemic of 1869-70. Alberta Historical Review, 11, no. 2 (1963): 13-19.

Anonymous. Tuberculosis survey: James and Hudson Bays. Arctic Circular, 4 (1951): 45-47.

Averkieva, Iŭlia P. Okhotnich'i plemena Amerikanskogo severa. By Iŭ. P.

Averkieva and E. E. Blomkvist. In A. V. Efimov and S. A. Tokarev, eds. Narody Ameriki. Vol. 1. Moskva, Izdatel'stvo Akademiia Nauk SSSR, 1959: 171-193.

Ballantyne, R. M. Hudson's Bay, 2d ed.: 41-69. Edinburgh, 1848.

Ballantyne, Robert M. Hudson's Bay; or, Every-day life in the wilds of North America during six years' residence in the territories of the Honourable Hudson's Bay Company. Rutland, Vt., C. E. Tuttle, 1972. 22, 328 p. illus.

Barbeau, C. Marius. Indian days on the western prairies. Ottawa, Queen's Printer, 1960. 6, 234 p. illus., end maps. (Canada, National Museum, Bulletin, 163)

Beardsley, G. Notes on Cree medicines. Michigan Academy of Science, Arts and Letters, Papers, 27 (1941): 483-496.

Belcourt, George Antoine. Hunting buffalo on the northern Plains: a letter from Father Belcourt. North Dakota History, 38 (1971): 332-348.

Bell, C. N., ed. Journal of Henry Kelsey. Historical and Scientific Society of Manitoba, Transactions, n.s., 4 (1928): 1-43.

Bell, R. Report on an exploration of portions of the At-ta-wa-pish-kat and Albany Rivers, Lonely Lake to James Bay, 1886. Canada, Geological Survey, Report of Progress, pt. G (1886): 1-38.

Bell, R. The history of the Che-che-puy-ew-tis. Journal of American Folklore, 10 (1897): 1-8.

Bennett, John W. Northern plainsmen: adaptive strategy and agrarian life. Chicago, Aldine, 1970. 352 p. illus., maps.

Bishop, Charles A. Demography, ecology and trade among the Northern Ojibwa and Swampy Cree. Western Canadian Journal of Anthropology, 3, no. 1 (1972): 58-71.

Bloomfield, L. Plains Cree texts. American Ethnological Society, Publications, 16 (1934): 1-309.

Bloomfield, L. Sacred stories of the Sweet Grass Cree. Canada, Department of Mines, National Museum of Canada, Bulletin, 60 (1930): 1-346.

Bloomfield, L. The Plains Cree language. International Congress of Americanists, Proceedings, 22, vol. 2 (1926): 427-431.

Bloomfield, L. The story of the bad owl. International Congress of Americanists, Proceedings, 22, vol. 2 (1926): 23-34.

Boas, F. Zur Anthropologie der nordamerikanischen Indianer. Berliner Gesellschaft für Anthropologie, Ethnologie und Urgeschichte, Verhandlungen (1895): 367-411.

Boulanger, Tom. An Indian remembers, my life as a trapper in northern Manitoba. Winnipeg, Peguis, 1971. 85 p. illus., map.

Bowen, P. Serum protein polymorphisms in Indians of Western Canada: gene frequencies and data on the Gc/albumin linkage. By P. Bowen, F. O'Callaghan and Catherine S. N. Lee. Human Heredity, 21 (1971): 242-253.

Boyle, D. The killing of Moostoos, the Wehtigoo. Annual Archaeological Report, being Part of Appendix to the Report of the Minister of Education, Ontario (1903): 126-138.

Braroe, Niels Winther. Reciprocal exploitation in an Indian-White community. Southwestern Journal of Anthropology, 21 (1965): 166-178.

Breen, David H. "Timber Tom" and the North-West rebellion. Alberta Historical Review, 19, no. 3 (1971): 1-7.

Bryan, Alan L. An alternative hypothesis for the origin of the name Blackfoot. Plains Anthropologist, 15 (1970): 305-306.

Buck, Ruth Matheson. Tanning hides. By Ruth Matheson Buck and Edward Ahenakew. Beaver, 303, no. 1 (1972/1973): 46-48.

Burpee, L. J., ed. Journals and letters of Pierre Gaultier de Varennes de la Vérendrye and his sons. Champlain Society, Publications, 16 (1927): 1-548.

Bushnell, D. I. Sketches by Paul Kane in the Indian Country, 1845-1848. Smithsonian Miscellaneous Collections, 99, no. 1 (1940): 1-25.

Cadzow, D. A. Peace-pipe of the Prairie Cree. Indian Notes, 3 (1926): 82-89.

Cadzow, D. A. Smoking tipi of Buffalo-Bull the Cree. Indian Notes, 4 (1927): 271-280.

Cadzow, D. A. The Prairie Cree tipi. Indian Notes, 3 (1926): 19-27.

Cameron, D. The Nipigon country. In L. F. R. Masson, ed. Les Bourgeois de la Compagnie du Nord-Ouest. Vol. 2. Quebec, 1890: 231-265.

Cameron, W. B. Blood red the sun. Calgary, 1950. 225 p.

Campbell, H. C. Radisson's journal: its value in history. State Historical Society of Wisconsin, Proceedings, 43 (1896): 88-116.

Campbell, Robert. The private journal of Robert Campbell. Edited by George R. Brooks. Missouri Historical Society, Bulletin, 20 (1963/1964): 3-24, 107-118.

Chaboillez, Charles Jean Baptiste. Journal of Charles Jean Baptiste Chaboillez, 1797-1798. Edited by Harold Hickerson. Ethnohistory, 6 (1959): 265-316, 363-427.

Chance, Norman A. Community adjustment to rapid change among the Eskimo and Cree. By Norman A. Chance and John Trudeau. North, 11, no. 1 (1964): 34-39.

Chance, Norman A. Social organization, acculturation, and integration among the Eskimo and the Cree: a comparative study. By Norman A. Chance and John Trudeau. Anthropologica, n.s., 5 (1963): 47-56.

Chance, Norman A., ed. Conflict in culture: problems of developmental change among the Cree. Ottawa, 1968. 104 p. illus., map. (Saint Paul University, Canadian Research Centre for Anthropology, Document, 2)

Chappell, E. Narrative of a voyage to Hudson's Bay. London, 1817. 279 p.

Chappell, Edward. Narrative of a voyage to Hudson's Bay in His Majesty's ship Rosamond. Toronto, Coles, 1970. 279 p. illus., map.

Chown, B. and M. Lewis. The blood group genes of the Cree Indians and the Eskimos of the Ungava District of Canada. American Journal of Physical Anthropology, n.s., 14 (1956): 215-224.

Clay, C. Indians as I know them. Canadian Geographical Journal, 8 (1934): 43-50.

Clay, C. Swampy Cree legends. Toronto, 1938. 95 p.

Clay, C. The Cree legend of creation. Alberta Folklore Quarterly, 2 (1946): 69-71.

Cocking, M. An adventurer from Hudson Bay. Ed. by L. J. Burpee. Royal Society of Canada, Proceedings and Transactions, ser. 3, 2, pt. 2 (1908): 89-121.

Cooper, J. M. Field notes on Northern Algonkian magic. International Congress of Americanists, Proceedings, 23 (1928): 513-518.

Cooper, J. M. Is the Algonquian family hunting ground system pre-Columbian? American Anthropologist, n.s., 41 (1939): 66-90.

Cooper, J. M. Northern Algonkian scrying and scapulimancy. In Festschrift P. W. Schmidt. Wien, 1928: 205-217.

Cooper, J. M. Tete-de-Boule Cree. International Journal of American Linguistics, 11 (1945): 36-44.

Cooper, J. M. The Cree witiko psychosis. Primitive Man, 6 (1933): 20-24.

Cooper, J. M. The Northern Algonquian supreme being. Catholic University of America, Anthropological Series, 2 (1934): 1-78.

Cooper, J. M. The shaking tent rite among Plains and Forest Algonquians. Primitive Man, 17 (1944): 60-84.

Cooper, John M. The Cree witiko psychosis. In Alan Dundes, ed. Every Man His Way. Englewood Cliffs, Prentice-Hall, 1968: 288-292.

Corrigan, C. Medical practice among the Bush Indians of northern Manitoba. Canadian Medical Association Journal, 54 (1946): 220-223.

Coues, E., ed. Manuscript journals of Alexander Henry and of David Thompson. New York, 1897. 3 v.

Cox, D. W. Two ceruplasmin variants in Canadian Indians and West-Indian Negroes. American Journal of Human Genetics, 22, no. 6 (1970): 13A-14A.

Cresswell, J. R. Folk-tales of the Swampy Cree. Journal of American Folklore, 36 (1923): 404-406.

Curtis, E. S. The North American Indian, Vol. 18: 55-87, 129-135, 152-158, 205-210. Norwood, 1928.

Darby, tr. The epistle to the Romans in the Cree language. Oonikup, N.W. Territory, 1897. 67 p.

Darnell, Regna. Two trails: a proposal for Cree educational television. By Regna Darnell and Anthony L. Vanek. Prince Albert, Sask., Saskatchewan Newstart, 1971. 65 p. illus.

Darnell, Regna, ed. Linguistic diversity in Canadian society. Edmonton, Instant

Printers, 1971. 307 p. (Linguistic Research, Inc., Sociolinguistics Series, 1)

Davidson, D. S. Decorative art of the Tetes de Boule of Quebec. Indian Notes and Monographs, 10 (1928): 115-153.

Davidson, D. S. Notes on Tete de Boule ethnology. American Anthropologist, n.s., 30 (1928): 18-46.

Davidson, D. S. Some Tete de Boule tales. Journal of American Folklore, 41 (1928): 262-274.

Davies, Kenneth G., ed. Letters from Hudson Bay 1703-40. Edited by K. G. Davies, assisted by A. M. Johnson. London, 1965. 68, 455 p. (Hudson's Bay Record Society, Publications, 25)

Denig, Edwin T. Five Indian tribes of the Upper Missouri: Sioux, Arickaras, Assiniboines, Crees, Crows. Edited by John C. Ewers. Norman, University of Oklahoma Press, 1961. 217 p. illus.

Denmark, D. E. James Bay beaver conservation. Beaver, 279 (1948): 38-43.

Dever, Harry. The Nicolet myth. Michigan History, 50 (1966): 318-322.

Diamond, D. James Bay and the Cree. Recherches Amérindiennes au Québec, 2, no. 4/5 (1972): 33-35.

Dillenberg, H. A preventive approach to impetigo of Treaty Indians using staphylococcus polyvalent somatic antigen vaccine. By H. Dillenberg and M. P. D. Waldron. Canadian Medical Association Journal, 89 (1963): 947-949.

Drier, Roy W. The Michigan College of Mining and Technology Isle Royale excavations, 1953-1954. In James B. Griffin. Lake Superior Copper and the Indians: Miscellaneous Studies of Great Lakes Prehistory. Ann Arbor, University of Michigan, 1961: 1-7. (Michigan, University, Museum of Anthropology, Anthropological Papers, 17)

Dunn, J. History of the Oregon Territory, 88-100. London, 1846.

Edwards, Allan M. Observations on juvenile hypothyroidism in native races of Northern Canada. By Allan M. Edwards and Gordon C. Gray. Canadian Medical Association Journal, 84 (1961): 1116-1124.

Eggan, Fred. Northern Woodland ethnology. In Jacob W. Gruber, ed. The Philadelphia Anthropological Society; Papers Presented on Its Golden Anniversary.

New York, distributed by Columbia University Press for Temple University Publications, 1967: 107-124.

Eggleston, Edward. George W. Northrup: the Kit Carson of the Northwest; the-man-that-draws-the-handcart. Edited by Louis Pfaller. North Dakota History, 33 (1966): 4-21.

Ellis, C. Douglas. A note on Okima•hka•n. Anthropological Linguistics, 2, no. 3 (1960): 1.

Ellis, C. Douglas. Cree verb paradigms. International Journal of American Linguistics, 37 (1971): 76-95.

Ellis, C. Douglas. Spoken Cree; west coast of James Bay. Toronto, Anglican Church of Canada, Department of Missions, 1962. [411 p.]

Ellis, C. Douglas. Tagmemic analysis of restricted Cree text. Canadian Journal of Linguistics, 6 (1960/1961): 35-51.

Ellis, C. Douglas. The missionary and the Indian in central and eastern Canada. Arctic Anthropology, 2, no. 2 (1964): 25-31.

Ellis, C. Douglas. The so-called interrogative in Cree. International Journal of American Linguistics, 27 (1961): 119-124.

Ellis, H. A voyage to Hudson's-Bay, 181-198. London, 1748.

Ewers, J. C. Edwin T. Denig's "Of the Crees or Kristeneau". Missouri Historical Society, Bulletin, 9 (1952): 37-69.

Ewers, J. C. Three ornaments worn by Upper Missouri Indians a century and a quarter ago. New York Historical Society Quarterly, 41 (1957): 24-33.

Faraud, H. J. Dix-huit ans chez les sauvages. Bruxelles, 1866. 456 p.

Faries, R., ed. A dictionary of the Cree language. Toronto, 1938. 530 p.

Fay, George E., ed. Charters, constitutions and by-laws of the Indian tribes of North America. Part IIa: The Northern Plains. Greeley, 1967. 6, 141 l. maps. (University of Northern Colorado, Museum of Anthropology, Occasional Publications in Anthropology, Ethnology Series, 3) ERIC ED051923.

Flannery, R. Cross-cousin marriage among the Cree and Montagnais of James Bay. Primitive Man, 11 (1938): 29-33.

Flannery, R. Gossip as a clue to attitudes. Primitive Man, 7 (1934): 8-12.

Flannery, R. Some aspects of James Bay recreative culture. Primitive Man, 9 (1937): 49-56.

Flannery, R. The position of women among the Eastern Cree. Primitive Man, 8 (1935): 81-86.

Fortescue, J. Les Indiens Cris de l'Amérique du Nord. Société Américaine de France, Archives, n.s., 3 (1883): 31-66.

Foster, John E. Program for the Red River Mission: the Anglican clergy 1820-1826. Histoire Sociale, 4 (1969): 49-75.

Francine, J. The forgotten land. Canadian Geographical Journal, 18 (1939): 52-57.

Frank E. Price and Associates, Limited. A sociological study of the Saskatchewan River delta; a study of Indian and Metis attitudes to potential development in the Cumberland House area. Winnipeg, 1967. 86 p.

Franklin, J. Narrative of a journey to the shores of the Polar Sea. London, 1823.

Fraser, W. B. Big Bear, Indian patriot. Alberta Historical Review, 14, no. 2 (1966): 1-13.

Fraser, William Bernard. Big Bear, Indian patriot. Calgary, Historical Society of Alberta, 1966. 15 p. illus.

Gates, R. R. Pedigree study of Amerindian crosses in Canada. Royal Anthropological Institute of Great Britain and Ireland, Journal, 68 (1928): 511-532.

Gibbon, Mary. Trapper's wife. Beaver, 292, no. 4 (1961/1962): 38-42.

Giliarevskiĭ, R. S. Opredelitel' iazykov mira po pis'mennostiam. By R. S. Giliarevskiĭ and V. S. Grivnin. Moskva, Izdatel'stvo Nauka, 1965. 375 p.

Goddard, Ives. Notes on the genetic classification of the Algonquian languages. In Contributions to Anthropology: Linguistics I. Ottawa, Queen's Printer, 1967: 7-12. (Canada, National Museum, Bulletin, 214)

Goddard, P. E. Notes on the sun dance of the Cree in Alberta. American Museum of Natural History, Anthropological Papers, 16 (1919): 295-310.

Godsell, P. H.   Red hunters of the snows.
Toronto, 1938.   324 p.

Gold, Dolores.   Psychological changes
associated with acculturation of
Saskatchewan Indians. Musk-Ox, 2 (1967):
37-45.

Graham, Andrew.   Andrew Graham's
observations on Hudson's Bay, 1767-91.
Edited by Glyndwr Williams. London,
1969. 72, 423 p. illus., maps.
(Hudson's Bay Record Society,
Publications, 27)

Grant, J. C. B.   Anthropometry of the
Chipewyan and Cree Indians of the
neighborhood of Lake Athabaska. Canada,
Department of Mines, National Museum of
Canada, Bulletin, 64 (1930): 1-59.

Grant, J. C. B.   Anthropometry of the Cree
and Saulteaux Indians in northeastern
Manitoba. Canada, Department of Mines,
National Museum of Canada, Bulletin, 59
(1929): 1-73.

Grant, J. C. B.   Anthropometry of the Lake
Winnipeg Indians. American Journal of
Physical Anthropology, 7 (1924): 299-
315.

Grant, J. C. B.   Progress in an
anthropometric survey of the Canadian
aborigines. Pacific Science Congress,
Proceedings, 5, vol. 4 (1933): 2715-
2721.

Gray, C. G.   Some orthopaedic problems in
Indians and Eskimos. Canadian Journal of
Occupational Therapy, 27 (1960): 45-50.

Greenlees, S.   Indian canoe makers.
Beaver, 285 (Summer 1954): 46-49.

Greenlees, S.   The caribou hunters. Forest
and Outdoors, 48, no. 11 (1952): 12-13,
20.

Guinard, J. E.   Witiko among the Tete-de-
Boule. Primitive Man, 3 (1930): 69-71.

Hady, Walter M.   Indian migrations in
Manitoba and the West. Historical and
Scientific Society of Manitoba, Papers,
ser. 3, 17 (1960/1961): 24-53.

Hallowell, A. I.   Cross-cousin marriage in
the Lake Winnipeg area. Philadelphia
Anthropological Society, Publications, 1
(1937): 95-110.

Hallowell, A. I.   Kinship terms and cross-
cousin marriage of the Montagnais-
Naskapi and the Cree. American
Anthropologist, n.s., 34 (1932): 171-
199.

Hallowell, A. I.   The incidence,
character, and decline of polygyny among
the Lake Winnipeg Cree and Saulteaux.
American Anthropologist, n.s., 40
(1938): 235-256.

Hallowell, A. I.   Was cross-cousin
marriage practised by the North-Central
Algonkian? International Congress of
Americanists, Proceedings, 23 (1928):
519-544.

Hamilton, H.   Life at Eastmain. Beaver,
274 (1943): 42.

Hamilton, J. C.   Two Algonquin legends.
Journal of American Folklore, 7 (1894):
201-204.

Hamilton, T. M.   A Cree bow with sinew
backing; its possible relationship to
the bows of the Arctic and the High
Plains. Museum of the Fur Trade
Quarterly, 5, no. 3 (1969): 4-8.

Hanzeli, Victor E.   Missionary linguistics
in New France; a study of seventeenth-
and eighteenth-century descriptions of
American Indian languages. The Hague,
Mouton, 1969. 141 p. illus., map.
(Janua Linguarum, Series Maior, 29)

Hanzeli, Victor E.   The Algonquin R-
dialect in historical records. In
International Congress of Linguists,
10th. 1967, Bucarest. Proceedings.
Vol. 2. Bucarest, Éditions de
l'Académie de la République Socialiste
de Roumanie, 1970: 85-89.

Hardisty, R. G.   The last sun dance.
Alberta Folklore Quarterly, 2 (1946):
57-61.

Harmon, D. W.   A journal of voyages and
travels in the interior of North
America, 269-353. Ed. by W. L. Grant.
Toronto, 1911.   269-353.

Harper, Francis.   The friendly Montagnais
and their neighbors in the Ungava
Peninsula. Lawrence, University of
Kansas, Museum of Natural History, 1964.
5, 121 p. illus. (Kansas, University,
Museum of Natural History, Miscellaneous
Publication, 37)

Harris, Barbara.   Plant and animal names
of Indian origin in British Columbia. By
Barbara Harris and Leopoldina Hrubant.
Syesis, 4 (1971): 223-225.

Haworth, J. C.   Familial chronic acidosis
due to an error in lactate and pyruvate
metabolism. By J. C. Haworth, J. D.
Ford, and M. K. Younoszai. Canadian
Medical Association Journal, 97 (1967):
773-779.

Hayden, F. V. Contributions to the
ethnography and philology of the Indian
tribes of the Missouri Valley. American
Philosophical Society, Transactions,
n.s., 12 (1862): 234-248.

Hector, J. and W. S. W. Vaux. Note of the
Indians seen by the exploring expedition
under the command of Captain Palliser.
Ethnological Society (London),
Transactions, n.s., 1 (1861): 245-261.

Helm, June. The hunting tribes of
subarctic Canada. By June Helm and
Eleanor Burke Leacock. In Eleanor Burke
Leacock and Nancy Oestreich Lurie, eds.
North American Indians in Historical
Perspective. New York, Random House,
1971: 343-374.

Henry, A. Travels and adventures in
Canada, 339-342. Ed. by M. M. Quaife.
Chicago, 1921. 339-342.

Henry, Alexander. Travels and adventures
in Canada and the Indian territories,
between the years 1760 and 1776. New ed.
New York, B. Franklin, 1969. 33,
347 p. illus., maps.

Henry, Alexander. Travels and adventures
in Canada and the Indian territories,
between the years 1760 and 1776. Edited
by James Bain. Edmonton, M. C. Hurtig,
1969. 46, 347 p. illus., maps.

Hewitt, Oliver H. Recent studies on blue
and lesser snow goose populations in
James Bay. North American Wildlife
Conference, Transactions, 15 (1950):
304-309.

Hickerson, Harold. Some implications of
the theory of the particularity, or
"atomism," of Northern Algonkians.
Current Anthropology, 8 (1967): 313-345.
[With comments].

Hicks, Joseph. With Hatton's scouts in
pursuit of Big Bear. Alberta Historical
Review, 18, no. 3 (1970): 14-23.

Hind, H. Y. Narrative of the Canadian Red
River exploring expedition. London,
1860. 2 v.

Hind, H. Y. North-West Territory.
Toronto, 1859. 201 p.

Hind, H. Y. Of some of the superstitions
and customs common among the Indians in
the valley of the Assiniboine and
Saskatchewan. Canadian Journal, n.s., 22
(1859): 253-262.

Hind, Henry Youle. Narrative of the
Canadian Red River exploring expedition
of 1857 and of the Assiniboine and
Saskatchewan exploring expedition of

1858. Rutland, Vt., Tuttle, 1971.
illus.

Hislop, D. M. C. A case of Dubin-Johnson
syndrome in a North American Cree Indian
with a suggestive evidence of familial
occurrence. Medical Services Journal,
Canada, 20 (1964): 61-64.

Hockett, Charles F. What Algonquian is
really like. International Journal of
American Linguistics, 32 (1966): 59-73.

Hoffman, Hans. Culture change and
personality modification among the James
Bay Cree. Alaska, University,
Anthropological Papers, 9 (1960/1961):
81-91.

Hoffmann, Hans. Assessment of cultural
homogeneity among the James Bay Cree.
Dissertation Abstracts International, 32
(1971/1972): 1332B. UM 71-22,722.

Holmes, E. M. Medicinal plants used by
the Cree Indians. Pharmaceutical Journal
and Transactions, ser. 3, 15 (1884):
302-304.

Honigmann, J. J. Attawapiskat--blend of
traditions. Anthropologica, 6 (1958):
57-67.

Honigmann, J. J. Culture patterns and
human stress. Psychiatry, 13 (1950): 25-
34.

Honigmann, J. J. European and other tales
from the Western Woods Cree. Journal of
American Folklore, 66 (1953): 309-331.

Honigmann, J. J. Incentives to work in a
Canadian Indian community. Human
Organization, 8, no. 4 (1949): 23-28.

Honigmann, J. J. Intercultural relations
at Great Whale River. American
Anthropologist, 54 (1952): 510-522.

Honigmann, J. J. Social organization of
the Attawapiskat Cree Indians.
Anthropos, 48 (1953): 809-816.

*Honigmann, J. J. The Attawapiskat Swampy
Cree. Alaska, University,
Anthropological Papers, 5, no. 1 (1956):
23-82.

Honigmann, J. J. The logic of the James
Bay survey. Dalhousie Review, 30 (1951):
378-386.

Honigmann, J. J. and R. Carrera. Another
experiment in sample reliability.
Southwestern Journal of Anthropology, 13
(1957): 99-102.

Honigmann, J. J. and P. Carrera. Cross-
cultural use of Machover's Figure

Drawing Test. American Anthropologist, 59 (1957): 650-654.

*Honigmann, John J.   Foodways in a muskeg community: an anthropological report on the Attawapiskat Indians. Ottawa, 1961. 4, 216 p. illus. (Canada, Department of Northern Affairs and National Resources, Northern Co-ordination and Research Centre, NCRC-62:1)

Honigmann, John J.   Indians of Nouveau-Québec. In Jean Malaurie and Jacques Rousseau, eds. Le Nouveau-Québec. Paris, Mouton, 1964: 315-373.

Horden, J.   A grammar of the Cree language. London, 1881. 238 p.

Horden, J., tr.   Bible and gospel history. London, 1892. 64 p.

Howse, J.   A grammar of the Cree language. London, 1844. 324 p.

Hunter, J.   A lecture on the grammatical construction of the Cree language. London, 1875. 267 p.

Irvine, A. G.   A parley with Big Bear. Alberta Historical Review, 11, no. 4 (1963): 19.

Iserhoff, Sam R.   Bear customs among Indians. Beaver, 5, no. 4 (1924/1925): 174-175.

Iserhoff, Sam R.   The good old days. Beaver, 6, no. 1 (1925/1926): 8-9.

Jeanes, C. W. L.   Inactivation of isoniazid by Canadian Eskimos and Indians. By C. W. L. Jeanes, O. Shaefer, and L. Eidus. Canadian Medical Association Journal, 106 (1972): 331-335.

Jefferson, R.   Fifty years on the Saskatchewan. Canadian North-West Historical Society, Publications, 1, no. 5 (1929): 1-160.

Jenkins, Dale W.   Ecological survey of the mosquitoes of southern James Bay. By Dale W. Jenkins and Kenneth L. Knight. American Midland Naturalist, 47 (1952): 456-468.

Jérémie, N.   Account of Hudson Strait and Bay. Ed. by R. Douglas and J. N. Wallace. Ottawa, 1926. 42 p.

Johnston, Alexander, comp. The battle of Belly River; stories of the last great Indian battle. Lethbridge, Historical Society of Alberta, Lethbridge Branch, 1966. 22 p. illus., maps.

Kelkar, Ashok R.   Participant placement in Algonquian and Georgian. International Journal of American Linguistics, 31 (1965): 195-205.

Kennedy, G. A.   The last battle. Alberta Folklore Quarterly, 1 (1945): 57-60.

Kidd, K. E.   Trading into Hudson's Bay. Beaver, 288, no. 3 (1957): 12-17.

Koolage, William W., Jr.   Adaptation of Chipewyan Indians and other persons of native background in Churchill, Manitoba. Dissertation Abstracts International, 32 (1971/1972): 681B.   UM 71-20,978.

Lacombe, A.   Dictionnaire de la langue des Cris. Montreal, 1874. 709 p.

Lacombe, A.   Grammaire de la langue des Cris. Montreal, 1874. 190 p.

Lagasse, Jean H.   Community development in Manitoba. Human Organization, 20 (1961/1962): 232-237.

Laidlaw, G. E.   Gambling amongst the Crees with small sticks. American Antiquarian and Oriental Journal, 23 (1901): 275-276.

Lance, B. C. L.   When the Crees moved west. Annual Archaeological Report, being Part of Appendix to the Report of the Minister of Education, Ontario, 34 (1923): 25-34.

Lane, C.   The sun dance of the Cree Indians. Canadian Record of Science, 2 (1887): 22-26.

Lanegraff, T. G.   Pioneering among the Indians. Utica, N.Y., N. T. Lewis, 1961. 20 p. illus.

Latourelle, R.   Étude sur les Écrits de Saint Jean de Brébeuf. Montreal, 1953. 271 p.

Lawrence, V. A.   Pioneer recollections. Alberta Historical Review, 20, no. 3 (1972): 30.

Leden, C.   Unter den Indianern Canadas. Zeitschrift für Ethnologie, 44 (1912): 811-831.

Leechman, D.   The savages of James Bay. Beaver, 276 (1945): 14-17.

Leechman, D.   The trappers. Beaver, 288, no. 3 (1957): 24-31.

Leechman, John Douglas. The Swampy Cree. Beaver, 283 (Dec. 1952): 26-27.

Leguerrier, Jules, ed. Livre de prières en langue crise à l'usage des Indiens de la côte ouest de la Baie James. Edited by Jules Leguerrier and A. Lavoie. Lac Sainte-Anne, 1952. 167 p.

Leith, Charles K. A summer and winter on Hudson Bay. By Charles K. Leith and A. T. Leith. Madison, Cartwell, 1912. 203 p. illus., map.

Liebow, Elliot. A preliminary study of acculturation among the Cree Indians of Winisk, Ontario. By Eliot Liebow and John Trudeau. Arctic, 15 (1962): 190-204.

Light, Douglas W. Tattooing practices of the Cree Indians. Calgary, Glenbow-Alberta Institute, 1972. 23 p. illus. (Glenbow-Alberta Institute, Occasional Paper, 6)

Linderman, F. B. Indian old-man stories. New York, 1920. 169 p.

Linderman, F. B. Indian why stories. New York, 1915. 236 p.

Logan, R. A. The precise speakers. Beaver, 282, no. 1 (1951): 40-43.

Logan, Robert A. Cree language notes. Lake Charlotte, Nova Scotia, Loganda, 1958. 2, 14 p.

Logan, Robert A. Cree-English dictionary and remarks on the Cree language. Duluth, 1964. 2 v. [1,044 p.].

Loggie, Margaret. Fort Dunvegan. Alberta Historical Review, 7, no. 1 (1959): 18-26.

Longacre, R. E. Quality and quantity in Cree vowels. Canadian Linguistic Association, Journal, 3 (1957): 66-70.

Lowie, R. H. The military societies of the Plains Cree. International Congress of Americanists, Proceedings, 31, no. 1 (1955): 3-9.

MacEwan, John W. G. Portraits from the Plains. Toronto, McGraw-Hill of Canada, 1971. 287 p. illus., map.

Macfie, J. Crafts of the Cree. Beaver, 288, no. 2 (1957): 53-57.

Macfie, John. The Coast Crees. Beaver, 298, no. 3 (1967/1968): 13-21.

MacKeevor, Thomas. A voyage to Hudson's Bay, during the summer of 1812. London, printed for Sir R. Phillips and Co., 1819. 2, 76 p. (New Voyages and Travels, 3d Series, 2, no. 2)

Mackenzie, A. Voyage from Montreal. Ed. by M. M. Quaife. Chicago, 1931.

Mackintosh, W. A. Prairie settlement. Toronto, 1934.

Mandelbaum, D. G. Boom periods in the history of an Indian tribe. Social Forces, 16 (1937): 117-119.

Mandelbaum, D. G. Friendship in North America. Man, 36 (1936): 205-206.

*Mandelbaum, D. G. The Plains Cree. American Museum of Natural History, Anthropological Papers, 37 (1940): 155-316.

Mandelbaum, David G. Anthropology and people: the world of the Plains Cree. Saskatoon, 1967. 14 p. (Saskatchewan, University, University Lectures, 12)

Mandelbaum, David Goodman. Changes in an aboriginal culture following a change in environment, as exemplified by the Plains Cree. Dissertation Abstracts International, 33 (1972/1973): 542B. UM 72-22,282.

Mason, Leonard. The Swampy Cree: a study in acculturation. Ottawa, Queen's Printer, 1967. 11, 75 p. illus., maps. (Canada, National Museum, Anthropology Papers, 13)

Matson, G. A. Blood groups and ageusia in Indians of Montana and Alberta. American Journal of Physical Anthropology, 24 (1938): 81-89.

McDonnell, J. Some account of the Red River. In L. F. R. Masson, ed. Les Bourgeois de la Compagnie du Nord-Ouest. Vol. 1. Quebec, 1889: 265-295.

McDougall, J. Pathfinding on plain and prairie. Toronto, 1898. 277 p.

McLean, J. Notes of a twenty-five years' service in the Hudson's Bay territory. Ed. by W. S. Wallace. Champlain Society, Publications, 19 (1932): 1-402.

McLean, John. Notes of a twenty-five years' service in the Hudson's Bay territory. New York, Greenwood Press, 1968. 36, 402 p. map. (Champlain Society, Publication, 19)

Melvill, C. D. Report on the east-coastal fisheries of James Bay. Canada, Department of the Naval Service, Reports on Fisheries Investigations in Hudson and James Bays (1914): 3-28.

Michelson, T. Linguistic classification of Cree and Montagnais-Naskapi dialects.

U.S. Bureau of American Ethnology, Bulletin, 123 (1939): 67-95.

Michelson, T. Plains Cree kinship terms. American Anthropologist, n.s., 40 (1938): 531-532.

Michelson, T. The linguistic classification of the Tete de Boule. American Anthropologist, n.s., 35 (1933): 396.

Michelson, Truman. A report on a linguistic expedition to James and Hudson's Bay. American Anthropologist, n.s., 38 (1936): 685-686.

Millar, J. Some observations on haemoglobin levels of an Indian population. Canadian Medical Association Journal, 67 (1952): 414-417.

Mooney, J. Maskegon. U.S. Bureau of American Ethnology, Bulletin, 30, vol. 1 (1907): 813-814.

Mooney, J. Têtes de Boule. U.S. Bureau of American Ethnology, Bulletin, 30, vol. 2 (1910): 735-736.

Mooney, J. and C. Thomas. Cree. U.S. Bureau of American Ethnology, Bulletin, 30, vol. 1 (1907): 359-362.

Moore, P. E., et al. Medical survey of nutrition among the northern Manitoba Indians. Canadian Medical Association Journal, 54 (1946): 223-233.

Morgan, L. H. Systems of consanguinity and affinity. Smithsonian Contributions to Knowledge, 17 (1871): 291-382.

Morgan, L. H. The Indian journals, 1859-62, p. 111-113, 115, 117, 120. Ann Arbor, 1959.

Morin, Leopold. Moosonee Indians' integration. Moosonee, Ont., 1971. 56 p.

Morrissette, Hugues, ed. Problèmes nordiques des façades de la Baie de James. Edited by Hugues Morrissette and Louis-Edmond Hamelin. Québec, 1967. 179 l. illus., maps. (Laval, Université, Centre d'Études Nordiques, Travaux Divers, 18)

Morton, Desmond, ed. Telegrams of the North-West Campaign 1885. Edited by Desmond Morton and Reginald H. Roy. Toronto, 1972. 103, 431 p. illus., maps. (Champlain Society, Publications, 47)

Nichols, Johanna. Diminutive consonant symbolism in western North America. Language, 47 (1971): 826-848.

Oaks, Abel. The boy and the buffalo. Indian Historian, 1, no. 4 (1967/1968): 29.

O'Brodovich, Lloyd S. Historical analysis: 19th century; the establishment of Cree culture in the Plains area. Na'páo, 2, no. 1 (1969): 5-23.

Orchard, W. C. Old porcupine-quillwork. Indian Notes, 1 (1924): 157-161.

Orr, R. B. The Crees of New Ontario. Annual Archaeological Report, being Part of Appendix to the Report of the Minister of Education, Ontario (1923): 9-24.

Osmond, Humphry. Peyote night. In Bernard S. Aaronson and Humphry Osmond, eds. Psychedelics: the Uses and Implications of Hallucinogenic Drugs. Garden City, Doubleday, 1970: 67-86.

Palliser, J. Further papers. London, 1860. 325 p.

Palliser, J. Papers. London, 1859. 325 p.

Parker, John. The fur trader and the emerging geography of North America. Museum of the Fur Trade Quarterly, 2, no. 3 (1966): 6-10; 2, no. 4 (1966): 7-11.

Peel, Bruce. The coal fleet. Alberta Historical Review, 12, no. 4 (1964): 8-14.

Peeso, F. E. The Cree Indians. Museum Journal, 3 (1912): 50-57.

Perrot, N. Memoir on the manners, customs and religion of the savages of North America. In E. H. Blair, ed. The Indian Tribes of the Upper Mississippi Valley. Vol. 1. Cleveland, 1911: 25-272.

Perrot, N. Mémoire sur les moeurs, coutumes et religion des sauvages de l'Amérique septentrionale. Paris, 1864. 341 p.

Petitot, E. F. S. De Carlton-House au Fort Pitt. Société Neuchâteloise de Géographie, Bulletin, 11 (1899): 176-195.

Petitot, E. F. S. Légendes et traditions des Cris. Littératures Populaires de Toutes les Nations, 23 (1886): 445-488.

Petitot, E. F. S. On the Athabasca district of the Canadian North-West Territory. Canadian Record of Science, 1 (1884): 27-53.

Pierce, Joe E. Possible electronic
computation of typological indices for
linguistic structures. International
Journal of American Linguistics, 28
(1962): 215-226.

Pike, Kenneth L. Conflated field
structures in Potawatomi and in Arabic.
By Kenneth L. Pike and Barbara Erickson.
International Journal of American
Linguistics, 30 (1964): 201-212.

Pittman, Richard S. The fused subject and
object pronouns of Red Pheasant Cree.
Linguistics, 13 (1965): 34-38.

Poirier, Jean. Les êtres supernaturels
dans la toponymie amérindienne du
Québec. Revue Internationale
d'Onomastique, 21 (1969): 287-300.

Preston, Richard J. Ritual hangings; an
aboriginal 'survival' in a northern
North American trapping community. Man,
64 (1964): 142-144.

Preston, Richard Joseph, III. Cree
narration: an expression of the personal
meanings of events. Dissertation
Abstracts International, 32 (1971/1972):
6798B. UM 72-18,443.

Proulx, Jean Baptiste. À la baie
d'Hudson, où récit de la première visite
pastorale de Mgr. N. Z. Lorrain.
Montréal, Librairie Saint-Joseph,
Cadieux and Derome, 1886. 284 p.

Prud'homme, L.-A. Carmel, une légende de
la tribu des Cris. Royal Society of
Canada, Proceedings and Transactions,
ser. 3, 13, sect. 1 (1919): 95-100.

Ray, Arthur Joseph, Jr. Indian
exploitation of the forest-grassland
transition zone in Western Canada, 1650-
1860: a geographical view of two
centuries of change. Dissertation
Abstracts International, 32 (1971/1972):
3432B. UM 71-28,359.

Raymond, M. Notes ethnobotaniques sur les
Têtes-de-boule de Manouan. Montréal,
Université, Institut Botanique,
Contributions, 55 (1945): 113-135.

Raynor, W. Windigo woman. Beaver, 288,
no. 1 (1957): 32-33.

Richardson, Boyce. 'Progress' comes to
James Bay. Living Wilderness, 36,
no. 119 (1972): 10-19.

Richardson, J. Arctic searching
expedition, Vol. 2: 33-60, 387-395.
London, 1851.

Rogers, E. S. Down the Rupert's River.
Beaver, 279 (1948): 29-33.

Rogers, Edward S. Band organization among
the Indians of eastern subarctic Canada.
In Contributions to Anthropology: Band
Societies. Ottawa, Queen's Printer,
1969: 21-55. (Canada, National Museums,
Bulletin, 228)

Rogers, Edward S. Changing settlement
patterns of the Cree-Ojibwa of northern
Ontario. Southwestern Journal of
Anthropology, 19 (1963): 64-88.

Rogers, Edward S. Natural environment--
social organization--witchcraft: Cree
versus Ojibwa--a test case. In
Contributions to Anthropology:
Ecological Essays. Ottawa, Queen's
Printer, 1969: 24-39. (Canada, National
Museums, Bulletin, 230)

Rogers, Edward S. Plains Cree. Beaver,
300, no. 2 (1969/1970): 56-59.

Rogers, Edward S. Subsistence areas of
the Cree-Ojibwa of the eastern
Subarctic: a preliminary study. In
Contributions to Ethnology V. Ottawa,
Queen's Printer, 1967: 59-90. (Canada,
National Museum, Bulletin, 204)

Rogers, Edward S. The fur trade, the
government and the central Canadian
Indian. In Deward E. Walker, Jr., ed.
The Emergent Native Americans. Boston,
Little, Brown, 1972: 337-342.

Rogers, Edward S. The fur trade, the
government and the central Canadian
Indian. Arctic Anthropology, 2, no. 2
(1964): 37-40.

Rogers, Edward S. The Indians of the
Central Subarctic of Canada. By Edward
S. Rogers and Father John Trudeau. In
Internationale Amerikanistenkongress,
38th. 1968, Stuttgart-München.
Verhandlungen. Band 3. München, Klaus
Renner, 1971: 133-149.

Rohrl, Vivian J. A nutritional factor in
windigo psychosis. American
Anthropologist, 72 (1970): 97-101.

Rohrl, Vivian J. Comment on "The cure and
feeding of windigos: a critique".
American Anthropologist, 74 (1972): 242-
244.

Roming, John H. James Bay geese. Beaver,
277 (Sept. 1946): 22-25.

Rordam, Vita. The woman who spoke to a
dog. Beaver, 298, no. 3 (1967/1968): 54.

Rossignol, M. Cross-cousin marriage among
the Saskatchewan Cree. Primitive Man, 11
(1938): 26-28.

Rossignol, M. Property concepts among the Cree of the Rocks. Primitive Man, 12 (1939): 61-70.

Rossignol, M. The religion of the Saskatchewan and western Manitoba Cree. Primitive Man, 11 (1939): 67-71.

Rousseau, J. J. Les voyages du Père Albanel au Lac Mistassini et la Baie James. Revue d'Histoire de l'Amérique Française, 3 (1950): 556-586.

Rousseau, J. J. Mokouchan. Forêt et Conservation, 2 (1950): 683-687.

Rousseau, J. J. Persistance paiennes chez les Amérindiens de la Forêt Boréale. Cahiers des Dix, 17 (1952): 183-208.

Roy, Chunilal. The prevalence of mental disorders among Saskatchewan Indians. By Chunilal Roy, Adjit Choudhuri, and Donald Irvine. Journal of Cross-Cultural Psychology, 1 (1970): 383-392.

Rue, Leonard Lee, III. Barriere Indians. Beaver, 292, no. 2 (1961/1962): 27-32.

Russell, F. Explorations in the far north, 21-40, 168-186, 201-220. Iowa City, 1898.

Saindon, J. E. Mental disorders among the James Bay Cree. Primitive Man, 6 (1933): 1-12.

Saindon, J. Emile. Two Cree songs from James Bay. Primitive Man, 7 (1934): 6-7.

Sanderson, James F. Indian tales of the Canadian prairies. Calgary, Historical Society of Alberta, 1965. 15 p. illus.

Sanderson, James F. Indian tales of the Canadian prairies. Alberta Historical Review, 13, no. 3 (1965): 7-21.

Saunders, L. G. A survey of helminth and protozoan incidence in man and dogs at Fort Chipewyan, Alberta. Journal of Parasitology, 35 (1949): 31-34.

Schmidt, W. Die Ostzentral-Algonkin. In his Die Ursprung der Göttesidee. Bd. 2. Münster i. W., 1929: 459-474.

Schmidt, W. Die Ostzentral-Algonkin. In his Die Ursprung der Göttesidee. Bd. 5. Münster i. W., 1934: 531-554, 887.

Schoolcraft, H. R. Kenistenos. In his Information respecting the History, Condition, and Prospects of the Indian Tribes of the United States. Vol. 5. Philadelphia, 1855: 164-172.

Schubert, Josef. Verbal regulation of behavior and IQ in Canadian Indian and White children. By Josef Schubert and A. J. Cropley. Developmental Psychology, 7 (1972): 295-301.

Schultz, Hart Merriam (Lone Wolf). Lone Wolf returns . . . to that long ago time. Edited by Paul Dyck. Montana, the Magazine of Western History, 22, no. 1 (1972): 18-41.

Scott, Simeon. The origin of the Muskegon Cree. Beaver, 300, no. 1 (1969/1970): 62.

Scull, G. D. Voyages of Peter Esprit Radisson. Boston, 1885. 385 p.

Sevareid, Arnold Eric. Canoeing with the Cree. Reprint ed. St. Paul, Minnesota Historical Society, 1968. 15, 206 p. illus., maps.

Shave, H. John West, Peguis and P. Rindisbacher. Beaver, 288, no. 1 (1957): 14-19.

Shearwood, Mrs. F. P. By water and the word. Toronto, Macmillan of Canada, 1943. 12, 216 p. illus.

Shera, John W. Poundmaker's capture of a wagon train. Pioneer West, 1 (1969): 7-9.

Shipley, N. Frances and the Crees. Toronto, 1957. 181 p.

Siebert, Frank T., Jr. Discrepant consonant clusters ending in *-k in Proto-Algonquian, a proposed interpretation of saltatory sound changes. In Contributions to Anthropology: Linguistics I. Ottawa, Queen's Printer, 1967: 48-59. (Canada, National Museum, Bulletin, 214)

Simms, S. C. Myths of the Bungees or Swampy Indians of Lake Winnipeg. Journal of American Folklore, 19 (1906): 334-340.

Simms, S. C. The metawin of the Bungees or Swampy Indians of Lake Winnipeg. Journal of American Folklore, 19 (1906): 330-333.

Simpson, Nancy E. Polyacrylamide electrophoresis used for the detection of C5+ cholinesterase in Canadian Caucasians, Indians, and Eskimos. American Journal of Human Genetics, 24 (1972): 317-320.

Skinner, A. A visit to the Ojibway and Cree of central Canada. American Museum Journal, 10 (1910): 9-18.

Skinner, A. Bear customs of the Cree and other Algonkin Indians of northern

Ontario. Ontario Historical Society, Papers and Records, 12 (1914): 203-209.

*Skinner, A. Notes on the Eastern Cree and Northern Saulteaux. American Museum of Natural History, Anthropological Papers, 9 (1911): 1-116.

Skinner, A. Notes on the Plains Cree. American Anthropologist, n.s., 16 (1914): 68-87.

Skinner, A. Ojibway and Cree of central Canada. American Museum Journal, 10 (1908): 9-18.

Skinner, A. Plains Cree tales. Journal of American Folklore, 29 (1916): 341-367.

Skinner, A. Political organization, cults and ceremonies of the Plains-Cree. American Museum of Natural History, Anthropological Papers, 11 (1914): 513-542.

Skinner, A. The sun dance of the Plains-Cree. American Museum of Natural History, Anthropological Papers, 16 (1919): 283-293.

Skinner, Alanson B. Some remarks on the culture of eastern near-Arctic Indians. Science, n.s., 29 (1909): 150-152.

Skinner, Mark. The Seafort Burial Site (FcPr100), Rocky Mountain House (1835-1861): life and death during the fur trade. Western Canadian Journal of Anthropology, 3, no. 1 (1972): 126-145.

Sluman, Norma. Poundmaker. Toronto, Ryerson Press, 1967. 301 p.

Smith, J. G. E. Rousseau's review of "Material culture of the Mistassini": a comment. American Anthropologist, 71 (1969): 710.

Somogyi-Csizmazia, W. Three-rooted mandibular first permanent molars in Alberta Indian children. By W. Somogyi-Csizmazia and A. J. Simons. Canadian Dental Association, Journal, 37 (1971): 105-106.

Spry, Irene M., ed. The papers of the Palliser Expedition 1857-1860. Toronto, 1968. 138, 694 p. illus., map. (Champlain Society, Publications, 44)

Stallcop, Emmett A. A religious effigy of the Cree of Rocky Boy Reservation. Plains Anthropologist, 17 (1972): 68-70.

Stevens, James R. Sacred legends of the Sandy Lake Cree. Toronto, McClelland and Stewart, 1971. 12, 144 p. illus.

Stewart, J. Rupert's Land Indians in the olden time. Annual Archaeological Report, being Part of Appendix to the Report of the Minister of Education, Ontario (1904): 89-100.

Swindlehurst, F. Folk-lore of the Cree Indians. Journal of American Folklore, 18 (1905): 139-143.

Teeter, Karl V. Consonant harmony in Wiyot (with a note on Cree). International Journal of American Linguistics, 25 (1959): 41-43.

Teit, J. A. Two Plains Cree tales. Journal of American Folklore, 34 (1921): 320-621.

Thompson, David. David Thompson's narrative 1784-1812. Edited by Richard Glover. Toronto, 1962. 102, 410 p. map. (Champlain Society, Publications, 40)

Thwaites, R. G., ed. Radisson and Groseilliers in Wisconsin. State Historical Society of Wisconsin, Collections, 11 (1888): 64-96.

Thwaites, R. G., ed. The Jesuit Relations and allied documents. Cleveland, 1896-1901. 74 v.

Trudeau, Jean. Culture change among the Swampy Cree Indians of Winisk, Ontario. Dissertation Abstracts, 27 (1966/1967): 2968B-2969B. UM 67-1842.

Trudeau, John. [Review of] "Foodways in a Muskeg Community" by John Honigmann. Anthropologica, n.s., 5 (1963): 86-90.

Tyrrell, J. B., ed. David Thompson's narrative of his explorations in western America. Champlain Society, Publications, 12 (1916): 78-127.

Tyrrell, J. B., ed. Documents relating to the early history of Hudson Bay. Champlain Society, Publications, 18 (1931): 1-419.

Uhlenbeck, C. C. Ontwerp van eene vergelijkende vormleer van eenige Algonkin-talen. Amsterdam, Koninklijke Akademie van Wetenschappen, Afdeeling Letterkunde, Verhandelingen, n.s., 11, no. 3 (1910): 1-67.

Umfreville, E. The present state of Hudson's Bay. London, 1790.

Vivian, R. Percy, et al. The nutrition and health of the James Bay Indian. Canadian Medical Association, Journal, 59 (1948): 505-518.

Walker, Willard. Notes on native writing systems and the design of native literacy programs. Anthropological Linguistics, 11, no. 5 (1969): 148-166.

Wallace, James Nevin. Early explorations along the Bow and Saskatchewan Rivers. Alberta Historical Review, 9, no. 2 (1961): 12-21.

Watetch, Abel. Payepot and his people. By Abel Watetch as told to Blodwen Davies. Regina, Saskatchewan History and Folklore Society, 1959. 66 p. illus.

Watkins, E. A. A dictionary of the Cree language. London, 1865. 460 p.

Watkins, E. A. A dictionary of the Cree language. Toronto, 1938. 534 p.

White, M. C. David Thompson's journals relating to Montana and adjacent regions, 1808-1812. Missoula, 1950. 507 p.

Whitney, C. On snow-shoes to the barren grounds. New York, 1896. 324 p.

Willians, Milton. Twice disappointed. Alberta Historical Review, 11, no. 4 (1963): 15-18.

Wiltshire, E. Bevan. Draw-a-Man and Raven's Progressive Matrices (1938): intelligence test performance of reserve Indian children. By E. Bevan Wiltshire and John E. Gray. Canadian Journal of Behavioural Science, 1 (1969): 119-122.

Wissler, C. The excess of females among the Cree Indians. National Academy of Sciences, Proceedings, 22 (1936): 151-153.

Wissler, Clark. Population changes among the Northern Plains Indians. New Haven, Yale University Press, 1936. 20 p. (Yale University Publications in Anthropology, 1)

Wissler, Clark. Population changes among the Northern Plains Indians. New Haven, Human Relations Area Files Press, 1970. 20 p. (Yale University Publications in Anthropology, 1)

Wolfart, H. Christoph. Plains Cree internal syntax and the problem of noun-interpretation. In Internationale Amerikanistenkongress, 38th. 1968, Stuttgart-München. Verhandlungen. Band 3. München, Klaus Renner, 1971: 511-518.

Wolfart, Hans Christoph. An outline of Plains Cree morphology. Dissertation Abstracts International, 31 (1970/1971): 1255A. UM 70-17,442.

Wood, W. J. Tularemia. Manitoba Medical Association, Review, 31 (1951): 641-644.

Woodward, J. A. A leisure time activity of the Plains Cree. By J. A. Woodward and V. C. Woodward. Anthropological Journal of Canada, 8, no. 4 (1970): 29-31.

Woodward, John A. Plains Cree beadwork. Masterkey, 43 (1969): 144-150.

Woolworth, Nancy L. The Grand Portage Mission: 1731-1965. Minnesota History, 39 (1964/1965): 301-310.

Wright, James V. Cree culture history in the Southern Indian Lake region. In Contributions to Anthropology VII: Archaeology and Physical Anthropology. Ottawa, Queen's Printer, 1971: 1-31. (Canada, National Museums, Bulletin, 232)

Wuttunee, William I. C. Peyote ceremony. Beaver, 299, no. 1 (1968/1969): 22-25.

Young, E. R. By canoe and dog-train among the Cree and Salteaux Indians. London, 1890. 267 p.

Young, E. R. On the Indian trail. New York, 1897. 214 p.

Young, E. R. Stories from Indian wigwams and northern Camp-fires. New York, 1893. 293 p.

Zaslow, Morris, ed. Rendezvous at Moose Factory, 1882. Ontario History, 53 (1961): 81-94.

11-05   Malecite

Ray, Roger B. The Indians of Maine: a bibliographical guide. Portland, Me., Maine Historical Society, 1972. 44 p.

Adney, E. Tappan. The Malecite Indian's names for native berries and fruits, and their meanings. Acadian Naturalist, 1 (1943/1944): 103-110.

Alger, A. L. A collection of words and phrases taken from the Passamaquoddy tongue. American Philosophical Society, Proceedings, 21 (1885): 240-255.

Alger, A. L. In Indian tents. Boston, 1897. 139 p.

Anonymous. Ontario Indians: their fisheries and fishery appliances. Annual Archaeological Report, being Part of

Appendix to the Report of the Minister of Education, Ontario (1917): 24-43.

Anonymous. Supersititions of the Passamaquoddies. Journal of American Folklore, 2 (1889): 229-231.

Anonymous. Wood and wood products: their uses by the prehistoric Indians of Ontario. Annual Archaeological Report, being Part of Appendix to the Report of the Minister of Education, Ontario (1918): 25-48.

Barratt, Joseph. Key to the Indian language of New-England [!] in the Etchemin, or Passamaquoddy tongue, spoken in Maine and St. Johns, New Brunswick. Middletown, Conn., C. H. Pelton, 1850. 8 p.

Barratt, Joseph. The Indian of New-England, and the north-eastern provinces. 3d ed. Middletown, Conn., C. H. Pelton, 1851. 24 p.

Brown, Mrs. W. W. "Chief-making" among the Passamaquoddy Indians. Journal of American Folklore, 5 (1892): 57-59.

Chamberlain, M. Indians in New Brunswick in Champlain's time. Acadiensis, 4 (1904): 280-295.

Chamberlain, M. The origin of the Maliseets. New Brunswick Magazine, 1 (1898): 41-45.

Clarke, George F. Someone before us; our Maritime Indians. Fredericton, N.B., Brunswick Press, 1968. 240 p. illus.

Dionne, N. E. Étude archéologique: le Fort Jacques-Cartier et la Petite Hermine. Montreal, 1891.

Dodge, E. S. An early nineteenth century Passamaquoddy bark box. Massachusetts Archaeological Society, Bulletin, 14 (1953): 77-78.

Eckstorm, F. H. Old John Neptune and other Maine Indian shamans. Portland, 1945. 209 p.

Ede, M. C. Diabetes and the way of life on an Indian reservation. London, Guy's Hospital Reports, 115 (1966): 455-461.

Feest, Christian F. Lukas Vischers Beiträge zur Ethnographie Nordamerikas. Archiv für Völkerkunde, 22 (1968): 31-66.

Fergusson, Charles Bruce. Pre-revolutionary settlements in Nova Scotia. Nova Scotia Historical Society, Collections, 37 (1970): 5-22.

Fewkes, J. W. A contribution to Passamaquoddy folk-lore. Journal of American Folklore, 3 (1890): 257-280.

Fidelholtz, James Lawrence. Micmac morphophonemics. Dissertation Abstracts International, 34 (1973/1974): 2595A. UM 73-25,772.

Ganong, W. F. Historical-geographical documents relating to New Brunswick. New Brunswick Historical Society, Collections, 5, no. 13 (1930): 76-128.

Ganong, W. F. The economic mollusca of Acadia: wampum among the New Brunswick Indians. New Brunswick, Natural History Society, Bulletin, 8 (1889): 3-116.

Goddard, Ives. Notes on the genetic classification of the Algonquian languages. In Contributions to Anthropology: Linguistics I. Ottawa, Queen's Printer, 1967: 7-12. (Canada, National Museum, Bulletin, 214)

Goodwin, W. L. Notes on an old Indian encampment. Canadian Record of Science, 5, no. 5 (1893): 284-285.

Hadlock, W. S. and E. S. Dodge. A canoe from the Penobscot River. American Neptune, 8 (1948): 289-301.

Hadlock, Wendell S. The significance of certain textiles found at Redbank, New Brunswick, in relation to the history of the culture area. Acadian Naturalist, 2, no. 8 (July 1947): 49-62.

Hoffman, B. G. The Souriquois, Etechemin and Wegesh. Ethnohistory, 2 (1955): 65-87.

Kellogg, E. Vocabulary of words in the language of the Quoddy Indians. Massachusetts Historical Society, Collections, ser. 3, 3 (1833): 181-182.

Leland, C. G. The Algonquin legends of New England. Boston, 1884. 379 p.

Leland, C. G. and J. D. Prince. Kulóskap the master, and other Algonquin poems. New York, 1902. 370 p.

Leland, Charles G. The Algonquin legends of New England. Detroit, Singing Tree Press, 1968. 15, 379 p. illus.

Lescarbot, M. Histoire de la Nouvelle-France. Paris, 1609. 888 p.

Lescarbot, M. Nova Francia. New ed., 145-330. London, 1928.

Lescarbot, M. The history of New France. Ed. by L. Grant. Toronto, 1907-1914. 3 v.

Maillard, A. S. Account of the customs and manners of the Micmakis and Maricheets. London, 1758. 138 p.

Maine, Laws, Statutes, etc. A compilation of laws pertaining to Indians. Rev. Prepared by the Department of Indian Affairs. Augusta, 1969. 30 p.

Maine, State Department of Health and Welfare. Indians of Maine. Augusta, 1964. 14 p. ERIC ED031364.

McFeat, Tom F. S. The Algonkian project. In his Museum Ethnology and the Algonkian Project. Ottawa, Queen's Printer, 1962: 15-80. (Canada, National Museum, Anthropology Papers, 2)

McFeat, Tom F. S. Two Malecite family industries: a case study. Anthropologica, n.s., 4 (1962): 233-271.

Mechling, W. H. Malecite tales. Canada, Department of Mines, Geological Survey, Memoirs, 49 (1914): 1-133.

Mechling, W. H. Maliseet tales. Journal of American Folklore, 26 (1913): 219-258.

*Mechling, W. H. The Malecite Indians, with notes on the Micmacs. Anthropologica, 7 (1958): 1-160; 8 (1959): 161-274.

Michelson, T. The Passamaquoddy Indians of Maine. Smithsonian Institution, Explorations and Field-Work (1934): 85-88.

Mooney, J. and C. Thomas. Malecite. U.S. Bureau of American Ethnology, Bulletin, 30, vol. 1 (1907): 793-794.

Morgan, L. H. Systems of consanguinity and affinity. Smithsonian Contributions to Knowledge, 17 (1871): 291-382.

Nicholas, Andrew. New Brunswick Indians-- conservative militants. In Waubageshig, ed. The Only Good Indian. Toronto, new press, 1972: 36-43.

Pratson, Frederick John. Land of the four directions. Old Greenwich, Conn., Chatham Press, 1970. 131 p. illus.

Prince, J. D. A Passamaquoddy aviator. American Anthropologist, n.s., 11 (1909): 628-650.

Prince, J. D. A Passamaquoddy tobacco famine. International Journal of American Linguistics, 1 (1917): 58-63.

Prince, J. D. Algonquins (Eastern). In J. Hastings, ed. Encyclopaedia of Religion and Ethics. Vol. 1. New York, 1908: 319-321.

Prince, J. D. Notes on Passamaquoddy literature. New York Academy of Sciences, Annals, 13 (1901): 381-386.

Prince, J. D. Notes on the language of the Eastern Algonkin tribes. American Journal of Philology, 9 (1888): 310-316.

Prince, J. D. Passamaquoddy texts. American Ethnological Society, Publications, 10 (1921): 1-85.

Prince, J. D. Some Passamaquoddy documents. New York Academy of Sciences, Annals, 11 (1898): 369-377.

Prince, J. D. Some Passamaquoddy witchcraft tales. American Philosophical Society, Proceedings, 38 (1899): 181-189.

Prince, J. D. The morphology of the Passamaquoddy language. American Philosophical Society, Proceedings, 53 (1914): 92-117.

Prince, J. D. The Passamaquoddy wampum records. American Philosophical Society, Proceedings, 36 (1897): 479-495.

Prince, J. D. The Passamaquoddy wampum records. New York State Museum Bulletin, 184 (1916): 119-125.

Raymond, W. O. The old Meductic fort. New Brunswick Historical Society, Collections, 1 (1896): 221-272.

Reade, J. Some Wabanaki songs. Royal Society of Canada, Proceedings and Transactions, 5, pt. 2 (1887): 1-8.

Skinner, Vincent P. The children of the forgotten: the Indians of Maine. Contemporary Education, 42 (1970/1971): 284-289.

*Smith, N. N. Notes on the Malecite of Woodstock, New Brunswick. Anthropologica, 5 (1957): 1-40.

Sockabasin, Allen J., comp. Off-reservation Indian survey Me P-74. Compiled by Allen J. Sockabasin and John G. Stone. Augusta, Maine Department of Indian Affairs, 1971. 67 p.

Speck, F. G. An Algonkian myth. Museum Journal, 1 (1910): 49-52.

Speck, F. G. Game totems among the Northeastern Algonkians. American Anthropologist, n.s., 19 (1917): 9-18.

Speck, F. G. Kinship terms and the family band among the Northeastern Algonkian.

American Anthropologist, n.s., 20
(1918): 143-161.

Speck, F. G. Malecite tales. Journal of
American Folklore, 30 (1917): 479-485.

Speck, F. G. Reptile-lore of the Northern
Indians. Journal of American Folklore,
36 (1923): 273-280.

Speck, F. G. The Eastern Algonkian
Wabanaki Confederacy. American
Anthropologist, n.s., 17 (1915): 492-
508.

Speck, F. G. and R. W. Dexter.
Utilization of animals and plants by the
Malecite Indians of New Brunswick.
Washington Academy of Sciences, Journal,
42 (1952): 1-7.

Speck, F. G. and W. S. Hadlock. A report
on tribal boundaries and hunting areas
of the Malecite Indian of New Brunswick.
American Anthropologist, n.s., 48
(1946): 355-374.

Stamp, H. A Malecite tale. Journal of
American Folklore, 28 (1915): 243-248.

Szabó, László. Malecite prosodics. In
André Rigault and René Charbonneau, eds.
International Congress of Phonetic
Sciences, 7th. 1971, Montreal.
Proceedings. The Hague, Mouton, 1972:
1032-1034. (Janua Linguarum, Series
Maior, 57)

Szabó, László. Stress and vowel length in
Malecite. American Philosophical
Society, Proceedings, 116 (1972): 338-
342.

Teeter, Karl V. Preliminary report on
Malecite-Passamaquoddy. In Contributions
to Anthropology: Linguistics I. Ottawa,
Queen's Printer, 1967: 157-162.
(Canada, National Museum, Bulletin, 214)

Teeter, Karl V. The main features of
Malecite-Passamaquoddy grammar. In Jesse
Sawyer, ed. Studies in American Indian
Languages. Berkeley and Los Angeles,
University of California Press, 1971:
191-249. (California, University,
Publications in Linguistics, 65)

Thwaites, R. G., ed. The Jesuit Relations
and allied documents. Cleveland, 1896-
1901. 74 v.

Treat, J. Etchemins. American Antiquarian
Society, Transactions and Collections, 2
(1836): 305-367.

Trueman, Stuart. The ordeal of John
Gyles. Toronto, McClelland and Stewart,
1966. 9, 155 p.

Van Wart, A. F. The Indians of the
Maritime Provinces, their diseases and
native cures. Canadian Medical
Association Journal, 59 (1948): 573-577.

Vetromile, E. The Abnakis and their
history. New York, 1866. 171 p.

*Wallis, W. D. and R. S. Wallis. The
Malecite Indians of New Brunswick.
National Museum of Canada, Bulletin, 148
(1957): 1-58.

Watson, L. W. The origin of the
Melicites. Journal of American Folklore,
20 (1907): 160-162.

Weer, P. Passamaquoddy and Quapaw
mnemonic records. Indiana Academy of
Science, Proceedings, 55 (1946): 29-32.

Welsh, David. The Passamaquoddy Indians.
Ramparts, 5 (Mar. 1967): 40-45.

Williamson, W. D. The history of the
state of Maine, Vol. 1: 453-514.
Hallowell, 1832.

Wilson, G. L. Indian hero tales. New
York, 1906. 203 p.

11-06 Micmac

Adrien, P. Conservatisme et changement
chez les Indiens Micmacs.
Anthropologica, 2 (1956): 1-16.

Alger, A. L. In Indian tents. Boston,
1897. 139 p.

Barratt, Joseph. The Indian of New-
England, and the north-eastern
provinces. 3d ed. Middletown, Conn., C.
H. Pelton, 1851. 24 p.

Baxter, J. P. A memoir of Jacques
Cartier. New York, 1906. 464 p.

Boas, F. Zur Anthropologie der
nordamerikanischen Indianer. Berliner
Gesellschaft für Anthropologie,
Ethnologie und Urgeschichte,
Verhandlungen (1895): 367-411.

Bock, Philip K. Social time and
institutional conflict. Human
Organization, 25 (1966): 96-102.

*Bock, Philip K. The Micmac Indians of
Restigouche; history and contemporary
description. Ottawa, 1966. 9, 95 p.
map. (Canada, National Museum,
Bulletin, 213)

Bromley, W. A general description of Nova
Scotia, 44-58. Halifax, 1823.

Cameron, J. A craniometric study of the Micmac skull. Nova Scotian Institute of Natural Science, Proceedings and Transactions, 15 (1919): 1-31.

Campbell, D. Nova Scotia, 17-26. Montreal, 1873.

Chamberlain, A. F. Indians of the eastern provinces of Canada. Annual Archaeological Report, being Part of Appendix to the Report of the Minister of Education, Ontario (1905): 122-136.

Chamberlain, M. Indians in New Brunswick in Champlain's time. Acadiensis, 4 (1904): 280-295.

Chiasson, L. P. Fingerprint pattern frequencies in the Micmac Indians. Canadian Journal of Genetics and Cytology, 2 (1960): 184-188.

Chiasson, L. P. Gene frequencies of the Micmac Indians. Blood groups and other inherited characters. Journal of Heredity, 54 (1963): 229-236.

Clark, J. S. Uktce-bal-lok, a Micmac legend. Acadiensis, 3 (1903): 301-303.

Clarke, George F. Someone before us; our Maritime Indians. Fredericton, N.B., Brunswick Press, 1968. 240 p. illus.

Crevel, Jacques. Honguedo, ou l'histoire des premiers Gaspésiens. By Jacques Crevel and Maryvonne Crevel. Québec, Éditions Garneau, 1970. 211 p. illus., maps.

*Denys, N. The description and natural history of the coasts of North America. Ed. by W. F. Ganong. Champlain Society, Publications, 2 (1908): 399-452, 572-606.

*Denys, Nicolas. Description and natural history of the coasts of North America (Acadia). New York, Greenwood Press, 1968. 16, 625 p. illus., maps.

Dixon, R. B. The migrations of the Indians of New England and the Maritime Provinces. American Antiquarian Society, Proceedings, n.s., 24 (1914): 65-76.

Eckstorm, F. H. Old John Neptune and other Maine Indian shamans. Portland, 1945. 209 p.

Elder, W. The aborigines of Nova Scotia. North American Review, 112 (1871): 1-30.

Fauset, A. H. Folklore from the halfbreeds in Nova Scotia. Journal of American Folklore, 38 (1925): 300-315.

Fergusson, Charles Bruce. Pre-revolutionary settlements in Nova Scotia. Nova Scotia Historical Society, Collections, 37 (1970): 5-22.

Fewkes, J. W. A pictograph from Nova Scotia. American Naturalist, 24 (1890): 995-999.

Frye, Col. Indians in Acadie, A.D. 1760. Massachusetts Historical Society, Collections, ser. 1, 10 (1809): 115-116.

Ganong, W. F. The economic mollusca of Acadia: wampum among the New Brunswick Indians. New Brunswick, Natural History Society, Bulletin, 8 (1889): 3-116.

Ganong, W. F. Upon aboriginal pictographs from New Brunswick. New Brunswick, Natural History Society, Bulletin (1904): 175-178.

Gates, R. R. The blood groups and other features of the Micmac Indians. Royal Anthropological Institute of Great Britain and Ireland, Journal, 68 (1938): 283-298.

Gatschet, A. S. Micmac fans and games. Pennsylvania, University, Free Museum of Science and Art, Bulletin, 2 (1900): 190-194.

Gilpin, J. B. Indians of Nova Scotia. Nova Scotian Institute of Natural Science, Proceedings and Transactions, 4 (1877): 260-281.

Gilpin, J. B. On the stone age of Nova Scotia. Nova Scotian Institute of Natural Science, Proceedings and Transactions, 3 (1873): 220-231.

Hadlock, Wendell S. The significance of certain textiles found at Redbank, New Brunswick, in relation to the history of the culture area. Acadian Naturalist, 2, no. 8 (July 1947): 49-62.

Hagar, S. A melange of Micmac notes. American Association for the Advancement of Science, Proceedings, 44 (1895): 257-258.

Hagar, S. Micmac customs and traditions. American Anthropologist, 8 (1895): 31-42.

Hagar, S. Micmac magic and medicine. Journal of American Folklore, 9 (1896): 170-177.

Hagar, S. The celestial bear. Journal of American Folklore, 13 (1900): 92-103.

Hagar, S. Weather and the seasons in Micmac mythology. Journal of American Folklore, 10 (1897): 101-105.

Haliburton, R. G. On the festival on the dead. Nova Scotian Institute of Natural Science, Proceedings and Transactions, 1, no. 1 (1863): 61-85.

Hanzeli, Victor E. Missionary linguistics in New France; a study of seventeenth- and eighteenth-century descriptions of American Indian languages. The Hague, Mouton, 1969. 141 p. illus., map. (Janua Linguarum, Series Maior, 29)

Harper, J. R. Micmac arm bands. Pennsylvania Archaeologist, 27 (1957): 135-136.

Harper, J. R. Two seventeenth century Micmac "copper kettle" burials. Anthropologica, 4 (1957): 11-36.

Hoffman, B. G. Historical ethnography of the Micmac of the sixteenth and seventeenth centuries. Ethnohistory, 3 (1956): 190-191.

Hoffman, B. G. The Souriquois, Etechemin and Wegesh. Ethnohistory, 2 (1955): 65-87.

Howard, James H. Photo feature. Micmac Indians of Nova Scotia. By James H. Howard and Stephen J. Gluckman. South Dakota, University, Museum, Museum News, 26, nos. 3/4 (1965): 14-20.

Howard, James H. The Micmac bowl game. By James H. Howard and Stephen J. Gluckman. American Indian Tradition, 8, no. 5 (1962): 206-209.

Howard, James H. The St. Anne's Day celebration of the Micmac Indians, 1962. South Dakota, University, Museum, Museum News, 26, nos. 3/4 (1965): 5-13.

Hutton, Elizabeth Ann. Indian affairs in Nova Scotia, 1760-1834. Nova Scotia Historical Society, Collections, 34 (1963): 33-54.

Isaac, Morris. Funny--I'm still looking for that place. Anthropologica, n.s., 13 (1971): 23-36.

Johnson, F. Notes on Micmac shamanism. Primitive Man, 16 (1943): 53-80.

Johnson, Micheline Dumont. Apôtres ou agitateurs; la France missionaire en Acadie. By Micheline Dumont-Johnson. Trois-Rivières, Boréal Express, 1970. 150 p. illus., maps.

Kroeber, A. L. Micmac. In Encyclopaedia Britannica, 14th ed. Vol. 15. 1929: 426.

Le Clercq, C. Language of the Gaspesians. Historical Magazine, ser. 1, 5 (1861): 284-285.

*Le Clercq, C. Nouvelle relation de la Gaspésie. Paris, 1691. 572 p.

*Le Clercq, Chrétien. New relation of Gaspesia. Translated and edited by William F. Ganong. New York, Greenwood Press, 1968. 15, 452 p. illus., maps. (Champlain Society, Publications, 5)

*Le Clercq, C. New relation of Gaspesia. Ed. by W. F. Ganong. Champlain Society, Publications, 5 (1910): 1-452.

Leland, C. G. The Algonquin legends of New England. Boston, 1884. 379 p.

Leland, C. G. and J. D. Prince. Kulóskap the master and other Algonkin poems. New York, 1902. 370 p.

Leland, Charles G. The Algonquin legends of New England. Detroit, Singing Tree Press, 1968. 15, 379 p. illus.

Lescarbot, M. Histoire de la Nouvelle-France. Paris, 1866. 3 v.

Lescarbot, M. The history of New France. Ed. by L. Grant. Toronto, 1907-1914. 3 v.

Maillard, A. S. An account of the customs and manners of the Micmakis and Maricheets. London, 1758. 138 p.

Maillard, A. S. Grammar of the Mikmaque language. New York, 1864. 101 p.

Maillard, A. S. and Pacifique. Le catéchisme micmac. Ristigouche, P.Q., 1906. 128 p.

McFeat, Tom F. S. The Algonkian project. In his Museum Ethnology and the Algonkian Project. Ottawa, Queen's Printer, 1962: 15-80. (Canada, National Museum, Anthropology Papers, 2)

McGee, Harold Franklin, Jr. Windigo psychosis. American Anthropologist, 74 (1972): 244-246.

McLeod, R. R. In the Acadian land, 140-155. Boston, 1899.

McLeod, R. R. Markland or Nova Scotia, 166-175. Chicago, 1903.

Mechling, W. H. The Malecite Indians, with notes on the Micmacs. Anthropologica, 7 (1958): 1-160; 8 (1959): 161-274.

Michelson, T. Micmac tales. Journal of American Folklore, 38 (1925): 33-54.

Mooney, J. and C. Thomas. Micmac. U.S. Bureau of American Ethnology, Bulletin, 30, vol. 1 (1907): 858-859.

Morgan, L. H. Systems of consanguinity and affinity. Smithsonian Contributions to Knowledge, 17 (1871): 291-382.

Nicholas, Andrew. New Brunswick Indians--conservative militants. In Waubageshig, ed. The Only Good Indian. Toronto, new press, 1972: 36-43.

Pacifique. Le pays des Micmacs. Société de Géographie (Québec), Bulletin, 21 (1927): 111-117, 165-185; 22 (1928): 43-55, 140-145, 270-277; 23 (1929): 37-45; 25 (1931): 96-106; 27 (1933): 34-64; 28 (1934): 105-147.

Pacifique. Leçons grammaticales théoriques et pratiques de la langue micmaque. Ristigouche, P.Q., 1939.

Pacifique. Notes supplémentaires sur les traités de langue micmaque. Association Canadienne-Française pour l'Avancement des Sciences, Annales, 6 (1940): 271-277.

Pacifique. Quelques traits caracteristiques de la tribu des Micmacs. International Congress of Americanists, Proceedings, 15, vol. 1 (1906): 315-328.

Pacifique. Traité theorique et pratique de la langue micmaque. Association Canadienne-Française pour l'Avancement des Sciences, Annales, 4 (1938): 213-333; 5 (1939): 159-276.

Parsons, E. C. Half-breed. Scientific Monthly, 18 (1924): 144-148.

Parsons, E. C. Micmac folklore. Journal of American Folklore, 38 (1925): 55-133.

Parsons, E. C. Micmac notes. Journal of American Folklore, 39 (1926): 460-485.

Patterson, G. Antiquities of Nova Scotia. Smithsonian Institution, Annual Reports of the Board of Regents (1881): 673-677.

Patterson, G. History of the County of Pictou, Nova Scotia, 26-37. Montreal, 1877.

Patterson, G. The stone age in Nova Scotia. Nova Scotian Institute of Natural Science, Proceedings and Transactions, 7 (1889): 231-252.

Peterson, M. S. Some Scandinavian elements in a Micmac swan maiden story. Scandinavian Studies and Notes, 11 (1930): 135-138.

Pierronet, T. Specimen of the Mountaineer or Sheshatapooshshoish, Skoffie, and Micmac languages. Massachusetts Historical Society, Collections, 6 (1798): 16-33.

Piers, H. Aboriginal remains of Nova Scotia. Nova Scotian Institute of Natural Science, Proceedings and Transactions, 7 (1889): 276-290.

Piers, H. Brief account of the Micmac Indians. Nova Scotian Institute of Natural Science, Proceedings and Transactions, 13 (1912): 99-125.

Piers, H. Relics of the stone age in Nova Scotia. Nova Scotian Institute of Natural Science, Proceedings and Transactions, 9 (1895): 26-58.

Pratson, Frederick John. Land of the four directions. Old Greenwich, Conn., Chatham Press, 1970. 131 p. illus.

Prince, J. D. A Micmac manuscript. International Congress of Americanists, Proceedings, 15, vol. 1 (1906): 87-124.

Prince, J. D. Notes on the language of the Eastern Algonquin tribes. American Journal of Philology, 9 (1888): 310-316.

Quinn, D. B. The voyage of Etienne Bellenger to the Maritimes in 1583: a new document. Canadian Historical Review, 43 (1962): 328-343.

Rand, S. T. A short statement of facts relating to the history, manners, customs, language, and literature of the Micmac tribe of Indians. Halifax, 1850. 40 p.

Rand, S. T. Dictionary of the language of the Micmac Indians. Halifax, 1888. 286 p.

Rand, S. T. Glooscap, Cuhkw and Coolpurjot. American Antiquarian and Oriental Journal, 12 (1890): 283-286.

Rand, S. T. Legends of the Micmacs. New York, 1894. 452 p.

Rand, S. T. Micmac place-names in the Maritime Provinces and Gaspé Peninsula. Ottawa, 1919.

Rand, S. T. Rand's Micmac dictionary. Charlottetown, P.E.I., 1902.

Rand, S. T. The beautiful bride. American Antiquarian and Oriental Journal, 13 (1890): 156-159.

Rand, S. T. The coming of the White Man revealed. American Antiquarian and Oriental Journal, 13 (1890): 155-156.

Rand, S. T. The legends of the Micmacs.
American Antiquarian and Oriental
Journal, 12 (1890): 3-14.

Rand, S. T. The Micmac Indians. Our
Forest Children, 2 (1888): 10-12.

Rand, S. T. The Micmac language. Canadian
Science Monthly, 3 (1885): 142-146.

Rand, Silas T. Legends of the Micmacs.
New York, Johnson Reprint, 1971. 46,
452 p. illus.

Rousseau, J. J. Ethnobotanique et
ethnozoologie gaspéssienne. Archives de
Folklore, 3 (1948): 51-64.

Rousseau, J. J. Notes sur
l'ethnobotanique d'Anticosti. Archives
de Folklore, 1 (1946): 60-71.

Schmidt, W. Die Nordost Algonkin. In his
Die Ursprung der Göttesidee. Bd. 2.
Münster i. W., 1929: 449-458.

Shaw, A. A Micmac Glengarry. New
Brunswick Museum, Art Bulletin, 2, no. 3
(1954): 3-4.

Shaw, B. H. H. The Indians of the
Maritimes. Canadian Magazine, 58 (1922):
343-350.

Shea, John G. Micmac or Recollect
hieroglyphics. Historical Magazine,
ser. 1, 5 (1861): 289-292.

Silver, Shirley. Natick consonants in
reference to Proto-Central Algonquian.
International Journal of American
Linguistics, 26 (1960): 112-119, 234-
241.

Smith, H. I. and W. J. Wintemberg. Some
shell-heaps in Nova Scotia. Canada,
Department of Mines, National Museum of
Canada, Bulletin, 47 (1929): 1-192.

Sockabasin, Allen J., comp. Off-
reservation Indian survey Me P-74.
Compiled by Allen J. Sockabasin and John
G. Stone. Augusta, Maine Department of
Indian Affairs, 1971. 67 p.

Speck, F. G. Beothuk and Micmac. Indian
Notes and Monographs, ser. 2, 22 (1921):
1-187.

Speck, F. G. Kinship terms and the family
band among the Northeastern Algonkian.
American Anthropologist, n.s., 20
(1918): 143-161.

Speck, F. G. Micmac slate image. Indian
Notes, 1 (1924): 153-154.

Speck, F. G. Reptile-lore of the Northern
Indians. Journal of American Folklore,
36 (1923): 273-280.

Speck, F. G. Some Micmac tales from Cape
Breton Island. Journal of American
Folklore, 28 (1915): 59-69.

Speck, F. G. The Eastern Algonkian
Wabanaki Confederacy. American
Anthropologist, n.s., 17 (1915): 492-
508.

Speck, F. G. The family hunting band as
the basis of Algonkian social
organization. American Anthropologist,
n.s., 17 (1915): 289-305.

Speck, F. G. and R. W. Dexter.
Utilization of animals and plants by the
Micmac Indians of New Brunswick.
Washington Academy of Sciences, Journal,
41 (1951): 250-259.

St. Croix, S. The Micmacs of
Newfoundland. In J. R. Smallwood, ed.
The Book of New Foundland. Vol. 1. St.
John's, 1937: 284-286.

St. Hilaire, Theodore J. Pedagogy in the
wilderness. Oregon Historical Quarterly,
63 (1962): 55-60.

Stoddard, Natalie B. Micmac foods.
Halifax, Nova Scotia Museum, 1967.
7 p. illus.

Szabó, László. Malecite prosodics. In
André Rigault and René Charbonneau, eds.
International Congress of Phonetic
Sciences, 7th. 1971, Montreal.
Proceedings. The Hague, Mouton, 1972:
1032-1034. (Janua Linguarum, Series
Maior, 57)

Thwaites, R. G., ed. The Jesuit Relations
and allied documents. Cleveland, 1896-
1901. 74 v.

Uhlenbeck, C. C. Ontwerp van eene
vergelijkende vormleer van eenige
Algonkin-talen. Amsterdam, Koninklijke
Akademie van Wetenschappen, Afdeeling
Letterkunde, Verhandelingen, n.s., 11,
no. 3 (1910): 1-67.

Van Wart, A. F. The Indians of the
Maritime Provinces, their diseases and
native cures. Canadian Medical
Association Journal, 59 (1948): 573-577.

Vernon, C. W. Indians of St. John Island.
Acadiensis, 3 (1903): 110-115.

Vetromile, E. The Abnakis and their
history. New York, 1866. 171 p.

Wallis, W. D. Medicines used by the Micmac Indians. American Anthropologist, n.s., 24 (1922): 24-30.

Wallis, W. D. and R. S. Wallis. Culture loss and culture change among the Micmac of the Canadian Maritime Provinces, 1912-1950. Kroeber Anthropological Society, Publications, 8/9 (1953): 100-129.

*Wallis, W. D. and R. S. Wallis. The Micmac Indians of eastern Canada. Minneapolis, 1955. 530 p.

Wallis, Wilson D. Historical background of the Micmac Indians of Canada. In Contributions to Anthropology 1959. Ottawa, Queen's Printer, 1961: 42-63. (Canada, National Museum, Bulletin, 173)

Watson, L. W. The origin of the Malicites. Journal of American Folklore, 20 (1907): 160-162.

West, J. A journal of a mission to the Indians of the British provinces of New Brunswick and Nova Scotia, 235-255. London, 1827.

Whitby, Barbara. The Beothucks and other primitive people of Newfoundland: a review. Anthropological Journal of Canada, 5, no. 4 (1967): 2-19.

Wilson, G. L. Indian hero tales. New York, 1906. 203 p.

Witthoft, J., et al. Micmac pipes, vase-shaped pipes, and calumets. Pennsylvania Archaeologist, 23 (1953): 89-107.

11-07 Montagnais

Carrière, Gaston. Catalogue des manuscrits en langues indiennes conservés aux archives oblates, Ottawa. Anthropologica, n.s., 12 (1970): 151-179.

Cooke, Alan, comp. Bibliographie de la peninsule du Québec-Labrador. Compiled by Alan Cooke and Fabien Caron. Boston, G. K. Hall, 1968. 2 v.

Feit, H., et al. Bibliography: native peoples, James Bay region. Recherches Amérindiennes au Québec, 2, no. 1, suppl. (1972): 1-62.

Achard, Eugène. Le royaume du Saguenay. Montréal, Librairie Générale Canadienne, 1942. 207 p. illus.

Anderson, James Watt. Fur trader's story. Toronto, Ryerson Press, 1961. 15, 245 p. illus.

Anderson, James Watt. The Rupert River brigade. Beaver, 266, no. 3 (1935): 13-17, 66.

Anderson, William Ashley. Angel of Hudson Bay; the true story of Maude Watt. New York, Dutton, 1961. 217 p. illus., map.

Angers, Lorenzo. Guerres des Iroquois contre les Montagnais. Bulletin de Recherches Historiques, 45, no. 4 (1939): 102-110.

Anonymous. Nascapee. U.S. Bureau of American Ethnology, Bulletin, 30, vol. 2 (1910): 30-32.

Anonymous. Tuberculosis survey: James and Hudson Bays. Arctic Circular, 4 (1951): 45-47.

Arkle, P. W. A study of the Nascapi in Labrador. Oral Hygiene, 33 (1943): 202-206.

Banfield, Alexander William Francis. Dermoid cysts a basis of Indian legends. Journal of Mammalogy, 39 (1958): 451-452.

Barbeau, M. The kingdom of Saguenay. Toronto, 1936. 170 p.

Barger, Kenneth. Differential adaptation to northern town life by the Eskimos and Indians of Great Whale River. by Kenneth Barger and Daphne Earl. Human Organization, 30 (1971): 25-30.

Barriault, Yvette. Mythes et rites chez les Indiens montagnais. [n.p.] Société Historique de la Côte Nord, 1971. 14, 165 p. maps.

Basile, Marie-Jeanne. Atanukana. Légendes montagnaises. By Marie-Jeanne Basile and Gerard E. McNulty. Québec, Université Laval, Centre d'Études Nordiques, 1971. 6, 37 p. (Coll. "Nordicana", 31)

Bell, Robert. The Labrador Peninsula. Scottish Geographical Magazine, 11 (1895): 335-361.

Biays, P. Conditions et genres de vie au Labrador Septentrionale. Québec, 1955. 33 p.

Biays, Pierre. Les marges de l'oekoumène dans l'est du Canada. Québec, Presses de l'Université Laval, 1964. 29, 760 p. illus. (Laval, Université, Centre d'Études Nordiques, Travaux et Documents, 2)

Bishop, Charles A. The emergence of
hunting territories among the Northern
Ojibwa. Ethnology, 9 (1970): 1-15.

Blumberg, Baruch S., et al. Blood groups
of the Naskapi and Montagnais Indians of
Schefferville, Quebec. Human Biology, 36
(1964): 263-272.

Boas, F. Zur Anthropologie der
nordamerikanischen Indianer. Berliner
Gesellschaft für Anthropologie,
Ethnologie und Urgeschichte,
Verhandlungen (1895): 367-411.

Bond, E. W. How to build a birchbark.
Natural History, 64 (1955): 242-246.

Brochu, Michel. A preliminary study of
the establishment of equalization prices
for the pelts of fur-bearing animals in
New-Quebec. Musk-Ox, 9 (1971): 42-52.

Brochu, Michel. Étude préliminaire sur
l'établissement d'un prix de péréquation
des peaux d'animaux à fourrure au
Nouveau-Québec. Actualité Économique, 46
(1970/1971): 287-315.

Bruemmer, Fred. The Belcher Islands.
Beaver, 302, no. 1 (1971/1972): 4-13.

Bruet, E. Le Labrador et Le Nouveau-
Québec. Paris, 1949. 346 p.

Burgesse, J. A. Lake St. John and the big
beaver. Beaver, 284 (Dec. 1953): 48-49.

Burgesse, J. A. Les Indiens du Saguenay.
Société Historique du Saguenay,
Bulletin, 2 (1946): 2-11.

Burgesse, J. A. Montagnais cross-bows.
Beaver, 274, no. 4 (1943): 37-39.

Burgesse, J. A. Montagnais-Naskapi
nomenclature. Primitive Man, 16 (1943):
44-48.

Burgesse, J. A. Property concepts of the
Lac-St-Jean Montagnais. Primitive Man,
18 (1945): 1-25.

Burgesse, J. A. The Montagnais hunter.
Beaver, 273, no. 2 (1942): 43-45.

Burgesse, J. A. The spirit wigwam.
Primitive Man, 17 (1944): 50-53.

Burgesse, J. A. The woman and child among
the Lac-St-Jean Montagnais. Primitive
Man, 17 (1944): 1-18.

Burgesse, J. A. Tribal laws of the
woodlands. Beaver, 272 (1942): 18-21.

Burgesse, J. Allan. Our abused
aborigines. Beaver, 271 (Dec. 1940): 35-
38.

Burgesse, J. Allan. Saguenay
celebrations. Beaver, 278 (Sept. 1947):
44-45.

Burgesse, J. Allan. Seven Islands, P.Q.
Beaver, 282, no. 1 (1951): 30-33.

Burgesse, J. Allan. Snowshoes. An outline
of the various types of Eastern Indian
snowshoes and their development with the
aid of steel tools. Beaver, 271, no. 4
(1941): 24-28.

Burgesse, J. Allan. Windigo! Beaver, 277
(Mar. 1947): 4-5.

Cabot, W. B. In Northern Labrador.
Boston, 1912. 292 p.

Cabot, William Brooks. The Indians. In
Wilfred T. Grenfell, et al. Labrador.
New ed. New York, Macmillan, 1922: 184-
255.

Caldwell, Dorothy J. The Big Neck affair:
tragedy and farce on the Missouri
frontier. Missouri Historical Review, 64
(1969/1970): 391-412.

Chamberlain, A. F. Indians of the Eastern
Provinces of Canada. Annual
Archaeological Report, being Part of
Appendix to the Report of the Minister
of Education, Ontario (1905): 122-136.

Chambers, E. T. D. The Ouananiche and its
Canadian environment, 301-329. New
York, 1896.

Champlain, Samuel de. Voyages and
discoveries made in New France, from the
year 1615 to the end of the year 1618.
Translated and edited by H. H. Layton
and W. F. Ganong. Toronto, The
Champlain Society, 1929. illus., maps.
(The Works of Samuel de Champlain, 3)

Chance, Norman A. Implications of
environmental stress: strategies of
developmental change in the North.
Archives of Environmental Health, 17
(1968): 571-577.

Chance, Norman A. The changing world of
the Cree. Natural History, 76, no. 5
(1967): 16-23.

Chance, Norman A., ed. Conflict in
culture: problems of developmental
change among the Cree. Ottawa, 1968.
104 p. illus., map. (Saint Paul
University, Canadian Research Centre for
Anthropology, Document, 2)

Chance, Norman A., et al. Developmental
change among the Cree Indians of Quebec
(summary report). Ottawa, Dept. of
Regional Expansion, 1970. map.

Comeau, N. A. Life and sport on the north shore of the lower St. Lawrence and Gulf. 2d ed. Quebec, 1923. 440 p.

Cooke, Alan. A woman's way. Beaver, 291, no. 1 (1960/1961): 40-45.

Cooper, J. M. Field notes on Northern Algonkian magic. International Congress of Americanists, Proceedings, 23 (1928): 413-418.

Cooper, J. M. Northern Algonkin scrying and scapulimancy. In Festschrift P. W. Schmidt. Wien, 1928: 205-217.

Cooper, J. M. Some notes on the Waswanipi. International Congress of Americanists, Proceedings, 22, vol. 2 (1926): 459-461.

Cooper, J. M. The Northern Algonquian supreme being. Catholic University of America, Anthropological Series, 2 (1934): 1-78.

Cooper, J. M. The shaking tent rite among Plains and Forest Algonquians. Primitive Man, 17 (1944): 60-84.

David, C. E. Les Montagnais du Labrador. International Congress of Americanists, Proceedings, 15, vol. 1 (1906): 205-211.

Davidson, D. S. Family hunting territories of the Waswanipi Indians. Indian Notes, 5 (1928): 42-59.

Davies, Kenneth G., ed. Letters from Hudson Bay 1703-40. Edited by K. G. Davies, assisted by A. M. Johnson. London, 1965. 68, 455 p. (Hudson's Bay Record Society, Publications, 25)

Davies, Kenneth G., ed. Northern Quebec and Labrador journals and correspondence 1819-35. Edited by K. G. Davies, assisted by A. M. Johnson. London, 1963. 79, 415 p. maps. (Hudson's Bay Record Society, Publications, 24)

Davies, W. H. A. Notes on Esquimaux Bay and the surrounding country. Literary and Historical Society of Québec, Transactions, 4, pt. 1 (1843): 70-94.

Davies, W. H. A. Notes on Ungava Bay and its vicinity. Literary and Historical Society (Quebec), Transactions, 4 (1854): 119-137.

Desbarats, Peter. What they used to tell about; Indian legends from Labrador. Toronto, McClelland and Stewart, 1969. 92 p.

Diamond, D. James Bay and the Cree. Recherches Amérindiennes au Québec, 2, no. 4/5 (1972): 33-35.

Douglas, F. H. A Naskapi painted skin shirt. Denver Art Museum, Material Culture Notes, 10 (1939): 38-42.

Dragon, Antonio. Trentes robes noires au Saguenay. Edited by Adrien Pouliot. Chicoutimi, Québec, 1971. 387 p. illus., maps. (Société Historique du Saguenay, Publications, 24)

Dryfoos, Robert J., Jr. Mermen, mermaids and Indians: a psychocultural interpretation. Man in the Northeast, 3 (1972): 49-54.

Dyke, A. P. Montagnais-Naskapi or Montagnais and Nascaupi? An examination of some tribal differences. Ethnohistory, 17 (1970): 43-48.

Eggan, Fred. Northern Woodland ethnology. In Jacob W. Gruber, ed. The Philadelphia Anthropological Society; Papers Presented on Its Golden Anniversary. New York, distributed by Columbia University Press for Temple University Publications, 1967: 107-124.

Ellis, C. Douglas. The missionary and the Indian in central and eastern Canada. Arctic Anthropology, 2, no. 2 (1964): 25-31.

Evans, G. Heberton, III. Eastmain sod houses. Beaver, 302, no. 2 (1971/1972): 30-33.

Faillon, Abbé. The Indian tribes on the St. Lawrence at the time of the arrival of the French. Translated by John Squair. Toronto, Ontario Provincial Museum, Annual Archaeological Report, 34 (1923): 82-88.

Feit, H. A. L'ethno-écologie des cris waswanipis, ou comment des chasseurs peuvent aménager leurs ressources. Recherches Amérindiennes au Québec, 1, no. 4/5 (1971): 84-93.

Flannery, R. Cross-cousin marriage among the Cree and Montagnais of James Bay. Primitive Man, 11 (1938): 29-33.

Flannery, R. Some aspects of James Bay recreative culture. Primitive Man, 9 (1937): 49-56.

Flannery, R. The shaking-tent rite among the Montagnais of James Bay. Primitive Man, 12 (1939): 11-16.

Flannery, Regina. Infancy and childhood among the Indians of the east coast of James Bay. Anthropos, 57 (1962): 475-482.

Flannery, Regina. Some magico-religious concepts of the Algonquians on the East

Coast of James Bay. By Regina Flannery-Herzfeld. In Mario D. Zamora, et al., eds. Themes in Culture. Quezon City, Kayumanggi, 1971: 31-39.

Francine, J. The forgotten land. Canadian Geographical Journal, 18 (1939): 52-57.

Gaines, R. A Montagnais prayer-book and a Mohawk primer. Indian Notes, 6 (1929): 138-147.

Garigue, P. The social organization of the Montagnais-Naskapi. Anthropologica, 4 (1957): 107-136.

Garigue, Philippe. Une enquête sur l'industrialisation de la Province de Québec: Schefferville. Actualité Économique, 33 (1957): 419-436.

Gille, J. Die Montagnais in 1535. In H. Plischke, ed. Göttingen Völkerkundliche Studien. Leipzig, 1939: 263-267.

Gille, J. Montagnais und Canadiens. Anthropos, 35 (1940): 153-165.

Gordon, John M. Michigan journal, 1836. Edited by Douglas H. Gordon and George S. May. Michigan History, 43 (1959): 10-42, 129-149, 257-293, 433-478.

Graburn, Nelson H. H. Takamiut Eskimo kinship terminology. Ottawa, Department of Northern Affairs and National Resources, Northern Co-ordination and Research Centre, 1964. 6, 222 p. illus., map. (NCRC-64-1)

Greenman, Emerson F. The Upper Palaeolithic and the New World. Current Anthropology, 4 (1963): 41-91.

Grenfell, W. T. Labrador, 184-225. New York, 1909.

Hallowell, A. I. Kinship terms and cross-cousin marriage of the Montagnais-Naskapi and the Cree. American Anthropologist, n.s., 34 (1932): 171-199.

Hallowell, A. I. The physical characteristics of the Indians of Labrador. Société des Américanistes, Journal, n.s., 21 (1929): 337-371.

Hanzeli, Victor E. Missionary linguistics in New France; a study of seventeenth- and eighteenth-century descriptions of American Indian languages. The Hague, Mouton, 1969. 141 p. illus., map. (Janua Linguarum, Series Maior, 29)

Hanzeli, Victor E. The Algonquin R-dialect in historical records. In International Congress of Linguists, 10th. 1967, Bucarest. Proceedings.

Vol. 2. Bucarest, Éditions de l'Académie de la République Socialiste de Roumanie, 1970: 85-89.

Harp, E. An archaeological survey in the Strait of Belle Isle area. American Antiquity, 16 (1951): 203-220.

Harper, Francis. The friendly Montagnais and their neighbors in the Ungava Peninsula. Lawrence, University of Kansas, Museum of Natural History, 1964. 5, 121 p. illus. (Kansas, University, Museum of Natural History, Miscellaneous Publication, 37)

Hartweg, Raoul. La dentition des Esquimaux de l'Ungava et des Indiens Wabemakustewatsh de la côte orientale de la Baie d'Hudson. Québec, 1966. 156 l. illus., map. (Laval, Université, Centre d'Études Nordiques, Travaux Divers, 13)

Hartweg, Raoul. Les malpositions dentaires des Indiens Wabemakustewatsh de la cote orientale de la Baie d'Hudson. Société des Américanistes (Paris), Journal, n.s., 54 (1965): 123-126.

Helm, June. The hunting tribes of subarctic Canada. By June Helm and Eleanor Burke Leacock. In Eleanor Burke Leacock and Nancy Oestreich Lurie, eds. North American Indians in Historical Perspective. New York, Random House, 1971: 343-374.

Henriksen, Georg. The transactional basis of influence: White Men among Naskapi Indians. In Robert Paine, ed. Patrons and Brokers in the East Arctic. St. John's, Memorial University of Newfoundland, 1971: 22-33. (Newfoundland Social and Economic Papers, 2)

Hickerson, Harold. Some implications of the theory of the particularity, or "atomism," of Northern Algonkians. Current Anthropology, 8 (1967): 313-345. [With comments].

Hind, Henry Youle. Explorations in the interior of the Labrador Peninsula, the country of the Montagnais and Nasquapee Indians. London, Longman, Roberts and Green, 1863. 2 v.

Hoffman, Hans. Culture change and personality modification among the James Bay Cree. Alaska, University, Anthropological Papers, 9 (1960/1961): 81-91.

Honigmann, John J. Five Canadian Arctic and Subarctic towns: their native populations. In Internationale

Amerikanistenkongress, 38th. 1968, Stuttgart-München. Verhandlungen. Band 3. München, Klaus Renner, 1971: 125-132.

Honigmann, John J. Indians of Nouveau-Québec. In Jean Malaurie and Jacques Rousseau, eds. Le Nouveau-Québec. Paris, Mouton, 1964: 315-373.

Honigmann, John J. Social networks in Great Whale River: notes on an Eskimo, Montagnais-Naskapi, and Euro-Canadian community. Ottawa, Queen's Printer, 1962. 6, 110 p. illus., map. (Canada, National Museum, Bulletin, 178)

Huard, Victor Alphonse. Labrador et Anticosti. Montréal, Beauchemin, 1897. 15, 505 p. illus., map.

Johnson, William D. An exploratory study of ethnic relations at Great Whale River. Ottawa, 1962. 21 p. (Canada, Department of Northern Affairs and National Resources, Northern Co-ordination and Research Centre, NCRC-62-7)

Kenton, E., ed. The Indians of North America. New York, 1927. (Vol. 1) 103-210 (Vol. 2) 412-424.

Kleivan, H. Labrador i Støpeskjeen. Polarboken (1956): 65-98.

Knight, Rolf. A re-examination of hunting, trapping, and territoriality among the Northeastern Algonkian Indians. In Anthony Leeds and Andrew P. Vayda, eds. Man, Culture, and Animals. Washington, D.C., 1965: 27-42. (American Association for the Advancement of Science, Publication, 78)

Knight, Rolf. Ecological factors in changing economy and social organization among the Rupert House Cree. Ottawa, Queen's Printer, 1968. 112 p. map. (Canada, National Museum, Anthropology Papers, 15)

Knowles, N. The torture of captives by the Indians of eastern North America. American Philosophical Society, Proceedings, 82 (1940): 151-225.

Kranck, Ernst Hakan. Med motor och hammare längs Labradorküsten. Helsingfors, Söderström, 1940. 170 p. illus., map.

Kupferer, Harriet J. Impotency and power: a cross-cultural comparison of the effect of alien rule. In Marc J. Swartz, et al., eds. Political Anthropology. Chicago, Aldine, 1966: 61-71.

Lacasse, Zacharie. Trois contes sauvages. Québec, Imprimerie de "La Verité", 1882. 55 p.

Lacroix, Lianne. Distribution of ABO and Rh blood groups among Cree Indians at Ft. George, Quebec. By Lianne Lacroix and Edward O. Dodson. Journal of Heredity, 60 (1969): 271-272.

*Lane, K. S. The Montagnais Indians, 1600-1640. Kroeber Anthropological Society, Publications, 7 (1952): 1-62.

Laplante, L. Essai d'analyse d'un chant montagnais. By L. Laplante and J. Mailhot. Recherches Amérindiennes au Québec, 2, no. 2 (1972): 2-19.

Laure, R. P. Mission du Saguenacy. Edited by Arthur E. Jones. Montréal, Archives du Collège Ste-Marie, 1889. 72 p.

Leacock, E. Matrilocality in a simple hunting economy. Southwestern Journal of Anthropology, 11 (1955): 31-47.

Leacock, E. Status among the Montagnais-Naskapi of Labrador. Ethnohistory, 5 (1958): 200-209.

*Leacock, E. The Montagnais hunting territory and the fur trade. American Anthropological Association, Memoirs, 78 (1954): 1-71.

Leacock, Eleanor B. The Montagnais-Naskapi band. In Contributions to Anthropology: Band Societies. Ottawa, Queen's Printer, 1969: 1-20. (Canada, National Museums, Bulletin, 228)

Lee, Thomas E. The Naskapi. Anthropological Journal of Canada, 4, no. 3 (1966): 12-14.

Lefebvre, Madeleine. Tshakapesh, récits montagnais-naskapi. Québec, Ministère des Affaires Culturelles, 1971. 171 p. illus.

Legoff, L. Dictionnaire français-montagnais. Lyon, 1916. 1,058 p.

Legoff, L. Histoire de l'ancien testament racontée aux Montagnais. Montreal, 1889. 214 p.

Leith, Charles K. A summer and winter on Hudson Bay. By Charles K. Leith and A. T. Leith. Madison, Cartwell, 1912. 203 p. illus., map.

Lemoine, G. Dictionnaire Français-Montagnais. Boston, 1901.

Lenton, Lloyd. Indians of Canada. América Indígena, 20 (1960): 15-23.

Leonard, John N. Grand Lake Mistassini.
Beaver, 269, no. 1 (1938): 30-33.

Lewis, Arthur. Life and work of the Rev.
E. J. Peck among the Eskimos. New York,
A. C. Armstrong and Son, 1904. 16,
349 p. illus.

Lips, Eva. Die gegenwärtige
Akkulturationssituation der Montagnais-
Naskapi-Indianer von Lake St. John,
Kanada. In Internationale
Amerikanistenkongress, 34th. 1960, Wien.
Akten. Horn-Wien, Berger, 1962: 514-
521.

Lips, Eva. Vorläufiger Kurzbericht über
eine Forschungsreise nach Kanada, 1959
(Lake St. John-Gebiet). Ethnographisch-
Archäologische Zeitschrift, 1 (1960):
65-66.

*Lips, J. E. Naskapi law. American
Philosophical Society, Transactions,
n.s., 37 (1947): 379-492.

*Lips, J. E. Naskapi trade. Société des
Américanistes, Journal, 31 (1939): 129-
195.

*Lips, J. E. Notes on Montagnais-Naskapi
economy. Ethnos, 12 (1947): 1-78.

Lips, J. E. Public opinion and mutual
assistance among the Montagnais-Naskapi.
American Anthropologist, n.s., 39
(1937): 222-228.

Lips, J. E. Tents in the wilderness.
Philadelphia, 1942. 297 p.

Lips, J. E. Trap systems among the
Montagnais-Naskapi Indians of Labrador.
Stockholm, Statens Etnografiska Museum,
Smärre Meddelanden, 13 (1936): 1-28.

Lips, Julius E. Zelte in der Wildnis;
Indianerleben in Labrador. Wien,
Danubia, 1947. 253 p. illus.

Low, A. P. Report on explorations in the
Labrador Peninsula. Canada, Geological
Survey, Annual Reports, n.s., 8 (1896):
44L-51L.

MacKeevor, Thomas. A voyage to Hudson's
Bay, during the summer of 1812. London,
printed for Sir R. Phillips and Co.,
1819. 2, 76 p. (New Voyages and
Travels, 3d Series, 2, no. 2)

Magnan, Hormidas. Notes historiques sur
le nord de la province de Québec, le
baie d'Hudson, l'Ungava. Bulletin des
Recherches Historiques, 25, no. 4
(1919): 105-119.

Mailhot, J. Le maître de poisson chez les
Montagnais-Naskapi: mouche à chevreuil

ou tortue painte? Recherches
Amérindiennes au Québec, 1, no. 2
(1971): 51-55.

Mailhot, José. North West River; étude
ethnographique. By José Mailhot and
Andrée Michaud. Québec, Université
Laval, 1965. 120 p. illus. (Laval,
Université, Centre d'Études Nordiques,
Travaux Divers, 7)

Malaurie, Jean, ed. Le Nouveau-Québec.
Contribution à l'étude de l'occupation
humaine. Edited by Jean Malaurie and
Jacques Rousseau. Paris, Mouton, 1964.
466 p. illus.

Marcotte, Eugène. Les missions indiennes
du Québec. Études Oblates, 4 (1945):
193-198.

Mason, John Alden. A Naskapi Indian robe.
Pennsylvania, University, University
Museum Bulletin, 2, no. 3 (1931): 98-99.

Mattox, W. G. Fort Nascopie on
Petitsikapau Lake. McGill University,
Sub-Arctic Research Laboratory, Research
Papers, 18 (1964): 1-24.

McFeat, Tom F. S. The Algonkian project.
In his Museum Ethnology and the
Algonkian Project. Ottawa, Queen's
Printer, 1962: 15-80. (Canada, National
Museum, Anthropology Papers, 2)

*McGee, John T. Cultural stability and
change among the Montagnais Indians of
the Lake Melville region of Labrador.
Washington, D.C., 1961. 8, 159 p.
illus., map. (Catholic University of
America, Anthropological Series, 19)

McKenzie, J. The King's posts. In L. F.
R. Masson, ed. Les Bourgeois de la
Compagnie du Nord-Ouest. Vol. 2.
Quebec, 1890: 401-454.

McLean, J. Notes of a twenty-five year's
service in the Hudson's Bay Territory.
Ed. by W. S. Wallace. Champlain Society,
Publications, 19 (1932): 258-265.

McLean, John. Notes of a twenty-five
years' service in the Hudson's Bay
territory. New York, Greenwood Press,
1968. 36, 402 p. map. (Champlain
Society, Publication, 19)

Melvill, C. D. Report on the east-coastal
fisheries of James Bay. Canada,
Department of the Naval Service, Reports
on Fisheries Investigations in Hudson
and James Bays (1914): 3-28.

Michelson, T. Linguistic classification
of Cree and Montagnais-Naskapi dialects.
U. S. Bureau of American Ethnology,
Bulletin, 123 (1939): 67-95.

Michelson, T. Some linguistic features of Speck's "Naskapi". American Anthropologist, n.s., 39 (1937): 370-372.

Michelson, T. Studies among the Montagnais-Naskapi Indians of the northern shore of the St. Lawrence River. Smithsonian Institution, Explorations and Field-Work (1937): 119-122.

Michelson, Truman. A report on a linguistic expedition to James and Hudson's Bay. American Anthropologist, n.s., 38 (1936): 685-686.

Michelson, Truman. The linguistic classification of Rupert House and East Main Cree. American Anthropologist, n.s., 26 (1924): 295.

Miller, E. C. Aksunai. Canadian Geographical Journal, 51 (1955): 256-263.

Mooney, J. and C. Thomas. Mistassin. U.S. Bureau of American Ethnology, Bulletin, 30, vol. 1 (1907): 912.

Mooney, J. and C. Thomas. Montagnais. U.S. Bureau of American Ethnology, Bulletin, 30, vol. 1 (1907): 933-934.

Moore, Omar Khayyam. Divination--a new perspective. American Anthropologist, 59 (1957): 69-74.

Moore, Omar Khayyam. Divination--a new perspective. In Andrew P. Vayda, ed. Environment and Cultural Behavior. Garden City, Natural History Press, 1969: 121-129.

Morrissette, Hugues, ed. Problèmes nordiques des façades de la Baie de James. Edited by Hugues Morrissette and Louis-Edmond Hamelin. Québec, 1967. 179 l. illus., maps. (Laval, Université, Centre d'Études Nordiques, Travaux Divers, 18)

Moussette, M. La dichotomie tce 'mentu et metci 'mentu d'après quelques documents anciens. Recherches Amérindiennes au Québec, 1, no. 2 (1971): 46-50.

Murphy, Robert F. Tappers and trappers: parallel process in acculturation. By Robert F. Murphy and Julian H. Steward. Economic Development and Cultural Change, 4 (1956): 335-355.

Neilson, J. M. The Mistassini territory of northern Quebec. Canadian Geographical Journal, 37 (1948): 144-157.

Nouvel, Henry. A canoe trip to Midland in 1675. Edited and with an introduction by Harold W. Moll. Michigan History, 46 (1962): 255-274.

Paine, Robert. Animals as capital: comparisons among northern nomadic herders and hunters. Anthropological Quarterly, 44 (1971): 157-172.

Parker, John. The fur trader and the emerging geography of North America. Museum of the Fur Trade Quarterly, 2, no. 3 (1966): 6-10; 2, no. 4 (1966): 7-11.

Peacock, F. W. The Newfoundland Government and the Eskimos of Labrador. North, 11, no. 4 (1964): 1-4.

Pierronet, T. Specimen of the Mountaineer or Sheshatapooshshoish, Skoffie, and Micmac languages. Massachusetts Historical Society, Collections, 6 (1798): 16-33.

Poirier, Jean. Les êtres supernaturels dans la toponymie amérindienne du Québec. Revue Internationale d'Onomastique, 21 (1969): 287-300.

Pothier, Roger. Relations inter-ethniques et acculturation à Mistassini. 2. tirage. Québec, 1967. 154 l. illus., map. (Laval, Université, Centre d'Études Nordiques, Travaux Divers, 9)

Preston, R. J. Problèmes humains reliés au développement de la baie James. Recherches Amérindiennes au Québec, 1, no. 4/5 (1971): 58-68.

Preston, Richard J. Functional politics in a Northern Indian community. In Internationale Amerikanistenkongress, 38th. 1968, Stuttgart-München. Verhandlungen. Band 3. München, Klaus Renner, 1971: 169-178.

Proulx, Jean Baptiste. À la baie d'Hudson, où récit de la première visite pastorale de Mgr. N. Z. Lorrain. Montréal, Librairie Saint-Joseph, Cadieux and Derome, 1886. 284 p.

Quimby, G. I. Habitat, culture, and archaeology. In Essays in the Science of Culture in Honor of Leslie A. White. New York, 1960: 380-389.

Ritzenthaler, R. and M. Sellars. Indians in an urban situation. Wisconsin Archeologist, 36 (1955): 147-161.

Robbins, Richard Howard. Drinking behavior and identity resolution. Dissertation Abstracts International, 31 (1970/1971): 4466B-4467B. UM 71-3592.

Robinson, J. C., et al. Serum alkaline phosphatase types in North American Indians and Negroes. Journal of Medical Genetics, 4 (1967): 96-101.

Rogers, Edward S. Down the Rupert's River. Beaver, 279 (Sept. 1948): 29-33.

Rogers, Edward S. Indian time. Ontario Fish and Wildlife Review, 4, no. 4 (1965): 23-26.

Rogers, Edward S. Leadership among the Indians of eastern Subarctic Canada. Anthropologica, n.s., 7 (1965): 263-284.

Rogers, Edward S. Les Indiens de la baie James et l'énergie hydroélectrique. Recherches Amérindiennes au Québec, 1, no. 4/5 (1971): 44-57.

Rogers, Edward S. Mistassini Cree. Beaver, 301, no. 1 (1970/1971): 22-25.

Rogers, Edward S. Mistassini hunting groups and hunting territories. Dissertation Abstracts, 19 (1958/1959): 2715. UM 59-332.

Rogers, Edward S. Notes on snowshoes among the Montagnais-Naskapi. Toronto, Royal Ontario Museum, Annual Report (1961): 57-66.

Rogers, Edward S. Subsistence areas of the Cree-Ojibwa of the eastern Subarctic: a preliminary study. In Contributions to Ethnology V. Ottawa, Queen's Printer, 1967: 59-90. (Canada, National Museum, Bulletin, 204)

Rogers, Edward S. The canoe-sled among the Montagnais-Naskapi. Toronto, Royal Ontario Museum, Annual Report (1962): 74-76, 125.

*Rogers, Edward S. The hunting group--hunting territory complex among the Mistassini Indians. Ottawa, 1963. 4, 95 p. maps. (Canada, National Museum, Bulletin, 195)

Rogers, Edward S. The Indians of the Central Subarctic of Canada. By Edward S. Rogers and Father John Trudeau. In Internationale Amerikanistenkongress, 38th. 1968, Stuttgart-München. Verhandlungen. Band 3. München, Klaus Renner, 1971: 133-149.

Rogers, Edward S. The individual in Mistassini society from birth to death. By Edward S. Rogers and Jean H. Rogers. In Contributions to Anthropology 1960. Part II. Ottawa, Queen's Printer, 1963: 14-36. (Canada, National Museum, Bulletin, 190)

*Rogers, Edward S. The material culture of the Mistassini. Ottawa, 1967. 11, 156 p. illus. (Canada, National Museum, Bulletin, 218)

Rogers, Edward S. The Mistassini Cree. In Mario G. Bicchieri, ed. Hunters and Gatherers Today. New York, Holt, Rinehart, and Winston, 1972: 90-137.

Rogers, Edward S. The Naskapi. Beaver, 300, no. 3 (1969/1970): 40-43.

Rogers, Edward S. The Nemiscan Indians. Beaver, 296, no. 1 (1965/1966): 30-35.

Rohrl, Vivian J. Comment on "The cure and feeding of windigos: a critique". American Anthropologist, 74 (1972): 242-244.

Ross, William Gillies. Human geography. McGill Sub-Arctic Research Laboratory, Annual Report, 1955/56, Supplement, 1 (1955/1956): 34-43.

Rouillard, Eugène. A travers le pays. Croisière et explorations dans le golfe St.-Laurent. Société de Géographie de Québec, Bulletin, 13 (1919): 214-217.

Rouillard, Eugène. Betsiamites. Quelle est la véritable orthographie de ce nom. Société de Géographie de Québec, Bulletin, 13 (1919): 149-150.

Rouillard, Eugène. La Côte Nord du Saint-Laurent et le Labrador canadien. Québec, Laflamme and Proulx, 1908. 188 p. illus.

Rouillard, Eugène. Une tribu sauvage au Labrador. Les Nascapis. Société de Géographie de Québec, Bulletin, 3 (1908): 54-57.

Rousseau, J. J. A travers l'Ungava. Actualité Économique, 25 (1949): 83-131.

Rousseau, J. J. Autour de la marmite des Mistassini. Gastronomie, 8 (1946): 9-12.

Rousseau, J. J. Chez les Mistassini. Institut Français d'Amérique Latine, Revue, 2 (1945): 64-91.

Rousseau, J. J. Dans l'Ungava. Explorateur, 79 (1951): 25-28; 80 (1951): 25-28; 81 (1951): 25-28; 82 (1951): 25-28; 83 (1951): 25-29.

Rousseau, J. J. Ethnobotanique des Mistassini. Association Canadienne-Française pour l'Avancement des Sciences, Annales, 13 (1947): 118.

Rousseau, J. J. La crainte des Iroquois. Revue d'Histoire de l'Amérique Française, 2 (1948): 13-26.

Rousseau, J. J.   La religion primitive des Montagnais et des Hurons. International Congress of Americanists, Proceedings, 30 (1955): 151-154.

Rousseau, J. J.   Le caribou et le renne dans la Québec Arctique et Hémiarctique. Revue Canadienne de Géographie, 4 (1950): 60-89.

Rousseau, J. J.   Le dualisme religieux chez les Mistassini. Association Canadienne-Française pour l'Avancement des Sciences, Annales, 13 (1947): 118-119.

Rousseau, J. J.   Le nom du caribou chez les Montagnais-Naskapi et les Esquimaux de l'Ungava. Anthropologica, 1 (1955): 212-214.

Rousseau, J. J.   Le partage du gibier dans la cuisine des Montagnais-Naskapi. Anthropologica, 1 (1955): 215-217.

Rousseau, J. J.   Mistassini calendar. Beaver, 280 (1949): 33-37.

Rousseau, J. J.   Notes ethnologiques. Forêt et Conservation, 2 (1950): 683-687.

Rousseau, J. J.   On human and animal adaptation. Canadian Geographer, 6 (1955): 17-20.

Rousseau, J. J.   Rites paiens de la forêt quebecoise. Cahiers des Dix, 18 (1953): 129-155.

Rousseau, J. J. and J. P. Currier.   Notes sur le folklore zoologique des Mistassini et particulièrement la pêche. Association Canadienne-Française pour l'Avancement des Sciences, Annales, 13 (1947): 117-118.

Rousseau, J. J. and M. Raymond.   Le folklore botanique de Caughnawaga. Montréal, Université, Institut Botanique, Contributions, 55 (1945): 7-74.

Rousseau, M.   La crainte de l'Iroquois au Lac Mistassini. Association Canadienne-Française pour l'Avancement des Sciences, Annales, 13 (1947): 119-120.

Rousseau, M. and J. J. Rousseau.   La cérémonie de la tente agitée chez les Mistassini. International Congress of Americanists, Proceedings, 28 (1947): 307-315.

Roy, Joseph Edmond.   In and around Tadoussac. Levis, Mercier, 1891. 246 p.

Rupert, Thomas.   Tales of Chikapash. Told by Thomas Rupert to George W. Bauer. Beaver, 296, no. 4 (1965/1966): 53-54.

Ryerson, John.   Hudson' Bay; or, A missionary tour in the territory of the Honourable Hudson's Bay Company. Toronto, Sanderson, 1855.   24, 190 p. illus.

Savard, Rémi.   Carcajou et le sens du monde; récits montagnais-naskapi. Québec, Ed. Officiel du Québec, 1971. 141 p.   illus.   (Collection "Civilisation du Québec. Série Cultures Améridiennes", 3)

Savard, Rémi.   Note sur le mythe indien de ayašew à partir d'une version montagnaise. Recherches Amérindiennes au Québec, 2, no. 1 (1972): 3-16.

Schmidt, W.   Die Ostzentral-Algonkin. In his Die Ursprung der Göttesidee. Bd. 5. Münster i. W., 1934: 531-554.

Schmidt, W.   Die Ostzentral-Algonkin. In his Die Ursprung der Göttesidee. Bd. 2. Münster i. W., 1929: 459-474.

Schmidt, W.   Die Ostzentral-Algonkin. In his Die Ursprung der Göttesidee. Bd. 7. Münster i. W., 1940: 727-760.

Simard, Hidalla.   La Côte-Nord. Esquisse de la région et des moeurs de ses habitants. Société de Géographie de Québec, Bulletin, 11 (1917): 203-216.

Sirois, L.   Montagnais sans maître: Ilnoimun e kakatshishkotomoakent. Saguenay, 1936.   135 p.

Skinner, Alanson B.   Some remarks on the culture of eastern near-Arctic Indians. Science, n.s., 29 (1909): 150-152.

Smith, J. G. E.   Rousseau's review of "Material culture of the Mistassini": a comment. American Anthropologist, 71 (1969): 710.

Soper, P. J.   Amateur doctor. Beaver, 273 (Sept. 1942): 46-47.

Speck, F. G.   An incident in Montagnais winter life. Natural History, 26 (1926): 61-67.

Speck, F. G.   Analysis of Eskimo and Indian skin-dressing methods in Labrador. Ethnos, 2 (1937): 345-353.

Speck, F. G.   Central Eskimo and Indian dot ornamentation. Indian Notes, 2 (1925): 151-172.

Speck, F. G.   Culture problems in northeastern North America. American

Philosophical Society, Proceedings, 65
(1926): 274-282.

Speck, F. G. Dogs of the Labrador
Indians. Natural History, 25 (1925): 58-
64.

Speck, F. G. Ethical attributes of the
Labrador Indians. American
Anthropologist, n.s., 35 (1933): 559-
594.

Speck, F. G. Family hunting territories
of the Lake St. John Montagnais.
Anthropos, 22 (1927): 387-403.

Speck, F. G. Family hunting territories
of the Waswanipi Indians. Indian Notes,
5 (1928): 42-59.

Speck, F. G. Game totems among the
Northeastern Algonkians. American
Anthropologist, n.s., 19 (1917): 9-18.

Speck, F. G. Hunting charms of the
Montagnais and Mistassini. Indian Notes
and Monographs, ser. 2, 13 (1921): 1-19.

Speck, F. G. In Montagnais country. In E.
C. Parsons, ed. American Indian Life.
New York, 1925: 87-97.

Speck, F. G. Indian and Eskimo
backgrounds in southern Labrador.
General Magazine and Historical
Chronicle, University of Pennsylvania,
30 (1935/1936): 1-17, 143-163.

Speck, F. G. Kinship terms and the family
band among the Northeastern Algonkian.
American Anthropologist, n.s., 20
(1918): 143-161.

Speck, F. G. Mammoth or "stiff-legged
bear". American Anthropologist, n.s., 37
(1935): 159-163.

Speck, F. G. Medicine practices of the
Northeastern Algonquians. International
Congress of Americanists, Proceedings,
19 (1915): 303-321.

Speck, F. G. Mistassini hunting
territories. American Anthropologist,
n.s., 25 (1923): 452-471.

Speck, F. G. Mistassini notes. Indian
Notes, 7 (1930): 410-457.

Speck, F. G. Modern and classical soul
philosophy among stone age savages of
Labrador. General Magazine and
Historical Chronicle, University of
Pennsylvania, 28 (1926): 112-117.

Speck, F. G. Montagnais and Naskapi
tales. Journal of American Folklore, 38
(1925): 1-32.

Speck, F. G. Montagnais art in birch-
bark. Indian Notes and Monographs, 11
(1937): 45-157.

Speck, F. G. Montagnais-Naskapi bands and
early Eskimo distribution in the
Labrador Peninsula. American
Anthropologist, n.s., 33 (1931): 557-
600.

Speck, F. G. More Algonkian scapulimancy
from the North. Ethnos, 4 (1939): 21-28.

*Speck, F. G. Naskapi. Norman, 1935.
236 p.

Speck, F. G. Reptile-lore of the Northern
Indians. Journal of American Folklore,
36 (1923): 273-280.

Speck, F. G. Some Naskapi myths from
Little Whale River. Journal of American
Folklore, 28 (1915): 70-77.

Speck, F. G. Spiritual beliefs among the
Labrador Indians. International Congress
of Americanists, Proceedings, 21, vol. 1
(1924): 266-275.

Speck, F. G. Swimming-paddles among
Northern Indians. American
Anthropologist, n.s., 39 (1937): 726-
727.

Speck, F. G. The double-curve motive in
Northeastern Algonkian art. Canada,
Department of Mines, Geological Survey,
Memoirs, 42 (1914): 1-17.

Speck, F. G. The Montagnais Indians.
Southern Workman, 38 (1909): 148-154.

Speck, F. G. The Montagnais of Labrador.
Home Geographic Monthly, 2, no. 1
(1932): 7-12.

Speck, F. G. and G. G. Heye. Hunting
charms of the Montagnais and the
Mistassini. Indian Notes and Monographs,
ser. 2, 13 (1921): 5-19.

Speck, F. G. and L. C. Eiseley.
Montagnais-Naskapi bands and family
hunting of the central and southeastern
Labrador Peninsula. American
Philosophical Society, Proceedings, 85
(1942): 215-242.

Speck, Frank G. Bird-lore of the Northern
Indians. Pennsylvania, University,
Public Lectures by the Faculty, 7
(1919/1920): 349-380.

Speck, Frank G. One of Caesar's anecdotes
among the Indians of North America.
Pennsylvania, University, Alumni
Register, 19, no. 9 (1917): 686-690.

Spencer, Miles. Notes on the breeding habits of certain mammals, from personal observations and enquiries from Indians. In Albert P. Low. Report on Explorations in James' Bay and Country East of Hudson Bay. Montreal, W. F. Brown, 1888: 76-79. (Canada, Geological Survey, Annual Report, n.s., 3(J))

Stearns, W. A. Labrador, 259-268. Boston, 1884.

Stephen, C. N. Kosoak River brigade. Beaver, 272 (1941): 36-43.

Stewart, T. D. Anthropometric observations on the Eskimos and Indians of Labrador. Field Museum, Anthropological Series, 31 (1939): 1-163.

Strong, W. D. A stone age culture from northern Labrador. American Anthropologist, n.s., 32 (1930): 126-144.

Strong, W. D. Cross-cousin marriage and the culture of the Northeastern Algonkian. American Anthropologist, n.s., 31 (1929): 277-288.

Strong, William Duncan. North American traditions suggesting a knowledge of the mammoth. American Anthropologist, n.s., 36 (1934): 81-88.

Strong, William Duncan. Notes on mammals of the Labrador interior. Journal of Mammalogy, 11 (1930): 1-10.

Tanner, A. Existe-t-il des territoires de chasse? Recherches Amérindiennes au Québec, 1, no. 4/5 (1971): 69-83.

Tanner, V. Folkrörelser och kulturväxlingar pa Labrador-halvön. Svensk Geografisk Arsbok, 15 (1939): 80-126.

Tanner, V. Outlines of the geography, life and customs of Newfoundland-Labrador. Acta Geographica, 8, vol. 1 (1944): 437-891.

Tanner, Vainö. Folk och kulturer på Labrador. Helsinki, 1939. 54 p. illus., maps. (Finska Vetenskaps-societeten, Årsbok-Vuosikirja, 17B, no. 2)

Tantaquidgeon, G. Notes on the origin and uses of plants of the Lake St. John Montagnais. Journal of American Folklore, 45 (1932): 265-267.

Tantaquidgeon, Gladys. How the summer season was brought north: abstract of a Montagnais tale. Journal of American Folk-Lore, 54 (1941): 203-204.

Thériault, Yves. Roi de la Côte Nord. Montréal, Éditions de l'Homme, 1960. 125 p. illus.

Thomas, Gordon W. Carcinoma among Labrador Eskimos and Indians. Canadian Journal of Surgery, 4 (1960/1961): 465-468.

Thwaites, R. G., ed. The Jesuit Relations and allied documents. Cleveland, 1896-1901. 74 v.

Townsend, C. W., ed. Captain Cartwright and his Labrador journal. Boston, 1911. 385 p.

Tremblay, Victor. Une épopée ignorée: l'évangélisation du Saguenay par les Jésuites de 1641 à 1782. Société Canadienne d'Histoire de l'Église Catholique, Rapport (1944/1945): 37-49.

Treude, Erhard. Die gegenwärtige Siedlungs- und Wirtschaftsstruktur Nordlabradors. In Internationale Amerikanistenkongress, 38th. 1968, Stuttgart-München. Verhandlungen. Band 3. München, Klaus Renner, 1971: 151-162.

Trigger, Bruce G. Champlain judged by his Indian policy: a different view of early Canadian history. Anthropologica, n.s., 13 (1971): 85-114.

*Turner, L. M. Ethnology of the Ungava District. U.S. Bureau of American Ethnology, Annual Reports, 11 (1890): 159-184, 267-350.

Turner, L. M. On the Indians and Eskimos of the Ungava District. Royal Society of Canada, Proceedings and Transactions, 5, pt. 2 (1887): 108-119.

Turner, L. M. Scraper of the Naskopie (Naynaynots) Indians. American Anthropologist, 1 (1888): 186-188.

Turner, L. M. The single-headed drum of the Naskopie. United States National Museum, Proceedings, 11 (1888): 433-434.

Twomey, Arthur C. Needle to the North, the story of an expedition to Ungava and the Belcher Islands. By Arthur C. Twomey and Nigel Herrick. Boston, Houghton Mifflin, 1942. 8, 360 p. illus., map.

Twomey, Arthur C. Ungava expedition. Beaver, 270, no. 1 (1939): 44-49.

Vaillancourt, Émile. Au Labrador canadien. Société de Géographie de Québec, Bulletin, 13 (1919): 287-295.

Vinay, Jean-Paul. La vie au Mistassini, le Labrador québécois. Club Musical et

Littéraire de Montréal (1947/1948): 78-99.

Vivian, R. Percy, et al. The nutrition and health of the James Bay Indian. Canadian Medical Association, Journal, 59 (1948): 505-518.

Walker, L. J. Indian burial customs. Journal of American Folklore, 63 (1950): 239-240.

Walker, L. J. Jawinikom's tale. Midwest Folklore, 5 (1955): 35-36.

Wallace, Anthony F. C. The value of the Speck papers for ethnohistory. In The American Indian. Philadelphia, American Philosophical Society, 1968: 20-34. (American Philosophical Society, Library Publication, 2)

Wallace, D. The long Labrador trail. New York, 1907. 315 p.

Watt, Maud. Chimo days. Beaver, 270, no. 2 (1939): 30-35.

Waugh, F. The Naskopi Indians of Labrador and their neighbors. Women's Canadian Historical Society of Ottawa, Transactions, 9 (1925): 126-136.

Webber, Alika Podolinsky. A painting tool. Beaver, 299, no. 2 (1968/1969): 24-26.

Webster, Gordon. By river from Chimo. Beaver, 269 (June 1938): 27-29.

Whitby, Barbara. The Beothucks and other primitive people of Newfoundland: a review. Anthropological Journal of Canada, 5, no. 4 (1967): 2-19.

Williams, Glyndwr. James Clouston's journey across the Labrador Peninsula in 1820. Beaver, 297, no. 1 (1966/1967): 4-15.

Wilson, Clifford P. Tadoussac, the Company and the King's Posts. Beaver, 266, no. 1 (1935): 8-12, 66.

Wintrob, Ronald M. Education and identity conflict among Cree Indian youth: a preliminary report, annex 3. By Ronald M. Wintrob and Peter S. Sindell. Montreal, McGill University, 1968. 120 p. ERIC ED039063.

11-08 Ojibwa

Carrière, Gaston. Catalogue des manuscrits en langues indiennes conservés aux archives oblates, Ottawa.
Anthropologica, n.s., 12 (1970): 151-179.

Fay, George E. Bibliography of the Indians of Wisconsin. Wisconsin Indians Research Institute, Journal, 1, no. 1 (1965): 107-132.

Minnesota Historical Society. Chippewa and Dakota Indians; a subject catalog of books, pamphlets, periodical articles, and manuscripts in the Minnesota Historical Society. St. Paul, 1969.

Adam, L. Esquisse d'une grammaire comparée de la langue des Chippeways et de la langue des Crees. International Congress of Americanists, Proceedings, 1, vol. 2 (1875): 88-148.

Adam, L. Examen grammatical comparé de seize langues américaines. International Congress of Americanists, Proceedings, 2, vol. 2 (1877): 161-244.

Adams, Ian. The poverty wall. Toronto, McClelland and Stewart, 1970. 154 p.

Anderson, David D. John Disturnell introduces the Great Lakes to America. Inland Seas, 18 (1962): 96-106.

Anonymous. Fur trade in Minnesota--1856. Museum of the Fur Trade Quarterly, 1, no. 1 (1965): 9-10.

Anonymous. More lessons from Red Lake. Lancet, 2 (1970): 251-252.

Anonymous. Wisconsin Indian state legislation 1955-1965. Wisconsin Indians Research Institute, Journal, 2, no. 2 (1966): 68-72.

Armstrong, Benjamin G. Reminiscences of life among the Chippewa. Wisconsin Magazine of History, 55 (1971/1972): 172-194, 287-309.

Armstrong, Benjamin G. Reminiscences of life among the Chippewa. Wisconsin Magazine of History, 56 (1972/1973): 37-58.

Armstrong, H. G. Early life among the Indians. Ashland, 1892. 266 p.

Assiniwi, Bernard. Anish-nah-be; contes adultes du pays algonkin. By Bernard Assiniwi and Isabelle Myre. Montréal, Leméac, 1971. 105 p. illus.

Astrov, M., ed. The winged serpent, 75-79. New York, 1946.

Atwater, C.   Remarks made on a tour to
Prairie du Chien.   Columbus, 1831.
296 p.

Babbitt, F. E.   Illustrative notes
concerning the Minnesota Odjibwas.
American Association for the Advancement
of Science, Proceedings, 36 (1887): 303-
307.

Babcock, W. M.   The Minnesota Indian and
his ·history. Minnesota Archaeologist, 19
(1954): 18-25.

Babcock, Willoughby M.   With Ramsey to
Pembina; a treaty-making trip in 1851.
Minnesota History, 38 (1962/1963): 1-10.

Baldwin, W. W.   Social problems of the
Ojibwa Indians in the Collins area in
northwestern Ontario. Anthropologica, 5
(1957): 51-124.

Balikci, A.   Note sur le midewiwin.
Anthropologica, 2 (1956): 165-217.

Ball, A. E.   White Earth Consolidated
Agency. In United States, Department of
the Interior, Census Office, Eleventh
Census, Report on Indians Taxed and
Indians not Taxed.   Washington, D.C.,
1890: 339-351.

Baner, J. G. R. and J. L. Bellaire.
Kitch-iti-ki-pi. Manistique, Michigan,
1933.   61 p.

Baraga, F.   A dictionary of the Otchipwe
language. New ed.   Montreal, 1878-1880.
2 v.

Baraga, F.   A lecture delivered in 1863.
Acta et Dicta, 5 (1917).

Baraga, F.   A theoretical and practical
grammar of the Otchipwe language. 2d ed.
Montreal, 1878.   422 p.

Baraga, Friedrich.   A dictionary of the
Otchipwe language, explained in English.
New ed.   Minneapolis, Ross and Haines,
1966.

Baraga, Friedrich.   Zgodovina, značaj,
nravi in šege severnoameriških
Indijancev. Celje, Mohorjeva Družba,
1970.   134 p.   illus.

Barnouw, V.   A psychological
interpretation of a Chippewa origin
legend. Journal of American Folklore, 68
(1955): 73-85, 211-223, 341-355.

Barnouw, V.   Acculturation and personality
among the Wisconsin Chippewa. American
Anthropological Association, Memoirs, 72
(1950): 1-152.

Barnouw, V.   Reminiscences of a Chippewa
mide priest. Wisconsin Archeologist, 35
(1954): 83-112.

Barnouw, V.   The phantasy world of a
Chippewa woman. Psychiatry, 12, no. 1
(1949): 67-76.

Barnouw, Victor.   A Chippewa Mide priest's
description of the Medicine Dance.
Wisconsin Archeologist, n.s., 41 (1960):
77-97.

Barnouw, Victor.   Chippewa social atomism.
American Anthropologist, 63 (1961):
1006-1013.

Barrett, S. A.   The dream dance of the
Chippewa and Menominee Indians of
northern Wisconsin. Public Museum of the
City of Milwaukee, Bulletin, 1 (1911):
251-406.

Beauchamp, W. M.   Indian nations of the
Great Lakes. American Antiquarian and
Oriental Journal, 17 (1895): 321-325.

Beaulieu, David.   The formal education of
Minnesota Indians; historical
perspective until 1934.   Minneapolis,
University of Minnesota, Training Center
for Community Programs, 1971.   38 l.
maps.   ERIC ED050873.

Bebchuk, William.   Chronic ulcerative
colitis in a North American Indian. By
William Bebchuk, Arnold G. Rogers, and
J. L. Downey. Gastroenterology, 40
(1961): 138-140.

Becker, David A.   Enteric parasites of
Indians and Anglo-Americans, chiefly on
the Winnebago and Omaha Reservations in
Nebraska. Nebraska State Medical
Journal, 53 (1968): 293-296, 347-349,
380-383, 421-423.

Belcourt, G. A.   Department of Hudson's
Bay. Minnesota Historical Society,
Collections, 1 (1872): 227-236.

Belcourt, G. A.   Principles de la langue
des sauvages appelés Sauteux.   Quebec,
1839.   146 p.

Belcourt, George Antoine.   Hunting buffalo
on the northern Plains: a letter from
Father Belcourt. North Dakota History,
38 (1971): 332-348.

Beltrami, J. C.   A pilgrimage in Europe
and America, Vol. 2: 227-300.   London,
1828.

Benndorf, Helga, ed.   Indianer
Nordamerikas 1760-1860 aus der Sammlung
Speyer. Edited by Helga Benndorf and
Arthur Speyer.   Offenbach a.M.,

Deutsches Ledermuseum, Deutsches Schuhmuseum, 1968. 141 p. illus.

Benson, Maxine. Schoolcraft, James, and the "White Indian". Michigan History, 54 (1970): 311-328.

Bernard, M. Religion and magic among the Cass Lake Ojibwa. Primitive Man, 2 (1929): 52-55.

Bishop, Charles A. Demography, ecology and trade among the Northern Ojibwa and Swampy Cree. Western Canadian Journal of Anthropology, 3, no. 1 (1972): 58-71.

Bishop, Charles A. The emergence of hunting territories among the Northern Ojibwa. Ethnology, 9 (1970): 1-15.

Bishop, Charles Aldrich. The Northern Chippewa: an ethnohistorical study. Dissertation Abstracts International, 30 (1969/1970): 2513B. UM 69-20,556.

Black, M. B. Mythes et structures sémantiques: ambiguités référentielles au lac Weagamow, Ontario. Recherches Amérindiennes au Québec, 2, no. 2 (1972): 20-28.

Black, Mary B. A note on gender in eliciting Ojibwa semantic structures. Anthropological Linguistics, 11 (1969): 177-186.

Black, Mary B. On Ojibwa question constructions. International Journal of American Linguistics, 37 (1971): 146-151.

Black, Mary Rose Bartholomew. An ethnoscience investigation of Ojibwa ontology and world view. Dissertation Abstracts, 28 (1967/1968): 772B-773B. UM 67-11,020.

Blackbird, A. J. History of the Ottawa and Chippewa Indians of Michigan. Ypsilanti, 1887. 128 p.

Blackburn, George M. Foredoomed to failure: the Manistee Indian station. Michigan History, 53 (1969): 37-50.

Blackburn, George M. George Johnston, Indian agent and copper hunter. Michigan History, 54 (1970): 108-121.

Blackwood, B. Tales of the Chippewa Indians. Folk-Lore, 40 (1929): 315-344.

Bleeker, S. The Chippewa Indians. New York, 1955. 157 p.

Blessing, F. K. A Southern Ojibwa glossary. Minnesota Archaeologist, 19, no. 1 (1954): 2-57.

Blessing, F. K. An exhibition of mide magic. Minnesota Archaeologist, 20, no. 4 (1956): 9-13.

Blessing, F. K. Contemporary costuming of Minnesota Chippewa Indians. Minnesota Archaeologist, 20, no. 4 (1956): 1-8.

Blessing, F. K. Miscellany. Minnesota Archaeologist, 20, no. 4 (1956): 14-17.

Blessing, F. K. Some observations on the use of bark by the Southern Ojibwa Indians. Minnesota Archaeologist, 19, no. 4 (1954): 3-14.

Blessing, F. K. Some uses of bone, horn, claws and teeth by Minnesota Ojibwa Indians. Minnesota Archaeologist, 20, no. 3 (1956): 1-11.

Blessing, F. K. The physical characteristics of Southern Ojibwa woodcraft. Minnesota Archaeologist, 18, no. 4 (1952): 9-21.

Bloomfield, L. Eastern Ojibwa. Ann Arbor, 1957. 282 p.

Boas, F. Zur Anthropologie der nordamerikanischen Indianer. Berliner Gesellschaft für Anthropologie, Ethnologie und Urgeschichte, Verhandlungen (1895): 367-411.

Boggs, S. T. An interactional study of Ojibwa socialization. American Sociological Review, 21 (1956): 191-198.

Boggs, S. T. Culture change and the personality of Ojibwa children. American Anthropologist, 60 (1958): 47-58.

Bolt, Robert. Reverend Leonard Slater in the Grand River Valley. Michigan History, 51 (1967): 241-251.

Breck, J. L. Chippeway pictures from the Territory of Minnesota. Hartford, 1910. 29 p.

Brogan, D. Wild rice harvest. Frontiers, 20, no. 5 (1956): 131-135.

Brown, D. M. Wisconsin Indian corn origin myths. Wisconsin Archeologist, n.s., 21 (1940): 19-27.

Brown, Dorothy M. Indian legends of historic and sceneic Wisconsin. Madison, 1969. 69 p.

Brown, Dorothy M. Wisconsin Indian place-name legends. Madison, 1948. 30 p.

Brown, James Allison, et al. The Gentleman Farm Site, La Salle County, Illinois. Springfield, 1967. 6, 48 p.

illus., maps. (Illinois, State Museum, Report of Investigations, 12)

Brown, T. T. Plant games and toys of Chippewa children. Wisconsin Archeologist, n.s., 9 (1930): 185-186.

Burden, H. N. Manitoulin. London, 1895. 164 p.

Burnford, Sheila. Without reserve. Toronto, McClelland and Stewart, 1969. 242 p. illus.

Burton, F. R. American primitive music. New York, 1909. 281 p.

Burton, Frederick R. American primitive music; with special attention to the songs of the Ojibways. Port Washington, Kennikat Press, 1969. 284, 73 p.

Bushnell, D. I. An Ojibway ceremony. American Anthropologist, n.s., 7 (1905): 69-73.

Bushnell, D. I. Burials of the Algonquian, Siouan and Caddoan tribes. U.S. Bureau of American Ethnology, Bulletin, 83 (1927): 2-6.

Bushnell, D. I. Ojibway habitations and other structures. Smithsonian Institution, Annual Reports of the Board of Regents (1917): 609-617.

Bushnell, D. I. Sketches by Paul Kane in the Indian Country, 1845-1848. Smithsonian Miscellaneous Collections, 99, no. 1 (1940): 1-25.

Bushnell, D. I. Villages of the Algonquian, Siouan and Caddoan tribes. U.S. Bureau of American Ethnology, Bulletin, 77 (1922): 8-17.

Cadzow, D. A. Bark records of the Bungi Midewin Society. Indian Notes, 3 (1926): 123-134.

Calkins, H. Indian nomenclature of northern Wisconsin, with a sketch of the manners and customs of the Chippewas. State Historical Society of Wisconsin, Collections, 1 (1854): 119-126.

Cameron, D. The Nipigon country. In L. F. R. Masson, ed. Les Bourgeois de la Compagnie du Nord-Ouest. Vol. 2. Quebec, 1890: 231-265.

Campbell, G. M. Original Indian dictionary of the Ojibway or Chippewa language. Minneapolis, 1940. 80 p.

Campbell, Robert. The private journal of Robert Campbell. Edited by George R. Brooks. Missouri Historical Society, Bulletin, 20 (1963/1964): 3-24, 107-118.

Canfield, Francis X. A diocese so vast: Bishop Rese in Detroit. Michigan History, 51 (1967): 202-212.

Cappel, J. L'S. Chippewa tales. Los Angeles, 1928. 64 p.

Cardenal, Ernesto, tr. Poesía de los indios de Norteamérica. América Indígena, 21 (1961): 355-362.

Carlson, E. J. Indian rice camps. Indians at Work, 2, no. 7 (1934): 16-23.

Carson, W. Ojibway tales. Journal of American Folklore, 30 (1917): 491-493.

Carver, J. Travels through the interior parts of North America. London, 1778. 360 p.

Casagrande, J. B. John Mink, Ojibwa informant. Wisconsin Archeologist, 36 (1955): 106-127.

Casagrande, J. B. Ojibwa bear ceremonialism. International Congress of Americanists, Proceedings, 29, vol. 2 (1952): 113-117.

Casagrande, J. B. The Ojibwa's psychic universe. Tomorrow, 4, no. 3 (1956): 33-40.

Cass, Elizabeth. Why dogs hate cats. Beaver, 299, no. 1 (1968/1969): 51.

Cass, Lewis. A memorandum of Lewis Cass: concerning a system for the regulation of Indian affairs. Edited by Francis Paul Prucha and Donald F. Carmony. Wisconsin Magazine of History, 52 (1968/1969): 35-50.

Caudill, W. Psychological characteristics of acculturated Wisconsin Ojibwa children. American Anthropologist, n.s., 51 (1949): 409-427.

Cervenka, Jaroslav. Cleft uvula in Chippewa Indians: prevalence and genetics. By Jaroslav Cervenka and Burton L. Shapiro. Human Biology, 42 (1970): 47-52.

Chaboillez, Charles Jean Baptiste. Journal of Charles Jean Baptiste Chaboillez, 1797-1798. Edited by Harold Hickerson. Ethnohistory, 6 (1959): 265-316, 363-427.

Chamberlain, A. F. A Mississaga legend of Naniboju. Journal of American Folklore, 5 (1892): 291-292.

Chamberlain, A. F. Maple sugar and the Indians. American Anthropologist, o.s., 4 (1891): 381-384.

Chamberlain, A. F. Nanibozhu amongst the Otchipwe, Mississagas, and other Algonkian tribes. Journal of American Folklore, 4 (1891): 193-213.

Chamberlain, A. F. Notes on the history, customs, and beliefs of the Mississagua Indians. Journal of American Folklore, 1 (1888): 150-160.

Chamberlain, A. F. Tales of the Mississaguas. Journal of American Folklore, 2 (1889): 141-147; 3 (1890): 149-154.

Chamberlain, A. F. The language of the Mississagas of Skugog. Philadelphia, 1892. 84 p.

Chamberlain, A. F. The two brothers: a Mississagua legend. American Association for the Advancement of Science, Proceedings, 38 (1889): 353.

Chatfield, W. The Midewiwin songs of Fine-Day. South Dakota, University, William H. Over Museum, Museum News, 15, no. 10 (1954): 1-2.

Cleve, H., et al. Two genetic variants of the group-specific component of human serum: Gc Chippewa and Gc Aborigine. American Journal of Human Genetics, 15 (1963): 368-379.

Coatsworth, E. S. The Indians of Quetico. Toronto, 1956. 68 p.

Cocks, J. Fraser, III. George N. Smith: reformer on the frontier. Michigan History, 52 (1968): 37-49.

Coleman, B. Decorative designs of the Ojibwa of northern Minnesota. Catholic University of America, Anthropological Series, 12 (1947): 1-125.

Coleman, B. Religion and magic among the Cass Lake Ojibwa. Primitive Man, 2 (1929): 52-53.

Coleman, B. The Ojibwa and the wild rice problem. Anthropological Quarterly, 1 (1953): 79-88.

Coleman, B. The religion of the Ojibwa of northern Minnesota. Primitive Man, 10 (1937): 33-57.

Coleman, Bernard. Ojibwa myths and legends. By Sister Bernard Coleman, Ellen Frogner, and Estelle Eich. Minneapolis, Ross and Haines, 1962. 135 p. illus.

Coon, Carleton S. The hunting peoples. Boston, Little, Brown, 1971. 21, 413 p. illus., maps.

Cooper, J. M. Field notes on Northern Algonkian magic. International Congress of Americanists, Proceedings, 23 (1928): 513-518.

Cooper, J. M. Notes on the ethnology of the Otchipwe of the Lake of the Woods and of Rainy Lake. Catholic University of America, Anthropological Series, 3 (1936): 1-29.

Cooper, J. M. The shaking tent rite among Plains and Forest Algonquians. Primitive Man, 17 (1944): 60-84.

Copway, G. Indian life and Indian history. Boston, 1860. 266 p.

Copway, G. The life, letters and speeches of Kah-ge-ga-gah-bowh, 11-48. New York, 1850.

Copway, G. The traditional history and characteristic sketches of the Ojibway nation. London, 1850. 298 p.

Coues, E., ed. Manuscript journals of Alexander Henry and of David Thompson. New York, 1897. 3 v.

Crawford, Dean A., et al. Minnesota Chippewa Indians, a handbook for teachers. St. Paul, Upper Midwest Regional Education Laboratory, 1967. 114 p. ERIC ED017383.

Culkin, W. E. Tribal dance of the Ojibway Indians. Minnesota History Bulletin, 1 (1915): 83-93.

Cumming, John. A Puritan among the Chippewas. Michigan History, 51 (1967): 213-225.

Dailey, Robert C. The Midewiwin, Ontario's first medical society. Ontario History, 50 (1958): 133-138.

Dally, N. Tracks and trails. Walker, 1931. 138 p.

Davidson, J. F. Ojibwa songs. Journal of American Folklore, 58 (1945): 303-305.

Davidson, J. N. In unnamed Wisconsin. Milwaukee, 1895. 314 p.

Davis, Edward W. Seegwin; a legend of the fur trade. Minnesota History, 37 (1960/1961): 235-254.

De Geyndt, Willy. Health behavior and health needs of American Indians in Hennepin County. By Willy De Geyndt and Linda M. Sprague. Minneapolis, University of Minnesota, 1971. 67 p. ERIC ED052850.

Delisle, Gilles Louis. Universals and
person pronouns in Southwestern
Chippewa. Dissertation Abstracts
International, 33 (1972/1973): 5703A.
UM 73-10,541.

Delorme, D. P. Emancipation and the
Turtle Mountain Chippewas. American
Indian, 7, no. 1 (1954): 11-20.

Densmore, F. An Ojibwa prayer ceremony.
American Anthropologist, n.s., 9 (1907):
443-444.

*Densmore, F. Chippewa customs. U.S.
Bureau of American Ethnology, Bulletin,
86 (1929): 1-204.

Densmore, F. Chippewa music. U.S. Bureau
of American Ethnology, Bulletin, 45
(1910): 1-209.

Densmore, F. Chippewa music. U.S. Bureau
of American Ethnology, Bulletin, 53
(1913): 1-334.

Densmore, F. Material culture among the
Chippewa. Smithsonian Miscellaneous
Collections, 70, no. 2 (1919): 114-118.

Densmore, F. Music of the Winnebago,
Chippewa, and Pueblo Indians.
Smithsonian Institution, Explorations
and Field-Work (1930): 217-224.

Densmore, F. Poems from Sioux and
Chippewa songs. Washington, D.C., 1917.
23 p.

Densmore, F. Study of Chippewa material
culture. Smithsonian Miscellaneous
Collections, 68, no. 12 (1918): 95-100.

Densmore, F. The importance of the mental
concept in Indian art. Masterkey, 22
(1948): 86-99.

Densmore, F. The native art of the
Chippewa. American Anthropologist, n.s.,
43 (1941): 678-681.

Densmore, F. The rhythm of Sioux and
Chippewa music. Art and Archaeology, 9
(1920): 59-67.

Densmore, F. Uses of plants by the
Chippewa Indians. U.S. Bureau of
American Ethnology, Annual Reports, 44
(1927): 275-397.

Densmore, Frances. Chippewa music. New
York, Da Capo Press, 1972. 2 v. illus.

Dever, Harry. The Nicolet myth. Michigan
History, 50 (1966): 318-322.

Dewdney, Selwyn. Ecological notes on the
Ojibway shaman-artist. Artscanada, 27
(Aug. 1970): 17-28.

Dixon, Joseph M. Young Joe Dixon in the
Flathead Country. Edited by Jules
Alexander Karlin. Montana, the Magazine
of Western History, 17, no. 1 (1967):
12-19.

Doty, J. Northern Wisconsin in 1820.
State Historical Society of Wisconsin,
Collections, 7 (1876): 195-206.

Dougherty, P. A Chippewa primer. New
York, 1844. 84 p.

Dougherty, P. Ojibwa of Grand Traverse
Bay. In H. R. Schoolcraft, ed.
Information respecting the History,
Condition, and Prospects of the Indian
Tribes of the United States. Vol. 2.
Philadelphia, 1852: 458-469.

Douglas, F. H. The Ojibwa or Chippewa
Indians. Denver Art Museum, Indian
Leaflet Series, 36 (1931): 1-4.

Drier, Roy W. The Michigan College of
Mining and Technology Isle Royale
excavations, 1953-1954. In James B.
Griffin. Lake Superior Copper and the
Indians: Miscellaneous Studies of Great
Lakes Prehistory. Ann Arbor, University
of Michigan, 1961: 1-7. (Michigan,
University, Museum of Anthropology,
Anthropological Papers, 17)

Ducatel, J. J. A fortnight among the
Chippewas of Lake Superior. In W. W.
Beach, ed. Indian Miscellany. Albany,
1877: 361-378.

Duluth, Daniel Greysolon de. Capital
punishment in Michigan, 1683: Duluth at
Michilimackinac. Michigan History, 50
(1966): 349-360.

Duncan, K. J. Tom Pahbewash's visions.
Anthropologica, n.s., 6 (1964): 237-243.

Dunn, Marty. Red on White: the biography
of Duke Redbird. Toronto, New Press,
1971. 121 p. illus.

Dunning, R. W. Rules of residence and
ecology among the Northern Ojibwa.
American Anthropologist, 61 (1959): 806-
816.

*Dunning, R. W. Social and economic change
among the Northern Ojibwa. Toronto,
1959. 227 p.

Dunning, R. W. Some implications of
economic change in Northern Ojibwa
social structure. Canadian Journal of
Economics and Political Science, 24
(1958): 562-566.

Dunning, Robert W. Ethnic relations and
marginal man in Canada. Human
Organization, 18 (1959/1960): 117-122.

Dunning, Robert W. Some problems of reserve Indian communities: a case study. Anthropologica, n.s., 6 (1964): 3-38.

Eastman, C. A. Life and handicrafts of the Northern Ojibwas. Southern Workman, 40 (1911): 273-278.

Edmonson, Munro S. A measurement of relative racial difference. Current Anthropology, 6 (1965): 167-198. [With comments].

Eggan, Fred. Northern Woodland ethnology. In Jacob W. Gruber, ed. The Philadelphia Anthropological Society; Papers Presented on Its Golden Anniversary. New York, distributed by Columbia University Press for Temple University Publications, 1967: 107-124.

Eggleston, Edward. George W. Northrup: the Kit Carson of the Northwest; the-man-that-draws-the-handcart. Edited by Louis Pfaller. North Dakota History, 33 (1966): 4-21.

Elliott, R. R. The Chippewas and Ottawas. American Catholic Quarterly Review, 22 (1897): 18-46.

Elliott, R. R. The Chippewas of Lake Superior. American Catholic Quarterly Review, 21 (1896): 354-373.

Ellis, C. Douglas. The so-called interrogative in Cree. International Journal of American Linguistics, 27 (1961): 119-124.

Emmert, Darlene Gay. The Indians of Shiawassee County. Michigan History, 47 (1963): 127-155, 243-272.

Engelhardt, Z. Anishinabe Neganiod. Harbor Springs, Michigan, 1901.

Evatt, H. The red canoe. Indianapolis, 1940. 137 p.

Farrell, David. Settlement along the Detroit frontier, 1760-1796. Michigan History, 52 (1968): 89-107.

Fay, George E., ed. Charters, constitutions and by-laws of the Indian tribes of North America. Part II: The Indian tribes of Wisconsin (Great Lakes Agency). Greeley, 1967. 6, 124 l. illus., map. (University of Northern Colorado, Museum of Anthropology, Occasional Publications in Anthropology, Ethnology Series, 2) ERIC ED046552.

Fay, George E., ed. Charters, constitutions and by-laws of the Indian tribes of North America. Part XIV: Great Lakes Agency: Minnesota-Michigan.

Greeley, 1972. 4, 84 l. map. (University of Northern Colorado, Museum of Anthropology, Occasional Publications in Anthropology, Ethnology Series, 15)

Fay, George E., ed. Charters, constitutions and by-laws of the Indian tribes of North America. Part IIa: The Northern Plains. Greeley, 1967. 6, 141 l. maps. (University of Northern Colorado, Museum of Anthropology, Occasional Publications in Anthropology, Ethnology Series, 3) ERIC ED051923.

Fay, George E., ed. Charters, constitutions and by-laws of the Indian tribes of Wisconsin. Wisconsin Indians Research Institute, Journal, 3, no. 1 (1967): 1-124.

Fay, George E., ed. Treaties between the Menominee Indians and the United States of America, 1817-1856. Wisconsin Indians Research Institute, Journal, 1, no. 1 (1965): 67-104.

Federal Writers' Projects. Wisconsin Indian place legends, 26-27, 40-50. Milwaukee, 1936.

Fiero, Charles. Ojibwa language course. Red Lake, Ont., Northern Light Gospel Mission, 1965.

Fiero, Charles E. Ojibwa assimilation. Freeport, Pa., Fountain Press, 1967.

Fiero, Charles E. Ojibwa assimilation. Red Lake, Ontario, 1964. 47 p.

Fitting, James E. Settlement analysis in the Great Lakes region. Southwestern Journal of Anthropology, 25 (1969): 360-377.

Flanagan, John T., ed. From La Pointe to the Falls of St. Anthony in 1846. Minnesota History, 41 (1968/1969): 137-144.

Flannery, R. The cultural position of the Spanish River Indians. Primitive Man, 13 (1940): 1-25.

Foster, John E. Missionaries, mixed-bloods and the fur trade: four letters of the Rev. William Cockran, Red River Settlement, 1830-1833. Western Canadian Journal of Anthropology, 3, no. 1 (1972): 94-125.

Foster, John E. Program for the Red River Mission: the Anglican clergy 1820-1826. Histoire Sociale, 4 (1969): 49-75.

Friedl, E. A note on birchbark transparencies. American Anthropologist, n.s., 46 (1944): 149-150.

Friedl, E.   Persistence in Chippewa culture and personality. American Anthropologist, 58 (1956): 814-825.

Fruth, Alban.   A century of missionary work among the Red Lake Chippewa Indians 1858-1958.   Redlake, Minn., St. Mary's Mission, 1958.   5, 127 p.

Furlan, William P.   In charity unfeigned; the life of Father Francis Xavier Pierz. St. Cloud, Diocese of St. Cloud, 1952. 10, 270 p.

Galbraith, John S.   British-American competition in the border fur trade of the 1820s. Minnesota History, 36 (1958/1959): 241-249.

Gates, R. R.   Pedigree study of Amerindian crosses in Canada. Royal Anthropological Institute of Great Britain and Ireland, Journal, 58 (1928): 511-532.

Gilfillan, J. A.   Ojibwa characteristics. Southern Workman, 31 (1902): 260-262.

Gilfillan, J. A.   The Ojibways of Minnesota. Minnesota Historical Society, Collections, 9 (1901): 55-128.

Gillin, J.   Acquired drives in culture contact. American Anthropologist, n.s., 44 (1942): 545-554.

Gillin, J. and V. Raimy.   Acculturation and personality. American Sociological Review, 5 (1940): 371-380.

Gilman, Rhoda R.   Last days of the Upper Mississippi fur trade. Minnesota History, 42 (1970/1971): 123-140.

Gilmore, M. R.   Some Chippewa uses of plants. Michigan Academy of Science, Arts and Letters, Papers, 17 (1933): 119-143.

Godsell, P. H.   The Ojibwa Indian. Canadian Geological Journal, 4 (1932): 51-66.

Gordon, John M.   Michigan journal, 1836. Edited by Douglas H. Gordon and George S. May. Michigan History, 43 (1959): 10-42, 129-149, 257-293, 433-478.

Gould, John.   Portfolio from Pikangikum. Beaver, 299, no. 4 (1968/1969): 34-39.

Gower, Calvin W.   The CCC Indian division: aid for depressed Americans, 1933-1942. Minnesota History, 43, no. 1 (1972): 3-13.

Grant, J. C. B.   Anthropometry of the Cree and Saulteaux Indians in northeastern Manitoba. Canada, Department of Mines,

National Museum of Canada, Bulletin, 59 (1929): 1-73.

Grant, J. C. B.   Anthropometry of the Lake Winnipeg Indians. American Journal of Physical Anthropology, 7 (1924): 299-315.

Grant, P.   The Sauteux Indians. In L. F. R. Masson, ed. Les Bourgeois de la Compagnie du Nord-Ouest. Vol. 2. Quebec, 1890: 303-366.

Greenlees, S.   Indian canoe makers. Beaver, 285, no. 1 (1954): 46-49.

Greenman, E. F.   Chieftainship among Michigan Indians. Michigan History Magazine, 24 (1940): 361-379.

Grewe, John M., et al.   Prevalence of malocclusion in Chippewa Indian children. Journal of Dental Research, 47 (1968): 302-305.

Gringhauis, Richard H.   Lore of the Great Turtle; Indian legends of Mackinac retold.   Mackinac Island, Mackinac Island State Park Commission, 1970.   5, 89 p.   illus.

Hady, Walter M.   Indian migrations in Manitoba and the West. Historical and Scientific Society of Manitoba, Papers, ser. 3, 17 (1960/1961): 24-53.

Hall, G. L.   Me papoose sitter.   New York, 1955.   243 p.

Hallowell, A. I.   Acculturation processes and personality changes as indicated by the Rorschach technique. Rorschach Research Exchange, 6 (1942): 42-50.

Hallowell, A. I.   Aggression in Saulteaux society. Psychiatry, 3 (1940): 395-407.

Hallowell, A. I.   Concordance of Ojibwa narratives in the published works of Henry R. Schoolcraft. Journal of American Folklore, 59 (1946): 136-153.

Hallowell, A. I.   Cross-cousin marriage in the Lake Winnipeg area. Philadelphia Anthropological Society, Publications, 1 (1937): 95-110.

*Hallowell, A. I.   Culture and experience. Philadelphia, 1955.   450 p.

Hallowell, A. I.   Culture and mental disorder. Journal of Abnormal and Social Psychology, 29 (1934): 1-9.

Hallowell, A. I.   Fear and anxiety as cultural and individual variables in a primitive society. Journal of Social Psychology, 9 (1938): 25-47.

Hallowell, A. I. Freudian symbolism in the dream of a Saulteaux Indian. Man, 38 (1938): 47-48.

Hallowell, A. I. Magic: the role of conjuring in Saulteaux society. In M. A. May, ed. Papers Presented before the Monday Night Group, 1939-40. New Haven, 1940: 94-115.

Hallowell, A. I. Myth, culture and personality. American Anthropologist, n.s., 49 (1947): 544-556.

Hallowell, A. I. Notes on the material culture of the Island Lake Saulteaux. Société des Américanistes, Journal, n.s., 30 (1938): 129-140.

Hallowell, A. I. Notes on the northern range of Zizania in Manitoba. Rhodora, 37 (1935): 302-304.

Hallowell, A. I. Ojibwa personality and acculturation. International Congress of Americanists, Proceedings, 29, vol. 2 (1952): 105-112.

Hallowell, A. I. Pagan tribe in Ontario. El Palacio, 33 (1932): 204-205.

Hallowell, A. I. "Popular" responses and cultural differences. Rorschach Research Exchange, 9 (1945): 153-168.

Hallowell, A. I. Psychic stresses and culture patterns. American Journal of Psychiatry, 92 (1936): 1291-1310.

Hallowell, A. I. Shabwan: a dissocial Indian girl. American Journal of Orthopsychiatry, 8 (1938): 329-340.

Hallowell, A. I. Sin, sex and sickness in Saulteaux belief. British Journal of Medical Psychology, 18 (1939): 191-197.

Hallowell, A. I. Some empirical aspects of Northern Saulteaux religion. American Anthropologist, n.s., 36 (1934): 389-404.

Hallowell, A. I. Some European folktales of the Berens River Saulteaux. Journal of American Folklore, 52 (1939): 155-179.

Hallowell, A. I. Some psychological aspects of measurement among the Saulteaux. American Anthropologist, n.s., 44 (1942): 62-77.

Hallowell, A. I. Temporal orientation in Western civilization and in a preliterate society. American Anthropologist, n.s., 39 (1937): 647-670.

Hallowell, A. I. The incidence, character, and decline of polygyny among the Lake Winnipeg Cree and Saulteaux. American Anthropologist, n.s., 40 (1938): 235-256.

Hallowell, A. I. The passing of the Midewiwin in the Lake Winnipeg region. American Anthropologist, n.s., 38 (1928): 32-51.

Hallowell, A. I. The role of conjuring in Saulteaux society. Philadelphia Anthropological Society, Publications, 2 (1942): 1-96.

Hallowell, A. I. The Rorschach method as an aid in the study of personalities in primitive society. Character and Personality, 9 (1941): 235-245.

Hallowell, A. I. The Rorschach technique in the study of personality and culture. American Anthropologist, n.s., 47 (1945): 195-210.

Hallowell, A. I. The social function of anxiety in a primitive society. American Sociological Review, 6 (1941): 869-881.

Hallowell, A. I. The spirits of the dead in Saulteaux life and thought. Royal Anthropological Institute of Great Britain and Ireland, Journal, 70 (1940): 29-51.

Hallowell, A. I. The use of projective techniques in the study of the socio-psychological aspects of acculturation. Journal of Projective Techniques, 15 (1951): 27-44.

Hallowell, A. I. Values, acculturation and mental health. American Journal of Orthopsychiatry, 20 (1950): 732-743.

Hallowell, A. I. Was cross-cousin marriage practised by the North-Central Algonkian? International Congress of Americanists, Proceedings, 23 (1928): 519-544.

*Hallowell, A. Irving. Culture and experience. New York, Schocken Books, 1967. 14, 434 p. map.

Hallowell, A. Irving. Intelligence of Northeastern Indians. In Robert Hunt, ed. Personalities and Cultures. Garden City, Natural History Press, 1967: 49-55.

Hallowell, A. Irving. Ojibwa ontology, behavior, and world view. In Stanley Diamond, ed. Primitive Views of the World. New York, Columbia University Press, 1964: 49-82.

Hallowell, A. Irving. Ojibwa ontology, behavior, and world view. In Stanley Diamond, ed. Culture in History. New York, Columbia University Press, 1960: 19-52.

Hallowell, A. Irving. Ojibwa personality and acculturation. In Paul Bohannan and Fred Plog, eds. Beyond the Frontier. Garden City, Natural History Press, 1967: 227-237.

Hallowell, A. Irving. Ojibwa world view and disease. In Iago Galdston, ed. Man's Image in Medicine and Anthropology. New York, International Universities Press, 1963: 258-315.

Hallowell, A. Irving. On being an anthropologist. In Solon T. Kimball and James B. Watson, eds. Crossing Cultural Boundaries. San Francisco, Chandler, 1972: 51-62.

Hallowell, A. Irving. The role of conjuring in Saulteaux society. New York, Octagon Books, 1971. 14, 96 p. illus.

Hallowell, A. Irving. The role of dreams in Ojibwa culture. In Gustav E. von Grunebaum and Roger Caillois, eds. The Dream and Human Societies. Berkeley, University of California Press, 1966: 267-292.

Hallowell, A. Irving. Values, acculturation and mental health. In Deward E. Walker, Jr., ed. The Emergent Native Americans. Boston, Little, Brown, 1972: 584-594.

Hamilton, J. C. The Algonquin Manabozho and Hiawatha. Journal of American Folklore, 15 (1903): 229-233.

Hamilton, Raphael. The Marquette death site: the case for Ludington. Michigan History, 49 (1965): 228-248.

Hamilton, Raphael N. Jesuit mission at Sault Ste. Marie. Michigan History, 52 (1968): 123-132.

Hammond, J. H. The Ojibway of Lakes Huron and Simcoe. Annual Archaeological Report, being Part of Appendix to the Report of the Minister of Education, Ontario (1904): 71-73.

Hamp, Eric P. Assimilation and rule application. Language, 43 (1967): 179-184.

Hannin, Daniel. Selected factors associated with the participation of adult Ojibway Indians in formal voluntary organizations. Dissertation

Abstracts, 28 (1967/1968): 4717A. UM 67-16,954.

Hanzeli, Victor E. Missionary linguistics in New France; a study of seventeenth- and eighteenth-century descriptions of American Indian languages. The Hague, Mouton, 1969. 141 p. illus., map. (Janua Linguarum, Series Maior, 29)

Hanzeli, Victor E. The Algonquin R-dialect in historical records. In International Congress of Linguists, 10th. 1967, Bucarest. Proceedings. Vol. 2. Bucarest, Éditions de l'Académie de la République Socialiste de Roumanie, 1970: 85-89.

Harkins, Arthur M. Attitudes and characteristics of selected Wisconsin Indians. By Arthur M. Harkins and Richard G. Woods. Wisconsin Indians Research Institute, Journal, 4, no. 1 (1968): 64-130.

Harkins, Arthur M. Attitudes and characteristics of selected Wisconsin Indians. By Arthur M. Harkins and Richard G. Woods. Minneapolis, University of Minnesota, Training Center for Community Programs, 1969. 89 p. ERIC ED032174.

Harkins, Arthur M. Attitudes of Minneapolis agency personnel toward urban Indians. By Arthur M. Harkins and Richard G. Woods. Minneapolis, University of Minnesota, Training Center for Community Programs, 1968. 87 p. ERIC ED030515.

Harkins, Arthur M. Chippewa children at the primary level. Journal of American Indian Education, 8, no. 1 (1968/1969): 17-25.

Harkins, Arthur M. Education-related preferences and characteristics of college-aspiring urban Indian teenagers: a preliminary report. By Arthur M. Harkins and Richard G. Woods. Minneapolis, University of Minnesota, Training Center for Community Programs, 1969. 32 p. ERIC ED030514.

Harkins, Arthur M. Public education on a Minnesota Chippewa reservation. Final report. Lawrence, Kansas University, 1968. 6 v. (641 p.) (U.S., Office of Education, Bureau of Research, Bureau, BR-7-8138) ERIC ED025338.

Harkins, Arthur M. Public education on a Minnesota Chippewa reservation. Dissertation Abstracts International, 30 (1969/1970): 846A. UM 69-11,219.

Harmon, D. W. A journal of voyages and travels in the interior of North

America. Ed. by W. L. Grant. Toronto,
1911. 269-334.

Harrington, M. R. You can't rush an
Indian. Masterkey, 27, no. 1 (1953): 29-
30.

Harstad, Peter T. Disease and sickness on
the Wisconsin frontier: smallpox and
other diseases. Wisconsin Magazine of
History, 43 (1959): 253-263.

Hart, I. H. The story of Beengwa.
Minnesota History, 9 (1928): 319-330.

Hasketh, J. History of the Turtle
Mountain Chippewa. North Dakota State
Historical Society Collections, 5
(1923): 85-124.

Hay, Thomas H. The windigo psychosis:
psychodynamic, cultural, and social
factors in aberrant behavior. American
Anthropologist, 73 (1971): 1-19.

Hay, Thomas Hamilton. Ojibwa emotional
restraint and the socialization process.
Dissertation Abstracts, 29 (1968/1969):
1912B. UM 68-17,091.

Henry, A. Travels and adventures in
Canada. Ed. by M. M. Quaife. Chicago,
1921. 340 p.

Henry, Alexander. Travels and adventures
in Canada and the Indian territories,
between the years 1760 and 1776. Edited
by James Bain. Edmonton, M. C. Hurtig,
1969. 46, 347 p. illus., maps.

Henry, Alexander. Travels and adventures
in Canada and the Indian territories,
between the years 1760 and 1776. New ed.
New York, B. Franklin, 1969. 33,
347 p. illus., maps.

Henry, George, tr. Nu-gu-mo-nun O-je-boa
an-oad ge-ë-se-üu-ne-gu-noo-du-be-üng.
Translated by George Henry and James
Evans. New York, D. Fanshaw, 1837.
392 p.

Hickerson, H. The genesis of a trading
post band: the Pembina Chippewa.
Ethnohistory, 3 (1956): 289-345.

Hickerson, H., ed. Journal of Charles
Jean Baptiste Chaboillez, 1797-1798.
Ethnohistory, 6 (1959): 265-320, 363-
427.

Hickerson, Harold. Land tenure of the
Rainy Lake Chippewa at the beginning of
the 19th century. Washington, D.C.,
Smithsonian Press, 1967. 4, 41-63 p.
map. (Smithsonian Contributions to
Anthropology, 2, no. 4)

Hickerson, Harold. Notes on the post-
contact origin of the Midewiwin.
Ethnohistory, 9 (1962): 404-423.

Hickerson, Harold. Some implications of
the theory of the particularity, or
"atomism," of Northern Algonkians.
Current Anthropology, 8 (1967): 313-345.
[With comments].

Hickerson, Harold. The Chippewa and their
neighbors: a study in ethnohistory. New
York, Holt, Rinehart and Winston, 1970.
10, 133 p. illus., maps.

Hickerson, Harold. The Chippewa of the
Upper Great Lakes: a study in
sociopolitical change. In Eleanor Burke
Leacock and Nancy Oestreich Lurie, eds.
North American Indians in Historical
Perspective. New York, Random House,
1971: 169-199.

Hickerson, Harold. The Feast of the Dead
among the seventeenth century Algonkians
of the Upper Great Lakes. American
Anthropologist, 62 (1960): 81-107.

Hickerson, Harold. The genesis of a
trading post band: the Pembina Chippewa.
In Deward E. Walker, Jr., ed. The
Emergent Native Americans. Boston,
Little, Brown, 1972: 270-300.

Hickerson, Harold. The genesis of
bilaterality among two divisions of
Chippewa. American Anthropologist, 68
(1966): 1-26.

Hickerson, Harold. The sociohistorical
significance of two Chippewa
ceremonials. American Anthropologist, 65
(1963): 67-85.

Hickerson, Harold. The Southwestern
Chippewa: an ethnohistorical study.
Menasha, American Anthropological
Association, 1962. 6, 110 p. maps.
(American Anthropological Association,
Memoir, 92)

Hickerson, Harold. William T. Boutwell of
the American Board and the Pillager
Chippewa: the history of a failure.
Ethnohistory, 12 (1965): 1-29.

Hickerson, Harold E. The Virginia deer
and intertribal buffer zones in the
Upper Mississippi Valley. In Anthony
Leeds and Andrew P. Vayda, eds. Man,
Culture, and Animals. Washington, D.C.,
1965: 43-65. (American Association for
the Advancement of Science, Publication,
78)

Hildebrand, Carol L. Maternal-child care
among the Chippewa: a study of the past
and the present. Military Medicine, 135
(1970): 35-43.

*Hilger, I. Chippewa child life and its cultural background. U.S. Bureau of American Ethnology, Bulletin, 146 (1951): 1-218.

Hilger, M. I. A social study of one hundred fifty Chippewa Indian families. Washington, D.C., 1939. 251 p.

Hilger, M. I. Ceremonia para dar nombre a un niño chippewa. Sociedad de Geografía e Historia, Anales, 22 (1947): 166-171.

Hilger, M. I. Ceremonia para dar nombre a un niño indio chippewa. América Indígena, 4 (1944): 237-242.

Hilger, M. I. Chippewa burial and mourning customs. American Anthropologist, n.s., 46 (1944): 564-568.

Hilger, M. I. Chippewa customs. Primitive Man, 9 (1936): 17-24.

Hilger, M. I. Chippewa hunting and fishing customs. Minnesota Conservationist, no. 2/3 (April 1936): 17-19.

Hilger, M. I. Chippewa interpretations of natural phenomena. Scientific Monthly, 45 (1937): 178-179.

Hilger, M. I. Chippewa pre-natal food and conduct taboos. Primitive Man, 9 (1936): 46-48.

Hilger, M. I. In the early days of Wisconsin. Wisconsin Archeologist, n.s., 16 (1936): 32-49.

Hilger, M. I. Indian women making birch-bark receptacles. Indians at Work, 3, no. 3 (1935): 19-21.

Hilger, M. I. Indian women preparing bulrush mats. Indians at Work, 2, no. 2 (1935): 41.

Hilger, M. I. Letters and documents of Bishop Baraga extant in the Chippewa country. American Catholic Historical Society of Philadelphia, Records, 47 (1936): 292-302.

Hilger, M. I. Naming a Chippewa Indian child. Wisconsin Archeologist, 39 (1958): 120-126.

Hilger, M. I. Some phases of Chippewa material culture. Anthropos, 32 (1937): 780-782.

Hilger, M. Inez. Some customs of the Chippewa on the Turtle Mountain Reservation of North Dakota. North Dakota History, 26 (1959): 123-132.

Hill, H. C., ed. A dictionary of the Chippewa Indian language. Flint, 1943. 16 p.

Hind, H. Y. Narrative of the Canadian Red River Exploring Expedition. London, 1860. 2 v.

Hind, H. Y. North-West Territory. Toronto, 1859. 201 p.

Hind, Henry Youle. Narrative of the Canadian Red River exploring expedition of 1857 and of the Assiniboine and Saskatchewan exploring expedition of 1858. Rutland, Vt., Tuttle, 1971. illus.

Hindley, J. I. Indian legends. Barrie, Ontario, 1885. 22 p.

Hockett, C. F. The conjunct modes in Ojibwa and Potawatomi. Language, 26 (1950): 278-282.

Hockett, Charles F. What Algonquian is really like. International Journal of American Linguistics, 32 (1966): 59-73.

Hoffman, W. J. Notes on Ojibwa folk-lore. American Anthropologist, 2 (1889): 215-223.

Hoffman, W. J. Pictography and shamanistic rites of the Ojibwa. American Anthropologist, 1 (1888): 209-229.

Hoffman, W. J. Remarks on Ojibwa ball play. American Anthropologist, 3 (1890): 133-135.

Hoffman, W. J. The Midewiwin or "Grand Medicine Society" of the Ojibwa. U.S. Bureau of American Ethnology, Annual Reports, 7 (1886): 143-300.

Hofstrand, Richard H. Wild ricing. Natural History, 79, no. 3 (1970): 50-55.

Holbert, Victoria L., et al. Indian Americans at Mille Lacs. Minneapolis, University of Minnesota, Training Center for Community Programs, 1970. 44 p. ERIC ED044194.

*Holmer, N. M. The Ojibway on Walpole Island, Ontario. Uppsala Canadian Studies, 4 (1954): 1-91.

Honigmann, J. J. Attawapiskat-blend of traditions. Anthropologica, 6 (1957): 57-68.

Horsman, Reginald. Wisconsin and the War of 1812. Wisconsin Magazine of History, 46 (1962): 3-15.

Houghton, F. The Indian occupancy of the Niagara Frontier. Buffalo Society of Natural Sciences, Bulletin, 9 (1909): 263-374.

Houston, James A. Ojibwa summer. Barre, Mass., Barre Publishers, 1972. 96 p. illus.

Howard, J. H. The sun dance of the Turtle Mountain Ojibwa. North Dakota Historical Quarterly, 19 (1952): 249-264.

Howard, James H. The Henry Davis drum rite: an unusual drum religion variant of the Minnesota Ojibwa. Plains Anthropologist, 11 (1966): 117-126.

Howard, James H. The identity and demography of the Plains-Ojibwa. Plains Anthropologist, 6 (1961): 171-178.

Howard, James H. The identity and demography of the Plains-Ojibwa. Hamburg, Völkerkundliche Arbeitsgemeinschaft, Nachrichtenblatt, 4 (1963): 91-100.

*Howard, James H. The Plains-Ojibwa or Bungi, hunters and warriors of the northern prairie, with special reference to the Turtle Mountain Band. Vermillion, 1965. 5, 165 p. illus. (South Dakota, University, South Dakota Museum, Anthropological Papers, 1)

*Howard, James H. The Plains-Ojibwa or Bungi, hunters and warriors of the northern prairies with special reference to the Turtle Mountain Band. South Dakota, University, Museum, Museum News, 24, nos. 11/12 (1963): 1-18; 25, nos. 1/2 (1964): 2-24; 25, nos. 3/4 (1964): 2-28; 25, nos. 5/6 (1964): 2-24; 25, nos. 7/8 (1964): 2-15; 25, nos. 9/10 (1964): 2-15; 25, nos. 11/12 (1964): 1-22; 26, nos. 1/2 (1965): 1-26.

Howard, James H. The Turtle Mountain 'Chippewa'. North Dakota Quarterly, 26, no. 2 (1958): 37-46.

Howard, James H. Two war bundles from the Bungi or Plains-Ojibwa. American Indian Tradition, 8, no. 2 (1962): 77-79.

Hrdlička, A. Anthropological work among the Sioux and Chippewa. Smithsonian Miscellaneous Collections, 46, no. 17 (1917): 92-99.

Hrdlička, A. Anthropology of the Chippewa. In Holmes Anniversary Volume. Washington, D.C., 1916: 198-227.

Hrdlička, A. Trip to the Chippewa Indians of Minnesota. Smithsonian Miscellaneous Collections, 66, no. 3 (1916): 71-75.

Hudson's Bay Company. Saskatchewan journals and correspondence: Edmonton House 1795-1800; Chesterfield House 1800-1802. Edited by Alice M. Johnson. London, 1967. 102, 368, 14 p. map. (Hudson's Bay Record Society, Publications, 26)

Hugolin. L'idée spiritualiste et l'idée morale chez les Chippewas. International Congress of Americanists, Proceedings, 15, vol. 1 (1906): 329-335.

Hurlburt, T. A memoir on the inflections of the Chippewa tongue. In H. R. Schoolcraft, ed. Information respecting the History, Condition, and Prospects of the Indian Tribes of the United States. Vol. 4. Philadelphia, 1854: 385-396.

Hurt, Wesley R. Factors in the persistence of peyote in the Northern Plains. Plains Anthropologist, 5 (1960): 16-27.

Hymes, Dell H. Some North Pacific Coast poems: a problem in anthropological philology. American Anthropologist, 67 (1965): 316-341.

James, Bernard J. Continuity and emergence in Indian poverty culture. Current Anthropology, 11 (1970): 435-452. [With comments].

James, Bernard J. Social-psychological dimensions of Ojibwa acculturation. American Anthropologist, 63 (1961): 721-746.

James, E., ed. A narrative of the captivity and adventures of John Tanner. New York, 1830. 426 p.

Jenks, A. E. Indian-White amalgamation. Minnesota, University, Studies in the Social Sciences, 6 (1916): 1-24.

Jenks, A. E. The bear-maiden. Journal of American Folklore, 15 (1902): 33-35.

Jenks, A. E. The childhood of Ji-shib, the Ojibwa. Madison, 1900.

Jenks, A. E. The wild rice gatherers of the Upper Lakes. U.S. Bureau of American Ethnology, Annual Reports, 19, (1898): 1013-1137.

*Jenness, D. The Ojibwa Indians of Parry Island. Canada, Department of Mines, National Museum of Canada, Bulletin, 78 (1935): 1-115.

Joblin, E. E. M. The education of the Indians of western Ontario. Ontario, College of Education, Department of Educational Research, Bulletin, 13 (1948): 1-138.

Johnson, F.   Notes on the Ojibwa and Potawatomi of the Parry Island Reservation. Indian Notes, 6 (1929): 193-216.

Johnson, Roy P.   Fur trader Chaboillez at Pembina. North Dakota History, 32 (1965): 83-99.

Johnston, G.   Ojibwa of St. Mary's. In H. R. Schoolcraft, ed. Information respecting the History, Condition, and Prospects of the Indian Tribes of the United States. Vol. 2.   Philadelphia, 1852: 458-469.

Jones, J. A.   The political organization of the Three Fires. Indiana Academy of Science, Proceedings, 63 (1953): 46.

Jones, P.   History of the Ojebway Indians. London, 1861.   278 p.

Jones, P.   Life and journals of Kah-ke-wa-quo-na-by.   Toronto, 1860.   435 p.

Jones, Peter.   History of the Ojebway Indians, with especial reference to their conversion to Christianity. Freeport, N.Y., Books for Libraries Press, 1970.   6, 278 p.   illus.

Jones, V. H.   A Chippewa method of manufacturing wooden brooms. Michigan Academy of Science, Arts and Letters, Papers, 20 (1934): 23-30.

Jones, V. H.   Notes on the manufacture of cedar-bark mats by the Chippewa Indians. Michigan Academy of Science, Arts and Letters, Papers, 32 (1946): 341-363.

Jones, V. H.   Notes on the preparation and the uses of basswood fiber by the Indians of the Great Lakes region. Michigan Academy of Science, Arts and Letters, Papers, 22 (1936): 1-14.

Jones, V. H.   Some Chippewa and Ottawa uses of sweet grass. Michigan Academy of Science, Arts and Letters, Papers, 21 (1935): 21-31.

Jones, W.   Central Algonkin. Annual Archaeological Report, being Part of Appendix to the Report of the Minister of Education, Ontario (1905): 136-146.

Jones, W.   Ojibwa tales from north shore of Lake Superior. Journal of American Folklore, 29 (1916): 368-391.

Jones, W.   Ojibwa texts. American Ethnological Society, Publications, 7, no. 1 (1917): 1-501; 7, no. 2 (1919): 1-771.

Josselin de Jong, J. P. B. de.   A few Otchipwe-Songs. Internationales Archiv für Ethnographie, 20 (1912): 189-190.

Josselin de Jong, J. P. B. de.   Original Odzibwe-texts. Baessler-Archiv, Beiheft 5 (1913): 1-54.

Keating, W. H.   Narrative of an expedition to the source of St. Peter's River, Vol. 2: 151-173.   Philadelphia, 1824.

Keller, R. H., Jr.   On teaching Indian history: legal jurisdiction in Chippewa treaties. Ethnohistory, 19 (1972): 209-218.

Kerckhoff, Alan C.   Anomie and achievement motivation: a study of personality development within cultural disorganization. Social Forces, 37 (1959): 196-202.

Kidd, K. E.   Burial of an Ojibwa chief, Muskoka District, Ontario. Pennsylvania Archaeologist, 21, no. 1/2 (1951): 3-8, 31-32.

King, Cheryl Mills.   Ojibwa Indian legends.   Marquette, Northern Michigan University Press, 1972.   20 p.   illus.

Kinietz, W. V.   Birch bark records among the Chippewa. Indiana Academy of Science, Proceedings, 49 (1940): 38-40.

*Kinietz, W. V.   Chippewa village. Cranbrook Institute of Science, Bulletin, 25 (1947): 1-259.

Kinietz, W. V.   The Indian tribes of the western Great Lakes. Michigan University, Museum of Anthropology, Occasional Contributions, 10 (1940): 317-329.

Kinietz, W. V. and V. H. Jones.   Notes on the manufacture of rush mats among the Chippewa. Michigan Academy of Science, Arts and Letters, Papers, 27 (1941): 525-537.

Koeninger, R. C.   An experiment in intercultural education. Michigan Academy of Science, Arts and Letters, Papers, 33 (1947): 407-412.

Kohl, J. G.   Kitchi-Gami.   London, 1860.   428 p.

Kohl, J. G.   Kitchi-Gami.   Minneapolis, 1956.   451 p.

Kohl, J. G.   Kitschi-Gami.   Bremen, 1859.   2 v.

Kohl, Johann Georg.   Kitschi-Gami; oder, Erzählungen vom Obern See.   Graz,

Akademische Druck- und Verlagsanstalt, 1970.

Kroska, Rita A. Comparative appraisal of bone, fat, and muscle development of Minnesota White and Indian school children. Minnesota Academy of Sciences, Journal, 35 (1968): 52-56.

Kroska, Rita Caroline Ann. Comparative physical growth study of Minnesota White and Indian children age 6 through 12 years: appraisal of leanness-fatness. Dissertation Abstracts, 27 (1966/1967): 1023B-1024B. UM 66-9610.

Kurath, G. P. Chippewa sacred songs in religious metamorphosis. Scientific Monthly, 79 (1954): 311-317.

Kurath, G. P. Wild rice gatherers of today. American Anthropologist, 59 (1957): 713.

Lafleur, L. J. On the Midé of the Ojibway. American Anthropologist, n.s., 42 (1940): 705-707.

Lagasse, Jean H. Community development in Manitoba. Human Organization, 20 (1961/1962): 232-237.

Laidlaw, G. E. Ojibwa myths and tales. Annual Archaeological Report, being Part of Appendix to the Report of the Minister of Education, Ontario (1914): 77-79; (1915): 71-90; (1916): 84-92; (1918): 74-110; (1920): 66-85; (1921/1922): 84-99; (1924/1925): 34-80.

Laidlaw, G. E. Ojibway myths and tales. Wisconsin Archeologist, n.s., 1 (1922): 28-38.

Lambert, Bernard. Mission priorities: Indians or miners? Michigan History, 51 (1967): 323-334.

*Landes, R. Ojibwa sociology. Columbia University Contributions to Anthropology, 29 (1937): 1-144.

Landes, R. The abnormal among the Ojibwa. Journal of Abnormal and Social Psychology, 33 (1938): 14-33.

Landes, R. The Ojibwa of Canada. In M. Mead, ed. Cooperation and Competition among Primitive Peoples. New York, 1937: 87-126.

*Landes, R. The Ojibwa woman. Columbia University Contributions to Anthropology, 31 (1938): 1-247.

Landes, R. The personality of the Ojibwa. Character and Personality, 6 (1937): 51-60.

Landes, Ruth. Ojibwa religion and the Midéwiwin. Madison, University of Wisconsin Press, 1968. 8, 250 p. illus.

*Landes, Ruth. Ojibwa sociology. New York, AMS Press, 1969. 144 p. illus.

*Landes, Ruth. The Ojibwa woman. New York, AMS Press, 1969. 8, 247 p.

Lathrop, S. E. A historical sketch of the old mission. Ashland, Wisconsin, 1905.

Layrisse, Miguel. The Diego system--steps in the investigation of a new blood group system. Further studies. By Miguel Layrisse and Tulio Arends. Blood, 12 (1957): 115-122.

League of Women Voters of Minnesota. Indians in Minnesota. 2d ed. St. Paul, 1971. 165 p. illus., maps.

Leekley, Thomas B. The world of Manabozho. New York, Vanguard Press, 1965. 128 p. illus.

Leitch, A. Porcupine crafts. Canadian Geographical Journal, 51 (1955): 128-129.

Levi, M. C. Chippewa Indians of yesterday and today. New York, 1956. 385 p.

Lieberman, Leonard. Labor force mobility in the underclass: opportunities, subculture and training among Chippewa and poor White. Dissertation Abstracts International, 31 (1970/1971): 2514A-2515A. UM 70-20,488.

Lincoln, J. S. The dream in primitive cultures. London, 1935. 359 p.

Linderman, F. B. Indian old-man stories. New York, 1920. 169 p.

Linderman, F. B. Indian why stories. New York, 1915. 236 p.

Lips, E. Das Indianerbuch. Leipzig, 1956. 443 p.

*Lips, E. Die Reisernte der Ojibwa-Indianer. Berlin, 1956. 406 p.

Lips, E. Wanderungen und Wirtschaftsformen der Ojibwa-Indianer. Leipzig, Universität, Wissenschaftliche Zeitschrift, Gesellschafts- und Sprachwissenschaftliche Reihe, 1 (1951/1952): 1-38.

Lips, E. Zizania Aquatica als bestimmender Faktor im Leben der Ojibwa-Indianer von Nett Lake (Minnesota). In Huitième Congrès Internationale de Botanique, Rapports et Communications parvenus avant le Congrès au Sections 14, 15 et 16.   Paris, 1954: 45-49.

Lips, J. E.   Notes on some Ojibway-traps. Ethnos, 2 (1937): 354-360.

Lloyd, T.   Wild rice in Canada. Canadian Geographical Journal, 19 (1939): 288-300.

Long, J. K.   Voyages and travels of an Indian interpreter and trader. Ed. by M. M. Quaife.   Chicago, 1922.   238 p.

Long, John.   Voyages and travels of an Indian trader.   Toronto, Coles, 1971. 10, 295 p.   map.

Lowie, R. H.   Ojibwa. In J. Hastings, ed. Encyclopaedia of Religion and Ethics. Vol. 9.   New York, 1917: 454-458.

Lugthart, Douglas W.   The Burnt Bluff rock paintings. In James E. Fitting, ed. The Prehistory of the Burnt Bluff Area.   Ann Arbor, University of Michigan, 1968: 98-115.   (Michigan, University, Museum of Anthropology, Anthropological Papers, 34)

Lurie, Nancy Oestreich.   Comments on Bernard J. James's analysis of Ojibwa acculturation. American Anthropologist, 64 (1962): 826-833.

Lurie, Nancy Oestreich.   Wisconsin: a natural laboratory for North American Indian studies. Wisconsin Magazine of History, 53 (1969/1970): 3-20.

Lyford, C. A.   The crafts of the Ojibwa. Indian Handcrafts, 5 (1943): 1-216.

MacDonald, R. A.   Poliomyelitis epidemic on a Minnesota Indian reservation. Minnesota Medicine, 43 (1960): 842-844.

Macfie, John.   Ojibwa craftsman. Beaver, 290, no. 3 (1959/1960): 34-37.

Massie, Dennis.   Jacob Smith in the Saginaw Valley. Michigan History, 51 (1967): 117-129.

Matson, G. A., et al.   A study of the hereditary blood factors among the Chippewa Indians of Minnesota. American Journal of Physical Anthropology, n.s., 12 (1954): 413-426.

Maxted, W. R.   Streptococcus pyogenes, type 49. A nephritogenic streptococcus with a wide geographical distribution. By W. R. Maxted, Cherry A. M. Fraser, and M. T. Parker. Lancet, 1 (1967): 641-644.

Mayer, Catherine M., et al., comps. Minnesota Indian resources directory. 2d

ed.   Minneapolis, University of Minnesota, Center for Urban and Regional Affairs, 1970.   173 p.   ERIC ED043435.

McDonnell, J.   Some account of the Red River. In L. F. R. Masson, ed. Les Bourgeois de la Compagnie du Nord-Ouest. Vol. 1.   Quebec, 1889: 265-295.

McGee, W J.   Ojibwa feather symbolism. American Anthropologist, 11 (1898): 177-180.

McKenney, T. L.   Memories, official and personal.   New York, 1846.   490 p.

McKenney, T. L.   Sketches of a tour of the Lakes.   Baltimore, 1827.   493 p.

McKenney, Thomas L.   Sketches of a tour to the lakes, of the character and customs of the Chippeway Indians . . . .   Barre, Mass., Imprint Society, 1972.   20, 414 p.   illus.

McLean, J.   Notes of a twenty-five years' service in the Hudson's Bay Territory. Ed. by W. S. Wallace. Champlain Society, Publications, 19 (1932): 1-402.

McLean, John.   Notes of a twenty-five years' service in the Hudson's Bay territory.   New York, Greenwood Press, 1968.   36, 402 p.   map.   (Champlain Society, Publication, 19)

Meakins, C.   Old Albert of Chemung. Forest and Stream, 91 (1921): 5-7, 34-38, 64-65, 85-87.

Means, P. A.   Preliminary survey of the remains of the Chippewa settlements on La Pointe Island. Smithsonian Miscellaneous Collections, 66, no. 14 (1917): 1-15.

Merwin, B. W.   Some Ojibway buffalo robes. Museum Journal, 7 (1916): 93-96.

Michelson, T.   Maiden sacrifice among the Ojibwa. American Anthropologist, n.s., 36 (1934): 628-629.

Michelson, T.   Ojibwa tales. Journal of American Folklore, 24 (1911): 249-250.

Michelson, T.   Studies of the Fox and Ojibwa Indians. Smithsonian Miscellaneous Collections, 78, no. 1 (1926): 111-113.

Michon, Jean-Louis.   La Grande Médecine des Ojibways. Société Suisse des Américanistes, Bulletin, 36 (1972): 37-72.

Michon, Jean-Louis.   La Grande Médecine des Ojibways. Société Suisse des

Américanistes, Bulletin, 27 (1964): 33–34; 28 (1964): 13–14.

Miller, Frank C. Chippewa adolescents: a changing generation. By Frank C. Miller and D. Douglas Caulkins. Human Organization, 23 (1964): 150–159.

Miller, Frank C. Humor in a Chippewa tribal council. Ethnology, 6 (1967): 263–271.

Miller, Frank C. Involvement in an urban university. In Jack O. Waddell and O. Michael Watson, eds. The American Indian in Urban Society. Boston, Little, Brown, 1971: 312–340.

Minnesota, Governor's Human Rights Commission. Minnesota's Indian citizens, yesterday and today. St. Paul, 1965. 136 p. map.

Minnesota, Governor's Human Rights Commission. Race relations in Minnesota; reports of the commission. St. Paul, 1948. illus., maps.

Minnesota, Governor's Human Rights Commission. The Indian in Minnesota; a report to Governor C. Elmer Anderson of Minnesota by the Governor's Interracial Commission. Rev. St. Paul, 1952. 79 p.

Minnesota, Governor's Human Rights Commission. The Indian in Minnesota; a report to Governor Luther W. Youngdahl of Minnesota by the Governor's Interracial Commission. St. Paul, 1947. 80 p. map.

Minnesota Historical Society. The Ojibway people. St. Paul, 1972. 18 p. illus. (Gopher Historian Leaflet Series, 6)

Minnesota, Indian Affairs Commission. Report. St. Paul, 1967. 51 p.

Minnesota, Interim Commission on Indian Affairs. Report of the Interim Commission on Indian Affairs. St. Paul, 1957. 18 p.

Minnesota, Interim Commission on Indian Affairs. Report submitted to the Legislature of the State of Minnesota. St. Paul, 1961. 27 l.

Monckton, E. The white canoe. New York, 1904. 138 p.

Mooney, J. and C. Thomas. Chippewa. U.S. Bureau of American Ethnology, Bulletin, 30, vol. 1 (1907): 277–281.

Mooney, J. and C. Thomas. Missisauga. U.S. Bureau of American Ethnology, Bulletin, 30, vol. 1 (1907): 909–910.

Moran, G. Ojibwa of Saganaw. In H. R. Schoolcraft, ed. Information respecting the History, Condition, and Prospects of the Indian Tribes of the United States. Vol. 2. Philadelphia, 1852: 458–469.

Morgan, Fred. Friday night drum. Beaver, 293, no. 2 (1962/1963): 52–55.

Morgan, Fred. Wild rice harvest. Beaver, 291, no. 2 (1960/1961): 24–31.

Morgan, L. H. Systems of consanguinity and affinity. Smithsonian Contributions to Knowledge, 17 (1871): 291–382.

Morgan, L. H. The Indian journals, 1859–62, p. 82–84, 114–115. Ann Arbor, 1959.

Morriseau, Norval. Legends of my people, the great Ojibway. Edited by Selwyn Dewdney. Toronto, Ryerson Press, 1965. 22, 130 p. illus.

Morse, J. A report to the Secretary of War. New Haven, 1822. 400 p.

Morse, R. F. The Chippewas of Lake Superior. State Historical Society of Wisconsin, Collections, 3 (1856): 338–369.

*Müller, W. Die blaue Hütte. Studien zur Kulturkunde, 12 (1954): 1–145.

Myers, F. A. The bear-walk. Inland Seas, 9 (1953): 12–18, 98–103, 169–174, 250–254.

Myers, Frank A. Historic sites marked in Manitoulin Island region. Inland Seas, 16 (1960): 196–202.

Myers, Frank A. History of the Hudson Bay Company post at Little Current, Ontario. Inland Seas, 15 (1959): 88–96, 222–232, 276–282; 16 (1960): 47–59.

Myers, Frank A. How Little Current got its name. Inland Seas, 16 (1960): 119–122.

Nasatir, A. P. Before Lewis and Clark. St. Louis, 1952. 2 v. (882 p.)

Neill, E. D. History of the Ojibways. Minnesota Historical Society, Collections, 5 (1885): 395–510.

Neumeyer, Elizabeth. Michigan Indians battle against removal. Michigan History, 55 (1971): 275–288.

Nicollet, Joseph N. The journals of Joseph N. Nicollet. Translated by André Fertey. Edited by Martha Coleman Bray. St. Paul, Minnesota Historical Society, 1970. 18, 288 p. illus., maps.

Norman, Howard. Ojibwa pictures and song-
pictures. Alcheringa, 3 (1971): 64-67.

O'Brien, F. G. Minnesota pioneer
sketches. Minneapolis, 1904. 372 p.

Orr, R. B. The Chippewa Indians. Annual
Archaeological Report, being Part of
Appendix to the Report of the Minister
of Education, Ontario (1918): 9-23.

Orr, R. B. The Mississaugas. Annual
Archaeological Report, being Part of
Appendix to the Report of the Minister
of Education, Ontario (1915): 7-18.

Owl, F. M. Seven chiefs rule the Red Lake
Band. American Indian, 6, no. 3 (1952):
3-12.

Paredes, J. Anthony. Toward a
reconceptualization of American Indian
urbanization: a Chippewa case.
Anthropological Quarterly, 44 (1971):
256-271.

Paredes, James Anthony. Chippewa
townsmen: a study in small-scale urban
adaptation. Dissertation Abstracts
International, 31 (1970/1971): 1671B.
UM 70-19,708.

Parker, Seymour. Eskimo psychopathology
in the context of Eskimo personality and
culture. American Anthropologist, 64
(1962): 76-96.

Parker, Seymour. The Wiitiko psychosis in
the context of Ojibwa personality and
culture. American Anthropologist, 62
(1960): 603-623.

Patterson, E. Palmer, II. Arthur E.
O'Meara, friend of the Indians. Pacific
Northwest Quarterly, 58 (1967): 90-99.

Perlman, Lawrence V., et al.
Poststreptococcal glomerulonephritis. A
ten-year follow-up of an epidemic.
American Medical Association, Journal,
194 (1965): 63-70.

Perrot, N. Memoir on the manners,
customs, and religion of the savages of
North America. In E. H. Blair, ed. The
Indian Tribes of the Upper Mississippi
Valley. Vol. 1. Cleveland, 1911: 25-
272.

Perrot, N. Mémoire sur les moeurs,
coustumes et relligion des sauvages de
l'Amérique septentrionale. Paris, 1864.
341 p.

Petersen, Karen Daniels. Chippewa mat-
weaving techniques. Washington, D.C.,
Government Printing Office, 1963. 211-
285 p. illus. (U.S., Bureau of
American Ethnology, Anthropological

Papers, 67. U.S., Bureau of American
Ethnology, Bulletin, 186)

Pfaller, Louis. Indian scare of 1890.
North Dakota History, 39, no. 1 (1972):
4-17.

Pfaller, Louis. The peace mission of
1863-1864. North Dakota History, 37
(1970): 293-313.

Piper, W. S. The eagle of Thunder Cape.
New York, 1924. 235 p.

Plischke, H. Eine Bilderschrift auf
Birkenrinde, Odjibeway-Indianer.
Zeitschrift für Ethnologie, 82 (1957):
171-173.

Potherie, B. de la. History of the savage
peoples who are allies of New France. In
E. H. Blair, ed. The Indian Tribes of
the Upper Mississippi Valley. Vol. 2.
Cleveland, 1912: 13-136.

Potherie, B. de la. History of the savage
peoples who are allies of New France. In
E. H. Blair, ed. The Indian Tribes of
the Upper Mississippi Valley. Vol. 1.
Cleveland, 1911: 273-372.

Pruitt, O. J. A tribe of Chippewa
Indians. Annals of Iowa, 3d ser., 33
(1955/1957): 295-297.

Query, William T. Aggressive responses to
the Holtzman Inkblot technique by Indian
and White alcoholics. By William T.
Query and Joy M. Query. Journal of
Cross-Cultural Psychology, 3 (1972):
413-416.

Quimby, G. I. New evidence links Chippewa
to prehistoric cultures. Chicago Natural
History Museum, Bulletin, 29, no. 4
(1958): 7-8.

Quimby, George I. A year with a Chippewa
family, 1763-1764. Ethnohistory, 9
(1962): 217-239.

Quimby, George I. Alexander Henry in
Central Michigan, 1763-64. Michigan
History, 46 (1962): 193-200.

Quimby, George I. The Pic River Site. In
James B. Griffin, ed. Lake Superior
Copper and the Indians: Miscellaneous
Studies of Great Lakes Prehistory. Ann
Arbor, University of Michigan, 1961: 83-
89. (Michigan, University, Museum of
Anthropology, Anthropological Papers,
17)

Radin, P. An introductive enquiry in the
study of Ojibwa religion. Ontario
Historical Society, Papers and Records,
12 (1914): 210-218.

Radin, P. Ethnological notes on the Ojibwa of southeastern Ontario. American Anthropologist, n.s., 30 (1928): 659-668.

Radin, P. Ojibwa and Ottawa puberty dreams. In Essays in Anthropology Presented to A. L. Kroeber. Berkeley, 1936: 233-264.

Radin, P. Ojibwa ethnological chit-chat. American Anthropologist, n.s., 26 (1924): 491-533.

Radin, P. Some aspects of puberty fasting among the Ojibwa. Canada, Department of Mines, Geological Survey, Museum Bulletin, 2 (1914): 69-78.

Radin, P. Some myths and tales of the Ojibwa of southeastern Ontario. Canada, Department of Mines, Geological Survey, Memoirs, 48 (1914): 1-83.

Radin, P. and A. B. Reagan. Ojibwa myths and tales. Journal of American Folklore, 41 (1928): 61-146.

Reagan, A. B. Flood myths of the Bois Fort Chippewas. Kansas Academy of Science, Transactions, 30 (1921): 437-443.

Reagan, A. B. Hunting and fishing of various tribes of Indians. Kansas Academy of Science, Transactions, 30 (1921): 443-448.

Reagan, A. B. Medicine songs of George Farmer. American Anthropologist, n.s., 24 (1922): 332-369.

Reagan, A. B. Picture writings of the Chippewa Indians. Wisconsin Archeologist, n.s., 6 (1927): 80-83.

Reagan, A. B. Plants used by the Bois Fort Chippewa. Wisconsin Archeologist, n.s., 7 (1928): 230-248.

Reagan, A. B. Rainy Lakes Indians. Wisconsin Archeologist, n.s., 2 (1923): 140-147.

Reagan, A. B. Some Chippewa medicinal receipts. American Anthropologist, n.s., 23 (1921): 246-249.

Reagan, A. B. Some games of the Bois Fort Ojibwa. American Anthropologist, n.s., 21 (1919): 264-278.

Reagan, A. B. Some plants of the Bois Fort Indian Reservation and vicinity in Minnesota. Illinois State Academy of Science, Transactions, 14 (1921): 61-70.

Reagan, A. B. The Bois Fort Chippewa. Wisconsin Archeologist, n.s., 3 (1924): 101-132.

Reagan, A. B. The flood myth of the Chippewas. Indiana Academy of Science, Proceedings, 29 (1919): 347-352.

Reagan, A. B. The O-ge-che-dah or Head-Men Dance of the Bois Fort Indians. Americana, 28 (1934): 302-306.

Redbird, Duke. Tobacco burns. In Waubageshig, ed. The Only Good Indian. Toronto, new press, 1972: 1.

Redsky, James. Great leader of the Ojibway: Mis-quona-queb. Edited by James R. Stevens. Toronto, McClelland and Stewart, 1972. 127 p. illus.

Reid, A. P. Religious beliefs of the Ojibois or Sauteux Indians. Royal Anthropological Institute of Great Britain and Ireland, Journal, 3 (1873): 106-113.

Reid, Dorothy M. Tales of Nanabozho. New York, H. Z. Walck, 1963. 128 p. illus.

Richardson, J. Arctic searching expedition, 262-277. New York, 1852.

Riddiough, Norman. Treaty time. Beaver, 293, no. 1 (1962/1963): 10-13.

Riggs, S. R. Protestant missions in the Northwest. Minnesota Historical Society, Collections, 6 (1894): 117-188.

Ritzenthaler, R. Chippewa preoccupation with health. Public Museum of the City of Milwaukee, Bulletin, 19 (1953): 175-258.

Ritzenthaler, R. Impact of war on an Indian community. American Anthropologist, n.s., 45 (1943): 325-326.

Ritzenthaler, R. The acquisition of surnames by the Chippewa Indians. American Anthropologist, n.s., 47 (1945): 175-177.

Ritzenthaler, R. The building of a Chippewa Indian birch-bark canoe. Public Museum of the City of Milwaukee, Bulletin, 19 (1950): 53-99.

Ritzenthaler, R. The ceremonial destruction of sickness by the Wisconsin Chippewa. American Anthropologist, n.s., 47 (1945): 320-322.

Ritzenthaler, R. The Chippewa Indian method of securing and tanning deerskin. Wisconsin Archeologist, n.s., 28 (1947): 6-13.

236   11   EASTERN CANADA

Ritzenthaler, R.   Totemic insult among the
Wisconsin Chippewa. American
Anthropologist, n.s., 47 (1945): 322-
324.

Ritzenthaler, Robert E.   Primitive
therapeutic practices among the
Wisconsin Chippewa. In Iago Galdston,
ed. Man's Image in Medicine and
Anthropology. New York, International
Universities Press, 1963: 316-334.

Ritzenthaler, Robert E.   The Woodland
Indians of the western Great Lakes. By
Robert E. Ritzenthaler and Pat
Ritzenthaler. Garden City, Natural
History Press, 1970. 16, 178 p.
illus., map. (American Museum Science
Books, B21)

Robb, Wallace H.   Arrayed-in-Wampum.
Toronto, Ontario Department of Lands and
Forests, 1966. 46 p.

Roddis, L. H.   The Indian wars of
Minnesota. Cedar Rapids, 1956. 329 p.

Rogers, Edward S.   Band organization among
the Indians of eastern subarctic Canada.
In Contributions to Anthropology: Band
Societies. Ottawa, Queen's Printer,
1969: 21-55. (Canada, National Museums,
Bulletin, 228)

Rogers, Edward S.   Changing settlement
patterns of the Cree-Ojibwa of northern
Ontario. Southwestern Journal of
Anthropology, 19 (1963): 64-88.

Rogers, Edward S.   Leadership among the
Indians of eastern Subarctic Canada.
Anthropologica, n.s., 7 (1965): 263-284.

Rogers, Edward S.   Natural environment--
social organization--witchcraft: Cree
versus Ojibwa--a test case. In
Contributions to Anthropology:
Ecological Essays. Ottawa, Queen's
Printer, 1969: 24-39. (Canada, National
Museums, Bulletin, 230)

Rogers, Edward S.   Subsistence areas of
the Cree-Ojibwa of the eastern
Subarctic: a preliminary study. In
Contributions to Ethnology V. Ottawa,
Queen's Printer, 1967: 59-90. (Canada,
National Museum, Bulletin, 204)

Rogers, Edward S.   The dugout canoe in
Ontario. American Antiquity, 30
(1964/1965): 454-459.

Rogers, Edward S.   The fur trade, the
government and the central Canadian
Indian. In Deward E. Walker, Jr., ed.
The Emergent Native Americans. Boston,
Little, Brown, 1972: 337-342.

Rogers, Edward S.   The fur trade, the
government and the central Canadian
Indian. Arctic Anthropology, 2, no. 2
(1964): 37-40.

Rogers, Edward S.   The Indians of the
Central Subarctic of Canada. By Edward
S. Rogers and Father John Trudeau. In
Internationale Amerikanistenkongress,
38th. 1968, Stuttgart-München.
Verhandlungen. Band 3. München, Klaus
Renner, 1971: 133-149.

*Rogers, Edward S.   The Round Lake Ojibwa.
Toronto, 1962. illus., maps. (Royal
Ontario Museum, Art and Archaeology
Division, Occasional Paper, 5)

Rogers, Edward S.   The yearly cycle of the
Mistassini Indians. By Edward S. and
Jean H. Rogers. Arctic, 12 (1959): 131-
138.

Rogers, Jean H.   Survey of Round Lake
Ojibwa phonology and morphology. In
Contributions to Anthropology 1961-62.
Part II. Ottawa, Queen's Printer, 1964:
92-154. (Canada, National Museum,
Bulletin, 194)

Rogers, John.   A Chippewa speaks. By Chief
Snow Cloud. Hollywood, Calif., Snow
Cloud Publishers, 1957. 131 p. illus.

Rohr, J. F.   Ojibway trails. Ottawa,
Illinois, 1928. 33 p.

Rohrl, Vivian J.   A Chippewa funeral.
Wisconsin Archeologist, n.s., 48 (1967):
137-140.

Rohrl, Vivian J.   A nutritional factor in
windigo psychosis. American
Anthropologist, 72 (1970): 97-101.

Rohrl, Vivian J.   Comment on "The cure and
feeding of windigos: a critique".
American Anthropologist, 74 (1972): 242-
244.

Rohrl, Vivian J.   Some observations on the
Drum Society of Chippewa Indians.
Ethnohistory, 19 (1972): 219-225.

Rohrl, Vivian J.   The Drum Societies in a
Southwestern Chippewa community.
Wisconsin Archeologist, n.s., 49 (1968):
131-137.

Rohrl, Vivian Joyce Lober.   The people of
Mille Lacs: a study of social
organization and value orientations.
Dissertation Abstracts, 28 (1967/1968):
2244B. UM 67-14,645.

Rokala, Dwight Allen.   The anthropological
genetics and demography of the
Southwestern Ojibwa in the Greater Leech
Lake-Chippewa National Forest area.

Dissertation Abstracts International, 32 (1971/1972): 4375B-4376B. UM 72-5574.

Roy, Chunilal. The prevalence of mental disorders among Saskatchewan Indians. By Chunilal Roy, Adjit Choudhuri, and Donald Irvine. Journal of Cross-Cultural Psychology, 1 (1970): 383-392.

Sagatoo, M. A. Wah Sash Kah Moqua. Boston, 1897. 140 p.

Sanderson, James F. Indian tales of the Canadian prairies. Calgary, Historical Society of Alberta, 1965. 15 p. illus.

Sanderson, James F. Indian tales of the Canadian prairies. Alberta Historical Review, 13, no. 3 (1965): 7-21.

Schmidt, W. Die Ojibwa. In his Die Ursprung der Göttesidee. Bd. 5. Münster i. W., 1934: 555-564.

Schmidt, W. Die Ojibwa. In his Die Ursprung der Göttesidee. Bd. 2. Münster i. W., 1929: 475-507.

Schmirler, A. A. A. Wisconsin's lost missionary: the mystery of Father Rene Menard. Wisconsin Magazine of History, 45 (1961): 99-114.

Schoolcraft, H. R. Algic researches. New York, 1839. 2 v.

Schoolcraft, H. R. Mythology, superstitions and languages of the North American Indians. New York Theological Review, 2 (1835): 96-121.

Schoolcraft, H. R. Narrative journal of travels from Detroit northwest through the great chain of American Lakes. Albany, 1821. 419 p.

Schoolcraft, H. R. Narrative of an expedition through the Upper Mississippi to Itasca Lake. New York, 1834. 307 p.

Schoolcraft, H. R. Oneóta, or characteristics of the red race of America. New York, 1845. 512 p.

Schoolcraft, H. R. Personal memoirs of a residence of thirty years with the Indian tribes on the American frontiers. Philadelphia, 1851. 703 p.

Schoolcraft, H. R. Summary narrative of an exploratory expedition to the sources of the Mississippi River. Philadelphia, 1855. 596 p.

Schoolcraft, H. R. The myth of Hiawatha. Philadelphia, 1856. 343 p.

Schoolcraft, H. R. Travels in the central portions of the Mississippi valley. New York, 1825. 459 p.

Schwarz, Herbert T. Windigo, and other tales of the Ojibways. Toronto, McClelland and Stewart, 1969. 40 p. illus.

Shack, William A. Hunger, anxiety, and ritual: deprivation and spirit possession among the Gurage of Ethiopia. Man, n.s., 6 (1971): 30-43.

Sheehan, John F. Carcinoma of the cervix in Indian women. By John F. Sheehan, George J. Basque, and Harle V. Barrett. Nebraska State Medical Journal, 50 (1965): 553-558.

Sheldon, Alexander J. The Kalamazoo Mound: a letter from Alexander J. Sheldon. Edited by Alexis A. Praus. Michigan History, 44 (1960): 384-400.

Shields, J. Thrilling adventures among the Sioux and Chippewas. Missouri Historical Society, Bulletin, 13 (1957): 275-282.

Shimpo, Mitsuru. Socio-cultural disintegration among the fringe Saulteaux. By Mitsuru Shimpo and Robert Williamson. Saskatoon, University Campus Centre for Community Studies, 1965. 11, 291 p. illus., maps. (Saskatchewan, University, Extension Publication, 193)

Sieber, S. A. The Saulteaux Indians. St. Boniface, Man., 1948. 160 p.

Sieber, S. A. The Saulteaux, Penobscot-Abenaki, and the concept of totemism. International Congress of the Anthropological and Ethnological Sciences, Acts, 4, vol. 2 (1955): 325-329.

Simms, S. C. Myths of the Bungees or Swampy Indians of Lake Winnipeg. Journal of American Folklore, 19 (1906): 334-340.

Simms, S. C. The Metawin Society of the Bungees or Swampy Indians of Lake Winnipeg. Journal of American Folklore, 19 (1906): 330-333.

Skinner, A. A visit to the Ojibway and Cree of Central Canada. American Museum Journal, 10 (1910): 9-18.

Skinner, A. Bear customs of the Cree and other Algonkin Indians of Northern Ontario. Ontario Historical Society, Papers and Records, 12 (1914): 203-209.

Skinner, A. European tales from the
Plains Ojibwa. Journal of American
Folklore, 29 (1916): 330-340.

Skinner, A. Medicine ceremony of the
Menomini, Iowa and Wahpeton Dakota.
Indian Notes and Monographs, 4 (1920):
309-326.

*Skinner, A. Notes on the Eastern Cree and
Northern Saulteaux. American Museum of
Natural History, Anthropological Papers,
9 (1911): 117-177.

Skinner, A. Ojibway and Cree of Central
Canada. American Museum Journal, 10
(1908): 9-18.

Skinner, A. Plains Ojibwa tales. Journal
of American Folklore, 32 (1919): 280-
305.

Skinner, A. Political and ceremonial
organization of the Plains-Ojibway.
American Museum of Natural History,
Anthropological Papers, 11 (1914): 475-
511.

Skinner, A. The cultural position of the
Plains Ojibway. American Anthropologist,
n.s., 16 (1914): 314-318.

Skinner, A. The sun dance of the Plains-
Ojibway. American Museum of Natural
History, Anthropological Papers, 16
(1919): 311-315.

Slight, B. Indian researches. Montreal,
1844. 179 p.

Smith, H. H. Botanizing among the Ojibwe.
Public Museum of the City of Milwaukee,
Yearbook, 3 (1923): 38-47.

Smith, H. H. Ethnobotany of the Ojibwe
Indians. Public Museum of the City of
Milwaukee, Bulletin, 4 (1932): 327-525.

Smith, H. I. An Ojibwa cradle. American
Antiquarian and Oriental Journal, 16
(1894): 302-303.

Smith, H. I. Certain shamanistic
ceremonies among the Ojibwas. American
Antiquarian and Oriental Journal, 18
(1896): 282-284.

Smith, H. I. Some Ojibwa myths and
traditions. Journal of American
Folklore, 19 (1906): 215-230.

Smith, H. I. The monster in the tree: an
Ojibwa myth. Journal of American
Folklore, 10 (1897): 324-325.

Snelling, W. J. Early days at Prairie du
Chien. Wisconsin State Historical
Society, Reports and Collections, 5,
no. 1 (1868): 123-153.

Snelling, W. J. Tales of the Northwest.
Boston, 1830. 294 p.

Speck, F. G. Family hunting territories
and social life of various Algonkian
bands of the Ottawa valley. Canada,
Department of Mines, Geological Survey,
Memoirs, 70 (1915): 11-30.

Speck, F. G. Kinship terms and the family
bands among the Northeastern Algonkian.
American Anthropologist, n.s., 20
(1918): 143-161.

Speck, F. G. Myths and folk-lore of the
Timiskaming Algonquin and Timiskaming
Ojibwa. Canada, Department of Mines,
Geological Survey, Memoirs, 71 (1915):
28-87.

Speck, F. G. The family hunting band as
the basis of Algonkian social
organization. American Anthropologist,
n.s., 17 (1915): 289-305.

Speck, F. G. and F. I. Speck. Ojibwa,
Hiawatha's people. Home Geographic
Monthly, 1, no. 4 (1932): 7-12.

Spindler, G. D. Research design and
Ojibwa personality persistence. American
Anthropologist, 60 (1958): 934-936.

Stark, Matthew. Project Awareness:
Minnesota encourages the Chippewa
Indians. Journal of American Indian
Education, 6, no. 3 (1966/1967): 6-13.

Stebbins, Catherine L. The Marquette
death site. Michigan History, 48 (1964):
333-368.

Steinbring, Jack. Acculturational
phenomena among the Lake Winnipeg Ojibwa
of Canada. In Internationale
Amerikanistenkongress, 38th. 1968,
Stuttgart-München. Verhandlungen. Band
3. München, Klaus Renner, 1971: 179-
187.

Steinbring, Jack. Culture change among
the Northern Ojibwa. Historical and
Scientific Society of Manitoba,
Transactions, ser. 3, 21 (1964/1965): 3-
24.

Steinbring, Jack. The manufacture and use
of bone defleshing tools. American
Antiquity, 31 (1965/1966): 575-581.

Stewart, O. C. Cart-using Indians of the
American Plains. International Congress
of the Anthropological and Ethnological
Sciences, Acts, 5 (1960): 351-355.

Stickney, G. P. Indian use of wild rice.
American Anthropologist, 9 (1896): 115-
121.

Stobie, Margaret. Backgrounds of the dialect called Bungi. Historical and Scientific Society of Manitoba, Transactions, ser. 3, 24 (1967/1968): 65-75.

Stowe, G. C. Plants used by the Chippewa. Wisconsin Archeologist, n.s., 21 (1940): 8-13.

Suelflow, Roy A. Lutheran missions in the Saginaw Valley. Michigan History, 51 (1967): 226-240.

Summerfield, J. Sketch of grammar of the Chippeway language. Cazenovia, 1834. 35 p.

Swanton, J. R. Some neglected data bearing on Cheyenne, Chippewa, and Dakota history. American Anthropologist, n.s., 32 (1930): 156-160.

Sweet, G. W. Incidents of the threatened outbreak of Hole-in-the-Day. Minnesota Historical Society, Collections, 6 (1894): 401-408.

Szathmary, Emoke J. E. Caucasian admixture in two Ojibwa Indian communities in Ontario. By Emoke J. E. Szathmary and T. Edward Reed. Human Biology, 44 (1972): 655-671.

Tanner, John. Dreissig Jahre unter den Indianern. Translated by Eva Lips. Weimar, Kiepenheuer, 1968. 379 p. map.

Taylor, J. Garth. Northern Ojibwa communities of the contact-traditional period. Anthropologica, n.s., 14 (1972): 19-30.

Teeter, Karl V. The Algonquian verb: notes toward a reconsideration. International Journal of American Linguistics, 31 (1965): 221-225.

Telford, C. W. Test performance of full and mixed-blood North Dakota Indians. Journal of Comparative Psychology, 14 (1932): 123-145.

"The Engages". Maple sugar in the fur trade. Museum of the Fur Trade Quarterly, 7, no. 1 (1971): 6-9.

Thistle, Johnson L., et al. Prevalence of gallbladder disease among Chippewa Indians. Mayo Clinic, Proceedings, 46 (1971): 603-608.

Thompson, L. Attitudes and acculturation. American Anthropologist, n.s., 50 (1948): 200-215.

Thompson, S. The Indian legend of Hiawatha. Modern Language Association, Publications, 37 (1928): 128-140.

Thomson, William D. History of Fort Pembina: 1870-1895. North Dakota History, 36 (1969): 5-39.

Thwaites, R. G., ed. The French regime in Wisconsin. State Historical Society of Wisconsin, Collections, 16-18 (1902-1908).

Thwaites, R. G., ed. The Jesuit Relations and allied documents. Cleveland, 1896-1901. 74 v.

Todd, Evelyn Mary. A grammar of Ojibwa: the Severn dialect. Dissertation Abstracts International, 31 (1970/1971): 4147A. UM 71-3606.

Tomkins, W. Universal Indian sign language. San Diego, 1927. 96 p.

Uhlenbeck, C. C. Ontwerp van eene vergelijkende vormleer van eenige Algonkin-talen. Amsterdam, Koninklijke Akademie van Wetenschappen, Afdeeling Letterkunde, Verhandelingen, n.s., 11, no. 3 (1910): 1-67.

U.S., Congress, Senate, Committee on Interior and Insular Affairs, Subcommittee on Indian Affairs. Federal lands in trust for tribes in Minnesota and Wisconsin. Hearing, Ninety-second Congress, first session, on S. 1217 . . . S. 1230 . . . March 26, 1971. Washington, D.C., Government Printing Office, 1971. 3, 72 p.

Van Dusen, C. The Indian chief. London, 1867. 216 p.

Verwyst, Chrysostom. Chippewa exercises. Minneapolis, Ross and Haines, 1971. 13, 494, 6 p. illus.

Verwyst, F. C. Chippewa exercises. Harbor Springs, 1901.

Verwyst, F. C. Geographical names in Wisconsin, Minnesota and Michigan having a Chippewa origin. State Historical Society of Wisconsin, Collections, 12 (1892): 390-398.

Verwyst, F. C. Life and labors of Rt. Rev. Frederic Baraga. Milwaukee, 1900. 476 p.

Verwyst, F. C. Missionary labors of Fathers Marquette, Menard, and Allouez. Chicago, 1886. 262 p.

Vizenor, Gerald. The Anishinabe. Indian Historian, 4, no. 4 (1971): 16-18.

Vizenor, Gerald R. The everlasting sky; new voices from the people named Chippewa. New York, Crowell-Collier Press, 1972. 22, 140 p. illus.

Voegelin, E. W. Notes on Ojibwa-Ottawa pictography. Indiana Academy of Science, Proceedings, 51 (1941): 44-47.

Vogel, Virgil J. The missionary as acculturation agent: Peter Dougherty and the Indians of Grand Traverse. Michigan History, 51 (1967): 185-201.

Walker, Willard. Notes on native writing systems and the design of native literacy programs. Anthropological Linguistics, 11, no. 5 (1969): 148-166.

Warren, W. W. History of the Ojibways. Minnesota Historical Society, Collections, 5 (1885): 21-394.

Warren, W. W. Oral traditions respecting the history of the Ojibwa Nation. In H. R. Schoolcraft, ed. Information respecting the History, Condition, and Prospects of the Indian Tribes of the United States. Vol. 2. Philadelphia, 1852: 135-167.

Watrall, Charles R. Virginia deer and the buffer zone in the Late Prehistoric-Early Protohistoric periods in Minnesota. Plains Anthropologist, 13 (1968): 81-86.

Wax, Murray L., et al. Indian communities and Project Head Start. Summary and observations in the Dakotas and Minnesota, together with an appraisal of possibilities for a Head Start program among the Potawatomi Indians of Kansas. Washington, D.C., 1967. 65 p. (U.S., Office of Economic Opportunity, Report, 520) ERIC ED016510.

Weisenburger, Francis P. Caleb Atwater: pioneer politican and historian. Ohio Historical Quarterly, 68 (1959): 18-37.

West, G. A. Uses of tobacco and the calumet by Wisconsin Indians. Wisconsin Archeologist, 10 (1911): 5-64.

Westermeyer, Joseph. Chippewa and majority alcoholism in the twin cities: a comparison. Journal of Nervous and Mental Disease, 155 (1972): 322-327.

Westermeyer, Joseph. Options regarding alcohol use among the Chippewa. American Journal of Orthopsychiatry, 42 (1972): 398-403.

Westermeyer, Joseph John. Alcohol related problems among Ojibway people in Minnesota: a social psychiatry study. Dissertation Abstracts International, 32 (1971/1972): 409B-410B. UM 71-18,837.

Whipple, H. B. Civilization and christianization of the Ojibways of Minnesota. Minnesota Historical Society, Collections, 9 (1901): 129-142.

Wiens, Agnes A. Nursing service on a Chippewa reservation. American Journal of Nursing, 61, no. 4 (1961): 92-93.

Wilcox, A. T. The Chippewa sugar camp. Michigan History Magazine, 37 (1953): 276-285.

Wilford, L. History of the Chippewa. Minnesota Archaeologist, 17, no. 2 (1951): 3-10.

Wilson, E. F. Missionary work among the Ojebway Indians. London, 1886. 255 p.

Wilson, E. F. The Ojebway language. Toronto, 1874. 412 p.

Winchell, N. H. The aborigines of Minnesota, 580-743. St. Paul, 1911.

Wisconsin, Governor's Commission on Human Rights. Handbook on Wisconsin Indians. Compiled and written by Joyce M. Erdman. Madison, 1966. 103 p. illus., maps. ERIC ED033816.

Wood, W. J. Tularemia. Manitoba Medical Association, Review, 31, no. 10 (1951): 641-644.

Woods, Richard G. Indian employment in Minneapolis. By Richard G. Woods and Arthur M. Harkins. Minneapolis, University of Minnesota, Training Center for Community Programs, 1968. 44, 48 l. ERIC ED021659.

Woods, Richard G. Indians in Minneapolis. Minneapolis, League of Women Voters, and University of Minnesota, Training Center for Community Problems, 1968. 110 p. ERIC ED022578.

Woolworth, Nancy L. The Grand Portage Mission: 1731-1965. Minnesota History, 39 (1964/1965): 301-310.

Wright, Dana. The Sibley trail of 1863. North Dakota History, 29 (1962): 283-296.

Wright, J. C. The great myth. Lansing, 1922. 170 p.

Wright, James V. A regional examination of Ojibwa culture history. Anthropologica, n.s., 7 (1965): 189-227.

Wright, James V. An archaeological survey along the north shore of Lake Superior. Ottawa, Queen's Printer, 1963. 9 p. map. (Canada, National Museum, Anthropology Papers, 3)

Wright, James V. Michipicoten site. In Contributions to Anthropology: Archaeology and Physical Anthropology. Ottawa, Queen's Printer, 1969: 1-85. (Canada, National Museum, Bulletin, 224)

Wright, James V. The application of the direct historical approach to the Iroquois and the Ojibwa. Ethnohistory, 15 (1968): 96-111.

Wright, James V. The Pic River Site: a stratified Late Woodland site on the north shore of Lake Superior. In Contributions to Anthropology V: Archaeology and Physical Anthropology. Ottawa, Queen's Printer, 1967: 54-99. (Canada, National Museum, Bulletin, 206)

Yarnell, Richard Asa. Aboriginal relationships between culture and plant life in the Upper Great Lakes region. Ann Arbor, University of Michigan, 1964. 6, 218 p. (Michigan, University, Museum of Anthropology, Anthropological Papers, 23)

Yarnell, Richard Asa. Aboriginal relationships between culture and plant life in the Upper Great Lakes region. Dissertation Abstracts, 24 (1963/1964): 2217-2218. UM 64-914.

Young, E. R. Algonquin Indian tales. New York, 1903. 256 p.

Young, E. R. By canoe and dog-train among the Cree and Salteaux Indians. London, 1890. 267 p.

Young, E. R. On the Indian trail. New York, 1897. 214 p.

Young, E. R. Stories from Indian wigwams and northern camp-fires. New York, 1893. 293 p.

Zschokke, H. Ein Besuch bei den Chippewas-Indianern in der Reservation White Earth in Nordamerika. Leopoldinenstiftung in Kaiserthume Oesterreich, Berichte, 51 (1881).

11-09   Ottawa

Bauman, R. F. Pontiac's successor. Northwest Ohio Quarterly, 26 (1954): 8-38.

Bauman, R. F. The last Ottawa. Northwest Ohio Quarterly, 24 (1951/1952): 4-9.

Bauman, R. F. The migration of the Ottawa Indians from the Maumee Valley to Walpole Island. Northwest Ohio Quarterly, 21 (1949): 86-112.

Bauman, Robert F. Ottawa fleets and Iroquois frustration. Northwest Ohio Quarterly, 33 (1960/1961): 6-40.

Bauman, Robert F. The Ottawas of the Lakes; 1615-1766. Part 2, the heyday of the Ottawa supremacy over the Great Lakes fur trade; 1660-1701. Northwest Ohio Quarterly, 35 (1962/1963): 69-100.

Beauchamp, W. M. Indian nations of the Great Lakes. American Antiquarian and Oriental Journal, 17 (1895): 321-325.

Benson, Maxine. Schoolcraft, James, and the "White Indian". Michigan History, 54 (1970): 311-328.

Bibaud, F. M. Biographie des sagamos illustrés de l'Amérique Septentrionale, 213-221. Montréal, 1848.

Blackbird, A. J. History of the Ottawa and Chippewa Indians of Michigan. Ypsilanti, 1887. 128 p.

Blackburn, George M. Foredoomed to failure: the Manistee Indian station. Michigan History, 53 (1969): 37-50.

Boas, F. Zur Anthropologie der nordamerikanischen Indianer. Berliner Gesellschaft für Anthropologie, Ethnologie und Urgeschichte, Verhandlungen (1895): 367-411.

Bolt, Robert. Reverend Leonard Slater in the Grand River Valley. Michigan History, 51 (1967): 241-251.

Canfield, Francis X. A diocese so vast: Bishop Rese in Detroit. Michigan History, 51 (1967): 202-212.

Chaboillez, Charles Jean Baptiste. Journal of Charles Jean Baptiste Chaboillez, 1797-1798. Edited by Harold Hickerson. Ethnohistory, 6 (1959): 265-316, 363-427.

Chamberlain, A. F. Nanibozhu amongst the Otchipwe, Mississagas, and other Algonkian tribes. Journal of American Folklore, 4 (1891): 193-213.

Chamberlain, M. E. The twenty-one precepts of the Ottawa Indians. Journal of American Folklore, 5 (1892): 332-334.

Charron, Yvon. Monsieur Charles de Bellefeuille, missionaire de l'Outawais (1836-1838). Revue d'Histoire de l'Amérique Française, 5 (1950/1951): 193-226.

Cleland, Charles E., ed. The Lasanen Site: an historic burial locality in Mackinac County, Michigan. East Lansing, 1971. 11, 147 p. illus.

(Michigan State University, Museum, Publications, Anthropological Series, 1, no. 1)

Cocks, J. Fraser, III. George N. Smith: reformer on the frontier. Michigan History, 52 (1968): 37-49.

Collins, Harriet Whitney. The life history of Harriet Whitney Collins. As related by herself to her daughter, Harriet Collins Perry.

Downes, R. C. The Ottawa Indians and the Erie and Kalamazoo Railroad. Northwest Ohio Quarterly, 24 (1952): 136-138.

Draper, Lyman S. Material in Draper "S" on 18th- and early 19th-century Indians of the Old Northwest. Ethnohistory, 8 (1961): 281-288.

Drier, Roy W. The Michigan College of Mining and Technology Isle Royale excavations, 1953-1954. In James B. Griffin. Lake Superior Copper and the Indians: Miscellaneous Studies of Great Lakes Prehistory. Ann Arbor, University of Michigan, 1961: 1-7. (Michigan, University, Museum of Anthropology, Anthropological Papers, 17)

Duluth, Daniel Greysolon de. Capital punishment in Michigan, 1683: Duluth at Michilimackinac. Michigan History, 50 (1966): 349-360.

Elliott, R. R. The Chippewas and Ottawas. American Catholic Quarterly Review, 22 (1897): 18-46.

Emmert, Darlene Gay. The Indians of Shiawassee County. Michigan History, 47 (1963): 127-155, 243-272.

Engelhardt, Z. Anishinabe Neganiod. Harbor Springs, Michigan, 1901.

Ettawageshik, F. Ghost suppers. American Anthropologist, n.s., 45 (1943): 491-493.

Ettawageshik, J. Three true tales from L'Arbre Croche. Midwest Folklore, 7 (1957): 38-40.

Farrell, David. Settlement along the Detroit frontier, 1760-1796. Michigan History, 52 (1968): 89-107.

Fay, George E., ed. Charters, constitutions and by-laws of the Indian tribes of North America. Part VI: The Indian tribes of Oklahoma (cont'd.). Greeley, 1968. 5, 129 l. map. (University of Northern Colorado, Museum of Anthropology, Occasional Publications in Anthropology, Ethnology Series, 7) ERIC ED046556.

Fitting, James E. Settlement analysis in the Great Lakes region. Southwestern Journal of Anthropology, 25 (1969): 360-377.

Foreman, G. The last trek of the Indians, 89-92, 190-193. Chicago, 1946.

Gordon, John M. Michigan journal, 1836. Edited by Douglas H. Gordon and George S. May. Michigan History, 43 (1959): 10-42, 129-149, 257-293, 433-478.

Greenman, E. F. Chieftainship among Michigan Indians. Michigan History Magazine, 24 (1940): 361-379.

Hallowell, A. I. Was cross-cousin marriage practised by the North-Central Algonkian? International Congress of Americanists, Proceedings, 23 (1928): 519-544.

Hamelin. Ottawas. American Antiquarian Society, Transactions and Collections, 2 (1836): 305-367.

Hamilton, J. C. The Algonquin Manabozho and Hiawatha. Journal of American Folklore, 15 (1903): 229-233.

Hamilton, Raphael. The Marquette death site: the case for Ludington. Michigan History, 49 (1965): 228-248.

Hamilton, Raphael N. Jesuit mission at Sault Ste. Marie. Michigan History, 52 (1968): 123-132.

Hanzeli, Victor E. Missionary linguistics in New France; a study of seventeenth- and eighteenth-century descriptions of American Indian languages. The Hague, Mouton, 1969. 141 p. illus., map. (Janua Linguarum, Series Maior, 29)

Hanzeli, Victor E. The Algonquin R-dialect in historical records. In International Congress of Linguists, 10th. 1967, Bucarest. Proceedings. Vol. 2. Bucarest, Éditions de l'Académie de la République Socialiste de Roumanie, 1970: 85-89.

Harris, Kate. Parkersburg; history of city from time of its settlement to the present in gripping narrative from the pen of the late Miss Kate Harris. West Virginia History, 25 (1963/1964): 241-264.

Hickerson, H. The feast of the dead among the seventeenth century Algonkians of the upper Great Lakes. American Anthropologist, 62 (1960): 81-107.

Hilger, M. I. In the early days of Wisconsin. Wisconsin Archeologist, 16 (1936): 32-49.

Holmes, Norman G. The Ottawa Indians of
Oklahoma and Chief Pontiac. Chronicles
of Oklahoma, 45 (1967): 190-206.

Hootkins, H. Some notes on the Ottawa
dialect. Michigan Academy of Science,
Arts and Letters, Papers, 26 (1940):
557-560.

Humphrey, N. B. The mock battle greeting.
Journal of American Folklore, 54 (1941):
186-190.

Hunter, A. F. Wampum records of the
Ottawas. Annual Archaeological Report,
being Part of Appendix to the Report of
the Minister of Education, Ontario
(1901): 52-56.

James, E., ed. A narrative of the
captivity and adventures of John Tanner.
New York, 1830. 426 p.

Jenks, A. E. The wild rice gatherers of
the Upper Lakes. U.S. Bureau of American
Ethnology, Annual Reports, 19 (1898):
1013-1137.

Jones, J. A. The political organization
of the Three Fires. Indiana Academy of
Science, Proceedings, 63 (1953): 46.

Jones, V. H. Some Chippewa and Ottawa
uses of sweet grass. Michigan Academy of
Science, Arts and Letters, Papers, 21
(1935): 21-31.

Keller, Kathryn M. Scene: Toledo; time:
1837. Northwest Ohio Quarterly, 34
(1961/1962): 52-70.

Kenton, E., ed. The Indians of North
America, Vol. 2: 164-167, 371-374. New
York, 1927.

*Kinietz, W. V. The Indian tribes of the
western Great Lakes. Michigan,
University, Museum of Anthropology,
Occasional Contributions, 10 (1940):
226-307.

Kurath, G. P. Catholic hymns of Michigan
Indians. Primitive Man, 30 (1957): 31-
44.

Lambert, Bernard. Mission priorities:
Indians or miners? Michigan History, 51
(1967): 323-334.

Laning, Paul L. Colonial trail blazers
around western Lake Erie. Inland Seas,
19 (1963): 266-276.

Lincoln, J. S. The dream in primitive
cultures. London, 1935. 359 p.

Martin, Helen M. How people came to
Mackinac. Michigan History, 44 (1960):
401-404.

Massie, Dennis. Jacob Smith in the
Saginaw Valley. Michigan History, 51
(1967): 117-129.

Maxwell, T. J. Pontiac before 1763.
Ethnohistory, 4 (1957): 41-46.

McCoy, I. History of Baptist missions.
Washington, D.C., 1840. 611 p.

McDowell, John E. Madame La Framboise.
Michigan History, 56 (1972): 271-286.

Meeker, J. Ottawa first book. 2d ed.
1850. 128 p.

Michelson, T. Note on the gentes of the
Ottawa. American Anthropologist, n.s.,
13 (1911): 338.

Michelson, T. Three Ottawa tales. Journal
of American Folklore, 44 (1932): 191-
195.

Mooney, J. and J. N. B. Hewitt. Ottawa.
U.S. Bureau of American Ethnology,
Bulletin, 30, vol. 2 (1910): 167-172.

Morgan, L. H. Systems of consanguinity
and affinity. Smithsonian Contributions
to Knowledge, 17 (1871): 291-382.

Morgan, L. H. The Indian journals, 1859-
62, p. 37-40. Ann Arbor, 1959.

Myers, F. A. The bear-walk. Inland Seas,
9 (1953): 12-18, 98-103, 169-174, 250-
254.

Myers, Frank A. Historic sites marked in
Manitoulin Island region. Inland Seas,
16 (1960): 196-202.

Myers, Frank A. History of the Hudson Bay
Company post at Little Current, Ontario.
Inland Seas, 15 (1959): 88-96, 222-232,
276-282; 16 (1960): 47-59.

Myers, Frank A. How Little Current got
its name. Inland Seas, 16 (1960): 119-
122.

Nasatir, A. P. Before Lewis and Clark.
St. Louis, 1952. 2 v. (882 p.).

Neumeyer, Elizabeth. Michigan Indians
battle against removal. Michigan
History, 55 (1971): 275-288.

Nouvel, Henry. A canoe trip to Midland in
1675. Edited and with an introduction by
Harold W. Moll. Michigan History, 46
(1962): 255-274.

O'Leary, Mrs. James L. Henry Chatillon.
Missouri Historical Society, Bulletin,
22 (1965/1966): 123-142.

Orr, R. B. The Ottawas. Annual
Archaeological Report, being Part of
Appendix to the Report of the Minister
of Education, Ontario (1916): 7-25.

Parkman, F. The conspiracy of Pontiac and
the Indian war after the conquest of
Canada. Boston, 1886. 2 v.

Peckham, H. H. Pontiac and the Indian
uprising. Princeton, 1947. 346 p.

*Perrot, N. Memoir on the manners,
customs, and religion of the savages of
North America. In E. H. Blair, ed. The
Indian Tribes of the Upper Mississippi
Valley. Vol. 1. Cleveland, 1911: 25-
272.

*Perrot, N. Mémoire sur les moeurs,
coustumes et relligion des sauvages de
l'Amerique septentrionale. Paris, 1864.
341 p.

Pruitt, O. J. John Y. Nelson: plainsman.
Annals of Iowa, 35 (1960): 294-303.

Quimby, George I. A year with a Chippewa
family, 1763-1764. Ethnohistory, 9
(1962): 217-239.

Quimby, George I. The voyage of the
Griffin: 1679. Michigan History, 49
(1965): 97-107.

Radin, P. Ojibwa and Ottawa puberty
dreams. In Essays in Anthropology
Presented to A. L. Kroeber. Berkeley,
1936: 233-264.

Ritzenthaler, Robert E. The Woodland
Indians of the western Great Lakes. By
Robert E. Ritzenthaler and Pat
Ritzenthaler. Garden City, Natural
History Press, 1970. 16, 178 p.
illus., map. (American Museum Science
Books, B21)

Schmidt, W. Die Potawatomie (und Ottawa).
In his Die Ursprung der Göttesidee.
Bd. 5. Münster i. W., 1934: 565-579.

Schmidt, W. Die Potawatomie (und Ottawa).
In his Die Ursprung der Göttesidee.
Bd. 2. Münster i. W., 1929: 508-515.

Schoolcraft, H. R. Algic researches. New
York, 1839. 2 v.

Sheldon, Alexander J. The Kalamazoo
Mound: a letter from Alexander J.
Sheldon. Edited by Alexis A. Praus.
Michigan History, 44 (1960): 384-400.

Smith, James. An account of the
remarkable occurrences in the life and
travels of Col. James Smith, during his
captivity with the Indians in the years
1755, '56, '57, '58, and '59, with an

appendix of illustrative notes. Edited
by Wm. N. Darlington. Cincinnati, R.
Clarke, 1870. 12, 190 p. (Ohio Valley
Historical Series, 5)

Stebbins, Catherine L. The Marquette
death site. Michigan History, 48 (1964):
333-368.

Szczepański, Jan. Czarne wampumy głoszą
wojnę; powstanie Pontiaka, 1763-64.
Warszawa, Czytelnik, 1970. 165 p.
illus., maps.

Thwaites, R. G., ed. The Jesuit Relations
and allied documents. Cleveland, 1896-
1901. 74 v.

Townes, Caleb. From Old Vincennes, 1815.
Indiana Magazine of History, 57 (1961):
141-154.

Voegelin, E. W. Notes on Ojibwa-Ottawa
pictography. Indiana Academy of Science,
Proceedings, 51 (1941): 44-47.

Vogel, Virgil J. The missionary as
acculturation agent: Peter Dougherty and
the Indians of Grand Traverse. Michigan
History, 51 (1967): 185-201.

Weer, P. Ethnological notes on the
Ottawa. Indiana Academy of Science,
Proceedings, 49 (1940): 23-27.

Weisenburger, Francis P. Caleb Atwater:
pioneer politican and historian. Ohio
Historical Quarterly, 68 (1959): 18-37.

Wilson, E. F. The Ottawa Indians. Our
Forest Children, 3 (1889): 1-6.

Wright, J. C. The crooked tree. 3d ed.
Harbor Springs, 1917. 148 p.

Yarnell, Richard Asa. Aboriginal
relationships between culture and plant
life in the Upper Great Lakes region.
Ann Arbor, University of Michigan, 1964.
6, 218 p. (Michigan, University, Museum
of Anthropology, Anthropological Papers,
23)

Young, Chester Raymond. The stress of war
upon the civilian population of
Virginia, 1739-1760. West Virginia
History, 27 (1965/1966): 251-277.

Zoltvany, Yves F. New France and the
West, 1701-1713. Canadian Historical
Review, 46 (1965): 301-322.

Ethnonymy

Arctic-Subarctic Ethnonymy

An ethnonymy is a list of names of ethnic groups, together with alternate names and variant spellings. The ethnonymy on the following pages was prepared by the compilers of this bibliography to assist them in making decisions as to where to assign individual books, journal articles, etc. within the bibliography. Thus, it was designed primarily as a classificatory device for purposes unique to this bibliography. The basic ethnonymy was prepared before the compilation of this edition was begun, using as a base list the "Index of Tribal Names" compiled by Professor Murdock and published in the 1960 edition. The present compilers consulted a number of basic reference tools and added a large number of names of ethnic groups, reservations and reserves, and headings, such as Pan-Indianism, to this basic list. New names were also added as they were encountered in the literature. The resulting ethnonymy is comparatively extensive, but in reality contains a relatively small percentage of the total possible number of names found in the literature. However, the present list was generally sufficient for our needs in compiling this bibliography. We have supplied citations to a small number of reference works, below, which contain further listings and descriptions. The synonymy in Hodge (1907-1910) is particularly notable for the large number of variant names and spellings it gives, and should be the first source to be consulted for information on any name which is not in the present ethnonymy.

As noted in the General Introduction, there are now 269 individual ethnic group bibliographies in this work. In addition, there are bibliographies for each of the fifteen culture areas distinguished, as well as bibliographies for North America as a whole, Pan-Indianism, Urban Indians, Canadian Indians, United States government relations with the Native Peoples, and Canadian government relations with the Native Peoples. Adding these together gives a grand total of 290 individual bibliographies, i.e. there are 290 possible places in which bibliographic citations on a particular ethnic group might be found. The ethnonymy acts as a locator device for finding the particular bibliography which might have the citations needed by the user. The names in the ethnonymy are keyed to individual bibliographies by a four-digit code. The first two digits in the code refer to the culture area in which the group is located. The third and fourth digits in the code refer to the particular bibliography within the culture area to which citations on that particular ethnic group have been assigned. The two sets of digits have been separated by a hyphen for ease in reading. As an example, in the ethnonymy we may find the name and code "Navaho 15-21." This indicates that any bibliographic references to the Navaho which have been processed have been assigned to individual bibliography 15-21. This means that all bibliographic citations to the Navaho have been assigned to the twenty-first bibliography within culture area number 15, which on inspection turns out to be the Navajo bibliography within the Southwest culture area. Note that in this case, "Navaho" is a variant spelling of the name "Navajo." The latter name is the one used to denote this particular bibliography. Similarly, the name and code "Back River Eskimo 01-09" means that bibliographic citations on this group have been placed in the ninth bibliography within culture area number 1, which is the Netsilik Eskimo bibliography within the Arctic Coast area. Note that locating the name of an ethnic group in the ethnonymy does not necessarily mean that bibliographic references on that particular ethnic group will actually be found in the bibliography. The presence of a name in the ethnonymy simply means that *if* the compilers found a bibliographic reference on the Back River Eskimo, for example, they would include it in bibliography 01-09. If *no* references on the Back River Eskimo were located, none would be in bibliography 01-09.

The following ethnonymy contains the names and numerical codes for this volume only, that is, only those names and numerical codes applying to ethnic groups living in the arctic and Subarctic will be found here. The first two digits of each numerical code will be one of three combinations: 01-, 02- or 11-. These two-digit numbers refer to the Arctic Coast, Mackenzie-Yukon, and Eastern Canada bibliographies respectively. The third and fourth digits of the numerical codes refer to the individual bibliographies within each of the three major divisions of this volume. Thus, 01-06 refers to the Iglulik Eskimo bibliography, 02-01 refers to the Ahtena bibliography, and 11-06 refers to the Ojibwa bibliography.

The reference works which were found most useful in compiling the ethnonymy are listed below:

Canada, Department of Indian Affairs and Northern Development, Indian Affairs Branch. Linguistic and cultural affiliations of Canadian Indian bands. Ottawa, 1967.

Hodge, Frederick Webb, ed. Handbook of American Indians north of Mexico. Washington, D.C., Government Printing Office, 1907-1910. 2 pts. (U.S., Bureau of American Ethnology, Bulletin, 30). (SuDocs no. SI2.3:30) [reprint editions available]

Swanton, John R. The Indian tribes of North America. Washington, D.C., Government Printing Office, 1952. (U.S., Bureau of American Ethnology, Bulletin, 145) (SuDocs no. SI2.3:145) [reprint editions available]

U.S., Department of Commerce. Federal and State Indian reservations and Indian trust areas. Washington, D.C., 1974. (SuDocs no. C1.8/3:In2)

The following is a schedule of the code numbers of the individual bibliographies which will be found in each of the five volumes of the complete bibliography:

Volume 1, General North America, contains bibliographies for code numbers 01-00, 02-00, 03-00, 04-00, 05-00, 06-00, 07-00, 08-00, 09-00, 10-00, 11-00, 12-00, 13-00, 14-00, 15-00, 16-00, 16-01, 16-02, 16-03, 16-04, and 16-05.

Volume 2, Arctic and Subarctic, contains bibliographies for *all* code numbers beginning with 01-, 02-, and 11-.

Volume 3, Far West and Pacific Coast, contains bibliographies for *all* code numbers beginning with 03-, 04-, 05-, 06-, 07-, and 08-.

Volume 4, Eastern North America, contains bibliographies for *all* code numbers beginning with 10-, 12-, and 13-.

Volume 5, Plains and Southwest, contains bibliographies for *all* code numbers beginning with 09-, 14-, and 15-.

A

Abenaki   11-01
Abenaki Indian Village   11-01
Abenaki, Saint Francis   11-01
Abenakis of Becancour   11-01
Abenakis of Odanak   11-01
Abitibi   11-02
Abitibi Dominion   11-00
Abnaki   11-01
Abnaki, Western   11-01
Acadia   11-06
Afton   11-06
Aggomiut   01-06
Aglemiut   01-12
Agomiut   01-06
Agto   01-15
Ahagmiut   01-04
Ahtena   02-01
Ahtnakhotana   02-01
Aishihik   02-12
Aivilik   01-06
Aivilingmiut   01-06
Aivilirmiut   01-06
Aivillirmiut   01-06
Aivitimiut   01-07
Aivitumiut   01-07
Akianimiut   01-02
Aklavik   02-12
Akudnirmiut   01-02
Akuliarmiut   01-02
Akulliakatagmiut   01-04
Akunermiut   01-15
Alaskan Eskimo   01-00
Albany   11-04
Alderville   11-08
Aleut   01-01
Aleut, Commander   01-01
Aleut, Komandorskiy   01-01
Alexander   11-04
Alexandria   02-04
Alexis Creek   02-04
Algonkin   11-02
Algonquin   11-02
Alkatcho   02-03
Amaseconti   11-01
Ammasalik   01-05
Ammassalimiut   01-05
Ammassalingmiut   01-05
Androscoggin   11-01
Angmagsalik   01-05
Angmagsalingmiut   01-05
Annapolis Valley   11-06
Anvik-Shageluk   02-10
Arctic Coast   01-00
Arctic Highlanders   01-11
Arctic Red River   02-12
Argonaut   11-02
Arosaguntacook   11-01
Arsuk   01-15
Arveqtormiut   01-09
Arvertormiut   01-09
Arviligjuarmiut   01-09
Arviligyuarmiut   01-09
Asiagmiut   01-04
Asiaqmiut   01-03

Atawapiskat   11-04
Athabaska   02-05
Athabaskans   02-00
Athabaskans, Canadian   02-00
Athabaskans, Northern   02-00
Atka   01-01
Atnah   02-01
Atnas   02-01
Atnatana   02-01
Attawapiskat   11-04
Attu   01-01
Auvagmiut   01-08
Avangnamiut   01-15
Avitimiut   01-07
Avitumiut   01-07

B

Babine   02-03
Babine, Lake   02-03
Babine, River   02-03
Back River Eskimo   01-09
Bad River Reservation   11-08
Baffinland Eskimo   01-02
Barren Ground Cree   11-04
Barren Ground Naskapi   11-07
Barren Lands   02-05
Barrière   11-04
Barrière   11-02
Barriere Lake   11-02
Barter Island Eskimo   01-10
Batchewana   11-08
Bay Mills Reservation   11-08
Bear River   11-06
Beardy's and Okemasis   11-04
Beausoleil   11-08
Beaver   02-02
Beaver Lake   11-04
Beaver of Horse Lakes and
   Clear Hills   02-02
Becancour Abenakis   11-01
Belcher Island Eskimo   01-07
Beothuk   11-03
Berens River   11-08
Bering Island   01-01
Bersimis   11-07
Big Cove   11-06
Big Grassy   11-08
Big Island   11-08
Big Plume's Band   02-15
Big River Cree   11-04
Big River Naskapi   11-07
Bigstone   11-04
Birch Creek Kutchin   02-12
Black River Kutchin   02-12
Bloods   02-15
Bloodvein   11-04
Bonasila   02-10
Boyer River   02-02
Broad Grass   02-15
Brokenhead   11-08
Brunswick House   11-08
Buctouche   11-06
Buffalo Point   11-08
Bums Lake   02-03
Bungee   11-08
Bungi   11-08

Burnt Church   11-06

C

Canadian Athabaskans   02-00
Canadian Eskimo   01-00
Caniba   11-01
Canoe Lake   11-04
Cape Croker   11-08
Cape York Eskimo   01-11
Caribou Eskimo   01-03
Caribou Lake   11-04
Caribou-eaters   02-05
Carmacks   02-12
Carrier   02-03
Carrier, Northern   02-03
Carrier, Southern   02-03
Central Eskimo   01-00
Champagne   02-12
Chandalar River Kutchin   02-12
Chapel Island   11-06
Chapleau Cree   11-04
Chapleau Ojibway   11-08
Chaplino   01-16
Chemahawin   11-04
Cheslatta   02-03
Chicoutimi   11-07
Chilcotin   02-04
Chilcotin, Stone   02-04
Chingigmiut   01-14
Chintagottine   02-09
Chipewyan   02-05
Chipewyan, Cold Lake   02-05
Chipewyan, Fort McMurray   02-05
Chipewyan, Snowdrift   02-05
Chipewyan, Yellowknife   02-05
Chippewa   11-08
Chippewa, Kansas   11-08
Chippewa, Minnesota   11-08
Chippewa, Rocky Boy's   11-08
Chippewa, Southeastern   11-08
Chippewa, Southwestern   11-08
Chippewa, Turtle Mountain   11-08
Chippewa, Wisconsin   11-08
Chippewas of Georgina Island   11-08
Chippewas of Kettle and
   Stony Point   11-08
Chippewas of Rama   11-08
Chippewas of Samia   11-08
Chippewas of the Thames   11-08
Chippewayan   02-05
Chisedec   11-07
Chitra-Gottineke   02-13
Chnagmiut   01-14
Chuckbuckmiut   01-07
Chugach   01-12
Chugachigmiut   01-12
Churchill   02-05
Clark Lake   02-20

Cockburn Island 11-08
Cold Lake Chipewyan 02-05
Cold Lake Cree 11-04
Commander Aleut 01-01
Constance Lake 11-04
Copper Eskimo 01-04
Copper Indians 02-24
Copper River Indians 02-01
Copperknife Indians 02-24
Cote 11-08
Couchiching 11-08
Cowessess 11-04
Coyukon 02-06
Crane River 11-08
Credit Mississaugas 11-08
Cree 11-04
Cree, Barren Ground 11-04
Cree, Big River 11-04
Cree, Chapleau 11-04
Cree, Cold Lake 11-04
Cree, Fort McMurray 11-04
Cree, Gordon 11-04
Cree, Lowland 11-04
Cree, Missanabie 11-04
Cree, Muscowpetung 11-04
Cree, Okanese 11-04
Cree, Pasqua 11-04
Cree, Paul 11-04
Cree, Peguis 11-04
Cree, Plains 11-04
Cree, Poplar River 11-04
Cree, River 11-04
Cree, Rocky 11-04
Cree, Rocky Boy's 11-04
Cree, Sucker Creek 11-04
Cree, Sunchild 11-04
Cree, Swampy 11-04
Cree, Western Wood 11-04
Cree, Whitebear 11-04
Cree, Whitefish Lake 11-04
Cree, Woodland 11-04
Cross Lake 11-04
Crow River Kutchin 02-12
Crow-Chief's Band 02-15
Crow-Child's Band 02-15
Cumberland House 11-04
Cumberland Sound Eskimo 01-02
Curve Lake 11-08

D

Dalles 11-08
Davis Inlet 11-07
Dawson 02-12
Day Star 11-04
Deer Creek Reservation 11-08
Deer Lake 11-04
Delinigotini 02-16
Deonedhekkenadé 02-05
Desnedekenade 02-05
Desnedheyarèlottiné 02-18
Dihai 02-12
Diomedes 01-16
Disko 01-15
Dogrib 02-07

Dogrib, Eastern 02-07
Dogrib, Lac La Martre 02-07
Dogrib, Portage 02-07
Dogrib, Rae 02-07
Dokis 11-08
Driftpile 11-04
Dumoine 11-02
Duncan's 11-04
Dunvegan 02-02
Dutagotine 02-09

E

Eagle 02-08
Eagle Lake 11-08
East Greenland Eskimo 01-05
Eastern Canada 11-00
Eastern Canadian Indians 11-00
Eastern Dogrib 02-07
Eastern Nahane 02-11
Eastmain 11-07
Ebb and Flow 11-08
Edjiérétroukkenadé 02-05
Edmundston 11-05
Eel Ground 11-06
Eel River 11-06
Egedesminde 01-15
Ehtagottiné 02-13
Ekaluktogmiut 01-04
Eléidlingottiné 02-18
Eleidlinottine 02-18
English River 02-05
Enoch 11-04
Ermineskin 11-04
Esbataottine 02-11
Escoumains 11-07
Eskasoni 11-06
Eskimo 01-00
Eskimo, Alaskan 01-00
Eskimo, Back River 01-09
Eskimo, Baffinland 01-02
Eskimo, Barter Island 01-10
Eskimo, Belcher Island 01-07
Eskimo, Canadian 01-00
Eskimo, Cape York 01-11
Eskimo, Caribou 01-03
Eskimo, Central 01-00
Eskimo, Copper 01-04
Eskimo, Cumberland Sound 01-02
Eskimo, East Greenland 01-05
Eskimo, Great Whale River 01-07
Eskimo, Greenland 01-00
Eskimo, Iglulik 01-06
Eskimo, Labrador 01-07
Eskimo, Mackenzie 01-08
Eskimo, Netsilik 01-09
Eskimo, North Alaska 01-10
Eskimo, Pelly Bay 01-09
Eskimo, Point Barrow 01-10
Eskimo, Point Hope 01-10
Eskimo, Polar 01-11
Eskimo, Port Harrison 01-07

Eskimo, Saint Lawrence Island 01-16
Eskimo, Siberian 01-16
Eskimo, Smith Sound 01-11
Eskimo, South Alaska 01-12
Eskimo, Southampton Island 01-13
Eskimo, Ungava 01-07
Eskimo, Vrangel 01-16
Eskimo, West Alaska 01-14
Eskimo, West Greenland 01-15
Espatotena 02-11
Etatchogottine 02-16
Etatcinlagotini 02-16
Etatcogotini 02-16
Etchaottine 02-18
Etchareottine 02-18
Etchemin 11-05
Etcheridiegottine 02-18
Etchimin 11-05
Etheneldeli 02-05
Étheneltèli 02-05
Ettchéridiegottiné 02-18
Ewigotini 02-16
Eyak 02-01

F

Fairford 11-08
Fetutlin 02-08
Finlay River 02-17
Fisher River 11-08
Fishing Lake 11-08
Fiskernaes 01-15
Fitz/Smith 02-05
Flying Post 11-08
Fond du Lac 02-05
Fond du Lac Reservation 11-08
Fort Albany 11-04
Fort Alexander 11-08
Fort Chimo 11-07
Fort Chipewyan 02-05
Fort Folly 11-06
Fort Franklin 02-09
Fort George 02-03
Fort George 11-07
Fort Good Hope 02-09
Fort Hope 11-08
Fort Liard 02-18
Fort McKay 02-05
Fort McMurray 02-00
Fort McMurray Chipewyan 02-05
Fort McMurray Cree 11-04
Fort McPherson 02-12
Fort Nelson 02-18
Fort Norman 02-18
Fort Providence 02-18
Fort Saint John 02-02
Fort Severn 11-04
Fort Simpson 02-18
Fort Vermilion 11-04
Fort William 11-08
Fort Wrigley 02-18
Fox Lake 11-04

Frances Lake   02-11
Fraser Lake   02-03
Frederikshaab   01-15
French Canadians   11-10
Frog Lake   11-04

G

Gamblers   11-08
Garden River   11-08
Gaspe   11-06
Georgina Island Chippewas
   11-08
Godbout   11-07
Godhavn   01-15
God's Lake   11-04
Godthaab   01-15
Golden Lake   11-02
Goontdarshage   02-19
Gordon   11-00
Gordon Cree   11-04
Gordon Ojibwa   11-08
Grand Lac Victoria   11-02
Grand Lake Victoria Indians
   11-02
Grand Portage Reservation
   11-08
Grand Rapids   11-04
Grassy Narrows   11-08
Great Bear Lake Indians   02-
   16
Great Whale River   11-07
Great Whale River Eskimo
   01-07
Greenland Eskimo   01-00
Grouard   11-04
Gull Bay   11-08

H

Han   02-08
Haneragmiut   01-04
Haningayormiut   01-09
Hankutchin   02-08
Hare   02-09
Hare 4   02-18
Harvaqtormiut   01-03
Hauheqtormiut   01-03
Hay River   02-18
Heart Lake   02-02
Henvey Inlet   11-08
Hiawatha   11-08
Hollow Water   11-08
Holstenborg   01-15
Holy Cross-Georgetown   02-10
Horse Lakes and Clear Hills
   Beaver   02-02
Hudson Hope   02-02
Hunter's Point   11-02
Hwitsiwoten   02-03
Hwotsotenne   02-03

I

Igdlorssuit   01-15
Igluligmiut   01-06
Iglulik Eskimo   01-06
Iglulingmiut   01-06
Iglulirmiut   01-06
Iglumiut   01-07
Ikogmiut   01-14
Iliamna   02-20
Iluilermiut   01-09
Indian Island   11-06
Indian Township Reservation
   11-05
Indians, Copper   02-24
Indians, Copper River   02-01
Indians, Copperknife   02-24
Indians, Eastern Canadian
   11-00
Indians, Grand Lake Victoria
   11-02
Indians, Great Bear Lake
   02-16
Ingalik   02-10
Inukjuamiut   01-07
Inupiaq   01-00
Inupik   01-00
Inutjuamiut   01-07
Isabella Reservation   11-08
Island   11-08
Island Lake   11-04
Islington   11-08
Ita   01-11
Itanese   01-11
Itivimiut   01-07
Ivigtut   01-15
Iyiniwok   11-04

J

Jackhead   11-08
Jakobshavn   01-15
James Bay   11-04
James Smith   11-04
Janvier   02-05
John Smith   11-04
Joseph Bighead   11-04
Julianehaab   01-15

K

Kachemak Bay   02-20
Kagmalirmiut   01-10
Kahkewistahaw   11-04
Kaialigamiut   01-14
Kaialigmiut   01-14
Kaiyuhkhotana   02-06
Kaktovik   01-10
Kalatdlitmiut   01-15
Kangamiut   01-15
Kangatsiak   01-15
Kangerdlugsiatsiak   01-15
Kanghiryuarmiut   01-04
Kangiamiut   01-15

Kaniagmiut   01-12
Kañianermiut   01-10
Kaniapiskau   11-07
Kanithlualukshuamiut   01-07
Kansas Chippewa   11-08
Kaska   02-11
Katagottine   02-09
Katcogotine   02-09
Katshikotin   02-08
Kaviagmiut   01-14
Kawchodinne   02-09
Kawchogottine   02-09
Kawchottine   02-09
Keeseekoose   11-08
Keeseekowenin   11-08
Kehewin   11-04
Kenai   02-20
Kenaitz   02-20
Kenisteno   11-04
Kennebec   11-01
Kepiskari   11-04
Kesagami   11-04
Kettle and Stony Point
   Chippewas   11-08
Kevalingamiut   01-10
Keweenaw Bay Reservation
   11-08
Key   11-08
Kfwetragottine   02-13
Kiatagmiut   01-12
Kichespirini   11-02
Kidlinungmiut   01-07
Kigiktagmiut   01-07
Kigirktarugmiut   01-10
Kiglinirmiut   01-04
Kikitarmiut   01-10
Killinermiut   01-10
Killinunmiut   01-07
Killirmiut   01-10
Kilusiktomiut   01-04
Kingnaitmiut   01-02
Kingsclear   11-05
Kinistino   11-08
Kinugmiut   01-14
Kinugumiut   01-14
Kipawa   11-02
Kiskakon   11-09
Kitcisagi   11-02
Kittegaryumiut   01-08
Kittigazuit   01-08
Kivalinaqmiut   01-10
Kkpaylongottine   02-13
Klokkègottine   02-13
Klondike   02-08
Klowanga   02-15
Kluane   02-12
Kluskus   02-03
Knaiakhotana   02-20
Knisteneau   11-04
Kogloktogmiut   01-04
Koksoakmiut   01-07
Kolchan-Teneyna   02-10
Komandorskiy Aleut   01-01
Kongithlushuamiut   01-07
Koniag   01-12
Konithlushumiut   01-07
Konyag   01-12
Kopagmiut   01-10
Kowagmiut   01-10

Koyuhkhotana 02-06
Koyukon 02-06
Koyukukhotana 02-06
Kristinaux 11-04
Kugmiut 01-10
Kukparungmiut 01-10
Kûngmiut 01-05
Kungmiut 01-09
Kunmiut 01-10
Kupugmiut 01-08
Kurugmiut 01-08
Kuskokwagmiut 01-14
Kuskowagamiut 01-14
Kuskwogmiut 01-14
Kustsheotin 02-03
Kutcha Kutchin 02-12
Kutchin 02-12
Kutchin, Birch Creek 02-12
Kutchin, Black River 02-12
Kutchin, Chandalar River
  02-12
Kutchin, Crow River 02-12
Kutchin, Kutcha 02-12
Kutchin, Mackenzie Flats
  02-12
Kutchin, Nakotcho 02-12
Kutchin, Natsit 02-12
Kutchin, Netsi 02-12
Kutchin, Peel River 02-12
Kutchin, Takkuth 02-12
Kutchin, Tatlit 02-12
Kutchin, Tennuth 02-12
Kutchin, Tetlit 02-12
Kutchin, Tranjik 02-12
Kutchin, Tukkuth 02-12
Kutchin, Upper Porcupine
  River 02-12
Kutchin, Vunta 02-12
Kutchin, Yukon Flats 02-12
Kuuvakmiut 01-10

L

Labrador Eskimo 01-07
Lac Courte Oreilles
  Reservation 11-08
Lac des Mille Lacs 11-08
Lac des Quinze 11-02
Lac du Flambeau Reservation
  11-08
Lac La Croix 11-08
Lac la Hache 02-05
Lac La Martre Dogrib 02-07
Lac la Ronge 11-04
Lac Saint Jean 11-07
Lac Seul 11-08
Lac Simon 11-02
Lake Babine 02-03
Lake Manitoba 11-08
Lake Saint John 11-07
Lake Saint Joseph 11-08
Lake Saint Martin 11-08
Lakweip 02-19
L'Anse Reservation 11-08
Leech Lake Reservation 11-
  08
Lennox Island 11-06

Liard River 02-11
Lintchare 02-07
Little Black Bear 11-04
Little Black River 11-08
Little Grand Rapids 11-08
Little Pine 11-04
Little Red River 11-04
Little Saskatchewan 11-08
Long Lake No. 58 11-08
Long Lake No. 77 11-08
Long Plain 11-08
Long Point 11-02
Loon Lake 11-04
Loucheux 02-12
Louis Bull 11-04
Lower Inlet 02-20
Lowland Cree 11-04
Lthautenne 02-03
Lubican Lake 11-04
Lucky Man 11-04

M

Mackenzie Eskimo 01-08
Mackenzie Flats Kutchin 02-
  12
Mackenzie-Yukon 02-00
Magemiut 01-14
Magnetawan 11-08
Magnettawan 11-08
Malecite 11-05
Malemiut 01-14
Mamikininiwug 11-04
Manitoulin Island 11-08
Maniwaki 11-02
Manowan 11-02
Many Horses' Band 02-15
Maple Creek 11-04
Maria Micmacs 11-06
Maritime Provinces 11-00
Martin Falls 11-08
Maskegon 11-04
Matachewan 11-08
Mathias Colomb 11-04
Mattagami 11-08
Mayo 02-12
McGrath 02-10
McLeod Lake 02-17
Meadow Lake 11-04
Medny Island 01-01
Métis, Northern 02-25
Michikamau 11-07
Michipicoten 11-08
Micmac 11-06
Micmac, Restigouche 11-06
Micmacs of Maria 11-06
Middle Inlet 02-20
Middle River 11-06
Midnoosky 02-01
Miduusky 02-01
Mille Lacs Reservation 11-
  08
Mingan 11-07
Minnesota Chippewa 11-08
Minnesota Ojibwa 11-08
Missanabie Cree 11-04
Missiassik 11-01

Missisauga 11-08
Mississaugas of the Credit
  11-08
Mistassini 11-07
Mistawasis 11-04
Moisie 11-07
Mole Lake Reservation 11-08
Monsoni 11-04
Montagnais 11-07
Montana Cree Reserve 11-04
Montreal Lake 11-04
Moose 11-04
Moose Deer Point 11-08
Moose Factory 11-04
Moose Lake 11-04
Moosomin 11-04
Moricetown 02-03
Mountain 02-13
Mountain People 01-10
Muscowekwan 11-08
Muscowpetung 11-00
Muscowpetung Cree 11-04
Muscowpetung Ojibwa 11-08
Muskeg Lake 11-04
Musquarro 11-07

N

Nabesna 02-14
Nabesna River Head 02-14
Nabesna River Mouth 02-14
Nabesnatana 02-14
Nagssugtormiut 01-06
Nagyuktogmiut 01-04
Nahane 02-11
Nahane, Eastern 02-11
Nahane, Western 02-19
Nahani 02-11
Naicatchewenin 11-08
Nakotcho Kutchin 02-12
Nakraztlitenne 02-03
Naloten 02-19
Nanortalik 01-15
Napaktomiut 01-10
Napaskiak 01-14
Naskapi 11-07
Naskapi, Barren Ground 11-
  07
Naskapi, Big River 11-07
Naskoten 02-19
Naskotin 02-03
Nassauaketon 11-09
Nataotin 02-03
Natashquan 11-07
Nataskwan 11-07
Natliatin 02-03
Natlotenne 02-03
Natsit Kutchin 02-12
Naukan 01-16
Nazkhutenne 02-03
Nazko 02-03
Necoslie 02-03
Nedlungmiut 01-11
Nelagotine 02-09
Nellagottine 02-09
Nelson 02-11
Nelson House 11-04

Nemaska   11-04
Nemiah Valley   02-04
Nemiscau   11-07
Nemiskari   11-07
Neoskweskari   11-07
Nepissing   11-02
Netcetumiut   01-07
Netsi Kutchin   02-12
Netsilik Eskimo   01-09
Netsilingmiut   01-09
Netsilirmiut   01-09
Nett Lake Reservation   11-08
New Post   11-04
Nichikun   11-07
Nicickousemenecaning   11-08
Nigottine   02-09
Nikolski   01-01
Nikozliautin   02-03
Nipigon   11-08
Nipissing   11-02
Nitutinni   02-03
Noahonirmiut   01-04
Noatagmiut   01-10
Noatak   01-10
Norridgewock   11-01
North Alaska Eskimo   01-10
Northern Athabaskans   02-00
Northern Carrier   02-03
Northern Métis   02-25
Northern Saulteaux   11-08
Northwest Angle No. 33   11-08
Northwest Angle No. 37   11-08
Northwest River   11-07
Norway House   11-04
Ntshaautin   02-03
Nuajarmiut   01-06
Nuataqmiut   01-10
Nugsuak   01-15
Nugsuak   01-11
Nugumiut   01-02
Nunamiut   01-10
Nunatagmiut   01-10
Nunengmiut   01-07
Nunenumiut   01-07
Nunivagmiut   01-14
Nunivak   01-14
Nushagagmiut   01-14
Nushagak   01-14
Nushagamiut   01-14
Nut Lake   11-08
Nutcatenna   02-03
Nutšatenne   02-03
Nutzotin   02-14
Nuvorugmiut   01-08
Nuvugmiut   01-07
Nuwukmiut   01-10

O

Obedjiwan   11-02
Ochapowace   11-04
O'Chiese   11-04
Odanak Abenakis   11-01
Ogoki   11-08
Ogulmiut   01-12

Ojibwa   11-08
Ojibwa, Gordon   11-08
Ojibwa, Minnesota   11-08
Ojibwa, Muscowpetung   11-08
Ojibwa, Okanese   11-08
Ojibwa, Parry Island   11-08
Ojibwa, Pascua   11-08
Ojibwa, Peguis   11-08
Ojibwa, Plains   11-08
Ojibwa, Poplar River   11-08
Ojibwa, Sucker Creek   11-08
Ojibwa, Walpole Island   11-08
Ojibwa, Whitebear   11-08
Ojibwa, Whitefish Lake   11-08
Ojibwa, Wisconsin   11-08
Ojibway, Chapleau   11-08
Okagamiut   01-07
Okanese   11-00
Okanese Cree   11-04
Okanese Ojibwa   11-08
Oklahoma Ottawa   11-09
Okomiut   01-02
Old Factory   11-07
Old Sarcee's Band   02-15
Omineca   02-03
One Arrow   11-04
Onion Lake   11-04
Ononchataronon   11-02
Ontonagon Reservation   11-08
Oromocto   11-05
Osnaburgh   11-08
Ossipee   11-01
Ottawa   11-09
Ottawa, Oklahoma   11-09
Ottawa, Sucker Creek   11-09
Ottawa, Whitefish Lake   11-09
Oturkagmiut   01-10
Ouchestigouetch   11-07
Oumamiwek   11-07
Oxford House   11-04

P

Pabineau   11-06
Padlermiut   01-03
Padlimiut   01-03
Padliqmiut   01-03
Papinachois   11-07
Parry Island Ojibwa   11-08
Pascua Ojibwa   11-08
Paskwawininiwug   11-04
Pasqua   11-00
Pasqua Cree   11-04
Passamaquoddy   11-05
Paul Cree   11-04
Pays Plat   11-08
Peace River Crossing   02-02
Pedro Bay   02-20
Peel River Kutchin   02-12
Peepeekeesis   11-04
Peguis Cree   11-04
Peguis Ojibwa   11-08
Pekangekum   11-08
Pelican Lake   11-04

Pelly Bay Eskimo   01-09
Pembina   11-08
Penobscot   11-01
Penobscot Reservation   11-01
People Who Hold Aloof   02-15
Pequawket   11-01
Peter Ballantyne   11-04
Peter Pond Lake   02-05
Petiskapau   11-07
Piapot   11-04
Pic Heron Bay   11-08
Pic Mobert   11-08
Pictou Landing   11-06
Pikangikum   11-08
Pilingmiut   01-02
Pine Creek   11-08
Pingangnaktogmiut   01-04
Pintce   02-03
Plains Cree   11-04
Plains Ojibwa   11-08
Pleasant Point Reservation   11-05
Point Barrow Eskimo   01-10
Point Grondin   11-08
Point Hope Eskimo   01-10
Polar Eskimo   01-11
Poorman   11-04
Poplar River Cree   11-04
Poplar River Ojibwa   11-08
Port Harrison Eskimo   01-07
Portage Dogrib   02-07
Portage la Loche   02-05
Poundmaker   11-04
Povernitormiut   01-07
Povungnituk   01-07
Pröven   01-15
Puivlirmiut   01-04
Puthlavamiut   01-07
Putlavamiut   01-07

Q

Qaermiut   01-03
Qaernermiut   01-03
Qaumauangmiut   01-02
Qeqertarsuarmiut   01-15
Qinguamiut   01-02
Qiqiktamiut   01-07
Quavaitmiut   01-15
Quesnel   02-04
Quoddy   11-05

R

Rabbitskins   02-09
Rae Dogrib   02-07
Rainy River   11-08
Rama Chippewas   11-08
Rat Portage   11-08
Red Bank   11-06
Red Cliff Reservation   11-08
Red Earth   11-04
Red Lake Reservation   11-08
Red Pheasant   11-04
Red Rock   11-08

Resolution 02-05
Restigouche Micmac 11-06
River Babine 02-03
River Cree 11-04
River Desert Indians 11-02
Rocameca 11-01
Rocky Bay 11-08
Rocky Boy's Chippewa 11-08
Rocky Boy's Cree 11-04
Rocky Cree 11-04
Rolling River 11-08
Romaine 11-07
Roseau River 11-08
Ross River 02-11
Rupert House 11-07

S

Sabaskong 11-08
Sable 11-09
Saddle Lake 11-04
Sadlirmiut 01-13
Sagaiguninini 11-02
Sagdlirmiut 01-13
Saginaw-Chippewa Indian
  Tribe 11-08
Saint Augustin 11-07
Saint Croix Communities
  Reservation 11-08
Saint Francis Abenaki 11-01
Saint Lawrence Island Eskimo
  01-16
Saint Marguerite 11-07
Saint Mary's 11-05
Sakawininiwug 11-04
Sakimay 11-04
Sallumiut 01-07
Samia Chippewas 11-08
Samson 11-04
Sandpoint 11-08
Sandy Bay 11-08
Sandy Lake 11-04
Santotin 02-14
Sarcee 02-15
Sarsi 02-15
Saschutkenn 02-17
Sasignan 01-01
Sasuchan 02-17
Sasuten 02-17
Satchogottine 02-09
Satudene 02-16
Saugeen 11-08
Saulteaux, Northern 11-08
Saulteaux, Southern 11-08
Saumingmiut 01-02
Sawridge 11-04
Saxozuegotini 02-16
Scoresbysund 01-05
Scottie Creek-Snag 02-14
Scugog 11-08
Seine River 11-08
Sekani 02-17
Sékannais 02-17
Selawigmiut 01-10
Selkirk 02-12
Serpent River 11-08
Seven Islands 11-07

Shammatawa 11-04
Shawanaga 11-08
Sheguiandah 11-08
Shelter Bay 11-07
Sheshegwaning 11-08
Shoal Lake 11-04
Shoal Lake No. 39 11-08
Shoal Lake No. 40 11-08
Shoal River 11-08
Shubenacadie 11-06
Siberian Eskimo 01-16
Sidarumiut 01-10
Siilivikmiut 01-10
Sikanee 02-17
Sinabo 11-09
Sinimiut 01-09
Sipiwininiwug 11-04
Sireniki 01-16
Sirqinirmiut 01-07
Slave 02-18
Slaves of Upper Hay River
  02-18
Smith Sound Eskimo 01-11
Snowdrift Chipewyan 02-05
Sokaogon Chippewa Community
  11-08
Sokoki 11-01
Souriquois 11-06
South Alaska Eskimo 01-12
South Bay 11-08
Southampton Island Eskimo
  01-13
Southeastern Chippewa 11-08
Southern Carrier 02-03
Southern Saulteaux 11-08
Southern Tutchone 02-23
Southwestern Chippewa 11-08
Spanish River No. 1 11-08
Spanish River No. 2 11-08
Spanish River No. 3 11-08
Spanish River No. 4 11-08
Split Lake 11-04
Stangecoming 11-08
Star Blanket 11-04
Stelatin 02-03
Stellaquo 02-03
Stone Chilcotin 02-04
Stonies 02-04
Stony Creek 02-03
Stony Rapids 02-05
Stuart-Trembleur Lake 02-03
Sturgeon Lake 11-04
Sucker Creek Cree 11-04
Sucker Creek Ojibwa 11-08
Sucker Creek Ottawa 11-09
Suhinimiut 01-07
Sukinninmiut 01-07
Sukkertoppen 01-15
Sunchild Cree 11-04
Susitna 02-20
Swampy Cree 11-04
Swan Lake 11-08
Swan River 11-04
Sweet Grass 11-04
Sydney 11-06

T

Tadousac 11-07
Tahagmiut 01-07
Tahltan 02-19
Takamiut 01-07
Takfwelottine 02-07
Takkuth Kutchin 02-12
Takla Lake 02-03
Takon 02-08
Takulli 02-03
Talagotine 02-09
Talakoten 02-19
Talirpingmiut 01-02
Tallcree 11-04
Tanaina 02-20
Tanana 02-21
Tanana, Upper 02-14
Tanotenne 02-03
Taqagmiut 01-07
Taremiut 01-10
Tasiusak 01-15
Tatcinegotine 02-09
Tatlatan 02-01
Tatlazan 02-01
Tatlit Kutchin 02-12
Tatsanottine 02-24
Tatsanottine 02-05
Tatshiautin 02-03
Tatshikotin 02-03
Tautin 02-03
Taxtlowedi 02-19
Tchiglit 01-08
Tchippewayan 02-05
Temiscaming 11-02
Ten'a 02-06
Tenankutchin 02-21
Tennuth Kutchin 02-12
Tents Cut Down 02-15
Tête-de-Boule 11-04
Tetlin Lake 02-14
Tetlit Kutchin 02-12
Thames Chippewas 11-08
The Pas 11-04
Thessalon 11-08
Thilanottine 02-05
Thlingchadine 02-07
Thule 01-11
Thunderchild 11-04
Tigara 01-10
Tikaihoten 02-19
Tikeramiut 01-10
Tikiraqmiut 01-10
Timagami 11-08
Timiskaming 11-02
Tishotina 02-19
Tlathenkotin 02-04
Tlaztenne 02-03
Tlepanoten 02-19
Tleskotin 02-04
Tlotona 02-17
Tobique 11-05
Togiagamiut 01-14
Togiagmiut 01-14
Toosey 02-04
Tranjik Kutchin 02-12
Trochutin 02-08
Trout Lake 11-04

Truro 11-06
Tsantieottine 02-07
Tsattine 02-02
Tsekani 02-17
Tseloni 02-17
Tseottine 02-07
Tsethaottine 02-13
Tsetsaut 02-22
Tsilkotin 02-04
Tukkuth Kutchin 02-12
Tunît 01-13
Tununermiut 01-06
Tununerusirmiut 01-06
Tununirmiut 01-06
Tununirusirmiut 01-06
Turtle Mountain Chippewa
   11-08
Turtle Mountain Reservation
   11-08
Tutchone 02-23
Tutchone, Southern 02-23
Tutchonekutchin 02-23
Tyonek 02-20

                    U

Uel'kal' 01-16
Ugalakmiut 01-12
Ugyuligmiut 01-09
Ukkusiksaligmiut 01-09
Ulkatcho 02-03
Umanak 01-15
Unakhotana 02-06
Unalakleet 01-14
Unalaska 01-01
Unaligmiut 01-14
Ungalaqlingmiut 01-14
Ungava 11-07
Ungava Eskimo 01-07
Ungavamiut 01-07
Upernavik 01-15
Upper Hay River Slaves 02-
   18
Upper Inlet 02-20
Upper Liard 02-11
Upper Porcupine River
   Kutchin 02-12
Upper Tanana 02-14
Uqumiut 01-07
Uterus 02-15
Utkiavigmiut 01-10
Utkiavingmiut 01-10
Utkiavinmiut 01-10
Utkuhighalingmiut 01-09
Utkuhiksalingmiut 01-09
Utukamiut 01-10

                    V

Valley River 11-08
Vermilion 02-02
Viger 11-05
Vrangel Eskimo 01-16
Vunta Kutchin 02-12

                    W

Wabanaki 11-01
Wabasca 11-04
Wabauskang 11-08
Wabemakustewatsh 11-07
Wabigoon 11-08
Wahnapitae 11-08
Wallirmiut 01-04
Walpole Island Ojibwa 11-08
Waswanipi 11-07
Waterhen 11-08
Waterhen Lake 11-04
Wawenoc 11-01
Wawenock 11-01
Wawenok 11-01
Waywayseecappo 11-08
Weenusk 11-04
Weskarini 11-02
West Alaska Eskimo 01-14
West Bay 11-08
West Greenland Eskimo 01-15
Western Abnaki 11-01
Western Nahane 02-19
Western Wood Cree 11-04
Wewenoc 11-01
Weymontachie 11-02
White Earth Reservation 11-
   08
White Whale River 11-07
Whitebear Cree 11-04
Whitebear Ojibwa 11-08
Whitefish Bay 11-08
Whitefish Lake Cree 11-04
Whitefish Lake Ojibwa 11-08
Whitefish Lake Ottawa 11-09
Whitefish River 11-08
Whitehorse 02-11
Whitesand 11-08
Whycocomagh 11-06
Winisk 11-04
Wisconsin Chippewa 11-08
Wisconsin Ojibwa 11-08
Witchekan Lake 11-04
Wolfe Lake 11-02
Woodland Cree 11-04
Woodstock 11-05

                    Y

Yellowknife 02-24
Yellowknife Chipewyan 02-05
Yetaottine 02-05
York Factory 11-04
Young Buffalo Robe 02-15
Yugyt 01-16
Yuit 01-16
Yukon Flats Kutchin 02-12
Yukonikhotana 02-06
Yupigyt 01-16
Yupik 01-00
Yutuwichan 02-17

General Ethnic Map of Native North America

1 TSETSAUT
2 BELLABELLA
3 BELLACOOLA
4 CHILCOTIN
5 LILLOOET
6 COWICHAN
7 KLALLAM
8 QUILEUTE
9 QUINAULT
10 TWANA
11 SNUQUALMI
12 THOMPSON
13 NICOLA
14 SANPOIL
15 SPOKAN
16 KALISPEL
17 COEUR D'ALENE
18 WALLAWALLA
19 CAYUSE
20 UMATILLA
21 TENINO
22 MOLALA
23 WISHRAM
24 KLIKITAT
25 CHEHALIS
26 KWALHIOQUA
27 CHINOOK
28 TLATSKANAI
29 TILLAMOOK
30 ALSEA
31 SIUSLAW
32 COOS
33 CHASTACOSTA
34 TOLOWA
35 TAKELMA
36 KLAMATH
37 ACHOMAWI
38 YANA
39 SHASTA
40 KAROK
41 CHIMARIKO
42 HUPA
43 YUROK
44 WIYOT
45 WAILAKI
46 YUKI
47 WINTUN
48 POMO
49 WAPPO
50 OLAMENTKE
51 COSTANO
52 SALINA
53 TUBATULABAL
54 KAWAIISU
55 CHUMASH
56 GABRIELINO
57 LUISENO
58 CAHUILLA
59 KAMIA
60 COCOPA
61 YUMA
62 MARICOPA
63 HALCHIDHOMA
64 MOHAVE
65 HAVASUPAI
66 HOPI
67 ZUNI
68 MANSO
69 ACOMA
70 ISLETA

71 QUERES
72 TANO
73 TEWA
74 JEMEZ
75 TAOS
76 KIOWA APACHE
77 HIDATSA
78 MISSOURI
79 WINNEBAGO
80 SOUTHAMPTON ESKIMO
81 PENNACOOK
82 MASSACHUSET
83 MOHEGAN
84 METOAC
85 NANTICOKE
86 POWHATAN
87 TUSCARORA
88 PAMLICO
89 CUSABO
90 APALACHEE
91 ALABAMA
92 CHARCHIUMA
93 TUNICA
94 BILOXI
95 ACOLAPISSA
96 HUMA
97 CHITIMACHA
98 KARANKAWA
99 TARAHUMARA
100 CHINIPA
101 GUASAVE
102 HUICHOL
103 TAMAULIPECO
104 JANAMBRE
105 HUAXTEC
106 TOTONAC
107 CHINANTEC
108 ZAPOTEC
109 TEQUISTLATECO
110 HUAVE
111 CHIAPANEC